GW00419715

The Subject, Capitalism, and Religion

NEW APPROACHES TO RELIGION AND POWER

Series editor: Joerg Rieger

While the relationship of religion and power is a perennial topic, it only continues to grow in importance and scope in our increasingly globalized and diverse world. Religion, on a global scale, has openly joined power struggles, often in support of the powers that be. But at the same time, religion has made major contributions to resistance movements. In this context, current methods in the study of religion and theology have created a deeper awareness of the issue of power: Critical theory, cultural studies, postcolonial theory, subaltern studies, feminist theory, critical race theory, and working class studies are contributing to a new quality of study in the field. This series is a place for both studies of particular problems in the relation of religion and power as well as for more general interpretations of this relation. It undergirds the growing recognition that religion can no longer be studied without the study of power.

Series editor:

Joerg Rieger is Wendland-Cook Professor of Constructive Theology in the Perkins School of Theology at Southern Methodist University.

Titles:

*No Longer the Same: Religious Others and the Liberation of
    Christian Theology*
David R. Brockman

*The Subject, Capitalism, and Religion: Horizons of Hope in
    Complex Societies*
Jung Mo Sung

The Subject, Capitalism, and Religion

Horizons of Hope in Complex Societies

Jung Mo Sung

First published in 2011 by
PALGRAVE MACMILLAN®
in the United States—a division of St. Martin's Press LLC,
175 Fifth Avenue, New York, NY 10010.

Where this book is distributed in the UK, Europe and the rest of the world,
this is by Palgrave Macmillan, a division of Macmillan Publishers Limited,
registered in England, company number 785998, of Houndmills,
Basingstoke, Hampshire RG21 6XS.

Palgrave Macmillan is the global academic imprint of the above companies
and has companies and representatives throughout the world.

Palgrave® and Macmillan® are registered trademarks in the United States,
the United Kingdom, Europe and other countries.

ISBN: 978–0–230–11975–8

Library of Congress Cataloging-in-Publication Data

Sung, Jung Mo, 1958–
     The subject, capitalism, and religion : horizons of hope in complex
societies / Jung Mo Sung.
          p. cm.—(New approaches to religion and power)
     Includes bibliographical references and index.
     ISBN 978–0–230–11975–8 (hardback)
      1. Liberation theology. 2. Church work with the poor. 3. Poor—Social
conditions. 4. Poor—Religious life. I. Title.

BT83.57.S865 2011
230'.0464—dc23   2011019623

A catalogue record of the book is available from the British Library.

Design by Newgen Imaging Systems (P) Ltd., Chennai, India.

First edition: November 2011

10 9 8 7 6 5 4 3 2 1

Printed and bound in Great Britain by
CPI Antony Rowe, Chippenham and Eastbourne

Also by Jung Mo Sung

Beyond the Spirit of Empire
Deus em nós: o reinado que acontece no amor solidário aos pobres
Cristianismo de libertação: espiritualidade e luta social
Desire, Market, and Religion
Educar para reencantar a vida
Sementes de esperança: a fé em um mundo em crise
Competência e sensibilidade solidária: educar para esperança
Teologia e economia: repensando a teologia da libertação e utopias

Contents

Series Editor's Preface:
Faith Communities, Labor, and Desire[1]

Joerg Rieger

One of the things that are becoming clearer today is that there can be no study of religion or theology in abstract terms. Studies of religion and theology increasingly consider particular contexts and concrete phenomena, although there are still some who refuse to deal with their location and claim universality.

Latin American liberation theology, the tradition in which Jung Mo Sung writes and to which he has made major contributions, has been among the pioneering methods of contextual and concrete studies of religion and theology. Nevertheless, early generations of liberation theologians still maintained a certain level of abstraction that has been challenged repeatedly. Talk about the poor in general, for instance, did not allow for an in-depth understanding of lower-class people and for an in-depth understanding of the power relations that constitute the class system. Talk about economics was often too general as well, as Jung himself has pointed out.[2] Differences along the lines of gender, sexuality, and ethnic background have been addressed by subsequent generations of liberation theologians.

The issues discussed by Jung Mo Sung in this book are located in the context of history, life, and ultimately in the context of faith communities. Jung himself is involved in the day-to-day struggles along these lines not only as observer but as participant, living and working in São Paulo, Brazil. His involvement in faith communities is not limited to the Roman Catholic Church and its base communities, his spiritual home, but extends to new religious communities, which include charismatics, Pentecostals, and a Japanese religious community in São Paulo, the so-called World Messianic Church in Brazil. These involvements do not make his work less astute—the opposite is the case: the depth of his insight is tied to being involved.

Jung's definition of theology as hermeneutics of history, as an effort to understand the dynamic of human life in view of a God in solidarity with those who are marginalized, plays out in the midst of history itself. Perhaps the most important lesson here is that there is no other place in which scholars of religion and theologians can write than in the midst of history; that there is no place for us outside of history and the world. What has sometimes been called a "God's-eye view" is not available to human beings, and even Godself seems to have renounced it again and again, particularly in the Christian tradition of the incarnation. By the same token, not even the academy provides a place outside of history and the world, contrary to the myth of academic objectivity. The decisive question then becomes not whether we are located in history or not, but where in history we locate ourselves. Since Jung is addressing this question primarily from the perspective of Latin America and the Global South, in this introduction I will address it from the perspective of the United States and the Global North.

Communities of Faith

In response to *Beyond the Spirit of Empire*, a book co-authored by Jung Mo Sung, Néstor Míguez (an Argentinean liberation theologian), and myself, a colleague wondered where the church was discussed in this project.[3] Since our book deals with theology, politics, and the future of liberation theology, this question is crucial because it asks about the location of religious and theological reflection in relation to communities of faith. This question, of course, is bigger than the question whether specific communities of faith are addressed in a particular book—the question also has to do with the scholars' own involvement in such communities and what difference scholarship makes to such communities. Scholarship in religious studies often shies away from these sorts of accounts, but scholarship in theology is often not doing much better in identifying its social location. The good news is, however, that the current climate in both religious studies and theology is more open to this issue than in the past.

In either case, in *Beyond the Spirit of Empire* we were perhaps not as forthcoming about the church and communities of faith as we might have been. But, speaking as one of the co-authors, I wonder whether there was a certain hesitance as well in addressing this issue. The reason for this hesitance has nothing to do with a lack of connection to communities of faith and churches, but that too often even talk about churches and communities of faith serves as one more level of abstraction. While there is broad agreement that academia often confines itself to the proverbial ivory towers, too often churches and communities of faith inhabit their very own ivory towers. To be sure, the real problem with these ivory towers is not that they do not allow for connections to the outside, as is commonly assumed. The real problem with these ivory towers is that the existing connections to the broader community and to the world go unrecognized or are covered up. This was one of Antonio Gramsci's critiques of those academics whom he called "traditional intellectuals," who "put themselves forward as autonomous and independent of the dominant social group,"[4] while in reality their work is tied to the status quo without being aware of it.

The unfortunate truth is that many faith communities have become tied to the status quo without being aware of it. This phenomenon can be observed, for instance, in the fact that many faith communities have become self-referential. What matters in these cases are the exclusive interests of the community and its members, its projects, and its welfare. Moreover, this self-centeredness takes on a particular shape, as the basic concerns of the community are commonly influenced by those who hold the most power and often the most wealth in the wider context in which the community finds itself. In other words, those who are endorsed by the wider context due to their social standing are commonly also the ones who determine the shape of faith communities, thus integrating them effectively into this status quo. Even so-called outreach projects, as the charitable and missionary actions of churches today are often called, frequently fail to push beyond this self-referential nature of religious communities. The problem is that frequently such outreach has nothing to do with opening up to the outside but is designed to integrate others into the community, or to shape others in one's own image.

In this context, dealing with communities of faith and with churches does not necessarily help to make the sorts of connections that theologians and religious scholars need to make. An engagement with faith communities and churches only pushes beyond the ivory towers when we investigate how these entities are located in the world and in history, especially in regard to is struggles and tensions. It is for these reasons that in *Beyond the Spirit of Empire* we discussed the complex notion of empire and the challenges this empire poses to our world and to history, which includes challenges to religious and ecclesial communities. The difference between democracy and laocracy, for instance, applies not only to political and other communities but to communities of faith as well.[5] In other words, the difference between a rule of the people that is focused on the elites (democracy) and a rule of the people that truly incorporates the common people (laocracy) has implications not just for politics and economics but also for the church and for other communities of faith.

Once this broader perspective has been established, based on examinations of the tectonics of power in the larger context in which we find ourselves, it is then possible to talk about specific religious and ecclesial communities in ways that go deeper and acknowledge both the complexity of these communities (a growing concern in contemporary studies of religion) and the flow of power in these communities (a growing concern in liberative discourses of religion and theology).

In this introduction, I will discuss how desire—one of the major concepts with which Jung Mo Sung has engaged with in several of his books, including the present one—can be addressed in religious communities that are aware of how they function in a broader context, pushing beyond moralism and romanticism. The relation of religion and labor will serve as an example. This relation is important for various reasons, not the least of them is a deep affinity between the Judeo-Christian traditions and people who work for a living. Moreover, many of the power structures at the core of global capitalism are negotiated between those who have no choice but to work for a living in some form or fashion (which includes the unemployed, the casually employed, and even small businesspeople) and those whose wealth works for them. Finally, the relation of religion and labor helps us understand in the Global North some of the struggles that people of faith are living through in the Global South.

Religion and Labor: What is Going On?

In the global economy, both in the North and in the South, the topics of labor and worker justice are arguably among the most burning issues of our time, tied to record unemployment and concomitant pressures on those who retain the remaining jobs.

Many of the mainline denominations support issues of labor and worker justice, including collective bargaining rights.[6] Nevertheless churches, especially in the United States, have often been highly reluctant to deal with labor and worker justice, and these issues are largely absent from theological reflection. What is the reason for this discrepancy?

Key reasons for the lack of engagement of churches and theologians in matters of labor include a fundamental lack of understanding of the relation of labor and religion. In the United Sates, these reasons also include a widespread misunderstanding that sees labor as a special interest concern, a pervasive lack of understanding of matters of socioeconomic class, and acquiescence to a climate of systemic increase of pressures leveled against workers.

Common Interest

Labor is misunderstood as a special interest concern, for instance, when it is seen as the occupation of mostly white and male blue-collar workers. Furthermore, labor is misunderstood as special interest when it is overlooked that labor is one of the pillars of life in the world today, without which there is no production, no subsistence, and no human flourishing.[7] In response to these misunderstandings it should be noted that the working class makes up the majority of the population in the United States, and that contemporary labor includes large numbers of women, ethnic and racial minorities, and immigrants. Moreover, labor includes many white-collar workers who have little control over their work. Economist Michael Zweig has pointed out that in the United States 62 percent belong to the working class, 36 percent to the middle class, and only 2 percent to the ruling class.[8]

This has direct implications for religious communities, whose constituencies resemble this statistics. This means that even in the United States, which has high rates of participation in religious communities, a large part of the membership is not middle class but working class. Even the common assumption that mainline religion, and mainline Christianity in particular, is mostly made up by members of the middle and upper classes will have to be reevaluated. And while the mainline may be constituted more heavily of members of a middle class background, the question is with whose interests the interests of the middle class are aligned. The default assumption is that the middle class and the ruling class share many interests in common, but in the current climate it is becoming more obvious that this may not be the case. While both classes own stocks, for instance, the amount of stocks owned is vastly different. The so-called Great Recession that is moving into the second decade of the twenty-first century has produced a number of economic winners, but the middle class has for the most part been among the losers, paralleling the fate of the working class rather than the ruling class. In the United States, many well-paying middle-class jobs have been lost, only to be replaced with less well-paying jobs.[9] Many middle class families know intuitively that their children will not be able to maintain their economic standing.

Class analysis is thus a crucial matter, not only in order to understand economic and political registers but also to understand religious ones. Before we turn to this topic, the implications for communities of faith need to be pointed out. At present, many communities of faith are shaped by the interests of those members in their midst who represent relative power and wealth, and these members are usually in the minority. In other words, a dominant minority is able to assure that its interests, rather than the interests of the majority of the members of the church, are pursued. Many examples could be given. Why would churches in Texas, for instance, be afraid to tackle issues of economics, labor, and even universal health care, especially at a time when so many of its members are hurting in these areas, and when the institutions themselves are suffering economic losses? Moreover, why would churches in this context be afraid to have conversations about the so-called Employee Free Choice Act, a proposal before the United States Congress that would eliminate some of the considerable hurdles that prevent workers from forming unions?

In a climate when even the topic of universal health care is anathema in most mainline churches, support of labor issues is almost unimaginable. The strangeness of this situation can be seen in stark relief in light of the fact that most mainline churches officially support collective bargaining rights and the formation of labor unions, and that matters of health and work are key issues in the Jewish-Christian traditions. Jesus' healing ministry, for example, provides what might be considered free health care for the least of these, and his concern for working people is hard to dismiss. All this points to the fact that the interests dominating the religious communities that block discussions of labor and health care for all are the interests of a minority rather than the majority. Here, our sense for what is common and what is special interest shifts.

Class

Socioeconomic class is arguably one of the most misunderstood subjects in the United States. When class is discussed at all, it is mostly done in terms of economic stratification. While there is much to be gained from information about income levels and about the distribution of income in society, what such discussions overlook is the question of how class relates to power.

When class is discussed in terms of power rather than in terms of income levels, one of the key questions is what control people have over their own work and their lives. The power people have over their work and their lives is an important clue as to their place in an economic system where some hold enormous powers and others very little. This power is, of course, also reflected in the financial benefits of work, as those in power consistently make hundreds or thousands of times more than others.[10] In terms of this definition, those who have little power over their work belong to the working class, which includes many white-collar workers as well. Here, work is constrained by regulations, which are increasingly determined by the ideal of "lean and mean production," which result in increasing the speed of work and in lowering its benefits. Those who have the most power over their own work, including the work of others, belong to the ruling class. Here, work means setting the parameters for the work of others and thus the ability to control what is going on, at least to some degree.

To the middle class belong those who are in between these two groups, with some power over their work. This includes, for instance, small business people and professionals. Here, work still allows for some creativity, although even the life of professionals is more and more regulated and subject to an increasing number of "performance reviews." Life in the middle, therefore, is not as comfortable as it looks, especially in an economic climate where the middle class is losing ground. Under pressure to work more while earning less, and receiving fewer benefits, even medical doctors in the United States are now forming and joining unions. And even the work of professors at colleges and universities is increasingly under pressure from business models that stress efficiency and evaluation of academic production in terms of measurable outcomes.

In this context, the interests of those who lack power at work matter less and less. According to United States law, corporations are not accountable for the well-being of their workers but for the production of wealth for their stock holders. If the interests of those who lack power at work are to continue to matter at all, they will need to organize in order to prevent existing imbalances of power from deepening. This insight is relevant for communities of faith and churches because these imbalances of power are reproduced not just in the economic realm but in the realm of religion as well. To put it bluntly, the ministry of too many churches and the imagination of too many theologians are shaped by positions of power and wealth, for the most part without even being aware of it. God is invariably located at the top, wielding power from the top down in the manner of the powerful and wealthy.

Here is an excerpt from a letter I wrote to a pastor in Dallas, who wrote to me about how a recent series of presentations on religion and economics at church was well received by the majority but met with the active resistance of a small number of wealthy and powerful families:

> Thanks for your note, which I received the other day. I know exactly what you are talking about, as the same thing seems to be happening anywhere I look. Anything that really challenges the current status quo, especially when it addresses power and wealth, is quickly brushed off the table. The actors are always the same: people who enjoy a certain power and wealth, although they are not necessarily the ones who benefit from the overall economic climate the most. At the same time, many of our church members are open and would like to hear and do more. They are the ones who are getting it, but unfortunately the pastors are left hanging in the middle. One way to address this would be to organize the common membership, just like labor needs to organize if it wants to make a dent.

In other words, there is a class struggle being waged from the top down, not only in society but also in the realm of religion, which has tremendous implications for the future of communities of faith and churches. Yet not all is lost: once this is acknowledged, alternatives can be envisioned.

This problem is not limited to Texas, where the interests of the ruling class exert enormous pressures on the labor movement that are unmatched in most other states in the United States.[11]

This problem can be encountered in many other places as well, both in the Global North and the Global South. Furthermore, and more closely related to the topic of this introduction, the interests of the ruling class exert pressure on communities of faith as well, often represented vicariously by members of the middle class and even the working class who mistakenly see their interests aligned with those of the ruling class.

Since pastors and other religious professionals are dependent on these powers—through their salaries and their ranking in a system that decides on merit and the next steps in their careers—their performance is severely handicapped. Rarely are they in a position where they can present many challenges, and thus even their training in religious studies and theology is often rendered irrelevant to their profession, especially where it contains a critique of the status quo. Of course, training in religious studies and theology itself is frequently designed to adapt to these power structures, which is why those approaches that present fewer challenges, whether they insist on strict objectivity or make efforts to provide what they consider balance, enjoy a higher currency.[12]

Acquiescence

Taken-for-granted accomplishments like eight-hour workdays, weekends off work, benefits, and basic protections for working people exist because they were negotiated by organized labor in the United States and elsewhere, which understood that common interest is built from the bottom up. "An injury to one is an injury to all" is one of the time-honored mottos of organized labor. This insight reflects the well-known words of the apostle Paul: "If one member suffers, all suffer together with it" (1 Cor. 12:26). Common interest is pursued where the weakest members and those who have been injured are taken into consideration. Since the well-being of the whole body is at stake, we can argue that the interest of the middle and of the ruling classes is at stake in the interest of the working class as well.

Unfortunately, these accomplishments are now under attack from corporations and politicians alike, especially in the United States, where conservative politicians have launched all-out attacks against labor, with little resistance from their more progressive colleagues, and sometimes with their support. In this situation, the corporations are able to play off against each other workers in other locations around the world and U.S. workers, eroding standards of labor everywhere and discouraging worker solidarity both globally and locally. Under current law, the United States restricts the opportunities to organize new trade unions more severely than most other countries: as many as 60 million U.S. workers want to organize, while only 500,000 are permitted to do so every year.[13] In this context of increasing pressures leveled against labor, communities of faith and churches will need to reevaluate their own positions, as acquiescence means to support this status quo.

Communities of faith in the current climate tend to look at these things from the outside, as if they were not directly affected by what is going on. One of the key insights of liberation theology, reflecting ancient wisdom, is that this is not true: religion, faith, and life can never be separated. This is especially striking in the southern parts of the United States, where this separation is often assumed in a situation where faith and life are even more closely related than elsewhere. Here, communities of faith are more directly affected by labor issues than elsewhere, as many workers are also members of churches. In Europe, by contrast, most members of the working class gave up on the church decades ago. At a recent Labor Day breakfast organized by the Dallas AFL-CIO, more than 75 percent of the 500 union leaders in attendance raised their hands when asked whether they were members of religious communities.

Such close relations of religion and labor, even when there is less direct involvement of workers in the church, carry tremendous potential. Unfortunately, the vast majority of union leaders and their fellow workers who are members of faith communities are likely to find themselves in situations where labor issues are never addressed at any level. This situation leads to a tacit endorsement of the powers that be, which results in the increasing reduction of benefits for workers, reductions of wages, and an increasing loss of the last semblances of human decency at the workplace. Separating religion and labor in this way creates the impression not only that communities of faith have no interests in matters of labor, but that they have nothing of value to contribute. At the level of theological reflection, the same assumption is also made about God: God appears to have no interest in labor and nothing of value to contribute. When religion and labor are thus separated, the status quo wins every time.

This separation of religion and labor, which results in the acquiescence of faith communities to the status quo, has severe consequences, as worsening conditions of labor are becoming matters of life and death. Ultimately, the worsening conditions of labor in the global economy are reproduced in communities of faith and churches themselves. Benefits for religious workers, including some of the leaders, are cut back all the time. Even time-honored traditions like guaranteed pastoral appointments in The United Methodist Church, which are closely related to its appointment system and the theology that backs it up, are now under attack.

Religion and Labor: Next steps

When issues of religion and labor are discussed rather than repressed, matters are usually framed in terms of a one-way street: What might faith communities do in support of labor? The reverse question, however, is equally important, if not more so: What might labor do in support of faith communities? This leads us to the question of what happens when faith communities, theologians, and scholars of religion are introduced to the problems of labor (which includes their own labor) and to an understanding that these problems are not natural catastrophes but socially produced.

Rather than speculating about the answer to this question, let me introduce some insights generated in the context of the work of a local Workers' Rights Board in Dallas, Texas.[14] This board, whose members include community leaders, pastors, teachers, academics, and members of faith communities, holds regular hearings on labor issues. These hearings bring to the surface particular labor struggles that are taking place in the local scene, a reality that is dramatically underreported in any of the news media. The mission of the Workers' Rights Board is to address these struggles, by understanding the nature of the conflict, meeting with workers and employers and their representatives, working on matters of labor rights with politicians, and many other avenues. Yet perhaps the most important mission of the Workers' Rights Board is to develop a deeper understanding of these conflicts, both for the members of the board who seek to investigate what is going on and what the deeper roots of the problem are, and for the wider public. Thus, one part of the mission of the Workers' Rights Board is to publicize these labor struggles in various ways: the hearings are open to the public and the media are invited, board members write letters to the editor and news reports on the hearings that are distributed to media outlets, and findings are disseminated in other ways as well. Finally, these issues are beginning to find their way back into communities of faith and the theological production of the members of the Workers' Rights Board who are involved in faith communities, whether they are members or leaders or academics.[15]

To give a specific example: Learning about the plight of immigrant construction workers, for instance, who are forced to work in the extremely hot summers in the Southern United States without water and safety equipment, creates a basic understanding for the situation of labor in our context, as well as a sense for the life-and-death urgency of labor issues. Furthermore, learning how these concerns are often played down and shrugged off by the employers when they are approached by delegations of the Workers' Rights Board and workers, creates a new feel for the power differentials at work in labor from the perspective of those who hold little formal power. And dealing with the media, which often fail to report on these grave violations and never discuss their real causes, creates a sense of the marginal place which these issues occupy in our society.

It is only in this context that theological and religious reflections on the importance of labor begin to make sense. One of the first surprising discoveries that communities of faith make in this context is that the causes of labor and workers have been at the core of many religious traditions. In Christianity, for instance, Jesus' parables present a perspective that takes seriously the concerns of workers, including service workers, fishermen, peasants, and working women. The parable of the unforgiving servant, to name but one example, makes sense only from the perspective of labor: in the unusual situation where a master gives up control over the servant by forgiving debt, the logical response for the servant would be to forgive the debt of his fellow servant. After all, solidarity among servants is much more valuable for the well-being of the community than a little pocket money (Matthew 18:23–34).

The Jewish religion presents the traditions of Moses in terms of divine solidarity with laboring slaves. God's mysterious revelation, speaking out of a burning bush, makes sense only in this context, as the mission given to Moses is a specific one: "The cry of the Israelites has now come to me; I have also seen how the Egyptians oppress them. So come, I will send you to Pharaoh to bring my people, the Israelites, out of Egypt" (Exodus 3:9–10). Islam, too, promotes the fair treatment of workers and insists on the importance of fair pay (see, for instance, the Qur'an, Sura LXX). Issues of labor are indeed of central importance to many faith communities. In the Christian traditions that understand Jesus as divine, this connection of labor and religion is part of the inner sanctum, beginning with the incarnation of God in Jesus Christ: Here, Godself is born as a day laborer in construction (Mark 6:3; this is what the Greek word often translated as "carpenter" means), and the first to acknowledge this miracle are day laborers who tend the sheep of other people (Luke 2:8–20).

Throughout the history of the Christian church, there have been movements embodying relations of religion and labor. Even in the United States there is a long tradition of religion and labor that often goes unrecognized, for instance, in the Roman Catholic Worker movements, the Social Gospel, and in more recent organizations like Interfaith Worker Justice (IWJ) and Clergy and Laity United for Economic Justice (CLUE). Even in unlikely places like Texas there have been prominent religion and labor movements in the past. In the early 1900s, Christian socialist camp meetings attracted 10,000 people in Northeast Texas and Southeastern Oklahoma. Today, the Dallas Workers' Rights Board and various other organizations like the Worker Defense Project in Austin and another Interfaith Worker Justice-related worker center in Houston continue the religion and labor tradition, which include efforts to work with particular faith communities. All of these traditions help rediscover some genuine truths about the Christian faith that are mostly forgotten in contemporary Christianity.

The question of why to engage labor and religion in the first place can now be addressed at a deeper level. We are obviously not dealing with a special-interest topic here, as the question is not merely what to do about labor issues. The question is how attention to labor issues and struggles might help us to reform communities of faith and churches in such a way that they become more faithful to the core of their own traditions. Understanding that all of us are invariably engaged in these issues, whatever social class we belong to, we are now able to examine on a broader scale what various religious traditions might contribute to more just relations of labor and what more just relations of labor might contribute to religious traditions and theologies. Many religious traditions reveal deeper levels of meaning when retold from the perspectives of labor, as many of them originated in such contexts.[16]

Even the theological question of God, often considered to be an abstract metaphysical question, is raised here in new ways. If God takes sides in the hermeneutics of history, as various religious traditions hold, the question of God needs to be rethought in the context of labor. Without having to identify God and labor, there are some major lessons to be learned here. As several Christian theologians have reminded us in recent years, many of the biblical traditions portray Godself as a worker, beginning with the creation stories in the book of Genesis.[17]

Conclusion: Reevaluating Desire

We are now ready to return to a key issue that Jung Mo Sung raises from a Latin American perspective. When Jung notes the problem of consumption and limitless desire—in the United States we talk about consumerism as an attitude that makes consumption appear limitless—he digs deeper than the common popular critiques in the North. Consumption, he notes, is not primarily about what some have called "materialism," that is, the acquisition of more and more material goods. Consumption has to do with the ideals and higher values that we pursue, as the things that we acquire do not take on the roles of ends in themselves. Buying a new car every two years for instance, a common practice in the recent history of the United States, is more about ideals like feeling safe and secure and manifestations of self-appreciation and love than about the actual car itself. These ideals are crucial for the formation of personal identity, as consumers define a sense of their self-worth and the character of their personalities in this way. Subjectivity, another major concept in Jung's work, is closely tied to this dynamic. What is more, our deepest desires are shaped and reshaped in this context of consumption.

This analysis of consumption and desire helps us understand the all-pervasiveness of the problem. The success of a capitalist economy depends to a large degree on producing desire and the concomitant ideals that keep people focused on consumption. Moreover, the production of limitless desire and consumption is not only one of the main pillars on which a capitalist economy rests; Jung also notes how this relates to faith in the market and the resulting absolutization of the market, which can be observed not only in the Global South but also in the Global North. Communities of faith are not immune to these dynamics and the idolatrous faith that is produced here.

In this context, one of the most common critiques of consumerism in the United States, often pronounced from within faith communities and churches, only makes things worse. The complaint that people are "materialist," that they constantly seek to acquire more stuff, covers up the deeper motivations and the role of faith and ideals in consumerism. What is commonly called "materialism" is not really a focus on material things but a focus on misguided ideals and misguided faith, a certain "spiritualism," as material things are acquired not for themselves but in the search for higher values and ultimate truth. Moreover, the use of the notion of "materialism" in this context covers up the deeper problem of the absolutization of ideals that are not absolute, and thus idolatry—the worship of false gods. When Jung talks about the spiritual or spirituality, he seeks to present alternatives to this problem, as the spiritual that he promotes is not the lofty absolute of false consciousness but worked out in the midst of the struggle for life where God is at work.

On the basis of what has been said in this introduction, a more appropriate response to consumerism and desire can now be imagined through the relation of religion and labor. Here, desire can be seen in a new light and, as a result, can be kept in check to some degree. While Jung is right that desire is shaped in consumption, related to a utopian horizon that has become an idol, the perspective of labor and production is what helps us see that desire itself is not ultimate reality. Rather, desire in a capitalist economy needs to be produced in order to keep the world of production going. Without the relentless production of desire via the ever-expanding advertising industry, the production of goods and services would stagnate. In other words, the success of capitalism is dependent on the ongoing production of desire and an aggressive enticement of consumerism in order to maintain an increase in production. This is why blaming consumers for their consumerism, the typical approach in the United States pursued frequently by well-meaning communities of faith, is putting the cart before the horse.[18]

Even an understanding of consumerism in terms of a search for ideals and ultimate values does not go far enough if it overlooks the need to keep production going. It is at this point that an alternative view of production, as it emerges from the world of labor, might help. While production is still one of the major places for the creation of profit in a capitalist economy (despite the role of virtual capital and stock markets) and thus part of its mythology, production looks different from the perspective of those who have little power in the process because they have little else to bring to the bargaining table than their labor. Here, some major insights can be gained and new spiritualities, grounded in real life, develop. Through listening to perspectives from labor, even the members of the Workers' Rights Board discussed above, although they are not employed in production themselves, are beginning to understand the limits of production and the consequences of production that becomes meaner and leaner all the time. These limits have to with the limits of workers, the limits of exploitation, and the limits of nature and the environment of which we are becoming more aware today.

If production is, thus, not without limits, neither can desire be without limits. When this is taken into account, we begin to understand that both unlimited production and the satisfaction of unlimited desire are impossible and ultimately harmful and deadly. As religion gets back in touch with labor, these insights become clearer again. Godself is not the warrant for unlimited desire, unlike the "invisible hand of the market" that guarantees apparently unlimited success. Faith communities that are developing an understanding of these mechanisms and their limits can help make a real difference in reshaping desire.

Desire does not have to be given up at this point, but it is reshaped in light of its limitations. Moreover, from the perspective of those who labor in production and those who stand in solidarity with them, desire can now be linked to what people really need. These needs include not only the basic ones like food, shelter, and clothing, but also the need to engage in constructive labor and to produce new spiritualities, grounded in real life. Such labor can then be valued again for what it is: not a mere tool for the production of economic surplus by those who hire labor, but a way of life that mirrors divine production which is geared at sustaining the life of communities and the globe as a whole. Such labor ultimately creates more hopeful desires, which can flourish by engaging their limitations.

Notes

1. I want to thank Ph.D. students Kevin Minister and Peter Jones for their valuable contributions to this chapter.
2. See, for instance, for instance, Jung Mo Sung, *Economia: Tema Ausente En La Teología de La Liberación* (San José: DEI, 1994); and Jung Mo Sung, *Teologia e Economia: Repensando A Teologia da Libertação e Utopias* (Petrópolis: Vozes, 1994). *La Liberación* (San José: DEI, 1994); and the Portuguese version: Jung Mo Sung, *Teologia e Economia: Repensando A Teologia da Libertação e Utopias* (Petrópolis: Vozes, 1994).

3. This was part of the response of Nancy Bedford, as part of a panel reviewing Néstor Míguez, Joerg Rieger, and Jung Mo Sung, *Beyond The Spirit of Empire: Theology and Politics in a New Key*, Reclaiming Liberation Theology Series (London: SCM Press, 2009), at the Annual Meeting of the American Academy of Religion in Atlanta in October 2010.

4. Antonio Gramsci, "The Intellectuals," in *Selections from the Prison Notebooks*, ed. and trans. Quintin Hoare and Geoffrey Nowell Smith (New York: International Publishers, 1971), 7.

5. Míguez, Rieger, and Jung, *Beyond the Spirit of Empire*, 176–78.

6. See, for instance, "Economic Justice for All: A Pastoral Letter on Catholic Social Teaching and the U.S. Economy," the United States Conference of Roman Catholic Bishops, 1986. The Social Principles, in: *The Book of Discipline of the United Methodist Church 2008* (Nashville: United Methodist Publishing House, 2008). *Message from the Tenth Assembly* (Winnipeg, Canada:Lut heranWorldFederationTenthAssembly, July 2003), 17–18, http://www.lwf-assembly.org/PDFs/LWF_Assembly_Message-EN.pdf. *Covenanting for Justice in the Economy and the Earth*, document-GC23-e (Accra, Ghana: World Alliance of Reformed Churches, 24th General Council, July 30–August 13, 2004), http://warc.jalb.de/warcajsp/ news_file/doc-181-1.pdf. For other religious positions on the organizations of unions, see "What Faith Groups Say about the Right to Organize," compiled by Interfaith Worker Justice (IWJ) (Chicago, IL: Interfaith Worker Justice), http://iwj.org/template/page.cfm?id=62.

7. The relation of labor and human flourishing is pointed out by Darby Kathleen Ray, *Working: Christian Explorations of Daily Living* (Minneapolis: Fortress Press, 2011).

8. Michael Zweig, *The Working Class Majority* (Ithaca, N.Y.: ILR, 2000), 20, 34–35.

9. See Zachary Roth, "Jobs returning—but good ones not so much," Yahoo News (March 9, 2001), on the web: http://news.yahoo.com/s/yblog_thelookout/20110309/ts_yblog_thelookout/jobs-returning-but-good-ones-not-so-much.

10. See the numbers in Joerg Rieger, *No Rising Tide: Theology, Economics, and the Future* (Minneapolis: Fortress Press, 2009), 9.

In 2006, the average CEO made 364 times more than an average worker in the United States, down from over 500 times a few years earlier. At the same time, the difference between the salary of an average worker and the top twenty private-equity and hedge-fund managers in the United States is much higher: these top-investors earned 22,255 times the pay of the average worker.

11. For good reasons, only 5.4 percent of workers in Texas were members of unions in 2010, compared to 24.2 percent in the State of New York and 17.5 in the State of California. See: http://www.bls.gov/news.release/union2.t05.htm.

12. The problem is, thus, not just that the church would restrict pastors from teaching what they learned in seminary, as Jack Good, *The Dishonest Church* (Haworth, NY: St. Johann Press, 2008) has pointed out. The problem is also that the seminaries submit to these pressures and adjust curricula and theology accordingly.

13. See Michael Payne, "Unionization: A Private Sector Solution to the Financial Crisis," Dissent (Spring 2009): 59. The AFL-CIO estimates that 60 million workers would like to be organized in unions, while opponents of the Employee Free Choice Act reduce this number to a still sizable figure of 25 million workers.

14. For more information, see: http://wrbdallas.blogspot.com/.

15. My own work as a theologian has been greatly informed by this work.

16. This is one of the key points of my book *No Rising Tide*.

17. See the recent books by Darby Ray, *Working: Christian Exploration of Daily Living* (Minneapolis: Fortress Press, 2011), and David Jensen, *Responsive Labor: A Theology of Work* (Philadelphia: Westminster John Knox, 2006).

18. See also Rieger, *No Rising Tide*, chapter 4.

Acknowledgments

Many ideas presented here matured in the seminars of the Center for Religious Studies at the IFAN Society (the Franciscan Institute of Anthropology) at the University of St. Francis (Universidade de São Francisco), where I was a researcher. This book is a part of IFAN's effort in thinking about the possible ways of overcoming the social exclusion that marks our time. I want especially to express my thanks to my friend Luciano Glavina, who read the chapters and enthusiastically discussed them with me; to Peter L. Jones, who has invested much time in the study of my texts and in the translation of this work; to Kevin Minister, who has prepared the index; and to Joerg Rieger, who has contributed an introduction and who was instrumental in bringing about the publication of this work in the United States. Finally, I am grateful to Orbis Press for permission regarding "The Human Being as Subject: Defending the Victims" from *Latin American Liberation Theology: The Next Generation*, edited by Ivan Petrella. A new translation of the text on which it is based appears here as chapter 2, "The Subject and the Defense of the Life of the Victims."

Registry of the Texts' Origins

Chapter 1: "Teología y la vida de los pobres." In *Panorama de la Teología Latinoamericana*, edited by Juan José Tamayo and Juan Bosch, 371–88. Estella, Espanha: Verbo Divino, 2001.

Chapter 2: "Sujeito e defesa da vida das vítimas." In *Terra Prometida: Movimento Social, Engajamento Cristão e Teologia*, edited by Luiz Carlos Susin, 225–47. Petrópolis: Vozes/SOTER, 2001.

Chapter 3: "Sujeito como transcendentalidade ao interior da vida real – Um diálogo com o pensamento de Franz Hinkelammert." *Cadernos do IFAN* 20 (2000): 47–66.

Chapter 4: "Novas formas de legitimação da economia." In *Teologia em Diálogo*, edited by Degislando N. Lima and Jacques Trudel, 19–51. São Paulo: Paulinas, 2002.

Chapter 5: An enlarged and modified version of the article, "Ética e economia," written in honor of Fr. Carlos Josaphat, for his seventieth birthday.

Chapter 6: "Sensibilidade solidária e a condição humana." In *Cultura Vozes* 95, no. 6 (2001): 51–66.

Introduction

Can anyone live without dreams or hopes? Can a people or social group live without hope or without a utopian horizon? Perhaps there are people living without dreams or hopes, but such lives become dull, without feeling, and without grace. To dream and have hopes are necessities almost as vital as eating and drinking, as we are biological and symbolic beings, and we need to discover a meaning and reason for living.

A great majority of persons share the dreams, hopes, and the utopias offered by the dominant sectors of society. This is always the case. However, the capacity of the dominant classes and the social system itself to manipulate the dreams and hopes of people was never so great as it is today. Specialists in marketing and advertising understand that, in our consumer culture, the most important thing in the act of consuming is not the characteristics of the product or its capacity to satisfy the necessities or desires of the consumer, but the personal, interpersonal, and social significance of the act of consuming certain brands and goods. That is, the primary social function of goods stops being the satisfaction of the desires of consumers and comes to be the communication of meaning.[1] The dreams and hopes of a large part of the world's population today have to do with consuming certain symbols. The most profound meanings and yearnings of human existence are expressed through brands and consumer goods.

Happily, not all resign themselves to consuming only those dreams offered through the market. There are still those who look for other dreams, other hopes, and other utopias. Yes, other utopias, because neoliberal capitalism not only produces dreams and hopes, but itself possesses and promulgates a utopia: the utopia of a world completely dominated by the logic of the market. In a horizon founded on the desire of consumption, there is no significant place for the suffering of the poor and socially excluded. When they "cross" that horizon, they are seen as intruders, and end up being ignored, expelled, or even exterminated.

It is because there exists in the "depths of our soul" a desire and hope for a more human world that we are still touched by the suffering of others and that we become capable of feeling ethical indignation in the face of the injustices of the world that affect, not just myself and or ourselves, but others. It is this compassion, this feeling in ourselves the pain of the other, that leads us to set out from resignation and from passivity and to desire that a new world that we imagine become reality. How great is this compassion, this desire for change, and this haste and feeling of urgency. However, if we are not careful we will fall into the mistake of believing, because we want to, that it is possible, simply because we desire it, to construct a world in the image and likeness of our desires.

Whoever believes in this possibility of a world configured by desire itself is accustomed to simplifying natural and social realities and believing in the notion of a "messianic" subject (individual or collective) capable of molding history according to the desire to establish definitively the Good and the Just within human history. The simplification of social reality or the reduction of the complexity of history and society to simple laws is the first fundamental step, since on it depends the very possibility of the messianic action of the historical subject. Perhaps that is why we find, among groups deeply committed to the cause of social justice, phrases like these: "The economy is simple. Economese is complicated, precisely in order to keep the crowds from understanding the rules of the game and beginning to be suspicious of what the cartels say."[2] No, it is not true that the economy is so simple, especially the economies of large, globalized, and complex societies like ours.

To recognize the complexity of a social reality is to recognize human limits. The human being is incapable of fully knowing reality, just as it is incapable of controlling all the effects of its actions and of producing a society according to its projects and desires. At the same time, however, to recognize the complexity of the human being itself is also to recognize that we are capable of desiring a world beyond what exists, of creating symbols that name and indicate that desired world, of elaborating utopias that express more systematically our horizons of hope and our commitment to good and just causes that give a more human meaning to our existence.

Many, however, prefer the "all-or-nothing" game: it is possible to construct the utopia of a perfect world or it is not worth thinking about social commitments and utopian horizons. With that, some cling to ancient dogmatic formulas that no longer explain anything or mobilize many persons; and others completely abandon the notion of the subject and of social transformation. I think that it is fundamental that we overcome these two extremes.

In order that our desire for a more human world is not lost in unjust simplifications, dogmatisms, or "postmodern cynicisms," it is necessary that we return frequently to discuss the complex relation between the notion of the subject, complex societies, and utopian horizons. It is necessary to rethink the concept of the subject and the concepts with which we analyze social problems and elaborate alternatives. Many of those concepts depend on theories elaborated in the nineteenth century, with strong mechanistic and reductive connotations, theories that have already shown themselves to be insufficient or useless. We need new concepts and notions, like self-organization, spontaneous order, emergent new properties, dissipative structures, autopoiesis, the ecology of action, and more, for an analysis more appropriate to complex societies and to rethink seriously our utopias and action strategies. A friend of mine, an old "activist" in the causes of the poor, told me that we need to perform an autopsy on our old utopias. I don't know if we need to go so far, but we certainly need to rethink the way in which we understand utopias and utopian horizons.

In our study of these themes and this relation, we must keep in mind that hope and utopian horizons are not subject to empirical analysis, as they are still nonexistent realities. They are imaginary or theoretical constructs that are, at the same time, the objects of a wager, of faith, and the criteria or models from which we interpret and intervene in reality. I am not using here the concept of faith in a strictly religious sense but in a broader anthropological sense.

The horizons that give meaning to existence and to human actions are always objects of a wager, of faith, since, obviously, we still cannot come close to proving empirically the validity and goodness of that horizon. Horizons, by their own characteristic properties, are out of reach, since they always remain ahead of us, however much we walk in their direction. That is to say, the faith and myths (explicitly religious or apparently secularized) that sustain this wager are unavoidable aspects and themes in a critical reflection on the capitalist course and utopia dominant today, as well as on possible alternative utopias.

Celso Furtado, analyzing the options for development in Latin America, wrote something similar:

> Myths have exercised an undeniable influence over the minds of men as they strive to understand the social reality.... [S]ocial scientists have always searched for support in some postulate rooted in a system of values that they rarely come close to making explicit. Myth brings together hypotheses that cannot be tested.... [T]he principal function of the myth is to orient, on

an intuitive plane, the construction of what Schumpeter called the vision of the social process, without which analytic work makes no sense.[3]

Juan Luis Segundo, in turn, commenting on the anthropological dimension of faith, says that faith, in its most broad sense, "constitutes an indispensable component—a dimension—of all human existence" and that "faith is not only the way of endowing our perception with value, with obligation. It is also a cognitive principle that makes us perceive certain things and not perceive others, equally evident."[4]

To say that hope and faith, by their own internal structure, are not subject to empirical analysis does not mean that we must not critique them theoretically, whether those critiques arise from anticapitalist groups or from neoliberals. (As we will see more systematically in chapter 4, the form of the theory of evolution and self-organization being used to justify the neoliberal market system is based on an act of faith in the providential character of evolution and "the invisible hand" of the market.) We must understand, for a pertinent theoretical critique of the faiths and hopes that ground the visions of the world and political economies, that modern social theories are not always sufficient. I think that a dialogue between the social and human sciences with theology can be quite fruitful; which implies a transdisciplinary approach beyond the established rules and frontiers of the modern sciences.

So that there are no misunderstandings or preconceptions on the part of readers not accustomed to this type of proposal, I want to make it clear that theology is not understood here as a "science" of God or supernatural realities, nor as a theory that systematizes and defends the dogmas of some specific religious confession. Theology is understood here as a hermeneutic of history that makes explicit and reflects critically on the foundations that support the hopes and the visions of the world's theories and societies, foundations that, it is necessary to emphasize, are not placed on firm ground, or based on scientific proof or proven evidence, as such things do not exist, but are supported by a wager, by a fundamental faith.

That said, I think that it is more honest and explanatory for me to make explicit in this introduction my own fundamental wagers, which orient my critical analyses and interpretations. My understanding of theology as a critical hermeneutic of history has much to do with the notion of theology presented by Max Horkheimer. According to him, consciousness of our finitude, and of our human condition, cannot be considered as proof of the existence of God, "except that only it can produce the hope that there is an absolute positive" and that "we cannot represent the absolute, we cannot, when speaking of the absolute, affirm much more than this: the world in which we live is something relative."[5] This affirmation concerning the relativity of our "knowledge" of God and the relativity of the world is fundamental for our avoiding as well as critiquing the idolatries that dominate our world. As Horkheimer says: "Any limited being—and humanity is limited—that considers itself as the ultimate, the most high, and the unique, makes itself into an idol hungry for blood sacrifices, and that has, moreover, a demonic capacity to change identity and to allow in things a different meaning."[6] That said, I want to make Horkheimer's words my own:

> In no way is theology here considered the science of the divine or the science of God.
> Theology here signifies the consciousness that the world is a phenomenon, that it is not the absolute or ultimate truth. Theology is—expressing myself with prudence—the hope that the injustice that characterizes the world cannot remain, that injustice cannot be considered the last word.[7]

Aside from that hermeneutical principle, my reflection is marked by my personal and intellectual history within the

Christian tradition. I make, principally in chapters 1 and 2—texts written for a Christian audience—explicit references to my status as a Christian. However, as there are many conceptions of Christianity, I think that it is important to explain my vision of the essential characteristic of Christianity. For that, I want to use the words of Hugo Assmann:

> The essential novelty of the Christian message, precisely because it has introduced into history the fraternal love of all, consists in the central affirmation: the victims are innocent and no excuse justifies their victimization.[8]

That recognition of the innocence of the victims and of the sacrificial character of the system that victimizes them leads us to assume together the commitment of solidarity toward the victims who are around us and throughout the world. It may seem strange to many that we must defend the innocence of the victims, since if they are victims then they are not guilty. However, the logic of domination requires considering its victims as guilty and those dominating/sacrificing as innocent. It is what we can call sacrificial inversion.

Those hermeneutical principles that orient my reflection—the critique of idolatry, the hope that injustice cannot be the last word, and the defense of the innocence of the victim, which leads us to solidarity—are "reasonable" principles that do not need to be founded and justified by theology and do not demand the support of a religious confession. This is the reason why readers uninterested in theology in the classical sense can also read with profit chapters 1 and 2, which are those that dialogue the most with theology.

After that digression concerning theology as a hermeneutic of history, we return to the challenge of seriously rethinking the relation between the subject, complex societies, and utopian horizons. It was with the objective of contributing to that task that I resolved to bring together and revise some of my recent texts concerning those themes. They are texts that complement each other and show the diverse aspects and facets of this relation. As they were written and published separately, each chapter has the advantage of possessing a beginning, middle, and end that makes it possible for the reader to take the liberty of not following the order of the chapters, or reading only those that presently interest the reader. The counterpart of that advantage is some inevitable repetition. However, those repetitions can also serve, counting on the goodwill of the reader, to reinforce some ideas that are fundamental to the book as a whole.

I think that it would have been better if I, instead of selecting and organizing texts, wrote a book from beginning to end treating the same themes in a more systematic and developed way. However, that would demand much more of my time and patience. Theoretical reflections and analyses demand time and patience for their maturation. On the other hand, the suffering of millions of excluded persons from the minimal conditions of a dignified life and the difficulties in social struggles cry out with urgency.

Whoever makes of theoretical reflection a social commitment with the victims of history must respond to two contradictory demands in the face of the suffering of innocent persons, especially children, where we come to understand what they want to say: "The time is urgent!" While we search for concepts and theories that can help us better understand what is happening in the world and with persons and that permit us to glimpse into and elaborate alternatives, we are conscious that the rhythm of theory is slow. This book bears the marks of that tension.

Another characteristic of the book is the unending attempt to produce a synthesis between the intellectual vocation and social commitment. That appears in the tension between the existential *imminence* that I assume in order to treat various themes and the epistemological *distance* of searching for as much objectivity as possible. It is clear that many times I am unable to maintain a healthy tension between these two postures. The first chapter is the one that is the most existential in character. It was written, in 1999, for a book that presented a panorama of Latin American theology. The editors explicitly requested that the text have a dimension of personal testimony. Therefore, it is a distinct chapter that is out of place with the others in terms of style and content. I decided to include it in this volume, after much indecision, thinking that it shows more clearly the existential aspect of my reflection, an aspect that many times we relegate to the background.

The second chapter is a text presented at a conference of SOTER, the Brazilian Society of Theology and Religious Studies, and presents a more panoramic vision of the themes tackled in the book.

The third treats the concept of the subject and is a dense and fundamental text for understanding my critiques of the concept of the historical subject and the negation of the subjectity (the quality of being a subject) of the individual by neoliberalism.

In the fourth chapter, I analyze, fundamentally, the mythico-theological way in which the ideologues of capitalism are using the theory of evolution and biology in order to legitimate the market system and social exclusion.

In the fifth chapter, I study the relation between ethics and economics. I analyze the problem of ethics and businesses, the limits of the notion of the social responsibility of businesses, and the challenges that the introduction of the notion of self-organizing economic systems brings to ethical reflection.

In the sixth chapter, I present reflections concerning how the acceptance of our human condition can help us in the reduction of social insensitivity and in the increase of social solidarity. This is the most anthropological and existential chapter, which takes up in another way the more existential character of the first chapter.

CHAPTER 1

Theology and the Life of the Poor

This chapter addresses a difficult challenge: to give an account of one's theological path, showing the connection between our human trajectory and theological work. Giving an account of this path has to do with memory. And, in my opinion, theology also has very much to do with memory. It is in the name of the memory of the biblical people and the women and men who followed Jesus that we practice our theology. Memory is not a simple recounting of the facts, but always a reinterpretation and reorganization of the facts of the past from the perspective of the present in which we are living. It is always a creative exercise, yet, at the same time, we try to be faithful to the past.

For that, I'm going to try to articulate an account of memory in view of some of my present theological preoccupations. It will be like a web that does not follow a timeline, just as our lives do not unfold in a linear fashion. I hope that the reader does not become lost in this intersecting labyrinth of memories and theological reflections.

The Children's Faces and Accounts Payable

Two experiences profoundly marked my adolescence, and they helped me to understand some of the existential reasons that lead me to concentrate my theoretical reflections on the theological critique of the economy.

When I was 15 years old, I began to participate in a group of young people from the Catholic Church in the old center of the city of São Paulo. Aside from the meetings where we would discuss the Gospel and other typical activities of a church group, we were doing aid work with an institution maintained by the government in order to protect migrant newcomers to the city. It was the beginning of the 1970s, a time in which there was a great exodus from the rural parts of Brazil.

On Sunday mornings we walked for more than 30 minutes in order to assist in the celebration of mass, presided over by a priest who was a friend of ours, after which we would facilitate some activities for the children. Basically, we would play with them. When we arrived, we found the children's faces pressed to the gate, waiting for us anxiously, a yearning that would turn to smiles and shouts when we arrived. We would not do many things beyond playing, and giving and receiving affection. Our group did not have, as we say today, a social or political conscience.

It was difficult for me to explain that gratifying experience, which was the only thing that would make me wake up early without complaining every Sunday. Years later, I would explain that experience as an experience of grace born in the encounter with the other, in a "face-to-face" relationship.

At the same time that I was experiencing grace in relation to the gratitude with those children and with other young members of the group on Sunday, I was living, during the week, in a world ruled by a totally different logic. As the oldest son in a family of Korean immigrants, I began to work very early in my family's small business. I began as a translator for my father, who was not fluent in Portuguese, and slowly I took on more responsibilities. When I was 18 years old, I was already managing part of the business and various administrative activities.

When you are responsible for the operational parts of a business, especially when your family depends on that business, you learn that good words do not solve concrete problems. When there are bills to pay, there is no point in trying to seek refuge in poetry, in daydreams about the future, the meaning of human existence and of the universe, or to critique the injustices of the world; it is necessary to arrange money to pay the bills.

It was an experience both contradictory and complementary. I was living in the "cold" and calculating world of business, having responsibilities with defined dates and numbers, and at the same time, I was experiencing the mystery of gratitude, of the face-to-face encounter with the Other, who is revealed in the face of a poor child. It is clear that at that time I did not succeed in making a satisfactory synthesis. I was living in two parallel "worlds," but with little understanding (to put it bluntly) that experiences as outstanding as that of grace are fundamental for giving meaning and joy to our lives, although they are not sufficient to pay our bills, that is, in order to reproduce our concrete and immediate lives. It was a lesson more unconscious than conscious, but, in any case, it was a process of training that profoundly marked my way of seeing the world.

Later, I was better able to explain this tension with the theological concept (or mystery) of the incarnation, the God who became incarnate, or of the grace of God within the limits of human history.

Theological Lessons in the School of Business Administration

As a "natural" extension of my professional activities, I enrolled in the school of business administration in a public university marked by the positivist anticlerical tradition and with an outstanding presence of Marxists in the student body. It was my first experience of an environment where religious arguments were not only not accepted, but despised.

Whoever does not understand that area of the economic and administrative sciences is accustomed to think that there is no fundamental difference between economics and business administration. But, in my opinion, there is a fundamental difference: their postures toward the scientific method and reality.

On the one hand, economists have, as the object of analysis, the economy, which is an abstract concept or a macrosocial reality. Therefore, the theoretical work—and, through that, their academic formation—is fundamentally bibliographic and focused on the analysis of economic data based on mathematical models. This is why economics claims to be the most "exact" of the human and social sciences.

As the object studied is an abstraction of reality or a macro-reality, feedback has a small role, or at least not an immediate one, within the theoretical system. That is, if the "economic reality" appears not to act in accordance with the theory, economists can offer more diverse interpretations of the subject, from denying the reality itself (which, basically, is also the fruit of an organization and interpretation of data) to saying that the anticipated result will occur in the near future. In this way, they can maintain for a longer period of time the truth and self-sufficiency of their economic theories or beliefs.

On the other hand, a business administrator works with an object more concrete and of an infinitely smaller scale, a business. The administrator must show concrete results on the balance sheet every three months or year and on reports to the shareholders. Feedback is more rapid and bears much greater powers of persuasion: the dismissal or promotion of the executive, the success or failure of the business. Being thus, the administrators, even their theoreticians, are not so attached to the "scientific-ness" of their theories and are much more open to dialogue with other sciences or branches of knowledge. An administrator with minimal practical experience knows that the business cannot function like a machine, as it is composed fundamentally of people, with their cultural mechanisms, and also knows that consumers don't function as "economic man" (a purely rational being, motivated by the calculus of cost and benefit), as many economists believe. Therefore, "the science of administration" is not seen by many as a science, in classical terms, since it is formed by a collection of sciences; like economics, mathematics, psychology, sociology, accounting, and, as it will likely remain, administration *theory*.

I digress over this difference between economics and administration in order to emphasize the importance for my theological reflection of this interdisciplinary experience I had in the school of administration. Today, I believe that the transdisciplinary is a more satisfactory approach than the interdisciplinary.

Beyond that epistemological posture, two other lessons from the administration courses were important in the formation of my theological thinking. They came from the course on marketing. In the first class, the professor justified the relevance of his course by saying that the marketing department is the most important part of a business because it determines what and how much a business must produce. For that, one does market research and consults socioeconomic classes A, B, and C in order to discover the preferences and desires of consumers. If the business sells products more cheaply, it must also inquire about the upper part of class D. The lower part of class D and class E are not consulted because they do not exist in the market, that is, they are outside the consumer market. Today we call them "the excluded."

Capitalism is an economic and social system based on the free market, that is, a system where the absolute majority of economic agents belong to private initiative and produce for the market, within the laws of supply and demand. That implies that the demands of those outside the market are not captured by those investigations, and therefore will not be answered by the market.

Clearly, when I had that lesson I did not draw all those conclusions. The professor's argument seemed logical to me and I continued to find it logical within the rationality of the market, but, at the same time, something was telling me that it was not quite correct. I was going to need several years in order to understand the reason for that paradox.

One other lesson was about the diverse aspects of a commodity. Another professor of marketing taught us that a product for sale has four aspects: (a) the product in itself; (b) its use; (c) what the consumer thinks about the product; and (d) what others come to think of him or her, the consumer, possessing this product. He concluded the lesson by saying that the most important aspects are not (a) or (b), as many might think, but (c) and (d). I was grasping that the economy, the production and commercialization of material goods, was not a merely material problem, but was profoundly symbolic and, in a certain sense, spiritual.

Philosophy and Crisis

I abandoned my study of business administration in the third year and decided to become a priest. I had much interest in religious and theological subjects, and people I knew indicated to me that the seminary was a natural course for me. In that time, the shape of lay theology was not well known in Brazil, much less in my circles. When I discovered that it was possible to be a theologian without necessarily being a priest, I left the seminary and continued my theological studies as a layman.

As a Catholic seminarian, I studied philosophy before moving onto theology. My contact with logical reasoning and the critique of philosophies marked me profoundly. I was thrilled with the arguments but also had to put up with the crisis that these arguments were provoking in me, principally in my religious beliefs. My world was collapsing. The religious beliefs that had led me to the seminary were coming undone, like bubbles that could not sustain contact with the hardness, the materiality, of the reality represented by the logical and critical modes. But, at the same time, I could not simply deny those theories, as if they had no value or consistency. I recognized in them something true and honest.

I survived these theoretical-existential crises with two fundamental lessons for myself. The first is: the foundation stone of our faith cannot simply be a belief or doctrine assimilated through a catechetical process, but the spiritual experience of grace that must impress upon the most profound part of our being. Only this experience can tolerate and defeat the theoretical, existential, ecclesial, and other crises that all committed Christians face. The second lesson happened as part of the first: in the face of questions and critiques, some justified and others not, we need to learn to offer explanations if not rational, since faith always transcends reason, at least reasonable. That is, explanations that can be understood and accepted as rational and good, even by those who do not share in our faith, because they have not had the same experience as us, or having experienced it explain it in a different way because they belong to other spiritual and/or cultural traditions.

In a modern pluralistic world like ours (without entering into a discussion here about postmodernity or hypermodernity), those reasonable explanations are also important for us Christians. We should not articulate the reason for our hope and faith, with gentleness and respect, only for those who question us, but also for ourselves.

Beyond that contact with the rigor of philosophical thought, contact with Marxism was another great lesson of my philosophy course. Studying Marx and other Marxists, like Gramsci, I discovered that poverty has more profound and invisible structural causes. History was no longer for me the unfolding of God's omnipotent will, but the result of human action, of conflicts between groups' interests and social classes. Poverty stopped being to me a cross imposed by God for the salvation of souls. So, overcoming poverty would not come from prayers or the conversion of hearts, but from structural transformations in society. I was beginning to be freed from a sacrificial vision of God.

The discovery of those ideas revolutionized my mind and prepared me to assimilate the concept of "the option for the poor" of liberation theology, which I would study with passion in the department of theology. Nevertheless, I was gradually facing a very serious theological problem: if poverty has resulted from conflicts of interests of social classes within history and if the liberation of the poor will come with the structural transformation of society brought about by popular movements then what is the role of God's action in human history? How and for what has God revealed God's self in history?

"Dialogue" with Authors Who Have Influenced Me

I make no claim to respond to those questions as I am fully conscious that I am not capable of that. I present them because they are questions that often accompany my reflection, like "background noise," and always end up resurfacing in my texts.

This explanation complete, deterring the reader from seeking out answers to such questions in this work, I want to present briefly the principle influences in my formation process. I know that to present, in a short chapter, a list like this is always dangerous because invariably we do injustice to many people. However, in an exercise like this we have a rare opportunity to pay homage to thinkers that influence us in a special way.

Enrique Dussel

The first author whose thought I studied systematically was Enrique Dussel. His reflections on "totality," "exteriority," and "alterity" were fundamental for my first steps into theological reflection. Having been trained in his books on ethics and philosophy, those concepts served as a base so that I could give a "reasonable" explanation of my faith, an explanation based in the "face-to-face" experience with poor children in my youth and with other poor persons in the course of my study of theology. They are concepts that allow me to introduce the faith in God who reveals God's self in the faces and outcries of the poor, as the Bible teaches us, in a reasonable way to my interlocutors, whether they are Christian or not, believers or not.

Beyond those fundamental concepts, Dussel marked in a special way the path of my theological reflection with an article that I regard as one of the most important in the history of liberation theology: "The Bread of the Eucharistic Celebration as a Sign of Justice in the Community."[1] In that text he introduces in a clear and didactic way the intrinsic relation between the economy (the production and circulation of the goods necessary for the reproduction of life) and the celebration of the Eucharist. Studying this article, I had the conviction that one cannot do theology without taking into consideration the economy and I moved my studies more firmly in the direction of what today one calls "theology and economics."

Franz Hinkelammert

One of the principle names in theology and economics is Franz Hinkelammert. His book *The Ideological Weapons of Death* is a landmark in reflections on theology and economics.[2] In that book, he showed how fetishism marks the spirit of the institutions and analyzed brilliantly the fetishism of the market, money, and capital in capitalist societies. Gilberto Gorgulho (who was my professor when he introduced me to Hinkelammert's work), referring to that book, wrote:

> The understanding of the reality of 'fetish' in the dynamism of society marked a new beginning for reflection. Theology has the job of discerning between 'fetish' and 'Spirit'. In that way,

the act of theology is an act of discernment or spiritual appropriation as much of the text as of praxis in order to penetrate more deeply both into the mechanisms of death and domination and the power of the resurrection and the full life of God's people in the world. Hermeneutics is a discernment of the ideological weapons of death and a search for the power of the Spirit of life (cf. 1 Jn 4).[3]

After the conclusion of my master's in theology (with the thesis *The Idolatry of Capital and the Death of the Poor: A Theological Reflection on External Debt*[4]) I spent a semester at the Ecumenical Department of Research (DEI—Departamento Ecuménico de Investigaciones) studying with Hinkelammert and Pablo Richard in the "Formation of New Researchers" program.[5] There I was able to go deeper into a central concept in Hinkelammert's thought: "utopian reason."[6] I learned that utopian reason is a capacity that enables us to visualize an intervention and transformation, but that as a limit concept its realization is impossible. This applies to the concept of the perfectly free market for liberals, the perfect planning of the Soviets, and even the Kingdom of God in the world for Christians. That is, it is impossible to construct a society with a totally free market without any social regulation, a society with no market as radical socialists claim, or a society without any domination, oppression, or inequality as many Christians demand. I learned that sacrificialism is born when a group or institution presents itself as the effective way to that utopia.

While I was going deeper into the critique of the sacrificialism of the neoliberal market, I also learned that the recognition of human limits or of the historical nonrealizability of our utopias was a demand of common sense and, more importantly, a condition for social and political action on behalf of the poor and oppressed. Only when we stop demanding the realization of the impossible (the utopia) are we able to struggle to realize the best possible (viable historical projects). To avoid misunderstanding: I do not want to say that we must give up our utopias, as utopias are like horizons that give meaning to our struggles, but that we must give up the desire to construct historically those utopias. It is fundamental that we differentiate the utopia (the horizon) from the historical or institutional project.

That theory helped me to synthesize the experience of grace and the world of concrete business operations, the tension that I had experienced in my youth, and allowed me to open my horizon towards the eschatological hope based on faith in the resurrection of Jesus. The utopian dream and desire for a fully fraternal world is not abandoned, but expected as the gift of God in the Parousia. In this way, eschatological hope does not become disassociated from "historical reason," nor do social and political struggles close off eschatological hope.

Júlio de Santa Ana

I ended my period of study at DEI with a question: Why have well-known sectors of liberation theology not entered into the discussion concerning economics as a logical step of its option for the poor? Many pages were written in order to say that the poor in question were not "poor in spirit," but poor in the ordinary sense of the word; that is, economically poor. The liberation sought would necessarily pass through the economic question. That question was the object of research in my doctoral dissertation, in the religious studies program at the Methodist University of São Paulo, under the direction of Professor Júlio de Santa Ana (a Uruguayan Methodist).

In my dissertation—which was published with the title *Theology and the Economy: Rethinking Liberation Theology and Utopias* in Brazilian and Spanish editions,[7] and in Costa Rica with a different title, *The Economy: The Missing Theme in Liberation Theology*[8]—I tried to critique liberation theology beginning with its own fundamental epistemological principles. I believed that my contribution was in the direction of showing that the near absence of reflection on the economy in many of the books of liberation theology has to do with the difficult epistemological question of the place of theology in the modern world, and in particular in the dialogue between theology and the social sciences. One other important point was to try to show that the transcendental illusion of the modern world (the illusion that one can construct utopias) has not been properly critiqued by various liberation theologians, who, therefore, ended up reproducing some of the mistakes resulting from that illusion in their reflections on "the construction of the Kingdom of God."

In the elaboration of that thesis, I learned many things from my director. Among them, I want to highlight two points. Júlio de Santa Ana surprised me one day with an affirmation that upset me. He told me that liberation theology, which had become excessively Catholic, was no longer dealing with God as a theology must do, but was basically preoccupied with the church. The principle projects had as their object the life of and in the church, whether in its "dispute" with the Vatican, or around base communities. At first, I was perplexed, but later agreed with him. The second great lesson was to understand theology not as a "scientific" discourse about God, but as a "hermeneutic of history."

At first glance those two ideas can seem contradictory, but they are not. St. Thomas Aquinas had already said that we know more what God is not than what God is. In that sense, we must, especially after the consistent critiques of the pretensions of human reason by diverse modern and postmodern thinkers, recognize that we cannot know God *in se*. But, at the same time, theology cannot lose its specificity and identity as theory and dissolve amid so many human and social sciences that claim to analyze and interpret human and social reality. To do theology as a hermeneutic of history is to try to understand the dynamic of human history, the functioning of societies and interpersonal relations, in view of the God who reveals God's self in the "historical memory of the poor" (Pablo Richard) preserved in the Bible.

Hugo Assmann

A significant example of this way of understanding theology is found in the book *The Idolatry of the Market* by Hugo Assmann and Franz Hinkelammert.[9] In that book, Assmann critiques theologically the rendering of the market as an idol, which occurs in liberal and neoliberal economic theories. I believe that it is opportune to reaffirm here that Assmann, as well as Hinkelammert or Júlio de Santa Ana, do not critique the market as such, as many people mistakenly hold. They do not propose a society without commercial relations, as this is impossible in modern and complex societies. What they critique is the absolutization of the market and the faith that the market will always produce beneficial nonintentional effects for society, from which arises a demand for the sacrifice of human lives (in economic terms, "social costs") in the name of the laws of the market. The idol is the human institution elevated to the category of the absolute that demands the sacrifice of human lives.

Beginning with the recognition of the impossibility of doing away with the market or with social goals and plans and the critique of the idolatry of the market, Assmann has offered diverse themes for reflection that have marked me in recent years. I want only to present two so that the reader may have some idea of my present preoccupations.

First is the critique of the anthropological optimism of leftists, including Christians committed to the poor. Often the Left does not take into consideration that human beings are capable of solidarity, but also are egoistic; they are often motivated by conflicting interests and are beings of desire and necessity. All this signifies that in the same way after "the" revolution, people are not going to be totally in solidarity, nor will they be free of the desires that are beyond social or historical possibility.

To what point is the human being capable of solidarity with people and social groups that are outside of one's circle of

relationships? How can we institutionalize the "spirit of solidarity" so that it functions in an efficient way in a complex
society, in a globalized world? These are some serious questions that we must face. And yet, if we add to all this the fact
that our actions always produce unintended effects, it is easy
to conclude that it is humanly impossible to construct a society
without suffering, injustice, or domination.

The second theme is linked to what today is known as the
theory or paradigm of complexity. Concepts such as self-
organization, self-regulation, autopoiesis, dissipative structures
(which come from new theories of biology, chemistry, and
physics), or themes like system and environmental relations,
the hologramatic principle, the brain-mind relation, and many
others have profoundly transformed not only the natural sciences but also the human and social sciences. Assmann has
worked with those concepts and themes from within his main
present preoccupation, the field of education, but has not lost
opportunities to make a point concerning theology and the
economy.

Those concepts and themes have in themselves and at the
same time bring about a new idea concerning life, as much
biological as human and social. And we must not forget that
one of the key ideas of Latin American liberation theology is
the notion that our God is the God of Life. Theologies of liberation up to now have placed the emphasis on the first part
of the expression, the notion of God; perhaps it is time that
we explore more attentively the notion of "life" for an understanding more realistic and useful for our political, social, and
ecclesial practices in favor of the life of the poor.

Juan Luis Segundo

Continuing from Assmann's preoccupation with the education
process (a fundamental theme in the present society based in
knowledge), I want to say something about Juan Luis Segundo.

Of the many lessons that I have learned from his work, I want to cite here a small text that was fundamental for consolidating my option for this form of doing theology, which I am, in a fragmentary way, presenting: "The 'divine revelation' is not a deposit of correct information, but a true pedagogical process. . . . It is a 'process,' a growth of humanity, and in it man does not learn 'things'. He learns to learn."[10]

If God's revelation is a pedagogical process, then theology cannot be the systematization of truths formulated a priori, whether about God *in se* or the process of the liberation of the poor. Instead of that, it must be a critical discernment of the processes of the creation of idols, whether within religions and Churches or in economics or politics, and a reflection that is going to signal and make possible better readings of the humanization processes that occur in diverse spaces of our lives and societies. In other words, it must be a hermeneutic of history.

René Girard

When I was still working on my doctoral thesis, I received an invitation from Hugo Assmann that was another landmark in my life. The invitation was to participate in a dialogue with René Girard and some liberation theologians around the theme of sacrificialism. Of course, I immediately accepted. I was already working on a critique of the sacrificialism of the market and also knew the work of Girard. That encounter was in the city of Piracicaba, in the state of São Paulo, from July 25–29 in 1990, and participating, among others, were Leonardo Boff, Hugo Assmann, Júlio de Santa Ana, Franz Hinkelammert, and Gilberto Gorgulho. Needless to say, it was a magnificent week in all senses.

Some years later, during the examination for my doctoral thesis, I don't remember very well if it was Hugo Assmann or Júlio de Santa Ana, but one of the two asked me about my future theoretical projects. I answered that I had long wished to compare and, if possible, synthesize the theories of sacrificialism of Girard and Hinkelammert.

I think that Girard's theories concerning the relation between violence and the sacred, which becomes more visible in sacrifice, and his explanations rooted in mimetic desire are really very stimulating. In one of my terms at DEI, I began to articulate those questions with a theory already defended many times by Celso Furtado. For him, one of the fundamental reasons for the social dualism and exclusion that exist in Latin America is the desire of our elites to imitate the patterns of consumption of the elites in rich countries. That mimetic desire is not only the cause of social dualism, the concentration of income, and social exclusion but also impedes the effort to overcome poverty in our countries. On the other hand, for Friedrich A. von Hayek, the "pope" of neoliberalism, that desire to imitate consumption is the engine of economic growth. These are two apparently contradictory positions, but which are actually complementary. In truth, the imitation of consumption patterns has generated in Latin America exclusive economic growth and concentrated wealth.

It is necessary to be clear that in a consumer society like ours the pressure to consume more and more is not merely a problem of "materialism," in the sense that people are judged and located in society according to their patterns of consumption. Personal identity is today profoundly linked to consumption. In order to be recognized as *being* it is necessary *to have* certain consumer goods. When someone looks to consume in the same market where the "models" of society consume, one is not simply looking to have something but is looking "to be" someone.

This theme of mimetic desire in consumption has also appeared in important documents and studies regarding ecological and social crises all over the world. There is an emerging consensus among critics of the current economic model that this pattern of consumption is threatening the environment and generating social crises. And therefore it is urgent that one move away from the current pattern of consumption and break this process of imitation.

The current process of mimetic desire in consumption leads to sacrifices of human life and, at the same time, to speak of a change in desire is to approach the field of spirituality. These are fundamental theological questions. It falls to theology to make its contribution to this debate that is occurring on many and diverse levels around the world.

One partial result of these investigations of mine was published in my more recent book, *Desire, Market, and Religion*.[11] I believe that the articulation between theology, economics, and anthropology (with the theme of desire) is the most original contribution among my published works.

Why do Theology?

Initially I thought about placing in this last section a summary of my current preoccupations and investigative projects. I see, however, that I have already presented them in the course of my recollections. It is an account that was good for me. I ended up returning to some places in my memory that were forgotten.

I uncovered (do you think?) why I continue doing theology in spite of all the struggles of the Left in Latin America and in the world, growing levels of social exclusion, and churches more preoccupied with increasing the numbers of their followers and focusing less and less on serious theological reflection and social involvement and on prophetic commitment with the "least of these" (cf. Mt 25). I think that I continue doing theology because of the faces of the poor children pressed to the gate hoping for people who will love them freely, worry about their problems, and help them overcome or diminish their sufferings.

Only that those sufferings are many. Those and many other sufferings have their origins in the insensibility of people, in the lack of public officials seriously committed to the poor, in the lack of education appropriate for our technological and cultural standards, in programs of economic adjustments imposed by international economic organizations, in the current form of economic globalization, in the desires of people who want to consume more and more. It is clear that theology will never have the answers for all these questions, but I firmly believe that if Christianity, as a religious and spiritual tradition, is not able to offer its specific contribution to minimize the sufferings of "the least," it will lose the true spirit that moves it and opens it toward the great horizon of the Kingdom of God and will survive only through "social inertia."

And that contribution must be "reasonable," it must be comprehensible and believable to those who do not share in our faith. This is the task of theology.

CHAPTER 2

The Subject and the Defense of the Life of the Victims

If the historical situation of dependence and domination of two thirds of humankind, with its 30 million dead from hunger and malnutrition each year, does not become the point of departure of any Christian theology today, even in the rich and dominant countries, theology will not be able to situate and concretize historically its fundamental themes. Its questions will not be real questions. It will pass by the real person. Therefore, as one participant observed at the meeting in Buenos Aires, "it is necessary to save theology from its cynicism." Because really, facing the problems of today's world, many theological writings are reduced to cynicism.[1]

Theology and Ethical Indignation

At the beginning of the 1970s, a group of Latin American theologians presented to the world and to the Christian churches a theology with two epistemological novelties: a new methodology and the perspective of the poor. This theology received, as we know, the name liberation theology. In this current moment of profound crisis for this theology, I think that the essence of the theological proposal was not and is not its name, nor the historical objective present in the name: the *liberation* of the poor. Rather, those two epistemological novelties are the key.

From the beginning, liberation theologians have made it
very clear that the theology of liberation was and is a second
moment. The first moment is the *praxis* of liberation that grows
out of ethical indignation in the face of situations in which
human beings are reduced to a subhuman condition. Ethical
indignation, strong enough to lead people to assume the risks
and pains of others, was understood as a spiritual experience:
the encountering of the person of Jesus Christ in the faces of
the crushed and oppressed.

This intrinsic relation between liberation theology and
praxis was seen as one of the fundamental differences between
liberation theology and other theologies. Clearly, it was recognized that traditional theologies also propose a relation with
Christian practice. But, as Assmann said, "The fundamental
structures of traditional theological language are not historical. Its determinant categories seek to establish truth in itself,
without the intrinsic connection with praxis. Praxis is seen as
something happening later, as the 'application' of pre-existing
'truth' to reality."[2]

I think that rescuing or recalling this fundamental and original intuition of liberation theology is fundamental, since we
are frequently tempted to seek only in books (even if it is the
"Sacred Book") or in "fashionable" theories some truth prior to
or disassociated from the concrete problems of praxis that can
illuminate for us and help us overcome the crisis into which
Latin American theology is now plunged. In other words, liberation theology cannot desire to resolve its difficulties through
analyses and/or deductions from the concept of God or from
some other concept, but in beginning with the experiences of
God within history and through the critical analysis of the
concepts with which we interpret those experiences.

To propose to do a theology linked intrinsically to praxis
does not mean abandoning the rigor of thought, quite to
the contrary. According to Gustavo Gutiérrez, for example,
this theology must be, "a critical reflection on humankind,

on basic human principles" with "a clear and critical attitude regarding economic and sociocultural issues in the life and reflection of the Christian community" so that in this way it is necessarily "a criticism of society and the Church insofar as they are called and addressed by the Word of God."[3] In this sense, he was saying that theology carries out its liberative function relative to the human being and the Christian community to the extent that it preserves them "from fetishism and idolatry."[4]

To speak of this intrinsic relation between the praxis of liberation and liberation theology can seem somewhat "out of fashion" as few still use the expression "praxis of liberation" or even "the liberation of the poor." The collapse of the socialist bloc, the crisis of popular movements in Latin America, the daily bombardment in the media of the announcement that there is no escape from or alternative to the capitalist market system, and the desire to imitate the success of "religious spectacles" seems to have buried forever these expressions. Certainly, we must recognize that there was an exaggerated expectation regarding the liberation of the poor, a point to which we shall later return. However, the first moment of liberation theology was never this expectation; or, at least, it was not that to which theologians were referring. The first moment was always the practice of what was at that time called liberation, which grew out of the spiritual experience of encountering Jesus Christ in the faces of the oppressed. In other words, the first moment was and is the service of the defense of the life and dignity of the poor and the victim. In the 1970s and 1980s, this service was seen and labeled as the praxis of liberation, however, this labeling does not exhaust the richness and the possibilities that can arise from that experience, and neither is there a single way to interpret this expression. In the words of Gutiérrez, "theology is reflection, a critical attitude"; first, there is *real charity, action, and commitment* to the service of others," and "theology *follows*, it is the second step."[5]

This estrangement in relation to the "languages of libera-tion" shows us that we live in an era very different from the 1970s and 1980s. Moreover, it reveals to us the insufficiency of the "traditional" language of liberation theology for interpret-ing and expressing the faith experiences of people, who today feel ethical indignation in the face of the massive social exclu-sion of certain groups, of other forms of human oppression, and with the destruction of the environment. At the end of the 1960s, the era in which liberation theology was gestating, Rubem Alves, in *A Theology of Human Hope*, says that

> man's language is a mirror of his historicity. It not only emerges out of the metabolism which goes on between him and his world but is uttered as a response to the concrete situations in which he finds himself.... It contains *man's interpretation* of the message and challenge that his world addresses to him and expresses *man's response* to this message and challenge. It tells from within, through his eyes, how he understands himself in this world, what he believes to be his vocation, place, possibili-ties, direction, and function in his world.[6]

Further, "the appearance of a new language announces, there-fore, the coming into being of a new experience, a new self-understanding, a new vocation, and, consequently, a different man and community, a new subject."[7] Liberation theology was this new discourse of an emerging self-understanding on the part of the Christian community in Latin America and the world. However, we experience today a certain exhaustion of this language in the form in which it was constructed in the 1970s.

I particularly believe that it is possible to renew this lan-guage, since some of the structural problems of liberation the-ology have been resolved.[8] However, I also think that most important is not the "survival" of liberation theology, but the continuity of the theological production that reflects critically on the practice of the charity and service born of the ethical indignation in the face of situations and logics that reduce the human being to a subhuman condition, and which for that maintains the perspective of the victims in doing its theology. That is, more important is the formulation of religious and theological languages that make possible a better expression and critical understanding of the experience of faith, ethical indignation, and commitment to the defense of the life of the victims.

For that, we must accept the permanent challenge of critically reflecting on our presuppositions and concepts. In this text I want to contribute to this task with a few considerations of the concept of the "historical subject" that was always associated with the liberation of the poor.

Ethical Indignation and the Subject

The founding experience that liberation theology calls the first moment is, as we saw, ethical indignation. However grave the social problem, not everyone feels this ethical indignation. There are those who do not feel this indignation because they no longer encounter the victims, or simply because the victims are outside their field of vision, or because they no longer consider them persons. There are also those who are uncomfortable at the sight of the suffering of the victims, but for whom that discomfort does not become ethical indignation, and with the passing of time they forget.

What happens when someone feels this ethical indignation? It is clear that it is impossible to answer this question fully. Each experience is different from another and presupposes the worlds and histories of the people involved. However, I want to point out two aspects for our reflection.

So that a person may be indignant in the face of a situation in which someone is being treated or reduced to a subhuman condition it is necessary that the person recognize the humanity of the other. Without this recognition there is no ethical indignation since no one is indignant in the face of the situation in which a subhuman being is being treated as a subhuman. Many people are not indignant in the face of these situations because they do not "see" or recognize the humanity of these people.

This difficulty in recognizing the humanity of the victims in these situations has to do with the difficulty in differentiating the social location and role of these people from their dignity as human beings. More and more, people confuse human dignity with social location. In a consumer culture, the pattern of consumption is the determining factor in the definition of identity and in recognizing the dignity of individuals. Nonconsumers are seen as nonpersons. The lower the place one occupies in the socioeconomic hierarchy, the less human one is. There is, in ethical indignation, the recognition of the humanity of people apart from their social role or location. People are freely recognized, that is, recognized as human, independent of their capacity to consume and their social condition, sex, ethnicity, religion, and more. In the extreme case, for example, if in our society we encounter an individual who is poor, black, a woman, a lesbian, a prostitute, AIDS-infected, disabled, ugly, and old, and can still see a human being with her fundamental dignity, then we can truly be said to have had a spiritual experience of grace (recognizing freely, beyond all social convention) and faith (seeing what is invisible to the "eyes of the world").

In our society, which is marked by the unfettered search for success as a way to "justify" human existence, such gratuitous recognition between subjects in the subject-to-subject, "face-to-face," relation is truly a spiritual experience of grace and justification by faith. It is an experience that justifies the existence not only of the oppressed person, but also the person who feels the indignation. This is why this experience is perceived as liberating as much for the one who feels the indignation as for the one who is the victim and is recognized as a person. That is why the experience of ethical indignation that leads to social commitment was and must be interpreted as a truly spiritual experience.

A second important aspect is the utopian horizon of desire that is presupposed in ethical indignation. It is the utopian horizon of a reality where people are recognized and respected independently of their social condition that makes us see the real situation as ethically unacceptable and as a situation that must be transformed. Without this desire for a distinct world we would not feel the indignation. At the same time, it is the indignation that makes us "see" this utopian horizon.

Initially, this horizon appears to us as a utopian vision, that is, as the dream of a world free of all forms of oppression and objectification of the human being. Then, this dream is developed and is presented to us as a "project" for a new human society. Sometimes, in Christian environments, it is presented as "God's project."

To the extent that this horizon (imaginative or "utopian project") is what permits us to understand the present reality as unacceptable and malleable and is, at the same time, an object of desire, we start to believe—because we desire it—that it is possible to fully realize this project within history. From the desire that it be possible, we start to believe that it is possible. And, sometimes, desire leads us to believe that not only is it possible, but that it is also inevitable.

And in believing that it is realizable, we are faced with the need for a subject that realizes or "constructs" this horizon/project within history. Here appears the use of such concepts as "historical subject," "subjects of history," and "protagonist of history."

These two aspects of ethical indignation, these complementary and intrinsically related aspects, present us with two notions or facets of the subject: (a) the subject who is recognized and recognizes itself beyond all social roles and locations; and (b) the subject constructing or realizing fully the utopian horizon or project for a totally new society, a new world, and a new human being.

I want here to set out some reflections on this concept of the subject.

The Historical Subject and the Human Condition

The concept of the historical subject so profoundly marked liberation theology and the Christian communities committed to the life of the poor that when this concept entered into crisis, beginning with the fall of the socialist bloc, several attempts to rescue it appeared. Perhaps the most common form of this was the use of the expression "new historical subjects" or "new emergent subjects." Recognizing the crisis of the concept of the historical subject, which had referred to the working class or the poor, many presented other social groups (like women, blacks, indigenous...) as new subjects. With that, they retained the concept of the historical subject, and only modified the concrete definition of who is this subject.

Another form of trying to preserve this concept came from the dialogue with new theories in physics. Frei Betto, one of the most influential people of the Latin American Christian Left, is one of the authors following this line. He, for example, in his article "Indetermination and Complementarity," proposes a dialogue with quantum physics so that we might formulate new paradigms to see beyond the crisis of utopias.[9] And in the final part of the article, which has a meaningful subtitle "The Quantum Rescue of the Historical Subject," he implies that this subject has the mission of "confronting the great challenge of ensuring that capital—in the form of money, technology, and knowledge—is at the service of human happiness, breaking the barriers of racial, social, ethnic, and religious discrimination. Then, we will rediscover the paths that lead to the Garden of Eden."

We do not want to discuss here whether we are really witnessing the crisis of utopias or the victory of one utopia—capitalism—over others; or whether it is possible for the human being to arrive at the Garden of Eden, that is, to construct a fully paradisiacal and just society; or even whether the theories of quantum physics can be transposed so directly to the sphere of human and social relations. What we want to call attention to with this text is the weight and the importance of the concept of the historical subject in the modern tradition, particularly among Latin American Christians committed to the liberation of the poor.

The modern concept of the historical subject has its roots in the Judeo-Christian tradition that elaborated a notion of God as "the subject of history," as a God who is outside history and the world and directing or determining it. The transcendent God, who is beyond the limits of the human world, was seen as the subject, and history was seen as the object of God's will and action. The modern world substituted this notion of God as the subject of history with the notion of the human being as the subject of history. Secularization, in this sense, can be understood as a process of disenchantment of the world and the reenchantment of the human being. Modernity takes from God the image of the subject and transfers it to the human being. In this sense, Alain Touraine says: "In entering into Modernity, religion explodes, but its components do not disappear. *The subject, ceasing to be divine, or to be defined as Reason, becomes human, personal*, becomes a certain kind of relation of the individual or group to themselves," and that the "subject of modernity is none other than the secularized descendent of the subject of religion."[10]

With this profound transformation and veritable anthropological revolution, history comes to be seen as an object in relation to the human being. In the construction of the concept of the subject of history there occurs, at the same time, the construction of the concept of history as the object to be constructed by the human subject. In the earliest days of the human race, the notion of destiny written by gods or spirits of nature predominated, there still being no notion of history. With time appeared the notion of moral evil, sin, and with that the notion of human liberty, giving rise to the notion of history. The Old Testament is an example of this cultural rupture, of the vision of history as a tension between divine and human will. However, for the most part, human history was seen as defined by gods or by reason. With modernity arose this novelty: the perception of history as being constructed by human subjects.

Agnes Heller says that with the Renaissance arose a dynamic concept of humankind and the notion of a history of personal development and the development of society. And, with that, "the relation between the individual and the situation becomes fluid: the past, present, and future are transformed into human creations. This 'humanity,' however, constitutes a generalized and homogenous concept. It is in this moment, that 'liberty' and 'fraternity' arise as inherent ontological categories. Time and space are humanized, the infinite is transformed into a social reality."[11]

In the construction of history by the modern human subject, reason plays a central role. The individual becomes a subject to the extent that he or she creates a world regulated by rational laws and intelligible to human thought. This creation of a rational world is seen as the realization of the progress that would lead us to "the Garden of Eden." God, the organizer of the world and of history, is substituted by the human subject, the organizer of the world and history according to reason.

Not only do the concepts of the human being, the subject, and history change, but also the "localization" of Paradise, the utopian horizon. The historical subject is the constructor of the history that must lead to plentitude. The medieval Paradise, which was expected beyond human history, is placed within history, in the future. There is a process to making medieval eschatology immanent. The human subject "constructs" history, "ordains" it, so that through progress we move beyond all human and social contradictions to full harmony between human beings and nature. What Marx called the construction of the realm of freedom many Christians called the *construction* of the Kingdom of God.

I think that the insistence to maintain, recover, or reform the concept of the "historical subject" without questioning its presuppositions has everything to do with this profound desire to see realized within our history this utopian horizon.

Authors like Franz Hinkelammert and Hugo Assmann have already written many texts criticizing this "transcendental illusion": the belief that it is possible with finite human actions to construct a perfect world, which presupposes infinite knowledge, time, and space. This illusion is at the heart of the project of the perfect market of neoliberalism, the perfect planning of Soviet model of socialism, and even of many projects "to construct the Kingdom of God." The problem with that illusion is not reducible to theory, this illusion generates systemic sacrifices: social systems and institutions demand the sacrifice of human lives as "the necessary cost" to attain "Paradise," the "redemption" of history and humanity.

Beyond this "transcendental illusion" and the resulting sacrificialism, there is an underlying theological problem that we are going to treat briefly. The notion of God that at the beginning, and, in a certain way, continues underlying the notion of the human being as the subject of history, is a notion of God as the organizer of the world and history. All plentitude, any fully harmonious social or natural order, is understood as an order free of evil and conflict.

Western thought, or a good part of it, is influenced by one of the important characteristics of Greek philosophy: the search for God as the foundation of order. In this perspective, Greek philosophy thought that the human being would realize its destiny to the extent that it occupied its place in the cosmic order, submitting itself to the universal order established and moved by God. However, ethical indignation is not an indignation that arises because of one's awareness that one's "destiny" or the preestablished order is unrealized. Ethical indignation—and

here I want to emphasize the ethical character of indignation—
arises from the recognition of the humanity of the person that
is being denied in a relationship and/or social system. It is
from the "face-to-face" experience that the contestation of the
injustices and the evils of the world arise. The indignation that
arises from some theory, without this basic face-to-face experience, cannot endure very long, it is forgotten or disappears in
the midst of some pragmatic rationalization.

It is from the experience of mutual recognition, from the
subject-subject relationship beyond any and all necessary institutionalization of life and society, which the conviction arises that
in this ethical indignation we experience the grace of God, who
is Love. The experience of God as Love, which can only occur
in unconditional and free relationships, cannot be explained
and systematized by philosophies or other theories that require,
by their constitution, necessarily logical relationships. The God
experienced by the people of the Bible is different from the gods
of philosophies or theologies that know only the concept of God
and seek in God the basis of the perfect order.

As José Comblin says, "In the Bible, however, everything
is different because God is love. Love does not found order,
but disorder. Love breaks any structure of order. Love founds
freedom and, consequently, disorder. Sin is the consequence of
God's love."[12] To say that God is Love is to say that the human
vocation is freedom and that we realize ourselves as human
beings living in freedom and love.

There is freedom only if it is possible that we can err. There
is love only if we are capable of forgiving the errors of beloved
persons. The perfect social order, a new society without suffering, oppression, and injustice, of perfect harmony, is not only
impossible to construct within history, but also must not be
desired. Precisely! We must not desire to construct this "perfect" social order. What we desire is *a utopian horizon* of God's
kingdom, and we must always remember that this horizon,
like any horizon, is only attainable through eyes of desire, but

cannot be obtained by our human actions. What we can and must construct is a more just, more human, more fraternal society, but which always comes with the possibility of errors and problems, intentional or not.

Christianity is not a proposal to withdraw from the world, from the contradictions and possibilities inherent to the human condition, but, on the contrary, to love our human condition and to live in freedom and love in the face of the limits of the human condition. It is the experience of the definitive and absolute within the provisional nature of human history. It is the proposal of faith in a God who emptied God's self of God's divinity to become human, to become a slave (Phil. 2:7). This is the scandal of Christianity!

I sometimes have the impression that in liberation theology, in our revalorizing of the Exodus event in Christian theology, we frequently end up overestimating historical possibilities. One of the greatest contributions of the Old Testament to the history of thought was to relocate the center of God's revelation from nature to ethical relations. That is, to pass from a conception of destiny toward the notion of human history. God was no longer sought primarily in nature, but in the relations of justice within human history. An important rupture of Christianity in relation to Judaism does not occur in the turn to nature or to destiny but in the recognition of the limits of human history. In other words: in recognizing the one defeated, crucified, and resurrected as the promised Messiah, Christianity recognizes that God does not break with the limits of history and the human condition. It recognizes that the liberation promised by God cannot exceed human freedom or the human condition, since, if it did, this liberation would not bring us freedom nor be a liberation enjoyed by human beings. Christianity is founded on the paradox of a crucified God, of a defeated liberator-Messiah, as is the proposal that we struggle for the life and dignity of the victims of dominant—that is, victorious—social systems, even if we know more defeats than victories in the political and social arenas. In other words, instead of reading the Christ event through the paradigm of the Exodus, we must read Exodus from the crucifixion and resurrection event of Jesus of Nazareth.

If these reflections have any basis, and I think that they are not totally mistaken, this obligates us to reconsider seriously the concept of the historical subject in our theology and in our social and pastoral practices.

The Subject and Self-Organization

A second problematic aspect of the notion of the historical subject is that the concept of the subject appears counterposed to history as an object. History is seen as an object to be constructed or molded by human actions. The social sciences already have for a long time criticized this underlying notion of many political and social theories. History or society is a very peculiar "object" to the extent that the subject is a part of it; that is, the subject is within the "object," history or society. At the same time, the subject is influenced or determined (depending on the stream of thought) by this same object, whether the object of study or of transformation. Therefore, the subject-object relation could no longer be applied to the field of history or society as a whole.

New concepts are acquiring strength in the fields of the social and natural sciences that question even further this notion of the historical subject, or of the subject as constructor of history. These are concepts like self-organization, self-regulation, autopoiesis, and dissipative structures that come from diverse fields of knowledge, like biology, physics, chemistry, and cybernetics, and are influencing human and social sciences.[13]

It is not the objective of this chapter to develop reflections on these new theories but to highlight some key ideas.

Hugo Assmann, in his excellent glossary that occupies the central part of the book *Re-enchanting Education*, begins the entry for "self-organization" by saying that this concept refers to the "dynamic of spontaneous emergence from patterns of order and chaos in a system due to recurring relations within the system itself and/or the interactions of the same with its environment. With the rise of these emergent qualities, complexity increases."[14] This is strange language for those not familiar with these new theories.

These concepts and theories are being used as new metaphors or as instruments of analysis of social phenomena and dynamics. However, we would do well to remember that this theory of spontaneous order is very old and has a long tradition in the history of social thought. It preceded Darwin's concept of evolution but only acquired strength in social thought beginning in the 1970s. The theory of spontaneous order is based on the notion that most things that produce general benefits in social systems or that make possible their reproduction are the fruit of the unintended effects of human actions, that is, they are not under the conscious control and direction of people or conscious plans.

This notion of self-organization or of spontaneous order poses an important question to our challenge of rethinking the notion of the subject underlying our practices in favor of the life and dignity of the victims (which were understood earlier as practices of liberation) and our theologies.

To be brief, I will cite a provocative text of Assmann's, assuming the challenges set out by him. Assmann, who in the 1970s was radically against the market, says the following:

Among the undeniable things, in the area of human interactions in complex societies, is the existence and functionality of partially self-regulating dynamic systems, in which one refers to human behaviors. In the economy, this question has a name, which was rejected by many sectors of the left until today: the market. Do we know how to join social consciousness and the ethical subject with the (partial) self-regulation of the market?

To accept, critically but positively, the market, without giving up the goals of solidarity, demands a new reflection on the very concept of the ethical subject, individual and collective. . . . It is a question of jointly considering individual ethical options and the objectification, material and institutional, of values, under the form of normatization of human conviviality with strong self-regulating connotations.[15]

In order to prevent possible misunderstandings, it is important to emphasize here a fundamental difference between the use of concepts like self-organization, self-regulation, or spontaneous order made by Assmann and by neoliberal or liberal authors, like Paul Krugman. For the latter group, the market is a spontaneous order that always produces the best results possible. Assmann, in contrast, while recognizing the existence of self-regulation in complex systems (social or natural) and their positive aspects also critiques the neoliberal's blind faith in the market that does not permit them to see the negative effects of this very process. This is why he criticized the idolatry of the market, that is, the sacralization of the market, but not the market as such.[16]

The Subject, the Social Agent, and Liberation

We saw above that the experience of the subject-subject, face-to-face relation is one of the basic aspects of the founding experience to which we are referring and comprises one of the two ways of understanding the concept of the subject in the praxis of liberation. To this point, we have considered more the notion of the subject as the constructor of history; but now we want to take up again some of the aspects of the notions of the subject that refer to the face-to-face relationship.

To speak of the subject as a subject, that is, of the subject being that we experience in the face-to-face relation, is an impossible task. So, "when one speaks of the subject, it is treated as an object even in the moment in which the subject speaks of itself. When one acts in the institutional environment, one is acting in relation to people transformed into institutional objects, even if dealing with the person designated as the superior of the entire institutional system."[17]

That does not mean that it is impossible for the subject to survive, but only that all theory and any institution is, in a way, bad theory and a bad institution because they treat the human subject as an object. However, since we cannot live without a language and without the institution, we can and must make a distinction between the concept of the subject and the social agent, the individual "living out" a social role in a given institutionalized relation. The human being, the individual, is a subject who transcends all its objectifications in language and institutions. The individual cannot live without institutions and social roles, but the subject is not the sum of these roles, much less is identified with a single role. Totalitarian systems, oppressive systems, try to deny the subjectity (the quality of being a subject) of the individual by reducing it to a social role or set of roles, objectifying it within the system.[18]

Let us take as an example the reduction of the individual to an economic agent. When the capitalist market system tells a person excluded from the market that he or she does not have the right to eat, because the individual is not a consumer (not having the money to live out the role of the consumer), the subjectity of that person is denied and is reduced to an economic role. The same occurs when a worker is treated as a mere object in the chain of production.

In the face of such situations, it is not rare to hear the poor protesting: "I am poor, but I am also a child of God!" That is, they claim to be subjects prior to any and all institutionalizations that objectify them in social roles.

The subject being is not manifest in the mundane, when we live out our social roles as citizens, spouses, professors, or consumers. The subject being is manifest in resistance to concrete forms of domination, when the individual resists being reduced to a mere social role or set of roles. This is worth as much to those who occupy a high place within the institution as those who are on a lower level.

For that resistance to be able to occur, the person must deny the legitimizing rationalizations produced by institutions.

Rationalization is irrational, since it reduces the subject to an object. Therefore, some authors, like Hinkelammert, are considering the concept of liberation not only as the anticipation of the Kingdom of God but also as the recovery of the human being as subject. In Hinkelammert's words: "When we speak today of the turn to the repressed and crushed subject, we speak of the human being as the subject of this rationality, who is confronted with the irrationality of the rationalized. In this perspective, *liberation* becomes the recovery of the human being as *subject*."[19]

When one is manifest and experienced as a subject in resistance to oppressive relations, one can recognize oneself as a subject and, at the same time, recognize the subjectity of other people beyond any and all social roles. It is what we were speaking of earlier as the experience of gratuity in the face-to-face relation. If we cannot speak of the subject as a subject or construct institutions where people are not objectified, we can live out our subject being in the resistance/struggle and in the subject-subject relation.

That is to say that being a subject is intimately connected to resistance and struggle against oppressive and domineering institutions. The problem is that, to struggle, we must "channel" our resistance and struggle through some social or ecclesial group or movement. That is, in order to live out our subjectity in the resistance and struggle against oppressive institutions we must participate in some institution, we must act as social agents. It is clear that we must struggle so that this institution is less oppressive and domineering than the institution or social system against which we are struggling. But, to participate in an institution is to live out a social role and to obey, at least minimally, the institutional rules that objectify us. In doing that, the subject is again reduced to a social agent, to a role of transformer of social relations, which are the "reducers" of one's subjectity. It is impossible to overcome this tension. Therefore, being a subject in the full sense is also out of reach within our history.

In the case of social groups, when people are united to protest and resist the negation of their human dignity, we can say, analogously, that they form a subject-community. But when this social group begins the struggle in order to stand up for their rights, it goes on to act as a collective social agent.

The only way for us to preserve our subjectity is not to accept being reduced to any social role, however important, "holy," or "revolutionary" this role may be; and not to accept the sacralization of any social institution or system. It is the necessity of the critiques of idolatry and fetishism, which we saw above in the Gutiérrez text.

The Tension between the Micro- and Macrosocial

The experience of being a subject in the face-to-face encounter and in the struggle for the dignity of oneself and others is a very gratifying experience and the giver of a deep and human meaning to our existence. It is a spiritual experience of grace. The most propitious environment for these experiences is, without doubt, the communitarian environment and in local social struggles. It is in these environments that we have more opportunities for face-to-face relations, for the simple reason that we can only cultivate interpersonal relationships in small environments in which not too many people are involved.

From this fact, two temptations can arise. The first is the temptation for us to withdraw into communitarian environments and into local, microsocial struggles. To the extent that large institutions and social struggles do not permit these immediate and face-to-face relationships, the temptation is great to believe that the solutions to religious and social problems are only on the communitarian and microsocial level. Nonetheless, however much we are tempted to deny it, the reality of economic globalization, the web of global communication, and other globalized relations continue impacting our lives. A financial crisis in the Far East can mean unemployment in our communities here in Brazil.

Another temptation is for us to desire that large religious, economic, and political institutions function like our small communities; or to struggle for the project of a society that is simply the quantitative amplification of our communitarian relations. That is, to desire that society functions as a community. This is the desire for a harmonious society where everyone is respected and in relationships with everyone else like they know each other and live in the same community, a society where there is no need for laws and regulating institutions and is, therefore, without repressors.

These two temptations are fully understandable, for these relations and experiences are at the foundation of social commitment and are sources of strength for continuing in the struggle and the "guarantee" that liberation is possible. However, we must return to the theme of the "incarnation" so that we might remember that it is within the human and historical conditions that we must struggle and seek solutions.

The temptation to withdraw into communities or the microsocial environment is the temptation to shut out the wind of the Spirit that "drives" us, calls us, to go out from our community and face the challenges of the world.

However, the temptation of desiring a society that would be a community is the result of a quite common error: that of not recognizing the qualitative differences that emerge when we pass from one level to another and, similarly, when we make linear projections from the microsocial level in the direction of the macrosocial. New properties emerge when we pass from one level to another, whether from a microsocial level to a macrosocial, or from the level of physics to the biological. It is this emergence of new properties that allows us to perceive that we pass from one level to another. If we are capable of perceiving this passage, we must recognize that on this new level the system functions in a different way and, therefore, things that were functioning well on the prior level do not function in the same way or may even no longer function.

These observations bring us the challenge of thinking about the relation between our actions and experiences on the microsocial communitarian level and the macrosocial aspects of our problems and solutions. It is clear that this question must be considered by taking into account other concepts, such as self-organization and autopoiesis, as we just saw above.

Final Words

Latin American theology is living in a moment of the delimitation of its challenges. Innumerable meetings of theologians, across Latin America, to assess the path and discuss our challenges, reveal as much. It also shows that the first moments of the crisis are being overcome. As no theological tradition can account for all questions, it is essential that we be able to delimit and define well our challenges. In the course of this chapter, I have already proposed some themes and questions. In conclusion, I want only to point out some others that are related to the previous ones.

For many people who have long been on the path, for those who in the name of faith participated in the hope that liberation or significant changes—in the churches and in the world—were near, it is important to find responses to disenchantment. It is the same disenchantment of the disciples at Emmaus: "We had hoped that it was he who would redeem Israel." (Luke 24:21) We must find responses to the crisis of the failed messiah, of the failure of our expectations.

An easy response, that which the disciples and many Christians of our time assume, is this: if he failed, he was not the Messiah (the disciples of Emmaus); or if we lost, and there is no chance of victory, we were mistaken (as with many ex-activists today).

The disciples were able to overcome this easy and immediate response and came to understand the paradox of the defeated Messiah. Even after 2000 years of Christianity, that second response is not easily found and understood. It is necessary that our generation elaborate our response, which is faithful at the same time to the experience of the disciples and to our experience. It is necessary for us to find the meaning of the struggle in favor of the lives of the "least of these" without certainties or promises of victory; and often without counting on the understanding and support of our churches.

Therefore, I think that it is fundamental that we continue deepening our reflections to elaborate and revise concepts and ways of thinking that help people "of good will" perceive how, in ethical indignation and in the struggle for the lives of the "least of these," with all its contradictions and limits, we can live out the most profound of spiritual experiences: the experience of God's grace that is among us.

Finally, there is a challenge that flows from the previous reflections. Latin American theology has as one of its central themes the God of Life. Much was written to show how the God of the Bible is the God of Life. But the second part of the expression, "life," was assumed as something obvious. It is easy to identify who is alive or dead. To define life is much more difficult. I think that we must, in dialogue with the life sciences and with the human and social sciences, assume this challenge to understand better what life is and how it functions (in the biological, personal, social, and ecological spheres), so that we can in the same way better understand what it means to say God of Life, and to help in a more efficient way defend threatened life.

CHAPTER 3

The Subject as Transcendentality within Real Life

"When we speak today of the return of the repressed and crushed subject, we speak of the human being as the subject of this rationality, who is confronted with the irrationality of the rationalized. In this perspective liberation becomes the recovery of the human being as *subject*."[1] With these words, Franz Hinkelammert reveals an inflection important not only in his thought, but also in the tradition of thought that is articulated around the Ecumenical Department of Research (DEI) in Costa Rica: liberation is no longer considered solely or principally about the construction of a new society, but it is also about the concept of the subject.

The theme of the subject and subjectivity has been the object of reflection for diverse authors of the Marxist tradition or influence in recent years. In the area of Latin-American theology, these two themes, especially that of subjectivity, was the path taken by some authors for a (self-)critique of liberation theology and even of the notion of liberation itself. However, the text cited above presents the theme in a very particular way.

The reason for this new perspective from the "DEI school" cannot be credited only to the failure of the socialist bloc, to the utopian crisis of Latin-American leftists, or to the weakening of popular social and political movements throughout Latin-America. Beyond these facts, it is also a result of the development of Hinkelammert's thought and of the dialogue between him and other thinkers of that "school."

This theme of the subject is not new in Hinkelammert's thought. One of his most important books, *Critique of Utopian Reason* (1984), already had an entire chapter, the final one, dedicated to this theme. In the preface of the book he says that "politics as the art of the possible contains, therefore, a *critique of utopian reason* without which it is not possible to establish it. That 'is not possible' is not something given but something discovered.... In this sense, the critique of utopian reason is not the rejection of the utopia but rather its transcendental conceptualization. It flows into the discussion of the landmark categories within which social thoughts are elaborated."[2] It was within this objective of analyzing and criticizing social thoughts that he approached the problem of the subject, dealing with the relation between the empirical sciences, the human subject, and the reproduction of real life. According to Hinkelammert, "at the root of empirical sciences is found the human subject who is approximated from reality with determined ends and acts as a function of those ends."[3] But as the human subject can only determine its ends and work to attain those ends if he or she is alive, the reproduction of real life, that is, the satisfaction of necessities, becomes or must be a point of departure. That does not happen in neoliberalism, which hides the denial of the satisfaction of necessities in the name of the satisfaction of consumer preferences.

His critique, however, is not restricted to neoliberalism but is directed at all social theories or political projects (as, for example, Soviet socialism, anarchism, and conservatism) that do not recognize the nonrealizability of their utopias and transcendental concepts, concepts that are necessary for reflection, but impossible to be reached, that is, historically not possible.

There is an insuperable tension between the utopia desired and necessary for social thought and the possible institutions and political projects, which in being implemented in anticipation of these utopias end up denying them through their institutional dynamics. This tension also appears in the concept of the subject. Hinkelammert shows that when one speaks of the subject, it is treated as an object even when the subject speaks of itself; and when the subject acts in the environment of institutions, it is acting as a subject transformed into the object of itself and others. This is a problem presented by any theory or institution. Therefore Hinkelammert says that, "the subject being a subject and not an object, its treatment as an object is in itself inadequate, because it can never correspond to the subjective being of the subject, which is an unattainable plenitude. Therefore, any theory is a bad theory and any institution is a bad institution."[4]

This recognition does not mean, for Hinkelammert, the denial of any and all theory or institution, but the recognition of an insuperable dialectical tension. Along these lines, he says that "the subject, therefore, transcends all of its objectifications, yet cannot exist without them. The subject also transcends, therefore, all forms of the subject that appear to treat the subject as an object."[5]

Despite constant reflections on the concept of the subject in his book from the 1980s and in other texts, it is with his 1998 book *The Cry of the Subject* that Hinkelammert makes this theme one of the central themes of his reflection and, at the same time, the perspective through which he critiques capitalism and the current process of globalization. This "new" course in his thought stood out so much that the expression "the cry of the subject" came to be an expression shared and repeated in the texts of diverse authors who dialogue with Hinkelammert's thought. The Meeting of Social Scientists and Theologians on the Problem of the Subject in the Context of Globalization, held in December of 1999 at the DEI, can be considered a landmark that made public this new course assumed by the group. In a text that returns to the ideas presented at that meeting, Hinkelammert presents two paragraphs that synthesize, in my opinion, some of the fundamental points of his thought on the concept of the subject:

> The human being is not a subject, but there is a process in which it is revealed that it is not possible to live without becoming a subject. There is no survival because the process, which is developed in the functioning of the inertia of the system, is self-destructive. It crushes the subject, which gains consciousness of being called to be a subject as this destructivity is resisted. One must oppose that inertia of the system if one wants to live, and in the opposing, one develops as a subject.
>
> The call to be a subject is revealed in the course of a process. *Therefore, the subject being is not one before the process, but turns out to be one afterwards.* The human being as subject is neither any substance *nor a prior transcendental subject. It reveals itself as a necessity to the extent that the inertia of the system is self-destructive.* It turns out, then, that the subject being is a human potentiality and not a positive presence. It is revealed as a lack that shouts and that is present, but it is as an absence. *As such the absence beseeches. To become a subject is to respond to this absence positively, because that absence is in turn a solicitation. It is a question of responding positively to the absence, without eliminating it as an absence. It answers.* In this sense, the human being is a part of the system as an agent or calculating individual. While the subject is facing the system, it transcends it.[6]

Let us distinguish some ideas:

(1) the subject is not a substance;
(2) the human being is revealed as a subject to the extent that it confronts the inertia of the system that crushes it, therefore the subject is revealed in the cry, it is revealed as an absence;

(3) the human being is called to respond to this cry as a social agent or calculating individual within the system;

(4) the human being as subject always transcends the system.

I want to develop some reflections around the questions presented by Hinkelammert with the intention of conversing with his thought and other authors who also dialogue with him. The expression "reflections around" can be taken in the quite literal sense, as I will be going around this theme, examining its diverse facets. I would like to make clear that the reflections presented here are still quite provisory and are marked, as it could not otherwise be, by my manner of reading and interpreting Hinkelammert's work.

The Subject is Not a Substance

I think that when Hinkelammert affirms that "the human being as subject is not a substance" he is affirming something a little different than the ideas presented by Augusto Serrano in his article "The Subject and the Web."[7] Serrano also critiques the concept of the subject as a substance, as presented by the Western tradition. For him,

> There is no original subject, still free of determinations, identical to itself, imperturbable, grounded beyond time, which is later adorned with mutating predicates. The subject is the integration of all its predicates.... Each subject is a center of convergence of the relations (call them predicates or accidents) that constitute them. Each subject is what it is through the relations that cross it and, therefore, form it. Each subject is a node of the great universal web in which everything and everyone are caught.[8]

Therefore, he affirms that "social beings are not the nodes of a flat web but of a multidimensional web: a web of webs. The web is not prior to or exterior to the subjects that, centering rays on themselves, simultaneously exist in and give form to the web. Neither are there subjects outside of it, for there is no exteriority possible in the web."[9]

Serrano does not differentiate the concept of "the subject" from the concept of "the social being," but uses them interchangeably, and therefore he affirms that there are no subjects and there is no exteriority outside the web.

Continuing Serrano's line of thought, Elsa Tamez also critiques the essentialist and abstract divisions underlying the concept of the subject as substance. She relies on an analogy with grammar (also present in Serrano's work), where the predicate is not an appendix of speech but the concretization of the subject in speech, in order to say that one can only speak of the living subject considering its concrete manifestation through its experience of gender and race.

"The challenge then is how to articulate in a convincing manner the cries of the subject who is 'racialized' and 'genderized' in a global society and whose rationality, in the words of Hinkelammert, is irrational for its self-destructive effects."[10] Therefore, she proposes an approach transversing the constitution of new subjects and the critique of the economic theory dominant today because "that plurality [of the subject] . . . disappears on the frontier of economic theory."[11]

Hinkelammert, Serrano, and Tamez agreed on the critique of a substantialist and abstract conception of the subject. Nevertheless, it is necessary to note that there is a fundamental difference between Hinkelammert and the other two authors. For Serrano—and it seems that Tamez is also going in the same direction—there are no subjects outside the web, because there is no exteriority possible outside the web. What Serrano and Tamez propose is a transversal vision of the subject capable of giving account of the complexity of the reality woven as a web of webs.

Hinkelammert, meanwhile, affirms that the subject is revealed as an absence and that the subject is not—in the sense used by Serrano and Tamez—in the system, since it transcends it. The concept used by Hinkelammert is not that of the web of webs, but of the system. Nevertheless, I believe that this difference is not important at the moment. Since the notion of a web of webs can also be treated through the theory of systems, according to which there would be a complex system formed of interrelated subsystems of a complex and transversal mode. In any case, what is emphasized here is that the concept of the subject in Hinkelammert does not refer to something present within the system or the web, but to something that is present as an absence and that transcends the system.

This difference is important, since if the concept of the "subject" is understood in the sense presented by Serrano and Tamez, as a center of convergence of those relations that cross and, thereby, constitute it, then it does not make much sense for them to speak of negated subjects or to say that "liberation becomes the recovery of the human being as subject." A web is not maintained as such, beyond having its reproduction compromised, if its centers of convergence are denied. The struggle for the recovery of the human being as subject presupposes a difference between the concepts "human being" and "subject." If we were to express Serrano's thought in Hinkelammert's terms, we could say that the human being (and not the subject = social being) is a center of convergence of the relationships that form it.

It is that difference between the concepts of the human being, the subject, and the social agent that permits Hinkelammert a point of departure from which to criticize the concrete way in which the human being lives within a social system, its "crushed" and "negated" condition. Meanwhile Tamez, for example, by not clearly differentiating these concepts, critiques the present situation beginning with the idea that systems of domination—whether patriarchal or of the market—objectify the human being. That critique presupposes the possibility of a nonobjectifying relation within a system or institution.

Now, systems and institutions function because the people that make them up obey the social roles that are expected of them. In other words, it is not possible for institutions to function without any process of objectifying human beings, or without the dynamic itself of the system or of the institution determining or delimiting the roles to be lived by the people that make it up. The problem does not consist of this inevitable determination or objectification in any system, but in the reduction of the human being to determined roles. This reduction denies other potentialities of the human being.

In order to avoid this reduction and also the illusion that it is possible for us to live without any form of institutionality and objectification of the human being—the eternal anarchistic dream of humanity that is also present in liberation theology and in base communities, as also in many other groups of "the Left"—is why Hinkelammert says that the subject transcends the system. He had already written in the 1980s: "Institutions cannot direct themselves to the subject without treating it as an object. Institutions cannot be the environment of recognition between subjects, because such recognition ruptures, as it takes place, institutional logic."[12] To say that the subject transcends the system is to say that no system, no web of webs, exhausts the potentiality and subjectity (the quality of being a subject) of the human being; while affirming the necessity of institutional systems: "the subject . . . transcends all its objectifications, yet cannot exist without them."[13]

The Human Being as Subject and Social Agent

Hinkelammert begins his chapter "The Return of the Repressed Human Subject in the Face of the Strategy of Globalization" saying: "That the human being is a subject is a determination that arises with modernity."[14] With this affirmation he distinguishes clearly the concept of the human being and the subject.

Moreover, he links the concept of the subject with modernity. Hinkelammert has already treated this theme in an earlier text: "The Reformation and the consequent substitution of the feudal relations of production began with the affirmation of the subject far beyond any hierarchy, whether ecclesiastical or political-economic."[15]

With this affirmation Hinkelammert shows us two important things: (a) the modern world and the bourgeoisie, in the beginning of their movement, were bearers of a "revolutionary" proposal; and (b) the concept of the subject appears with the affirmation of the human being as subject beyond any hierarchical or legal system. The concept of the subject does not appear simply as an opposition to a given social system, but as an opposition to any and all hierarchies.

The problem of bourgeois modernity was not the loss of this concept of the subject, but the way its realization was conceived. According to Hinkelammert, the affirmation of the subject profoundly modified the medieval image of heaven. "Heaven ceases to be a feudal court and is transformed into a heaven of souls, all enjoying equal happiness. . . . And in anticipation of this new heaven the subject is transformed into the bourgeois individual."[16] Here he makes a distinction between the subject and the bourgeois individual, the latter understood as a social agent. This necessity comes from the human condition itself. "As subject, the human being conceives ends and is referred to the set of its possible ends. Yet, one cannot realize all the ends that seem possible under a means-ends calculation."[17] If it were possible to attain the ends without the need for concrete action and a means-end calculus, perhaps there would be no need for the human being to be determined as a social agent. But this immediate realization, without any sociohistorical mediation, is not humanly possible. Hinkelammert's frequent critique of the reduction of reason to a means-end calculus cannot lead us to the mistake of thinking that he critiques the means-end calculus in itself. He is not proposing the end of means-end calculations, but the nonreduction of reason to this calculus, which is very different.

This explanation is necessary as many of Hinkelammert's readers, and also those of Hugo Assmann and other theologians who critique the idolatry of the market, still confuse the critique of the idolatry of the market with the critique of the market in itself. What these authors criticize is the absolutization of the market, not the market in itself. They do not propose the end of the market, since this is not possible in a society so large and complex, and neither is it desirable.[18] The same occurs with respect to the reduction of reason to the concept of efficiency (means-ends calculus).

Therefore, Hinkelammert says: "Seeing the human being as a subject who in the face of its ends is transformed into an agent of means-end action, the subject is the totality of its potential and possible ends."[19] For him the concept of the "subject" is not a concept that describes or refers to the concrete human being who exists in social and human relationships (as it seems to be in the thought of Serrano, Tamez, and others), but is a concept that synthesizes human potentiality. Therefore the subject is not a substance—something that exists and subsists by itself alone or in relations inside systems or "webs"—but is an "absence that cries out," a potentiality or set of potentialities that make it possible for the human being to oppose and resist the attempted reduction by the dominant social system.

The affirmation of the human being as subject in the face of social systems—which aim to objectify the human being and reduce it to a piece of the system—demands for its manifestation social and/or political action. This action can only be realized to the extent that the human being takes part in a social movement and/or a social structure (like a party or syndicate), that is, to the extent that it is transformed into a social agent within an institution and utilizes means-end calculus. In this sense, the problem of the bourgeois revolution was not the determination of the subject as a bourgeois individual but the identification of the bourgeois individual with the subject. That is to reduce the totality of its potentialities to a determined form of the subject's objectification, the bourgeois individual (social agent).

This identification/reduction does not occur in an immediate or direct way. It is the result of the identification of the laws of the market with the laws of history, an identification made by liberalism and, in a much more radical way, by neoliberalism. The laws of the market, which result from the interactions of the unintended effects of the fragmented actions of the bourgeois social agent, are identified as the metaphysical laws of history. With that, the possibility of a subject beyond the laws of the market, a subject that transcends the market system, was denied.

It is this identification of the human being with a determined social role within the market system that denies the human being as subject. This is why the human being affirms itself as a subject in crying out; in opposing this reduction that makes its life unsupportable. Nevertheless, the denied victim who cries out to affirm itself as subject cannot prescind from acting on the social and institutional plane as a social agent. That is, for the human being to affirm itself as a subject, it must objectify itself as a social agent in institutionalized social relations. Therefore, for Hinkelammert, "the subject . . . transcends all its objectifications, yet cannot exist without them."[20]

If we identify the human being acting in a social movement—as a social agent—with the "subject" being or the "new subject," we will not be able to escape from the trap: the reduction of human potentiality to the social role; even if this role is understood as multifaceted or transversely (gender, ethnicity, social class, political option, sexual orientation, et cetera) in a liberative perspective or as transformer of reality. With that, one ends up absolutizing a given type of social movement or institution and denying the subjectity of the "activist." The differentiation of these concepts permits us to see better that, regardless of however "liberative" or "open" a social move-ment may be, it is not possible to give an account of the set of possibilities and desires of the people who participate in the movement.

Another side of the coin of this type of trap occurs when one criticizes in an abstract way social movements or diverse forms of popular resistance. If some end up absolutizing determined social or political movements with the reduction of the subject to the social agent, there are also those who, by demanding that the social movements or institutions be expressions of the totality of human possibilities, that is, be spaces of experiencing the fullness of human subjectity, end up negating or criticiz-ing in an abstract and total way all possible concrete proposals and struggles. And, with that, they paralyze concrete actions and struggles that might improve people's lives, in particular those of the very poor. The nondifferentiation of the concepts of the human being, the subject, and the social agent can lead to those two kinds of mistakes.

Having recognized the difference in the relation between the subject and social agent, we must remember that the human being as social agent can only act in a fragmented way. Since, to the extent that a perfect understanding of all the factors that make up natural, human, and social reality is impossible, all action is fragmentary. And, as Hinkelammert says, "the agents, in their behaving in an atomistic manner—that is, fragmentarily—cre-ate the inevitability of the market. But, in acting in the market, they create the laws that are imposed onto the agents. One cause implies the other. However, both inevitabilities are produced as unintended effects of intentional action. The code itself of bour-geois privilege does not create that atomistic individual, but to the contrary confirms and legalizes it."[21]

These laws that act behind the backs of people and "the compulsive strength of the facts" are "expressions of the unin-tended effects of intentional action that return to the agent himself and exert on him a compulsive effect."[22] This dynamic does not function only in capitalism or with the bourgeois individual, but also with all people who affirm themselves as subjects and, therefore, necessarily act as social agents. The difference between the bourgeois individual who is devoted to these laws and the individuals or groups who resist is that the latter, in this resistance, affirm themselves as solidarious subjects. Nevertheless, we cannot again fall into a romantic and noninstitutional vision of solidarity. Solidarity on the social level demands actions in the institutional arena, which brings us back to the human being-subject-social agent circuit.[23]

In Hinkelammert's thought, the relation that exists between the concept of the subject and social agent is analogous to the relationship that exists between the utopia (the transcendental concept) and the sociohistorical project. The utopia is an unrealizable horizon that gives meaning to concrete historical projects. These projects cannot be identified with the utopia or else risk becoming totalitarian. Moreover, we cannot forget that these projects, in being introduced, deny the very utopia that they claim to anticipate or concretize. This denial is the result of the dynamic itself of sociocultural institutions and the human condition. Nevertheless, the utopia cannot be anticipated without a historical project that denies it. This dialectic between the utopia and the historical project is, without doubt, one of Hinkelammert's major theoretical contributions.[24]

The Subject and Transcendentality within Real Life

Paraphrasing Hinkelammert with respect to the concept of the reign of freedom in Marx, we can say that the concept of the person as subject in Hinkelammert is the result of his method. It is a concept necessary for being able to analyze and critique the condition of the human being "crushed" and "negated" by the social system dominant today. For one cannot describe human conditions and relationships within the capitalist system or in another social model without an analysis of that which they are not. "By considering what human relationships are not . . . it is possible to arrive at what they are."[25]

There is in the commercial and social relations within capitalism a lack or absence that cries out but which the appearances of these same relations hide. Without the perception and the analytical comprehension of this absence it is not possible to have a principle of intelligibility for unmasking the reduction of the human being to an "economic cog," under the appearance of "Rational Economic Man," or to a simple object to be discarded or sacrificed in economic adjustment programs or in the present model of globalization, or to the abstract concept of the human being without physical needs. The concept of "the subject" is, for Hinkelammert, the principle of intelligibility that permits the unmasking and critique of the condition in which the human being is being subjected. One can only interpret the present condition of the poor human being as "crushed" and "negated" to the extent that one knows what this condition is not.

The concept of the subject that is revealed as an absence is an end that is "a transcendentality existing within real material life."[26] It is an end not in the sense of something attainable at the end of the road but as a horizon with which we establish a logical and epistemological relation. It is a vision of an existence full of human possibilities that, upon revealing what is not, reveals what the social and human relations are within capitalism and, with that, drives the struggles for more humanizing concrete historical projects. It is, therefore, a transcendentality within real life. I think that it is never too much to remember that those more humanizing historical projects will always be on this side of the vision and in contradiction with it, as the concept of the subject, like that of the reign of freedom, is beyond human realizability.

We can say that, for Hinkelammert, the concept of the subject, like that of the reign of freedom or the Kingdom of God, emerges "out of the search the search for this Archimedean point...which, as an absence, can make history and commodity relationships intelligible."[27]

Continuing Hinkelammert's thought, we can say that when a community or collectivity "cries out," as a form of resistance to the system that reduces the subjectity of the people to a determined role, we have the revelation of the community or collectivity as subject. But, when the group moves to social or political action it no longer acts as subject, but as a collective social agent. And as social agent it must orient its actions and strategies to means-end calculations, to the search for efficient means to attain its specific objectives. The "cry of the subject," which was important in order to resist the oppressing system and reveal the subjectity of the community, now no longer serves as a criterion for the actions of the social agent. And in acting as a collective social agent—in order to achieve the objectives that are announced in "the cry of the subject"—we do not have "emergent subjects" or "a racialized and gendered subject," but emergent, racialized, and genderized social agents.

The Subject and the Transcendental Illusion

What is the importance of emphasizing this difference between Hinkelammert's thought and the thoughts of others who are in conversation with him? I think that it is important so that we do not lose sight of one of Hinkelammert's fundamental contributions: the critique of the transcendental illusion and the sacrificialism inherent in this illusion.

As mentioned earlier, one of Hinkelammert's principle contributions is his idea of "utopian reason." For him the utopian concept (like the perfect market of capitalism or the perfect planning of Soviet socialism, or the Kingdom of God of the Christianity that makes the option for the poor) is a condition for understanding reality and intervening in it. One can only understand what the social reality is to the extent that one also understands what it is not. And one can only act socially having in view a perfect social model (utopia) that serves as a horizon to be achieved or approximated.

However, no horizon is achievable. It is always in the distance as we approach it. So also it is with the utopia. The difference is that the utopia is not just any horizon but a horizon desirable in itself and which also gives meaning to our struggles and existence. That is why we have such difficulty in accepting the impossibility of our utopias: we often prefer self-deception and continue to think that it is possible to reach this society so desired.

In premodern societies religion was the great bearer of the promise to bring near this utopia. Today, after the fall of the socialist bloc, the liberal or neoliberal market system is presented as the only bearer of those promises. In a sense, the "total market" is presented as the historical messianic subject that will fulfill the metaphysical laws of history. The great problem of these institutions, which are presented as efficient instruments for reaching the utopia, is the demand for sacrifices of human lives being presented as necessary. It is the promise of "paradise" that transforms murder into "sacrifices necessary for redemption."

There is no other way to criticize radically the thesis of "necessary sacrifices" except by reaffirming the impossibility of realizing the utopia within history. Utopia is a transcendental concept that plays an important role within concrete life but in being transcendental remains impossible, not fully realizable. From there comes the importance of understanding utopia as transcendentality within concrete life.

From the utopia we must elaborate an institutional historical project. We must not forget, however, that this project that appears as an instrument of anticipation and approximation of the utopia, through its necessarily institutional character, denies the utopia itself. It is now quite common in Latin American theology to criticize the idolatry of the market. In a sense, we can say—paraphrasing Marx—that in Latin American theology, the critique of the idolatry of the market is settled. (In spite of many still confusing the critique of the idolatry of the market with the critique of the market itself.) Nevertheless, the denial of the realizability of the neoliberal utopia does not always signify the acceptance of the impossibility of all utopias, including here the utopia of the Kingdom of God or a fully just and fraternal society within history. It is easier to deny the utopia of our adversaries and continue believing that our own utopias are not utopian in the sense of being impossible. It is clear that nowadays there is not as much confidence or optimism that there once was among the Latin American left, Christian or not, with respect to the construction of the Kingdom of God or the reign of freedom, nor in socialism as "the" way to this utopia. Nevertheless, it seems to me that the desire for fullness is alive in some of the "new" conversations concerning the subject.[28]

Let us take as an example, from among many, the proposal of Rui Manuel Graça das Neves presented at the already mentioned Meeting of Social Scientists and Theologians on the Problem of the Subject held at the DEI. After saying that liberation theology needs to dialogue with new epistemologies, he affirms: "There cannot be partial subjects. The subject is integral or it is not. It is not enough to be an economic subject, it is necessary also to be a political, cultural, epistemic, human subject."[29]

As this text is taken from the summary of the meeting, we cannot analyze precisely the words of Rui Manuel; nevertheless his central idea is clearly expressed. He is going in the same direction as Serrano and Tamez: the subject must be assumed in the integrality of its relations. However, when a subject (human being) is acting as a political subject (or agent) it cannot experience all these qualities at the same time and with the same intensity. In the case of political action, the person must privilege the political space and the qualities necessary for efficient political action. Without that, the person's desire to face the dominant system or overcome a situation of oppression cannot be set in motion in an effective way.

If, in the name of an effective operationalization, the person chooses the political institutional arena—a political party or something similar—for political action, he or she must act according to the logic of that arena and its institutions. And the arena of politics is the arena of struggles for possible objectives, of tension between ends, ethics, and means-end calculus. If that person were at the same time a poet, he or she cannot confuse the cultural space of poetry with that of the political-institutional arena and must differentiate poetry (where the only limits are words) from political action. It is clear that sometimes politicians are also called to be poets. This occurs because the subjectity of this person is not exhausted by his or her political role. Outside that environment he or she can exist in other roles, like being a professor or parent. What one cannot do is desire or demand that one live out all the roles at the same time. It is important not to reduce the human being to a single role, or confuse its multiple roles.

Affirmations like these: "There cannot be partial subjects. The subject is integral or it is not. It is not enough to be an economic subject, it is necessary also to be a political, cultural, epistemic, human subject"; can be the fruits of conceptual imprecision. It seems to me, however, that more than a simple conceptual imprecision is involved. My hypothesis is that it reveals a romantic-anarchist vision of reality, which does not take into consideration insoluble contradictions of the human condition, and of the also insoluble dialectical tension between utopia and institution. Even more, it is a way of persisting—even if unconsciously—in the dream of the full realization of the Kingdom of God or the reign of freedom within history. As it is only in a society without any institutionalization that we can conceive the possibility of a human being who fully realizes his or her subjectity or, in the words of Rui Manuel, is an integral subject.

To desire that people be this "integral subject" or to desire "to construct the subject from the perspective of the poor and the construction of the poor itself as subject" is, in my understanding, to fall again into the transcendental illusion of the construction of the Kingdom of God or the reign of freedom, now in form of a transcendental illusion in terms of the "integral" subject or of the idea of a subject who does not experience any form of objectification.[30] This is an illusion caused by the nondifferentiation between the concepts of the human being, subject, and social agent.

We know that transcendental illusions bring with them sacrificialism.[31] If my analyses have any basis, the question that arises is this: What is the concrete form that sacrificialism assumes in this transcendental illusion? Who are those sacrificed in the name of this "subject?" Finally, sacrificialism is not a privilege of the "Right."

If my hypothesis is wrong and if that way of understanding and proposing the integral subject does not end up becoming a transcendental illusion, there still remains another fundamental problem. The confusion or nondistinction between the concepts of the human being, subject, and social agent leads to operational inefficiency in the struggle for the defense of the life and dignity of the people excluded by the present process of economic globalization. This inefficiency is the result of the nonperception of the dialectical tension that exists between the utopia and the necessary institutional dynamics and between the "cry of the subject" and the necessary determinations and limits of the social agent who acts in the operational-institutional arena.

We must seriously assume the "cries of the subjects," the cries of the poor and of those who live under the judgment of any type of oppression, who affirm themselves as subjects in crying out, in resistance to the excluding and oppressing system, and so become a little more free. However, our (intellectuals committed to social causes and other readers of texts like this) commitment to the struggle for the dignified life of the poor cannot be only at the level of amplifying and giving a foundation to these cries. It is necessary to take a step forward and assume all the problems and contradictions that appear when starting from and in the name of those who cry out, as persons and collectivities who move on to act as social, individual, or collective agents. That is, we must help think of concrete strategies and actions that take into consideration the insoluble dialectical tension that exists between the utopia and the institutional project, between being a subject and being a social agent.

CHAPTER 4

A New Form of Legitimation of the Economy

I t is already a known fact that the dominant discourse today presents contemporary capitalism as a social system that has no alternative. Neoliberals and other pro-capitalist thinkers elaborate the most diverse theories in order to say the same thing: there is no alternative to the capitalist market system. However, this type of discourse is not a novelty in history. Every system of domination, whether an imperial or authoritarian regime, presents itself as a social model without alternative. This is because it would be an expression of the divine will, the evolution of nature, or the rational order of history, or simply because any other alternative would be impracticable. What varies is only the concrete form with which a dominant social system legitimates itself as being "without alternative."

Today, the presentation of capitalism, of the neoliberal sort, as a model without alternative occurs around the articulation of two fundamental concepts: self-organization and evolution. The legitimation and explication of the market system around these two concepts is not, in truth, a recent idea. Paul A. Samuelson, for example, in his introductory book *Economics*—one of the most influential and widely used textbooks in the formation of economists in the twentieth century, the first edition of which appeared in 1948—says:

> A market economy is an elaborate mechanism for unconscious coordination of people and businesses through a system of prices and markets. It is a communication device for pooling the knowledge and actions of millions of diverse individuals. Without a central intelligence, it solves a problem that today's largest computer could not solve, involving millions of unknown variables and relations. *Nobody designed it. It just evolved. Like human society, it is changing.* But it does meet the first test of any social organization—it can survive.[1]

In this text, despite not being explicitly utilized, two ideas appear clearly: self-organization and evolution. The first idea, the notion of the *unconscious coordination* of the knowledge and actions of millions of diverse individuals that act in the market, refers directly to the notion of self-organization, or to the theory of spontaneous order, which has a long tradition in the history of social thought, but which only acquired strength beginning in the 1970s. The theory of spontaneous order is based on the notion that the majority of the things that produce general benefits in social systems or that make possible their reproduction are not under the control of persons or conscious plans.

The second idea, Samuelson's affirmation that the market system "just evolved" and "like human society . . . is changing," is linked, as is easily observable, to the theory of the evolution of species.

The articulation of those two theories of self-organization and evolution, that is, the hypothesis that the system of the capitalist market is a self-organizing system that has naturally evolved, today occupies a central place as much in the analysis as in the discourse of the legitimation of capitalism.

"The Invisible Hand" of the Market and Self-Organization

Paul Krugman, one of the most influential economists in the world today, says that social scientists normally are suspicious, with good reason, of people who want to import concepts from physics or biology. However, he affirms that at present there is a very interesting interdisciplinary movement in which economists ought to participate. This movement focuses on the concept of self-organizing systems—complex systems in which randomness and chaos appears to evolve spontaneously toward an unexpected order—and has become in recent years a more and more influential idea, bringing together thinkers from many diverse areas, from artificial intelligence to chemistry, from evolution to geology. Krugman, however, recognizes that, for some reason, economists have not taken part in that movement and proposes that it be investigated as to how those new ideas can be applied to that immensely complex but indisputably self-organizing system that is called the economy.[2]

According to Krugman, when Adam Smith wrote about how the market guides its participants "as if by an invisible hand" to results that no one intended, he was describing nothing other than an emergent property, one of the fundamental characteristics of self-organizing systems. Krugman is not the only one who sees in Adam Smith's theory of the "invisible hand" the notion of self-organization. Fritjof Capra, a thinker quite critical of modernity and capitalism, holds a similar position. According to him, "throughout the history of the social sciences, numerous metaphors have been used in order to describe self-regulating processes in social life. Perhaps the most well known of them is the 'invisible hand' that regulates the market in the economic theory of Adam Smith."[3]

Krugman, like many other theorists who participate in what he calls the interdisciplinary movement around the concept of self-organization, affirms that "what links the study of embryos and hurricanes, of magnetic materials and collections of nerves, is that they are all self-organizing systems: systems that, even when they begin from an almost homogenous or random state, spontaneously form patterns on a grand scale."[4] And he concludes this reflection saying that the economy is, without doubt, a self-organizing system in this sense. In this way, Krugman, like many other authors, does not establish qualitative differences between physical, biological, or social systems in speaking of self-organization. It is as if new properties do not emerge in the passage from the physical level to the biological, and from this to the human and social levels that oblige us at least to adapt or qualify the concept of self-organization or self-organizing systems in order to account for those emergences that allow us to perceive differences on the physical, biological, and social levels.

An important point to emphasize in Krugman's thought is that, despite not making the distinction, at least not explicitly, between the physical, biological, and social levels, he does not consider self-organization as something necessarily or even presumably good. According to him, "self-organization is something that we observe and try to understand, not necessarily something that we desire."[5] With that, he does not legitimate the market as something good or irreplaceable through the simple fact of being self-organized. Nonetheless, in his book *The Accidental Theorist*, Krugman defends and legitimizes the market system with the affirmation that all other social systems are worse.[6]

Paulo Guedes, one of the most influential economists in Brazil today, is another example of how economists have more and more utilized concepts arising from physics or biology, like that of spontaneous order, self-organization, and evolution, and those who we can call interdisciplinarians.[7] He wrote, in his column in the magazine *Exame*, an article entitled "The

Biology of Business: Virtual Species Incapable of Adapting are Going to Disappear." Guedes begins this article saying:

> The great contribution of Adam Smith for the understanding of the ideas of competition in markets was the perception that extremely complex systems of coordination could result in decentralized mechanisms of decision-making. Biographers of Darwin suggest that the powerful image of the invisible hand sculpting complex instruments of coordination in apparently chaotic environments of conflicts between individual interests might have inspired the process of natural selection as a sculptor of the evolution of species. That historical approximation between Smith and Darwin suggests additional analogies between biology and the world of business.[8]

After setting out this analogy, Guedes sets out another between the "theory of punctuated equilibrium" of the biologist Stephen Jay Gould—the theory that questions the hypothesis of gradual evolution, without breaking with the theory of evolution—with the "theory of the long cycles of the economy," which says that periods of equilibrium based on the consolidation of old technologies are upset by a rapid acceleration of technological innovations. After developing some reflections on this analogy, Guedes concludes the article saying: "New technologies, like genetic mutations, depend on a competitive process of natural selection in order to be approved.... Great technologies in businesses without efficient corporate governance are like biomorphically well-designed animals, but without a cerebrum and threatened with extinction."[9]

From Instincts to the Institutions of the Market

There is also another movement in that "marriage" between biology and economics; the movement that comes from the area of biology. Matt Ridley is a typical example of the scientist in the area of biology who builds a bridge to economics. In his book, of a quite suggestive title, *The Origins of Virtue: Human Instincts and the Evolution of Cooperation*, he says that

> if biologists have not added to the theory proposed by Smith, they have at least tested it. Smith said two further things about the division of labor in society: that it increased with the size of the market and that in a market of a given size it increased with improvement in transport and communication. Both maxims prove to be true of simple societies of cells.... Virtually nothing else of interest has been written about the division of labor since Adam Smith, whether by biologists or by economists.[10]

Beginning with theories from the areas of biology and game theory, Ridley affirms that Smith's theory, in which social benefits result from private vices, is probably the least valued thought in the history of ideas and that "there is a beautiful parallel between what Smith meant and the human immune system.... The whole system is beautifully designed so that the self-interested ambitions of each cell can only be satisfied by the cell doing its duty for the body. Selfish ambitions are bent to the greater good of the body just as selfish individuals are bent by the market to greater good of society."[11] According to Ridley, "order emerges perfectly from chaos not because of the way people are bossed about, but because of the way individuals react rationally to incentives.... All without the slightest hint of central authority."[12] Moreover, "the human mind contains numerous instincts for building social cooperation and seeking a reputation for niceness. We are not so nasty that we need to be tamed by intrusive government, nor so nice that too much government does not bring out the worst in us, both as its employees and as its clients."[13]

From biology, the theory of evolution, and game theory, Ridley arrives at and concludes his book with a socioeconomic "truth" that, if not the same, is very close to the neoliberal proposal:

> If we are to recover social harmony and virtue, if we are to build back into society the virtues that made it work for us, it is vital that we reduce the power and scope of the state. That does not mean a vicious war of all against all. It means devolution: devolution of power over people's lives to parishes, computer networks, clubs, teams, self-help groups, small businesses— everything small and local. It means a massive disassembling of the public bureaucracy. . . . The roots of social order are in our heads, where we possess the instinctive capacities for creating not a perfectly harmonious and virtuous society, but a better one than we have at present. We must build our institutions in such a way that they draw out those instincts. Pre-eminently this means the encouragement of exchange between equals. Just as trade between countries is the best recipe for friendship between them, so exchange between enfranchised and empowered individuals is the best recipe for cooperation. We must encourage social and material exchange between equals for that is the raw material of trust, and trust is the foundation of virtue.[14]

The road to social harmony and virtue is, according to Ridley, the reduction of the state and the liberalization of the economy. The basis of this proposal is not taken from economic theories but from the biological sciences. The sources of the harmonious social order and social virtues are not, according to him, in conscious or planned social intervention on the part of the state and/or the larger institutions of civil society, but in the human instincts that we carry in ourselves. Social institutions favorable to the implementation of neoliberal politics are institutions that feed on these instincts, those instincts that would lead us to social harmony.

His proposal to devolve "power over people's lives to parishes, computer networks, clubs, teams, self-help groups, small businesses—everything small and local" is a romantic discourse of the past and the "local." Such discourse is, without doubt, in tune with many ecological groups with romantic tendencies, but it obfuscates the fundamental axis of his proposal: to make the "instinct" of exchange in the free market the criterion of everything and, most important, the foundation of virtue. When the virtue of social solidarity is sought only through free trade, there is no more to say about the virtues or solidarity. It is enough to do business in the free market, following our instincts.

Hayek and Faith in Evolution

The authors that we have considered up to this point provide an example of how the theories of self-organization and evolution go beyond their specific scientific areas or origins and are influencing more and more economic and social discourse. But, without doubt, the principal author of this thesis is Friedrich A. von Hayek.

First of all, it is important to emphasize here a fundamental difference between the thought of Adam Smith and Hayek regarding the market as a spontaneous order and producer of unintended beneficial effects. Smith and his followers understand the market to coordinate the personal interests of individuals in order to produce an unintended beneficial result for all. The emphasis is placed on the importance of the social division of labor as the producer of economic progress and in the market as the producer of the common good from self-interest.

Hayek shares this vision on the role of the division of labor and economic progress, but introduces the problem of knowledge that arises from the fact that the actions of a large socioeconomic system are dispersed among thousands or millions of economic agents. The coordination of the "division of knowledge" becomes as important as that of the division of labor. For

Hayek, the coordination of this diffuse knowledge by means of the market permits the use of a much greater quantity of knowledge than under known alternative social systems. Thusly, he speaks of the coordination of the actions of necessarily ignorant persons or persons with insufficient knowledge. The validity of his theory of spontaneous order, therefore, no longer depends on the so-called egoistic suppositions of traditional economic theory because the universal problem of coordination persists independently of whether persons are motivated by egoism or by altruism/solidarity. In other words, in the hypothesis of a society formed only by solidarious persons committed to the common good the problems of the coordination of the division of labor and the coordination of the necessarily fragmented knowledge of economic agents remain.

This is an important theme because one of the principal problems of Marxism and socialism was the presupposition that economic alienation and exploitation were products of the private ownership of the means of production. With that, it was believed, in the beginning, that the end of private property would be the primary path toward overcoming economic alienation and exploitation. With the establishment of socialist states it was verified that the end of the private ownership of the means of production did not resolve or overcome the problem of the coordination of the social division of labor. The attempted solution was that of centralized economic planning, seeking a more and more perfect plan for the economic system, which presupposes the possibility of perfect knowledge of all the factors involved in a large and complex economic system and the possibility of developing a perfect plan from this knowledge. These are humanly impossible things.[15]

Aside from the human impossibility of that knowledge, planning presupposes the stability or nonmodification of the factors involved for a time subject to being planned or executed. The problem is that while human material necessities are "stable" for a reasonable period, desires are not. Therefore, socialist economies of centralized planning were and still are very inefficient in the task of satisfying the desires of consumers in their population. Also, we must not forget that we human beings are beings of necessity and desires and that the desires of consumption are not only desires for objects-goods, but for symbols that have to do with social location and the meaning of existence.[16]

Returning to Hayek, the thesis that the market is the best form possible, if not the only possibility, for coordinating the actions of necessarily ignorant persons raises a problem: Who and how can one arrive at that judgment? If that thesis was scientifically proven by a person or scientific community then this would presuppose a level of knowledge that could measure and compare, from outside the market and other social systems, all the factors involved and come to an unequivocal conclusion about the efficiency of the market and other alternative models relative to the coordination of the division of labor and knowledge.

Hayek tries to argue for the validity of that judgment not by the demonstration of the truth of his affirmation but through the critique of the economic disorder supposedly provoked by conscious intervention, that is, planned intervention by governments or social institutions. In other words, it is not a direct proof in the sense of proving from the functioning of the market itself; rather, it is a proof through the negation of all the other alternatives. Put simply, it would be more or less like this: we do not have to prove that the market is the only efficient form of coordinating knowledge and the social division of labor, as this requires a knowledge that in itself is impossible, but we know that this thesis is true because all the other models of economic coordination that presuppose an intervention in the market create more economic disorder.

However, those economic disorders that are present under market systems are explained by Hayek as being caused by these interventions. One cannot prove this empirically in a definitive way, however, since that would break with the thesis that one cannot know all the factors that comprise the economy. Therefore, Hayek's thesis that the market system is the best economic model is founded on the hypothesis that any intervention can only provoke economic disorder and damage because intervention is based on the pretense of knowing what is impossible. It is a circular argument.

Even if we might disagree with Hayek's general proposal, we must accept the thesis that it is not possible to know all the factors and relations of the market, to the extent that this system is large and complex. However, from this same principle, we can arrive at a different conclusion: that we cannot, because of our ignorance in relation to the market, know if the market is or is not the best form of coordination, much less arrive at the conclusion that the market must be left untouched, without any intervention or control, since it will produce the best of the possible results. Ignorance itself in relation to the functioning of the market might lead us to the thesis that, through our inability to understand the outcomes of the market, we need to be mindful of the necessity of making corrections, that is, to intervene in the market.[17]

Hayek's conclusion, and that of many others, that the spontaneous order of the market is always the best possible is not comprehensible without a more expansive theory than the concept of self-organizing complex systems. It is necessary to move from the concept of self-organization or spontaneous order to the theory of evolution. It is necessary to link, to connect, the theory of spontaneous order or self-organization with the theory of evolution so that a necessarily positive judgment is possible and comprehensible. In other words, the connection between the theory of spontaneous order or self-organization with the always positive judgment of the neoliberal type over the market presupposes an inappropriate epistemological leap, an act of faith in a providential "invisible hand" guiding the evolution of living species. Let us look at this more closely.

Hayek, presenting the fundamental argument in his final book, says that "our civilization depends, not only for its origins but also for its preservation, on what can be precisely described only as the extended order of human cooperation, an order more commonly, if somewhat misleadingly, known as capitalism. To understand our civilization, one must appreciate that the extended order resulted not from human design or intention but spontaneously."[18] Thus, he presents capitalism not as a society or system of competition of all against all, as his critics are accustomed to pointing out, but as "an extended order of human cooperation." But he himself defines it not as an order of cooperation produced by an intentional solidarity or social accord, or things of this type, but as an order of spontaneous character. That is, cooperation is the result of the self-organization of the market system, not an intentional effect of the actions or intentions of groups or individuals.

The fact of not being produced by human intentionality does not mean that this order has nothing to do with the behavior and values of human beings. For Hayek, we live in a civilized society because of our "unintentionally conforming to certain traditional and largely moral practices, many of which men tend to dislike, whose significance they usually fail to understand, whose validity they cannot prove."[19] That is, for Hayek, those values and habits appeared and made possible the formation of civilized society, without the human being involved knowing what was happening and without their enjoying the results. In other words, it was a process not only unconscious, but also against the will of the individuals involved. And, as the unexpected result was civilization, we can deduce that this process of the generation of this spontaneous order was driven by a kind of "invisible hand/providence."

According to Hayek, the practice of those actions with nonpleasurable results, at least in the immediate term, and of unknown effectiveness were being spread through evolutionary processes based in selection, and this facilitated as much the population increase as material well-being for those groups that resigned themselves to accept this type of behavior. "The unwitting, reluctant, even painful adoption of these practices kept these groups together, increased their access to valuable information of all sorts, and enabled them to be 'fruitful, and multiply, and replenish the earth, and subdue it' (Genesis 1:28). This process is perhaps the least appreciated facet of human evolution."[20]

The question that then arises is this: How was it that those nonpleasurable and noncomprehensible traditions and values were transmitted and assumed? To try to explain this Hayek explicitly introduces the role of religion in this process. Since cultural qualities do not automatically transmit themselves like genes, he raised the hypotheses that "mythical beliefs of some sort may be needed to bring this about, especially where rules of conduct conflicting with instinct are concerned" and that, "like it or not, we owe the persistence of certain practices, and the civilization that resulted from them, in part to support from certain beliefs which are not true—or verifiable or testable—in the same sense as are scientific statements" but which are worthy of being called "symbolic truths" and which "even now the loss of these beliefs, whether true or false, creates great difficulties."[21]

Mythical beliefs, myths, and theologies of sacrificial character are presented as some of the foundation stones that explain the evolution of human societies to our societies with a large and complex market system. One of the "symbolic truths" that arises in this reflection is a notion of God or divine providence, whether in traditional religious language or a secularized pseudoscientific language, that is behind this law of evolution seen as the survival of the fittest or those most capable in market competitions. This is a notion of God that is manifest in the winner and transmitted through myths or sacrificial theologies.

As Norman Barry, a defender of liberal ideas, states, Hayek's "evolutionary gloss on the theory of spontaneous order distinguishes him from other writers in that tradition (for example,

Menger) who do not preclude the use of reason in the critical evaluation of the outcomes of an undesigned process."[22]

The mere recognition of the fact that large and complex social and economic systems are self-organizing systems does not mean that this determined system is good or desirable solely by this fact. We saw earlier the way that Krugman, a defender of the capitalist system, also recognizes this. The problem is that a simple analytic observation of that kind does not generate sufficient motivation for maintaining the social system's functioning in a reasonably cohesive way. For that, a belief is necessary. According to Serge Moscovici, "it matters less that this belief is sustained by a myth, an ideology, or a science, than that it exists. Humankind feels the vitality of the bond that unites them, the unique strength of their conviction, and the pull of finality that makes them act together."[23] Also, we must recognize, it is this belief in evolution-providence that gives firmness, political strength, and certain messianic aspects to the followers of neoliberalism.

This last critique cannot lead us mistakenly to consider every thesis of Hayek as totally unfounded and wrong. We cannot deny that complex systems do in fact function in a self-organizing way or, at least, that the evidence seems to demonstrate this. Moreover, Hayek makes a correct distinction between the microsocial and the macrosocial levels. He says: "If we were to apply the unmodified, uncurbed, rules of the micro-cosmos (i.e., of the small band or troop, or of, say, our families) to the macro-cosmos (our wider civilization), as our own instincts and sentimental yearnings often make us wish to do, *we would destroy it*. Yet if were always to apply the rules of the extended order to our more intimate groupings, *we would crush them*. So we must learn to live in two sorts of worlds at once."[24]

The problem is that he maintains this dichotomy in such a rigid way that he comes to affirm that "continued obedience to the command to treat all men as neighbors would have prevented the growth of an extended order. For those now living within the extended order gain from not treating one another as neighbors, and by applying, in their interactions, rules of the extended order—such as those of several property and contract—instead of the rules of solidarity and altruism."[25] With that he not only denies the notion of solidarity in the macrosocial environment but comes to say that proposing solidarity in this environment is to place at risk the future of humanity.

Challenges to Ethics and Theology

This new form of legitimating the market system and opposing the demand for solidarity in the macrosocial environment brings serious challenges to theology and ethical reflection. I want to point out here only some questions.

The first concerns the concept of self-organization, a concept that cannot be ignored in ethical and theological reflections today, and which calls into question the theory of causality that, in one way or another, is present in the majority of our theological and ethical reflections.[26] Concepts like "historical subject," whether individual or social, who would "construct" a new society or form history from their conscious actions, or social analysis that seeks the determination of the exact causes and persons responsible for social exclusion, for example, are fundamentally questioned by the theory of self-organization applied to social systems.

Hugo Assmann is of those authors who thoroughly reconsidered his theological and ethical reflections in view of the theory of self-organization. Known in the 1970s for his radical rejection of the market, he today presents to us a position at minimum interesting and polemical: "Among the undeniable things, in the area of human interactions in complex societies, is the existence and functionality of partially self-regulating dynamic systems, in which one refers to human behaviors. In the economy, this question has a name, which was rejected by many sectors of the left until today: the market."[27]

He recognizes not only the existence of self-regulating dynamic systems, but also the market as the name of this mechanism in the economy. Running the risk of being misunderstood by many on the "Left," he affirms, continuing with his critiques of the capitalist market system, that it is necessary "to accept, critically but positively, the market, without giving up the goals of solidarity" and that this "demands a new reflection on the very concept of the ethical subject, individual and collective. . . . It is a question of jointly considering individual ethical options and the objectification, material and institutional, of values, under the form of normatization of human conviviality with strong self-regulating connotations."[28]

That rethinking of ethics necessarily involves rethinking the ethical subject: "In practice, the ethical subject, in an economy-with-market, is always, on the one hand, involved in actually existing self-regulating levels (in the economy, politics, culture, education, and so on), or is, through its normatizations carried out on the objective plane; and, on the other hand, it is supposed that, in spite of objective pressures, something of the freedom of subjective self-determination survives in the ethical subject." For Assmann,

> this subjectivity is configured by the inseparable unity between necessities and desires. It is with bundles of passions and interests, and not without them, that one can be filled with sensitivity for neighbors. It is appropriate, therefore, to ask: in those circumstances, to what do we properly refer when speaking about an ethical option/action? Exclusively to the subjective aspect (for example, to intentional volition) or conjointly to subjective ethical intentionality while inserted in objective processes of (partial) self-regulation?[29]

It is important to reaffirm here, to avoid possible misunderstandings, that Assmann is not defending the capitalist market system in force today, but an "economy-with-market" together with social goals, which is very different.

The second question has to do with the qualitative difference between the micro- and macrosocial. It is true that the
norms and practices of small social groups do not function in
the same way in a macrosocial environment. This is because
the passage from one level to the other does not occur in a linear way, but in that process new properties emerge that modify
the functioning of the system. It is the emergence of these new
properties that enables us to perceive that we have passed from
one level to another. Therefore, practices of solidarity that
function in small communities do not function in the same
way or simply do not function at all in the environment of society, just as practices effective in small religious base communities become inefficient or impracticable in the environment
of far-reaching religious institutions. It is obvious that to take
refuge in the environment of small communities in order to
escape that problem is not a solution, to the extent that today
it is no longer possible to live in a community without being at
the same time within society, with all that this implies.

The great challenge is that the notion of solidarity and many
other theological and ethical concepts were, in large part,
forged in experiences of small communities or social groups,
which is not to say in premodern societies, and that they do not
function well in today's large and complex societies.[30]

The third question has to do with the concept of providence.
Perhaps here is one of the most fundamental challenges for a
theology committed to the life of the poor. As we saw earlier,
the theory of self-organization permits two approaches. One
that simply establishes the self-organizing function of complex societies, and the other that, beyond this, affirms that the
spontaneous orders that emerge are expressions of a biological-
human-social evolutionary process. This leap is based in an
act of faith, one joined to the metaphor of divine providence,
an "invisible hand" that governs history, perhaps all the evolution of the universe, a metaphor widely present in the Western
world.

Being a quite complex and difficult matter, which is beyond what is proposed in this chapter, we are only going to present briefly some problematizing questions.

Leonardo Boff is, without doubt, one of the Latin American authors working in the area of theology and ethical reflection who has assumed and worked more with concepts originating from new theories in physics and biology while professing a profound optimism in relation to the future and without denying the dramatic nature of the present. As an example of this optimism, let us take the following text: "The overall tendency of all beings and of the entire universe, as quantum physicists like Heisenberg have observed, is to pursue their tendency toward their own fulfillment and perfection. Violence is subject to this positive thrust, its overwhelming mysteriousness notwithstanding."[31]

On what does he base his faith in this "positive thrust" or benevolent logic that orients all evolution? He seeks this foundation as much in science as in theology. He says:

> There is a tiny range of measurements beyond which the stars would never have emerged nor life have exploded in the universe. This means that the universe is not blind but filled with purpose and intentionality. Even a well-known atheistic astrophysicist like Fred Hoyle recognizes that evolution can only be understood under the presumption that there is a supremely intelligent Agent. God, the name of this supremely intelligent Agent and Organizer, is umbilically involved in the evolutionary and cosmogenic process.[32]

According to Boff, the physical world shows us how that world is loaded with the purpose and intentionality of the organizing agent who is God and that the law or intentionality that governs the expansion of the universe is the same one that governs the evolutionary process. In fact, what makes him suppose that the universe is loaded with intentionality is not the physical world as such, but as he himself says is "this understanding" of the universe and the emergence of life.

Later in his reflection, he says that "the Spirit shapes its temple in the human spirit. Diversity notwithstanding, the universe remains one and constitutes an organic, dynamic, and harmonious whole. The Spirit is seen to be the driving force of the cosmogenic process, an arrow of time, charged with purpose and as convergence in diversity."[33] Further, that

> evolution needs to reach a certain convergence, to attain an omega point. Only then does the discourse on the incarnation make sense as Christians understand it, and only then does it allow for moving from the Christic to the Christological. This is the entry point of Christian faith, the spearhead of cosmic consciousness. Faith sees in the omega point of evolution the Christ of faith, he who is believed and announced as head of the cosmos and of the church, the *meeting point* of all beings. If what faith proclaims is not sheer ideology or insubstantial fantasy, then it must somehow be displayed in the evolutionary process of the universe.[34]

As the conclusion of this argument, we can cite this: "In terms of eco-spirituality, hope assures us that despite the threats of destruction that the human species' destructive machine has mounted and uses against Gaia, a good and kind future is assured because this cosmos and this Earth belong to the Spirit and the Word."[35]

These are quite optimistic words. An optimism so full of certainty, however, raises for us a question: If the universe is guided necessarily by a benevolent logic, where do the deaths and sufferings of the innocent fit in this evolution? Are they merely the pains of childbirth? If yes, is this not exactly, or almost exactly, what Hayek and others say in presenting the deaths of the poor and the weak as painful necessities, as non-pleasurable results of the process of an always benevolent evolution? Is this providential vision of evolution not just another form of recovering the historical metanarratives of modernity, which Boff himself criticizes? In this vision of history marked by the "necessity" of a good future, where remain contingency, human freedom, and sin?

Boff takes from the omega point of evolution, in which the Christian faith sees the Christ of faith, the meaning of the evolution of the cosmos and living species. It is an evolution that would confirm that "notwithstanding diversity, the universe does not stop being one, constituting an organic, dynamic, and harmonic totality." That is, there is an order behind everything. Even if the physical and biological worlds constitute this organic and harmonic totality—which is also debatable—is this a guarantee that there is an order that moves human consciousness and society toward that very harmony? Is it the case that, with the emergence of human consciousness, there is no emergence of new properties that do not permit this linear application of theories from the area of astrophysics or biology to the human-social area?

According to Freeman Dyson, the tyranny or determinism of genes over organisms lasted 3 billion years and was only precariously brought down in the last 100 million years with the emergence of Homo sapiens, who developed symbolic language and culture. With that, "our behavior patterns are now to a great extent culturally rather than genetically determined. We can choose to keep a defective gene in circulation because our culture tells us not to let hemophiliac children die. We have stolen back from our genes the freedom to make choices and to make mistakes."[36] That is to say, the supposed laws that regulate the expansion of the cosmos and the evolution of living species no longer determine or have lost their strength in the determination of such behavior and also thereby the future of humanity.

It is our capacity to produce symbols and culture that gave us the possibility of freedom (even if small, freedom nonetheless) and, with that, the capacity to dream and to desire a reality not yet existent. It is that which allows us to feel ethical indignation in the face of what is given, to face the world as it is. We are even capable of desiring and dreaming about things and relations that we are not able to realize, things and relations beyond human possibility. This liberty, clearly, also gives to us the possibility of erring, of failing and, therefore, reminds us that we are not guaranteed a necessarily harmonious and full future. Unless this (sparing) freedom is only an illusion and human history is only a farce that simply reproduces a plot preestablished by a superior being.

The ethical indignation that contests the injustices and evils of the world is born from a wager, from an act of faith that breaks with the notion of destiny (whether a malevolent or benevolent destiny), the logic of the dominant system, and the process of "evolution" that has guided the succession of cultures, civilizations, and empires.

For José Comblin, the biblical tradition differs from the Greek philosophy that sought in God the foundation of order and thought that the human being would realize its destiny by occupying its place in the cosmic order, submitting oneself to the universal order established and moved by God. "In the Bible, however, everything is different because God is love. A love that does not found order, but disorder. A love that breaks any structure of order. A love founded on freedom and, consequently, disorder. Sin is the consequence of God's love."[37]

When the Bible says that God is Love, it is affirming that the human vocation is freedom, that this is more than a quality or attribute of the human being, but is the proper reason for the being of humanity, the central axis of all human existence. "That God is Love and that the human vocation is freedom are two aspects of the same reality, two sides of the same movement."[38]

According to this perspective on God and the meaning of human existence, God, who is all-powerful, becomes impotent in the face of the free human being, and comes to the world, not with the omnipotent power to impose God's will on human history, but as one who "emptied God's self, and assumed the form of a slave, taking human likeness" (Phil 2:7).

As it is not possible to live in freedom without the possibility of evil (ethically speaking) and sin, God made the world such that sin is an inevitable possibility. Therefore, Comblin returns to a biblical text often cited by Juan Luis Segundo, "behold, I stand at the door and knock; if anyone hears my voice and opens the door, I will come in to him and will dine with him, and he with me" (Rev 3:20), and concludes: "if no one opens, God accepts defeat knowing that God's creation has failed. God created a world that could fail."[39]

In a more recent text, Leonardo Boff has continued professing optimism and certainty while at the same time opening space for doubt. On the one hand, he says: "Like it or not, one is already announcing the day in which globalization will not be solely economic. It will also come under the sign of ethics, of the feeling of universal compassion, of the discovery of the human family and persons of the most different peoples.... Everyone will be under the same rainbow of solidarity, respect, and the valorization of differences and moved by the love that makes everyone brothers and sisters."[40] This "like it or not" reveals the understanding of a history marked by necessity, a necessary direction that is independent of the will, support, or practices of human beings. It is probably an understanding profoundly marked by his desire for a harmonious world.

But, on the other hand, Boff also affirms in this same article that "this is the great lesson that we must take away: either we change or we perish. Either we take the Emmaus road of sharing and hospitality with all the inhabitants of spaceship Earth, or we will suffer the Babylonian road of tribulation and desolation. This time we are not permitted the illusion concerning the gravity of the present situation. Nonetheless, it strengthens in us an indescribable hope."[41]

Hope is not the same thing as optimism. We are optimists "because of," that is, we have scientific or religious reasons for our optimism. On the other hand, we have hope "in spite of," that is, without reasons for optimism. Hope is born from an act of faith.

A solution to the crux presented—whether beginning with science or theology—is far beyond my capacity and the scope of this article. I presented here two possible positions, only with the purpose of placing the challenge to rethink fundamental theological themes like divine providence, the incarnation, and the significance of Christ in history in the face of the new forms of legitimation of contemporary capitalism.

It is possible to understand faith in the incarnation of Christ as the foundation of an optimistic vision of the unfolding of the historical path to the omega point, but we can also understand the incarnation as an act of the "emptying of divinity," that is, the entry of a God without divine powers into human history. An incarnation that reveals the solidarity of God for the victims of history, but that does not guarantee the victory of the poor or the evolution—in the sense of a path toward fullness or qualitative development—of history. For these presuppose a divine strength that the Christ "emptied" already no longer possesses.

I present one final idea. Theological or ethical rationality is important in the founding of a new cosmic vision or a new set of ethical and moral values. However, it is not enough "to move multitudes," to change the direction in which our society and civilization is moving. We need people and groups who incarnate those values in their lives and religious and social practices and who, in that way, serve as models of desire, as catalysts of new social and religious movements. We need people who do not make certainty or victory the principal reason for their solidarious actions but who simply live out their human freedom responding to the appeal of solidarity that comes from the faces of other persons.

CHAPTER 5

Ethics and Complex Economic Systems

The themes of ethics and economics are becoming more and more familiar. Some discuss them in seeking greater productivity in business and others in seeking to overcome the brutal social inequality and unacceptable social exclusion that mark our time. The two groups, in spite of many differences in their objectives, share the same presupposition: the common good, whether of business or of society, is not obtained only with the defense of self-interest and the logic of the market. For the first group, a business does not succeed in obtaining better results only with individualistic values, whereas, for the second group, the market by itself cannot resolve the problem of poverty or generate a better situation for business.

It is common to find, in some social sectors preoccupied with overcoming social exclusion, theoretical positions that defend the "control" of the economy by ethics or the submission of economic logic to ethical values. It is as if the failure of the Soviet socialist model obliges them to find another controlling authority for the economy. That is, as a model of society failed where the state tried to control and direct the economy through centralized planning, there now appears the desire and the proposal that the economy, especially the dynamic of the market, be controlled and subjugated by ethical values.

"Ethics" would assume the role once attributed to the state or "good government."

It is necessary, without doubt, "to tame" the voracity with which capital tries to dominate and exploit every natural and human resource, and for that the debate concerning ethics and economics has an important role. However, the relation is not so simple to the point that we can simply demand that the economy be submitted to ethical values.

There is a small text by Paul Krugman in which he deals with what he calls the "mysterious triumph of capitalism over communism" that can help us make explicit some fundamental questions in the present debate over ethics and economics. In that article, he poses the following question: "Why did a system that functioned well enough to compete with capitalism in the 1940s and 50s collapse in the 1980s? What went wrong?"[1]

He does not accept explanations that appeal to the "laws of history," which supply a priori answers, as he also thinks that the thesis that technological change and economic globalization were central in the downfall of the Soviet model is not sufficient. Because the verification of those changes cannot explain the fact that the socialist economy not only fell behind technologically in relation to the West, but entered into decline and then into collapse.

For him, "the basic problem was not technical, but moral. Communism failed because the people stopped believing in it." That is, for Krugman, the socialist economy and social system itself can only function effectively to the extent that the people believe in them and assume the values proclaimed by the communist regime. Whereas "a market system, of course, works whether people believe in it or not.... Capitalism can run, even flourish, in a society of selfish cynics. But a non-market economy cannot."

The market system is therefore an economic system immune to variations in the society's morality. For him, the market system is efficient and successful precisely because its functioning is not bound to ethical or moral questions. This is a claim that Karl Polanyi, in his classic book *The Great Transformation*, called the self-regulating system of the market: "Market economy implies a self-regulating system of markets; in slightly more technical terms, it is an economy directed by market prices and nothing but market prices. Such a system capable of organizing the whole of economic life without outside help or interference would certainly deserve to be called self-regulating."[2]

Krugman does not want, with that thesis, to deny the fact that today more is said about the relation between ethics and economy, especially in businesses and schools of business administration. He recognizes that the monetary incentive is not enough to make a business good or successful and that it is necessary to construct a morality, a sense of mission so that employees seek the good of the business above what they think is good for themselves. However, the moral bankruptcy of one or various businesses, which can result in the economic bankruptcy of these businesses, does not take with it the whole of society. With that he clearly distinguishes the microeconomic level of businesses, where morality is necessary, from the macroeconomic level, that of the market as a self-organizing system, where there are no relations dependent on moral questions.[3]

He affirms in conclusion:

> Capitalism triumphed because it is a system that is robust to cynicism, which assumes that each man is out for himself. For much of the past century and a half men have dreamed of something better, of an economy that drew on man's better nature. But dreams, it turns out, can't keep a system going over the long term; selfishness can.[4]

I do not want to discuss here the validity of Krugman's analysis concerning the principal cause of the bankruptcy of the Soviet socialist model, nor that concerning the "benefit" of the market system. The objective of this chapter is to develop some reflections on two themes set out in Krugman's text: (a) the emphasis today on the relation between ethics and businesses, more than on the relation between ethics and the economy, and (b) ethics and a self-organizing economic system.

Ethics and Economics/Business

In recent years, the world's major schools of business administration have introduced courses in ethics as an obligatory discipline; this does not occur in schools of economics. Moreover, there have appeared in many countries associations of businesses and business persons defending an ethically and socially responsible posture on the part of businesses. The emergence of the SA 8000 certification, which verifies the social responsibility of a business (especially in relation to labor), is one of the examples of that preoccupation as much on the part of some sectors of the business community as consumers and citizens.[5]

That is a posture very different from the one defended in the 1970s by Milton Friedman (who received the Nobel Prize in economics in 1976), for whom the social responsibility of business is to increase its profits such that corporate executives have no moral obligation to ease the pressure to pursue profit maximization in order to further the broader interests of society.[6] This radical separation between the "mission" of businesses to obtain the maximum profit, meeting the demands of the market in the most efficient way, and the broader interests of society defended in the name of ethical values is founded, in the final instance, on the separation between economic science and ethics.

It is important to note that this separation, a notion important today for neoclassical and neoliberal business people and economists, is not found in the origins of liberal economic science. Adam Smith, known as the "father" of the modern economy, was not only a professor of moral philosophy at the University of Glasgow, but also considered economics as a branch of ethics. The relation between ethics and the economy was long accepted in the academic environment. According to Amartya Sen, Lionel Robbins, in the 1930s, was conscious that his theory that it is not logically possible to relate any form of ethics with the economy, but for mere juxtaposition, was contrary to the predominant vision.[7]

Denying the relation between ethics and economics or between business administration and ethics is not to say that businesses function or must function without any attention to practical moral or theoretical ethical questions. It is only to affirm that ethics and values external to the business and economy dynamic cannot dictate norms or restrict economic actions. Since, as Norman Barry says, "it is not difficult to show that business creates its own morality within a world of conventions that develop spontaneously and precede positive law."[8]

The recognition of the emergence of morality within businesses and moreover the explicit discussion concerning ethics in business and in major schools of business administration basically occurred for three reasons.

The first was the growing conflict of interests resulting from the separation of the owner or shareholder and the executives who manage the business. With the development of the stock market, there are fewer and fewer businesses of great size managed by their owners. In this situation, the interests of the business managers are not necessarily the same as that of the shareholders, provoking many opportunities for scandals in the business world, with managers looking out for their personal interests more than those of the shareholders. This type of problem raises the necessity of discussing the theme of ethics within businesses.

The second reason comes from the need to develop a team spirit within businesses. With the profound change in the manner of administrating businesses that occurred in the last three decades, one of the central points in the search for efficiency and the increase of productivity has become the creation and maintenance of a team spirit and "moral high ground." For many, the existence of common values shared by everyone in a business, from those at the bottom to the leaders at the top, and clear rules concerning acceptable and unacceptable conduct is fundamental. This is why the discussion of ethics within businesses has become nearly obligatory.

These two reasons are restricted to the relations within businesses or the business world. In this way, they are in accord with Barry's thesis presented earlier and do not enter into contradiction with the broader thesis that the economy must not be submitted to the values and dictates of ethics, understood as external and superior to the economic arena.

The third has to do with the financial and economic losses that businesses suffer with scandals, whether in the financial, ecological, or social areas. Oil spills in environmentally protected areas and denunciations of the use of child labor or slaves are scandals that impact the images of the businesses and their brands, which are today considered the most important goods of a business. With that, the ethical, social, and ecological preoccupations on the part of many businesses are attempts to protect and improve their images in the consumer market.

These preoccupations with ethics in the business world do not come from the goodwill of business persons, since from the beginning many saw this discussion as costly, but from the calculation of cost and benefit and from the pressure that comes from the increase in the ecological and social conscience of consumers and organized citizens in diverse forms.

As Laura Nash says, "the reasons for the newly elevated place of ethics in business thinking are many. Managers have seen the high costs that corporate scandals have exacted: heavy fines, disruption of the normal routine, low employee morale, increased turnover, difficulty in recruiting, internal fraud, and loss of public confidence in the reputation of the firm."[9] This is also one of the arguments presented by Adela Cortina to justify the importance of ethics in business: "*ethics is profitable*, among other things, because it reduces costs of external and internal coordination: it makes possible the identification with the corporation and a more efficient motivation."[10]

The preoccupation with ethics in the business world, on the microeconomic level (the level of businesses and relations among business persons), discussed up to this point is of an instrumental sort, that is, ethics as a means for achieving the principal objective of the business: the maximization of profits over the short and long terms. Therefore, Nash defines business ethics as "the study of how personal moral norms apply to the activities and goals of commercial enterprise."[11]

Clearly, this type of vision is not accepted by everyone. There are those who criticize the reduction of ethics to business logic and defend a more substantive notion of social responsibility, substantive in the sense that it has meaning and value in itself and not only as a function of the objectives of businesses, which would negate the meaning itself of social responsibility. However, to the extent that there is social pressure and businesses assume or claim to be preoccupied with their social responsibility, their images in the market have improved, and it is more difficult to say up to what point businesses and business persons who criticize that reductive vision really defend a more substantive vision. However, it is better that we live in a society where capitalist businesses feel pressured to assume their social responsibility than in a society where no one is preoccupied with that.

The Ethos Institute of Business and Social Responsibility is a significant example of this movement that exists in the business world. According to the institute, it was "created to help businesses understand and incorporate the concept of social responsibility in the daily life of its management. The practice of social responsibility is characterized by the permanent preoccupation with the ethical quality of the relations of the business with its diverse publics—collaborators, clients, suppliers, the environment, their communities, and public authorities."[12]

Founded in 1998 through the initiative of a group of business peoples, Ethos brought together, at the end of 2001, 517 business associations from all sectors and branches of activity, whose combined revenues were approximately R$ 250 billion (Brazilian Reais), or about 25 percent of Brazil's gross domestic product, and who employed approximately one million persons.

The Ethos Institute seeks to spread and promote the practice of corporate social responsibility by helping companies to:
1. understand and incorporate the concept of socially responsible corporate behavior in a progressive manner,
2. implement policies and practices that meet high ethical standards and in so doing contribute to the attainment of economic success in the long term,
3. assume their responsibilities towards all those affected by their activities (employees, clients, suppliers, the community, shareholders, public authorities and the environment),
4. show their shareholders how important the adoption of socially responsible behavior will be to a long-term return on their investments,
5. identify innovative and effective ways of working in partnership with the community towards a common state of well-being,
6. prosper while contributing to sustainable social, economic, and environmental development.[13]

These six points of the Ethos mission reveal a profound cultural change that is occurring in important sectors of the business community and society. More than simply calling business persons to take up their social responsibility, this proposal seeks to show that the long-term financial return of businesses depends also on its ethical conduct and its posture of social responsibility.

However the question that remains is this: Could it be that it is possible for businesses to maintain their competitiveness in the market and at the same time have economic practices based in ethics and social responsibility that are quantitatively significant? I do not want, with this question, to discredit or invalidate the effort of the Ethos Institute or other similar organizations. Quite to the contrary, I think that those initiatives are important and contribute to the solution or diminishment of grave and immense economic and social problems that afflict our people. My reflection concerns the limits of that type of initiative in order to avoid the error of thinking that we have at last found "the" solution to our social problems. Moreover, the recognition of limits makes possible a better use of its potential and opens the horizon to other complementary actions that must be realized by those same groups or by other sectors of society.

In this sense, I consider quite debatable Adela Cortina's thesis that

> our era is a *management era*, and our society, a *society of organizations*, in which business constitutes the paradigm for all the rest. So that some come close to affirming that now one cannot expect only from society the salvation of humankind, as the Rousseauian tradition desired, nor from the state, as the "real live socialism" of Eastern countries pretended, nor, ultimately, from the conversion of the heart, about which a certain Kantian tradition spoke, it is a *transformation of organizations* that can save us, the business being an example among them.[14]

This optimism of Cortina, with the almost messianic role attributed by her to "business ethics" in the construction of a just and socially and ecologically sustainable society, is due in part to her conception of the main objective of the business. For her, and for other authors who collaborated in the elaboration of the book, the "goal of *business activity* is the *satisfaction of human necessities*," and not the generation of profit for owners or shareholders through the satisfaction of consumers' desires in an efficient way.[15] In truth, businesses do not attend to human needs generally, as nonconsumers do not take part in the market and, therefore, private businesses do not attend to their needs. Moreover, businesses do not preoccupy themselves, in making their decisions, with whether the products or services desired by consumers-clients are human necessities or only desires and whims. What determines the path of businesses is principally the desires of consumers.

Norman Barry presents another position, one quite polemical, but which helps us to see the problem more clearly. Generally, businesses that assume, at least in public, their social responsibility also defend the maintenance of a competitive market, without large interventions of government and society. This position is justified in the name of the maintenance or improvement of competitiveness and efficiency. The defense of competition in the market means criticizing monopolies and other so-called imperfections of the market. But, counters Barry, "what they do not acknowledge is that the corporation can only be charitable and socially responsible the *less* competitive the market is," since, for him, "it is only the monopolist who has sufficient surplus to engage in charitable causes."[16] In other words, "charitable" and socially responsible economic and social actions that are qualitatively significant in society demand great funds and these can only be available to corporations that have great profits—so great as to be sufficient to remunerate well the shareholders, directors, and functionaries, to invest in new technologies and the constant modernization of the business, beyond safeguarding reserves for the future, and, finally, financing those social actions. Immense profits that can only be generated by monopolies or oligopolies.

Compared to this more skeptical vision of Barry's, some might say that many experiments of the engagement of businesses in the social problems of communities and also within the businesses themselves already exist and reveal their commitment to social responsibility. And that these practices are important not only for the businesses and for the communities that benefit, but also for creating a culture of greater solidarious sensibility in society. However, we must recognize that one cannot expect the solution of our great social and environmental problems with only the sum total, even if increasing, of those actions. Not only because it is mathematically impracticable, given the enormity of our problems, but also because the sum total of the actions and practices on the micro level does not signify a new social totality.

Society, like a complex system, cannot be reduced to the elements that comprise it: the properties of the system are inherent to the system as a whole and none of the parts possess them. Those properties emerge in the interactions and relations among the parts and therefore cannot be explained in terms of elements that constitute the system on the most basic level.[17] The whole is always different from the sum of its parts.

In this perspective, the social structure is seen as an emergent result not of intentional processes and their intentional effects, but of the process of the dissipation of intentions—processes of degradation of the intentions of the agents that interact in a social environment—and of the interactions of unintended effects.[18] That process, instead of having only a disorganizing function in social life, can, in certain conditions, generate relatively autonomous structures that are stable, far-reaching, and in a certain way, independent of the will of any individual.

Therefore, however important the actions of economic agents, we cannot consider the economic and social problems and, therefore, the relation between ethics and economics, only in terms of those practices. As Krugman says, the market system functions as an economic system with or without these practices of social responsibility on the part of businesses, and with or without a culture of solidarious sensibility in society. Without doubt, the growing debate about business and social responsibility or ethics and administration is an important step; but we must recognize that it is an insufficient step. Not only is it insufficient, but if reduced to that microeconomic level it becomes a theoretical error and a "trap" in terms of social and political struggles.

Ethics and the Self-Organizing Economic System

One of the principal problems in the discussion about ethics and economics, in my view, is that most authors concentrate basically on the ethical and moral problems of economic agents (in the majority of cases persons, like business persons and laborers, but also businesses) or on the actions of these agents, leaving aside the economic system. Basically, they bring to the reflection on ethics-economics the centrality that the theme "moral agent" has in traditional ethical theories.

Approaches of this type do not recognize that one of the fundamental novelties of modern economic theories, since Adam Smith, is the discovery that large and complex modern economic systems like the market are not a consequence of the conscious and intentional actions of economic agents, nor are they the sum total of those actions. The famous image of the "invisible hand" used by Adam Smith to explain the unintended results of the actions of economic agents in the market is the most well-known and influential metaphor in the area of economics that tries to synthesize this theoretical novelty. There is a fundamental qualitative difference between the level of concrete actions (conscious actions, with a certain intentionality) and the level of the economic system. In the passage from one level to the other, new properties emerge that allow us to perceive that we are dealing with a different level, though not necessarily a superior one in ethical terms. And this emergence of new properties modifies at the same time the system's ways of functioning. Therefore, strategies of action and ethical norms that functioned on one level no longer function in the same way on the other.

This is why Karl Homann, in writing the entry on "economic ethics" in a dictionary of economic ethics, relies on

Adam Smith to explain his fundamental thesis: "The systemic place—not the only one—of morality in the market economy is the system of arrangement. He tapped the business of competition so that consumers experience an increase in well-being. Wanting to harness the morality—or amorality—of the economy to the immediate reasons or interests of the agents in the concrete execution of business activity is a sign of a premodern social theory."[19]

This is not to say that the actions and intentions of economic agents are not important concerns for ethics but that these cannot be the sole focus of attention, much less the most important. Homann himself recognizes this and says that "the emphasis given to the ordering of the system does not render superfluous the moral engagement of individual agents. The observance of norms is demanded: vendor fairness, diligence, and trust as well as honesty, beyond other aspects."[20]

The problem with Homann's thesis is that he, like others, reduces the moral engagement of economic agents to the observance of norms established by the market. That is, in spite of his going beyond the discussion of ethics and business in setting out the theme of the system of the market, he does not question ethically this market and reduces the moral problem to the observance of the laws of the market and the moral norms that permit the good functioning of the market. With that, the market as a system is placed outside the jurisdiction of ethics.

However, as the unintended effects of intentional action must also be the objects of ethics, we cannot set aside the institutional structures that produce those unintended effects. In other words, ethical reflection cannot be restricted to the intentional actions of economic agents but must also consider the social structures as an ethically relevant space.

For this to become clearer, it is important for us to remember that the socioeconomic structure is "a habitat, a social form conditioning all human actions within which occurs intentional human action. The structure as something objectively given imposes limits on intentional human actions, which makes these actions also lead to consequences that did not result from the direct intentions of the agents and which therefore cannot be explained through the intentions of these agents."[21]

Amartya Sen, for example, already showed in his book *Poverty and Famines* that grave economic and social problems, like gigantic collective famines, can occur without the rights of anyone, like property rights, being violated.[22] This is because "horrors of *any* degree of seriousness—all the way from gigantic famines to regular undernourishment and endemic but nonextreme hunger—can be shown to be consistent with a system in which no one's libertarian rights are violated. Similarly, deprivation of other types (for example, the lack of medical care for curable diseases) can coexist with all libertarian rights (including rights of property ownership) being fully satisfied."[23]

It is not enough that we are honest and act in accord with moral values if the economic and social system in which we are inserted is an ethically perverse or socially excluding and oppressive system. With these reflections we want to emphasize an important distinction that we must make in ethical reflections concerning the economy: the level of actions within an economic system and the level of the system as such.

George Soros, the famous megainvestor in the international financial market, also proposes a similar distinction. He affirms that "we must make a distinction between making the rules and playing by those rules. Rule-making involves collective decisions, or politics. Playing by the rules involves individual decisions, or market behavior."[24] To reduce ethics to the moral behavior of individuals or businesses is to reduce ethics and socioeconomic analysis itself to the level of acting according to certain established rules. It is necessary to break this reduction and place the economic system itself, with its institutions and rules, as the object of analysis.

If the system as such has faults in its operations and/or ethical problems, Soros says, collective and political decision-action is necessary. In this sense, the problem of economic ethics cannot be restricted to the economic area because the decision and action of modifying the rules and values that govern the economic system in force is not a merely economic decision, but fundamentally a political and collective decision. That is, the debate concerning ethics and economy only makes sense if we recover the classical notion of the economy as political economy and recognize that the economic system is a subsystem within society.

In summary, ethics cannot be reduced to the discussion of the intentionality and concrete action of economic agents and, therefore, the economic structure, or, as we were saying above, the economic system—which delimits the possibilities of action of the agents and generates unintended effects—must be assumed as an ethically relevant space.

Liberation theology was one of the few currents of thought that assumed that challenge to reflect on ethics and economic systems. Nowadays, the theme of "structural sin" or "systemic sin" moves beyond the boundaries of liberation theology or Latin American theology, and is present in diverse sectors of Christianity and even of other religions. The concept of the "idolatry of the market"—a concept that has a more theological than ethical perspective, but that is in the same tradition of liberation theology of reflecting critically on economic systems—in turn, exceeded even the limits of the religious arena and is used by authors from other areas of knowledge.[25] As this chapter is tackling more the question of ethics, I think that it is worthwhile to return here to some questions concerning the concept of structural sin.

Structural Sin

Clodovis Boff, in an article written shortly after the collapse of the Soviet socialist bloc, says that it is impossible by the logic of capitalism to realize the central ethical principles set out by Pope John Paul II in his encyclical *Centesimus annus*: the primacy of labor over capital and the universal destination of goods as founding and limiting private property. He categorically affirms: "Capitalism is incapable of operating with those ethical demands independently of the good will of the individual capitalist. Not only is it incapable, it is founded exactly in its opposite."[26]

There are, in this affirmation, two ideas very important for our theme. First is the explicit distinction between the level of the will of the economic agent and the economic structure. The logic of the economic system functions and produces its results independently of the individual will of the agent. The economic system functions in an autonomous way and the results of this functioning are not subordinated to the intentions of individuals. In this way Boff introduces, even if not explicitly utilizing the concept, the notion of the self-organization of the capitalist economic system and also the difference between the systemic level and the level of the concrete action of economic agents, whether individuals or businesses.

The second idea is the ethical incompatibility between capitalism and the social teaching of the Roman Catholic Church or Christian ethics. "Between the 'ethic' (or 'logic') of capital that consists in seeking a reasonable profit, and the Christian ethic that privileges the interest of the community, one can truly speak of an 'impossible compromise.' . . . in order to be ethical, it is not enough that profit not be the *only* objective, but that it not be the *dominant* objective, which is ethical values."[27] As these ethical values are derived from the two principles expressed just above it is easy to understand how this reasoning leads to the conclusion of the qualitative incompatibility between capitalism and Christian ethics. The reason for which, Boff affirms:

> In that sense, the regime of wage capitalism has a moral stature analogous to that of ancient slavery and medieval servitude. As

structures joined by economic relations, all those systems are objectively immoral, though Christians are called to live out personal relations within them in a human way (as Peter and Paul taught in relation to the slaves) and, especially today, to struggle to overcome them as systems of sin.[28]

The affirmation that capitalism is a system of sin to be overcome demands the proposal of an alternative; even if it is in extremely generic terms. Boff presents it in a formulation that, in my opinion, still represents the thought of a significant portion of Christians and non-Christians committed to social justice:

> Now, it is to that point that one reappraises the solution of socialism, as at least one of the possible alternatives. This, in its ideal form, expresses exactly the proposal (still in good part utopian) to realize in economic structures the primacy of the common good, of labor, and ultimately of the human person. It is a question of a generous ideal, which possesses substantial ethical content, while capitalism only incorporates as much from ethics that its supreme constitutive law permits—profit. For that very reason, socialism requires virtue, as much for its creation as for its reproduction.[29]

It is curious to note that this affirmation of Boff is quite similar to that made by Krugman in his article concerning "the mysterious triumph of capitalism." For both of them, capitalism is a nonethical economic system, while socialism requires "ethical support" on the part of society in order to function. Moreover, Boff's critique of the instrumental use of ethics by capitalism is the very observation made by Barry and others.

Does this observation "prove" that Boff is right? The answer is not so simple. Since, as Krugman argues, the socialist bloc, even with all the ethical and social generosity of the "socialist utopia," was not able to survive in an economic environment where there were rapid and large technological and managerial transformations and that was globalizing more and more.

This means that an economic system must not be ethically and theologically judged only by its principles or ethical content. It also needs to be analyzed in its operational logic, in its structure that embodies certain ethical values. It is necessary to see if this structure, which is independent of the will and ethical values of its economic and political agents, is capable of producing at least what is sufficient for the material and symbolic reproduction of society and of being sufficiently agile to adapt itself to the technological, economic, and environmental changes that occur in the world. A just and ethical, but inefficient, socioeconomic system is also not an alternative.

Another important question, but into which we are not going to go deeper here, is the anthropology underlying that vision and the proposal of socialism. That is, the proposition of a "generous society" presupposes that persons and society as a whole are capable of living in a permanent way according to the virtues necessary for the creation and maintenance of that society. This anthropological optimism makes it difficult to see that persons, whether leaders or common citizens, are beings of passions and interests, capable of solidarity and egoism, of courage and cowardice, or of civilization and barbarity. And we have yet to touch on the fact that a social system, by its systemic character, does not depend exclusively on the generosity of its members.

There is another important question that I want to raise here as we deal with the theme of structural sin. One of the problems in the use of the concepts social sin, systemic sin, or structural sin (sometimes used by Latin American theologians as almost synonymous, and other times differentiated and with more emphasis on the latter two concepts) involves the question of the root or cause of this type of sin. Let us take as an example a formulation made by Antonio Moser upon treating the problem of responsibility in social sin: "Where does one find the ultimate root of social sin? Is it in persons or in society? . . . [I]s it the individual or collective egoisms that generate structures of sin?"[30] Moser proposes an answer that goes in the direction of a dialectic understanding in order to perceive the importance of the structures and the responsibility of persons and groups. He says that "in dealing with the undeniable co-responsibility of persons in social sin, we must distinguish at least three possibilities: introjection, reproduction, and omission."[31]

Gonzáles Faus also goes in this direction and says that "in speaking of 'structural sin,' we want to say that the personal malice that man commits *ends up condensing in those threads* that sustain the community fact; and is not condensed exclusively in the personal history of each one. Just as no man is simply an isolated 'monad' or an island, neither is the sinner exclusively a personal sinner but is, in a more general way at least, also a *social* sinner." From this definition, Faus affirms that "structural sin is always the result of a sinful attitude with which man approaches the *community fact* or the social fact."[32]

In turn, Marciano Vidal affirms that "structural sin pertains to the objective plane of culpability, while collective sin refers directly to the subjective plane. Evidently, responsibility exists for structural sin, but that responsibility can be as much individual as collective."[33]

These three authors converge in their conceptions of social or structural sin and point to the question concerning guilt or responsibility for structural sin. With that, it seems that they conceive of a causal relation between the sinful actions of individuals or collectivities and economic and social structures of sin. They do not take into account the possibility that between those actions and structures of sin there might not exist a direct causal relation, even if mediated, so that we might affirm so clearly that structural sin is caused by sinful human actions that concern the society or community. That is, they do not take into consideration that social structures emerge from the interaction of intended and unintended effects of individual and collective actions, and that social structures are constituted in breaking with the intentionality and ethical nature of the acts of individuals.

When Clodovis Boff says that "capitalism is incapable of operating with those ethical demands, independently of the goodwill of the capitalist individual" and says that capitalism is objectively a system of sin he accents this aspect of the emergence and self-organization of the capitalist economic system. Therefore, his is a notion of structural sin that is distinct from that of the other authors we considered above.

But, at the same time, we must not forget that "economic history reveals that the emergence of national markets was in no way the result of the gradual and spontaneous emancipation of the economic sphere from government control. On the contrary, the market has been the outcome of a conscious and often violent intervention on the part of government which imposed the market organization on society, for non-economic purposes."[34] In this sense, the question of the "causes" or sociohistorical origin of structural sin prevents us from accepting any longer the thesis of authors like Paul A. Samuelson that the market "just evolved [and] like human society, it is changing...it can survive."[35] Or also the more radical thesis of Hayek, that the processes of biological and cultural evolution, especially the system of market competition, "both rely on the same principle of selection: survival or reproductive advantage."[36]

This naturalization of the emergence of the market system and the identification of the capitalist system of market competition with the positive conception of the selection process in the evolution of the species leads Hayek, and others, to invert completely the debate concerning social justice, one of the central points of the discussion concerning ethics and economy. For him, solidarity is an animal instinct typical of small groups that must be overcome if human beings desire the continuation of development. According to him, "continued obedience to the command to treat all men as neighbors would have prevented the growth of an extended order."[37] For Hayek, therefore, those who defend the notion of social justice become, without knowing it, antisocial because social justice based on the concept of human solidarity is "irreconcilable with a competitive market order, and with growth or even maintenance of population and of wealth. Thus people have come, through such errors, to call 'social' what is the main obstacle to the very maintenance of 'society.'"[38] Social insensibility is defended here as a moral value since it is essential to the market economy.

It is true that the question about the "guilty" made by Moser, Vidal, and Faus helps us to avoid that naturalization of social problems, however, it is necessary to be careful so that we do not place too much emphasis on the search for those "guilty" for structural sin or systemic sin. For Vidal, for example,

> It is not correct to speak of "structural sin" without relating it to the person. Severing its link with the personal world, "structural sin" no longer concerns the category of guilt, which demands personal responsibility; it is, to the contrary, a concretion of faith in historical determinism or materialist structuralism.
>
> The culpability of structures consists "in the fruit, in the accumulation and concentration of many personal sins."[39]

We have in this affirmation two important points on which it is worth reflecting. The first deals with the relation between guilt and responsibility. For Vidal, without the notion of guilt one cannot demand personal responsibility in the face of structural sin. Therefore, in order to maintain the demand for personal responsibility he affirms that culpability for the structures comes from personal sins. With this premise that without guilt one cannot demand responsibility he does not take and could not take into consideration the possibility of the emergence of a social order qualitatively different from the sum total of the actions of individuals or groups and which functions independent of the good or ill will of individuals.

To get through this impasse we need to distinguish the notion of guilt from that of responsibility. The notion of guilt derives from the idea that we err morally, whether through ignorance, weakness, or the intention to do evil. Therefore, the relation of the subject with guilt is a correlate of the degradation or loss of the sense of ethical dignity. Responsibility, in turn, may or may not be tied to guilt. It is tied to guilt when we are agents of infraction or omission and depending on the sequence of disapproved effects. But we can be responsible for social problems that are not the results of our acts. Moreover, we can feel responsible in the face of structural injustices, structures of sin, and feel called to struggle for their transformation without having to assume guilt for the existence and functioning of those structures. In this sense, the notion of responsibility generates a conduct, attitude, or disposition for acting in a bigger and vaster way than mere culpability.

The second point that I want to emphasize in the insistence of Vidal concerning guilt is the relation that he establishes between culpability and the critique of historical determinism or materialist structuralism. For him, in the notion of structural sin, "there is no opposition between 'personal' and 'structural.' The personal is opposed, then, to the 'deterministic.'"[40] I think that the notions of unintended effects, system emergence, and self-organizing systems can help us to escape from these two extremes: that of personal culpability for structural sin and that of historical determinism. The latter is problematic not only because it denies human responsibility and creativity and with that the complexity of human societies, with their physico-bio-psycho-socio-ecological aspects, but mainly because it justifies in the name of a "higher law" the sufferings of the innocent and sacrificial logics and relations.[41]

Ethics and the Complexity Paradigm

Concepts like self-regulation, self-organization, and action with intended and unintended effects, which I have used up to now, refer us to or remind us of what some call the "complexity paradigm." Among diverse authors, Edgar Morin is without doubt one of the most well-known names of that current of thought and has also written about ethics beginning with the notion of complexity. In spite of his texts on ethics not being very extensive, I think that his influence in diverse sectors of Latin America makes a brief commentary worthwhile. That commentary, I want to make clear, is only an initial approximation with the objective of contributing to that rich discussion, but still in its beginnings in our environment.

Morin, in a small text on "Ethics and Society," says: it is "necessary to consider an ethic with no foundation other than itself. I mean to say, we cannot find the transcendent philosophical justification that would permit integrating ethics in itself."[42] The true problem for him is knowing how to ground an auto-ethic, an ethic based in itself, on the level of the autonomy of thought and personal liberty. But at the same time, if that ethic cannot have a foundation, it must be explained or illuminated by faith. Not a religious faith in the traditional sense, but a faith in fraternity, in love, and in community, which is not the foundation of the ethic, but its source of energy.

To summarize, says Morin,

> I do not believe that an ethic without faith exists. Let us take this word "faith" in every positive sense, not limiting it to the classical faith of the adherents of a revealed religion. That does not eliminate, in any way, the problems of the auto-ethic, which are, in my opinion, of three orders:
> - The first lies in ethical contradictions or in the confronting of antagonistic categorical imperatives;
> - The second is situated on the level of ethical uncertainties;
> - The third is the problematic of the "I" (of the "me") in relation to itself.[43]

Morin's proposal of an ethic without a foundation that is not itself, but which is illuminated by faith is the subject of much discussion. However, as it avoids our question, we are going to approach here only some aspects of the three problems he expressed that are of interest for our reflection on ethics and economics. The first problem refers to the fact that there are concrete situations in which there are in play two or more ethical imperatives and it is necessary to choose, that is, to assume a risk, which presupposes uncertainty on the part of the agent.

The second has to do with the ecology of action: the effects of an action are not necessarily those intended by the agent, being that many times they can take on a meaning opposite that which is desired. It is the problem of unintended effects and system/*habitat* that we saw above. This fact produces a problem of ethical uncertainty for, in our case, economic agents.

The third refers to the fact that however sincere and authentic we desire to be, there occur in us complex processes in which enter what is labeled *self-deception.*

What I want to call attention to here is the fact that all three of these problems raised by Morin concern the "subject." They are uncertainties of the subject who cannot have total and perfect understanding of reality because of its complexity and the insuperable limitation of our capacity to understand. Morin does not point to any ethical problem in relation to the social system in which we are inserted, even of the ethical uncertainty emerging from the limits of our understanding in relation to the social system. They are only uncertainties in relation to the deciding and acting of individuals or social groups.

Despite recognizing, in another text, that metaphorically "the culture of a society is a kind of complex calculating mega-unity that stores all the cognitive entries (information) and, through the use of almost logical properties, formulates the practical, ethical, and political norms of that society," he does not develop larger reflections on the validity and legitimacy of these ethical and political norms formulated by that culture.[44]

What I want to emphasize is that the majority of reflections on ethics made by defenders of the complexity paradigm do not succeed in overcoming fully the paradigm of modernity that places the accent on the "subject." And not placing the capitalist market system in the center of ethical reflection on the economy can give the impression that they do not clearly perceive that this system, even being a self-organizing system, is not "natural" or inevitable. And in that way they can reinforce, even if unintentionally, as an unintended effect of their theoretical actions, the attempt of neoliberals to avoid any ethical discussion on the market under the fallacy that there is no alternative to the market system or that "there is no salvation outside the market."

With this warning I do not mean to say that Morin does not propose any ethical reflection on the economy in a more structural sense or on the economic system. For example, he says that "the economy must be controlled and guided by anthropoetic norms. It is, therefore, the search for humanization that demands an ethic of development, so much more since there is no longer any promise or absolute certainty of a law of progress."[45] However, he does not go far beyond those abstract ethical demands; he does not enter into the analysis of the capitalist market system. That is, he does not ask if the economic system in force, the capitalist market system—in which we must seek to carry out our ethical actions—ceases to be controlled and directed by what he understands as anthropoetic norms. This question is placed, well or poorly, by Clodovis Boff, as we saw earlier, and others.

Morin is not the only one to ask that the economy be controlled and directed toward determined ends by ethical or anthropoetic values or norms. The problem in that type of proposal is that it presupposes a political superagent (a World State? the old desire for the "good and holy" king/governor?) with enough power and knowledge to impose those norms on the self-organizing dynamic of the globalized economy and with them control it. Even if the world progresses toward the constitution of a World State so powerful, we must not forget that the intervening actions of that government's political and economic agents may modify the economic structure in force, but will also create other unintended effects that will evade the control of those political agents and which will end up producing a new socioeconomic structure that will delimit their actions and produce new unintended effects. And this is to say nothing about the possibility of the holders of that centralized power imposing their own interests, and not the norms that Morin and others call ethical or anthropoetic.

Final Words

Upon recognizing that self-organizing social structures can be "structures of sin" or ethically perverse structures, we more clearly perceive that ethics cannot be reduced to the discussion concerning the intentionality and concrete actions of economic agents. The concrete economic structure, which delimits the possibilities and tendencies of the action of agents and produces unintended effects, must occupy one of the central places of ethical reflection.

This ethical reflection on economic systems is fundamental for our criticizing the attempt to naturalize the market system made by the ideologues now on duty. They utilize a providential and evolutionist vision in order to say that the market system is the fruit of an always benevolent evolution that began with the evolution of the species and approaches its apex with the evolution of social systems that lead to capitalism.

Ethical critique, by its own nature, only makes sense to the extent that this supposed necessary character and always beneficent evolution is denied. Therefore, the primary ethical question, or better, the fundamental ethical question must not be, which economic action is more in accord with ethical values, but what is my/our ethical posture in the face of the economic system in force. Persons who accept with no problem the market system will have different notions of what an ethical economic practice is than persons who have serious economic and ethical reservations in relation to the market system.

In our analyzing the concrete economic system, "the crucial question," as Hugo Assmann says, "is not in admitting that the market has self-regulating mechanisms, but in knowing up to what point they are inclusive or exclusive."[46] Further, this is approached without making the mistake of metaphysical critiques like those from certain anticapitalist sectors that only emphasize the excluding aspect, without also perceiving and valorizing the aspects of inclusion and efficiency in the solution of economic and social questions.

Beyond that, we cannot forget that complex social systems only come to be constituted and function for a long period to the extent that self-organizing mechanisms operate within them. In this sense, the challenge is in knowing how to combine social conscience and the ethical subject with the self-organization of the market.

We must also remember that abstract ethical principles, such as "defend the life of the poor" or "the right of everyone to a dignified life," must be embodied in social values, institutional mechanisms, and concrete economics. And in that process of "incarnation," we must always recall that the "emerging" of new social systems does not obey and cannot be controlled by our plans or good will, however "ethical" they may be. In other words, I think that ethical reflection, from the level of the foundation and ultimate principles up to the more operational-institutional level, must maintain a dialectical tension with economic rationality. I do not believe that ethics can control the economy or that an economy "controlled" by ethical values is possible. This would be to return to a type of idealism already shown to be insufficient. Human society is too complex to be controlled by a single rationality or by a single type of value or logic, and this is to say nothing of the dictatorial power that would be delegated to the group/governor responsible for imposing a given conception of ethics and economy.

It is not a merely theoretical tension, but a practical tension in the areas of economic, social, and political relations. It is a tension that is born of the social and political structures aiming at modifying the present economic and social structures, in the search for a new economy, without losing sight of the new theoretical and practical tensions that will be born and be necessary. Finally, those struggles will also generate unintended effects that will continue feeding the tension between ethical values and self-organizing and complex economic structures.

CHAPTER 6

Solidarity and the Human Condition

I take up again in this chapter a theme that, in one way or another, has always been present in my work: the problem of social exclusion and the insensibility of a significant part of society toward this exclusion. I think that what fascinates me, like so many others, is not the theme in itself, but the experiences that we carry inside of ourselves and that mark our memory: the encounter with a poor person and the feeling of indignation that is born through seeing a human being reduced to a subhuman condition of life.

Those who have ever been touched by a look from a poor person and allowed that look to penetrate into the depths of their being know that one can not escape "unhurt" from this experience. It is an experience that profoundly changes us, so much that many interpret it as an experience of God, a mystical-religious experience, or a fundamental ethical experience. This also is true for poor persons. When they are touched by other poor persons, they feel that something has changed within them. At bottom, I think it was this that the "founders" of liberation theology wanted to say when they insisted that liberation theology was born of a spiritual experience.

In this chapter, I want to treat the problem of social insensibility in the face of exclusion from a more anthropological point of view. Why do we human beings have such difficulty with being in solidarity with the victims of social exclusion?

Compassion and Indifference

I do not want to discuss here whether or not the concept of "social exclusion" is appropriate for understanding what is occurring today, but neither can one deny that repeated statistics show that there are more than 1 billion people in the world living on less than one dollar per day, while the number of billionaires increases startlingly (including in Brazil), which ought to offend everyone.[1] However, it seems that these facts do not offend as they should. Why?

Some might respond by saying that these are only numbers and numbers do not offend. But they are not only numbers. Today no one can avoid contact, real or "virtual," with those called the excluded. Whether because one cannot stop at an intersection in large cities without being approached by someone asking for or selling something, or because the high walls of closed communities reveal the invisible presence of the excluded, or also because televisions show, for example, scenes of starving children. Those called the excluded are a constant presence in our societies, whether in a visible or invisible way.

Social insensibility in the face of the phenomenon of massive social exclusion does not occur, therefore, as a result of lack of contact or ignorance of the problem. Are there people who by nature are incapable of feeling the pain and suffering of others, incapable of having compassion? This is a question that goes in the opposite direction from a certain anthropological optimism that was or still is present in many groups and persons who struggle for social justice and for a new society. According to those optimistic visions, "conscientious" people naturally tend toward solidarity and the search for the common good. That is, "conscientious" people do not tend to seek their personal interests above group interests and, after the creation of a new society, everyone would tend "naturally" to solidarity in the search for the common good. Therefore, there would be no need for us to think about creating mechanisms of control and coercion over people, leaders, and institutions in the new society. It would be a truly free society.

This anthropological optimism does not take into account what is happening in terms of social insensibility, much less the insensibility that we also find in many religious environments. Unhappily, in many religious communities (in the broad sense of the term) we can find insensibility in the face of the suffering of the excluded behind beautiful religious words. Such insensibility appears, for example, in the definition of priorities that exclude the problem of social exclusion. The grave problem is that the sufferings and the life of the excluded were excluded even from the list of "real" priorities, that is, from the list that could actually orient actions and investments in time, money, and personnel, and not that which serves only the rhetorical or propaganda purposes of many work plans of churches, missions, or political governments.

But let us return to our question: Are there people who are "naturally" insensitive to the sufferings of others? Or, is it the case that everyone is touched in one way or another by these sufferings and what actually varies is the way we respond to "being touched?"

This is a hot topic today, principally in the field of biology and other sciences that comprise what is today called the life sciences. I went "walking" in some of these areas in search of a satisfactory answer, since I think that certainty is beyond human capacity. And on one of those modest "walks" I found an answer that made an impression on me through its simplicity, clarity, and power of explanation. The interesting thing is that I was looking for answers to some other questions when I came across this idea presented by the current Dalai Lama:

When I speak of basic human feeling, I am not only thinking of something fleeting and vague, however, I refer to the capacity we all have to empathize with one another, which, in Tibetan, we call *shen dug ngal wa la mi sö pa*. Translated literally, this means "the inability to bear the sight of another's suffering." Given that this is what enables us to enter into, and to some extent participate, in others' pain, it is one of our most significant characteristics. It is what causes us to start at the sound of a cry for help, to recoil at the sight of some harm done to another, to suffer when confronted with others' suffering. And it is what compels us to shut our eyes when we want to ignore others' distress.[2]

When a person diverts their eyes in order not to see the suffering of others or responds in an aggressive way to a poor child who asks for change, he or she is not being indifferent. If that person were really indifferent or insensitive, he or she would not react by closing his or her eyes or diverting his or her sight, much less by being aggressive. These immediate reactions, most of the time unconscious or unplanned, show that the person was touched. The pain of the other person discomforts and he or she is unable to bear the sight of the suffering of another. The person reacts. Only that he or she reacts with an apparent indifference or aggressiveness as a way of defending oneself from the "discomfort," from the pain felt at the sight of the suffering of another. It is compassion.

For the Dalai Lama, this compassion or empathy is natural in the human being, although, clearly, in people with serious brain lesions that compromise their emotions there really may occur a total indifference to the pain of another. Even in those cases what we have are exceptions—treated as illnesses—that seem to confirm the validity of the rule. We can say the same for people who feel pleasure at the sight of the suffering of others. I do not know if it is possible to speak of a "human nature," but the immediate reaction even of the most indifferent shows us that we are all touched by the suffering of others. The difference is in how we perceive, interpret, and respond or react to that basic emotion of being touched by the pain of others.

There are people who feel impelled to solidarious action; others withdraw. This closing of the eyes or trepidation is a "preconscious" reaction to the emotion provoked by the sight of the suffering, for example, of a child. For us to understand this process a little better, let us look quickly at some ideas concerning emotion.

According to Antonio Damásio, there is a common biological center that founds all types of emotions (primary, secondary, and background emotions). Emotions are complex conjunctions of chemical and neural reactions that are bound to the life of an organism and their role is to assist the organism to conserve life. "Notwithstanding the reality that learning and culture alter the expression of the emotions and give emotions new meanings, emotions are biologically determined processes, depending on innately set brain devices, laid down by a long evolutionary history."[3]

There is a difference between emotion and feeling the emotion since "we only know that we feel an emotion when we sense that emotion is sensed as happening in our organism."[4] The feeling alerts the organism to the problem that the emotion already began, in a certain way, to resolve. "The simple process of feeling begins to give the organism *incentive* to heed the results of emoting (suffering begins with feelings, although it is enhanced by knowing, and the same can said for joy). The availability of feeling is also the stepping stone for the next development—*the feeling of knowing that we have feelings*. In turn, knowing is the stepping stone for the process of planning specific and nonstereotyped responses."[5]

For the subject we are treating here, it is fundamental that we take into account that "emotions are inseparable from the idea of reward or punishment, of pleasure or pain, of approach or withdrawal, of personal advantage and disadvantage. Inevitably, emotions are inseparable from the idea of good and evil."[6] That is, the ethical and or religious conception of the person plays an important role in the way he or she interprets the emotion provoked by the sight of the suffering of another.

There is in society a great diversity of cosmological visions, religious doctrines, or ethics that justify indifference. People who have difficulty living with the feeling of compassion have at their disposal the most diverse kinds of pseudoscientific doctrines or explanations for justifying the selection and/or blocking of emotions, particularly those that provoke more discomfort, like that of empathy with the excluded. Some people even say that it is more rational not to be carried along by the emotions and feelings, when we treat subjects so complex and difficult as that of social exclusion. They are people who generally defend positions contrary to those born of compassion and the desire for solidarity. Reason or rationality (in general economic or theological) is used to justify the blocking of the emotion that shows us our inability to see without reacting to the suffering of others.

"The poor deserve to be poor, as the rich/powerful merit their wealth"; "God knows what one does"; "one is paying for the sins of a past incarnation"; "there is no salvation of souls without sacrifices or without bearing the crosses that God gives us"; "economic problems are not part of our religious mission"; "these problems are so difficult . . . and I/we have so many other important things to do . . ."; "God will know how to sort out these problems." These are some of the innumerable explanations that we encounter in our society in order to justify diverting the eyes from the sufferings of the excluded.

Generally, these explanations have an a priori and abstract character, in the sense that they offer a global explanation to the history and life of persons without taking into consideration the specific context and history of the people or social group in question. The sufferings and joys of real people that do not fit into those systems of thought are simply denied or set aside.[7] Rationality without emotion was and continues to be the objective of many theorists, including many members of churches that consider themselves guardians of truth.

Studies of the mind-body relation, however, show that the

> selective reduction of emotion is at least as prejudicial for rationality as excessive emotion. It certainly does not seem true that reason stands to gain from operating without the leverage of emotion. On the contrary, emotion probably assists reasoning, especially when it comes to personal and social matters involving risk and conflict. . . . It is obvious that emotional upheaval can lead to irrational decisions. The neurological evidence simply suggests that selective absence of emotion is a problem. Well-targeted and well-deployed emotion seems to be a support system without which the edifice of reason cannot operate properly.[8]

This thesis is valuable for all areas and types of knowledge, but especially for the religious sphere. All religious experience holds something that is not reducible to reason. It is what specialists call the sacred or mystical dimension, which refers us to mystery. Mystery is not understood as something thus far undisclosed by reason and that, therefore, can be known in the future, but as something that is intrinsically irreducible to reason. I am not bringing up this theme in order to propose a vision of religion that approaches mysticism or even irrationality but in order to emphasize the limited character of human reason in the face of the human reality and, especially, in the face of religious experience.

For Christianity in particular, this is a fundamental subject. Christianity is not a religion of "mysterious" knowledge, in general irrational, that only the initiated or chosen can understand. To the contrary, as the Gospel of John says, "I no longer call you servants, because a servant does not know his master's business. Instead, I have called you friends, for everything that I learned from my Father I have made known to you" (John 15:15). (And "friends" here does not signify, naturally, a small group of the hierarchy of the Roman Catholic Church.) In other words, Christianity offers knowledge that is reasonable, that is comprehensible to people and that shows itself reasonable in the sense that people of good sense can recognize the validity and goodness of its propositions. When the First Letter of Peter asks Christians to be "always ready to give the reason for your hope," "with gentleness and respect" (1 Peter 3:15), certainly this is not referring to reason without emotion. Reason without emotion is not able to understand what it means to say that God is Love and that it is in loving that we understand God. Love, as we all know, goes far beyond mere rationality or religious dogmas.

The Fear of Our Human Condition and Love

What makes people search for "metaphysical" explanations (I argue, religious or not) in order to justify their apparent indifference to the suffering of others, or their aggressiveness in the face of those who suffer, or those who try to be in solidarity with them? The propagation and success of those justifications would not be so great if people did not reject so much the feeling of compassion, or feeling the suffering of the other, which is present in us. In other words, why do people avoid the feeling of compassion?

Christophe Dejours offers us a good clue:

Perceiving the suffering of others provokes a sensitive experience and an emotion from which thoughts are associated whose content depends on the particular history of the subject who perceives: guilt, aggressiveness, pleasure, etc. The mnemonic stabilization of perception necessary for the exercise of judgment...depends on the defensive reaction of the subject in the face of his or her emotion: rejection, denial, or repression. In the case of denial or rejection, the subject does not commit to memory the perception of the suffering of others—he or she loses consciousness of it.... Emotionally, he or she can then assume a posture of unavailability and *intolerance* towards the emotion provoked by the perception of the suffering of others. In this way, *emotional intolerance towards the relational emotion itself ends up leading the subject to separate him or herself from the suffering of others through an attitude of indifference—therefore, intolerance towards that which provokes their suffering.* In other words, consciousness of—or insensibility towards—the suffering of the unemployed [in our case, the excluded] inevitably depends on the relation of the subject to his or her own suffering.[9]

The manner in which the subject relates with his or her own suffering comes to determine the way he or she comes to react to the suffering of others. And the way people react to the suffering of others shows us how they relate with their own sufferings. Indifference and aggressiveness appear here as defense mechanisms against one's own sufferings and, we can add, one's own fears. Fear of what? Fear of making contact with one's pain and suffering and, at bottom, fear of the human condition itself. The lack of absolute certainty and security, inherent in the human condition, provokes in us a permanent fear of the unknown and the ambiguities and ambivalences of life. This is the reason why many people are always searching for certainties in the groups that present themselves as bearers of absolute certainties. Groups of the neo-Nazi type or dogmatic religious churches and groups—with their certainties concerning salvation and revealed truth—are the most visible, but not the only ones in our society.

In the desire to live without the ambivalence and ambiguity of life, people in societies end up creating a fortress or wall around their world and projecting their fears outside it. The enemies, in that case, are nothing other than the "incarnation" of one's own fears, one's internal demons.

In a culture of consumption like ours, the desire to live a life without submitting to the limits and ambiguities of the human condition makes people in societies see their enemies in the people excluded from consumption. For the excluded, with their sufferings, remind people of their human condition and, with that, of the fears, insecurities, and sufferings that they want to forget.

In the words of Zygmunt Bauman:

"Those 'left out of the game' (the *flawed consumers*...) are precisely the embodiment of the 'inner demons' specific to the consumer life."[10]

He continues:

"Increasingly, *being poor* is seen as crime; *becoming poor*, as the product of criminal predispositions or intentions—abuse of alcohol, gambling, drugs, truancy, and vagabondage. The poor, far from meriting care and assistance, deserve hate and condemnation—as the very incarnation of sin."[11]

For people who find in a certain religion or church the certainty that "saves" one from the ambivalence of life in the human condition, the enemies are those who live out religiosity in a different mode. Aggressiveness against them is more intense as more of these enemies reveal themselves fulfilled or happy in their different mode of living the religion.

Perhaps an example might help in the understanding of these ideas. At the end of the 1980s, I taught in a Catholic seminary focused on the formation of future priests of religious congregations. One of the seminary's donor congregations had two types of residences for seminarians. Initially there was only one type of formation house, in a comfortable house close to the theological institute. But a group of seminarians requested permission to move into a peripheral barrio of Greater São Paulo, in an experiment known as "imbedded community." They obtained permission and continued their studies normally, except for moving into a simpler house in a poor barrio and doing their pastoral work near this population. In the meetings of the congregation's seminarians, when all the seminarians from the two houses were brought together, the seminarians of the peripheral barrio felt a certain aggressiveness from their colleagues who lived in the other formation house. When questioned about the motives for the aggressiveness, the colleagues answered that they were simply "responding" to the aggressiveness of those who insist on speaking for the poor, as if those living in the barrio were accusing them of not making the option for the poor. Those who lived on the periphery were amazed with the reaction, since they had not spoken about the poor at this meeting and had never accused their colleagues of anything, at least not verbally and consciously.

I do not want to enter into the many details of this event. I only want to call attention to this type of aggressiveness that occurs in society and in churches against those who are in solidarity with the excluded. It is as if the ethical option and pastoral and/or social action of those people discomfort them. Why would doing good trouble those who consider themselves to be good people? Perhaps because the presence of the poor and of those in solidarity with the poor make them recall things that they want to forget or do not want to see. For example, that they are not as good as they think, or that their religious life is not as "full" as they think and would like it to be. This is to say nothing about speaking of the sufferings of the poor that make them recall their own sufferings and fears, and thusly reminding them of their human condition, which they want to forget and from which they want to be "liberated." "Liberation" is what is sought through one's self-image as "chosen" by God and, therefore, "protected" from the human condition.

What are the mechanisms that society offers to those kinds of people so that they delude themselves and think that they are "free" from the human condition and are able to achieve a condition of fullness and security? There are innumerable mechanisms, but I find that we can divide them into two large groups. The first is the illusion that unlimited consumption/ accumulation could lead us to plentitude. In a simple manner, we can say that the accumulation of money and all that one can buy is the path to overcoming the insecurity of the human condition. The fear of aging, for example, is overcome with the illusion that money can buy eternal youth (consider the prevalence of plastic surgery, exercise gyms, and vitamins) and immortality through the promises inherent, for example, in the genome project, which obviously will be accessible only to those who have enough money to pay.

The second is the certainty offered by religion. In adhering to a god (all powerful, of course), religious persons feel themselves chosen to be among the elite, the people who are above normal human conditions. There is not much difference between the discourses and promises of so many churches or religious groups. Almost all of them "sell" the promise of the supernatural power of God who will place the faithful outside the ambiguity and limits of the human condition. Many of the disputed religions do not go beyond the competition around who has more authority from God for their suprahuman promises. Salvation or the path to salvation is to negate the human condition.

But, as José Comblin says, this "escape to the eternal and absolute is a trick of the conscience to hide a weakness. The escape to the eternal relies on myths and uses them to try to deny the provisory reality and forget one's fragile character. Since for a human it is a challenge to have to permanently face the fragility of one's condition and the uncertainty of what is and can be."[12] In the case of Christianity, the escape to the absolute denies or is opposed to faith in the mystery of the incarnation of the Word. Paul of Tarsus presents us with the paradox of the incarnation of the Word saying that Jesus Christ "had the divine nature, and did not consider being equal to God as something to grasp consciously. But he emptied himself and assumed the condition of a servant, taking on human likeness" (Phil 2:6–7). Therefore, Comblin affirms that

> the novelty of Christianity is not the desire for the infinite, it is the love of finite things, the love of things that pass. The human was created, precisely, in order to experience the eternal, to love God, in the dimension of time. . . . The human was made to experience the eternal in the succession and in the instance that passes. It is not distancing oneself from things that pass that reunites one with God. To the contrary, it is plunging into them, picking them up, embracing them fully. Salvation does not come to transform that vocation. It comes to save it.[13]

These reflections serve to bring us closer to a conclusion: the apparent indifference in relation to the sufferings of the excluded and the aggressiveness against them and against those who struggle in solidarity on behalf of the excluded have much to do with defense mechanisms. If we want more people and groups to move beyond social insensibility and assume the cause of solidarity then we must dissolve or weaken those defensive "walls" that are created in society and in people's lives. Only when those defense mechanisms fail will those persons and social groups be able to live with the "inability to see the suffering of others" and search for new paths to solve this problem: the paths of solidarity and social transformation.

However, we must pay attention to one thing. People unconsciously create defense mechanisms because they feel fragile. Therefore, one should not knock down that defensive wall with more aggressiveness as that aggressiveness might come to be interpreted as more danger, which demands more of a defense. What we must always do, with others and with ourselves, is strengthen persons so that they can deal with their sufferings and pains, which the sufferings of others evoke in them/us.

What helps people to be strong in order to face their own sufferings and pains? Pain and suffering make people withdraw, from there arise "walls." Then, what opens these walls? What opens us to others? According to the biblical tradition, it is the Spirit of God, which is love. There is no better remedy than love, this gratifying experience of being loved freely, to help us set our feet and walk in the direction of the neighbor (of the fallen man, in the parable of the "Good Samaritan") and become close to the excluded. For some that can seem such a sentimental and simplistic thing. It is clear that for the great social changes that we require, the experience of love is not sufficient. But for the problem treated up to here, social insensibility and the generation of solidarious sensibility, the solution passes necessarily through love, that is, through the experience of being recognized freely as a person without needing to deny one's human condition. It is not for nothing that God was experienced and announced as Love by the first Christian communities and by other religious traditions. So that we might live with compassion, the foundation of solidarity, we must have spiritual strength to live with our suffering and with the suffering of others. And without the experience of being loved this is very difficult. Perhaps that is why the evangelists Matthew and Mark narrate for us that in the beginning, in the origin of the public life of Jesus is the experience of being loved by God (cf. Matt 3:17; Mark 1:11).

Put differently, it is not aggressiveness and personal critiques that come to make more people become solidarious with the excluded. It is the experience of being recognized as a person— independent of one's wealth or poverty, intellectual or professional capacity, religious creed or lack thereof, political option, sexuality, and so on—that leads people to have a solidarious sensibility, evoked by their own pain before the pain of others. When we feel accepted, recognized, and loved we find strength to face our insecurities and fears and open ourselves to more creative and human solutions.

The experience of meeting the person who suffers is also an inestimable source of strength for our continuing to dissolve even more our walls that defend us and separate us from others.

But we must not delude ourselves. These walls will never completely disappear from our lives. It is a constant and unending spiritual struggle. As Hugo Assmann has insisted, solidarity is not something easy and simple but is the fruit of constant conversion and spiritual perseverance.

Again a text of the Dalai Lama: "Compassion and love are not mere luxuries. As the source both of inner and external peace, they are fundamental to the continued survival of our species. On the one hand, they constitute nonviolence in action. On the other, they are the source of all spiritual qualities: of forgiveness, tolerance, and all the virtues. Moreover, they are the very thing that gives meaning to our activities and makes them constructive."[14]

Wisdom and Love

We live today in an era of information and knowledge. New technologies amaze us every day and things once unimaginable become routine for the generations that are born and growing up in this world of technology and information. Will it be that the great religious traditions still have something to offer and to "teach" to our world marked by the abundance of new information, technologies, and knowledge?

With so much information made possible by new information technologies and interconnected networks, like the Internet, people are confusing information with knowledge. And, among those who manage to acquire knowledge, few manage to see that knowledge is not necessarily wisdom that can lead us to a more human life.

In my opinion, one of the principal contributions that religions can offer to humanity today is their long experience in educating for the spread of wisdom, not simply religious information or theological knowledge (especially those that pretend to reveal divine secrets), but life wisdom that has been accumulating over so many years of traditions. It is clear that one cannot teach wisdom without transmitting at the same time information and knowledge. But, information and knowledge are not wisdom. The wisdom that needs to be taught and understood throughout the world is that which teaches us that one cannot be happy and truly love oneself if one is unable to open oneself to the suffering of other persons; if one is unable to have a solidarious sensibility. And that one cannot really live the solidarious sensibility if one is not capable of accepting, assuming, and loving oneself, in one's human condition and not in a false self-image of a supra- or infra-human being.

When persons love and feel loved, they recover and strengthen their self-esteem and sense of dignity, fundamental characteristics not only for solidarious actions but also for being capable of creativity and initiative, fundamental qualities for living well in the world today. In other words, the wisdom of love is not "useful" only for existential questions, but is also important for obtaining the economic means for a dignified life among economic relations more and more demanding and changing.[15]

I fear that, in proposing to assume our human condition and in insisting on the importance of love, there might occur problems in our communication. Therefore I want to make very clear that I am not proposing to abandon struggles and actions in the political and macrosocial areas, since that would be a great mistake. Especially now that we are passing through a process of economic globalization and a profound transformation of the role of nation-states and international organizations.

I am also not proposing that one turn to a more passive attitude in the name of a mistaken conception of love. To the contrary, the struggle for the dignified life of excluded people only perseveres in time, and is capable of going beyond defeats and frustrations, if it is a struggle moved by the profound experience of solidarity, of the ethical indignation that is born from compassion. In other words, if it is moved by love-solidarity. I think that we must take seriously one of the great intuitions of early Christianity, an intuition that is also present in other religious traditions: God is Love and whoever loves knows God and remains in God. God is not presented as power (even if it is on behalf of the poor), nor as a guarantor of salvation, much less as the one who negates our human condition. Love has a "logic" that often confounds us and, with certainty, is very different from the logic of the search for power and security.

The self-confidence, feeling of dignity, and spiritual strength to face our problems and fears are fundamental human qualities for living in a mature and continuous way in solidarity with the excluded. Only in this way can people assume their human condition and live with the pains of other people and with their own pains. And in this way they come to be capable of discovering happiness and grace, which is experienced in a relationship of mutual recognition and mutual solidarity. And this experience of grace feeds us in order to continue in solidarity/love.

The search for absolute security will not free us from our human condition; it only leads us to a new sensibility, to intolerance and self-deception. Where the Spirit is, security is not, but freedom and love are.

Our social and religious practices can and must provide spiritual experiences that help us to assume our human condition. In this way we will learn to love ourselves better, ourselves and the other, and to transform compassion into actions of solidarity. Parallel to that process of spiritual strengthening, it is also necessary to be deconstructing the metaphysical explanations that give apparent legitimacy and a tranquil conscience (always merely apparent) to the insensitive. It is necessary to criticize the metaphysic of the market elaborated by the ideologues of neoliberalism, as also it is necessary always to criticize religious and theological discourses that justify injustice and social insensibility.

The Desire Not to Transform Stone into Bread!

People who allow themselves to plunge into compassion, developing a solidarious sensibility and assuming struggles in defense of the life and dignity of the excluded, do not remain exempt from the temptation to deny the human condition. That temptation is only no longer in the form of "diverting the eyes," but in other forms of temptations that originate from the "urgency" that is born of ethical indignation and compassion.

Solidarious sensibility causes in us a new desire that articulates a new horizon of meaning for our lives and generates a utopian horizon and hope for a just and fraternal world. This new utopian horizon gives meaning to solidarious sensibility and reinforces our desire for a human, hospitable, and solidarious world. But, at the same time, indignation in the face of the injustices and sufferings of the people leads us to hope that our desire for a fully just and human world be realized in a rapid and direct way. In this desire, we often end up forgetting our human condition and assuming the messianic mission of constructing the Kingdom of God, or the mission of historical subjects (new, emergent, or old, it is not important) to construct the reign of freedom. And in this way we forget that we are not gods constructing the Kingdom of God, nor suprahuman beings capable of constructing a history without the contradictions and ambiguities inherent to our human condition.

Our ardent desire to see a new and different world can lead us to the temptation of magical solutions, solutions that do not take into account the limits of the human condition (like imagining societies where people do not have conflicting self-interests or desires, but are moved only by solidarity), or then do not take into account the inherent limits of all economic social and political systems. Often we do not want to see that certain desires of ours are not possible to be realized, however beautiful and just they are. We do not resign ourselves to seeing that history resists our most beautiful and just desires.

The evangelists tell us that the first temptation of Jesus in the desert was that of desiring to transform stones into bread. It is no wonder, as not only was he very hungry—since, according to the narrative, 40 days of fasting had passed—but he knew the hunger of the people. The people's urge to eat was so great that he was tempted to desire the transformation of stones into bread. And let us agree, what they were not lacking in Israel was stones. It was a perfect solution in order to obtain an abundance of food for the poor, one of the promises of the Kingdom. But, why was this desire—a well-intentioned desire, by the way—placed as a temptation in the mouth of the devil? Because it is a desire that denies the differences between stone and bread, that is, a desire for a magical solution capable of conforming the world to our desires. It is a desire that presupposes control of God or supernatural beings, the only beings capable of that miracle. But, the God of Jesus is not one of the gods of that type. Why not? Would it not be easier for everyone? Perhaps, but this is the mystery of the incarnation, of the God who emptied God's self of divinity to assume the human condition. A God full of love, but with little or almost no power.

It is interesting to note that, today, the best-selling books and most popular religious leaders are precisely those who promise to teach the formula for transforming all desires into realities. They promise blessings or secrets that would deny the difference between stones and bread, that would conform the world and life according to the desires of the consumers/faithful.

Not only do we have difficulty in accepting that reality resists our most beautiful desires, we also have difficulty in understanding why our social and political struggles seem to change so little in our social reality. It is not easy to comprehend the complex economic relations that occur in the process of economic globalization. We are not able to see clearly the real reasons for the increase in unemployment, lower salaries, the oscillations of the stock market, the intricate relations between municipal governments, states, nations, and international multilateral organizations (International Monetary Fund, World Bank, Bank for International Settlements, United Nations, and so on), the influence of the governments of the richest countries in the world, and many other things. We also have difficulty understanding why people with whom we work in communities or in social movements desire things without even being very conscious that they desire; or why the people are so distant from and discouraged with political subjects. There are so many things that confound us and only increase our pain.

Moreover, a tempting solution is to choose a scapegoat on whom we can unload all our rage and frustrations and accuse of being the culprit of all those things. In this way, beyond unloading our rage, we manage to simplify the functioning of our world, which we do not understand for being so complex. Today one of the favorite scapegoats is neoliberalism and its representatives. It seems that neoliberalism is the cause of everything bad that exists in the world, even those things that had existed before neoliberalism and that will continue to exist following the end of the neoliberal hegemony (which is not very distant in the countries of the First World). If we want to criticize anything or anyone, it is enough to associate them with neoliberalism.

It is obvious that neoliberalism, or better, the applications of neoliberal prescriptions have much to do with the increase of social exclusion in our world—I have already written enough on that to turn to the subject here—but we must have the good sense to recognize that neoliberalism is not the culprit for all the unjust and evil things that happen. Neoliberals are wrong to desire to absolutize the market—what theologians criticize as the idolatry of the market—but to want to absolutize in the negative sense neoliberalism or the market, making them "the" culprit for all those things is to reproduce the same neoliberal logic with the terms reversed.

I think that this obsessive search for a scapegoat has to do with the desire for a definitive solution for human and social problems. If there is a single culprit for all our ills, its death would mean the end of them all. But the definitive solution, a world without human and social problems, the utopia of our dreams, is the temptation to deny our human condition. What we can and must do is construct a society *more* human and just, but not a society *fully* just and harmonious.

The obsessive search for a scapegoat is generally accompanied by aggressiveness. When I see people in solidarious struggles act with aggressiveness in their pseudoprophetic denunciations, I think to myself about the reasons for that. I think that, many times, this aggressiveness has to do with the difficulty of living with the frustration of our unrealized desires, the difficulty of living with the pain and suffering of seeing the pain and suffering of other people. Basically, it is the difficulty of living with our human condition. They are pseudoprophetic denunciations because they are not capable of creating more human horizons and generating hope in the people. They nurture, without doubt, the self-image of the "radical prophet," but I do not believe that aggressiveness can generate hope and solidarious sensibility.

Others reduce their horizon of understanding or hope to small local and communitarian struggles, as if they were trying to forget that world so large, so complex, so difficult to understand and change. They reduce the "world" and the challenges to the microsocial environment and become skeptics in relation to social and political struggles of greater magnitude and, therefore, of longer duration. In that way, they end up creating a more hospitable "world" that responds more quickly to their actions. But, unhappily, life does not function in this way.

When those groups find themselves obliged to deal with the macrosocial reality, they project onto the macrosocial level their experiences of solidarity that function on the microsocial level. Their projects or critiques on the macrosocial level end up being a linear extension of their experiences on the microsocial level. In that way they do not want or do not manage to see that the values and ways of working in small communities do not always function in larger systems. What is certain in small communities, like cooperatives, does not always function well or in the same way when applied in macroeconomic relations. They nurture the desire and the illusion that if we could come to place in power some of our own, or if we could manage to convince all the people to assume our proposal, the whole world would function like our small communities or local initiatives, or like a network of solidarious communities/cooperatives. But society is not a "large" community, and therefore can only function in a way distinct from the functioning of small community networks.[16] All these temptations that are unconsciously denying our human condition place on our shoulders an enormous burden: the burden to carry out a suprahuman mission.

Spiritual Wisdom and the Human Condition

It seems that this desire to overcome our human condition is part of human "nature" itself. One of the reasons is our capacity for desiring beyond our possibilities. In premodern societies, people tended to accept better our limits and thusly placed in the hands of God and in life-after-death the full realization of our desires. Clearly, many took advantage of that in order to legitimize domination and repress attempts to transform society. With the advent of modernity, people began to believe that "where there's a will, there's a way" and to expect the full realization of their desires.

The way to overcome this temptation to deny our human condition cannot be to desire to make ourselves "super-persons" who no longer have this temptation, for this would be exactly to fall into temptation in the name of overcoming it. The only way for us to overcome—though never in a definitive way—this temptation is to assume that it is a part of our human condition and live with it. From there is born the necessity of permanent vigilance and continued conversation toward not denying our human condition. In other words, we can only assume our human condition to the extent that we reconcile ourselves with ourselves.

As Socrates has said, the wise man is not he who thinks he knows, but he who knows that he does not know or knows very little. Or, as I learned with my spiritual masters, the saint is not the one who does not sin or is conscious of being a saint, but the one who recognizes himself or herself as a sinner.

Knowing if we have or have not fallen into the temptation of denying our human condition is not the most important thing, but persevering in solidarious sensibility. This is the best way to keep ourselves reconciled with our human condition, since solidarious sensibility with those who suffer always reminds us that we are human.

When we recognize the potentialities and the limits of the human condition, a certain frustration is inevitable. Frustration gradually must be converted into wisdom. To recognize our human condition is to abdicate our dream of the full realization of our most beautiful dreams. But, when we abdicate the pretension of realizing those humanly impossible dreams, we *can* construct a better world, a world within our possibilities. What do we do with the dream of the full realization of our most beautiful desires? One part of Christianity—in which I include myself—hopes that God, in God's grace and mercy, grants us that fullness in our resurrection. It is a hope that is born of the faith in the resurrection of Jesus. No more than a hope.

The testimony of people who in their simplicity seek to live out, with hope and happiness, their solidarious sensibility and persevere acting in more diverse locations and struggles makes me see that it is still possible to live a life worth being lived. That is the most important thing.

Notes

Introduction

1. On this important theme see, for example, William Leiss, Stephen Kline, and Sally Jhally, *Social Communication in Advertising: Persons, Products, and Images of Well-Being*, 2nd ed. (New York: Routledge, 1997).
2. Frei Betto, "Manual da Crise," in *Contra Versões: Civilização or Barbárie na Virada do Século,* 2nd ed., ed. Emil Sader and Frei Betto (São Paulo: Boitempo, 2001), 176.
3. Celso Furtado, *O Mito do Desenvolvimento Econômico* (Rio de Janeiro: Paz e Terra, 1974), 15.
4. Juan Luis Segundo, *O Homem de Hoje diante de Jesus de Nazaré*, vol. 1 of *Fé e Ideologia* (São Paulo: Paulinas, 1985), 31 and 19.
5. Max Horkheimer, "La Añoranza de lo Completamente Otro," in *A la Búsqueda del Sentido,* Karl R Popper; Max Horkheimer; Herbert Marcuse (Salamanca: Sígueme, 1976), 103.
6. Ibid., 63.
7. Ibid., 106.
8. Hugo Assmann, "The Strange Imputation of Violence to Liberation Theology" (Conference on Religion and Violence, New York, Oct. 12–15, 1989). *Terrorism and Political Violence* 3, no. 4 (Winter 1991): 84.

1   Theology and the Life of the Poor

1. Enrique Dussel, "The Bread of the Eucharistic Celebration as a Sign of Justice in the Community." *Concilium* 152, no 2 (1982), 56–68.
2. Franz Hinkelammert, *The Ideological Weapons of Death: A Theological Critique of Capitalism* (Maryknoll: Orbis, 1986).

3. Gilberto Gorgulho, "Hermenêutica bíblica," in *Mysterium Liberationis: conceptos fundamentals de la teología de la liberación, Vol. 1*, ed. Ignacio Ellacuría and Jon Sobrino (Madri: Trotta, 1990), 181.

4. Jung Mo Sung, *A idolatria do capital e a morte dos pobres: uma reflexão teológica a partir da dívida externa* (São Paulo: Paulinas, 1989; San José: DEI, 1991).

5. The program has a new name: Seminario de Investigadores y Formadores (SIF). See http://www.dei-cr.org/?cat=4&lang=es&title=Programas, Seminarios y Cursos

6. See Franz Hinkelammert, *A crítica à razão utópica* (São Paulo: Paulinas, 1988).

7. Jung Mo Sung, *Teologia e economia: repensando a Teologia da Libertação e utopias* (Petrópolis: Vozes, 1994; Madri: Nueva Utopia, 1996).

8. Jung Mo Sung, *Economia: Tema Ausente en la Teologia de la Liberación* (San José: DEI, 1994).

9. Hugo Assmann and Franz Hinkelammert, *A Idolatria do Mercado. Ensaios Sobre Economia e Teologia* (São.Paulo: Editora Vozes, 1989).

10. Juan Luis Segundo, *El dogma que libera: fe, revelación, y magisterio dogmático* (Santander: Sal Terrae, 1989), 373.

11. *Desejo, mercado e religião* (Petropolis: Vozes, 1998). *Deseo, mercado y religion* (Santander: Sal Terrae, 1999; Mexico: Dabar, 1999). A Korean translation came out in 2001. An expanded edition was published in English in 2007 by SCM Press. After that book, I published another, in partnership with Hugo Assmann, *Competência e sensibilidade solidária: educar para esperança* (Petrópolis: Vozes, 2000). The latter came out of my post-doctorate work in education.

2 The Subject and the Defense of the Life of the Victims

1. Hugo Assmann, *Teología desde la praxis de la liberación: ensayo teológico desde la América dependiente,* 2nd ed. (Salamanca: Sígueme, 1976), 40. Assmann wrote this text—probably one of

his most widely quoted paragraphs in the world—in 1971. Forty years later, the text remains relevant.

2. Ibid., 63.

3. Gustavo Gutiérrez, *A Theology of Liberation*, rev. ed. (Maryknoll: Orbis, 1988), 9.

4. Ibid., 10. It is worth pointing out that the critique of idolatry and fetishism is not directed only at oppressing systems, but also at Christian communities and popular movements.

5. Ibid., 9. The first emphasis is mine.

6. Rubem Alves, *A Theology of Human Hope* (Washington: Corpus, 1969), 4. This is the published version of his doctoral dissertation, which was originally titled "Towards a Theology of Liberation."

7. Ibid., 5.

8. For some of these problems, see Jung Mo Sung, *Teologia e economia: repensando a TL e utopias*, 2nd ed. (Petrópolis: Vozes, 1994).

9. "Indeterminação e complementaridade," http://www.dhnet.org .br/direitos/militantes/freibetto/betto_indeterm.html (accessed March 23, 2011).

10. Alain Touraine, *Crítica da Modernidade* (Petrópolis: Vozes, 1994), 324 and 225.

11. Agnes Heller, *O Homen do Renascimento* (Lisboa: Ed Presença, 1982), 9.

12. José Comblin, *Cristãos rumo ao século XXI: nova caminhada de libertação* (São Paulo: Paulus, 1996), 65.

13. Niklas Luhman, Paul Krugman, Pablo Navarro, and Immanuel Wallerstein are examples of scientists who use or dialogue with these concepts. The latter two have several articles available on the Internet.

14. Hugo Assmann, *Reencantar a educação: rumo à sociedade aprendente* (Petrópolis: Vozes, 1998), 134.

15. Hugo Assmann, *Metáforas novas para reencantar a educação: epistemologia e didática* (Piracicaba: UNIMEP, 1996), 64.

16. See Hugo Assmann and Franz Hinkelammert, *A idolatria do mercado: ensaio sobre economia e teologia.* (São Paulo: Editora Vozes, 1989).

17. Franz Hinkelammert, *A crítica à razão utópica* (São Paulo: Paulinas, 1988), 282.
18. I am using the concept "subjectity" and not "subjectivity," as it is more common, because the way that the second concept is normally used causes problems in understanding the concept of the subject as developed in Franz Hinkelammert's work, on which I am drawing.
19. Franz Hinkelammert, *El sujeto y la ley: El retorno del sujeto reprimido* (Herédia, Costa Rica: EUNA, 2003), 494. Emphasis added. I develop this theme more amply in chapter 3.

3 The Subject as Transcendentality within Real Life

1. Franz Hinkelammert, *El sujeto y la ley: El retorno del sujeto reprimido* (Herédia, Costa Rica: EUNA, 2003), 494. Emphasis added.
2. Franz Hinkelammert, *Crítica a la razón utópica* (San José: DEI, 1984), 29.
3. Ibid., 231.
4. Ibid., 254.
5. Ibid.
6. Hinkelammert, *El sujeto y la ley*, 495–496. Emphasis added. A subject that deserves to be carefully considered, but which is not the object of discussion in this small text, is Hinkelammert's hypothesis that the process that develops as a function of the inertia of the capitalist system is self-destructive and leads humanity to suicide. I think that the present system sacrifices many lives, but is not necessarily self-destructive. The capitalist system shows an immense capacity to adapt to new economic and social conditions. The problem is that capitalism adapts, condemning millions of people to a life of poverty and death. It is clear that I also think that the capitalist system can be overcome by another type of social system, but to assume this possibility does not necessarily mean to agree with the hypothesis that it is self-destructive.

7. August Serrano, "El sujeto y la red." *Pasos* 85 (Sept/Oct 1999), 18–27.

8. Ibid., 21.

9. Ibid.

10. Elsa Tamez, "El sujeto viviente 'racializado' y 'generizado'." *Pasos* 88 (Mar/Apr 2000), 18.

11. Ibid., 20.

12. Hinkelammert, *Crítica a la razón utópica*, 263.

13. Hinkelammert, *Crítica a la razón utópica*, 254.

14. Hinkelammert, *El sujeto y la ley*, 485.

15. Franz Hinkelammert, *Democracia y totalitarismo* (San José: DEI, 1987), 243.

16. Ibid.

17. Franz Hinkelammert, *El mapa del emperador: determinismo, caos, sujeto* (San José: DEI, 1996), 23.

18. There is today a small difference between the critiques made by Hinkelammert and Assmann with respect to the idolatry of the market. Hinkelammert, even recognizing the impossibility of a modern economy without mercantile relations, privileges in his analysis the negative aspects of the capitalist market. With that, he gives, many times, the false impression that the market is essentially negative. Assmann, who in the 1970s denied the market in a much more radical way than Hinkelammert, today proposes a critical position, but at the same time positive in relation to some of the aspects of the market.

19. Hinkelammert, *El mapa del emperador*, 23.

20. Hinkelammert, *Crítica a la razón utópica*, 254.

21. Hinkelammert, *El mapa del emperador*, 254–255.

22. Ibid., 243.

23. On this problem, see Hugo Assmann and Jung Mo Sung, *Competência e sensibilidade solidária: educar para esperança* (Petropolis: Vozes, 2000), especially the first part.

24. There are two principle works of Hinkelammert on this subject: *Ideologías del desarrollo y dialéctica de la historia* (Santiago: Ed. Nueva Universidad, Universidad Católica de Chile, 1970) and *Crítica a la razón utópica*.

25. Franz Hinkelammert, *The Ideological Weapons of Death: A Theological Critique of Capitalism* (Maryknoll: Orbis, 1986), 58.
26. Ibid.
27. Ibid., 53.
28. In some authors we still find the promise of the realization of the great utopia, no longer based in the modern Marxist metanarrative, but in the (postmodern?) metanarrative of the evolution of the cosmic universe, a vision quite close to the thought of Teilhard de Chardin.
29. Rui Manuel Graça das Neves, "La crisis del sujeto y las nuevas epistemologías" *Pasos* 87 (Jan/Feb 2000), 18–19. This edition of *Pasos* presents a synthesis of the meeting itself.
30. Pablo Richard, "La construcción del sujeto en la Teología de la Liberación" *Pasos* 87 (Jan/Feb 2000), p. 33.
31. On this theme, see Hinkelammert, *Crítica a la razón utópica*.

4   A New Form of Legitimation of the Economy

1. Paul A. Samuelson, *Economics*, 11th ed. (New York: McGraw Hill, 1980), 38. Emphasis added. This textbook is now into its 19th edition (2009). The 11th edition was the last one authored exclusively by Samuelson.
2. See Paul Krugman, *The Self-Organizing Economy* (Malden-Oxford: Blackwell, 1996). The *Sante Fe Institute* (http://www .santafe.edu) is today one of the most important centers in the study of the application of the theories of complexity and self-organization in the area of economics. See, for example, W. Brian Arthur, Steven Durlauf, and David Lane, eds., *The Economy as an Evolving Complex System II* (Reading, MA: Addison-Wesley, 1997). The introduction is available on the Internet at http://tuvalu.santafe.edu/~wbarthur/Papers/ADLIntro.html (accessed March 25, 2011).
3. Fritjof Capra, *A teia da vida: uma nova compreensão científica dos sistemas vivos* (São Paulo: Cultix, 1997), 64.
4. Krugman, *The Self-Organizing Economy*, 3.
5. Ibid., 6.
6. Paul Krugman, *The Accidental Theorist* (New York: Norton, 1998).

7. Some other examples: John Henry Clippinger, ed., *The Biology of Business: Decoding the Natural Law of Enterprise* (San Francisco: Jossey-Bass, 1999); Kevin T. Kelly, *Out of Control: The New Biology of Machines, Social Systems, and the Economic World* (New York: Basic Books, 1994); Ken Baskin, *Corporate DNA: Learning from Life* (Boston: Butterworth-Heinemann, 1998); Pierre N.V. Tu, *Dynamical Systems: An Introduction with Applications in Economics and Biology*, 2nd rev. ed. (New York : Springer-Verlag, 1998); Gary F. Bargatze, *Exploring Corporate DNA in the Age of People: A Business Handbook for the New Millennium* (Torrance, CA: Griffin, 1999).

8. Paulo Guedes, "Biologia dos negócios: espécies virtuais incapazes de se adaptar vão desaparecer," *Exame* 279 (Dec. 13, 2001): 36.

9. Ibid.

10. Matt Ridley, *The Origins of Virtue: Human Instincts and the Evolution of Cooperation* (New York: Penguin, 1997), 43.

11. Ibid., 46.

12. Ibid., 238.

13. Ibid., 262.

14. Ibid., 264–65.

15. On that problem, see Hinkelammert's foundational text, *A crítica à razão utópica* (São Paulo: Paulinas, 1988), especially chapter 3, which is dedicated to the analysis of the Soviet model.

16. On the theme of desire, necessity, economics, and theology, see Jung Mo Sung, *Desire, Market, and Religion* (London: SCM Press, 2007).

17. George Soros, the mega-investor/speculator in the world financial market, defends, beginning with a rereading of Popper, similar ideas in his book *The Crisis of Global Capitalism: Open Society Endangered* (New York: Public Affairs, 1998).

18. Friedrich A. von Hayek, *The Fatal Conceit: The Errors of Socialism* (Chicago: University of Chicago Press, 1988), 6.

19. Ibid.

20. Ibid.

21. Ibid., 136–37.

22. Norman Barry, "The Tradition of Spontaneous Order." *Literature of Liberty* 5, no. 2 (1982). Online reprint: Library of Economics

and Liberty, under "Conclusion," http://www.econlib.org/library/Essays/LtrLbrty/bryTSO.html (accessed March 25, 2011).

23. Serge Moscovici, *A máquina de fazer deuses* (Rio de Janeiro: Imago, 1990), 27.
24. Hayek, *Fatal Conceit*, 18.
25. Ibid., 13.
26. See, for example, Juan Luis Segundo, *¿Qué mundo? ¿Qué hombre? ¿Qué Dios?* (Santander: Sal Terrae, 1993).
27. Hugo Assmann, *Metáforas novas para reencantar a educação: epistemologia e didática* (Piracicaba: UNIMEP, 1996), 64.
28. Ibid.
29. Ibid., 66.
30. On this theme, see for example, Hugo Assmann and Jung Mo Sung, *Competência e sensibilidade solidária: educar para esperança*, 2nd ed. (Petrópolis: Vozes, 2001), especially part one.
31. Leonardo Boff, *Cry of the Earth, Cry of the Poor* (Maryknoll: Orbis, 1997), 19.
32. Ibid., 146–47.
33. Ibid., 169.
34. Ibid., 178.
35. Ibid., 201.
36. Freeman Dyson, *Infinite in All Directions* (New York: Harper, 1988), 94.
37. José Comblin, *Cristãos rumo ao século XXI: nova caminhada de libertação* (São Paulo: Paulus, 1996), 65.
38. Ibid., 67.
39. Ibid., 66.
40. Leonardo Boff, "El pecado capital del ecocidio y del biocidio," in *Itinerário de la razón crítica: homenaje a Franz Hinkelammert en sus 70 años*, ed. José Duque and Germán Gutiérrez (San José, Costa Rica: DEI, 2001), 225.
41. Ibid., 227.

5 Ethics and Complex Economic Systems

1. Paul Krugman, *Capitalism's Mysterious Triumph*, under "Economic Theory," http://www.pkarchive.org (accessed March 25, 2011). The following quotations are from the same text.

2. Karl Polanyi, *The Great Transformation* (Boston: Beacon Press, 1957), 43. Polanyi's notion of the self-regulation of the market system refers more to the relation of the market with its "exterior," that is, the independence of the market system in relation to other systems or institutions of society and ethics itself. Whereas the concept of the self-regulating or self-organizing system presently used refers more to the internal aspect of the system, its internal functioning, without forgetting the relation of the system with its environment or surroundings.

3. See, for example, Paul Krugman, *The Self-Organizing Economy* (Malden-Oxford: Blackwell, 1996).

4. Krugman, *Capitalism's Mysterious Triumph.*

5. For more information on SA 8000, see the Social Accountability International website: http://www.sa-intl.org (accessed March 28, 2011).

6. Milton Friedman, "The Social Responsibility of Business is to Increase Its Profits," *The New York Times Magazine*, Sept. 13, 1970.

7. Amartya Sen, *On Ethics and Economics* (Oxford: Blackwell, 1987), 2. Robbins defended that thesis in his influential work *An Essay on the Nature and Significance of Economic Science* (London: Macmillan, 1932).

8. Norman Barry, "Do Corporations Have Any Responsibility Beyond Making a Profit?" *Journal of Markets and Morality* 3:1 (Spring 2000), http://www.acton.org/pub/journal-markets-morality/volume-3-number-1 (accessed March 29, 2011).

9. Laura Nash, *Good Intentions Aside: A Manager's Guide to Resolving Ethical Conflict* (Boston: Harvard Business School Press, 1993), 2.

10. Adela Cortina, *Ética de la empresa: Claves para uma nueva cultura empresarial* (Madrid: Trotta, 1994), 88.

11. Nash, *Good Intentions*, 5.

12. "Sobre O Ethos," Instituto Ethos de Empresas e Responsabilidade Social Ethos, under "O Instituto Ethos," www.ethos.org.br (accessed March 25, 2011).

13. "Missão," Instituto Ethos de Empresas e Responsabilidade Social Ethos, under "O Instituto Ethos" and "Quem Somos," www.ethos.org.br (accessed March 25, 2011).

14. Cortina, *Ética de la empresa*, 13.

156 • Notes

15. Ibid., 43.
16. Barry, "Do Corporations?"
17. On the concept of emergence in the social sciences see, for example, Geoffrey M. Hodgson, "The Concept of Emergence in Social Science: Its History and Importance," *Emergence* 2:4, 65–77.
18. On the theme of the dissipation of intentions, dissipative structures of action, see, for example, Pablo Navarro, "The Dissipative Structures of Action," http://www.netcom.es / pnavarro/Publicaciones/Amsterdam'97.html (accessed March 21, 2011). On the concept of dissipative structures in the natural sciences, see: Ilya Prigogine and Isabelle Stengers, *A nova aliança: Metamorphose da ciência*, 3rd ed. (Brasília: Ed UNB, 1997).
19. Karl Homann, "Ética da economia," in Georges Enderle et al., eds. *Dicionário de Ética Econômica* (São Leopoldo: Ed. Unisinos, 1997), 297.
20. Ibid.
21. Franz Hinkelammert, *Democracia y totalitarismo* (San José: DEI, 1987), 152.
22. Amartya Sen, *Poverty and Famines: An Essay on Entitlement and Deprivation* (Oxford: Oxford University Press, 1981).
23. Amartya Sen, *Development as Freedom* (New York: Random House, 1999), 66.
24. George Soros, *The Crisis of Global Capitalism: Open Society Endangered* (New York: Public Affairs, 1998), xxvi.
25. On the use of the concept "idolatry" in socioeconomic analysis see, for example, Jung Mo Sung, "Idolatria: uma chave de leitura da economia contemporânea," in *Religião ano 2000*, ed. Enio J. C. Brito and Gilberto S. Gorgulho, (São Paulo: Loyola PUC-SP, 1998), 109–29.
26. Clodovis Boff, "O capitalismo triunfante na visão atual de João Paulo II: leitura da 'Centesimus annus' a partir do Terceiro Mundo," *Revista Eclesiástica Brasileira* 51, no. 204 (December 1991): 844.
27. Ibid., 845.
28. Ibid.
29. Ibid. Michael Löwy and Frei Betto affirm in a text prepared for the 2002 World Social Forum, *Valores de uma nova civilização*,

the following: "I believe that the expression *civilization of solidarity* is a synthesis appropriated from this alternative project. This means not only a radically different economic and political structure but, especially, an alternative society that values the ideas of common good, public interest, universal rights, and gratuity. I propose to define this society with a term that summarizes almost two centuries of the aspirations of humanity for a new form of life, more free, more egalitarian, more democratic, and more solidarious. A term that—like all others (freedom, democracy, etc.)—was manipulated by deeply anti-popular and authoritarian interests but that, nonetheless, lost its original and authentic value: socialism." http://www.dhnet .org.br/direitos/militantes/freibetto/betto02.html   (accessed March 26, 2011).

30. Antônio Moser, "O pecado social em chave Latino-Americana," in *Temas Latino-Americanos de Ética*, ed. Márcio Fabri dos Anjos (Aparecida-SP: Santuário, 1988), 76–77.
31. Ibid., 78.
32. José Ignacio Gonzáles Faus and Marciano Vidal, "Pecado estrutural," in *Ética teológica: conceitos fundamentais*, ed. Mariano Vidal (Petrópolis: Vozes, 1999), 366.
33. Ibid. 373.
34. Polanyi, *Great Transformation*, 244.
35. Paul A. Samuelson, *Economics*, 11th ed. (New York: McGraw Hill, 1980), 38.
36. Friedrich A. von Hayek, *The Fatal Conceit: The Errors of Socialism* (Chicago: University of Chicago Press, 1988), 26.
37. Ibid., 12.
38. Ibid., 118.
39. Gonzáles Faus and Vidal, "Pecado estrutural," 376.
40. Ibid., 377.
41. On the theme of sacrificialism see: Franz Hinkelammert, *Sacafícios humanos e sociedade ocidental: Lúcifer e a Besta* (São Paulo: Paulus, 1995).
42. Edgar Morin, "Ética e sociedade," in *Edgar Morin: Ética, cultura e educação*, ed. Alfredo Pena-Veja, Cleide R. S. Almeida, and Izabel Petraglia (São Paulo: Cortez Editora, 2001), 40.
43. Ibid., 41.

44. Edgar Morin, "Cultura – conhecimento," in *O olhar do observador: contribuições para uma teoria do conhecimento construtivista*, eds. Paul Watzlawcik and Peter Krieg (São Paulo: Ed. Psy II, 1995), 72-73.

45. Edgar Morin and Anne B. Kern, *Terra-Pátria* (Lisbon: Insituto Piaget, 1993), 88.

46. Hugo Assmann, *Desafios e falácias: ensaios sobre a conjuntura atual* (São Paulo: Paulinas, 1991), 24.

6 Solidarity and the Human Condition

1. The World Bank's poverty indicators now set the international line of "extreme poverty" at 1.25 US$ per day. According to this new measure, around 1.4 billion people were living in extreme poverty in 2005. See http://go.worldbank.org/45FS30HBF0 (accessed March 28, 2011).

2. Bstan-'dzin-rgya-mtsho, Dalai Lama XIV, *Ethics for the New Millennium* (New York: Riverhead, 1999), 64.

3. Antonio Damasio, *The Feeling of What Happens: Body and Emotion in the Making of Consciousness* (New York: Harcourt Brace, 1999), 51.

4. Ibid., 279.

5. Ibid., 284–85.

6. Ibid., 55.

7. There is already good literature on these "metaphysical" explanations in the area of economy, especially, for example, Hugo Assmann and Franz Hinkelammert, *A Idolatria do mercado: ensaios sobre economia e teologia* (São.Paulo: Editora Vozes, 1989); Hugo Assmann, *Crítica à lógica da exclusão: ensaios sobre economia e teologia* (São Paulo, Paulus, 1994); Jung Mo Sung, *Desire, Market, and Religion* (London: SCM Press, 2007); Jung Mo Sung, "Idolatria: uma chave de leitura da economia contemporânea" in *Religião ano 2000*, ed. Enio J. C. Brito and Gilberto S. Gorgulho (São Paulo: Loyola PUC-SP, 1998), 109–29.

8. Damasio, *The Feeling of What Happens*, 41–42. See also his *Descartes' Error: Emotion, Reason, and the Human Brain*, rev ed. (London: Vintage, 2006).

9. Christophe Dejours, *A banalização da injustice social*, 2nd ed. (Rio de Janeiro: Ed. FGV, 1999), 45–46. Emphasis mine.

10. Zygmunt Bauman, *Postmodernity and Its Discontents* (Cambridge: Polity, 1997), 41–42.

11. Ibid., 43–44.

12. José Comblin, *O provisório e o definitivo* (São Paulo: Herder, 1968), 74.

13. Ibid., 72.

14. Dalai Lama, *Ethics*, 130–31.

15. On education, solidarious sensibility, and social exclusion see: Hugo Assmann and Jung Mo Sung, *Competência e sensibilidade solidária: educar para esperança* (Petrópolis: Vozes, 2000).

16. This is an important theme, but we cannot develop it further in this text. Therefore, I refer you to the text *Competência e sensibilidade solidária: educar para esperança*, which I co-wrote with Hugo Assmann.

Bibliography

Alves, Rubem. *A Theology of Human Hope.* Washington: Corpus, 1969.

Arthur, W. Brian, Steven Durlauf, and David Lane, eds., *The Economy as an Evolving Complex System II.* Reading, MA: Addison-Wesley, 1997.

Assmann, Hugo. *Teología desde la praxis de la liberación: ensayo teológico desde la América dependiente,* 2nd ed. Salamanca: Sígueme, 1976.

———. "The Strange Imputation of Violence to Liberation Theology." (Conference on Religion and Violence, New York, Oct. 12–15, 1989). *Terrorism and Political Violence* 3, no. 4 (Winter 1991): 80–99.

———. *Desafios e falácias: ensaios sobre a conjuntura atual.* São Paulo: Paulinas, 1991.

———. *Crítica à lógica da exclusão: ensaios sobre economia e teologia.* São Paulo, Paulus, 1994.

———. *Metáforas novas para reencantar a educação: epistemologia e didática.* Piracicaba: UNIMEP, 1996

———. *Reencantar a educação: rumo à sociedade aprendente.* Petrópolis: Vozes, 1998.

Assmann, Hugo and Franz Hinkelammert. *A Idolatria do mercado: ensaios sobre economia e teologia.* São Paulo: Editora Vozes, 1989.

Assmann, Hugo and Jung Mo Sung. *Competência e sensibilidade solidária: educar para esperança.* Petrópolis: Vozes, 2000.

Bargatze, Gary F. *Exploring Corporate DNA in the Age of People: A Business Handbook for the New Millennium.* Torrance, CA: Griffin, 1999.

Barry, Norman. "The Tradition of Spontaneous Order." *Literature of Liberty* 5, no. 2 (1982): 7–58. Online reprint: Library of Economics and Liberty, http://www.econlib.org/library/Essays/LtrLbrty / bryTSO.html (accessed March 28, 2011)

Barry, Norman. "Do Corporations Have Any Responsibility Beyond Making a Profit?" *Journal of Markets and Morality* 3, no.1 (Spring 2000), http://www.acton.org/pub/journal-markets-morality/volume-3-number-1 (accessed March 25, 2011).

Baskin, Ken. *Corporate DNA: Learning from Life*. Boston: Butterworth-Heinemann, 1998.

Bauman, Zygmunt. *Postmodernity and Its Discontents*. Cambridge: Polity, 1997.

Betto, Frei, "Indeterminação e complementaridade." http://www.dhnet.org.br/direitos/militantes/freibetto/betto_indeterm.html (accessed March 23, 2011).

———. "Manual da Crise." In *Contra Versões: Civilização or Barbárie na Virada do Século,* 2nd ed., edited by Emil Sader and Frei Betto, 176–78. São Paulo: Boitempo, 2001.

Betto, Frei and Michael Löwy. "Valores de uma nova civilização." http://www.dhnet.org.br/direitos/militantes/freibetto/betto02.html (accessed March 26, 2011).

Boff, Clodovis. "O capitalismo triunfante na visão atual de João Paulo II: leitura da 'Centesimus annus' a partir do Terceiro Mundo." *Revísta Eclesiástica Brasileira* 51, no. 204 (December 1991): 825–46

Boff, Leonardo. *Cry of the Earth, Cry of the Poor*. Maryknoll: Orbis, 1997.

———. "El pecado capital del ecocidio y del biocidio." In *Itinerário de la razón crítica: homenaje a Franz Hinkelammert en sus 70 años*, edited by José Duque and Germán Gutiérrez, 213–27. San José, Costa Rica: DEI, 2001.

Bstan-'dzin-rgya-mtsho, Dalai Lama XIV. *Ethics for the New Millennium*. New York: Riverhead, 1999.

Capra, Fritjof. *A teia da vida: uma nova compreensão cientifica dos sistemas vivos*. São Paulo: Cultix, 1997.

Clippinger, John Henry, ed. *The Biology of Business: Decoding the Natural Law of Enterprise*. San Francisco: Jossey-Bass, 1999.

Comblin, José. *O provisório e o definitivo*. São Paulo: Herder, 1968.

———. *Cristãos rumo ao século XXI: nova caminhada de libertação*. São Paulo: Paulus, 1996.

Cortina, Adela. *Ética de la empresa: Claves para uma nueva cultura empresarial*. Madrid: Trotta, 1994.

Damasio, Antonio. *The Feeling of What Happens: Body and Emotion in the Making of Consciousness.* New York: Harcourt Brace, 1999.

————. *Descartes' Error: Emotion, Reason, and the Human Brain*, rev. ed. London: Vintage, 2006.

Dejours, Christophe. *A banalização da injustice social*, 2nd ed. Rio de Janeiro: Ed. FGV, 1999.

Dussel, Enrique. "The Bread of the Eucharistic Celebration as a Sign of Justice in the Community." *Concilium* 172 no. 2 (1982): 56–68.

Dyson, Freeman. *Infinite in All Directions.* New York: Harper, 1988.

Furtado, Celso. *O Mito do Desenvolvimento Econômico.* Rio de Janeiro: Paz e Terra, 1974.

Friedman, Milton. "The Social Responsibility of Business is to Increase Its Profits." *The New York Times Magazine*, Sept. 13, 1970.

Gonzáles Faus, José Ignacio and Marciano Vidal, "Pecado estrutural." In *Ética teológica: conceitos fundamentais*, edited by Marciano Vidal. Petrópolis: Vozes, 1999.

Gorgulho, Gilberto. "Hermenêutica bíblica." In *Mysterium Liberationis: conceptos fundamentals de la teología de la liberación, Vol. 1*, edited by Ignacio Ellacuría and Jon Sobrino, 169–200. Madri: Trotta, 1990.

Graça das Neves, Rui Manuel. "La crisis del sujeto y las nuevas epistemologías." *Pasos* 87 (Jan./Feb. 2000): 18–20.

Guedes, Paulo. "Biologia dos negócios: espécies virtuais incapazes de se adaptar vão desaparecer." *Exame* 279 (Dec. 13, 2001): xx–xx.

Gutiérrez, Gustavo. *A Theology of Liberation*, rev. ed. Maryknoll: Orbis, 1988.

Hayek, Friedrich A. von. *The Fatal Conceit: The Errors of Socialism.* Chicago: University of Chicago Press, 1988.

Heller, Agnes. *O Homen do Renascimento.* Lisboa: Ed Presença, 1982.

Hinkelammert, Franz. *Ideologías del desarrollo y dialéctica de la historia.* Santiago: Ed. Nueva Universidad, Universidad Católica de Chile, 1970.

————. *Crítica a la razón utópica.* San José: DEI, 1984.

————. *The Ideological Weapons of Death: A Theological Critique of Capitalism.* Maryknoll: Orbis, 1986.

————. *Democracia y totalitarismo.* San José: DEI, 1987.

————. *A crítica à razão utópica.* São Paulo: Paulinas, 1988.

Hinkelammert, Franz. *Sacafícios humanos e sociedade ocidental: Lúcifer e a Besta.* São Paulo: Paulus, 1995.

———. *El mapa del emperador: determinismo, caos, sujeto.* San José: DEI, 1996.

———. "La vuelta del sujeto humano reprimido frente a la estrategia de globalización." In Franz Hinkelammert, *El sujeto y la ley: El retorno del sujeto reprimido.* Herédia, Costa Rica: EUNA, 2003.

Hodgson, Geoffrey M. "The Concept of Emergence in Social Science: Its History and Importance." *Emergence* 2, no. 4, 65–77.

Homann, Karl. "Ética da economia." In *Dicionário de Ética Econômica,* edited by Georges Enderle, et al. S. Leopoldo: Ed. Unisinos, 1997.

Horkheimer, Max. "La Añoranza de lo Completamente Otro." In *A la Búsqueda del Sentido,* Karl Popper, Max Horkheimer, and Herbert Marcuse, 67–124. Salamanca: Sígueme, 1976.

Kelly, Kevin. *Out of Control: The New Biology of Machines, Social Systems, and the Economic World.* New York: Basic Books, 1994.

Krugman, Paul. *The Self-Organizing Economy.* Malden-Oxford: Blackwell, 1996.

———. *The Accidental Theorist.* New York: Norton, 1998.

———. *Capitalism's Mysterious Triumph,* under "Economic Theory," http://www.pkarchive.org (accessed March 25, 2011).

Leiss, William, Stephen Kline, and Sally Jhally. *Social Communication in Advertising: Persons, Products, and Images of Well-Being,* 2nd ed. New York: Routledge, 1997.

Morin, Edgar. "Cultura – conhecimento." In *O olhar do observador: contribuições para uma teoria do conhecimento construtivista,* edited by Paul Watzlawick and Peter Krieg, 71–80. São Paulo: Ed. Psy II, 1995.

———. "Ética e sociedade." In *Edgar Morin: Ética, cultura e educação,* edited by Alfredo Pena-Veja, Cleide R. S. Almeida, and Izabel Petraglia, 39–45. São Paulo: Cortez Editora, 2001.

Morin, Edgar and Anne B. Kern. *Terra-Pátria.* Lisbon: Insituto Piaget, 1993.

Moscovici, Serge. *A máquina de fazer deuses.* Rio de Janeiro: Imago, 1990.

Moser, Antônio. "O pecado social em chave Latino-Americana." In *Temas Latino-Americanos de Ética,* edited by Márcio Fabri dos Anjos, 63–91. Aparecida-SP: Santuário, 1988.

Nash, Laura. *Good Intentions Aside: A Manager's Guide to Resolving Ethical Conflict.* Boston: Harvard Business School Press, 1993.

Navarro, Pablo. "The Dissipative Structures of Action," http://www .netcom.es/pnavarro/Publicaciones/Amsterdam'97.html (accessed March 21, 2011)

Polanyi, Karl. *The Great Transformation.* Boston: Beacon Press, 1957.

Prigogine, Ilya and Isabelle Stengers. *A nova aliança: Metamorphose da ciência,* 3rd ed. Brasília: Ed UNB, 1997.

Richard, Pablo. "La construcción del sujeto en la Teología de la Liberación." *Pasos* 87 (Jan./Feb. 2000): 31–34.

Ridley, Matt. *The Origins of Virtue: Human Instincts and the Evolution of Cooperation.* New York: Penguin, 1997.

Robbins, Lionel. *An Essay on the Nature and Significance of Economic Science.* London: Macmillan, 1932.

Samuelson, Paul. *Economics,* 11th ed. New York: McGraw Hill, 1980.

Segundo, Juan Luis. *O Homem de Hoje diante de Jesus de Nazaré.* Vol. 1 of *Fé e Ideologia.* São Paulo: Paulinas, 1985.

———. *El dogma que libera: fe, revelación, y magisterio dogmático.* Santander: Sal Terrae, 1989.

———. *¿Qué mundo? ¿Qué hombre? ¿Qué Dios?* Santander: Sal Terrae, 1993.

Sen, Amartya. *Poverty and Famines: An Essay on Entitlement and Deprivation.* Oxford/New York: Oxford University Press, 1981.

———. *On Ethics and Economics.* Oxford: Blackwell, 1987.

———. *Development as Freedom.* New York: Random House, 1999.

Serrano, August. "El sujeto y la red." *Pasos* 85 (Sept./Oct. 1999): 18–27.

Soros, George. *The Crisis of Global Capitalism: Open Society Endangered.* New York: Public Affairs, 1998.

Sung, Jung Mo. *A idolatria do capital e a morte dos pobres: uma reflexão teológica a partir da dívida externa.* São Paulo: Paulinas, 1989.

———. *Economia: Tema Ausente en la Teologia de la Liberación.* San José: DEI, 1994.

———. *Teologia e economia: repensando a Teologia da Libertação e utopias.* Petrópolis: Vozes, 1994; Madri: Nueva Utopia, 1996.

———. "Idolatria: uma chave de leitura da economia contemporânea." In *Religião ano 2000,* edited by Enio J. C. Brito and Gilberto S. Gorgulho, 109–29. São Paulo: Loyola PUC-SP, 1998.

Sung, Jung Mo. *Desejo, mercado e religião.* Petrópolis: Vozes, 1998.
———. *Desire, Market, and Religion.* London: SCM Press, 2007.
Tamez, Elsa. "El sujeto viviente 'racializado' y 'generizado.'" *Pasos* 88 (Mar./Apr. 2000): 18–25.
Touraine, Alain. *Crítica da Modernidade.* Petrópolis: Vozes, 1994.
Tu, Pierre N.V. *Dynamical Systems: An Introduction with Applications in Economics and Biology,* 2nd rev. ed. New York: Springer-Verlag, 1998.

Index

Fodor's 2001

Costa

Fodor's Travel Publications • New York, Toronto, London, Sydney, Auckland
www.fodors.com

CONTENTS

MAPS

Circled letters in text correspond to letters on the photographs. For more information on the sights pictured, turn to the indicated page number ⊄ on each photograph.

DESTINATION
COSTA RICA

Costa Rica's beauty would flatter a land ten times as large. The sheer plenty of flora and fauna packed into this tiny nation, combined with a wild variety of climates and landscapes, can make the senses reel. Riding horseback toward simmering volcanoes or tramping through coffee plantations, you can daydream about the next day's rain-forest trek or scuba jaunt off the coast—Pacific or Caribbean. And for all the enchanting ecozones, beach resorts and surf sites dot both shores, mixing revelry and relaxation; and dining and nightlife abound in the feisty capital, San José. Add white-water rafting, world-class birding, and antiquities and you can see why Costa Rica has become one of the hottest destinations in the Western Hemisphere.

Ⓐ 23

Nestled in the shadow of emerald mountain slopes, Costa Rica's urban hub is one of the most beautifully sited capitals on earth. As a boomtown, it has its share of quick-fix architecture, but

SAN JOSÉ

gems like the Ⓑ**Teatro Nacional** and the inside of the Ⓐ**Catedral Metropolitana** help redeem it, and you can always wander into an older barrio for a taste of the recent past. Aficionados of the distant past are dazzled by the city's gold and jade museums, packed with pre-Columbian artifacts. Local flavor fills the Ⓒ**Mercado Central,** and creative menus abound in San José's myriad restaurants. You can easily dart outside town for a day of horseback riding, rafting, or hiking, then plunge back into the fray for some nightlife, raucous or refined.

Ⓑ 25

Ⓒ 23

CENTRAL VALLEY: AROUND SAN JOSÉ

Ⓐ▷54

There's amusement for every taste in the culturally rich Central Valley—especially the taste for coffee. The golden bean forms the backbone of Costa Rica's economy, and the valley around San José is the heart of the industry. Sips are on the house at venerable plantations. For a different kind of jolt, sign up for a white-water rafting trip out of Turrialba on rivers where Olympic kayakers train, the Reventazón or the Pacuare. Although San José is within day-tripping distance, you may want to base yourself outside the city: Lodgings and restaurants in the valley are top-notch, and towns here retain an appealing whiff of history. Cartago, the nation's first capital, has a glorious cathedral, and Ⓐ**Sarchí** is a major crafts center, home to bazaars where you can watch local artisans work. Running the length of the valley is a string of exquisite peaks and parks, including the dreamy, two-mile-high Ⓑ**Volcán Irazú.** Just just about any drive through this region passes lush, green fields and charming farm communities.

Ⓑ▷57

NORTHERN GUANACASTE AND ALAJUELA

If, having come to Costa Rica to get away from it all, you want to get farther away from it all, head to the country's untrammeled northwestern

Ⓐ▷ 68

Ⓑ▷ 84

corner, where nature is pretty much untouched. Birds and birders flock here—up in the Ⓒ **Monteverde Cloud Forest** and the many other preserves that grace the region, you can flesh out your life list with once-in-a-lifetime sightings. Down by the sea, at Ⓑ**Santa Rosa National Park,** the cast of characters is different, and the critter-watching not a jot less sublime. Volcanoes, too, loom large on the ethereal landscape: Ⓐ**Lake Arenal** sits in the shadow of the great Volcán Arenal, whose molten show will humble you. On the very edge of northern Guanacaste, rocky bluffs overlook perfect Pacific bays. Come here to marvel at the grandeur of Earth itself.

Ⓒ▷ 79

Ⓐ 108

NICOYA PENINSULA

With world-class surfing, first-rate beach resorts, laid-back coastal hangouts, scads of nesting sea turtles, and the folkloric towns of Guaitil and Santa Cruz, the Nicoya Peninsula is for many the best of all Costa Rican worlds. It's drier here than in the rest of the country, so when it's inconveniently rainy elsewhere, you can still get voluntarily wet in sun-drenched Nicoya. One of the best places to submerge yourself is Ⓐ**Playa Pelada,** where the rocks create surreal snorkeling landscapes. Likewise, whoever named Ⓑ**Playa Hermosa**—Beautiful Beach—was telling it like it is. Whether you surf or sightsee, Nicoya will keep you breezily occupied.

Ⓑ 111

9

Fresh seafood alone would be reason to visit Costa Rica's central Pacific coast, but there's food for the soul here, too. As an ecological transition zone—between tropical dry forests to the north and wet forests to the south—the area teems with life, even by Costa Rican standards.

Marvel at everything from motmots to macaws in the Ⓐ**Carara Biological Reserve**, then go crocodile-watching on the Río Tárcoles and bed down in a forested bungalow. Plunk yourself down by the sea in the bustling, scenic town of Manuel Antonio for sea kayaking, skin diving, and coastal wildlife-peeping. And it's endless summer in the surfing town of Ⓑ**Jacó**.

CENTRAL PACIFIC

Ⓐ▷ **128**

Ⓑ▷ **130**

Ⓐ▷ 156

This is the land that developers forgot—which is just fine with those who like their settings heavy on outdoor beauty, hold the civilization. In the lush and enormous ⒶⒸ**Corcovado National Park,** hikers scamper past swamplands, jungle-thick riverbanks, unspoiled beaches, and heavenly virgin rain forest. If Costa Rica's geographic secret is to rise

Ⓑ▷ 158

SOUTHERN PACIFIC

quickly from sea to mountaintop—sprouting new habitats along the way—the southern Pacific region has perfected the trick. If you want to bond with nature but don't fancy sleeping outdoors in it, make for one of the sybaritic lodges in the heart of the forest. A boat ride in Ⓑ**Drake Bay,** meanwhile, shows you the same rugged coastline that Sir Francis saw when he paid a call. Divers dig these waters.

Ⓒ▷ 156

Ⓐ 180

Northeastern Costa Rica marches more to Caribbean drummers than to the Central American rhythms of San José. You'll find reggae, johnny-cakes, and fluent English-speakers in Ⓑ**Puerto Limón.** Natural sights explode here, both above and below sea level; experience both at Ⓐ**Cahuita National Park,** where you can snorkel or ride a glass-bottom boat around the coral reef or stroll the snowy-white, forest-edged

ATLANTIC LOWLANDS AND CARIBBEAN COAST

beach. At Tortuguero National Park, majestic green sea turtles come ashore to nest, having beaten nature's ferocious odds to make it as far as adulthood; the park also hides crocodiles, manatees, and a host of other species. Rustic Barra del Col-

Ⓑ 177

orado welcomes avid anglers. Inland and up in the clouds, the sprawling Ⓒ **Braulio Carrillo National Park** is the lush, com-fortable home of still more plants and animals, and you can soar above them all in the Rain Forest Aerial Tram.

Ⓒ 169

Ⓐ 198

PANAMA AND NICARAGUA

Because of its small size, Costa Rica yields an international bonus: Not far away, across its borders, are some of the prettiest places in Panama and Nicaragua—among them Panama's bucolic Chiriquí Province, dominated by Volcán Barú, and misty, fertile Ⓐ**Cerro Punta.** To kick back in salt air, aim for the Ⓒ**Bocas del Toro Archipelago** off Panama's Caribbean coast. In the other direction, a trip into Nicaragua rewards you with gems of colonial architecture—the entire city of Ⓑ**Granada,** founded in 1524, is like a museum. The crafts town of Masaya rewards shoppers. And a ferry ride on Lake Nicaragua brings you to the rain-forested island of Ometepe, where you can hike, hunt for petroglyphs, or just chill out.

Ⓑ 213

Ⓒ 202

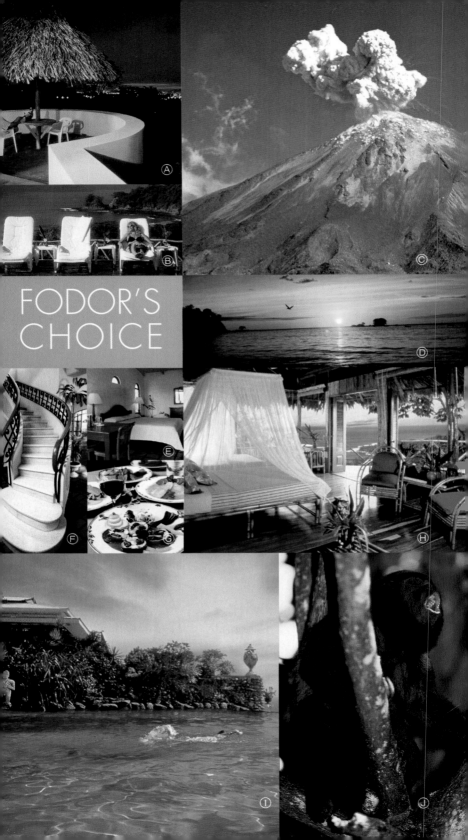

FODOR'S
CHOICE

Even with so many special places in Costa Rica, Fodor's writers and editors have their favorites. Here are a few that stand out.

NATURAL WONDERS

© **Volcán Arenal erupting at night.** Arenal's perfectly conical profile dominates the southern end of a lake, and thrills onlookers with regular incendiary performances. ☞ p. 76

ⓙ **Jungle rivers.** Slip into the rain forest the old-fashioned way. Adventures range from heart-stopping paddles down the hair-raising rapids of the Pacuare to lazy navigation of Caribbean canals or Pacific estuaries. With luck you'll spot a roseate spoonbill, purple gallinule, howler monkey, crocodile, or caiman on the way.

ⓓ **Pacific sunsets.** There's something about the cloud formations, colors, and settings that makes these exemplary crepuscular productions. Flocks of frolicking, diving pelicans, scarfing up sardines, often add foreground action.

ARCHAEOLOGY

Guayabo National Monument. Once home to 20,000 people, this ancient city was abandoned in the 15th century, and lay undiscovered until 1968. ☞ p. 62

FLAVORS

Ambrosia, San José. Fifteen minutes from downtown, this eclectic restaurant has long been popular among local epicureans thanks to its delicious inventions. $$$ ☞ p. 29

The Garden, Puerto Viejo de Limón. Chef-owner Vera Mabon's Indian-Canadian-Trinidadian background inspires sophisticated Costa Rican fusion cooking. $$–$$$ ☞ p. 181

Nogui's (Sunrise Café), Tamarindo. Local expats swear by this scruffy little joint, saying Nogui's *langostino* (small lobster) is the best in Guanacaste. Hearty American-style breakfast is also served. $$–$$$ ☞ p. 116

Café Mundo, San José. Set in a lovely old wooden house in historic Barrio Amón, this popular spot offers pastas, salads, and meat and seafood dishes at reasonable prices. The pastries are to die for. $$ ☞ p. 29

Chubascos, Volcán Poás. It's a winning combination: brisk mountain air, delicious *refrescos*, green surroundings, and platters packed with traditional Costa Rican taste treats. $$ ☞ p. 52

Miss Edith, Cahuita. Ticos and outsiders alike flock here for an outrageous Caribbean menu, including a variety of vegetarian dishes and herbal teas that owner Miss Edith claims will cure whatever ails you. $$ ☞ p. 179

COMFORTS

ⓑ **Punta Islita, Guanacaste, Nicoya Peninsula.** Overlooking the Pacific, this isolated resort offers comfortable rooms, splendid views, good food, and abundant peace and quiet. $$$$ ☞ p. 106

ⓔ **La Mariposa, Manuel Antonio.** Set high on a promontory, this elegant Spanish-style villa and series of private bungalows mix luxury, tranquility, and the best view in Manuel Antonio. $$$$ ☞ p. 136

ⓗ **Lapa Ríos, Cabo Matapalo.** Perched on a ridge in a private rain-forest reserve, with views of the surrounding jungle and the ocean beyond, Lapa Ríos is a small hotel that brings you close to nature without skimping on the amenities. $$$$ ☞ p. 158

ⓘ **Villa Caletas, Tárcoles.** Each of these exquisite bungalows on a forested promontory seems to enjoy a better view than the next. The scenery and isolation are only enhanced by the architecture, interior design, and cuisine. $$$$ ☞ p. 129

ⓐ **Xandari, Alajuela.** Whether you fix your vision on the clever design of the spacious villas or just watch birds and butterflies flit through the surrounding tropical gardens, its hard not to be enchanted by this unique inn. $$$$ ☞ p. 51

ⓖ **Grano de Oro, San José.** Built at the turn of the 20th century, this pink wooden house is now one of the capital's finest hotels, with interior gardens, a sundeck, and a first-class restaurant. $$$–$$$$ ☞ p. 32

Capitán Suizo, Tamarindo. Many consider this Swiss-run gem the finest beachfront lodging in Guanacaste, as its lush gardens provide a wonderful sense of seclusion not far from Tamarindo's resort-town amusements and gorgeous beach. $$$–$$$$ ☞ p. 117

Sueño del Mar, Playa Langosta. Susan Money's sweet little Mexican-style B&B has Balinese outdoor showers, fantastic breakfasts, charming gardens, and a perfect beach. Rooms are few, so the feel is intimate, but Susan's a high-energy charmer. Rent the whole place for a family reunion or a gathering of friends. $$$–$$$$ ☞ p. 119

Fonda Vela, Monteverde. Built with local hardwoods, these spacious rooms have plenty of windows, the better to enjoy the surrounding forest and distant Gulf of Nicoya. The restaurant serves food to match the view. $$$ ☞ p. 80

ⓕ **Le Bergerac, San José.** Deluxe rooms and extensive gardens have long kept this quiet, friendly hotel a notch above the competition, and the presence of L'Ile de France, one of the city's best restaurants, makes it that much more compelling. $$$ ☞ p. 32

Pacific Edge, Dominical. High in the hills south of town, these four simple cabins have wonderful views and get you quickly back to nature. $$–$$$ ☞ p. 149

Hotel Aranjuez, San José. Lush gardens, abundant common areas, hearty breakfasts, and low prices make this little B&B in the quiet Barrio Aranjuez a real bargain. $$ ☞ p. 33

1   SAN JOSÉ

Most trips to Costa Rica begin and end in
its capital, San José, home to excellent
cultural attractions as well as some of the
country's best hotels, restaurants, and
nightlife. From San José you can explore
the Central Valley and points beyond:
drive to the top of a nearby volcano,
raft white-water rapids, or zoom out to a
Pacific Ocean island.

Updated by
George
Soriano

D OWNTOWN SAN JOSÉ HAS MORE than its share of potholes and insipid architecture, but the city is not without its pleasures. San José's shady parks, quiet museums, and cobbled pedestrian mall offer needed respite from the traffic jams and gray office blocks that dominate the downtown grid, and its older neighborhoods and more affluent suburbs can be downright charming. San José is home to between 300,000 and 1 million Ticos (as Costa Ricans call themselves), depending on how many suburbs you include. It can boast such urban pleasures as fine dining and nightlife, but also suffers such urban problems as crime and exhaust fumes.

Still, downtown San José is a mere 40-minute drive from verdant, tranquil countryside. The city's best assets are its location and its climate. San José stands in a broad, fertile bowl at an altitude of more than 3,000 ft, bordered to the southwest by the jagged Cerros de Escazú (Escazú Hills), to the north by Volcán Barva (Barva Volcano), and to the east by lofty Volcán Irazú. In the dry season, these green uplands are almost never out of sight, and during rainy-season afternoons they're usually enveloped in cloudy mantles. Temperatures ranging from 15°C to 26°C (59°F to 79°F) create cool nights and pleasant days. The rainy season lasts from May to December, though mornings during this time are often sunny and brilliantly clear.

San José was founded in 1737 and replaced nearby Cartago as the capital of Costa Rica in 1823, shortly after the country won independence from Spain. San José grew relatively slowly during the following century, as revenues from the coffee and banana industries financed the construction of stately homes, theaters, and a trolley system that was later abandoned. The city mushroomed after World War II, when many old buildings were razed to make room for cement monstrosities, and it eventually sprawled to the point of connection to nearby cities. Today, San José dominates national life, and nearly one-third of Costa Rica's population lives in its metropolitan area. Industry, agribusiness, the national government, and the international diplomatic corps are headquartered here, and all the institutions required of a capital city—good hospitals, schools, the country's main university, theaters, restaurants, and nightclubs—flourish in close quarters.

Pleasures and Pastimes

Dining

Costa Rican specialties include *arroz con pollo* (chicken with rice), *ensalada de palmito* (heart-of-palm salad), *sopa negra* (black-bean soup), *gallo pinto* (rice with black beans), and *casados* (plates of rice, beans, fried plantains, salad, cheese, and fish or meat). Take advantage of the *plato del día* (plate of the day), a cheap lunch special that often includes a main course, *fresco natural* (fresh fruit drink), soup, and dessert. Tico food is often mild, but the capital has a smorgasbord of international restaurants, should you need some variety. To complement San José's selection, you might also want to dine in nearby Escazú (☞ Chapter 2).

Excursions

San José's central position in the Central Valley, and its relative proximity to both the Pacific coast and the mountains, invite day trips— you can be out in the countryside in just 20 to 30 minutes. The Central Valley is a boon for quick outdoor adventures, among them horseback tours on private ranches, mountain hikes, and white-knuckle rafting excursions down the Reventazón and Pacuare rivers. Most tours will pick you up at your San José hotel and drop you off the same day.

Festivals

Every other year the two-week Festival Internacional de las Artes brings dancers, theater groups, and musicians from Costa Rica and elsewhere to a dozen city venues in late March. The Festival de Coreógrafos is a dance festival held each December, and the Festival Internacional de Música enlivens July and August. A carnival parade heads down Avenida 2 every December 26, and a horse parade gets underway December 27. During Semana Universitaria (University Week), usually in April, students at the University of Costa Rica put their studies on hold to concentrate on drinking and dancing. The Día de la Virgen de Los Angeles honors Costa Rica's patron saint every August 2 with processions and a well-attended mass. On the eve of this holiday, nuns, athletes, families, and friends walk *la romaría*, a 22-km (14-mi) trek along the highway from San José to Cartago.

Lodging

San José packs every kind of accommodation, from luxury to bare necessity. You'll find massive hotels with all the modern conveniences and amenities, historic buildings with more atmosphere but fewer creature comforts, and smaller establishments with the simplicity (and prices) beloved of backpackers. Dozens of former homes in the city's older neighborhoods, such as Barrio Amón and Barrio Otoya, have been converted to bed-and-breakfasts, most moderately priced.

EXPLORING SAN JOSÉ

Costa Rica's capital is laid out on a grid: *avenidas* (avenues) run east and west, while *calles* (streets) run north and south. Avenidas north of the Avenida Central have odd numbers, and those to the south have even ones. On the western end of the city, Avenida Central becomes Paseo Colón; on the eastern end, at about Calle 31, it becomes an equally busy, though nameless, four-lane boulevard. Calles to the east of Calle Central have odd numbers; those to the west are even. This would be straightforward enough, except that Costa Ricans do not use street addresses. They rely instead on an archaic system of directions that makes perfect sense to them but tends to confuse foreigners. A typical Tico address could be "200 meters north and 50 meters east of the post office." The key to interpreting such directions is to keep track of east and west, and remember that a city block is 100 meters long.

Beyond the block and street level, downtown San José is divided into numerous barrios (neighborhoods), which are also commonly cited in directions. Some barrios are worth exploring; others you'll want to avoid. Barrio Amón and Barrio Otoya, northeast of the town center, are two of the city's oldest sections; some of their historic buildings are being transformed into charming hotels. Los Yoses and Barrio Escalante, east of downtown, are basically residential neighborhoods with some nice restaurants and galleries, and a few B&Bs. San Pedro, another pleasant area even farther east, is the home of the University of Costa Rica and numerous youth-oriented bars and restaurants.

San José's northwest quarter (everything west of Calle Central and north of Avenida 3) is a very different story. Called the Zona Roja, or red-light district, it's frequented by hard-luck prostitutes, drunks, and other delinquents and is best avoided unless you're headed to one of the bus companies there, in which case you should take a taxi. Much of the city's southern half—south of Avenida 4 between Calles Central and 14—is equally undesirable. If you follow Avenida Central west to where it becomes Paseo Colón, you'll enter a nice area, with plenty of restaurants, cinemas, and hotels. The farther west you head, the more exclusive the neighborhoods become. Escazú, in the hills west of San José, is a traditional town with relaxed ambience and numerous small inns and relatively upmarket, U.S.-style restaurants.

Most museums, shops, and restaurants are within walking distance of each other. If you're headed for a far-flung spot, or need to get from one end of the city to another, grab a taxi—they're abundant and inexpensive (U.S. $2–$3 for most trips).

On the whole, San José is a relatively safe city, but a growing influx of tourists has resulted in an increase in the number of thieves to prey on them, such as bag and backpack slitters, pickpockets, and distraction artists who usually work in pairs—one person molests you, or sprays something on you and helps you clean it off, while his or her partner gets your purse, wallet, backpack, camera, etc. Make sure you keep a photocopy of your passport and a list of credit-card phone numbers in your luggage, and never leave anything in an unguarded car.

Numbers in the text correspond to numbers in the margin and on the San José map.

Great Itineraries

San José has several interesting museums and theaters, more shops than you can shake a credit card at, and pleasant sidewalk amenities like newsstands and ice-cream vendors. If you're here during the rainy season, head out to the countryside in the morning and return to the city to shop and visit museums in the afternoon.

IF YOU HAVE 3 DAYS

Devote day one to exploring San José. Wander down the Avenida Central mall, pop into the Teatro Nacional and the Catedral Metropolitana, and visit the Museo Nacional, Museo de Oro, or Museo de Jade. The morning of day two, you may want to ride horseback in the mountains above town, visit a butterfly farm, or tour the Café Britt coffee plantation in Heredia (☞ Chapter 2), saving the afternoon for another museum. On day three you'll want to head up a volcano or, if it's cloudy, explore the Orosí Valley southeast of town.

IF YOU HAVE 5 DAYS

San José really deserves two days' exploration, since, in addition to attractions and shopping, it has enough nightlife to warrant some sleeping in. Take the walking tour below on your first day, making a proper visit to the Museo Nacional, Museo de Oro, or Museo de Jade. On day two, see another museum and enjoy places like the Serpentario and Jardín de Mariposas Spyrogyra. On day three, climb the Poás *or* Irazú volcano, stopping in the nearby towns of Alajuela and Cartago. Head to the Orosí Valley on day four: spend the morning in Parque Nacional Tapantí and the afternoon touring the valley. On day five, take a white-water rafting trip on the class III and IV rapids of the Río Pacuare (thrilling, but not so thrilling as to induce heart failure)— swimmable warm water and spectacular scenery make this a must for the moderately adventurous.

IF YOU HAVE 7 DAYS

Spend day one getting acquainted with San José, including at least one museum. On day two, hit one or two more museums and either the Serpentarium, Parque Zoológico Simón Bolívar, or Jardín de Mariposas Spyrogyra, the butterfly garden. On day three, go horseback-riding or tour a coffee plantation in the morning, then return to San José for more urban exploration. Venture out to the Orosí Valley on day four. By day five, you'll be ready to scale either Poás or Irazú. Though only hikers can reach the summit of Volcán Barva, you can drive along its green slopes and visit historic Heredia. Dedicate day six to a far-flung excursion: white-water rafting, say, or a cruise to Isla Tortuga. The Guápiles Highway enters Braulio Carrillo National Park (☞ Chapters 7 and 9) half an hour north of San José, making it an excellent day trip for day seven, easily combined with the Rain Forest Aerial Tram (☞ Chapter 7).

Downtown San José

A Good Walk

Start at the eastern end of the **Plaza de la Cultura** ①, where wide stairs lead down to the **Museo de Oro** ②, whose gold collection deserves a good hour or two. Next to the museum entrance, pop into the Instituto Costarricense de Turismo (tourist office) for a free map, bus schedule, and brochures. Wander around the bustling plaza and slip into the **Teatro Nacional** ③ for a look at the elegant interior and perhaps a cup of coffee in the lobby café. Leaving the theater, you'll be facing west, with the city's main eastbound corridor, Avenida 2, to your left. Walk 1½ blocks west along Avenida 2 to the **Parque Central** ④ and **Catedral Metropolitana** ⑤. Cross Avenida 2 and head north one block on Calle Central to Avenida Central, where you should turn left and follow the pedestrian zone to the small plaza next to the **Banco Central** ⑥. Continue west along the pedestrian zone to the **Mercado Central** ⑦, and shop or browse at your leisure. Head back east two blocks on the Avenida Central pedestrian zone; then turn left on Calle 2 and walk one block north to the green-and-gray stuccoed **Correos** ⑧, the central post office. From there, return to Avenida Central and walk east along the mall back to the Plaza de la Cultura.

From the eastern end of the Plaza de la Cultura, near the Museo de Oro, walk two blocks east on Avenida Central, turn left onto Calle 9, walk one block north, turn right, and slither halfway down the block to the **Serpentario** ⑨, home to an interesting collection of creepy crawlers. Turn left when you leave and head 1½ blocks west on Avenida 1 and one block north to **Parque Morazán** ⑩. Walk across the park— be careful crossing busy Avenida 3—and walk along the yellow metal school building to shady **Parque España** ⑪. On the north side of the park, on Avenida 7, is the modern Instituto Nacional de Seguros (INS) building, whose 11th-floor **Museo de Jade** ⑫ has an extensive American-jade collection and great city views.

From the INS building, continue east on Avenida 7 two blocks, passing the Cancilleria, or Foreign Ministry, and the Embajada de México (Mexican Embassy) on your left; then turn right on Calle 15 and walk a block south to the corner of **Parque Nacional** ⑬. Take a look at the Monumento Nacional at the center of the park, then head two blocks south to the entrance of the **Museo Nacional** ⑭, housed in the old Bellavista Fortress. On the west side of the fortress lies the terraced **Plaza de la Democracia** ⑮; from here you can walk west down Avenida Central to return to the Plaza de la Cultura.

TIMING

This walk can take an entire day if you pause to absorb each museum and monument and stop to shop here and there. You can, however, easily split the tour in half: see all the sights west of the Plaza de la Cultura (①–⑧) one day, and the remaining places (⑨–⑮) on another. Every stop on this tour is open Tuesday to Friday; if you're here on Monday or a weekend, check the hours listed below to make sure the sights you want to see are open.

San José

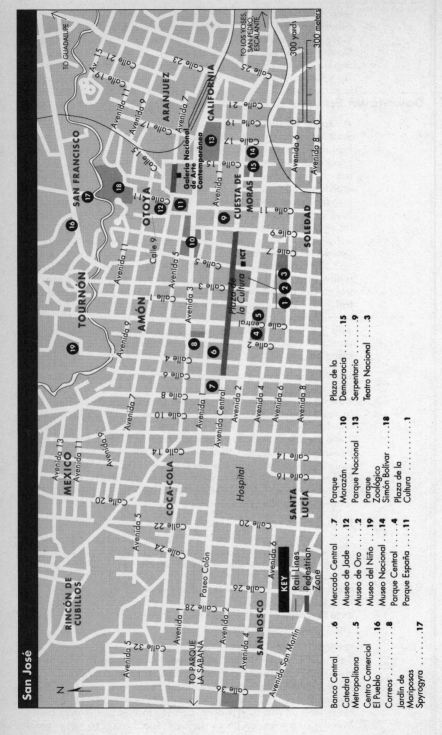

KEY

— Rail Lines

Pedestrian Zone

Banco Central **6**
Catedral
Metropolitana **5**
Centro Comercial
El Pueblo **16**
Correos **8**
Jardín de
Mariposas
Spyrogyra **17**

Mercado Central . . **7**
Museo de Jade **12**
Museo de Oro **2**
Museo del Niño . . . **19**
Museo Nacional . . . **14**
Parque Central **4**
Parque España **11**

Parque
Morazán **10**
Parque Nacional . . . **13**
Parque
Zoológico
Simón Bolívar **18**
Plaza de la
Cultura **1**

Plaza de la
Democracia **15**
Serpentario **9**
Teatro Nacional . . . **3**

Sights to See

❻ Banco Central (Central Bank). Outside the western end of Costa Rica's unattractive, modern federal reserve bank are 10 sculpted figures of bedraggled *campesinos* (peasants). The small, shady plaza south of the bank is popular with hawkers, money changers, and retired men and can be a good place to get a shoe shine and listen to street musicians. Beware: the money changers here are notorious for circulating counterfeit bills and using doctored calculators to shortchange unwitting tourists. ⊠ *Between Avdas. Central and 1 and Cs. 2 and 4.*

❺ Catedral Metropolitana (Metropolitan Cathedral). To the east of the park stands this not terribly interesting neoclassical structure, built in 1871, with a corrugated tin dome; inside, however, the cathedral has patterned floor tiles and framed polychrome bas-reliefs. The interior of the small chapel on the cathedral's north side is even more ornate than the cathedral itself, but it's usually closed. ⊠ *Between Avdas. 4 and 2 and Cs. Central and 1,* ☎ *221–3820.* ☼ *Daily 8–8 and for tours on weekdays 8–11, 1–3.*

❽ Correos (Central Post Office). The handsome, carved exterior of the post office, dating from 1917, is hard to miss among the bland buildings surrounding it. There's a display of first-day stamp issues upstairs, from where you can see the loading of *apartados* (post-office boxes) going on below: Ticos covet these hard-to-get boxes, as the city's lack of street addresses makes mail delivery a challenge. Opposite the post office is a small park shaded by massive fig trees, behind which is the marble facade of the exclusive, members-only Club Unión. The large building behind the Correos is the Banco Nacional, a state-run bank. ⊠ *C. 2 between Avdas. 1 and 3.* ☼ *Weekdays 8–6:30, Sat. 8–noon.*

❼ Mercado Central (Central Market). This block-long melting pot is a warren of dark, narrow passages flanked by stalls packed with spices (some purported to have medicinal value), fish, fruit, flowers, pets, and wood and leather crafts. You'll also see dozens of cheap restaurants and snack stalls, including the country's first ice-cream vendor. Be warned: the concentration of shoppers makes this a hot spot for pickpockets, purse snatchers, and backpack slitters. ⊠ *Avdas. Central and 1 and Cs. 6 and 8.* ☼ *Mon.–Sat. 6–6.*

★ **⓬ Museo de Jade** (Jade Museum). This is the world's largest collection of American jade—that's "American" in the hemispheric sense. Nearly all the items on display were produced in pre-Columbian times, and most of the jade dates from 300 BC to AD 700, before the local Indians learned goldsmithing. In the spectacular **Jade Room,** pieces are illuminated from behind so you can appreciate their translucency. A series of drawings explains how this extremely hard stone was cut using string saws with quartz-and-sand abrasive. Jade was used in a variety of jewelry designs, but it was most often carved into oblong pendants—evidently to represent ears of corn—that also functioned as knives. The museum also has other pre-Columbian artifacts, such as polychrome vases and three-legged metates (small stone tables for grinding corn), and a gallery of modern art. The final room on the tour holds a startling array of ceramic fertility symbols. ⊠ *11th floor of INS building, Avda. 7 between Cs. 9 and 11,* ☎ *223–5800, ext. 2584.* 🎟 *$5.* ☼ *Weekdays 8:30–3.*

★ **❷ Museo de Oro** (Gold Museum). The dazzling, modern museum of gold, in a three-story underground building, contains the largest collection of pre-Columbian gold jewelry in Central America—20,000 troy ounces in more than 1,600 individual pieces—all owned by the Banco Central. Many pieces are in the form of frogs and eagles, two animals perceived by the region's pre-Columbian cultures to have great spiritual significance. Most spectacular are the varied shamans, representing man's connection to animal deities. ⊠ *Eastern end of Plaza de la Cultura,* ☎ *243–4202.* 🎟 *$5.* ☉ *Tues.–Sun. 10–4:30.*

⑭ Museo Nacional (National Museum). Set in the whitewashed colonial interior of the **Bellavista Fortress,** dating from 1870, the National Museum gives you a quick and insightful lesson in Costa Rican culture from pre-Columbian times to the present. Exhibits feature pre-Columbian artifacts, period dress, colonial furniture, and photographs. Outside are a veranda and a pleasant, manicured courtyard garden. A former army headquarters, this now-tranquil building saw fierce fighting during the 1948 revolution, as the bullet holes pocking its turrets attest. ⊠ *C. 17 between Avdas. Central and 2,* ☎ *257–1433.* 🎟 *$5.* ☉ *Tues.–Sun. 8:30–4:30.*

❹ Parque Central (Central Park). Technically the city's nucleus, this simple tree-planted square has a gurgling fountain and cement benches. In the center of the park is a spiderlike, mango-color gazebo donated by former Nicaraguan dictator Anastasio Somoza. Several years ago a referendum was held to decide whether to demolish the despot's gift, but Ticos voted to preserve the bandstand for posterity. Across Avenida 2, to the north, stands the **Teatro Melico Salazar,** San José's second major performance hall (after the Teatro Nacional). The venerable **Soda Palace,** a restaurant and black-market exchange, is on the western end of that block. The fast-food outlet between the two was once a major movie theater. ⊠ *Between Avdas. 2 and 4 and Cs. 2 and Central.*

⑪ Parque España. This shady little park is one of the most pleasant spots in the capital. A bronze statue of Costa Rica's Spanish founder, Juan Vasquez de Coronado, overlooks an elevated fountain on its southwest corner; the opposite corner has a lovely tiled guardhouse. A bust of Queen Isabel of Castile stares at the yellow compound to the east of the park—a government liquor factory until 1994, this is now the **Centro Nacional de la Cultura** (National Center of Culture). Covering a double block, the complex houses the Ministry of Culture, two theaters, and the extensive **Museo de Arte y Diseño Contemporáneo** (Museum of Contemporary Art and Design), which hosts changing exhibits of work by artists and designers from all over Latin America. To the west of the park is a two-story, metal-sided school made in Belgium and shipped to Costa Rica in pieces more than a century ago. The yellow colonial-style building to the east of the modern INS building is the **Casa Amarilla,** home of Costa Rica's Foreign Ministry. The massive ceiba tree in front, planted by John F. Kennedy and the presidents of all the Central American nations in 1963, gives you an idea of how quickly things grow in the tropics. A few doors east is the elegant Mexican Embassy, once a private home. ⊠ *Between Avdas. 7 and 3 and Cs. 11 and 17.*

⑩ Parque Morazán. Anchored by a neoclassical bandstand, the largest park in downtown San José is somewhat barren, though the tabebuia trees on its northwest corner brighten things up when they bloom in the dry months. Avoid the park late at night, when prostitutes, drunks, and occasional muggers appear. Along the southern edge are a public school and two lovely old mansions, both with beautiful facades—one is a private home, the other a prostitute pickup bar. There's a park annex with a large fountain to the northeast, across busy Avenida 3, in front of the metal school building. ⊠ *Avda. 3 between Cs. 5 and 9.*

★ **⑬ Parque Nacional** (National Park). Large and leafy, the Nacional centers on a monument commemorating Costa Rica's battle against American invader William Walker in 1856. A pleasant block of downtown greenery, it's dominated by tall trees that often hide colorful parakeets in their branches. While enjoyable for relaxation by day, the park gets very dark at night, making it hospitable to muggers and best avoided then. The massive red building west of the park houses the **Registro Público** (National Registry) and the **Tribunal Supremo Electoral** (Electoral Tribunal), which keep track of voters and oversee elections. The modern building to the north is the **Biblioteca Nacional** (National Library), beneath which, on the western side, is the **Galería Nacional de Arte Contemporánea,** a small gallery featuring contemporary artists, mostly Costa Rican. Quality varies, but since admission is free, it's always worth taking a peek. The walled complex to the northwest is the Centro Nacional de Cultura (☞ Parque España, *above*). Across from the park's southwest end is the Moorish **Asamblea Legislativa** (Legislative Assembly), home to Costa Rica's congress. Next door is the **Casa Rosada,** a colonial-era residence now home to bureaucrats, and behind that is a more modern house used by the government for parties and special events. One block northeast of the park is the former Atlantic Railway Station, now a modest train museum. ⊠ *Between Avdas. 1 and 3 and Cs. 15 and 19.*

★ ❶ **Plaza de la Cultura.** This large cement square surrounded by shops and fast-food restaurants is somewhat sterile, but it's a nice place to feed pigeons and buy some souvenirs. It's also a favored performance spot for local marimba bands, clowns, jugglers, and colorfully dressed South Americans playing Andean music. The stately **Teatro Nacional** (☞ *below*) dominates the plaza's southern half, and its western edge is defined by the venerable **Gran Hotel Costa Rica** (☞ Lodging, *below*), with the 24-hour **Café Parisienne.** ⊠ *Between Avdas. Central and 2 and Cs. 3 and 5.*

❶❺ **Plaza de la Democracia.** President Oscar Arias built this terraced open space west of the Museo Nacional to mark 100 years of democracy, and to receive dignitaries during the 1989 hemispheric summit. The view west toward the dark-green Cerros de Escazú is nice in the morning and fabulous at sunset. The plaza is dominated by a statue of José "Pepe" Figueres, three-time president and leader of the 1948 revolution. Along the western edge, a string of stalls purvey jewelry, T-shirts, and crafts from Costa Rica, Guatemala, and South America. ⊠ *Between Avdas. Central and 2 and Cs. 13 and 15.*

🖐 ❾ **Serpentario** (Serpentarium). Don't be alarmed by the absence of motion within the display cases here—the inmates are very much alive. Most notorious in this collection of snakes and lizards is the terciopelo, responsible for more than half the poisonous snakebites in Costa Rica. The menagerie includes boa constrictors, Jesus Christ lizards, poison dart frogs, iguanas, and an aquarium full of deadly sea snakes as well as such exotic creatures as king cobras and Burmese pythons. ⊠ *Avda. 1 between Cs. 9 and 11,* ☎ *255–4210.* 🎟 *$5.* ☉ *Weekdays 9–6, weekends 10–5.*

★ ❸ **Teatro Nacional** (National Theater). Easily the most enchanting building in Costa Rica, the National Theater stands at the southwest corner of the Plaza de la Cultura. Chagrined that touring prima donna Adelina Patti bypassed San José in 1890, wealthy coffee merchants raised export taxes to hire Belgian architects to design this building, lavish with cast iron and Italian marble. The sandstone exterior is marked by Italianate arched windows, marble columns with bronze capitals, and statues of strange bedfellows Ludwig van Beethoven (1770–1827) and 17th-century Spanish golden-age playwright Pedro Calderón de la Barca (1600–1681). The Muses of Dance, Music, and Fame are silhouetted in front of a maroon iron cupola. Given the provenance of the building funds, it's not surprising that frescoes on the stairway inside depict coffee and banana production. The theater was inaugurated in 1894 with a performance of Gounod's *Faust,* featuring an international cast. The sumptuous Baroque interior sparkles thanks to an ongoing restoration project, begun after the theater was damaged in a 1991 earthquake. The theater closes occasionally for rehearsals. The stunning Belle Epoque **Café Britt,** just off the vestibule, serves upscale coffee concoctions, good sandwiches, and exquisite pastries. ⊠ *Plaza de la Cultura,* ☎ *221-1329.* ✉ *Entry $2.50, performance tickets $4–$40 ($10 average).* ☉ *Mon.–Fri. 9–5, Sat. 9–12, Sun. 1–5.*

North of Downtown

A Good Tour

The first two of these destinations are north of the city center, very close to each other. Take a taxi to the **Centro Comercial El Pueblo** ⑯, in Barrio Tournón. One block east and half a block south of El Pueblo is the **Jardín de Mariposas Spyrogyra** ⑰, a butterfly garden overlooking the greenery of Costa Rica's zoo, the **Parque Zoológico Simón Bolívar** ⑱. The best way to reach the zoo, however, is to walk north from the bandstand in the Parque Morazán (☞ *above*) along Calle 7 to the bottom of the hill, then turn right. The **Museo del Niño** ⑲, a children's museum and scientific and cultural center housed in an old jail, lies several blocks to the west. It's surrounded by dubious neighborhoods, so take a taxi there.

TIMING

You can visit all four of these sights in one morning. All are open daily except the Museo del Niño, which is closed Monday.

Sights to See

⑯ **Centro Comercial El Pueblo** (El Pueblo Shopping Center). This shopping center was built to resemble the kind of colonial village that Costa Rica lacks. "Pueblo" means "town," of course, and the cobbled passages, adobe walls, and tiny plazas are surprisingly convincing. Most of the commercial spaces are occupied by bars, restaurants, and discos—El Pueblo gets very busy at night, especially on weekends—but there are a few shops worth checking out. ⊠ *Barrio Tournón, Avda. 0.* ☉ *Daily 24 hrs.*

★ ℂ ⑰ **Jardín de Mariposas Spyrogyra** (Butterfly Garden). An hour or two at this magical garden is entertaining and educational for nature lovers of all ages. Self-guided tours enlighten you on butterfly ecology and give you a chance to see the winged creatures close up. Visitors watch an 18-minute video, then guide themselves through screened-in gardens along a numbered trail. Some 30 species of colorful butterflies flutter around, accompanied by several types of hummingbirds. Try to come when it's sunny, as butterflies are most active in the sun. The garden abuts the northern edge of the Parque Zoológico Simón Bolívar (☞ *below*), but you enter on the outskirts of Barrio Tournón, near El Pueblo Shopping Center. ⊠ *Half a block west and 1½ blocks south of main entrance to El Pueblo,* ☎ *222–2937.* ✉ *$5.* ☉ *Daily 8–4.*

⑲ **Museo del Niño.** San José's Children's Museum is housed in a former jail, and big kids may want to check it out just to marvel at the castle-like architecture and old cells, the latter of which have been preserved in an exhibit about prison life. The main halls in the complex are filled with eye-catching seasonal exhibits for kids, ranging in subject from local ecology to outer space. The exhibits are annotated in Spanish, but most are interactive, so language shouldn't be much of a problem. The museum's **Galería Nacional,** adjoining the main building, is more popular with adults; it usually shows fine art by Costa Rican artists free of charge. ⊠ *North end of C. 4,* ☎ *222-7485.* 🔳 *$5.* ⊙ *Mon.–Fri. 8–5, Sat.–Sun. 10–4.*

👆 ⑱ **Parque Zoológico Simón Bolívar.** Considering Costa Rica's mind-boggling diversity of wildlife, San José's zoo is rather modest in scope. It does, however, provide an introduction to some of the animals you might see in the jungle. The park is set in a forested ravine in historical Barrio Amón, providing soothing green space in the heart of the city. ⊠ *Avda. 11 and C. 11, Barrio Amón,* ☎ *233–6701.* 🔳 *$2.* ⊙ *Weekdays 8–3:30, weekends 9–4:30.*

DINING

Wherever you eat in San José, be it a small *soda* (café) or a sophisticated restaurant, dress is casual. Meals tend to be taken earlier than in other Latin American countries; few restaurants serve past 10 PM. Note that 23% is added to all menu prices—13% for tax and 10% for service. Because a gratuity is included, there's no need to tip; but if your service is good, it's nice to add a little money to the obligatory 10%. Except for those in hotels, most restaurants close between Christmas and New Year's Day and during Holy Week (Palm Sunday to Easter Sunday). Those that do stay open may not sell alcohol between Holy Thursday and Easter Sunday.

Downtown San José
CHINESE

$–$$ ✕ **Fulusu.** Some like it hot, and this Chinese place around the corner from the pink Hotel Presidente is one of the very few restaurants in Costa Rica where you can get a spicy food fix. The decor is mundane, with red-and-white tablecloths and Chinese prints, but the food is authentic and delicious. Start with some *empanadas chinas* (dumplings similar to pot stickers); then move on to a main course like *vainicas con cerdo* (green beans with pork) or *pollo estilo sichuan* (Szechuan chicken). Note that one entrée and two orders of rice are usually enough food for two people. ⊠ *C. 7 between Avdas. Central and 2,* ☎ *223–7568. Reservations not accepted. AE, MC, V. Closed Sun., around Easter, and last wk in Dec.*

COSTA RICAN

$$–$$$ ✕ **La Cocina de Leña.** In the charming Centro Comercial El Pueblo,
★ La Cocina serves up traditional Costa Rican fare amid white walls hung with old tools and straw bags to make you feel like you're down on the farm. Popular Tico dishes such as black-bean soup, ceviche, tamales, oxtail with yucca, and plantains cost more here than in the Mercado Central, but the quality and hygiene are more in keeping with the standards of the North American palate and stomach. The restaurant presents live marimba music several nights a week during the high season. This is one of the few places that don't close during Holy Week, but La Cocina does close every day between 3 and 5:30. ⊠ *Centro Comercial El Pueblo, Barrio Tournón,* ☎ *223–3704. AE, MC, V.*

$$ ✕ **El Cuartel de la Boca del Monte.** One of San José's more popular late-night spots, El Cuartel, in Barrio California, is actually a nice place to have a meal. If you dine here on a weekend, make for the more private room to the left, decorated with original art. The menu is filled with such Tico standards as *lomito encebollado* (tenderloin grilled with onions), sopa negra, and gallo pinto, though you have to order the eggs separately. You can also order plates of *bocas* (snacks), such as the *plato de gallos* (corn tortillas topped with beef, potatoes, and other fillings) and *piononos* (sweet plantains stuffed with cheese or beans and served with sour

San José Dining and Lodging

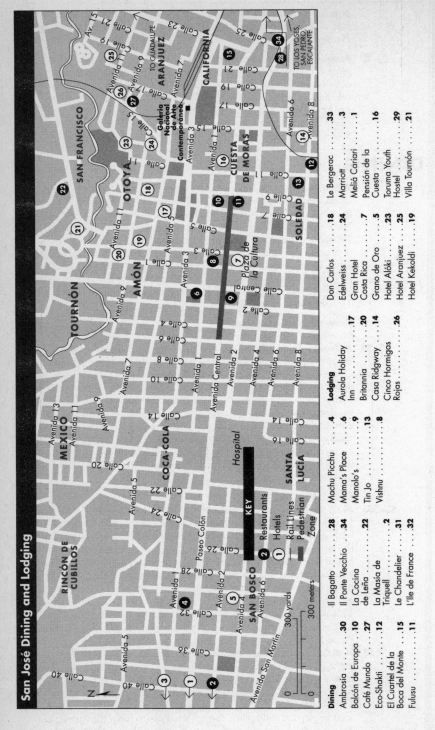

Dining

Ambrosia **30**
Balcón de Europa . . **10**
Café Mundo **27**
Eco-Shakti **12**
El Cuartel de la
Boca del Monte . . . **15**
Fulusu **11**

Il Bagatto **28**
Il Ponte Vecchio . . **34**
La Cocina
de Leña **22**
La Masia de
Triquell **2**
Le Chandelier **31**
L'Ile de France . . . **32**

Machu Picchu **4**
Mama's Place **6**
Manolo's **9**
Tin Jo **13**
Vishnu **8**

Lodging

Aurola Holiday
Inn **17**
Britannia **20**
Casa Ridgway **14**
Cinco Hormigas
Rojas **26**

Don Carlos **18**
Edelweiss **24**
Gran Hotel
Costa Rica **7**
Grano de Oro **5**
Hotel Alóki **23**
Hotel Aranjuez . . . **25**
Hotel Kekoldi **19**

Le Bergerac **33**
Marriott **3**
Meliá Cariari **1**
Pensión de la
Cuesta **16**
Toruma Youth
Hostel **29**
Villa Tournón **21**

KEY

- **2** Restaurants
- **1** Hotels
- ▬▬ Rail Lines
- Pedestrian Zone

cream). ⊠ *Avda. 1 between Cs. 21 and 23,* ☎ *221–0327. AE, MC, V. Closed around Easter and last wk in Dec. No lunch weekends.*

$–$$ ✕ **Mama's Place.** Mama's is a Costa Rican restaurant with a difference: The owners are Italian, so in addition to arroz con pollo and corvina *al ajillo* (sautéed with garlic), they serve homemade seafood chowder, an array of pastas, and meat dishes with delicate wine sauces. The brightly decorated coffee shop opens onto busy Avenida 1; the more subdued restaurant is upstairs. At lunchtime, it's usually packed with business types drawn to the delicious and inexpensive daily specials and perhaps the macrobiotic shakes. ⊠ *Avda. 1 between Cs. Central and 2,* ☎ *223– 2270. AE, MC, V. Closed Sun., around Easter, and last wk in Dec.*

$–$$ ✕ **Manolo's.** Within minutes of your entering this downtown eatery, management will ask where you come from. Don't be alarmed; they just want to add your nationality to the list on the blackboard, which lists the countries of origin of everyone dining at Manolo's at that moment. Outdoor seating on the bustling pedestrian thoroughfare is a great place to enjoy a meal or a cup of coffee. Choose from the restaurant's extensive international menu, featuring great Costa Rican dishes and sandwiches. Spanish favorites, such as *tortilla española* (a thick potato and onion omelet) and *churros con chocolate* (fried dough with hot-fudge sauce), add to the attractive fare. The restaurant never closes, and offers breakfast foods anytime. ⊠ *Avda. Central, between Cs. 0 and 2,* ☎ *221–2041,* ℻ *221–1153. AE, MC, V.*

ECLECTIC

$$$ ✕ **Ambrosia.** The navy-blue canopy of an open-air shopping mall her-
★ alds this chic restaurant in San Pedro. The menu is international, featuring inventive salads, soups, pasta, and fish dishes. Start with *sopa Neptuna* (a creamy fish soup with tomato and bacon), and follow with either the light fettuccine ambrosia (in a rich cream sauce with ham and oregano) or the corvina *troyana* (covered with a shrimp and tarragon sauce). The atmosphere is relaxed, and the informal decor matches the adventurous cooking: watercolors, wood and cane chairs, and plants. ⊠ *Centro Comercial de la C. Real, San Pedro,* ☎ *253–8012. AE, DC, MC, V. Closed around Easter and last wk in Dec. No dinner Sun.*

$$ ✕ **Café Mundo.** You could easily walk by this corner restaurant with-
★ out noticing its tiny sign behind the foliage. Walk in and up stairs, however, and you'll discover an elegant little eatery serving some excellent food. You can dine on the porch, on a garden patio, or in any of several dining rooms. The menu is a creative array of salads, pastas, pizzas, hot and cold sandwiches at lunchtime, and grill dishes for dinner. Start with the soup of the day and some fresh-baked bread, then opt for penne in a shrimp and vegetable cream sauce or *lomito en salsa de vino tinto* (tenderloin in a red-wine sauce). Save room for dessert— the pastries are to die for. ⊠ *C. 15 and Avda. 9, Barrio Otoya,* ☎ *222– 6190. AE, MC, V. Closed Sun. and around Easter.*

FRENCH

$$$$ ✕ **Le Chandelier.** In terms of decor, ambience, and cooking, this is San José's classiest restaurant, with wicker chairs, tile floor, original paintings, and formal service. The Swiss chef, Claude Dubuis, creates such unique dishes as corvina in a *pejibaye* (peach palm) sauce and the more familiar *pato a la naranja* (duck à l'orange). ⊠ *San Pedro, 1 block west and 1 block south of ICE,* ☎ *225–3980. AE, MC, V. Closed Sun. and last wk in Dec. No lunch Sat.*

$$$$ ✕ **L'Ile de France.** Long one of San José's most popular restaurants,
★ L'Ile de France is in the Le Bergerac hotel (☞ Lodging, *below*) in Los Yoses, where you can dine in a tropical garden courtyard. Chef and proprietor Jean-Claude Fromont offers a fairly traditional French menu with some interesting innovations. Start with the classic onion

soup or with *pâté de lapin* (rabbit liver pâté); then sink your teeth into a pepper steak or corvina in a spinach sauce. Save room for the profiteroles, puff pastries filled with vanilla ice cream and smothered in chocolate sauce. Reservations are recommended. ⊠ *C. 35 between Avdas. Central and 2, first entrance to Los Yoses,* ☎ *283–5812. AE, MC, V. Closed Sun. No lunch.*

ITALIAN

$$$ ✕ Il Ponte Vecchio. A simple, romantic setting and good food have kept this little Italian place in San Pedro popular for years. After a Caprese salad, tuck into one of the many homemade pasta specialties, such as seafood pasta with oysters and shrimp or traditional tomato lasagna. Cream sauces are excellent across the board. To top it all off, there's a wide array of Italian wines. ⊠ *100 m east and 25 m north of Fuente de la Hispanidad,* ☎ FAX *283–1810. AE, MC, V.*

$$–$$$ ✕ Balcón de Europa. In business since 1909, this restaurant was long owned and managed by chef Franco Piatti, who died in 1996. His widow now runs it with the same staff, so little has changed. The ambience has always been half the attraction, with hardwood floors and walls, old sepia photos of Costa Rica, and a strolling guitarist. Pasta dishes like the *plato mixto* (mixed plate with lasagna, tortellini, and ravioli) are among the house specialties, but you can also opt for quality Costa Rican fare, such as heart-of-palm salad or sautéed corvina. ⊠ *Avda. Central and C. 9,* ☎ *221–4841. AE, MC, V. Closed Sat. and Holy Week.*

$$–$$$ ✕ Il Bagatto. Ask one of Costa Rica's many Italian expatriates for the
★   name of their favorite San José restaurant and they're almost certain to answer, "Il Bagatto!" You don't have to be Italian, though, to appreciate these fresh pastas and top-heavy pizzas. Set in an old wooden house on the outskirts of town—and marked by a giant rotating sign— Il Bagatto has little in the way of decoration other than colorful tablecloths and some modern art on the walls. But it's the food that packs them in, dishes like *gnocchi alla Gorgonzola* (pasta dumplings with Gorgonzola cheese), homemade tagliatelle with any of a dozen sauces, and *lomito Il Bagatto* (tenderloin in a mushroom sauce). Choose from more than a dozen pizzas, or invent your own combination. Reservations are recommended. ⊠ *Across from Registro Nacional,* ☎ *224– 5297. AE, MC, V. Closed Mon., Easter wk, and Dec. 20–Jan. 10.*

PAN-ASIAN

$$ ✕ Tin Jo. There are two other Chinese restaurants on this block, but thanks
★   to its exceptional food, Tin Jo stands apart from them and from the vast majority of San José's other Asian eateries. Set in a former home, the restaurant achieves an elegant ambience with hardwoods, pastel tablecloths, and flowers on every table. The menu includes Cantonese, Szechuan, Thai, Japanese, and Indian dishes, among which are such treats as *kaeng* (Thai shrimp and pineapple curry in coconut milk), *mu shu* (a beef, chicken, or veggie stir-fry with crepes), *samosas* (stuffed Indian pastries), and sushi rolls. ⊠ *C. 11 between Avdas. 6 and 8,* ☎ *221–7605. AE, MC, V.*

PERUVIAN

$$–$$$ ✕ Machu Picchu. On a quiet street just north of Paseo Colón, this small
★   restaurant in a converted house is *the* place for excellent Peruvian cuisine or just a good pisco sour, a cocktail made with lime juice, egg whites, and pisco brandy. A few travel posters and a fishnet holding crab and lobster shells are the only real concessions to the idea of decor, but no matter: the food is anything but plain, and the seafood is excellent. The *pique especial de mariscos* (special seafood platter), big enough for two, presents you with shrimp, conch, and squid cooked four ways. The ceviche here is quite different, and better, than that served in the rest of the country. A blazing Peruvian hot sauce served on the side adds zip to any dish,

but be careful—apply it by the drop. ⊠ *C. 32, 150 m north of Kentucky Fried Chicken, Paseo Colón,* ☎ *222–7384. AE, DC, MC, V. Closed Sun.*

SPANISH

$$$–$$$$ ✗ **La Masía de Triquell.** San José's most authentic Spanish restaurant is appropriately housed in the Casa España, a Spanish cultural center. The dining room follows the theme with a tile floor; wood beams; red, green, and yellow walls; white tablecloths; and leather-and-wood Castilian-style chairs. *Champiñones al ajillo* (mushrooms sautéed with garlic and parsley) make a fine appetizer; *camarones Catalana* (shrimp in a tomato-and-garlic cream sauce) are a stand-out entrée. The long wine list is strongest in the Spanish and French departments. Reservations are a good idea. ⊠ *Sabana Norte, 50 m west and 150 m north of Burger King,* ☎ *296–3528. AE, DC, MC, V. Closed Sun., last wk in Dec., and around Easter.*

TURKISH

$$ ✗ **Aya Sofya.** This little no-frills Turkish place serves some of the tastiest food in town at very reasonable prices. Recent arrivals from Istanbul, the chef and one of the owners have imported excellent recipes for red peppers stuffed with spicy beef and rice, eggplant-tomato salad, and other Mediterranean treats. The less adventurous can opt for roast-chicken gyro sandwiches, with freshly baked pita-style bread, and a good selection of vegetable and green salads. Desserts include a scrumptious yogurt-and-honey *revani* cake as well as the beloved baklava. Beyond the obligatory evil-eye motif and a few wall hangings, there's little in the way of ambience, but good food and friendly staff make this a find, just east of downtown San José. ⊠ *Avda. Central and C. 21 (Barrio California),* ☎ *506/221–7185. MC, V. Closed Sun.*

VEGETARIAN

$ ✗ **Eco-Shakti.** Between the baskets of fruit and vegetables that at the entrance and the glass-topped terrarium tables, there's no doubt you're in a vegetarian joint. Serving breakfast and lunch, the restaurant offers soy burgers, pita sandwiches (veg or chicken, for carnivorous dining companions), macrobiotic shakes, and a hearty plato del día that comes with soup, green salad, and fruit beverage. The *ensalada mixta* is a meal in itself, and features a large variety of root vegetables native to Costa Rica. The atmosphere is on the bohemian side—incense burns throughout the afternoon. Good food makes this a popular alternative to the meat-based lunch specials around town. ⊠ *Avda. 8, between Cs. 13 and 11,* ☎ *222–4475. Reservations not accepted. No credit cards. Closed Easter and last wk in Dec. No dinner.*

$ ✗ **Vishnu.** Named after the Hindu god who preserves the universe, Vishnu has become a bit of an institution in San José. Even the ambience is institutional—sterile booths with Formica tables and posters of fruit on the walls—but the attraction is the inexpensive vegetarian food. Your best bet is usually the plato del día, which includes soup, beverage, and dessert, but the menu also offers soy burgers, salads, fresh fruit juices, and a yogurt smoothie called *morir soñando* (literally, "to die dreaming"). Vishnu keeps long hours. ⊠ *Avda. 1, just west of C. 3,* ☎ *222–2549. Reservations not accepted. No credit cards.*

LODGING

Downtown San José

$$$$ ▣ **Aurola Holiday Inn.** The upper floors of this 17-story mirrored-glass building, three blocks north of the Plaza de la Cultura, have the best views in town. Ignoring the view of downtown San José and its surroundings, however, you could just as soon be in Ohio, as the interior decoration betrays no local influence. The high-ceiling lobby is modern and airy, with lots of shiny marble. The good restaurant and casino are on the top floor, making full use of their vantage points. ⊠ *Avda. 5 and C. 5, Apdo. 7802–1000,* ☎ *222–242; 800/465–4329 in the U.S.,* FAX *223–0603. 188 rooms, 12 suites. Restaurant, bar, cafeteria, indoor pool, hot tub, sauna, exercise room, casino. AE, DC, MC, V.*

$$$–$$$$ 🏨 **Britannia.** On a busy corner in Barrio Amón, this pink house with a tiled porch has changed little since its construction in 1910, except for the addition of some rooms and the conversion of the old cellar into an intimate restaurant. Rooms in the newer wing are slightly small, with carpeting and hardwood furniture. Deluxe rooms and junior suites in the old house are spacious, with high ceilings and windows on the street side; they're worth the extra money but are close enough to the street that noise might be a problem if you're a light sleeper. The cellar restaurant, looking out on the interior gardens that separate the old and new wings, serves dishes such as cream of pejibaye soup and tenderloin with béarnaise sauce. ⊠ *C. 3 and Avda. 11, Apdo. 3742–1000,* ☎ *223–6667,* FAX *223–6411. 19 rooms, 5 junior suites. Restaurant. AE, MC, V.* 🍽

$$$–$$$$ 🏨 **Grano de Oro.** Two turn-of-the-century wooden houses on a quiet
★   side street on the western edge of San José have been converted into one of San José's most charming inns. New rooms have been added to the attractive space, which is decorated with old photos of the capital and paintings by local artists. A modest restaurant, run by a French chef, is surrounded by a lovely indoor patio and gardens. The old rooms are the nicest, especially the Garden Suite, with hardwood floors, high ceilings, and private garden. Standard rooms are a bit small, but tasteful. The hotel's sundeck has a spiffy view of both the city and the far-off volcanoes. ⊠ *C. 30 between Avdas. 2 and 4,* ☎ *255–3322,* FAX *221–2782. Box 025216, SJO 36, Miami, FL 33102–5216. 31 rooms, 3 suites. Restaurant, hot tub. AE, MC, V.* 🍽

$$$–$$$$ 🏨 **Hotel Alóki.** In a quiet, upscale residential neighborhood five blocks
★   from the city center, Hotel Alóki occupies an elegant turn-of-the-century manor house. Guest rooms surround a covered courtyard restaurant, whose wicker furniture and potted tropical plants spill onto multicolored glazed tiles. The antique furniture, gilt mirrors, and old prints in the rooms make this small, quiet place one of the most tasteful in San José. The Presidential Suite has a large drawing room. Breakfast is included. ⊠ *C. 13 between Avdas. 9 and 11,* ☎ *222–6702,* FAX *221–2533. 7 rooms, 1 suite. Restaurant, bar. MC, V.*

$$$ 🏨 **Don Carlos.** This rambling, multilevel gray villa was one of this city's
★   first guest houses and has been in the same family for four generations. Most guest rooms are in new additions, with ceiling fans, big windows, and lots of paintings; a few are air-conditioned. Those in the Colonial Wing have a bit more personality, and several newer rooms on the third floor have volcano views. The abundant public areas are adorned with orchids, pre-Columbian statues, and original art depicting scenes of Costa Rican life. The on-site souvenir shop, Boutique Annemarie, has the city's largest selection of crafts, curios, and Costa Rican music. Welcome cocktails and complimentary breakfast are served on the garden patio; the small restaurant serves lunch, dinner, and drinks. ⊠ *C. 9 and Avda. 9,* ☎ *221–6707,* FAX *255–0828. Box 025216, Dept. 1686, Miami, FL 33102-5216. 21 rooms, 12 suites. Restaurant, hot tub, travel services. AE, MC, V.* 🍽

$$$ 🏨 **Le Bergerac.** Set in the quiet, residential eastern neighborhood of
★   Los Yoses and surrounded by extensive green grounds, Le Bergerac is the cream of a growing crop of small upscale San José hotels. French owned and managed, it occupies two former private homes and is furnished with antiques. All rooms have custom-made wood-and-stone

dressers and writing tables; deluxe rooms have private garden terraces or balconies and large bathrooms. The hotel's restaurant, L'Ile de France (☞ Dining, *above*), is one of the city's best, so dinner reservations are essential, even for guests. Complimentary breakfast is served on a garden patio. ⊠ *C. 35, first entrance to Los Yoses, Apdo. 1107–1002,* ☎ *234–7850,* FAX *225–9103. 18 rooms. Restaurant, meeting room, travel services. AE, MC, V.* ✎

$$$ ▥ **Villa Tournón.** North of downtown, just two blocks from El Pueblo shopping center, the Tournón is popular with traveling businesspeople, who appreciate the peace, security, and reasonable rates. Sloping wooden ceilings and bare, redbrick walls may recall a ski chalet, but the kidney-shape pool out back is surrounded by tropical foliage. The carpeted rooms are snug and tastefully decorated, with pastel shades and prints. The restaurant is highly regarded, and the buffet breakfast is big enough to make you skip lunch. ⊠ *Barrio Tournón, Apdo. 6606–1000,* ☎ *233–6622,* FAX *222–5211. 80 rooms. Restaurant, pool. AE, MC, V.*

$$–$$$ ▥ **Edelweiss.** The interior may look more European than Latin American (one of the owners is Austrian), but this elegant little inn offers comfortable rooms in a charming corner of the city, near the Parque España, at very reasonable prices. Rooms have carved doors, custom-made furniture, small bathrooms, and ceiling fans. Most have hardwood window frames and floors; several have bathtubs. Complimentary breakfast is served in the garden courtyard, which doubles as a bar. ⊠ *Avda. 9 and C. 15, Barrio Otoya,* ☎ *221–9702,* FAX *222–1241. 27 rooms. Bar. AE, DC, MC, V.* ✎

$$–$$$ ▥ **Gran Hotel Costa Rica.** Opened in 1930, the grande dame of San José hotels remains a focal point of the city and is the first choice of travelers who want to be where the action is. It's a good deal for the money, but the flow of nonguests who frequent the 24-hour casino, Café Parisienne, restaurant, and bar reduces the intimacy quotient to zero. Rooms are large, with small windows, ceiling fans, and tubs in the tiled baths. Most overlook the Plaza de la Cultura, which can be a bit noisy, and the quieter interior rooms are pretty dark. The building is not air-conditioned. ⊠ *Avda. 2 and C. 3, Apdo. 527–1000,* ☎ *221–4000,* FAX *221–3501. 106 rooms, 4 suites. Restaurant, bar, café, casino. AE, DC, MC, V.*

$$ ▥ **Cinco Hormigas Rojas.** The name of this whimsical little lodge translates as "Five Red Ants." Behind the wall of vines that obscures it from the street is a wild garden that leads to an interior full of original art. Color abounds, from the bright hues on the walls right down to the toilet seats. Sure enough, the resident owner is an artist—Mayra Güell turned the house she inherited from her grandmother into San José's most original B&B–cum–art gallery. It's in the historic Barrio Otoya, one of San José's few pleasant neighborhoods, and the room price includes a hearty breakfast. ⊠ *C. 15 between Avdas. 9 and 11,* ☎ FAX *257–8581. 6 rooms, 1 with bath. Free parking. AE, MC, V.*

$$ ▥ **Hotel Aranjuez.** Hidden in the quiet residential neighborhood of Barrio Aranjuez, a short walk from most San José attractions, this family-run B&B occupies several old houses, with extensive gardens and cozy common areas. Every room is comfortable, but each is different—it pays to check out a few, as some have private gardens or little sitting rooms. Aranjuez is ecologically friendly, and offers such perks as free E-mail access, cable TV, and a discount tour service. The complimentary breakfast buffet makes lunch unthinkable. Reserve well in advance during high season. ⊠ *C. 19 between Avdas. 11 and 13,* ☎ *256–1825,* FAX *223–3528. 30 rooms, 22 with bath. Breakfast room, travel services, free parking. MC, V.*

$$ **Hotel Kekoldi.** This historic former home in charming Barrio Amón brings the color and spirit of the Caribbean to San José. Every wall has been painted to resemble the view from a beachside cabana, even though the nearest beach is two hours away. The artist went so far as to frame the false vista with striped drapes that appear to be blowing in the wind. Even the main staircase is fancifully painted in pastel pinks, blues, and yellows. The color continues into the clean, comfortable rooms, each furnished with restored hardwood floors, rattan chairs, and a simple wooden nightstand. The friendly, easy-going staff is happy to arrange tours. ⊠ *200 m north of Parque Morazán,* ☎ *223–3244,* ℻ *257–5476. 14 rooms. Breakfast room, laundry service, travel services. AE, MC, V. www.kekoldi.com.*

$$ **Pensión de la Cuesta.** Rooms in this laid-back, centrally located wooden villa on Cuesta de Nuñez have hardwood floors, brightly painted walls, and original art. Rooms in back are quieter, but those in front are brighter. You can lounge and read in the sunken sitting area (also used as the breakfast room), which has a high ceiling, a wall of windows, and cable TV. Breakfast is included in the price, and you're welcome to use the kitchen at other times. The nine rooms share four baths. A furnished apartment is also for rent. ⊠ *Avda. 1 between Cs. 11 and 15, Apdo. 1332,* ☎ *256–7946,* ℻ *255–2896. 9 rooms without bath, 1 apartment. Breakfast room. AE, DC, MC, V.* ✍

$ **Casa Ridgway.** Affiliated with the Quaker Peace Center next door,
★ Casa Ridgway is the budget option for itinerants concerned with peace, the environment, and social issues in general. Set in an old villa on a quiet street, the bright, clean premises include a planted terrace, a lending reference library, and a kitchen where you can cook your own food. There are three rooms with two bunk beds each, three rooms with single beds, and one with a double bed, all of which share three bathrooms. ⊠ *Avda. 6 Bis and C. 15, Apdo. 1507–1000,* ☎ ℻ *233–6168. 6 rooms without bath. Library, meeting room. No credit cards.*

$ **Toruma Youth Hostel.** The headquarters of Costa Rica's expanding hostel network is housed in an elegant colonial bungalow, built around 1900, in the eastern suburb of Los Yoses. The tiled lobby and veranda are ideal places for backpackers to hang out and exchange travel tales. Beds on the ground floor are in little compartments with doors; rooms on the second floor have standard bunks. There are also two private rooms for couples. The on-site information center offers discounted tours. ⊠ *Avda. Central between Cs. 29 and 31, Apdo. 1355–1002,* ☎ ℻ *224–4085. 2 rooms without bath, 80 beds. Dining room. MC, V.*

Northwest of San José

$$$$ **Marriott.** Towering over a coffee plantation west of San José, the
★ stately Marriott evokes an unusual colonial splendor. The building's thick columns, wide arches, and central courtyard are straight out of the 17th century, and hand-painted tiles and abundant antiques complete the historic ambience. Guest rooms are more contemporary, but they're elegant enough, with hardwood furniture and sliding glass doors that open onto tiny Juliet-type balconies. ⊠ *San Antonio de Belén,* ☎ *298–0055; 800/228–9290 in the U.S.,* ℻ *298–0011. 245 rooms, 7 suites. 2 restaurants, café, lobby lounge, 2 pools, beauty salon, driving range, putting green, 3 tennis courts, health club, business services, meeting rooms, travel services, car rental. AE, DC, MC, V.*

$$$$ **Meliá Cariari.** The low-rise Meliá Cariari was San José's original luxury hotel, and it remains popular for its wide range of facilities and out-of-town location. Just off the busy General Cañas Highway, about halfway between San José and the international airport, the Cariari is surrounded by thick vegetation that buffers it from traffic noise. Spacious, carpeted guest rooms in back overlook the pool area. The re-

laxed poolside bar, with cane chairs and mustard tablecloths, and nearby casino are popular spots. ⊠ *Autopista General Cañas, Apdo. 737–1007, just east of intersection for San Antonio de Belén,* ☎ *239– 0022; 800/227–4274 in the U.S.,* FAX *239–2803. 220 rooms. 2 restaurants, bar, cafeteria, pool, hot tub, golf privileges, 11 tennis courts, exercise room, casino. AE, DC, MC, V.*

NIGHTLIFE AND THE ARTS

The Arts

Film

Dubbing is rare in Costa Rica; films are screened in their original language, usually English, and subtitled in Spanish. There are theaters all over downtown San José, as well as in the malls outside the city. Check the local papers *La Nación* or the *Tico Times* (in English) for current listings. **Sala Garbo and Laurence Olivier** (⊠ Avda. 2 and C. 28, ☎ 222–1034) shows arty films, often in languages other than English (with, of course, Spanish subtitles). **Cine Variedades** (⊠ C. 5 between Avdas. Central and 1, ☎ 222–6108) is San José's other art house.

Theater and Music

The baroque **Teatro Nacional** (⊠ Plaza de la Cultura, ☎ 221–1329) is the home of the excellent National Symphony Orchestra, which performs on Friday evening and Sunday morning between April and December. The theater also hosts visiting musical groups and dance companies. San José's second main theater is the **Teatro Melico Salazar** (⊠ Avda. 2 between Cs. Central and 2, ☎ 221–4952). There are frequent dance performances and concerts in the **Teatro FANAL** and the **Teatro 1887**, both in the **Centro Nacional de la Cultura** (⊠ C. 13 between Avdas. 3 and 5, ☎ 257–5524; ☞ Exploring San José, *above*). Dozens of theater groups, including one that performs in English, hold forth in smaller theaters around town; check the English-language *Tico Times* for the latest.

Nightlife

Bars

No one could accuse San José of having too few watering holes, but outside the hotels, there aren't many places to have a quiet drink— Tico bars tend to be on the lively side. For a little taste of Mexico in Costa Rica, head to **La Esmeralda** (⊠ Avda. 2 between Cs. 5 and 7), a popular late-night spot where locals enjoy live mariachi music until the wee hours. If you want to watch a game and hang out with gringos, try the bar in the **Hotel del Rey** (⊠ Avda. 1 between Cs. 9 and 11), also a major pickup spot for San José's thriving prostitution trade. The second floor of the **Casino Colonial** (☞ Casinos, *below*) is a quieter, less racy place to watch a game.

A trendy place to see and be seen is **El Cuartel de la Boca del Monte** (⊠ Avda. 1 between Cs. 21 and 23), a large, low-ceiling bar where young artists and professionals gather to sip San José's fanciest cocktails and share plates of tasty bocas (snacks). It has live music Monday and Wednesday night. The **Jazz Café** (⊠ Avda. Central next to Banco Popular), in the eastern suburb of San Pedro, draws big crowds, especially for live jazz on Tuesday and Wednesday nights. The **Centro Comercial El Pueblo** (☞ Exploring San José, *above*) features a bar for every taste, from quiet pubs to thumping discos (☞ *below*). Several bars have live music on weekends; it's best to wander around and see what sounds good. **Café Mundo** (☞ Dining, Downtown San José, *above*) is a quieter spot frequented by gay men at night. **El Bochinche** (✉ C. 11 between Avdas. 10 and 12) and **Kashbah** (✉ C. Central between Avdas. 7 and 9) are two more of San José's many gay bars.

Casinos

The 24-hour **Casino Colonial** (✉ Avda. 1 between Cs. 9 and 11, ☎ 258–2827) has a complete casino, cable TV, bar, and restaurant, and a betting service for major U.S. sporting events. Most of the city's larger hotels also have casinos, including the Aurola Holiday Inn (the view from the casino is breathtaking), Meliá Cariari, Radisson Europa, and Gran Hotel Costa Rica.

Discos

El Tobogan, just outside town on the road north to Guápiles, is the place to watch the best in Latin dancing. Its oversize hall is always packed with dance fiends who swivel to live music on the weekends. For a more international scene, **Planet Mall,** on the top floor of the massive San Pedro Mall, is one of the city's most expensive dance bars. The Centro Comercial El Pueblo (☞ *above*) has two full-fledged discos: for Latin music head to **Cocoloco; Infinito** has two dance floors, one of which plays mostly techno, pop, and funk, and another that plays only Latin music. Across the parking lot from the Centro Comercial El Pueblo is **Plaza,** a larger, slightly more upscale disco that plays a good mix of northern and Latin music.

Déjà Vu (✉ C. 2 between Avdas. 14 and 16A) is a mostly gay, techno-heavy disco with two dance floors. A gay and lesbian crowd also dominates **La Avispa** (✉ C. 1 between Avdas. 8 and 10), which has two dance floors and a quieter upstairs bar with pool tables.

OUTDOOR ACTIVITIES AND SPORTS

Participant Sports

Fitness Centers

The Radisson Europa Hotel (✉ Avda. 15 between Cs. Central and 3, next to *La Republica* newspaper office, ☎ 257–3257) houses the downtown branch of the upscale, full-service gym **Multi Spa,** which offers daily rates. Other luxury hotels, like the Aurola Holiday Inn, Marriott, and the Meliá Cariari, have modern gyms for guests only. **Gimnasio Perfect Line** (✉ C. 1 and Avda. Central, 6th floor) is a full gym offering inexpensive one-month memberships. For a complete listing, look under "Gimnasios" in the *Páginas Amarillas* (Yellow Pages).

Horseback Riding

Most of San José's travel agencies can arrange one-day horseback tours to farms in the surrounding Central Valley. Several Central Valley hotels run their own horseback tours, one of the best of which is offered by **La Providencia Lodge** (☎ 380–6315; ☞ Chapter 2), near the top of Volcán Poás. The horseback tour at the **Sacramento Lodge** (✉ Just above Sacramento, ☎ 237–2116, FAX 237–2976), on the upper slopes of Volcán Barva, includes round-trip transportation, breakfast, lunch, and great views. A cheaper option is to get yourself to the **Centro Equestre Valle de Yos-Oy** (✉ 1 km/½ mi south on road to Salitral, ☎ 282–6934), outside the town of Santa Ana, where you pay by the hour for guided trail rides.

Running

Once San José's airport but now a eucalyptus-shaded park, **Parque La Sabana,** at the end of the Paseo Colón, is the city's best place to run, with 5-km (3-mi) routes on cement paths. Within the park are a sculpture garden and duck ponds.

White-Water Rafting
White-water trips down the Reventazón, Pacuare, Sarapiquí, and General rivers all leave from San José (☞ Guided Tours in San José A to Z, *below*). Nearly half a dozen licensed, San José–based tour companies operate similar rafting and kayaking trips of varying length and grade. The Reventazón's class III and IV–V runs are both day trips. You descend the General (class III–IV) on a three-day camping trip. You can run the Pacuare (class III–IV) in one, two, or three days, the Sarapiqué (class II–IV) in one day.

Accommodations for overnight trips on the General or Pacuare rivers are usually in tents, but Aventuras Naturales and Riós Tropicales have comfortable lodges on the Pacuare, making them the most popular outfitters for overnight trips on that river. The cost is around $70 to $90 per day, depending on the river. Two- and three-day packages with overnight stays are considerably more expensive. Try **Costa Rica Expeditions** (✉ Avda. 3 and C. Central, San José, ☎ 257–0766, FAX 255–4354), **Riós Tropicales** (✉ 50 m south of Centro Colón, San José, ☎ 233–6455, FAX 255–4354), **Aventuras Naturales** (✉ Behind Banco Nacional, San Pedro, ☎ 225–3939 or 224–0505, FAX 253–6934), and **Pioneer Raft** (✉ 2 blocks north of Bar La Luz, ☎ 225–8117 or 225–4735, FAX 253–4687).

Spectator Sports

Soccer
Professional soccer matches are usually played on Sunday morning or Wednesday night in either of two San José stadiums: the **Estadio Nacional,** on the western end of La Sabana park, and the **Estadio Ricardo Saprissa,** in the northern suburb of Tibás. Consult the Spanish-language daily *La Nación* or ask your hotel for details on upcoming games.

SHOPPING

Specialty Items

Antiques
Antigüedades Gobelino (✉ Avda. 9 between Cs. 3 and 5, ☎ 223–9552) sells antique paintings, ceramics, jewelry, and other small items. **Antigüedades Chavo** (✉ C. Central between Avdas. Central and 1, ☎ 258–3966) sells mostly furniture but has some smaller antiques.

Books and Maps
7th Street Books (✉ C. 7 between Avdas. Central and 1, ☎ 256–8251) has an excellent selection of new and used books in English, and is particularly strong on Latin America and tropical ecology. **Librería Internacional** has English translations of Latin American literature and myriad coffee-table books on Costa Rica. **Lehmann** (✉ Avda. Central between Cs. 1 and 3, ☎ 223–1212) has some books in English and a stock of large-scale topographical maps.

Coffee and Liquor
You can buy coffee in any souvenir shop or supermarket. The best brand is Café Rey Tarrazú; the second-best is Café Britt. Good, fresh-roasted coffee is also sold at **La Esquina del Café** (✉ Avda. 9 at C. 3 Bis, ☎ 257–9868). Costa Rica's best rum is the aged Centenario—pick up a bottle for about $6. There are also several brands of coffee liqueurs, the oldest of which is Café Rica, but the best of which is Britt. Buy these at any of San José's abundant supermarkets and liquor stores.

SAN JOSÉ A TO Z

Arriving and Departing

By Bus

A handful of private companies operate from San José, providing reliable, inexpensive bus service throughout much of Costa Rica from a variety of departure points (San José has no central bus station). For bus stops and companies, *see* Chapter 2.

By Car

San José is the hub of the national road system. Paved roads fan out from Paseo Colón south to Escazú and north to the airport and Heredia. For the Pacific coast, Guanacaste, and Nicaragua, take the Carretera Interamericana (Pan-American Highway) north (CA1). Calle 3 runs east into the highway to Guápiles, Limón, and the Atlantic coast. If you follow Avenidas Central or 2 east through San Pedro, you'll enter the Pan-American Highway south (CA2), which has a turnoff for Cartago, Volcán Irazú, and Turrialba before it heads southeast over the mountains toward Panama.

By Plane

AIRPORTS

All international and some domestic flights arrive at **Aeropuerto Internacional Juan Santamaría** (☎ 443–2942), 16 km (10 mi) northwest of downtown San José. Some domestic flights depart from **Aeropuerto Internacional Tobías Bolaños** (☎ 232–2820) in Pavas, 3 km (2 mi) west of the city center.

BETWEEN THE AIRPORT AND DOWNTOWN

A taxi from the airport to downtown San José costs around $12. Drivers do not expect tips, but beware of drivers eager to take you to a particular hotel—their only motive is a hefty commission. Far cheaper (about 40¢), and almost as fast, is the bus marked RUTA 200 SAN JOSÉ, which drops you at the west end of Avenida 2, close to the heart of the city. If you rent a car at the airport (☞ Car Rentals, *below*), driving time to San José is about 20 minutes, 40 if traffic is heavy or you get lost. Note that some hotels provide a free shuttle service—inquire when you reserve.

Getting Around

By Bus

Bus service within San José is absurdly cheap (20¢–25¢) and easy to use. For Paseo Colón and La Sabana, take buses marked SABANA-CEMENTERIO from stops on the southern side of the Parque Morazán, or on Avenida 3 next to the Correos building. For the suburbs of Los Yoses and San Pedro near the university, take one marked SAN PEDRO, CURRIDABAT, or LOURDES from Avenida Central, between Calles 9 and 11.

By Car

Almost every street in downtown San José is one-way. Try to avoid driving at peak hours, as traffic gets surprisingly congested. Parking lots, scattered throughout the city, charge around $1 an hour. Outside the city center, you can park on the street, but make sure someone guards your vehicle if you plan to leave it for a while.

By Taxi

Taxis are a good deal for transport within the city. You can hail one on the street (all taxis are red with a gold triangle on the front door) or call a cab company directly. It's best to recruit a Tico to call a cab for you, as cabbies tend to speak only Spanish and addresses are complicated. A 3-km (2-mi) ride costs around $1 (with rates increasing by

20% after 10 PM), and tipping is not the custom. Taxis parked in front of expensive hotels charge about twice the normal rate. By law, all cabbies must use their meters when operating within the metropolitan area; if one refuses, negotiate a price before setting off, or hail another. Cab companies include **San Jorge** (☎ 221–3434), **Coopetaxi** (☎ 235–9966), and, if you need to go to the airport, **Taxis Unidos** (☎ 221–6865).

Contacts and Resources

Car Rental
ADA (✉ Avda. 18 between Cs. 11 and 13, ☎ 233–7733 or 800/570–0671). **Budget** (✉ Paseo Colón and Calle 30, ☎ 223–3284 or 800/424–5431). **Dollar** (✉ Paseo Colón and Calle 32, ☎ 257–1585 or 800/800–4000). **Hertz** (✉ Paseo Colón and Calle 38, ☎ 221–1818 or 800/654–3001). **National** (✉ 1 km/½ mi north of Hotel Best Western Irazú, ☎ 290–8787 or 800/227–7368). Note: it's virtually impossible to rent a car in Costa Rica between December 20 and January 3. If you want to do so, reserve far in advance. Any other time of year, shop around for the best rate.

Embassies
Canada (✉ Oficentro La Sabana, Sabana Sur, ☎ 296–4149). **United Kingdom** (✉ Centro Colón, Paseo Colón between Cs. 38 and 40, ☎ 258–2025). **United States** (✉ In front of Centro Comercial del Oeste, Pavas, Apdo. 920–1200, ☎ 220–3939). The British Embassy handles inquiries for citizens of Australia and New Zealand.

Emergencies
You can dial ☎ 911 for just about any emergency. Some more-specific numbers: **Fire** (☎ 118). **Ambulance** (☎ 128). **Police** (☎ 117; 127 outside major cities). **Traffic Police** (☎ 222–9245).

Your embassy can provide you with a list of recommended doctors and dentists. Hospitals open to foreigners include **Clínica Bíblica** (✉ Avda. 14 between Cs. Central and 1, ☎ 257–0466 emergencies), which has a 24-hour pharmacy, and **Clínica Católica** (✉ Guadalupe, attached to San Antonio Church on C. Esquivel Bonilla St., ☎ 283–6616).

Guided Tours
ADVENTURE
Aventuras Naturales (✉ Behind Banco Nacional, San Pedro, ☎ 225–3939, FAX 253–6934) leads rafting and mountain-biking tours. **Costa Rica Expeditions** (✉ Avda. 3 at C. Central, San José, ☎ 222–0333, FAX 257–1665) is one of the country's most experienced rafting outfitters. **Horizontes** (✉ 150 m north of Pizza Hut, Paseo Colón, Apdo. 1780–1002, San José, ☎ 222–2022) will customize natural-history and soft adventure tours with expert guides to any Costa Rican itinerary. **Ríos Tropicales** (✉ 50 m south of Centro Colón, San José, ☎ 233–6455, FAX 255–4354) offers rafting, sea-kayaking, and mountain-biking tours. **Rain Forest Aerial Tram** (✉ Avda. 7 between Cs. 5 and 7, ☎ 257–5961) takes you floating through the treetops on a modified ski lift. **Tropical Bungee** (✉ Sabana Sur, 100 m west and 50 m south of Controlaría, Sabana, ☎ 232–3956) runs bungee jumps near San José on Sundays.

DAY TRIPS
Bay Island Cruises (✉ 125 m north of Toyota Paseo Colón, ☎ 258–3536, FAX 258–1189) and **Calypso** (✉ Arcadas building, 3rd floor, next to Gran Hotel Costa Rica, Apdo. 6941–1000, ☎ 256–2727, FAX 256–6767) run cruises to Isla Tortuga. The popular coffee tour run by **Café Britt** (✉ 900 m north and 400 m west of Comandancia, Heredia, ☎ 261–0707, FAX 260–1456), in Heredia, presents the history of coffee drinking via skits, a coffee-farm tour, and a tasting.

NATURAL HISTORY

Everyone is setting up ecological tours these days, but a few companies have more experience than most. Check out the following: **Camino Travel** (⊠ Between Avda. Central and 1, Calle 1, San José, ☎ 257-0107, FAX 257-0243); **Costa Rica Expeditions** (⊠ Avda. 3 at C. Central, San José, ☎ 222-0333, FAX 257-1665); **Costa Rica Sun Tours** (⊠ 200 m south of Toyota Paseo Colón, ☎ 255-3418, FAX 255-4410); **Horizontes** (☞ Adventure, *above*); **Tikal Tours** (⊠ Avda. 2 between Cs. 7 and 9, ☎ 222-6822, FAX 223-1916).

Travel Agencies

Galaxy (⊠ C. 3 between Avdas. 5 and 7, ☎ 233-3240). **Aviatica** (⊠ Avda. 1 and C. 1, ☎ 222-5630). **Intertur** (⊠ 50 m west of KFC, Avda. Central between Cs. 31 and 33, ☎ 253-7503).

Visitor Information

The **Instituto Costarricense de Turismo** (ICT; ⊠ C. 5 between Avdas. Central and 2, ☎ 222-1090) staffs a tourist-information office beneath the Plaza de la Cultura, next to the Museo de Oro. Pick up free maps, bus schedules, and brochures weekdays 9–12:30 and 1:30–5.

2 THE CENTRAL VALLEY: AROUND SAN JOSÉ

Defined by a ring of spectacular volcanoes, this agricultural area is densely planted with neat rows of coffee bushes and dotted with colorful farm towns. In its center is San José, a convenient base for heady excursions. Peer into the crater of a volcano, wander among radiant orchids, or visit colonial-era towns that prosper thanks to the *grano de oro* (golden bean).

By David
Dudenhoefer
and Justin
Henderson

Updated by
George
Soriano

HOVERING MORE THAN 3,000 FT ABOVE SEA LEVEL, the Meseta Central, or Central Valley, is Costa Rica's approximate geographic center. The valley is sandwiched between hulking mountain chains—the foothills of the Cordillera de Talamanca define the southern edge of the valley, and the Cordillera Central sweeps across its northern border. The fuming volcanoes along these chains, their summits protected within national parks, are within easy reach of San José: Volcán Irazú, Costa Rica's highest, towers to the east of San José; Poás, whose active crater often spews a plume of sulfuric smoke, stands to the northwest; and the older Volcán Barva looms between the two. Dramatic craters and thick cloud forests envelop these sleeping giants, while the slopes in their shadows hold a variety of coffee communities and charming agricultural hamlets.

The plateau is the cultural cradle of Costa Rica, with San José and other important cities sited here, and a total population of 1½ million. Though most of the region's colonial architecture has been destroyed by earthquakes and the ravages of time, several smaller cities preserve a bit more history than you'll find in San José. The central squares of Alajuela, Escazú, and Heredia, for example, are surrounded by architectural mixtures of old and new. Cartago, the country's first capital, has scattered historical structures and the impressive Basílica de Los Angeles. Beyond these small cities lie dozens of tiny farming communities, where lovely churches and adobe farmhouses look out onto coffee fields. You can easily tackle the Central Valley's attractions on a series of half- or full-day excursions from San José, but the abundance of excellent food and lodging in the valley's other towns invites you to base yourself here for a spell.

Pleasures and Pastimes

Dining

Restaurants in the Central Valley run the gamut, from rustic mountain lodges, where hearty meals are enhanced by the beauty of the natural surroundings, to the exceptional eateries in the hills above Escazú—fine dining with a backdrop of San José by night. Even if you keep your base in San José, consider venturing to this bedroom community for a meal or two.

Festivals

The Día de la Virgen de Los Angeles, which honors Costa Rica's patron saint, is celebrated in Cartago on August 2 with processions and a well-attended mass. The night before, tens of thousands of faithful worshippers walk *la romaría,* a 22-km (14-mi) trek east down the highway from San José to Cartago. April 11 is Día de Juan Santamaría in Alajuela, when a loud parade and other festivities get underway. July's Festival de los Mangos, also in Alajuela, celebrates this tropical fruit with nine days of music, parades, markets, and general merrymaking. On the second Sunday in March, the Día del Boyero (Oxcart-Driver Day) is marked with a colorful procession of carts through San Antonio de Escazú.

Lodging

The accommodations scattered across this area range from rustic *cabinas* (cottages) to elegant suites. San José has an ample selection of convenient hotels and restaurants, but it also has the crime, noise, and pollution that accompany crowds and traffic. If you want to get away from it all, lodging outside town can be an attractive option.

Volcanoes

Some of Costa Rica's most accessible volcanoes stand on the northern edge of the Central Valley, and paved roads run right to the summits of two, Poás and Irazú. Volcán Poás is very popular, as it has an extensive visitor center, an active crater, a luxuriant forest, and a jewel-like blue-green lake. Volcán Irazú, Costa Rica's highest, is topped by a desolate landscape (the result of violent eruptions in the early 1960s), but on a clear day the view is unparalleled. Barva, in the southern section of Braulio Carrillo National Park north of San José, is cloaked in an extensive cloud forest that resounds with the songs of colorful birds, such as the emerald toucanet and resplendent quetzal. You can visit all three volcanoes on day trips from San José; Poás and Irazú require only a morning, the summit of Barva a full day.

Exploring the Central Valley

The region has an extensive network of paved roads, many of which are in relatively good shape. The Pan-American Highway runs east–west through the valley (through the center of San José) and turns south at Cartago. Dozens of roads head off of this well-marked highway, but if you stray from the main travelers' routes, you may find a lack of road signs. If you do, don't despair—locals are always happy to point you in the right direction.

Numbers in the text correspond to numbers in the margin and on the Central Valley: Around San José map.

Great Itineraries

Most Central Valley towns stand in the shadows of volcanoes, so try to stop in one or two towns on your way down from the summit of any volcano you visit. To reach Volcán Poás, for example, you have to drive through Alajuela; Heredia lies on the road to Volcán Barva, and Cartago sits at the foot of Irazú. From Irazú you can take the serpentine roads eastward to Volcán Turrialba, Turrialba, and Guayabo National Monument, Costa Rica's most important archaeological site. Paraíso, just southeast of Cartago, is the gateway to the Valle de Orosi (Orosi Valley), southeast of San José.

IF YOU HAVE 2 DAYS

Drive up ⛰ **Volcán Poás** ⑤, where you can settle in for a night near the summit or just have a good lunch before returning to warmer ⛰ **Alajuela** ④ or San José. The next day, explore the Orosi Valley, stopping at the fascinating **Jardín Lankester** ⑪ on the way.

IF YOU HAVE 4 DAYS

Head north to ⛰ **Heredia** ② and the adjacent coffee communities, continuing up the slopes of **Volcán Barva** ③ for a picnic or gourmet lunch in the cool mountain air. If you have the energy, hike up to the crater lakes atop the volcano, or take a high-altitude horseback ride. Head northeast to spend the next day exploring **Cartago** ⑨ and the Orosi Valley, starting in the **Tapantí National Park** ⑭. Spend the night in the valley. Drive early the next morning to the summit of **Volcán Irazú** ⑩, then wind your way down its slopes to ⛰ **Turrialba** ⑮, stopping at **Guayabo National Monument** ⑯ on the way. Spend the night in Turrialba. Devote day four to white-water rafting, or return to the western Central Valley and spend the day at ⛰ **Volcán Poás** ⑤, visiting the towns of ⛰ **Grecia** ⑥ and **Sarchí** ⑦ in the afternoon.

IF YOU HAVE 6 DAYS

Spend a morning exploring ⛰ **Escazú** ①, then an afternoon in **Sarchí** ⑦ and ⛰ **Grecia** ⑥. On day two, hit the summit of ⛰ **Volcán Poás** ⑤, stopping at ⛰ **Alajuela** ④ and Zoo Ave, the bird zoo, afterward. Dedicate

The Central Valley: Around San José

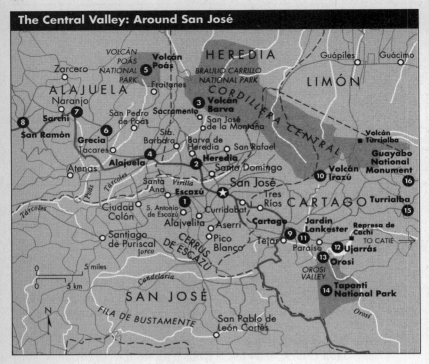

day three to horseback riding, hiking in the mountains above 🔲 **Heredia** ②, or exploring this historic city and the surrounding towns. Head for the Orosi Valley the following day, and explore (at least) the **Tapantí National Park** ⑭. Begin the fifth day with a trip up **Volcán Irazú** ⑩, after which you can wander through **Cartago** ⑨ and the **Jardín Lankester** ⑪, continuing east to 🔲 **Turrialba** ⑮. On day six explore **Guayabo National Monument** ⑯ and the tropical-research center CATIE, or go white-water rafting on the Río Reventazón or Río Pacuare.

When to Tour the Central Valley

From January to May it tends to be sunny and breezy here. On the upper slopes of the volcanoes, January and February nights can get quite cold. Afternoon downpours are common starting mid-May, dropping off a bit between July and September; from mid-September to December, precipitation picks up again. But don't rule out travel to Costa Rica during the rainy season—some days are spared rain, and when it does rain, it's usually during what you might call the siesta hours. Because few travelers visit during this period, you probably won't need reservations. The valley is swathed in green after the rains, but come January the sun begins to beat down, and by April the countryside is parched. Costa Ricans generally take their vacations during Holy Week (the week before Easter) and the last two weeks of the year, so it's essential to reserve cars and hotel rooms in advance for these periods.

THE WESTERN CENTRAL VALLEY

As you drive north or west out of San José, the city's suburbs and industrial zones quickly give way to arable land, most of which is given over to vast coffee plantations. Coffee has come to symbolize the prosperity of both the Central Valley and the nation as a whole; as such, this all-important cash crop has inspired a fair bit of folklore. Costa

Rican artists, for example, have long venerated coffee workers, and the painted oxcart, once used to transport coffee to the coast, has become a national symbol.

Within Costa Rica's coffee heartland are plenty of tranquil agricultural towns and two provincial capitals, Alajuela and Heredia, each of which holds some rare architectural treasures. Both cities owe their relative prosperity to the coffee beans cultivated on the fertile lower slopes of the Poás and Barva volcanoes. The upper slopes, too cold for coffee crops, are dedicated to dairy cattle, strawberries, ferns, and flowers, making for markedly different and thoroughly enchanting landscapes along the periphery of the national parks.

This area deserves at least two days: one for Alajuela, Grecia, Sarchí, and Volcán Poás, and one for Heredia and Volcán Barva. Escazú lies close enough to San José to be covered as a short side trip; alternately, it can serve as your base in the Central Valley. Since the hills above these towns hide some excellent restaurants and lodgings, rural overnights are a wonderful way to stretch out your exploration.

Escazú

❶ *5 km (3 mi) southwest of San José.*

A few minutes' drive west of San José takes you to Escazú, a traditional coffee-farming town and now a bedroom community at the foot of a small mountain range. Local lore has dubbed it the City of Witches, as it's thought to be popular with those spell-casting women. Escazú's ancient church faces a small plaza, surrounded in part by weathered adobe homes. Scattered amid the coffee fields that cover the steep slopes above town are well-tended farmhouses, often painted blue and white, with tidy gardens and the occasional oxcart parked in the yard—precisely the kind of scene that captured the attention of many a Costa Rican painter in the 20th century. There are also plenty of fancy homes between the humble farmhouses; Escazú has long been home to a wealthy mixture of Ticos and foreigners.

High in the hills above Escazú stands the tiny community of **San Antonio de Escazú,** famous for its annual oxcart festival held the second Sunday of March. The view from here—of nearby San José and distant volcanoes—is impressive by both day and night, but for even greater drama, head higher: virtually vertical roads wind up into the mountains toward **Pico Blanco,** the highest point in the Escazú Cordillera.

Dining and Lodging

$$$$ ✕ **Le Monastère.** The view from here is one of Escazú's best—a 270-degree panorama of ominous volcanoes. The restaurant's interior, that of a former chapel dressed up with antiques, is equally impressive, but Le Monastère would be popular even without its physical charm: the Belgian owner prepares outstanding classic French dishes and some original Costa Rican items, such as a grilled-caiman appetizer. If in doubt, try the grilled corvina smothered in a Provençal herb sauce. The restaurant only serves dinner, from 7 to 11 PM—and reservations are recommended—but the bar, La Cava, beneath the dining room is open and welcoming into the wee hours Tuesday through Saturday. ✉ *San Rafael de Escazú, take old road to Santa Ana, turn left 4 streets after U.S. ambassador's residence, and follow signs,* ☎ *289–4404. AE, DC, MC, V. Closed Sun. and Christmas. No lunch.*

$$$ ✕ **Hostaría Cerutti.** This little Italian restaurant on a busy intersection is the diva of San José's Italian eateries. Within a lovely, century-old adobe house, its whitewashed walls are adorned with antique prints. The extensive menu is heavy on seafood: start with octopus and as-

paragus in pesto, or ravioli with mushrooms in a truffle sauce; then sink your teeth into some grilled tuna or *cordero al horno* (rack of lamb roasted with vegetables). Reservations are recommended. ⊠ *Cruce de San Rafael de Escazú,* ☎ *228–4511. AE, MC, V. Closed Tues.*

$$$$ ⊞ **Alta.** This hotel is lofty in location and appearance as well as price. With barrel-tile roofs, ocher mixed into the stucco on the walls, and hand-painted bathroom tiles, its design evokes the Spanish colonial days. A high-ceilinged foyer leads into a sloping stairway lined with tall columns and palm trees, reminiscent of a narrow street in some ancient Iberian city. Above terra-cotta tile floors in the guest rooms are earth-tone fabrics and walls, colonial-style furniture, and a few paintings. Rooms on floors two through five have small balconies, and ground-floor rooms have garden terraces and direct pool access. The creations of the Californian chef have made the restaurant, La Luz, popular with the expat crowd. ⊠ *Old road to Santa Ana, Escazú,* ☎ *282–4160,* ᴁᴁ *282–4162;* ⊠ *Interlink 964, Box 02–5635, Miami, FL 33102,* ☎ *888/388–2582. 19 rooms, 4 suites. Restaurant, pool, sauna. AE, DC, MC, V.*

$$$$ ⊞ **Tara Resort Hotel.** Scarlett never had it so good. Modeled after the
  ★   famous fictitious mansion from *Gone With the Wind* and decorated in antebellum style, this luxurious little inn is near the top of Pico Blanco. Throughout the three-story white-and-green building, hardwood floors are covered with patterned area rugs. Guest rooms are decorated with floral spreads and lace curtains; French doors open onto the public veranda. At the Atlanta Dining Gallery, try the beef tenderloin in green-peppercorn sauce or chicken Tara in mango-avocado sauce. ⊠ *Apdo. 1459–1250, Escazú (head south from central church and follow signs),* ☎ *228–6992,* ᴁᴁ *228–9651. 12 rooms with bath, 1 suite, 1 bungalow. Restaurant, pool, hot tub, massage, spa. AE, MC, V.*

$$$ ⊞ **Costa Verde Inn.** Rooms at this B&B on the outskirts of Escazú make nice use of local hardwoods in their furniture and trim, and their white walls display traditional Peruvian art. South American art adorns the main building, where a large sitting area has comfortable chairs and a fireplace. The inn is surrounded by gardens, and at night you can see the lights of San José twinkling to the east. Complimentary breakfast is served on the shady patio. ⊠ *From southeast corner of second cemetery, 654 yards west and 109 m north,* ☎ *228–4080,* ᴁᴁ *289–8591;* ⊠ *SJO 1313, Box 025216, Miami, FL 33102-5216. 15 rooms with bath. Breakfast room, pool, hot tub, tennis court. AE, MC, V.*

$$$ ⊞ **Posada El Quijote.** At this friendly, family-run bed-and-breakfast perched on a hill in the Bello Horizonte neighborhood (on the San José side of Escazú), you'll find the best vantage point on the sundeck. The living room has big windows, a couch, a fireplace, and lots of modern art. Deluxe rooms have city views; superior rooms overlook the gardens. All rooms have queen-size beds and ceiling fans; complimentary breakfast is served on a covered interior patio. ⊠ *Bello Horizonte de Escazú,* ☎ *289–8401,* ᴁᴁ *289–8729;* ⊠ *Dept. 239–SJO, Box 025216, Miami, FL 33102-5216. 9 rooms, 2 apartments. Breakfast room, travel services. AE, MC, V.*

Heredia

❷ *15 km (9 mi) north of Escazú, 9 km (6 mi) north of San José.*

With a population of around 30,000, Heredia is the capital of one of Costa Rica's most important coffee provinces and perhaps the best-preserved colonial town in the country. It bears witness, however, to how little preservation can mean in an earthquake-prone country: Heredia has lost many of its colonial structures over the years. Still, the city retains an historic feel, with old adobe buildings scattered throughout downtown, and you'll see more in the charming nearby villages of Barva de Heredia, Santo Domingo, and San Rafael.

The tree-studded **Parque Central** holds some colonial appeal. At its eastern end stands the impressive stone **Catedral de Heredia,** dating back to 1797, whose thick walls, small windows, and squat buttresses have kept it standing through countless quakes and tremors. Unfortunately, the church's stained-glass work has not fared as well. The park has a simple kiosk and a cast-iron fountain imported from England in 1897. ⊠ *Parque Central,* ☎ *237–0779.* ☉ *Daily 6–6.*

Surrounding the park are some interesting buildings, such as the 1843 barrel-tile-roof **Casa de la Cultura,** which often houses art exhibits, and the brick **Municipalidad** (municipal building), behind which stands a strange, decorative tower called the *fortín,* or small fort.

Between Heredia and Barva is the **Museo de Cultura Popular** (Museum of Popular Culture), a turn-of-the-century farmhouse built with an adobelike technique called *bahareque.* Run by the National University, the museum is furnished with antiques and surrounded by a small garden and coffee fields. An inexpensive, open-air lunch restaurant serves authentic Costa Rican cuisine and can be a lively spot on weekends, when a more extensive menu is sometimes paired with marimba music and folk dancing. ⊠ *Between Heredia and Barva, follow signs for right turn,* ☎ *260–1619.* ☞ *$1.50.* ☉ *Daily 9–2, restaurant 11–2. No credit cards.*

Costa Rica's most popular export-quality coffee, **Café Britt,** welcomes visitors to its working coffee plantation. The tour highlights the history of coffee cultivation in Costa Rica through a theatrical presentation, a short walk through the coffee farm and processing plant, and a coffee-tasting session. ⊠ *900 m north and 400 m west of the Comandancia, Heredia,* ☎ *260–2748,* ℻ *238–1848.* ☞ *$15; $20 with transport from San José.* ☉ *Dec.–May, tours daily 9, 11, and 3; June–Nov., tours daily 9 and 11.*

Just northeast (about 2 km/1 mi) of Heredia lies **San Rafael,** a quiet, mildly affluent coffee town with a large church notable for its stained-glass windows and bright interior. The road north from the church winds its way up Volcán Barva to the Hotel Chalet Tirol (☞ Lodging *in* Volcán Barva, *below*) and the Monte de la Cruz. **Santo Domingo,** southeast of Heredia, is another attractive agricultural community with two churches, an abundance of adobe houses, and some traditional coffee farms on its outskirts.

The small community of **Barva de Heredia,** just north of Heredia proper (about 2 km/1 mi), has a wonderful Parque Central surrounded by old Spanish-tiled adobe houses on three sides and a white stucco church to the east. Flanked by royal palms, the stout, handsome church dates from the late 18th century; behind it is a lovely little garden shrine to the Virgin Mary. On a clear day you can see verdant Volcán Barva towering to the north, and if you follow the road that runs in front of the church, veering to the right, you'll reach the village of Sacramento. Here the road turns into a steep, dirt track leading to the Barva sector of Braulio Carrillo National Park.

Lodging

$$$$ 🏨 **Finca Rosa Blanca Country Inn.** There's nothing common about
★ this bed-and-breakfast overlooking the coffee farms west of Barva de Heredia; you need only step through the front door of the Gaudiesque main building to marvel at its soaring ceiling, white-stucco arches, columns, and polished wood. Each guest room is different, but all have original art, local hardwoods, colorful fabrics, and paintings. The spa-

COSTA RICA'S GOLDEN BEAN

WHEN COSTA RICA'S FIRST elected president, Juan Mora Fernandez, began encouraging his compatriots to cultivate coffee back in 1830, he could hardly have imagined how profound an impact the crop would have on his country. Over the last century, coffee has transformed Costa Rica from a colonial backwater into a relatively affluent and cosmopolitan republic.

It was the "golden bean" that financed the construction of most of the nation's landmarks. Founding families owned the largest plantations, creating a coffee oligarchy that has produced the majority of Costa Rican presidents. The bean also provided an economic incentive for tens of thousands of immigrant families from Europe and elsewhere in the Americas, who, during the 1800s and early 1900s, were given land in exchange for cutting down the forest and planting coffee. These farmers formed the backbone of a middle-class majority that has long distinguished Costa Rica from most of Latin America. Whether you credit the power of caffeine or the socioeconomic factors surrounding the crop, the tidy homes, colorful gardens, and orderly farms of the Central Valley make Costa Ricans look like the original coffee achievers.

Thanks to its altitude and mineral-rich volcanic soil, the Central Valley is ideal for growing coffee, and the crop covers nearly every arable acre of this region. Strangely, since it dominates the Central Valley's physical and cultural landscape, coffee is not actually native to Costa Rica: biologists claim the plant evolved in the mountains of Ethiopia. Arab nations were sipping the aromatic beverage as early as the 7th century—its scientific name is *Coffea arabica*—but it didn't catch on in Europe until the 1600s. Cof-fee plants first arrived in Costa Rica from the Caribbean, probably in the early 1820s.

The coffee-growing cycle begins in May, when the arrival of annual rains makes the dark-green bushes explode into a flurry of white blossoms—as close as it comes to snowing in Costa Rica. By November, the fruit starts to ripen, turning from green to red, and the busy harvest begins as farmers race to get picked "cherries" to *beneficios*, processing plants where the beans—two per fruit—are removed, washed, dried by machine, and packed in burlap sacks for export. Costa Rica's crop is consistently among the world's best, and most of the high-grade exports wind up in Europe and the United States.

Traditionally, coffee bushes are grown in the shade of trees, such as citrus or the nitrogen-fixing members of the bean family. Recently, however, many farmers have switched to sun-resistant varieties, cutting down shade trees to pack more coffee bushes into each acre. Shade farms provide habitats for migratory birds and other animals, but the new shadeless farms are practically biological deserts, which is why environmentalists are promoting a return to the old system by labeling shade coffee ECO-OK.

Ticos are fueled by an inordinate amount of coffee. They generally filter it through cloth bags, a method that makes for a stronger cup of java than your average American brew. The mean bean is even used in a favorite local dish: chicken roasted with coffee wood. Sadly, Ticos drink the low-grade stuff, often mixed with molasses, peanuts, or corn for bulk and roasted too long; you're best off buying such reliable brands as Café Rey's Tarrazú, Café Britt, Américo, Volio, and Montaña.

cious, two-story suite is out of a fairy tale, with a spiral staircase leading up to a window-lined tower bedroom. Out on the grounds—nicely planted with tropical flowers and shaded by massive fig trees—are two villas, each with two bedrooms. Four-course dinners are optional. ✉ *Barrio Jesus, 6 km (4 mi) west of Santa Barbara de Heredia,* ☎ *269–9392,* FAX *269–9555;* ✉ *SJO 1201, Box 025216, Miami, FL 33102–5216. 6 rooms, 2 villas. Restaurant, pool, horseback riding, airport shuttle, travel services. AE, MC, V.*

$$$ ★ 🏨 **Hotel Bougainvillea.** Here you'll soon forget that you're only 15 minutes from San José. Set amid the coffee farms of Santo Domingo de Heredia, the Bougainvillea has extensive grounds dominated by tall trees and brightened by plentiful flowers. The spacious, carpeted guest rooms are furnished with local hardwoods; the tiled bathrooms come with tub and hair dryer. Decorating the lobby and excellent restaurant are original pre-Columbian pieces and paintings by local artists. ✉ *Apdo. 69–2120, San José (from San José take Guápiles Hwy. to Tibas exit, then road to Santo Domingo, and follow signs),* ☎ *244–1414,* FAX *244–1313. 76 rooms, 4 suites. Restaurant, bar, pool, hot tub, sauna, tennis court. AE, MC, V.*

Volcán Barva

❸ *20 km (12 mi) north of Heredia, 30 km (19 mi) north of San José.*

North of Barva de Heredia the road grows narrow and steep as it winds its way up the verdant slopes of Barva Volcano, whose 9,500-ft summit is the highest point in **Braulio Carrillo National Park** (☞ Chapter 7). To the east a similar road climbs the volcano from San Rafael de Heredia, ending atop **Monte de la Cruz,** which borders the national park. Dormant for 300 years now, Barva is massive: its lower slopes are almost completely planted with coffee fields and hold about a dozen small towns. The upper slopes consist of pastures divided by exotic pines and the occasional native oak and cedar, giving way to the botanical diversity of the cloud forest near the top. The air is usually cool at the summit. Combined with the pines and pastures, the atmosphere here will surprise you if you've presumed that only rain-forest plants, bananas, and coffee beans can grow in Costa Rica.

Any vehicle can make the trip past San Rafael to the Monte de la Cruz, and even buses follow the loop above Barva via **San José de la Montaña;** but it's rough going if you want to get much higher than this. From San José de la Montaña to the crater, you can, in the dry months, take a four-wheel-drive vehicle over the extremely rocky road to the park entrance; alternately, leave your car and hike up on foot, a four-hour trip.

Barva's misty, luxuriant summit is the only part of the park where camping is allowed, and is a good place to see the rare resplendent quetzal if you're here early in the morning. Because it's somewhat hard to access, Barva receives a mere fraction of the crowds that flock to the summits of Poás and Irazú. A 30-minute hike in from the ranger station takes you to the main crater, which is about 200 m in diameter; its almost vertical sides are covered in poor man's umbrellas, a plant that thrives in the highlands, and oak trees laden with epiphytes. At the crater's lower edge is an otherworldly black lake; farther down the track into the forest lies another crater lake. Bring rain gear, boots, and a warm shirt, and stick to the trails—even experienced hikers who know the area have lost their way up here. ☎ *National Parks Service Information, 192 or 256–2717.* 🎟 *$6.* ☉ *Tues.–Sun. 7–4.*

Lodging

$$$$ 🏨 **Hotel Occidental La Condesa.** In keeping with the highland climate and scenery of Volcán Barva, the interior of this resort suggests a lodge

in a more northern latitude. The lobby is dominated by a stone fireplace surrounded by couches, armchairs, and a small bar. The central courtyard, topped by a giant skylight, is occupied by one of the hotel's three restaurants. A similarly enclosed pool area also holds a tropical garden. Guest rooms are carpeted and tastefully furnished, and each has a picture window. Junior suites and the Presidential Suite have bedroom lofts, sitting areas, and the best views. ⊠ *San Rafael de Heredia, next to the Castillo Country Club, 10 km (6 mi) north of Heredia,* ☎ *267–6000,* FAX *267–6200. 60 rooms with bath, 36 suites. 3 restaurants, 2 bars, indoor pool, hot tub, horseback riding, squash, meeting rooms, travel services, car rental. AE, MC, V.*

$$$ 🔝 **Hotel Chalet Tirol.** Amazingly enough, the Chalet Tirol's Austrian design doesn't seem out of place amid the pines, pastures, and cool air of Volcán Barva's upper slopes. The replica of a cobbled Tirolean town square—complete with fountain and church—may be a bit much, but the cozy, bright, two-story wooden chalets are quite charming, as is the restaurant, with its ivy, wooden ceiling, and elegant murals. Quality French cuisine makes this a popular weekend destination for Costa Ricans, and the hotel hosts occasional classical-music concerts. The suites have fireplaces and are more private than the separate chalets. Breakfast is complimentary. ⊠ *San Rafael de Heredia, 10 km (6 mi) north of Heredia,* ☎ *267–6222,* FAX *267–6229. 13 suites, 10 chalets. Restaurant, bar, 2 tennis courts. AE, DC, MC, V.*

$$-$$$ 🔝 **Las Ardillas.** Surrounded by old pines on a country road, these unpretentious log cabins are inviting oases for those looking to lock themselves up in front of a fireplace and tune out the world. The small on-site spa is one reason to venture from the comfortable, romantic rooms; the other is a meal at the restaurant, which specializes in meats roasted over a wood fire and has a nice selection of Spanish wines. Breakfast is complimentary. All rooms have modest wood furniture, kitchenettes, and queen-size beds. The spa features a sauna and hot tub, and offers massages and mud treatments. ⊠ *Apdo. 44–309, Barva, Guacalillo de San José de la Montaña,* ☎ *260–2172,* FAX *237–4119. 15 cabins. Restaurant, bar, kitchenettes, hot tub, sauna, spa. AE, MC, V.*

Outdoor Activities and Sports

HIKING

The upper slopes of Volcán Barva have excellent hiking conditions: cool air, vistas, and plentiful birds. The crater lakes topping the volcano can only be reached on foot, and if you haven't got a four-wheel-drive vehicle, you'll also have to trek from Sacramento up to the entrance of Braulio Carrillo National Park. **Hotel Chalet Tirol** leads an early-morning walk on a 4-km (2½-mi) trail through the cloud forest—an excellent trip for bird-watchers.

HORSEBACK RIDING

Horseback-riding tours along the upper slopes of Volcán Barva, near Braulio Carrillo National Park, combine views of the Central Valley with close exposure to the cloud forest and resident bird life. Reserve an excursion through the **Hotel Chalet Tirol,** the **Hotel Occidental La Condesa,** the **Sacramento Lodge** (just above Sacramento, in the mountains due north of Barva de Heredia; ☎ FAX 237–2116), or most San José travel agencies (☞ Contacts and Resources *in* San José A to Z, *in* Chapter 1).

Alajuela

❹ *20 km (13 mi) northwest of San José.*

Despite being Costa Rica's second-largest city (population 50,000) and a mere 30-minute bus ride from the capital, Alajuela has a decidedly provincial air. Architecturally it differs little from the bulk of Costa Rican towns: it's a grid plan of low-rise structures painted in primary colors. Alajuela's picturesque **Parque Central** is dominated by royal palms and mango trees, a lovely fountain imported from Glasgow, and cement benches where locals gather to chat. Surrounding the plaza is an odd mix of charming old buildings and sterile cement boxes. The large, neo-classical **cathedral,** badly damaged by a 1990 earthquake, has interesting capitals decorated with local agricultural motifs and a striking red dome. The interior, though spacious, is rather plain except for the ornate dome above the altar. ⊠ *C. Central between Avdas. 1 and Central,* ☎ *441–0769.* ⊙ *Daily 8–6.*

To the north of the park stands the **old jail,** which now houses the local offices of the Ministry of Education—an appropriate metaphor for a country that claims to have more teachers than police.

Alajuela was the birthplace of Juan Santamaría, the national hero who lost his life in a battle against the mercenary army of U.S. adventurer William Walker (1824–60) when the latter invaded Costa Rica in 1856 (☞ Santa Rosa National Park *in* Chapter 4). A statue of Santamaría stands in Alajuela's **Parque Juan Santamaría,** one block south of the Parque Central, and his deeds are celebrated in the **Museo Juan Santamaría,** one block north of Parque Central. The museum contains maps, compasses, weapons, and paintings, including an image of Walker's men filing past to lay down their weapons. The colonial building that houses the museum is more interesting than the displays, however. ⊠ *Corner of C. 2 and Avda. 3,* ☎ *441–4775.* ⊠ *Free.* ⊙ *Tues.–Sun. 10–6.*

Ⓒ Spread over the lush grounds of **Zoo Ave** (Bird Zoo) is a collection of large cages holding macaws, toucans, hawks, and parrots, not to mention crocodiles, monkeys, and other interesting critters. The zoo runs a breeding project for rare and endangered birds and mammals, all of which are destined for eventual release. To get here, head west from the center of Alajuela past the cemetery; then turn left after the stone church in Barrio San José. ⊠ *La Garita de Alajuela,* ☎ *433–8989.* ⊠ *$9.* ⊙ *Daily 9–5.*

Ⓒ The **Finca de Mariposas** (Butterfly Farm), in the suburb of La Guácima, offers a regular lecture on the ecology of these delicate insects and gives you a chance to observe and photograph them up close. In addition to an apiary exhibit, the farm comprises a variety of habitats housing 40 rare species of butterflies. Try to come here when it's sunny, as that's when butterflies are most active. The farm offers transportation from San José for $10. ⊠ *From San José, turn south (left) at the intersection just past Cariari Hotel, then right at church of San Antonio de Belén, then left, and then follow butterfly signs,* ☎ *438–0115.* ⊠ *$15.* ⊙ *Daily 9–5.*

Lodging

$$$$ 🏨 **Xandari.** Along a ridge about 5 km (3 mi) north of Alajuela, in the
★   middle of a coffee plantation and some well-tended gardens, the tranquil Xandari is a strikingly original inn. This brainchild of a talented couple—he's an architect, she's an artist—betrays aesthetic sensibility in everything from the design of the villas to the contemporary furniture and bold, colorful artwork that fill them. The villas are spacious, with plenty of windows, large terraces, and secluded lanais (sunbathing patios). Ultra villas are independent; the two Prima villas share one building. The attractive restaurant serves low-fat food, using some ingredients grown on the grounds. A trail through the hotel's forest reserve winds past five waterfalls. ⊠ *Apdo. 1485–4050, Alajuela,* ☎ *443–2020,* FAX *442–4847. 16 villas. Restaurant, bar, 2 pools, hot tub. AE, MC, V.*

$$$ ⚲ **Orquídeas Inn.** Shaded by tall trees and surrounded by polychrome tropical blossoms, the Orquídeas was once the home of a coffee farmer. The Spanish-style residence, complete with arches and a barrel-tile roof, now houses two suites; a third suite sits under a geodesic dome. Standard rooms, colored in pastels, have terra-cotta tile floors, Guatemalan bedspreads, and paintings by Central American artists. The Marilyn Monroe bar displays an impressive collection of posters and photos of Norma Jean and is a popular watering hole for American expats. Pet toucans, parrots, and macaws inhabit the wooded grounds, which means there's lots of squawking by the light of day. ⊠ *Apdo. 394, Alajuela (5 km/3 mi west of the cemetery)*, ☎ *433–9346*, ⨳ *433–9740. 20 rooms, 3 suites. Restaurant, bar, pool. AE, MC, V.*

Volcán Poás

❺ *37 km (23 mi) north of Alajuela, 57 km (35 mi) north of San José.*

The main crater of the Poás volcano, at nearly 1½ km (1 mi) across and 1,000 ft deep, is one of the largest active craters in the world. The sight of this vast, multicolored pit, gurgling with smoking fumaroles and a greenish-turquoise sulfurous lake, is simply breathtaking. All sense of scale is absent here, as the crater is devoid of vegetation. A paved road leads all the way to the 8,800-ft summit: The road from Alajuela winds past coffee fields, pastures, screened-in fern plantations, and, near the summit, thick cloud forest.

The peak is frequently enshrouded in mist, and many who come here see little beyond the lip of the crater. If you're faced with pea soup, wait a while, especially if some wind is blowing—the clouds can disappear quickly. The earlier in the day you go, the better your chance of a clear view. If you're lucky, you'll see the famous geyser in action, spewing a column of gray mud high into the air. Poás last had a major eruption in 1953 and is thought to be approaching another active phase; at any sign of danger, the park is closed to visitors. It can be very cold and wet up top, so dress accordingly. If you come ill equipped, you can duck under the poor man's umbrella plant. No one is allowed to venture onto the edge of the crater.

The 57-sq-km (22-sq-mi) **Volcán Poás National Park** protects the epiphyte-laden cloud forest on the volcano's slopes and the dwarf shrubs near the summit. One trail, which leads some 15 minutes off to the right of the main crater trail, winds through shrubs and dwarf trees toward the large and eerie **Laguna Botos** (Botos Lake), which occupies an extinct crater. The other trail, **Sendero Escalonia**, leads through a taller stretch of cloud forest from the picnic area back to the parking lot; boards along the way bear sentimental eco-poetry. Mammals are rare in this area, but you should see various birds, including insect-size hummingbirds and larger sooty robins. Quetzals have also been spotted in this park on occasion. Note that Volcán Poás is a popular sight and gets quite crowded, especially on Sunday. It's not a good choice if you want to commune with nature in solitude. ⊠ *From San José, take Pan-American Hwy. to Alajuela, Rte. 130 to Poás and follow signs.* ☎ *192 National Parks Service information; 290–8202.* ⬚ *$6.* ☉ *Daily 7–4.*

Dining and Lodging

$$ ✕ **Chubascos.** Set amid tall pines and colorful flowers on the upper
★   slopes of Poás Volcano, this popular restaurant has a limited menu of traditional Tico dishes and delicious daily specials. Pick from the full selection of *casados* (plates of white rice, beans, fried plantains, salad, cheese, and meat) and platters of *gallos* (a variety of fillings served on homemade tortillas). The *refrescos* (fresh fruit drinks) are top-drawer,

especially the ones made from locally grown *fresas* (strawberries) and *moras* (blackberries), served in milk. Reservations are recommended. ⊠ *West side of road to Poás Volcano National Park, between Fraijanes and Poásito,* ☎ *482–2069. AE, MC, V.*

$$$–$$$$ 🏨 **Poás Volcano Lodge.** Northern comforts abound at this former dairy farmhouse inspired by English and Welsh country homes. The rustic architecture, with rough stone walls and pitched beam roof, fits perfectly into the rolling pastures that surround this relaxing mountain retreat. The interior mixes Persian rugs with textiles from Latin America, and Guaitil Indian pottery with North American pieces. The lodge's most alluring feature is its oversize sunken fireplace, followed closely by the view of the Caribbean Lowlands from its 6,232-ft perch. All rooms are tasteful, but each is different, so look at a few before you decide. The master suite has an exquisite stone bathtub. ⊠ *Apdo. 5723–1000, San José (6 km/4 mi east of Churrascos Restaurant—☞ above—on road to Vara Blanca),* ☎ *482–2194,* ℻ *482–2513. 9 rooms, 7 with bath. Restaurant, Ping-Pong, billiards, travel services. MC, V.* 🐾

$$ 🏨 **La Providencia Lodge.** If you're looking for outdoor adventure,
★   tranquillity, and close contact with nature and you've rented a four-wheel-drive vehicle, this rustic, remote lodge perched on the northern edge of Poás Volcano National Park is just the place. Cabins scattered along the hillside have red cement floors, colorful quilts, and hot water. The walls in the restaurant are mostly glass. Trails wind through the lodge's 500-acre forest reserve, where you might spot quetzals and dozens of other birds, and the lodge's three horseback tours are among the best in Costa Rica. It can get very cold at night, so bring warm clothes and rain gear. ⊠ *Apdo. 10240–1000, San José (from the Poás Volcano National Park entrance, 2 km/1 mi to the left),* ☎ ℻ *380–6315. 6 cabins with bath. Restaurant, hiking, horseback riding. No credit cards.*

Outdoor Activities and Sports

HIKING

The footpaths in Poás Volcano National Park are rather short. Nearby **La Providencia Lodge** has more extensive trails for exploring the cloud forest.

HORSEBACK RIDING

La Providencia Lodge offers three different horseback tours, one of which leads around Volcán Poás to views of waterfalls and charred forests. You don't need to be a guest to join a tour, but you do have to call a day in advance to reserve your horse(s).

Shopping

A number of roadside stands on the way up Poás sell strawberry jam, *cajeta* (a pale fudge), and corn crackers called *biscoche*. The **Neotrópica Foundation** sells nature-theme T-shirts, cards, and posters in the national park's visitor center, and devotes a portion of the profits to conservation projects.

Grecia

❻ *26 km (16 mi) northwest of Alajuela, 46 km (29 mi) northwest of San José.*

Grecia's brick-red, prefabricated iron **Gothic church** overlooks a small **Parque Central,** where you might spot one of the resident sloths in the trees. The church was one of two buildings in the country imported from Belgium in the 1890s (the other is the metal schoolhouse next to San José's Parque Morazán), when some prominent Costa Ricans decided that metal structures would better withstand the periodic earthquakes that had taken their toll on so much of the country's architecture.

The pieces of metal were shipped from Antwerp to Limón, then transported by train to Alajuela—from which point the church was carried, appropriately, by oxcarts.

    At the **Mundo de las Serpientes** (World of Snakes), 50 varieties of serpents are kept in large outdoor cages. If you want to take one out for petting or photographing, just ask. ☒ *2 km (1 mi) east of Grecia, on road to Alajuela,* ☎ *494–3700.* ☜ *$11.* ☉ *Daily 8–4.*

Lodging

$$$$ 📷 **Vista del Valle Plantation Inn.** This lovely little B&B on an orange
★ and coffee plantation outside Grecia overlooks the canyon of the Río Grande. The simple cottages are beautiful, with wooden furniture and sliding French doors that open onto small porches. In the Japanese tradition, they have virtually no interior decoration, but each has its own personality; the Nido is the most romantic, while the Tea House is the largest and has the best views. The hotel has a forest reserve in the canyon, with an hour-long trail leading down to a waterfall. Complimentary breakfast is served by the pool or in the main house, where you can relax in a spacious living room. The owners are excellent cooks, and will accommodate special requests with advance notice. ☒ *Apdo. 1485–4050, Alajuela (on hwy. 1 km/ ½ mi west of Rafael Iglesia bridge on the right; follow sign),* ☎ *450–0800,* ☒ *451–1165. 1 room, 9 cottages. Restaurant, pool. V.* ✑

Sarchí

  ❼ *8 km (5 mi) west of Grecia, 53 km (33 mi) northwest of San José.*

Tranquil little Sarchí is spread over a collection of hills surrounded by coffee plantations. Though many of its inhabitants are farmers, Sarchí is also one of Costa Rica's centers for crafts and carpentry. People drive here from all over the Central Valley to shop for furniture, and caravans of tour buses regularly descend upon the souvenir shops outside town. Local artisans work native hardwoods into bowls, boxes, toys, platters, and even jewelry, but the area's most famous products are its brightly colored oxcarts—replicas of those traditionally used to transport coffee. Trucks and tractors have largely replaced oxcarts on Costa Rican farms, but the little wagons retain their place in local folklore, and can be spotted everywhere from small-town parades to postcards.

The vast majority of people who visit Sarchí spend all their time wandering through a crafts bazaar, but this traditional community is well worth poking around in more detail. The **church** dates only from the 1950s and is not particularly elaborate, but it is a colorful structure with several statues of angels alighted on its facade and a simple interior with some nice woodwork. Flanked by small gardens, the church faces a multilevel park in which a brightly decorated oxcart is displayed under its own roof. If you turn right when you leave the church, walk two blocks north, turn right again, and walk another block and a half, you'll see the town's only real oxcart factory on your left. **Taller Eloy Alfaro e Hijos** (Taller Eloy Alfaro and Sons) was founded in 1923, and its carpentry methods have changed little since then. The two-story wooden building housing the wood shop is surrounded by trees and flowers—usually orchids—and all the machinery on the ground floor is powered by a waterwheel at the back of the shop. Carts are painted in back, and although the factory's main product is a genuine oxcart—which sells for about $2,000—they also make some smaller mementos that can easily be shipped home. ☒ *2 blocks north and 1½ blocks east of church,* ☎ *no phone.* ☜ *Donation.* ☉ *Weekdays 8–4.*

Shopping

Sarchí is the best place in Costa Rica to buy miniature oxcarts, the larger of which are designed to serve as patio bars and can be broken down for easy transport or shipped to your home. Another popular item is a locally produced rocking chair with a leather seat and back. There's one store just north of town, and several larger complexes to the south. The nicest is the **Chaverri Factory,** a little over a mile south of Sarchí on the main road, and you can wander through its workshops (in back) to see the artisans in action. Chaverri is a good place to buy wooden crafts, but nonwood products, not to mention coffee and T-shirts, are cheaper in San José. Chaverri also runs a restaurant next door, Las Carretas, which serves international meals all day. The street behind the Taller Eloy factory (☞ *above*) comes alive on Friday for the local **farmers' market.**

San Ramón

❽ *23 km (14 mi) west of Sarchí, 59 km (36 mi) northwest of San José.*

Having produced a number of minor bards, San Ramón is known locally as the City of Poets, and you may well be tempted to wax lyrical yourself as you gaze at the facade of its church or stroll through its tidy Parque Central. As pleasant a little town as it may be, however, San Ramón hides its real attractions in the countryside to the north, on the road to La Fortuna, where comfortable nature lodges offer access to private nature preserves. Aside from the poets, the massive **Iglesia de San Ramón,** built in a mixture of the Romanesque and Gothic styles, is the city's claim to fame. In 1924 an earthquake destroyed the smaller adobe church that once stood here, and the city lost no time in creating a replacement—this great gray cement structure took a quarter of a century to complete, from 1925 to 1954. To ensure that the second church would be earthquake-proof, workers poured the cement around a steel frame that was designed and forged in Germany (by Krupp). Step past the formidable facade and you'll discover a bright, elegant interior. ⊠ *Across from Parque Central,* ☎ *455–5592.* ☉ *Daily 8–6.*

Lodging

$$$–$$$$ 🏨 **Villablanca.** Owned by former Costa Rican president Rodrigo Carazo, who is often around, this charming hotel is on a working dairy and coffee farm. The farmhouse contains the reception desk, bar, and restaurant; down the hill are lovely cottages called *casitas* ("little houses"), which are tiny replicas of traditional adobe farmhouses complete with whitewashed walls, tile floors, cane ceilings, and fireplaces. Resident guides lead nature walks through the adjacent cloud-forest reserve, which also holds a pulse-quickening canopy tour. Horses are available for exploring the rest of the farm. ⊠ *Apdo. 247–1250, Escazú (20 km (12 mi) north of San Ramón on road to La Fortuna),* ☎ *228–4603,* ℻ *228–4004. 48 casitas. Restaurant, bar, horseback riding. AE, DC, MC, V.* 🕭

$$$ 🏨 **Valle Escondido.** "Hidden Valley" lies within an ornamental plant farm in a long valley at the edge of a 250-acre forest preserve. Nature lovers could spend days exploring the 20 km (12 mi) of trails, which wind through primary forest past waterfalls and giant trees. The spacious rooms have panoramic views, ceiling fans, and small covered porches. The restaurant serves good international fare, particularly Italian. You're welcome to hike in the preserve even if you stop in just for lunch. ⊠ *32 km (19 mi) north of San Ramón,* ☎ *231–0906 or 460–1227,* ℻ *232–9591. 33 rooms with bath. Restaurant, pool, hot tub, hiking, horseback riding. AE, MC, V.* 🕭

THE EASTERN CENTRAL VALLEY

East of San José are Costa Rica's highest volcano and the remains of both the country's most important archaeological site and its oldest church. There are several interesting churches in the area, two in the scenic Orosi Valley, as well as the ecological attractions of a botanical garden and a protected cloud forest. Cartago, the country's first capital, has scattered historical structures and the impressive Basílica de Los Angeles. You can explore this area in two days, but only if you want to be on the road from dawn till dusk. For a more leisurely pace, dedicate at least three days to this end of the valley, visiting Volcán Irazú and Cartago one day, tackling the Orosi Valley on another, and ending up in the Turrialba area the third day.

Cartago

❾ *22 km (14 mi) southeast of San José.*

Capital of Costa Rica for almost three centuries, Cartago is much older than San José, but earthquakes have destroyed most of its colonial structures, leaving just a few interesting buildings among the concrete boxes. Cartago became Costa Rica's second city in 1923, when the seat of government was moved to San José, due in part to a major quake in 1910. The quake also prevented completion of the central Romanesque cathedral. **Las Ruinas** (the ruins) of this unfinished house of worship now stand in a pleasant central park planted with tall pines and bright bougainvillea. You'll see some attractive old buildings as you move through town, most of them erected after the 1910 quake. The majority of the architecture, however, is bland, with one impressive exception: the gaudy Basílica, on the eastern edge of town.

The spectacular **Basílica de Nuestra Señora de Los Angeles** (Basílica of Our Lady of the Angels) at the edge of Cartago, 10 blocks east of the central square, is a hodgepodge of architectural styles from Baroque to Byzantine, with a dash of Gothic. The interior is even more striking, with a colorful tile floor, intricately decorated wood columns, and lots of stained glass. It's also the focus of an amazing annual pilgrimage: the night of August 1 and well into the early morning hours of the 2nd, the road from San José clogs with worshippers, some of whom have traveled from as far away as Nicaragua, on their way to celebrate the 1635 appearance of La Negrita (the Black Virgin), Costa Rica's patron saint. At a spring behind the church, people fill bottles with water believed to have curative properties. Miraculous healing powers are attributed to the saint herself, and devotees have placed thousands of tiny symbolic crutches, ears, eyes, and legs next to her diminutive statue in recognition of her gifts. The constant arrival of tour buses and school groups, along with shops selling candles and bottles of holy water in the shape of La Negrita, add a bit of a circus atmosphere to the scene. The statue has twice been stolen, most recently in 1950 by José León Sánchez, now one of Costa Rica's best-known novelists, who spent 20 years on the prison island of San Lucas for having purloined the Madonna. ⊠ *C. 16 between Avdas. 2 and 4,* ☎ *551–0465.* ⊙ *Daily 8–6.*

En Route   Bear left where Irazú is signposted, 4 km (2½ mi) before Cartago, to bypass the city. Driving time from San José to the summit is just short of 1½ hours.

Volcán Irazú

① *31 km (19 mi) northeast of Cartago, 50 km (31 mi) east of San José.*

Volcán Irazú is Costa Rica's highest volcano, at 11,260 ft, and its summit has long been protected as a national park (☞ Chapter 9). The mountain looms to the north of Cartago, and its eruptions have dumped a considerable amount of ash on the city over the centuries. The most recent eruptive period lasted from 1963 to 1965, beginning the day John F. Kennedy arrived in Costa Rica for a presidential visit. Boulders and mud rained down on the countryside, damming rivers and causing serious floods. Although farmers who cultivate Irazú's slopes live in fear of the next eruption, they are also grateful for the soil's richness, a direct result of the volcanic deposits.

The road to the summit climbs past vegetable fields, pastures, and native oak forests. You'll pass through the villages of Potrero Cerrado and San Juan de Chicoá before reaching the bleak, gaping **crater** at the summit. Irazú is currently dormant, but the gases and steam that billow out from fumaroles on the northwestern slope are sometimes visible from the peak above the crater lookouts. This gray, lunar summit is one of the few places in Central America from which you can see both the Pacific Ocean and the Caribbean Sea (though clouds often obscure both from view). The **Area Recreativa de Prusia** (Prusia Recreation Area), halfway down, has hiking trails through oak and pine forest, and there are picnic areas in case you've brought your own supplies. Try to bring warm, waterproof clothing for your time on the summit, and leave San José very early in the day so as not to be thwarted by low clouds. ☎ *192 National Parks Service information; 290–8202. ☞ $6. ☉ Daily 8–3:30.*

Jardín Lankester

⑪ *7 km (4½ mi) east of Cartago, 57 km (35 mi) southeast of San José.*

If you're into plants, especially orchids, you'll definitely want to visit the Lankester Botanical Garden. Created in the 1950s by the English naturalist Charles Lankester to help preserve the local flora, it's now maintained by the University of Costa Rica. The lush garden and greenhouses contain one of the largest orchid collections in the world—more than 800 native and introduced species. Orchids are mostly epiphytes, meaning they use other plants for support without damaging them in the process. Bromeliads, heliconias, and aroids also abound, along with 80 species of trees including rare palms, bamboo, torch ginger, and other ornamentals. The diversity of plant life attracts a wide variety of birds. The best time to come here is January through April, when the most orchids are in bloom. To reach the gardens, drive through the center of Cartago, turn right at the Basílica, then left on the busy road to Paraíso and Orosi. After 6 km (4 mi), an orange sign on the right marks the garden's short dirt road. ✉ *Dulce Nombre, Cartago,* ☎ *552–3151. ☞ $3. ☉ Daily 9–3:30.*

$$ ✕ **Restaurant 1910.** Decorated with vintage photos of turn-of-the-20th-century buildings and landscapes, this restaurant documents the disastrous 1910 earthquake that rocked this area and all but destroyed the colonial capital of Cartago. The menu is decidedly Costa Rican, featuring traditional specialties like *pozol* (stew of corn and chicken)—hard to find in modern Tico kitchens. ✉ *300 m north of Jot Pacayas turnoff on the way to Volcán Irazú,* ☎ FAX *536–6063. AE, MC, V.*

Shopping

The gift shop in Jardín Lankester is one of the few places in Costa Rica where you can buy orchids that you can take home legally: along with the endangered plants comes a CITES certificate—a sort of orchid pass-port—that lets you ferry them across international borders without any customs problems.

THE OROSI VALLEY

The Orosi Valley, an area of breathtaking views and verdant landscapes 30 km (19 mi) south of San José, holds remnants of both the colonial era and the tropical forest that covered the country when the Spanish first arrived. The valley was one of the earliest parts of Costa Rica to be settled by Spanish colonists—in the 17th century, as ruins and a colonial church attest. Rich soil and proximity to San José have combined to make this an important agricultural area, with extensive plantations of coffee, chayote, and other vegetables. The valley is fed in the west by the confluence of the Navarro and Orosi rivers and drained in the east by the ferocious Reventazón. A dam built in the 1970s to create one of the country's first hydroelectric projects formed the Lago de Cachí, or Cachí Reservoir.

Two roads descend into the valley from Paraíso, an unattractive town 8 km (5 mi) east of Cartago. Both lead to a loop around the reservoir, passing tidy patchworks of cultivated crops, small towns, and the Represa de Cachí (Cachí Dam). Find the roads by turning right just before Paraíso's shady Parque Central. If you turn left at the *bomberos* (fire station), which houses some splendid old-style fire engines, you'll be on your way to Ujarrás; if you go straight, the road will lead you toward the town of Orosi and Tapanti National Park. Whichever route you choose, you'll eventually end up back at the same intersection. As you snake down into the valley, past coffee plantations, pastures, and patches of forest, keep your eyes open for the *mirador,* or lookout point, with covered picnic tables perched at the top of the canyon walls.

Ujarrás

⑫ *10 km (6 mi) southeast of Paraíso, 18 km (11 mi) southeast of Cartago.*

The ruins of Costa Rica's oldest church, **Iglesia de Ujarrás,** stand in a small park at the site of the former town of Ujarrás, on the floor of the Orosi Valley, just down the hill from Paraíso. Built between 1681 and 1693 in honor of the Virgin of Ujarrás, the church, together with the surrounding village, was abandoned in 1833 after a series of earthquakes and floods. An unlikely Spanish victory in 1666 over a superior force of invading British pirates was attributed to a prayer stop here. Today it's a pleasant monument surrounded by well-kept gardens and large trees, which often attract flocks of parakeets and parrots. ⊠ *Ujarrás.* ⊙ *Daily 8–5.*

Dining

$$$ ✕ **La Casona del Cafetal.** Set in a coffee plantation overlooking the Cachí
★   Reservoir, this restaurant is the best lunch stop in the valley. Housed in a spacious brick building with a high, barrel-tile roof, it has tables indoors and on a tiled portico on the lake side. Inventive twists on the local fare include *arroz tucurrique* (baked rice with cheese and heart of palm) and corvina *jacaranda* (stuffed with shrimp), as well as a variety of casados. Reservations are recommended for Sunday, when the restaurant is packed with Ticos out for a spin in the countryside. ⊠ *2 km (1 mi) southwest of Cachí Dam,* ☎ *533–3280. AE, DC, MC, V. Closed Mon.*

Shopping

The unique **Casa del Soñador** (House of the Dreamer; ☎ 533–3297), 1 km (½ mi) south of the Cachí Dam, was built by local wood sculptor Macedonio Quesada. Though Macedonio died several years ago, his son and a former apprentice are still here, carving interesting, often comical little statues out of coffee wood.

Orosi

13 *7 km (4 mi) south of Paraíso, 35 km (22 mi) southeast of San José.*

The town of Orosi, in the heart of the valley, has but one major attraction: a beautifully restored **colonial church.** Built in 1743, the structure has a low-slung whitewashed facade; the roof is made of cane overlaid with terra-cotta barrel tiles. Inside are an antique wooden altar and ancient paintings of the stations of the cross and the Virgin of Guadelupe, all brought to Costa Rica from Mexico. The **museum** in the cloister annex has a small collection of old religious regalia, multicolored wood carvings, and colonial furniture. ✉ *Across from soccer field,* ☎ *no phone.* 🎫 *Museum 50¢.* ☉ *Church daily 9–5; museum hrs fluctuate (ask around for someone to open it).*

South of town, some **thermal pools** fed by a hot spring are open to the public for a nominal fee.

En Route   From Orosi, veer right at the fork in the road for Tapantí. The road gets rougher as you near the park but is decent once you enter it.

Tapantí National Park

14 *12 km (7 mi) south of Orosi, 28 km (17 mi) southeast of Cartago.*

Tucked into a steep valley south of Orosi, Parque Nacional Tapantí (☞ *also* Chapter 9) encompasses a 47-sq-km (18-sq-mi) cloud-forest preserve teeming with birds. Drained by countless streams, this extremely lush forest provides refuge for more than 200 bird species, including the graceful, shy, and endangered resplendent quetzal. Quetzals are most readily visible in the dry season, when they mate; ask the park rangers where to look for them. The rough, 10-km (6-mi) track to Tapantí follows the course of the Río Orosi past coffee plantations, elegant *fincas* (farmhouses), and seasonal barracks for coffee pickers before it's hemmed in by the steep slopes of thick jungle. Stop at the large rangers' office and visitor center, on the right as you enter the park, to pay the entry fee. The road continues deep into the reserve; you can leave your vehicle at the heads of the various trails, the first of which leads to some small swimming holes in the chilly Río Orosi. Since the park tends to cloud up in the afternoon, it's best to get an early start. Taxis carrying up to six people make trips to the reserve from Orosi's soccer field. ☎ *192 National Parks Service information; 758–3996 Amistad Atlántico branch of the National Parks Service.* 🎫 *$6.* ☉ *Daily 7–4.*

Lodging

$$ 🏨 **Complejo Kiri.** Less than 1 km (½ mi) from the entrance to Tapantí,
★ this small lodge has its own 173-acre forest preserve, with more miles of hiking trails than the nearby national park. Guest rooms are in two cement buildings, with covered porches overlooking flower beds frequented by legions of hummingbirds. Forested hillsides rise in the background. Rooms in the upper building are a bit cramped. Complimentary breakfast is served in the lodge's bright restaurant. ✉ *Purisil, 11 km (6 mi) south of Orosi on road to Tapantí,* ☎ *284–2024. 6 rooms. Restaurant, hiking, horseback riding. AE, MC, V.*

TURRIALBA AND GUAYABO
NATIONAL MONUMENT

The tranquil town of Turrialba and the nearby Guayabo ruins lie considerably lower than the rest of the Central Valley, so they enjoy more-tropical climates. There are two ways to reach this area, both of which pass spectacular scenery. The more direct route, accessible by heading straight through both Cartago and Paraíso, winds through coffee and sugar plantations before descending abruptly into Turrialba. For the second route, turn off the road between Cartago and the summit of Irazú near the town of Cot. That narrow route twists along the slopes of Irazú and Turrialba volcanoes, passing some stunning scenery—pollarded trees line the road to form stately avenues, and white-girdered bridges cross crashing streams. From Santa Cruz a track leads up within hiking distance of the 10,900-ft summit of Volcán Turrialba. As you begin the descent to Turrialba town, the temperature rises, and neatly farmed coffee crops blanket the slopes.

Turrialba

⑮ *58 km (36 mi) east of San José.*

The relatively well-to-do agricultural center of Turrialba (population 30,000) suffered when the main San José–Puerto Limón route was diverted through Guápiles. The demise of the famous Jungle Train that connected these two cities was an additional blow. Though pleasant enough, Turrialba doesn't have much to offer, but the surrounding countryside hides some spectacular scenery, patches of rain forest, and a few excellent lodges. Turrialba is also near two of Costa Rica's best white-water rivers—the Pacuare and Reventazón—which explains why kayakers and rafters flock here ☞ Outdoor Activities and Sports, *below*). Serious enthusiasts, including the white-water Olympic kayaking teams from a handful of countries, stay all winter.

OFF THE BEATEN PATH   **CATIE** – Just outside Turrialba, on the road to Siquirres, is the Centro Agronómico Tropical de Investigación y Enseñanza (Center for Tropical Agricultural Research and Education), known by its Spanish acronym, CATIE. One of the leading tropical research centers in the world, CATIE draws students and experts from all over the Americas. The 8-sq-km (3-sq-mi) property includes modern labs and offices, landscaped grounds, seed-conservation chambers, greenhouses, orchards, experimental agricultural projects, a large swath of rain forest, and lodging for students and teachers. A muddy trail leads down into the forest behind the administration building, where you can see some of the biggest rapids on the Reventazón River. CATIE is also a good place to bird-watch; you might even catch sight of the yellow-winged jacana or purple gallinule in the lagoon near the main building. Call ahead to reserve a free tour. ☎ 556–6431 or 556–0169, 𝔽𝔸𝕏 556–1533. ⊙ Daily 7–4.

Lodging

$$$$ 🏨 **Casa Turrire.** Standing at the edge of a sugar plantation that's bordered by a man-made lake, this timeless hotel looks like a manor house that has survived mysteriously intact from the turn of the 20th century. In fact, it's the product of more recent imaginations. From the royal palms that line the driveway to the tall columns and tile floors, Casa Turrire is an exercise in elegance and attention to detail. High-ceilinged guest rooms feature tropical hardwoods, small balconies, and bright bathrooms with tubs. The central courtyard, complete with potted palms and marble-topped tables, and many sitting rooms are

excellent spots to relax after a day's adventure. ✉ *Apdo. 303–7150, Turrialba,* ☎ *531–1111,* FAX *531–1075. 12 rooms, 4 suites. Restaurant, bar, pool, hot tub, tennis court, horseback riding. AE, MC, V.*

$$$$ ⌐ **Rancho Naturalista.** Set within a 125-acre private nature reserve, Rancho Naturalista specializes in customized guided horseback and bird-watching tours for its guests. Three hundred species of birds and thousands of different moths and butterflies live on the reserve, and a resident ornithologist helps you see and learn as much as you want. The two-story lodge is upscale modern with rustic touches, as are its two separate cabins. Good home cooking is served in the indoor and outdoor dining rooms, both of which have beautiful views of Volcán Irazú and Turrialba Valley. ✉ *Southeast of Turrialba, 2½ km (1½ mi) up an unpaved road from Tuís,* ☎ *267–6014,* ☎ FAX *531–1516. Dept. 1425, Box 025216, Miami, FL 33102-5216. 9 rooms, 7 with bath. Dining room, horseback riding. No credit cards.* ✍

$$–$$$ ⌐ **Albergue Volcán Turrialba.** In the foothills of the volcano, accessible only by four-wheel-drive vehicle (which the lodge will arrange for a fee), the Volcán has comfortable rooms. You'll eat well, too: all meals are included in the room price, and the proprietors serve healthy, Costa Rican–style meals cooked on a wood-burning stove. Even more compelling are the tours, one of which goes deep into the Turrialba crater, and another of which visits the fumaroles and thermal waters of Volcán Irazú. Mountain biking, horseback riding, and a 10-hour trek from the Volcán Turrialba to Guápiles via Braulio Carrillo National Park can also be arranged. ✉ *Apdo. 1632–2050, San José (20 km/12 mi east of Cot, turn right from road to Irazú),* ☎ FAX *273–4335. 12 rooms. Bar, dining room. MC, V.*

$$ ⌐ **Turrialtico.** Eight kilometers (5 miles) out of Turrialba on the Limón road, a hedged drive winds its way up to this dramatically positioned, open-sided hotel. The second-floor rooms, handsomely designed with wood floors and Guatemalan spreads on firm beds, might be the best bargain in Costa Rica. Ask for a room on the west side—these have dazzling views toward Turrialba and, if you're in luck, Volcán Irazú. The restaurant serves a small selection of authentic Costa Rican cuisine cooked on a woodstove. A possible drawback is that Turrialtico is a breakfast stopover for tour and raft-trip buses. ✉ *Apdo. 121, Turrialba (take Hwy. 10 toward Limón 8 km/5 mi),* ☎ *556–1111,* FAX *556–1575. 14 rooms. Restaurant. AE, MC, V.*

Outdoor Activities and Sports

RAFTING AND KAYAKING

It's no coincidence that half a dozen Olympic kayaking teams use Turrialba as their winter training ground: it lies conveniently close to two excellent white-water rivers, the Reventazón and the Pacuare. And despite their appeal to the experts, these rivers can also be sampled by neophytes. The **Río Reventazón** flows right past Turrialba and has several navigable stretches; the most popular stretch has unfortunately been cut short by the construction of a dam (the Tucurrique section, class III). The Florida section (class III), above Turrialba, is a rip-roaring alternative for inexperienced rafters.

Just southeast of here is the **Río Pacuare,** Costa Rica's most spectacular white-water route, which provides rafters with an unforgettable, exhilarating, adrenaline-pumping experience. The 32-km (20-mi) Pacuare run includes a series of class III and IV rapids with evocative nicknames like Double Drop, Burial Grounds, and Magnetic Rock. The astoundingly beautiful scenery includes lush canyons where waterfalls plummet into the river, and vast expanses of rain forest—stretches of the Pacuare stood in for Africa in the otherwise forgettable 1995 film *Congo.* That riverine landscape is inhabited by an array of birds—toucans, kingfishers, aracaris, and *oropéndolas* (golden orioles) among them—along with blue morpho butterflies, the odd river otter, and other interesting critters. The rafting outfitters Aventuras Naturales and Ríos Tropicales have their own lodges on the river, making them the best options for two- and three-day trips that include jungle hikes.

For details, contact **Aventuras Naturales** (☎ 225–3939 or 224–0505, FAX 253–6934), **Costa Rica Whitewater** (☎ 257–0766, FAX 255–4354), **Ríos Tropicales** (☎ 233–6455, FAX 255–4354), **Ticos River Adventures** (☎ FAX 556–1231), and **Instinct** (☎ 556–2598).

Guayabo National Monument

16 *19 km (12 mi) north of Turrialba, 72 km (45 mi) east of San José.*

Nestled on the slopes of Volcán Turrialba is Monumento Nacional Guayabo, Costa Rica's most significant archaeological site. In 1968 a local landowner was out walking her dogs when she discovered what she thought was a tomb. A friend, archaeologist Carlos Piedra, began excavating the site and unearthed the base wall of the chief's house in what eventually turned out to be the ruins of a large city (around 20,000 inhabitants) covering 49 acres. The city was abandoned in AD 1400, probably due to disease or starvation. A guided tour in Spanish takes you through the rain forest to a mirador from which you can see the layout of the excavated circular buildings. Only the raised foundations survive, since the conical houses themselves were built of wood. As you descend into the ruins, notice the well-engineered surface and covered aqueducts leading to a trough of drinking water that still functions today. Next you'll pass the end of an 8-km (5-mi) paved walkway used to transport the massive building stones—abstract patterns carved on the stones continue to baffle archaeologists, but some clearly depict jaguars, which were revered by Indians as deities. The hillside jungle setting is captivating, and the trip is further enhanced by bird-watching possibilities: sacklike nests of oropéndolas hang from many of the trees. The last few miles of the road are in such bad shape that you'll need a four-wheel-drive vehicle to get here. ☎ *192 National Parks Service information; 290–8202.* ☞ *$6.* ☉ *Tues.–Sun. 8–4.*

THE CENTRAL VALLEY A TO Z

Arriving and Departing

By Bus

WESTERN CENTRAL VALLEY
Buses leave for **Escazú** from San José (⊠ Avda. 6 between Cs. 12 and 14) every 20 minutes. Buses begin the 25-minute trip to **Heredia,** from Calle 1 between Avenidas 7 and 9, every 10 minutes. For a 20-minute trip to Volcán Barva, take the Paso Llano bus from Heredia (**Rapidos Heredianos,** ⊠ C. 1 and Avdas. 7 and 9, ☎ 233–8392) and get off at Sacramento crossroads; the first bus is at 6:30 AM. Note: some of these buses go only as far as San José de la Montaña, adding an hour to the hike; check first. Departures for **Alajuela,** a 20-minute ride, are from Avenida 2 between Calles 12 and 14 (**TUASA,** ☎ 222–5325) daily every 10 minutes 6 AM–7 PM; every 40 minutes 7 PM–10:30 PM. An excursion bus for **Volcán Poás** departs San José daily at 8:30 AM from Calle 12 between Avenidas 2 and 4 (a 90-minute ride) and returns at 2:30 PM. Departures for the 40-minute trip to **Grecia,** from the Coca-Cola station, Calle 16 at Avenida 1, are every 30 minutes. For Sarchí, first take the 50-minute bus to Naranjo, which leaves from San José's Coca-Cola station (⊠ C. 16 between Avdas. 1 and 3) every 40 min-

utes 6 AM–6 PM. Buses to **Sarchí,** 15 minutes farther on, leave from Naranjo every half hour. Buses for the 60-minute ride to **San Ramón** (**Empresarios Unidos,** ⊠ C. 16 at Avda. 12, ☎ 222–0064) leave from the Puntarenas bus station, Calle 16 between Avenidas 10 and 12, every hour 6 AM to 7 PM.

EASTERN CENTRAL VALLEY
Buses leave San José for **Cartago,** a 45-minute trip, from Calle 5 and Avenida 18 (**SACSA,** ☎ 233–5350) every 10 minutes daily; it's more convenient, however, to catch the bus on Calle 9 at Avenida Central. An excursion bus departs San José for **Volcán Irazú,** a two-hour ride, every Saturday and Sunday at 8 AM from Avenida 2 between Calles 1 and 3, across from the Gran Hotel Costa Rica (**Metropoli,** ☎ 272–0651), and returns at 1 PM.

TURRIALBA AND GUAYABO NATIONAL MONUMENT
Buses leave for Turrialba, a two-hour trip, from Calle 13 between Avenidas 6 and 8 (**TRANSTUSA,** ☎ 556–0073) hourly 8–8.

By Car
WESTERN CENTRAL VALLEY
To reach **Escazú** from San José, turn left at the western end of Paseo Colón, take the first right, get off the highway at the first exit, and turn right at the traffic light. Turn right at the bottom of the hill for San Rafael and the old road to Santa Ana. The Paseo Colón ends at Parque La Sabana, on the west end of San José; turn right here for Alajuela and Heredia. For **Heredia,** turn right off the highway just before it heads onto an overpass, where the Hotel Irazú stands on the right; turn left at the Universidad Nacional for the center of Heredia, or continue straight for the town and volcano of Barva. The route to **Volcán Barva** heads north out of Heredia through the communities of Barva, San José de la Montaña, Paso Llano, and Sacramento. At Sacramento the paved road turns to dirt, growing worse as it nears the ranger station. A four-wheel-drive vehicle can make it all the way to the ranger station in the dry season. For **Alajuela,** take the highway all the way out to the airport and turn right. You can reach **Grecia** by continuing west on the highway past the airport—the turnoff is on the right—or by turning left just before the Alajuela cemetery. For **Sarchí,** take the highway well past the airport to the turnoff for Naranjo; then veer right just as you enter Naranjo. **San Ramón** is on the Pan-American Highway west of Grecia; head straight through town and follow the signs to reach the hotels to the north.

EASTERN CENTRAL VALLEY
All the attractions in the eastern Central Valley are accessible from San José by driving east on Avenida 2 through San Pedro, then following signs from the intersection to Cartago. Shortly before Cartago, a traffic light marks the beginning of the road up Irazú, with traffic to Cartago veering right. For the Jardín Lankester head straight through Cartago (entrance on right), turning right at the Basílica and left after two blocks.

OROSI VALLEY
For the Orosi Valley head straight through Cartago, turn right at the Basílica de Los Angeles, and follow the signs to Paraíso. Turn right at Paraíso's central plaza. A few blocks east, at the fire station, you can either turn left for Ujarrás or continue straight for Orosi and Tapantí National Park; either way takes you into the same loop around the valley.

The road through Cartago and Paraíso continues east to Turrialba, where you pick up another road a few blocks east of that town's central plaza. Marked by signs, this road leads north to the monument.

By Plane

The **Aeropuerto Internacional Juan Santamaría** (☎ 441–0744) is 16 km (10 mi) northwest of downtown San José.

BETWEEN THE AIRPORT AND CENTRAL VALLEY

You can taxis from the airport to any point in the Central Valley for between $5 and $50. Buses leave the airport for Alajuela several times an hour; from Alajuela you can catch buses to Grecia, Sarchí, and San Ramón. Less-frequent buses (one to three per hour) serve Heredia. To get from the airport to Escazú, Cartago, or Turrialba, you have to change buses in San José.

Getting Around

By Bus

WESTERN CENTRAL VALLEY

Buses travel between Alajuela and Heredia's main bus stations every half hour. To reach Zoo Ave, take the bus to La Garita, which departs every hour from the main bus station in Alajuela. Direct buses to Sarchí depart from Alajuela (✉ C. 8 between Avda. 1) every 30 minutes 6 AM–9 PM; the ride takes 90 minutes. Buses traveling between San José and Grecia or San Ramón pick up passengers on the southern edge of Alajuela. Departures for Grecia leave from Naranjo hourly 6 AM– 7 PM, a 15-minute hop.

EASTERN CENTRAL VALLEY

To visit Jardín Lankester, take the Paraíso bus, which leaves the south side of Cartago's Parque Central every 15 minutes daily.

OROSI VALLEY

Hourly buses (☎ 551–6810) depart from Cartago's southern side of Las Ruinas for a loop around the Orosi Valley, stopping at Orosi and Ujarrás. To reach Tapantí, you'll have to hire a taxi in Orosi.

TURRIALBA AND GUAYABO NATIONAL MONUMENT

The bus to Guayabo National Monument, a 50-minute ride, leaves once a day from one block south of the bus station in Turrialba, Monday to Saturday at 11 AM and Sunday at 9:30 AM.

By Taxi

Taxis parked near the central plazas in Alajuela, Cartago, and Heredia can take you to up Poás, Irazú, and Barva volcanoes, respectively, but the trips are quite expensive (about $50) unless you can assemble a group. If you don't have a car, the only way to get to Tapantí National Park is to take a cab from Orosi. Taxis parked near San Ramón's central plaza can take you to the nature lodges north of town.

Contacts and Resources

Car Rentals

See Car Rentals *in* San José A to Z, *in* Chapter 1.

Emergencies

General (☎ 911). **Fire** (☎ 118). **Police** (☎ 117). **Traffic Police** (☎ 222– 9330).

Guided Tours

Horizontes (✉ Paseo Colón, 150 m north of Pizza Hut, San José, ☎ 222–2022) offers expertly guided adventure and natural-history tours in the Central Valley and beyond. Most San José tour offices can also set you up with guided tours to the Poás and Irazú volcanoes or the Orosi Valley. **Swiss Travel** (✉ Meliá Corobicí Hotel lobby, San José, ☎ 231–4055) is one of the oldest operators in the country. For whitewater rafting outfitters, *see* Outdoor Activities and Sports *in* Turrialba, *above*.

Visitor Information

See Visitor Information *in* San José A to Z, *in* Chapter 1

3 NORTHERN GUANACASTE AND ALAJUELA

From Caño Negro's remote, bird-filled waters to the windsurfing mecca of Laguna de Arenal, Costa Rica's northernmost reaches are endlessly beguiling. Local wonders include astonishingly green Monteverde cloud forests; sparkling Pacific coast beaches; dusty, deforested uplands with cowboys and grazing cattle; exotic jungles alive with birds, monkeys, and butterflies; and a ragged row of fiercely beautiful volcanoes.

Updated by
Brad Weiss

WITH ONLY 65 INCHES OF RAINFALL a year, the northwest is Costa Rica's driest region. It's also home to countless natural wonders: large expanses of wet and dry forest, river deltas and estuaries bursting with life, and miles of sun-drenched beaches. The northwest offers you far more than the myriad ecosystems of the dry coastal plain; the territory contains the cloud and rain forests of Monteverde and other mountain preserves and the volcanoes and peaks of the Cordillera de Guanacaste, the Cordillera de Tilarán, and sections of the Cordillera Central. East of Guanacaste are the northern uplands and lowland plains of Alajuela, from the wetlands of Caño Negro Wildlife Refuge in the far north, down to the green farmlands and foothills around La Fortuna and Ciudad Quesada, east of Volcán Arenal.

Guanacaste is bordered by Nicaragua and the Pacific Ocean. The province derives its name from the broad ear-pod trees that shade the lounging white Brahman cattle so prevalent in the region. An independent province of Spain's colonial empire until 1787, when it was ceded to Nicaragua, Guanacaste became part of Costa Rica in 1814. After independence in 1821, both Nicaragua and Costa Rica claimed Guanacaste for their own. The Guanacastecos themselves were divided: the provincial capital, Liberia, wanted to return to Nicaragua, while rival city Nicoya favored Costa Rica. Nicoya got its way, helped by the fact that at the time the vote was taken, Nicaragua was embroiled in a civil war.

Guanacaste's far-northwestern coastline, still for the most part unblemished, offers everything the Nicoya Peninsula does and more: the dry forests and pristine sands of Santa Rosa National Park, the bird sanctuary of Isla Bolaños, the endless beaches of the Gulf of Santa Elena, and breezy Bahía Salinas. But tourist-driven development isn't limited to the Nicoya: a pair of new beachfront resort hotels have opened in Bahía Salinas, and others are in the works. Time will tell if this relatively untraveled stretch near the town of La Cruz and the Nicaraguan border finds itself home to the unnatural green of fairways and aqua-blue swimming pools.

East of the Carretera Interamericana (Pan-American Highway), Guanacaste's dry plains and forests slope upward into volcano country. Marching northwest to southeast in a rough, formidable line, the volcanoes of the Cordillera de Guanacaste include Orosí, Rincón de la Vieja and its nearby sister Santa Maria, Miravalles, Tenorio, and Arenal, looming over the southeast end of Laguna de Arenal. The northernmost peak in the Cordillera de Tilarán, Arenal ranks as one of the world's most active volcanoes. Below and between these active and not-so-active craters and calderas, the terrain ranges from dry forest to impassable jungle, from agricultural plain to roadless swamp.

A few of the parks and destinations in this area are relatively accessible from San José, even for day trips. Others require grueling hours of driving over pothole-scarred roads. As you contemplate spending time in this region—or anywhere in Costa Rica, for that matter—be sure to allow plenty of time for excruciatingly slow driving when and where necessary. That brief hop from the smooth pavement of the Pan-American Highway up to the famously lush cloud forests of Monteverde, for example, looks like 30 minutes behind the wheel when measured on the map. In reality, it's two hours of bone-jarring road, barely passable without high clearance or a four-wheel-drive vehicle.

Pleasures and Pastimes

Dining

Guanacaste's traditional foods derive from dishes prepared by pre-Columbian Chorotegan Indians. Typical fare includes *frito guanacasteco* (black beans, rice, vegetables, and meat), *pedre* (carob beans, pork, chicken, onions, sweet peppers, salt, and mint), *sopa de albóndigas* (meatball soup with chopped eggs and spices), and *arroz de maíz* (a kind of corn stew, sometimes made *con pollo*, with chicken). More prevalent at breakfast are eggs and *gallo pinto* ("spotted rooster," a mix of black beans and rice); at lunch and dinner you can always depend on a *casado*, the *típico* Costa Rican meal of rice and black beans served with meat, chicken, or fish. Seafood here is plentiful: *camarones* (shrimp), sautéed in garlic and butter and served with fries and salad; *langostinos* (a kind of lobster); and a fine variety of fish are available in most restaurants at reasonable prices (langostino dinners aside). Meat lovers, rejoice: the northwest, whose plains are covered with cattle ranches, produces the country's best steak.

Lodging

East and west of the mountains, Costa Rica's far northern zone offers a good mix of quality hotels, nature lodges, and more basic *cabinas* (cottages). In the areas of Monteverde and La Fortuna, a range of low- and mid-priced hotels, cabinas, and resorts fills the demand generated by visitors to Volcán Arenal and the cloud forest. Book ahead if you're headed to the coast during the dry season (December–April), especially for weekends, when Ticos flock to the beach.

Volcanoes

The sheer mass and power of Volcán Arenal, often ringed with an ominous haze, dominates Laguna de Arenal (Lake Arenal). It reiterates its presence at night, when you can see red-hot molten lava oozing from the cone, a flirtatious dance with disaster. It's easy to reach Arenal from the Pan-American Highway—watch for the turnoff at the town of Cañas—or from the east through La Fortuna. You may have to spend more than one day here, as the cone can be covered by clouds. Farther northwest, experienced hikers can trek to the lip of the steaming Rincón de la Vieja crater on trails through the namesake national park; less-active travelers can check out Las Pailas, a cluster of miniature volcanoes, fumaroles, and mud pots encircled by a relatively easy trail on the lower mountain slopes. Among the other (inactive) volcanoes are Orosí, in Guanacaste National Park, and Tenorio, which shares its name with yet another national park. Guanacaste National Park is minimally developed for tourism, and Tenorio as yet has no infrastructure whatsoever.

Windsurfing

When winter settles in up north, serious American windsurfers look to the south. These days many of them head to Laguna de Arenal, which many world-champion windsurfers have called "one of the world's top five windsurfing spots." From December through April, Caribbean trade winds sneak through a pass in the Cordillera Central, crank up to 80 kph (50 mph) or more, and blow from the east toward the northwest end of the lake, creating perfect conditions for high-wind freshwater sailing. The scenery here, too, is unmatched: watch the frequent volcanic eruptions while you glide along. The lake is somewhat choppy due to its narrow shape, but strong winds, fresh water, and hassle-free rigging and launch sites on both shores make it worthwhile.

Exploring Northern Guanacaste and Alajuela

Northern Guanacaste and Alajuela encompass the volcanic mountains of the Cordillera de Guanacaste, the northern section of the Cordillera de Tilarán, and the plains stretching west to the sea and north to Nicaragua. Most of the destinations on the west side of the mountains, including the coastal beaches, national parks, and the northwestern end of Laguna de Arenal, lie within easy reach of the Pan-American Highway. To reach La Fortuna, Volcán Arenal, the east end of Laguna de Arenal, and points farther east—including Caño Negro and Upala—the easiest drive is by way of Zarcero and Ciudad Quesada. Several roads pass through the mountains, linking these two distinct zones. Though they're mostly paved, these roads—one follows the northern shore of Laguna de Arenal and the other skirts the volcanoes along the nation's northern edge—still have poorly surfaced stretches and are subject to washouts and other difficulties. Always get a report on road conditions before setting out on long trips.

Numbers in the text correspond to numbers in the margin and on the Northern Guanacaste and Alajuela map.

Great Itineraries

As you plan your travels in this region, know that a fair amount of your time will be spent on the road. That is simply the reality of travel in Costa Rica, and particularly in these spread-out parts.

IF YOU HAVE 3 DAYS

Head northeast out of San José and through the mountains around **Zarcero** ①, en route to ⊞ **Ciudad Quesada** ② or ⊞ **La Fortuna** ③. The next day, hike to the La Fortuna waterfall; drive to ⊞ **Volcán Arenal** ⑤, checking out the Tabacón Resort's hot springs; or take a rafting trip on the Río Peñas Blancas, the Río Sarapiquí, or the Río Toro. Stay the night in an area hotel or continue north by northwest around Laguna de Arenal, with a stop at ⊞ **Tilarán** ⑦ or one of the lake-view hotels for a day or two of windsurfing, hiking, mountain biking, or volcano viewing.

IF YOU HAVE 5 DAYS TO SEE PARKS

Start from San José with a predawn drive to the ⊞ **Monteverde Cloud Forest Biological Reserve** ⑧ and spend a day hiking in the cloud forest. If Monteverde is too crowded, the compelling but smaller Santa Elena Reserve is just down the road (north). After overnighting in the area, another crack-of-dawn drive will take you to ⊞ **Tilarán** ⑦ by way of the mountain track (four-wheel-drive vehicle only) or the Pan-American Highway for an active day on Laguna de Arenal. Stay in Tilarán or in one of the lodges at the lake's northwesterly end. Early the next day return to the highway and drive north and then inland again for a day hike in ⊞ **Rincón de la Vieja National Park** ⑨. Stay at the mountain lodge, or return to the highway and head farther north for a night and a day at Hacienda Los Inocentes, the 100-year-old lodge on the northern border of ⊞ **Guanacaste National Park** ⑫. Stay a second night in the lodge, or late in the day head down to **Santa Rosa National Park** ⑩, being sure to tour the historic La Casona Hacienda. For a break from parks, your four-wheel-drive vehicle will safely deliver you to Playa Naranjo for a day at the beach.

IF YOU HAVE 5 DAYS FOR PARKS AND THE BEACH

After a pass through **Zarcero** ①, spend a day and night in the Laguna de Arenal area—⊞ **La Fortuna** ③, ⊞ **Nuevo Arenal** ⑥, or ⊞ **Tilarán** ⑦—and see the volcano (and its nocturnal performance), lake, Tabacón Resort, and/or the La Fortuna waterfall. From La Fortuna, head north to spend a day touring the **Caño Negro National Wildlife Refuge** ④.

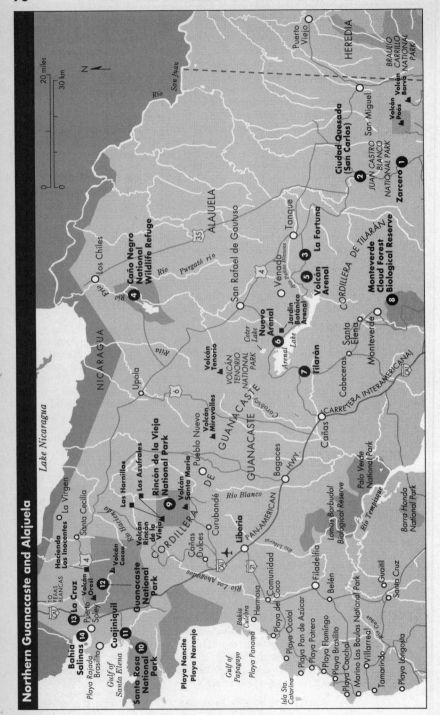

Northern Guanacaste and Alajuela

20 miles
30 km

N

Lake Nicaragua

NICARAGUA

Río

San Juan

Puerto Viejo

HEREDIA

BRAULIO CARRILLO NATIONAL PARK

Volcán Barva ▲

Volcán Poás ▲

San Miguel

San Carlos

Ciudad Quesada (San Carlos) **2**

JUAN CASTRO BLANCO NATIONAL PARK

Zarcero **1**

ALAJUELA

35

Los Chiles

Río

Purgató rio

Río

Caño Negro National Wildlife Refuge **4**

San Rafael de Guatuso

Tanque

La Fortuna **3**

4

Venado

Volcán Arenal **5**

CORDILLERA DE TILARÁN

Monteverde Cloud Forest Biological Reserve **8**

Upala

6

Cote Lake

Nuevo Arenal **6**

Jardín Botánico Arenal

Arenal Lake

Arenal

Tilarán **7**

Santa Elena

Monteverde

Cabeceras

Santa

CARRETERA INTERAMERICANA

Volcán Tenorio ▲

VOLCÁN TENORIO NATIONAL PARK

GUANACASTE

Volcán Miravalles ▲

Pueblo Nuevo

Corobicí

Bagaces

Cañas

PAN-AMERICAN HWY.

Santa Cecilia

La Virgen

Hacienda Los Inocentes

4

Volcán Orosí ▲

Río Sapoá

Las Hornillas

Los Azufrales

Rincón de la Vieja National Park

Volcán Santa María ▲

Volcán Rincón de la Vieja ▲ **9**

DE

Río Blanco

Curubandé

GUANACASTE

Lomas Barbudal Biological Reserve

Palo Verde National Park

Río Tempisque

Barra Honda National Park

PEÑAS BLANCAS

La Cruz **13**

CA1

Puerto Soley

Bahía Salinas **14**

Playa Rajada

Brasilito

Gulf of Santa Elena

Volcán Cacao ▲

Volcán Orosí ▲ **12**

Cuajiniquil **11**

Guanacaste National Park

CORDILLERA

Cañas Dulces

Liberia

Río Liberia

21

Filadelfia

Comunidad

Belén

Guaitil

Santa Cruz

Santa Rosa National Park **10**

Playa Nancite
Playa Naranjo

Gulf of Papagayo

Bahía Culebra

Isla Sta. Catarina

Playa Panamá

Hermosa

Playa del Coco

Playa Ocotal

Playa Pan de Azúcar

Playa Potrero

Playa Flamingo

Playa Brasilito

Playa Conchal

Marino Las Baulas National Park

Tamarindo

Villarreal

Río Cañas

Playa Longosta

Then take the road northwest that leads through the San Rafael de Guatuso area and continues around the Volcán Orosí. Stop for a mind-expanding look at Lago de Nicaragua from the *mirador* (lookout) at La Virgen, near Santa Cecilia, and then continue down the west slope of the mountains. Spend a night at Hacienda Los Inocentes, near ⚀ **Guanacaste National Park** ⑫, then a day hiking or horseback riding before continuing on to ⚀ **La Cruz** ⑬ and the resorts on the south shore of the half-moon-shape ⚀ **Bahía Salinas** ⑭. After a night (or two) here, work your way down to **Santa Rosa National Park** ⑩ for a day at the beach or take a day hike in the mixed environments of **Rincón de la Vieja National Park** ⑨. Either camp in the park or, more comfortably, tuck yourself into one of the nearby lodges or hotels.

When to Tour Northern Guanacaste and Alajuela

The areas in Guanacaste west of the Cordillera de Guanacaste are best toured in the dry season, from December to March. However, during the wet season, rain generally falls on this coastal plain for just an hour or two each day, so beyond the effect on the roads, problems with traveling are minimal. Farther inland, the northern uplands and lowlands offer a mixed climactic bag—the more easterly lowlands share the humid Caribbean weather of the east coast, while the uplands partake of the drier, cooler mountain clime. Given the larger numbers of tourists that visit Volcán Arenal and especially Monteverde, it might be wise to try an off-season, or edge-of-season, trip to avoid the crowds.

ARENAL AND THE CORDILLERA DE TILARÁN

Dense green cloud forests cloak the rugged mountains and rolling hills of the Cordillera de Tilarán extending northwest from San José. On the east side of the hills and on the plains below, logging and farming contend with tourism for dominance of the local economy. Still, there are great swaths of primary forest and jungle, including the marvelous cluster of reserves that straddle the continental divide at Monteverde. Farther north and west, Laguna de Arenal and the rolling green hills around it pay homage to the dark heart of this region—fiery, magnificent Volcán Arenal.

Laguna de Arenal has two distinct personalities: the northwest end is windsurf central—a row of power-generating windmills, with blades awhirl on the ridge above the Hotel Tilawa, signals another use for the relentless, powerful wind. The more sheltered southeast end, closer to the dam, is popular for other water sports, especially fishing for guapote. The southeast is also a marvelous place from which to view the volcano. If you took away the volcanoes, you might mistake the countryside of green, rolling hills for the English Lake District.

Zarcero

❶ *70 km (43 mi) northwest of San José.*

Ninety minutes from San José, the small town of Zarcero looks like it was designed by Dr. Seuss. For a fan of topiaries, this place is a must: Evangelisto Blanco's cypress shrubs in fanciful animal shapes—motorcycle-riding monkeys, a lightbulb-eyed elephant—enliven the park in front of the town church. The church interior is covered with elaborate pastel stencils and detailed religious paintings by Misael Solis, a local old-timer.

Shopping

Zarcero is renowned for its peach preserves and mild white cheese, both of which are sold in stores around town and along the highway.

SOUVENIRS

Stop at **El Tiesto Souvenir Shop,** across from the park, and talk politics with owner Rafael, a native Tico who lived in New Jersey for a while. He knows everything about the area and can arrange day trips to nearby waterfalls. At the tiny café-store **Super Dos** on the main road opposite the church in Zarcero, you can get a coffee and empanada *de piña* (of pineapple) while you mull over buying some of the excellent local peach preserves.

En Route   Passing through Sarchí (☞ Chapter 2) and Naranjo on your way to Zarcero, you'll wind upward through miles of coffee plantations, with spectacular views of the mountains, and come down the other side to the city of Ciudad Quesada. There are some hair-raising roadside chasms, particularly on the east slopes, but the road is paved all the way. The drive should take roughly 2½ to 3 hours.

Ciudad Quesada

❷ *45 km (28 mi) northwest of Zarcero.*

This lively, if not particularly picturesque, mountain market town (also known as San Carlos) is worth a stop for a soak in the soothing thermal waters of the Hotel El Tucano Resort and Spa (☞ Lodging, *below*). **Juan Castro Blanco National Park** (☞ Chapter 9) is also found nearby, though it has no facilities.

Lodging

$$$$ 🏨 **Hotel El Tucano Resort and Spa.** You come to El Tucano for the wa-
★   ters: the hotel abuts a river of hot, healing, marvelously invigorating natural springs. Two large outdoor hot tubs, the Olympic-size pool, natural steam room, and cool plunge are all fed by the Río Aguas Caliente, the cascading river that flows through the property. The hotel itself is somewhat overscale, and its public spaces suffer from the impersonality of any hotel subject to tour-group bookings. The food is ordinary at best. ⊠ *8 km/5 mi east of Ciudad Quesada (Apdo. 114–1017, San José),* ☎ *460–3141,* 🅵🅰🆇 *460–1692 or, in San José, 221–9095. 90 rooms. Restaurant, bar, pool, spa, steam room, 2 tennis courts, horse-back riding, laundry service. AE, DC, MC, V.* 🐾

La Fortuna

❸ *40 km (27 mi) east of Volcán Arenal, 10 km (6 mi) northwest of Ciudad Quesada.*

At the foot of towering, overpowering Volcán Arenal, the small farming community of La Fortuna de San Carlos (commonly called La Fortuna) attracts volcano watchers from around the world. The town overflows with restaurants, hotels, and tour operators. It's also the number one place to arrange trips to the Caño Negro refuge (☞ *below*). Tours vary in price and quality, so ask around, but all provide an easier alternative than busing up north to Los Chiles and hiring a boat to take you down through the rain forest on Río Frío.

Besides offering access to a multitude of outdoor adventures, La Fortuna also provides you with the opportunity for some serious pampering. Where else can you lounge in a natural hot-springs waterfall with a volcano spitting fireballs overhead? Kick back at the **Tabacón Resort,** a busy day spa and hotel (with 42 overnight cabinas in the $$$$ category). An inspired medley of gardens, waterfalls, swimming pools, swim-up bars, and dining facilities mingles in a florid Latin interpretation of grand European baths. Try to make an appointment a day in advance during the high season. ✉ *12 km (7 mi) northwest of La Fortuna on hwy. toward Nuevo Arenal,* ☎ *460–2020 or 256–1500,* FAX *221–3075.* ✉ *Entry $16; 45-min massage $40; mud-pack facial $20.* ☉ *Daily 8 AM–10 PM. MC, V.*

If Tabacón is full or if you want a less expensive spa alternative, head to **Baldi Termae.** The complex's five hot-springs pools vary in temperature but share views of Volcán Arenal. There's also a swim-up snack bar. ✉ *4 km (2½ mi) west of La Fortuna,* ☎ *479–9651.* ✉ *$7.* ☉ *Daily 10–10.*

A pleasant day hike from La Fortuna takes you to the 164-ft-high waterfall **Cataratas de la Fortuna.** The 6-km (4-mi) walk to the falls begins off the main road toward the volcano; look for the yellow sign marking the entrance (☞ Outdoor Activities and Sports, *below*). If you don't feel like walking, several operators in La Fortuna will take you on horseback or in a four-wheel-drive vehicle. If you've got your own wheels, use them: standard cars can also navigate the rocky road, but take it very slow—and double-check conditions in the rainy season.

OFF THE BEATEN PATH | **VENADO CAVES –** In 1945 a farmer in the mountain hamlet of Venado fell in a hole, and thus were discovered the Cavernas de Venado (Venado Caves). The limestone caves, 45 minutes (about 35 km/21 mi) north of La Fortuna and 15 km (9 mi) southeast of San Rafael, contain a series of eight chambers with an assortment of stalactites, stalagmites, underground streams, and other subterranean formations. Sunset Tours normally runs trips from La Fortuna (☞ Outdoor Activities and Sports, *below*). ☎ *Sunset Tours: 479–9415.* ✉ *Tours $35.* ☉ *Daily 7–8.*

Dining and Lodging

$–$$ ✕ **La Vaca Muca.** It isn't a posh place, but the food is good and the servings are generous. The exterior is draped with foliage, and the interior is bedecked with turquoise paneling and bamboo aplenty. Try the casado heaped with chicken or fish, rice, beans, fried egg, fried banana, cabbage salad—easily enough for two. ✉ *1 km (½ mi) west of La Fortuna,* ☎ *479–9186. V.*

$–$$ ✕ **Rancho la Cascada.** La Cascada's center-of-town location makes it a great place to grab breakfast before heading out on a rafting or riding trip. You can phone home, too: a bank of public phones (get phone cards at Sunset Tours) waits just outside the restaurant's high, palm-thatched roof. The festive upstairs contains a bar, whose large TV, neon signs, and flashing lights give it the appropriate ambience. Downstairs, the spacious dining room—decorated with foreign flags—serves basic, mid-priced Costa Rican fare as well as hearty, American-style breakfasts. ✉ *Across from northeast corner of Parque Central,* ☎ *479–9145. AE, MC, V.*

$$ ✕▥ **La Pradera.** La Pradera is a moderately priced roadside restaurant beneath a high thatched roof. The building next door contains 10 comfortable rooms, all with high ceilings, spacious bathrooms, and verandas. Five rooms are air-conditioned, and two have Jacuzzis. Beef lovers should try the restaurant's steak with jalapeño sauce—a fine, spicy dish. ✉ *Alajuela, about 2 km (1 mi) west of La Fortuna,* ☎ FAX *479–9167. 10 rooms. Restaurant, air-conditioning. AE, MC, V.*

$$$ ▥ **Chachagua Rain Forest Lodge.** At this ranch, intersected by a sweetly babbling brook, you can see caballeros at work, ride into the rain forest, and watch toucans in the open-air restaurant, which serves beef, milk, and cheese produced on the premises. Each cabina has a pair of double beds and a deck with a picnic table. Large, reflective windows enclos-

ing each cabina's shower serve a marvelous purpose: birds gather outside your window to watch their own reflections while you bathe and watch them. The lodge is downstream from the Children's Eternal Rainforest, San Ramon, and Monteverde reserves and 3 km (2 mi) up a rough track—four-wheel drive is recommended in rainy season—on the road headed south from La Fortuna to La Tigra. ✉ *Apdo. 476–4005, Ciudad Cariari, San José,* ☎ FAX *231–0356. 15 cabinas. Restaurant, bar, pool, sauna, tennis court, horseback riding, casino. AE, MC, V.* 🕭

$$$ ⊡ **Las Cabañitas Resort.** Each of the red-roof cabinas here has a terrace that looks out over landscaped grounds toward the volcano; have a seat in a rocking chair and enjoy the view. Inside, you'll find solid wood furnishings and quilted bedspreads. ✉ *Apdo. 5–4417, La Fortuna (1 km/½ mi east of La Fortuna),* ☎ *479–9400,* FAX *479–9408. 30 cabins. Restaurant, bar, pool, laundry service. AE, MC, V.* 🕭

$$$ ⊡ **Montaña de Fuego Inn.** Set on a grassy roadside knoll, this highly recommended collection of cabins affords utterly spectacular views of Volcán Arenal. The spacious, well-made hardwood structures are notable for their large porches. All rooms have ceiling fans and rustic decor. Management can arrange tours of the area. ✉ *6 km (4 mi) west of La Fortuna,* ☎ *460–1220,* FAX *460–1455. 22 cabinas. Laundry service. AE, MC, V.*

$$$ ⊡ **Tilajari Hotel Resort.** As a comfortable, upscale base, this elegantly landscaped (there's even a butterfly garden), 35-acre resort can't be beat. "Papaya on a stick" feeders hang just outside the open-air dining room, attracting an array of raucous toucans and parrots to entertain you while you sip your morning coffee. The cozy guest quarters have river-view balconies, satellite TV, and excellent bedside reading lights. The hotel organizes horseback tours through its own rain-forest preserve as well as other area tours. Note that the property is ½ hour outside of town, and there's no shuttle service—a real drawback if you're not part of a tour or don't have your own rental vehicle. ✉ *Apdo. 81, Ciudad Quesada,, La Fortuna (San Carlos Valley, just outside Muelle [follow signs], about 25 km/15 mi from La Fortuna),* ☎ *469–9091,* FAX *469–9095. 72 rooms, 4 suites. Restaurant, bar, air-conditioning, 2 pools, saunas, 4 tennis courts, basketball, horseback riding, racquetball, laundry service, meeting room. AE, DC, MC, V.* 🕭

$$–$$$ ⊡ **Arenal Observatory Lodge.** On your way to the observatory—the lodge closest to Arenal's base—you cross three large rivers whose bridges are regularly washed away, restricting access to those with four-wheel-drive vehicles. Built in 1987 for researchers, the lodge is rustic but comfortable; some bedrooms are dorms and some are doubles. The dining room has great views of the volcano and serves hearty food. ✉ *3 km (2 mi) east of dam on Laguna de Arenal (from La Fortuna, drive to Tabacon Resort and continue 4 km/3 mi past the resort to turnoff at base of volcano; turn and continue for 9 km/5½ mi,* ☎ *257–9489,* ☎ FAX *695–5033,* FAX *257–4220 in San José). John Aspinall, Arenal Observatory Lodge, Box 025216–1660, Miami, FL 33102-5216. 4 rooms with bath, 24 rooms and 1 cabina without bath. Restaurant, bar, laundry service. AE, MC, V.* 🕭

$$–$$$ ⊡ **Hotel San Bosco.** Covered in blue-tile mosaics, this two-story hotel
★ is certainly the most attractive and comfortable in the main part of town. Two kitchen-equipped cabinas (which sleep 8 or 14 people) are a good deal for families. The spotlessly clean, white rooms have polished wood furniture and firm beds and are linked by a long veranda lined with benches and potted plants. You pay a little more for air-conditioning. ✉ *220 m north of La Fortuna's gas station,* ☎ *479–9050,* FAX *479–9109. 34 rooms, 2 cabinas. Restaurant, air-conditioning, pool, hot tub, laundry service. AE, MC, V.* 🕭

Outdoor Activities and Sports

FISHING

The eastern side of Laguna de Arenal has the best freshwater fishing in Costa Rica, with guapote aplenty, although it is difficult to fish from the shore. Arenal Observatory Lodge (☞ Dining and Lodging *above*) is one of many hotels and tour companies in the area offering boats and guides.

HIKING

To take the 6-km (4-mi) day hike from La Fortuna to the **Cataratas de la Fortuna,** look for the yellow entrance sign off the main road toward the volcano. After walking 1½ km (1 mi) and passing two bridges, turn right and continue hiking straight until you reach the river turnoff. You'll go 10 or 15 minutes down a steep but very well-constructed step trail that has a few vertiginous spots along the way. Swimming in the pool under the waterfall is fairly safe. You can work your way around into the cavelike area behind the cataract for an unusual rear view, but you'll have to swim in turbulent waters and/or hike over slippery rocks. A $2 entrance fee is collected at the head of the trail, which is open daily 7–4.

HORSEBACK RIDING

If you're interested in getting up to Monteverde from the Arenal–La Fortuna area without taking the grinding four-hour drive, there's an alternative: the ever-ingenious Suresh Krishnan, a transplant from California, offers a wonderfully appealing adventure out of his tour agency, **Desafio** (✉ Central plaza (Apdo. 37–4417), La Fortuna, ☎ 479–9464)—a 4½-hour guided horseback trip around Volcán Arenal and up to Monteverde. The trip involves taxi service on both ends, as well as a boat ride across Laguna de Arenal. They'll take your luggage and drive your car up there if need be, all for $65 per person. (Note that several other agencies offer the same trip for less money, but they aren't 100% reliable.) You leave La Fortuna at 7:30 AM and arrive in Monteverde around 2:30 PM.

RAFTING

Desafio (☞ *above*) and several other La Fortuna operators offer class III and IV white-water trips on the Río Toro, Río Sarapiquí, and the Río Peñas Blancas. The narrow shapes of the Peñas Blancas and Toro rivers require the use of special, streamlined, U.S.-made boats that seat just four and go very fast. It costs $44–$55 per person for a half-day trip on Peñas Blancas, $69 for Toro trips, and $65–$80 for longer trips on the Sarapiquí.

SPELUNKING

Sunset Tours (✉ Across from Desafio, La Fortuna, ☎ 479–9415) will take you to the Venado Caves for $25, including an English-speaking guide, entrance fee, boots, and a lantern. Prepare to get wet and muddy.

En Route A paved road (Highway 4) leads northwest from Tanque, 10 km (6 mi) east of La Fortuna, passing through San Rafael de Guatuso; Upala; and several hamlets tucked in among forest preserves, farmland, and the reserves of the indigenous Guatuso peoples. The road winds west, roughly paralleling Costa Rica's northern border, and offers smooth, pothole-free driving except for one short, nasty stretch just east of Santa Cecilia. You'll see the eastern slopes of Guanacaste's volcanoes on the left and rolling farmland to the right. The dwellings visible here and there along the road are small and ramshackle, many lacking electricity. From Santa Cecilia, a short trip north on a dirt track leads to La Virgen, noteworthy for a nearby mirador with a spectacular view north across Lago de Nicaragua to the volcanoes beyond. From Santa Cecilia, the road descends toward the coast, skirting the northern edge of Guanacaste National Park. After passing citrus groves and the splendid **Hacienda Los Inocentes** (☞ Guanacaste National Park, *below*), the road terminates at the Pan-American Highway a few miles south of La Cruz. An alternative route south from Upala traverses the saddle between the Tenorio and Miravalles volcanoes, arriving at the Pan-American Highway just north of Cañas.

Caño Negro National Wildlife Refuge

④ *91 km (57 mi) northwest of La Fortuna.*

It might be miles off your planned itinerary, but the vast Lago di Caño Negro—in the 62-sq-km (38-sq-mi) Refugio Nacional de Vida Silvestre Caño Negro, in the far northern reaches of Alajuela—is an excellent place to watch such waterfowl as the roseate spoonbill, jabiru stork, and anhinga, as well as for observing a host of resident exotic animals (☞ *also* Chapter 9). In the dry season you can rent horses; in the rainy season you're better off renting a boat. Camp or stay in basic lodging for around $8, including meals. Approach via Upala—a bus from there takes 45 minutes. ⊠ $6. ☉ Daily 7–4.

Sunset Tours (☎ 479–9415), in La Fortuna, runs daylong tours down the Río Frío to Caño Negro for about $45. Bring your jungle juice: the mosquitoes are voracious.

Volcán Arenal

⑤ *17 km (11 mi) west of La Fortuna, 128 km (80 mi) northwest of San José.*

If you've never seen an active volcano, Arenal makes a spectacular first—its perfect conical profile dominates the southern end of Laguna de Arenal. Night is the best time to observe it as you can clearly see rocks spewing skyward and red-hot molten lava enveloping the top of the cone. Phases of inactivity do occur, however, so it's wise to check ahead. The volcano is also frequently hidden in cloud cover, so you may have to stay more than one day to get in a good volcano-viewing session.

Arenal lay dormant until 1968. On July 29 of that year an earthquake shook the area, and 12 hours later Arenal blew. Pueblo Nuevo to the west bore the brunt of the shock waves, poisonous gases, and falling rocks; 80 people perished. Since then, Arenal has been in a constant state of activity—eruptions, accompanied by thunderous grumbling sounds, are sometimes as frequent as one per hour. An enormous eruption in May 1998 put the fear back into the local community and led to closure of Route 42 and the evacuation of several nearby hotels. This earth-shaking event reminded everyone what it really means to coexist with an active volcano.

Hiking is possible on the volcano's lower slopes, but definitely not higher up; in 1988 two people were killed when they attempted to climb it. Ask at the Smithsonian Institute's **observatory** in the Arenal Observatory Lodge (☞ Dining and Lodging *in* La Fortuna, *above*), near the volcano's base, or at any one of the dozens of tour operators, such as Desafio (☞ Outdoor Activities and Sports *in* La Fortuna, *above*), working out of La Fortuna. They'll let you know how close you can safely approach or arrange a skilled guide.

Nuevo Arenal

⑥ *40 km (25 mi) west of La Fortuna.*

There's little reason to stop in Nuevo Arenal itself. Off the main road, the pleasant if nondescript little town was created in 1973 to replace the original Arenal, flooded when the lake was created. If you're staying overnight in the area make sure you find a hotel with a view of the volcano. On the north shore, between the dam and the town of Nuevo Arenal, there's one short stretch of road still unpaved, potholed, and at times quite dangerous; beware of deep, tire-wrecking washouts at all times. Be careful! A carload of American tourists went out of control on this road in 1998, resulting in one death and several severe injuries. This stretch adds a bone-jarring hour to an otherwise lovely drive with spectacular lake and volcano views all the way.

Five kilometers (3 miles) east of Nuevo Arenal, the elegantly organized **Jardín Botánico Arenal** (Arenal Botanical Gardens) exhibits more than 2,000 plant species from around the world. Countless orchids, bromeliads, heliconias, and roses; varieties of ferns; and a Japanese garden with a waterfall are among the many floral splendors laid out along well-marked trails. An accompanying brochure describes everything in delightful detail; well-placed benches and a fruit and juice stand provide resting places along the paths. ☎ 694–4273. ▣ $5. ☉ Daily 9–5.

Lodging

$$$–$$$$ 🏨 **Arenal Lodge.** Surrounded by macadamia trees and rain forest, this modern white bungalow is high above the dam, midway between La Fortuna and Nuevo Arenal. You need four-wheel drive to negotiate the steep 2-km (1-mi) drive, but the hotel will ferry you from the bottom for a small fee. The bedroom suites, some in a newer annex, are pleasantly furnished, and there are also cheaper, smaller, and darker rooms without volcano views. The interiors are finished in natural wood, with walls of louvered windows. The lodge's perks include manicured gardens, an extensive library, a small snooker table, breakfast with the price of a room, and a free hour of horseback riding. ✉ *Reserve through Apdo. 1139–1250, Escazú 1250, San José,* ☎ *383–3957,* ℻ *289–6798. 6 rooms, 18 suites. Dining room, hiking, horseback riding, fishing, library, laundry service. AE, MC, V.*

$$$ 🏨 **Hotel Joya Surena.** In the midst of a working coffee plantation, this property and its variously sized suites occupy a rather imposing three-story hacienda-style building surrounded by tropical gardens. It's fairly luxurious for up-country Costa Rica. Extensive trails in and around the place bring a rich diversity of plant, animal, and bird life to view. ✉ *1½ km (1 mi) down a rocky road that leads north from Nuevo Arenal,* ☎ *694–4057,* ℻ *694–4059. 28 rooms. Restaurant, pool, hot tub, massage, sauna, health club, hiking, boating, fishing, laundry service. AE, MC, V.* 🏊

$$$ 🏨 **Lake Coter Eco-Lodge.** This ruggedly handsome mountain hideaway is tucked into cloud forest. The lodge is associated with a tour company and tends to fill up with large groups, but hit it on a non-tour day and you'll have a choice of comfortable ridge-top cabinas. Clean, basic rooms are attached to the main brick-and-hardwood reception building, which has a friendly bar, dining facilities, a fireplace, and a pool table. The lodge offers canopy tours, hikes on 29 km (18 mi) of trails, kayaking and sailing on Laguna de Coter, and an extensive stable for trail rides through the cloud forest. ✉ *3 km/2 mi up a rough track off north shore of Laguna de Arenal* (✉ *Apdo. 85570–1000, San José*), ☎ *257–5075,* ℻ *257–7065. 23 rooms, 14 cabinas. Restaurant, bar, hiking, horseback riding, boating, laundry service, meeting rooms. AE, MC, V.* 🏊

Shopping

Toad Hall, an eclectic store on the road between Nuevo Arenal and La Fortuna, sells everything from indigenous art to maps to recycled paper. The owners can give you the lowdown on every tour and tour operator in the area; they also run a deli-café with stunning alfresco views of the lake and volcano. Toad Hall is open daily from 8:30 to 5.

Tilarán

❼ *22 km (14 mi) southwest of Nuevo Arenal, 62 km (38 mi) west of La Fortuna.*

Heading west around Laguna de Arenal, you'll pass a couple of small villages and several charming hotels ranging from the Cretan-inspired fantasy Hotel Tilawa to the rustic Rock River Lodge (☞ Dining and Lodging, *below*). The quiet whitewashed town of Tilarán, on the southwest side of Laguna de Arenal, is used as a base by bronzed windsurfers.

Dining and Lodging

$$$–$$$$ ✕⊞ **Hotel Tilawa.** Overlooking the windy western end of Laguna de
★ Arenal, this unique hotel is a knockoff of the Palace of Knossos on Crete. With its neoclassical murals, columns, and arches draped with flowering plants, scarily enough, it works. Spacious, comfortable rooms feature two queen-size beds with bright Guatemalan bedspreads beneath natural wood ceilings; the bathrooms are especially spacious. In the restaurant, you can enjoy renowned chef Ronnie Jimenez's varied delicacies with one of three types of microbrewed beer. Tilawa offers sailing tours in a 36-ft catamaran and runs a world-class windsurfing school and shop on the lake; packages include the use of windsurfing gear. ⊠ *Apdo. 92–5710, Tilarán (8 km/5 mi north of Tilarán),* ☎ *695–5050,* FAX *695–5766. 28 rooms. Restaurant, bar, pool, hiking, horseback riding, windsurfing, boating, mountain bikes, laundry service. AE, DC, MC, V.* ✉

$$–$$$ ✕⊞ **Rock River Lodge.** This handsome hotel perches on a grassy hill above the road leading from Tilarán to Nuevo Arenal. A long building houses half a dozen rustic wooden cabinas sharing a shaded front porch with views of the volcano. Eight Santa Fe–style cabinas are farther up the hill. The restaurant, bar, and lobby occupy another wood building a bit closer to the road, with plenty of porch space and lounging sofas, an open kitchen, and a welcoming fireplace. The owner, Norman List, is a dedicated windsurfer and rents gear; his launching site is across the lake from that of the Hotel Tilawa (☞ *above*). He also organizes innertube trips on the Sarapiquí and bird-watching excursions. The restaurant serves well-prepared food at reasonable prices. ⊠ *Apdo. 95, Tilarán,,* ☎ FAX *695–5644. 6 rooms, 8 cabinas. Restaurant, bar, horseback riding, windsurfing, fishing, mountain bikes, laundry service. V.*

$ ✕⊞ **Cabinas El Sueño.** Upstairs on a street just off Tilarán's central plaza, "The Dream" is probably the best low-priced deal in town—and for you budget-minded wind riders, it's a few scant miles from the pricier Hotel Tilawa's (☞ *above*) waterfront windsurfing center. The clean, quiet rooms surround a serene central courtyard with a fountain and a hammock for lounging. Downstairs, the hotel's Restaurant El Parque specializes in seafood dishes. ⊠ *Off Parque Central, Tilarán,* ☎ *695–5347. 12 rooms. Restaurant. MC, V.*

Outdoor Activities and Sports

HORSEBACK RIDING
Uncounted miles of good trails for horses cover a marvelous mix of terrain. **Hotel Tilawa** (☞ Dining and Lodging, *above*) and nearly every reputable hotel offer or can make arrangements for guided and unguided horseback treks.

MOUNTAIN BIKING
For those days when the windsurfers get "skunked" (the wind fails to blow), the **Hotel Tilawa** (☞ Dining and Lodging, *above*) rents moun-

tain bikes for riding a network of roads and trails in the area at the
north end of Laguna de Arenal.

WINDSURFING

Several hotels, including the Rock River Lodge (☞ Dining and Lodging, *above*), rent windsurfing equipment, but the best selection can be
found at **Tilawa Viento Surf** (☎ 695–5008), the lakefront shop associated with the Hotel Tilawa (☞ Dining and Lodging, *above*).

En Route   If your bones can take it, a very rough track leads from Tilarán via
Cabeceras to Santa Elena, near the Monteverde Cloud Forest Biological Reserve, doing away with the need to cut across to the Pan-American Highway. You may well need a four-wheel-drive vehicle—inquire
locally about the present condition of the road—but the views of
Nicoya Peninsula, Lake Arenal, and Volcán Arenal reward those will-
ing to bump around a bit. Note, too, that you don't really save much
time—it takes about 2½ hours as opposed to the three required via Cañas
and Río Lagarto on the highway.

Monteverde Cloud Forest Biological Reserve

★ ❽   *35 km (22 mi) southeast of Tilarán, 167 km (104 mi) northwest of San
José.*

In close proximity to several fine hotels, the Reserva Biológica Bosque
Nuboso Monteverde and Environs is one of Costa Rica's best-kept reserves, with well-marked trails, lush vegetation, and a cool climate. The
area's first residents were a handful of Costa Rican families fleeing the
rough-and-ready life of nearby gold-mining fields during the 1940s.
They were joined in the 1950s by Quakers from Alabama who came
in search of peace, tranquillity, and good grazing, but the cloud forest
that lay above their dairy farms was soon to attract the attention of
ecologists.

The collision of moist winds with the continental divide here creates
a constant mist whose particles provide nutrients for plants growing
at the upper layers of the forest. Giant trees are enshrouded in a cascade of orchids, bromeliads, mosses, and ferns, and, in those patches
where sunlight penetrates, brilliantly colored flowers flourish. The
sheer size of everything, especially the leaves of the trees, is striking.
No less astounding is the variety: 2,500 plant species, 400 species of
birds, 500 types of butterflies, and more than 100 different mammals
have so far been cataloged at Monteverde. A damp and exotic mixture of shades, smells, and sounds, the cloud forest is also famous for
its population of resplendent quetzals, which can be spotted feeding
on the *aguacatillo* (like an avocado) trees; best viewing times are early
mornings from January until September, and especially during the
mating season of April and May. Other forest-dwelling inhabitants include hummingbirds and multicolored frogs.

For those who don't have a lucky eye, a short-stay aquarium is in the
field station; captives here stay only a week before being released back
into the wild. Although the reserve limits visitors to 100 people at a
time, Monteverde is one of the country's most popular destinations and
gets very busy, so come early and allow a generous slice of time for
leisurely hiking to see the forest's flora and fauna; longer hikes are made
possible by some strategically placed overnight refuges along the way.
At the entrance to the reserve you can buy self-guide pamphlets and
rent gum boots; a map is provided when you pay the entrance fee. Note
that the Monteverde settlement has no real nucleus; houses and hotels
flank a 5-km (3-mi) road at intervals until you arrive at the reserve's
entrance. ☎ 645–5122. ☞ *Reserve $8, guide $15.* ☉ *Daily 7–4.*

Greet live Costa Rican reptiles at the **Serpentario Monteverde.** ⊠ *Just outside Santa Elena on road to Monteverde,* ☎ *645–5238.* ⊡ *$3.* ⊙ *Daily 8–5.*

Several conservation areas that have sprung up near Monteverde make attractive day trips for reserve visitors, particularly if the Monteverde reserve is too busy. The **Reserva Santa Elena,** just west of Monteverde, has a series of trails that can be walked alone or with a guide. ⊠ *5 km (3 mi) north of the town of Santa Elena,* ☎ *645–5014.* ⊡ *$5.* ⊙ *Daily 7–4.*

With tours operating out of the El Sapo Dorado hotel (☞ Dining and Lodging, *below*), the **Reserva Sendero Tranquilo** invites you to hike 200 acres containing four different stages of cloud forest, including one area illustrating the results of cloud-forest devastation. ⊠ *3 km (2 mi) north of park entrance,* ☎ *645–5010.* ⊡ *$20 (2-person minimum, 10-person maximum).*

☾ The **Jardín Mariposa** (Butterfly Garden) displays tropical butterflies in three enclosed botanical gardens with stunning views of the Golfo de Nicoya. A guided tour helps you understand the stages of a butterfly's life. The private **bird farm** next door has several trails through secondary forest. More than 90 bird species have been sighted here, from the crowned motmot to the resplendent quetzal. ⊠ *Near Pensión Monteverde Inn (take right-hand turnoff 4 km/2½ mi past Santa Elena on road to Monteverde; continue for 2 km/1 mi),* ☎ *645–5512.* ⊡ *$6.* ⊙ *Daily 9:30–4.*

Dining and Lodging

$$–$$$ ✕ **De Lucia.** Cordial Chilean owner José Belmar is the walking, talking (five languages) menu in this elegant, reasonably priced restaurant. He's always on hand to explain with enthusiasm such masterfully prepared dishes as fresh sea bass with garlic sauce and orange chicken. All the entrées are served with an impressive assortment of grilled vegetables and fried plantains. The handsome wooden restaurant with red mahogany tables is given a distinct South American flavor by an array of Andean tapestries and ceramics. An excellent dessert choice is the *torta de tres leches* (three-milk cake) with decaf coffee—a novelty in Costa Rica. ⊠ *Just off main road between Santa Elena and Monteverde, on turnoff to Jardín Mariposa,* ☎ *645–5337.* AE, DC, MC, V.

$$$ ✕🏠 **El Sapo Dorado.** Having begun life as a nightclub, El Sapo Do★ rado (The Golden Toad) became a popular restaurant and graduated into a very pleasant hotel. Geovanny Arguedas's family arrived here to farm 10 years before the Quakers did, and he and his wife, Hannah Lowther, have built secluded hillside cabins with polished paneling, tables, fireplaces, and rocking chairs. The restaurant is renowned for its pasta, pizza, vegetarian dishes, and fresh sailfish from Puntarenas. ⊠ *Apdo. 09–5655, Monteverde (6 km/4 mi northwest of park entrance),* ☎ *645–5010,* FAX *645–5180. 30 rooms. Restaurant, bar, massage, laundry service.* AE, MC, V. ✍

$$$ ✕🏠 **Fonda Vela.** The most innovatively designed of Monteverde's ho★ tels is also one of the closest to the reserve entrance. Owned by the Smith brothers, whose family were among the first American arrivals in the 1950s, these steep-roof chalets have large bedrooms with whitestucco walls, wood floors, and huge windows. Some have markedly better views of the wooded grounds, so specify when booking. Local and international recipes, prepared with flair, are served in the dining room or on the veranda. ⊠ *1½ km (1 mi) northwest of park entrance (Apdo. 70060–1000, San José),* ☎ *645–5125; 257–1413 in San José,* FAX *257–1416. 28 rooms. Restaurant, bar, refrigerators, horseback riding, meeting rooms.* AE, DC, MC, V. ✍

EYES AFLIGHT IN COSTA RICA

IF YOU VISIT A COSTA RICAN CLOUD forest, you'll probably have your eyes peeled for the emerald toucanet or the three-wattled bellbird, but if you're here between October and April, you'll actually be just as likely to see a Kentucky warbler. Experienced birders shouldn't be surprised to see that some of their feathered friends from home made similar vacation plans, but many people probably don't realize that when northern birds fly south for the winter, they don't all head to Miami.

Seasonal visitors are just part—about a quarter—of the amazing avian panorama in Costa Rica. Nearly 850 bird species have been identified here, more than the United States and Canada have between them—all in an area about half the size of Kentucky. The country is consequently a mecca for amateur ornithologists, who flock here by the thousands. Though the big attractions tend to be such spectacular species as the keel-billed toucan and resplendent quetzal, it is the diversity of shape, size, coloration, and behavior that makes bird-watching in Costa Rica so fascinating.

The country's avian inhabitants range in size from the scintillant hummingbird, standing a mere 2½ inches tall and weighing just over 2 grams, to the long-legged jabiru stork, which reaches a height of more than 4 ft and a weight of 14 pounds. The diversity of form and color varies from such striking creatures as the showy scarlet macaw and the quirky purple gallinule to the relatively inconspicuous, and seemingly ubiquitous, clay-color robin, which is, surprisingly enough, Costa Rica's national bird. These robins may look a bit plain, but their song is a melodious one, and since the males sing almost constantly toward the end of the dry season—the beginning of their mating season—local legend has it they call the rains, which play a vital role in a nation so dependent on agriculture.

Foreigners tend to ooh and aah at the sight of those birds associated with the tropics: parrots, parakeets, and macaws; toucans and toucanets; and the elusive but legendary resplendent quetzal. But there are many other equally impressive species flitting around, such as the motmots, with their distinctive racket tails; _oropéndolas_ (golden orioles), which build remarkable hanging nests; and an amazing array of hawks, kites, and falcons.

On the color scale, the country's tanagers, euphonias, manakins, cotingas, and trogons are some of its loveliest plumed creatures, but none of them match the iridescence of the hummingbirds and their hyperactive cousins. Costa Rica hosts 51 members of the hummingbird family, compared to the just one species for all of the United States east of the Rocky Mountains. A bit of time spent near a hummingbird feeder will treat you to an unforgettable display of accelerated aerial antics and general pugnacity.

You just might find that the more you observe Costa Rica's birds, the more interesting they get. Bird-watching can be done everywhere in the country—all you need is a pair of binoculars and a copy of _A Guide to the Birds of Costa Rica_, the excellent field guide by Stiles and Skutch. Wake up early, get out into the woods or the garden, focus those binoculars, and you'll quickly be enchanted by the beauty on the wing. For more information about Costa Rican birds, _see_ the Wildlife Glossary Background and Essentials.

$$$ ✕⛶ **Hotel Belmar.** Built into the hillside, Hotel Belmar resembles two
★ tall Swiss chalets and commands extensive views of the ·Golfo de
Nicoya and the hilly peninsula. The amiable Chilean owners have de-
signed both elegant and rustic rooms, paneled with polished wood; du-
vets cover the beds, and most rooms have balconies. In the dining room,
you can count on adventurous and delicious *platos del día* (daily spe-
cials) of Costa Rican and international fare. ✉ *Apdo. 5655, Monteverde,
Puntarenas (4 km/2½ mi north of Monteverde),* ☎ *645–5201,* FAX *645–
5135. 34 rooms. Restaurant, bar, basketball. DC, V.* ✿

$$$ ⛶ **Trapp Family Lodge.** Take a whiff in this cozy lodge and you can
imagine yourself in a lumberyard. The enormous rooms, with wood
paneling and ceilings, have lovely furniture marvelously crafted from—
you guessed it—wood. The architectural style is appropriate as the lodge
is surrounded by trees, just a 10-minute walk from the park entrance.
The friendly owners (distant relatives of the owners of Trapp Family
Lodge in Vermont) are always around to provide personalized service.
✉ *Apdo. 70–5655, Monteverde (on main road from park),* ☎ *645–
5858,* FAX *645–5990. 10 rooms. Restaurant, bar, laundry service. V.* ✿

$$ ⛶ **El Bosque.** Convenient to the Bajo Tigre nature trail and Meg's Sta-
bles (☞ Outdoor Activities and Sports, *below*), El Bosque is a popu-
lar shady diner with a veranda; the paneled dining room has a tile floor
and wood tables. A bridge from the veranda crosses a stream; a track
from there leads to the hotel. The quiet, simple rooms are grouped around
a central camping area with a volleyball court. ✉ *Apdo. 5655, Santa
Elena,* ☎ *645–5221 or 645–5158,* FAX *645–5129. 26 rooms. Restau-
rant, volleyball, laundry service. AE, DC, MC, V.* ✿

$ ⛶ **Pensión Monteverde Inn.** Situated on a 28-acre private preserve, the
cheapest inn in Monteverde is quite far from the park entrance. The
bedrooms are basic, but they have stunning views of the Golfo de Nicoya
and contain hardwood floors; firm beds; and powerful, hot showers.
Home cooking is served by the chatty David Savage and family. Their
dog, Bambi, warms up to guests soon enough. ✉ *5 km (3 mi) past But-
terfly Garden (on the turnoff road), Monteverde,* ☎ *645–5156. 10
rooms, 8 with bath. Dining room. No credit cards.*

Outdoor Activities and Sports

HIKING AND CANOPY TOURS

The Monteverde Conservation League's **Bajo del Tigre trail** (follow signs
along the highway to Monteverde) makes for a pleasant, 1½-km (1-
mi) hike through secondary forest. Admission to the trail is $5, and
it's open daily 8–4:30.

You can visit the Monteverde cloud forest from high in the air cour-
tesy of **Canopy Tours** (☎ 645–5243; in San José, 257–5149) which has
five platforms up in the trees that you arrive at using a cable-and-har-
ness traversing system, and another which you climb 40 ft inside a stran-
gler fig to reach. The tours last 2½ hours and are held at 7:30 AM, 10:30
AM, and 2:30 PM. The cost is $45.

Sky Walk (☎ 645–5238) lets you hike between treetops, up to a height
of 126 ft, by way of five hanging bridges connected from tree to tree.
The hour-long hike can be done anytime between 7 and 4 daily and
costs $12. Tours with an English-speaking guide leave at 8 and 1—be
sure to make reservations. At the same facility is the **Sky Trek**, which
has seven platforms and longer cables between them than the Canopy
Tour. Tours cost $35 and leave at 7:30, 9:30, 11:30, 1:30, and 2. The
company provides cheap transport to and from hotels when called a
few hours in advance.

HORSEBACK RIDING

Meg's Stables (✉ On main road, halfway between Santa Elena and Monteverde, ☎ 645–5052) offers horseback riding for everyone from toddlers to seasoned experts. Guided rides through the Monteverde area cost around $10 an hour, with prices dropping for longer rides. Reservations are a good idea in high season.

Shopping

In Monteverde, the **Cooperative de Artesanas Santa Elena y Monteverde** (CASEM; ☎ 645–5190), an artisans' cooperative open next door to the El Bosque hotel-restaurant (☞ Dining and Lodging, *above*), sells locally made crafts and books in English. The **Hummingbird Gallery**, near the reserve entrance, sells prints, slides, books, gifts, T-shirts, and great Costa Rican coffee.

FAR NORTHERN GUANACASTE

This area encompasses the mountains, plains, and Pacific coastline north of Liberia up to the border of Nicaragua. The primary town in the area, Liberia (☞ Chapter 4), serves as the capital of Guanacaste and home to Costa Rica's second-largest airport. You'll most likely pass through it on your way to the beaches west of the city and on the Nicoya Peninsula (☞ Chapter 4), or up north to the national parks of Rincón de la Vieja, Guanacaste, or Santa Rosa. Volcán Rincón de la Vieja, an active volcano that last erupted in 1991, is pocked with eerie wonders such as boiling creeks, bubbling mud pools, and vapor-emitting streams—look, but don't touch!

West of Rincón de la Vieja, on the coast, Santa Rosa National Park is a former cattle ranch where Costa Ricans defeated the invading mercenary army of American William Walker in 1857. Santa Rosa is also home to Playas Naranjo and Nancite, where hundreds of thousands of olive ridley turtles lay their eggs between August and November. Closer still to the Nicaraguan border are Guanacaste National Park and the town of La Cruz, overlooking the pristine beaches and new resorts of the lovely Golfo de Santa Elena and Bahía Salinas.

En Route   From Liberia, access to Rincón de la Vieja National Park is on 27 km (17 mi) of unpaved road. The road begins 6 km (4 mi) north of Liberia off the Pan-American Highway (follow signs for Albergue Guachipelín) or 25 km (15 mi) along the Colonia Blanca route northeast from Liberia, which follows the course of the Río Liberia to the Santa María park headquarters. A four-wheel-drive vehicle is recommended, though not essential, for either of these bone-rattling one- to 1½-hour rides.

Rincón de la Vieja National Park

❾ *27 km (17 mi) northeast of Liberia.*

Some compare the geysers, mud pots, and hot springs of Parque Nacional Rincón de la Vieja to those of Yellowstone National Park in the United States. The park's more than 177 sq km (54 sq mi) of protected land is primarily dry forest, much of which has been regenerated since the park's inception in 1973. The wildlife here is tremendously diverse: 200 species of birds, including keel-billed toucans and blue-crowned motmots, plus mammals such as brocket deer, tapirs, coatis, jaguars, sloths, armadillos, and raccoons. Needless to say, hiking here is fantastic, but it's wise to do some planning to know where to head. Trail maps and hiking information are available at the park headquarters by the entrance gate; alternatively, head to Rincón de la Vieja Mountain Lodge (☞ Lodging, *below*), which has guides for foot or horseback hiking available; call ahead to check availability. ☎ *661–8139.* 🎟 *$6.* ⊙ *Daily 7–4.*

The composite mass of **Volcán Rincón de la Vieja,** often enveloped in a mixture of sulfurous gases and cloud, dominates the scenery to the right of the Pan-American Highway as you head north. The volcano complex has two peaks: **Santa María** (6,284 ft) and **Rincón de la Vieja** (6,225 ft), to the northeast. The latter is barren and has two craters. Rincón de la Vieja is thought unlikely to erupt violently due to the profusion of fumaroles through which it constantly lets off steam. The last violent eruptions were between 1966 and 1970. If you want to explore the slopes of the volcano, go with a guide; the abundant hot springs and geysers have given unsuspecting visitors some very nasty burns. The upper slopes often receive fierce and potentially dangerous winds—check conditions at the ranger station before your ascent. **Las Hornillas** (The Kitchen Stoves), on the southern slope of the Rincón de la Vieja crater, is a 124-acre medley of mud cones, hot-water pools, bubbling mud pots, and vent holes most active during the rainy season. To the east, **Los Azufrales** are hot sulfur springs in which you can bathe; be careful not to get sulfur in your eyes.

Lodging

$$ 🏨 **Rincón de la Vieja Mountain Lodge.** Resting on the slopes of Rincón de la Vieja, this lodge has paneled cabins, small doubles, and comfy dormitory-style rooms. The sitting room has a TV with a VCR and a few movies. Meals of meat, fish, and vegetarian (made with homegrown produce) entrées are good, though on the pricey side. The affable staff of the owner, Alvaro, can take you to explore the park and volcano on foot or on horseback through the woods. Trails lead to a hot-water, sulfur bathing pool and a blue lake and waterfall. ✉ *Apdo. 114–5000, Liberia (2 km/1 mi northeast of park entrance),* ☎ FAX *661–8156. 38 rooms without bath. Dining room, bar, pool. AE, MC, V.* ♻

Outdoor Activities and Sports

From the Rincón de la Vieja Mountain Lodge (☞ Lodging, *above*), **Treetop Trails** runs four-hour canopy tours ($49.50) that include a forest-floor hike and canopy observation from 16 cable-linked treetop platforms. A more elaborate seven-hour tour ($77) also includes horseback riding to the park's blue lake and waterfall.

Santa Rosa National Park

❿ *48 km (30 mi) south of the Nicaraguan border, west of the Pan-American Highway at Km 269.*

Parque Nacional Santa Rosa was established in 1971 to protect **La Casona Hacienda,** scene of the famous 1856 battle in which a ragged force of ill-equipped Costa Ricans routed the superior army of William Walker. A U.S. filibuster from Tennessee, Walker had established himself as chief of staff of the Nicaraguan army as part of his Manifest Destiny–influenced scheme to create a slave empire in the region. In 1857, the hostilities having continued onto Nicaraguan soil, Juan Santamaría, a drummer boy from Alajuela, threw burning wood into the building where Walker and his henchmen were gathered, so ending the war and thereby winning undying national fame for himself. (Walker was later turned over to Honduras and shot by a firing squad.) The rambling colonial-style farmstead of La Casona stands as a monument to this national triumph and contains an interesting museum, with maps, weapons, uniforms, and furniture. The start of a short explanatory nature trail is visible just out front. Keep an eye out for the number of large green parrots inhabiting the trees around the farmstead. ☎ 666–5051. 🖃 $6. ⏱ Daily 8–4:30.

For ecologists, Santa Rosa has a more important role—protecting and regenerating 495 sq km (191 sq mi) of forest land, both moist, basal-belt transition and deciduous, tropical dry forests. The central administrative area is a hive of scientific activity. Much of the research here has been into forest propagation, the fruits of which are evident in former cattle pastures where windblown seeds have been allowed to establish themselves. Bush fires are a constant hazard in the dry season, making firebreaks a necessity. Typical dry-forest vegetation includes oak, wild cherry, mahogany, calabash, bullhorn acacia, hibiscus, and gumbo-limbo, with its distinctive reddish-brown bark. Because of its less luxuriant foliage, the park is a good one for viewing wildlife, especially if you station yourself next to water holes during the dry season. Inhabitants include spider, white-faced, and howler monkeys, as well as deer, armadillos, coyotes, tapirs, coatis, and ocelots. Ocelots, commonly known as *manigordos* ("fat paws") on account of their large feet, are striped wildcats that have been brought back from the brink of extinction by the park's conservation methods. These wildlands also define the southernmost distribution of many North American species such as the Virginia opossum and the *cantil* moccasin. Throughout the park it's wise to carry your own water, since water holes are none too clean. From the entrance gate, 7 km (4½ mi) of paved road leads to the **park headquarters**. ☎ 666–5020. 🖃 $6. ⏱ Daily 7–5.

Thirteen kilometers (8 miles) west of the administrative area—a two- to three-hour hike or one hour by four-wheel-drive vehicle—is the white-sand **Playa Naranjo,** popular for beachcombing thanks to its pretty shells and for surfing because of its near-perfect break. The campsite here has washing facilities, but bring your own drinking water. The lookout at the northern tip of the beach has views over the entire park.

Turtle *arribadas*—the phenomenon of turtles arriving on a beach to nest—do take place on Naranjo, but the big ones occur at a point reached by a two-hour walk north to **Playa Nancite,** also accessible by four-wheel-drive vehicle. It is estimated that 200,000 of the 500,000 turtles that nest each year in Costa Rica choose Nancite. Backed by dense hibiscus and button mangroves, the gray-sand beach is penned in by steep, tawny, brush-covered hills. Previously a difficult point to get to, it's now the world's only totally protected olive-ridley turtle arribada. The busy time is August to November, peaking in September and October. Olive ridleys are the smallest of the sea turtles (average carapace, or hardback shell, is 21–29 inches) and the least shy. The majority arrive at night, plowing the sand as they move up the beach and sniffing for the high-tide line, beyond which they use their hind flippers to dig the holes into which they lay their eggs. They spend an average of one hour on the beach before scurrying back to the sea. Hatching also takes place at night. The phototropic baby turtles naturally know to head for the sea, which is vital for their continued survival, since the brightest light is that of the shimmering ocean. Many of the nests are churned up during subsequent arribadas, and predators such as coatis, ghost crabs, raccoons, and coyotes lie in wait; hence just 0.2% of eggs reach the sea as young turtles. Permits are needed to stay at Nancite; ask at the headquarters.

Camping

$ ⛺ **La Casona.** Campers enjoy the rugged terrain and isolated feel of Santa Rosa National Park. The campsite, overhung by giant strangler figs, has no set sites—allowing you a choice of where to set up—and provides washing facilities and picnic tables. Be careful of snakes. Between Playas Naranjo and Nancite, another campground at Estero Real is available with tables only. ⊠ *Santa Rosa National Park,* ☎ *666–5051. Bathrooms, picnic tables. No credit cards.*

Cuajiniquil

⑪ *10 km (6 mi) north of Santa Rosa National Park.*

North from Santa Rosa on the Pan-American Highway is the left turn to Cuajiniquil, famous for its waterfalls. If you have time and a four-wheel-drive vehicle, Cuajiniquil has lovely views. The Golfo de Santa Elena is renowned for its calm waters, which is why it's now threatened by tourist development. Playa Blanca in the extreme west has smooth white sand, as its name implies. The rough track there passes through a valley of uneven width caused, according to geologists, by the diverse granulation of the sediments formerly deposited here. To the south rise the rocky Santa Elena hills (2,332 ft), bare except for a few chigua and nancite shrubs.

Guanacaste National Park

⑫ *32 km (20 mi) north of Liberia.*

To the east of the Pan-American Highway is Parque Nacional Guanacaste (☎ 695–5598), created in 1989 to preserve rain forests around **Volcán Cacao** (5,443 ft) and **Volcán Orosí** (4,877 ft), which are seasonally inhabited by migrants from Santa Rosa. Much of the park's territory is cattle pasture, which it is hoped will regenerate into forest. Three biological stations within the park have places for visitors to stay. The **Mengo Biological Station** (☎ no phone) lies on the slopes of Volcán Cacao at an altitude of 3,609 ft; accommodation is in rustic wood dormitories with bedding provided, but bring a towel. From Mengo one trail leads up Volcán Cacao, and another heads north to the modern **Maritza Station** (☎ no phone), a three-hour hike away at the base of Orosí, with more lodging available. You can also reach Maritza by four-wheel-drive vehicle. From Maritza you can trek two hours to **Llano de los Indios,** a cattle pasture dotted with volcanic petroglyphs. Farther north and a little east is rustic **Pitilla Station** (☎ 661–8150) and despite its lower elevation, it has views of the coast and Lago de Nicaragua.

Lodging

$$$ 🖽 **Hacienda Los Inocentes.** Built more than 100 years ago by the great-grandfather of Violeta Chamorra, the president of Nicaragua, this handsome, exquisitely maintained hardwood hacienda is in a private reserve along the northern border of Guanacaste National Park. A 14-km (8½-mi) drive on a smoothly paved road east from the Pan-American Highway takes you to the entrance of the working ranch, with its horses, cattle, and numerous birds. The hardwood-finished rooms are rustic but comfortable, with hot showers in bathrooms (some shared by two rooms) across the halls. Meals are included in most packages. Experienced ranch-hand guides, friendly horses, and miles of trails get you into the forests. ⊠ *Apdo. 228–3000, Heredia,* ☎ 🄵🄰🅇 *679–9190;* ☎ *265–5484 in San José; 888/613–2532 in the U.S.,* 🄵🄰🅇 *265–4385. 8 rooms without bath, 3 rooms with bath. Dining room, pool. AE, MC, V.* ⊜

La Cruz

⑬ *56 km (35 mi) north of Liberia, 20 km (12 mi) south of the Nicaraguan border.*

Farther north on the west side of the highway is a turnoff to La Cruz, noteworthy for the stunning views of Bahía Salinas (☞ *below*) from the restaurants and hotels along the bluff. It also serves as a gateway to the resorts and beaches on the south shore of Bahía Salinas, the hamlet of Puerto Soley, and the Golfo de Santa Elena.

Dining and Lodging

$$ ✕ **El Mirador Ehecatl.** You don't want to pass up a chance to have a drink at this two-story restaurant-bar with a cliffside promenade overlooking Bahía Salinas, Isla Bolaños, and the Nicaraguan coastline. Even better, the food is delicious: try anything with seafood—the ceviche is especially well prepared—or one of the many cheap, rice-based combination plates. The chef has a surprisingly refined hand. Ehecatl, by the way, means "god of the wind" in the old Chorotegan language, and the name suits, for Bahía Salinas is a very windy place. To find the restaurant, turn left and go around the La Cruz town square; at the "end" of the road veer slightly left rather than taking the steep downhill road that leads to Bahía Salinas. ☎ *No phone. V.*

$$ ✕🏠 **Colinas del Norte.** Nicaragua-bound adventurers will appreciate this outpost. On the Pan-American Highway halfway between La Cruz and the Nicaraguan border, 20 km (12 mi) north at Peñas Blancas, this rugged, two-story, hardwood hotel bills itself as a touring base for the surrounding dry tropical forest, but its most appealing feature appears to be its large pool, surrounded by shady palms. At the outdoor disco you can dance till you drop, then hop into the pool. The indoor-outdoor restaurant specializes in pizza and Italian food. Modest but comfortable upstairs rooms have private terraces. ✉ *Pan-American Hwy., about 6 km (4 mi) north of La Cruz (Apdo. 10493–1000, San José),* ☎ FAX *679–9132; 284–3972 in San José. 24 rooms. Restaurant, pool, miniature golf, dance club, laundry service. AE, MC, V.* ♺

$$ 🏠 **Amalia's Inn.** The late Lester Bounds, an American artist, and his Costa Rican wife, Amalia, created this breezy little inn on the cliff overlooking Bahía Salinas. Amalia now runs the inn with help from her brother. Bounds is also survived by his art—colorful modern paintings and prints that decorate the place and rooms. On the left (south) side of the road as you head into town, the inn features spacious rooms with private baths and balconies. The surrounding forest preserve was given to the town of La Cruz by Amalia's sister, who lives in and owns the magnificent Hacienda Quebrada de Agua, visible in the valley below La Cruz. Amalia's is a fine budget alternative to the pricier new resorts on the bay's south shore. ✉ *La Cruz, Guanacaste,* ☎ FAX *679–9181. 8 rooms. Pool, air-conditioning, laundry service. AE, MC, V.*

Bahía Salinas

⓮ *7 km (4½ mi) west of La Cruz.*

Several dirt and rock roads dead-end on different beaches along Bahía Salinas, the pretty little half-moon bay that lies at the very top of Costa Rica's Pacific coast—just turn right off the "main" road to the resorts. You'll probably end up on or near the beach, or in the hamlet of Puerto Soley, a tiny town tucked in off the bay—look for the salt flats to find the town, which is roughly 5–6 very slow-going km (3–4 mi) from La Cruz. There's public beach access along the bay.

The wind usually blows year-round, except in September and October, the height of the rainy season, so windsurfing here is supreme. Winds are generally not as powerful as at those at Laguna de Arenal, but they're strong enough to make this a viable alternative (stay on the south side for stronger winds), or accompaniment, to the Arenal experience. Ranking among the most beautiful beaches in all of Costa Rica are a couple of secluded, wind-sheltered strands, including the gorgeous, pristine **Playa Rajada,** with fine swimming and snorkeling. Just offshore is **Isla Bolaños,** a bird refuge and nesting site for thousands of endangered frigate birds as well as brown pelicans. The Bolaños Bay Resort (☞ Lodging, *below*) has a motor launch for Isla Bolaños tours, but don't try to land—it's against the law.

Lodging

$$$$ ⊞ **Bolaños Bay Resort.** On the approach to this resort, the first thing you'll spot is the high double rancho that shelters the reception area, bar, and restaurant. Given the winds that rocket across the bay, the resort's emphasis on windsurfing comes as no surprise. For windsurfing widows, a sheltered pool with a swim-up bar provides a diversion. The Belgium-based Three Corners Company, which runs the hotel, includes high-quality meals—especially hearty breakfasts—in the price of the room. Modest rooms are built into low-rise cabinas neatly arrayed across grassy lawns. ✉ *Take dirt road 3 km (2 mi) down the steep hill from La Cruz and follow signs for about 15 km/9 mi (Apdo. 1680–1250, Escazú, San José),* ☎ *679–9444,* [FAX] *679–9654; in San José, 228–4205. 36 rooms. Restaurant, 2 bars, pool, hot tub, windsurfing, laundry service. AE, MC, V.* ☜

$$$–$$$$ ⊞ **Ecoplaya Beach Resort.** On the same stretch of Bahía Salinas as the Bolaños Bay Resort (☞ *above*), the Ecoplaya emphasizes upscale luxury amenities. Every room has a small but fully equipped kitchen, a phone, air-conditioning, hot water, and custom hardwood furniture. The nearly 1-km-long (½-mi-long) beach fronting the hotel is flanked by bird- and wildlife-filled estuaries. Be warned, nonsailors: the wind blows hard here much of the time. ✉ *Reserve through Plaza Colonial, Escazú, No. 4, San José,* ☎ [FAX] *679–9380; in San José, 289–8920,* [FAX] *289–4536 in San José. 16 suites. Restaurant, bar, air-conditioning, pool, laundry service. AE, MC, V.*

Outdoor Activities and Sports

WATER SPORTS

The windsurfing **Pro Center** (☎ 679–9444) at Bolaños Bay Resort (☞ Lodging, *above*) is run by friendly, knowledgeable Bjorn Voigt. Charlie at La Cruz–based **Iyok Trips** (☎ 679–9444) at Bolaños Bay Resort (☞ Lodging, *above*) offers boat trips around Isla Bolaños, and snorkeling, fishing, and waterskiing trips to Playa Cuajiniquil and other spots in the Golfo de Santa Elena. Charlie promises sightings of nurse sharks, manta rays, and lots of large fish. Iyok's guides also lead horseback and mountain-biking tours of the area and know where the monkeys hang out in the woods.

NORTHERN GUANACASTE AND ALAJUELA A TO Z

Arriving and Departing

By Bus

ARENAL AND THE CORDILLERA DE TILARÁN

Buses run by **Auto Transportes Ciudad Quesada** (☎ 255–4318) leave San José for the three-hour trip to Ciudad Quesada daily from Calle 12 between Avenidas 7 and 9, every hour 5 AM–7:30 PM. From Ciudad Quesada you can continue to Arenal and Tilarán. **Auto Transportes** (☎ 460–5032) buses for Los Chiles (Caño Negro) depart from Calle 12, Avenida 9, daily at 5:30 AM and 3:30 PM; the trip takes an hour and a half.

Transportes Cañas (☎ 223–4193) has service to Cañas, and the turnoff for Tilarán and Arenal, daily at 8:30 AM, 10:30 AM, 12:30 PM, 1:20

PM, 2:30 PM, and 4:30 PM from Calle 16, between Avenidas 3 and 5. The trip to Cañas takes 3½ hours. **Transportes Tilarán** (☎ 222–3854) sends buses on the four-hour trip to Tilarán daily from Calle 12, between Avenidas 7 and 9, at 7:30 AM, 9:30 AM, 12:45 PM, 3:45 PM, and 6:30 PM. From Tilarán you can continue to Nuevo Arenal and Volcán Arenal. The company also makes the four-hour trip to Monteverde, departing weekdays at 6:30 AM and 2:30 PM. **Fantasy Bus** (☎ 800/326–8279) has daily service between San José and Arenal. Comfortable, air-conditioned buses leave San José at 8 AM and return at 2 PM. Tickets cost $19 and must be reserved a day in advance.

FAR NORTHERN GUANACASTE

Pulmitan (☎ 222–1650) has four-hour buses to Liberia that leave daily from Calle 14, Avenidas 3 and 4, every hour between 6 AM and 8 PM, with direct buses at 3 and 5 PM. Friday buses leave every hour from 1 PM to 8 PM, and Saturday they leave at 6, 7, 9, 10, and 11:30 AM. **Transportes Cañas** (☎ 233–4193) goes to La Cruz and Peñas Blancas, normally a six-hour trip that passes through Liberia; daily departures are at 5 AM, 1:20 PM, and 4:10 PM. Express buses cut the trip to 4½ hours; they leave from Calle 16, Avenidas 3 and 5, at 4:30 AM and 7 AM. The slower buses pass the entrance to Santa Rosa National Park after about five hours.

By Car

ARENAL AND THE CORDILLERA DE TILARÁN

Road access to the northwest is by way of the paved two-lane Pan-American Highway (Carretera Interamericana, CA1), which starts from the top of Paseo Colón in San José and runs northwest through Cañas and Liberia and to Peñas Blancas (Nicaraguan Border). The drive to Liberia takes about three to four hours. Turnoffs to Monteverde, Arenal, and other destinations are often poorly marked—drivers must keep their eyes open. The Monteverde turnoff is at Río Lagarto, about 125 km (78 mi) northwest of San José. (From here, an unpaved 30-km/19-mi track snakes dramatically up through hilly farming country; it takes 1½ to two hours to negotiate it, less by four-wheel-drive vehicle. At the junction for Santa Elena, bear right for the reserve.)

The turnoff for Tilarán and the northwestern end of Laguna de Arenal lies in the town of Cañas. At Liberia, Highway 21 west leads to the beaches of the northern Nicoya Peninsula (☞ Chapter 4). To reach Ciudad Quesada, La Fortuna, and Caño Negro, a picturesque drive (Highway 35) takes you up through the coffee plantations and over the Cordillera Central by way of Sarchí and Zarcero.

FAR NORTHERN GUANACASTE

On the Pan-American Highway (CA1) north of Liberia, the first turn for Rincón de la Vieja is easy to miss. Look for the Guardia Rural station on the right around 5 km (3 mi) north of town; turn inland and head for Curubande. Turnoffs for Santa Rosa National Park and La Cruz on CA1 are well marked.

By Plane

At press time, various charter companies were flying into Liberia on changing schedules. If your destination lies in Guanacaste, make sure your travel agent investigates the possibility of flying into Liberia instead of San José—you'll save some serious hours on the road. Locally, **Sansa** (✉ C. 42 and Avda. 3, San José, ☎ 506/221–9414) and **Travelair** (✉ Aeropuerto Internacional Tobías Bolaños, ☎ 506/220–3054) fly to Liberia from San José daily.

Getting Around

By Bus

ARENAL AND THE CORDILLERA DE TILARÁN
Buses to Ciudad Quesada continue to Tilarán and Arenal (☞ Arriving and Departing, *above*).

FAR NORTHERN GUANACASTE
Buses don't serve Rincón de la Vieja and Guanacaste national parks.

By Car

Four-wheel-drive vehicles are recommended, but not essential, for most roads. (If you don't rent a four-wheel-drive vehicle, at least rent a car with high clearance—you'll be glad you did.) The most important thing to know is that short drives can take a long time when the road is potholed or torn up. Plan accordingly. Most minor roads are unpaved and either muddy in rainy season or dusty in dry season—the pavement holds out only so far, and then dirt, dust, mud, potholes, and other impediments interfere with driving conditions and prolong hours spent behind the wheel.

ARENAL AND THE CORDILLERA DE TILARÁN
From this easterly zone (La Fortuna), you can head west by way of the road around Laguna de Arenal. For the paved road (Highway 4) that parallels the Nicaraguan border and loops west all the way to La Cruz, follow the signs out of Tanque (east of La Fortuna) northwest to San Rafael de Guatuso, Upala, and Santa Cecilia.

FAR NORTHERN GUANACASTE
The Pan-American Highway (CA1) and other paved roads run to the Nicaraguan border; paved roads run west to small towns like Filadelfia and La Cruz. The roads into Rincón de la Vieja are unpaved and very slow; figure on an hour from the highway, and be prepared to walk the last half mile to the Las Pailas entrance. The road into Santa Rosa National Park is smooth going as far as La Casona. Beyond that, it gets dicey and very steep in places. The national park service encourages you to walk, rather than drive, to the beach. A couple of dirt roads lead into various sections of Guanacaste National Park.

Contacts and Resources

Car Rentals

A few of the high-end resorts on the beach will arrange car rentals. Otherwise, *see* Contacts and Resources *in* San José A to Z *in* Chapter 1 *and* Contacts and Resources *in* Nicoya Peninsula A to Z *in* Chapter 4.

Emergencies

Ambulance: (☎ 221–5818). **Fire:** (☎ 118). **General Emergencies:** (☎ 911). **Police:** (☎ 117 in towns; 127 in rural areas). **Traffic Police:** (☎ 227–8030).

Guided Tours

SPECIAL-INTEREST TOURS
Tikal Tours (✉ Av. 2 between Cs. 7 and 9, San José, ☎ 223–2811) runs highly informative weeklong ecoadventure tours in Carara and Manuel Antonio (☞ Contacts and Resources *in* Nicoya Peninsula A to Z *in* Chapter 4), Santa Rosa, and Arenal. The excellent **Horizontes** (✉ 150 m north of Pizza Hut, Paseo Colón, San José, ☎ 222–2022) specializes in more independent tours with as few as eight people, including transport by four-wheel-drive vehicle, naturalist guides, and guest lectures.

Visitor Information

The tourist office in San José (☞ Visitor Information *in* San José A to Z, *in* Chapter 1) has information covering the northwest.

In Liberia, the **Casa de la Cultura** (3 blocks from Central Plaza, ☎ 666–4527) is open weekdays 8–noon and 1:30–5 and Saturday 8–noon and 1:30–4.

4 THE NICOYA PENINSULA

On this sun-drenched Pacific protrusion, expatriate California surfers wander endless golden beaches, coatimundis caper, monkeys howl in dry tropical forests, and turtles ride in on nocturnal high tides to lay their eggs. Combined with a burgeoning number of high-end resorts, these natural wonders make Nicoya a microcosm of Costa Rica.

L IMESTONE CAVERNS, BIRD-FILLED RIVER DELTAS, tracts of wet and dry forest, and miles of palm-flanked beaches are just some of the outdoor habitats on the Nicoya Peninsula. Separated from the mainland by the Gulf of Nicoya, the peninsula is a roughly thumb-shape spit of land comprising the southwestern section of the province of Guanacaste. Its southern end contains the Puntarenas province. Averaging just 65 inches of rain per year, the Nicoya Peninsula and much of Guanacaste constitute Costa Rica's driest zone.

Updated by
Brad Weiss

The Guanacastecos, descendants of the Chorotegan Indians and early Spanish settlers, started many of the traditions now referred to as typically Costa Rican, and a strong folkloric character is still evident in this region. As you travel down the peninsula, you might encounter traditional costumes, folk dancing, music, and meals made from recipes handed down from colonial times.

As a travel destination, Nicoya—especially the coastal areas—seems a bit confused at present: on one hand, politically correct ecotourists and their younger, backpack- and surfboard-toting cousins still hang out in search of environmental enlightenment or good waves; on the other hand, sun- and golf-seekers, content to admire caged toucans in plush hotel lobbies, are lured by azure pools and manicured putting greens bathed in tropical sun. Because the area has received huge amounts of investment and been somewhat developed, the endless miles of untracked beaches and thousands of acres of wilderness are occasionally interspersed with sprawling, all-inclusive behemoths.

Pleasures and Pastimes

Beaches

Graceful palms and elegant tamarindo trees line most Nicoya beaches, but the shrubby dry-forest vegetation of the northwestern Guanacaste coast contrasts sharply with the tropical beach backdrops you'll see farther south, in the Puntarenas province. The peninsula's great advantage is its climate, which in the rainy season is far drier than the inland regions and the Caribbean coast. Swimmers, however, should be careful of riptides, which are most common at beaches with high waves, such as the surfing area at Playa Grande. As a general rule, where you see surfers, beware of riptides.

Two strands near Coco (which itself is rather dirty) are worth checking out: Playa Ocotal, in a cove with snorkeling potential and good views, and Playa Hermosa, a curving gray-sand beach hemmed in by rocky outcrops. Playa Pan de Azúcar is deserted and has good snorkeling, but it's rather stony in the rainy season. Despite a few half-built condos and the Flamingo Beach Hotel, Playa Flamingo is still relatively low-key, and the beach is white and handsome. Playa Brasilito gives you a feel for life in a Costa Rican fishing village. Playa Conchal is famous for its tiny shells. Playa Grande, a restricted-access (at night) turtle-nesting beach stretching north 5 km (3 mi) from Tamarindo, is safest for swimming, except in the surfing area near the Hotel Las Tortugas. Tamarindo, a long white strand interrupted by the occasional rock formation, shelters a fleet of fishing and sailing boats on the lee side of Isla Capitán, a few hundred meters offshore. There are several good local beachfront bars here.

Playa Langosta, adjoining a bird sanctuary, has good surfing waves, nesting turtles at night, and few people. Playa Avellanes offers a kilometer (½ mi) of pristine sand, eight good surfing spots, and a river estuary and mangrove swamp close at hand for bird-watching. Playa Negra

is a mix of short sandy stretches and rocky outcrops and has some of
the best surfing waves in Costa Rica. Playa Junquillal features an uninterrupted 3-km (2-mi) stretch of grayish-white sand with low, shore-
break waves and very few buildings. Playa Pelada is a perfect jewel of
a beach hemmed in by rocks on both sides, great for snorkeling.
Nosara has a long beach backed by dense jungle where you might see
wildlife. The long, clean, smooth Playa Guiones has a good beach-break
surfing wave and a coral reef suitable for snorkeling. Playa Sámara offers some lively stretches near the Sámara community and quieter
stretches farther down the beach. Playa Carrillo sits on a deserted, highly
picturesque half-moon bay. Playa Cabo Blanco, on the southwestern
tip of the peninsula, is a pristine gem reached only by hiking through
the Reserva Natural Absoluta Cabo Blanco. Montezuma has several
colorful, shell-strewn beaches, some long and some short. Tambor, in
Bahía Ballena, edges calm swimming waters.

Dining

Seafood is plentiful here: *camarones* (shrimp), *langostinos* (a kind of
lobster), and a fine variety of fish are served in most restaurants at reasonable prices, though langostino dinners can get costly. Most places
serve international as well as local dishes, the latter centering on the
ubiquitous, moderate-priced *casados* (plates of white rice, beans, fried
plantains, salad, cheese, and meat).

Festivals

Santa Cruz celebrates its saint's day on January 15 with marimba
music, folk dances, and bullfights. On July 16 Puntarenas honors its
patron saint with a colorful regatta and carnival. The annexation of
Guanacaste is celebrated July 17–25 in Liberia with folk dances, bullfights, and rodeos. Nicoya's festival of La Yeguita features a solemn
procession, dancing, fireworks, and bullfights on December 12. Almost
every small town in Guanacaste has a rodeo fiesta once a year, complete with carnival rides, gaming, and the Costa Rican rodeo version
of bullfighting. It's wild! Guanacasteco cowboys ride the bulls, Amer-
ican-rodeo–style, while troupes of young men race around the ring dis-
tracting the bulls after they throw the riders, and cowboys with lariats
stand by on horseback to lasso the beasts should they get too ornery.
If you're in Guanacaste and aren't too squeamish, try to take in a rodeo;
just be warned the men do torment the bulls to get them riled up, and
that riders get thrown violently and are occasionally stomped or gored.
Ask around or read posters for details.

Lodging

Nicoya has a good mix of quality hotels, nature lodges, and more basic
cabinas (cottages). It's wise to reserve ahead for the dry season (December–April), especially weekends, when Ticos can fill beach hotels
to bursting. A number of luxury hotels line the coast, catering to an
upscale clientele.

Spelunking

The caves in Barra Honda National Park beckon you toward a serious plunge into the underworld. Terciopelo Cave, in particular, contains a vast assortment of oddly shaped rock formations, and some
stretches of the cave system are reputedly unexplored to this day.

Surfing

Costa Rica was "discovered" in the 1960s surf-film classic *The Endless Summer,* and revisited in the sequel. But with its miles of coastline
marked by innumerable points, rock reefs, river-mouth sandbars, and
other wave-shaping geological configurations, the Nicoya Peninsula
would have emerged as a surfer's paradise in any case. Warm water,

beautiful beaches, cheap beer, and relatively uncrowded waves—what more can a California boy or girl ask for?

Boca Barranca near Puntarenas—a somewhat dingy mainland town you might check out while waiting for the ferry to the peninsula's south end—has one of the world's longest lefts, but the water is dangerously polluted with sewage runoff from the nearby river. Tamarindo is a good base for some decent sandbar and rock-reef breaks, a superb low-tide river-mouth break, and the consistently high-quality, if at times over-crowded, Playa Grande beach break lies 5 km (3 mi) up the coast. Playa Grande's best waves usually break just south of the Hotel Las Tortu-gas; inquire at Iguana Surf, the surfboard shop in Tamarindo. Sámara, Giuones, and Nosara have decent beach breaks. Avellanes features a total of eight different surf spots, ranging from beach breaks to rock-reef breaks to river-mouth sandbar breaks. Witches Rock, in Santa Rosa National Park (☞ Chapters 3 and 9), has a right river-mouth, and Ollie's Point, a bit farther north, offers excellent right point-break waves. (In the summer, Witches Rock is not accessible by public transportation. You can drive or take the 1½-hour boat ride, informally chartered at Playa del Coco or other beaches along the Guanacaste coast. Ollie's Point is accessible primarily by boat.) For well-heeled wave riders, there's a good break directly in front of the Tango Mar Resort. Playa Negra, about a 45-minute dirt-road drive south from Tamarindo, is also gnarly, and its excellent right rock-reef break was showcased in *The Endless Summer II*. Playa Langosta, just south of Tamarindo, has a good river-mouth wave. Malpais, just above Cabo Blanco, is hit by some of the largest waves in Costa Rica. In all these places, be careful of rip-tides.

Turtle-Watching

The Nicoya Peninsula provides ace opportunities to watch the nesting rituals of several species of sea turtles. The olive ridley turtle nests year-round, but the peak nesting season runs July to October. Leatherbacks arrive between October and April, though nesting is largely over by mid-February. Occasionally you can see Pacific green turtles. Difficult to reach but worth the effort are Playa Nancite in Santa Rosa National Park (☞ Chapters 3 and 9) and the Ostional National Wildlife Refuge near Nosara. (For more information, *see also* Close Up: Tico Turtles *in* Chapter 7.) Both are prime for watching the mass *arribadas,* or nest-ings, of thousands of olive ridley turtles. More accessible are Playas Langosta and Grande—bookends for the resort town of Tamarindo—which teem with enormous, ponderous, yet exquisitely dignified leatherback turtles, who arrive with high tide to dig holes and deposit their eggs. Leatherbacks also show up at Junquillal and other beaches. Alas, word of mouth has it that locals at Junquillal and possibly Lan-gosta are still stealing turtle eggs as if there were an endless supply.

You can strike out on your own from Tamarindo to see Langosta tur-tles at night, but you've got to get across the Río San Francisco estu-ary—not something you should attempt at high tide. On the other hand, Playa Grande's turtle tours, now run by officially sanctioned guides drawn from the local populace, are very well organized.

If you want to venture out independently, you'll have to stay up very late, but many people find the arrival and egg-laying ritual of the leatherback mothers a singularly moving event. (It can get crowded, but the guides at the Playa Grande park entrance take people out in groups, and recent rule changes may limit the nightly numbers.) Others find the appearance of the babies, or hatchlings, even more charming, and you can see them during the day: Just walk down Playa Grande at dawn two to three months after the onset of the egg-laying season, and the hatchlings just might be making their amazing emergence from the sand. If you're like most ecotourists, you'll want to spend some time with these creatures, shepherding the tiny animals on their arduous, dangerous journey from the nest to the sea. If you don't perform this protective function, chances are you'll get to watch a less pleasant slice of life in the natural world, when a predatory frigate bird scoops your hatchling from the sand and eats it for breakfast.

If you do want to watch the turtles, it's best to go with a legitimate guide and follow the rules. It may be a little frustrating to experience this natural phenomenon governed by such unnatural rules, but these rules are critical for the health of the turtles. Finally, you're better off *not* trying to watch the turtles the week between Christmas and New Year's Day, when the crowds get heavy indeed.

Exploring the Nicoya Peninsula

Bear in mind that aside from the Carretera Interamericana (Pan-American Highway, or CA1), many of the roads in this region are of the pitted, pocked, rock-and-dirt variety, with the occasional river rushing over, rather than under, the pavement. Covering seemingly short distances can require long hours behind the wheel, and four-wheel drive is often essential. If you can swing it, we highly recommend flying; some beach resorts, such as Tamarindo, Carrillo, and Tambor, have nearby airstrips. Many northern beach resorts are most easily reached from the international airport at Liberia.

Numbers in the text correspond to numbers in the margin and on the Nicoya Peninsula map.

Great Itineraries

The ideal Nicoya Peninsula trip can be comfortably divided between lazy days on the beach, swims in the surf, and hikes and leisurely exploration of natural sights—caverns, forests, rivers, and estuaries. The beach towns and resorts can be clustered into three loose geographical groups based partly on location and partly on the routes you take to reach them: those on the south end of the peninsula, accessible by ferry from Puntarenas or by plane to Tambor; areas in the central peninsula, accessible by plane to Punta Islita, Carrillo, and Nosara or by car via the Tempisque Ferry and the roads through Carmona, Curime, and Nicoya; and towns on the northern part of the peninsula, accessible by plane to Tamarindo or Liberia or by car through Liberia and Comunidad. If your time is limited, consider whether you want, for example, lively surf or calm waters; turtle-watching options at night; an isolated resort or a more active beach town.

IF YOU HAVE 3–5 DAYS

Fly to ⊞ **Tambor** ④, ⊞ **Punta Islita** ⑫, ⊞ **Playa Carrillo** ⑬, ⊞ **Nosara** ⑯, *or* ⊞ **Tamarindo** ㉘ for a three-night stay at a beach resort. If you stay in Tambor or ⊞ **Montezuma** ⑤, a short drive takes you to Cabo Blanco, where you can hike through the **Cabo Blanco Strict Nature Reserve** ⑥ to deserted Playa Cabo Blanco, diving and frolicking ground for hundreds of pelicans. You can also visit the ⊞ **Curú National Wildlife Refuge** ③. If you surf and are staying at the Tango Mar Resort, hit the waves here or at Malpais, just north of Cabo Blanco, reputed home of the largest surfing waves in Costa Rica. If you have more time, head to ⊞ **Playa Naranjo** ②, near Naranjo—book a two- or three-day sea-kayaking adventure at the Hotel Oasis del Pacific, or just settle into a hotel for a few days of R&R.

If you choose a central Nicoya beach as your base, spend a day hiking, bird-watching, or spelunking at **Palo Verde National Park** ⑦ or

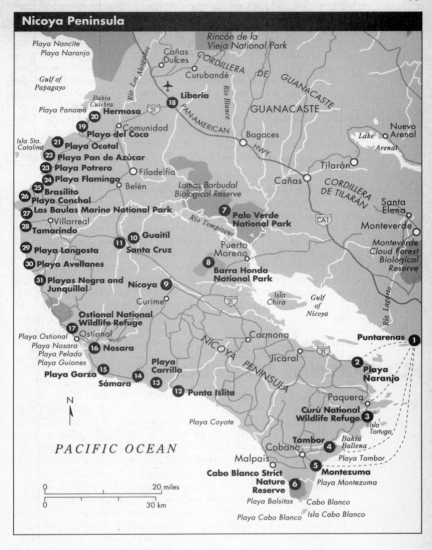

Nicoya Peninsula

Barra Honda National Park ⑧. On your second day, shop for pottery in **Guaitil** ⑩ and **Santa Cruz** ⑪. If you're here between July and October, stay up late to watch the arribada of the olive ridley turtles at **Ostional National Wildlife Refuge** ⑰.

A third option for a short stay on Nicoya is to come from Liberia, the hub to the north, and spend three to five nights at a beach between 🏨 **Tamarindo** ㉘ and 🏨 **Hermosa** ⑳. In season, you can also watch the leatherback turtles arrive by night at **Las Baulas Marine National Park** ㉗. For dedicated surfers, 🏨 **Playa Negra** ㉛ and 🏨 **Playa Avellanes** ㉚ offer great access to excellent waves and plenty of other recreational pastimes.

IF YOU HAVE 7 DAYS

Take the ferry from 🏨 **Puntarenas** ① to 🏨 **Playa Naranjo** ② and head for the 🏨 **Curú National Wildlife Refuge** ③, spending your nights in 🏨 **Tambor** ④ or 🏨 **Montezuma** ⑤. Around here you can hike, bird- and animal-watch, and swim in the lazy, sheltered waters of the southern Nicoya Peninsula. Alternately, stay in ☷ **Playa Naranjo** ② and spend a day or two sea-kayaking among the ruggedly beautiful islands in the gulf; then take Highway 21 north and swing east to Puerto Moreno to catch the Río Tempisque ferry and do some bird-watching on the river or in **Palo Verde National Park** ⑦. Spend the next day hiking and spelunking in **Barra Honda National Park** ⑧. Continue on through **Nicoya** ⑨ and **Santa Cruz** ⑪ and overnight in ☷ **Tamarindo** ㉘ or at one of the beach resorts to the north. Spend several days relaxing on the beach or exploring the Tamarindo and Río San Francisco estuaries north and south of Tamarindo, with nights watching turtles (in season) at **Las Baulas Marine National Park** ㉗. Head back to the highway via ☷ **Liberia** ⑱.

When to Tour the Nicoya Peninsula

The dry season, from December to April, is generally the best time to visit Costa Rica, but the northwest, especially the Nicoya Peninsula, is most appealing in the rainy season (barring only the *really* wet months of September and October). The Guanacastecos call the rainy season the "green" season, and that it is: the countryside—tending toward brown and arid the rest of the year—blooms lush and green from a few hours of rain each day. It's warm and sunny before and after the rain. The roads are muddy, but there are far fewer tourists in rainy season, and prices are lower everywhere. If you're bent on turtle-watching, you have to come during the dry season, but for most other activities any time of year will do. A good bet would be to travel in November, April, or May, around the edges of the dry season.

PUNTARENAS TO CABO BLANCO

Catch a ferry from Puntarenas to the southern tip of the Nicoya Peninsula and you'll be strokes away from gorgeous beaches—including Cocal, Cocalito, and Quizales—with waterfalls and tidal pools galore. Within the region are two quiet, well-preserved national parks where you can explore caves and pristine forests or travel by boat or sea kayak to remote islands and wildlife preserves for bird-watching, snorkeling, diving, and camping. Not too remote, and thus at times overcrowded, is Isla Tortuga, ringed by some of the most beautiful beaches in all of Costa Rica. If you like to mix nightlife with your outdoor adventures, the town of Montezuma and its nearby beaches are very often jammed with an international cast of hippies, mystics, musicians, and misfits of all sorts, from German boys in leather pants to Swedish girls in nothing at all. One wise guy has called this a gathering place for the "toxic youth of Europe."

Puntarenas

❶ *95 km (59 mi) west of San José.*

Five kilometers (3 miles) beyond Esparza, a popular truck stop about 90 km (56 mi) northwest of San José on the Pan-American Highway, is the turnoff to Puntarenas. This erstwhile coffee-shipping port sits on a narrow spit of sand protruding into the Gulf of Nicoya, with splendid views across to the peninsula. Most travelers stop here only to catch ferries to Playa Naranjo, Paquera, and Montezuma (pedestrians only) on the Nicoya Peninsula. The boardwalk is pleasant in a honky-tonk kind of way, but this downtrodden town suffers from rising crime and polluted water and is not worth a special trip. The grid-plan streets are lined with restaurants and markets, and the palm-lined promenade to the south is popular with day-trippers from San José (though the Ministry of Health warns against swimming here). On Saturday night the massive influx of urban weekenders presents a golden opportunity to watch the Costa Rican middle class at play. In summer, the **Casa de la Cultura** (⊠ 3 blocks from Parque Central, ☎ 661–1394) hosts a series of theater, music, and dance performances.

The murky estuary to the north is fringed with mangroves, and at its western end pelicans cast a watchful eye from the treetops over the Nicoya ferries. **Caldera,** 10 km (6 mi) southeast, has a modern harbor where cruise ships dock.

OFF THE BEATEN PATH | **ISLA TORTUGA** – Soft, bleached sand and casually leaning palms fringe Isla Tortuga, an island of tropical dry forest that makes a perfect day trip from Puntarenas, Montezuma, and other beach towns. Though state owned, the island is leased and inhabited by a Costa Rican family that funded efforts to reintroduce such species such as deer and wild pig to the island some years ago. A 40-minute hiking trail wanders past monkey ladders, strangler figs, bromeliads, orchids, and the fruit-bearing *guanabana* (soursop) and *marañón* (cashew) trees, and goes up to a lookout point with tantalizing vistas. You can take a short canopy tour on the beach. For information on getting to the island, *see* Guided Tours *in* The Nicoya Peninsula A to Z, *below*). ☎ *Hike $5; canopy tour $10.*

Dining and Lodging

$$–$$$ ✕ **La Caravelle.** Red-patterned tablecloths and dark-blue walls adorned with antique musical instruments create a chic ambience in this unexpectedly elegant French restaurant across the street from the sea. The cooking concentrates on sauces: try the corvina *al gratin con palmito* (with a white-wine sauce and hearts of palm) or fillet *con salsa oporto y hongos* (with a port-and-mushroom sauce). If you want to accompany any of this with claret, prepare to dig deep into your pocket. ⊠ *Paseo de los Turistas,* ☎ *661–2262. AE, MC, V. No lunch Mon.–Tues.*

$$$ 🏨 **Hotel Las Brisas.** This white, two-story motel-style building wraps around its pool at the west end of town, where the views of the sun setting over the Nicoya Peninsula are terrific. The hotel is across the street from the beach and not far from the ferry docks. Three of the simple rooms have balconies with views of the ocean; all are air-conditioned, though they're poorly lit. The restaurant serves decent, Greek-influenced seafood and meat. ⊠ *Paseo de los Turistas, Puntarenas,* ☎ *661–4040,* FAX *661–2120. 19 rooms. Restaurant, pool, air-conditioning, laundry service. AE, MC, V.*

$$$ 🏨 **Hotel Tioga.** The pastel-green and -yellow courtyard in this central hotel has the look of an ocean liner. Your best bets are the seven new guest rooms upstairs, overlooking the gulf—they're a bit bland, but each has a balcony, tile floor, quilted bedspread, and functional 1970s furniture, in addition to air-conditioning. The courtyard centers on a tiny pool with a sagging *guachepelín* tree growing from the islet in its center. ⊠ *Paseo de los Turistas, Apdo. 96–5400, Puntarenas,* ☎ *661–0271,* FAX *661–0127. 52 rooms. Restaurant, bar, air-conditioning, pool, casino, laundry service. AE, MC, V.* ☜

$$–$$$ 🏨 **Hotel Porto Bello.** Porto Bello's main asset is its thickly planted garden next to the wide estuary north of town. Guest rooms are housed in white stucco bungalow units with tile floors, zanily patterned bedspreads, air-conditioning, and verandas. Breakfast is complimentary. ⊠ *Apdo. 108, Puntarenas, 2 km (1½ mi) from downtown, 1 block north of main road,* ☎ *661–1322,* FAX *661–0036. 35 rooms. Restaurant, bar, air-conditioning, pool. AE, MC, V.*

Playa Naranjo

❷ *1½–2 hrs by ferry southwest of Puntarenas.*

Accessible by ferry from Puntarenas or by car from Nicoya, Playa Naranjo has an undeserved reputation as a kind of nowheresville en route from Puntarenas to Montezuma and points west. This is the best access point for the islands in the Gulf of Nicoya, and there's some excellent hiking, mountain biking, and sea kayaking nearby.

En Route If you want to drive around the tip of the peninsula, be prepared to spend some serious time in the car. The road to Nicoya's southern tip is partly paved and partly just gravel, and it winds up and down and around various bays. Much of the countryside is wild and wooded, though some has been turned into fruit farms or cattle pasture. Paquera, 45 minutes southeast of Playa Naranjo, is the closest town with shops and bars, and is also linked to Puntarenas by ferry. Heading north toward Nicoya, the road from Playa Naranjo (Highway 21) is paved, but it's rather badly potholed almost all the way.

Lodging

$$–$$$ 🏨 **Hotel Oasis del Pacific.** The enticing pier and coconut palms of these 12 roomy acres of waterfront are in the last cove on the left as you approach the Playa Naranjo ferry dock. Run by former ship's captain Lucky Wilhelm and his wife, Aggie, the hotel itself is a tad run-down, frayed around the edges, but you won't care once you're lazing in your hammock catching the afternoon breeze off the gulf. The indoor-outdoor restaurant-bar does a fine job with all three meals, and you can easily arrange fishing charters, sailing, horseback riding, and hiking. The hotel also offers sea-kayaking trips along the coast and among the islands in the gulf. ✉ *Apdo. 200–5400, Puntarenas,* ☎ FAX *661–1555. P.L. Wilhelm 1552, Box 025216, Miami, FL 33102-5216. 36 rooms. Restaurant, bar, pool, beach, dock, laundry service. AE, MC, V.* 🐢

Outdoor Activities and Sports

Ranging in length from one day to seven or more, sea-kayaking trips from a base near Playa Naranjo's ferry dock take you along the coast and among the islands of the Gulf of Nicoya. Kayakers at every level thus have a chance to explore wild islands, remote fishing villages, wildlife reserves, national parks, and more. Some of the more pristine islands include San Lucas, once a penal island, and Negritos, Guayabo, Venado, and Chira islands, home to isolated fishing villages and wildlife refuges. Reserve kayak trips through the Hotel Oasis del Pacific.

Curú National Wildlife Refuge

❸ *7 km (4½ mi) south of Paquera.*

South of the ferry dock at Paquera is the private Refugio Nacional de Vida Silvestre Curú, established by Federico Schutt in 1933 and given an indigenous name for the *pochote* and *guanacaste* trees, both native species. Trails lead through the forest and high-salinity mangroves, where you'll see hordes of phantom crabs on the beach, howler and white-faced monkeys in the banana trees, and plenty of hummingbirds, kingfishers, woodpeckers, trogons, and manakins (including the coveted long-tailed), to name a few birds. The refuge is working to reintroduce spider monkeys and scarlet macaws back into the wild. Some very basic accommodations, originally designed for students and researchers, are available by the beach; call ahead to arrange lodging, guides, and early-morning bird-watching walks. Take a passenger boat or ferry from Puntarenas to Paquera, where you can catch a bus to the refuge. ✉ *Schutt* *family, Curú, Paquera, 5370 Puntarenas, ☎ 710–8097. ⌨ $5; lodging $25 per person, including 3 meals and admission. ⊙ Daily 7–4.*

Tambor

❹ *20 km (14 mi) south of Curú National Wildlife Refuge, 27 km (17 mi) south of Paquera.*

The next village you reach after Curú is Tambor, nestled in the back of the large half-moon Bahía Ballena. This area is undergoing a land-sale frenzy similar to that at Tamarindo—you can see a golf course and housing development from the road, and signs of further development all around them. The hike from Tambor around the Piedra Amarilla point to Tango Mar Resort (☞ Lodging, *below*) is about 8 km (5 mi) long, and the trees along the way resound with the throaty utterings of male howler monkeys. You can also fly to Tambor from San José.

Lodging

$$$$ 🏨 **Tambor Tropical.** This collection of five cabinas, each with two
★   units, surrounds a pool in the palm trees off Playa Tambor in Bahía Ballena. The buildings themselves are remarkable: made from local hardwoods, they're embellished with exquisitely wrought designs. Each comfortable and spacious 1,000-sq-ft unit contains a living room, bedroom, bathroom with hot water, and fully equipped kitchen. ⌨ *Follow main street of Tambor toward water; hotel fronts beach,* ☎ 683–0011, FAX 683–0013; ✉ *867 Liberty St. NE (Box 12945), Salem, OR 97301,* ☎ *503/365–2872,* FAX *503/371–2471. 10 cabinas. Restaurant, bar, kitchenettes, pool, hot tub, horseback riding. AE, MC, V.* ✆

$$$$ 🏨 **Tango Mar Resort.** Here you can choose between rooms in the main
★   hotel and rustic, palm-thatch cabins on stilts. The latter are much more interesting; all have wood paneling, fans, and air-conditioners, and some have fully equipped kitchens. Rooms in the main hotel are luxurious by conventional standards but largely uninspired, though all have balconies and excellent sea views. The restaurant serves international cuisine. On the grounds are a spring-fed pool and an immaculate nine-hole golf course. The hotel is fronted by a good surfing wave. ⌨ *Apdo. 1–1260, Escazú, San José, 2 km (1 mi) west of Tambor,* ☎ *683–0002 or, in San José, 289–9328,* FAX *683–0003. 6 villas, 18 rooms, 12 suites. 2 restaurants, 2 bars, air-conditioning, in-room safes, refrigerators, pool, 9-hole golf course, 2 tennis courts, hiking, horseback riding, beach, boating, fishing. AE, DC, MC, V.* ✆

En Route   As you continue past the turn to Tango Mar, Cobano is the next real village, a collection of wooden bungalows straddling a crossroads and boasting a bank, gas station, and a group of cabinas for rent. The road to Malpais and Nicoya's other remote southern beaches runs west from here. Turn left (southeast) if you're headed to Montezuma and Cabo Blanco, bearing in mind that the final unpaved hill down to Montezuma is extremely steep and should not be attempted in a vehicle without four-wheel drive if the hill is wet.

Montezuma

❺ *7 km (4½ mi) southeast of Cobano, 45 km (28 mi) south of Paquera.*

Montezuma is beautifully positioned on a sandy bay, hemmed in by a precipitous wooded bank. At the bottom of the hill, the grubby but quaintly colorful town "center" consists of an oft-muddy crossroads with several shops, restaurants, bars, and hotels offering assorted diversions. Post-punk hipsters and other wanna-be bohemians seem to make this their first destination after touching down in San José, and if you don't mind entering the odd conversation on such *Mother Jones* subjects as yogurt and beat-the-system deals, this is an entertaining place to be. In years past, Montezuma was on the international vagabond circuit and its hippy-dippy aura had taken on a distinctly seedy quality; but in 1995, hotel owners banded together to form the **Cámara de Turismo de Montezuma** (CATUMA), an organization dedicated to cleaning up and improving the area. So far they've been fairly successful, and the town's image is on the mend. The beaches, in any case, are gorgeous. Just over a bridge 900 ft south, a path leads upstream to a 100-ft **waterfall,** a good swimming spot if overcrowded at times.

Lodging

$$$ ⬚ **Cabinas El Sano Banano.** This colony of distinctive domed bungalows
★ (each sleeping two) is set in the woods near the beach. Inside, the cozy bungalows look like well-outfitted igloos. Two have kitchen facilities, and all have refrigerators. The new pool with curvy mounds that form various waterfalls looks like something out of Disney World. The owners of the hotel have an excellent natural-foods restaurant by the same name, but it requires a 10-minute walk into town. It is a good place to get acquainted with the town's alternative atmosphere. Come for dinner at 7:30 and you'll take in a free movie. ⊠ *Montezuma, main road,* ☎ FAX *642–0068,* ☎ *642–0272 restaurant. 3 rooms, 8 bungalows. Restaurant, refrigerators, pool, hiking, beach, laundry service. AE, MC, V.*🐾

$$–$$$ ⬚ **Hotel Amor de Mar.** Take the time to walk 10 minutes outside "town"
★ to find this ruggedly handsome, two-story natural-wood hotel surrounded by trees and a grassy lawn stretching to the sea. Great breakfasts, a natural sea-fed pool, and immediate access to the waterfall hike make this perhaps the finest little hotel in Montezuma. The rooms are comfortable and simply furnished, with wood paneling. The dining room serves breakfast and lunch only. ⊠ *South of town on beach road,* ☎ FAX *642–0262. 11 rooms, 9 with bath. Restaurant, beach, laundry service. V.*

$$ ⬚ **Cabinas Mar y Cielo.** The advantage of this pleasant, old two-story wooden house is its quiet location—still on the beach but away from the boisterous bars. Each of the small, simple rooms has a balcony with excellent ocean views. The restaurant serves basic budget fare—casados and the like—with an emphasis on fresh seafood. Reserve ahead. ⊠ *Montezuma, 43 m from town center,* ☎ FAX *642–0261. 6 rooms. Restaurant, bar, beach. AE, MC, V.*

En Route   The 40- to 60-minute drive from Montezuma to Cabo Blanco follows a rough road and fords two streams on the way. If you're traveling in the rainy season, use a four-wheel-drive vehicle.

Cabo Blanco Strict Nature Reserve

❻   *10 km (6 mi) southwest of Montezuma, 55 km (43 mi) south of Paquera.*

Conquistadors named this area Cabo Blanco on account of its white earth and cliffs, but it was a more benevolent pair of foreigners who bestowed the other half of Cabo Blanco's name. Covering 12 sq km (4½ sq mi) in all, the Reserva Natural Absoluta Cabo Blanco was created by the pioneering efforts of Nils Olof Wessberg and his wife, Karen, who arrived here from Sweden in 1950. Appalled by the first clear-cut in the Cabo Blanco area in 1960, the couple launched an international appeal to save the forest. In time their efforts and those of their supporters led not only to the creation of the reserve in 1963 but also to the founding of Costa Rica's national park service. Olof Wessberg was murdered on the Osa Peninsula in 1975 while researching the area's potential as a national park.

Because the reserve gets more rain than other parts of the peninsula, its vegetation is properly described as tropical moist forest. There are more evergreen species here than in the sparsely vegetated Santa Rosa (☞ Chapters 3 and 9), and the greenery is somewhat lusher. The most abundant trees are strawberry, *apamate,* brazilwood, cow tree, *capulen, pochote,* and *sapodilla.* Sapodillas produce a white latex used to make gum; you'll often see V-shape scars where the trees have been cut to allow the latex to run into containers placed at the base. The wildlife is quite diverse considering the relatively small size of the reserve. Olof Wessberg cataloged a full array of animals here: porcupine, hog-nosed skunk, spotted skunk, gray fox, anteater, cougar, and jaguar. Resident birds include coastal pelicans, white-throated magpies, toucans, cattle egrets, green herons, parrots, and turquoise-browed motmots. A fairly strenuous 4-km (2½-mi) hike, about two hours in each direction, follows a trail from the reserve entrance to **Playa Cabo Blanco.** The beach is magnificent, with hundreds of pelicans flying in formation, dive-bombing for fish, and paddling in the calm waters offshore; and you can wade right in and join them. Trickling down a cliff behind the beach is a stream of potable water. Off the tip of the cape is the 7,511-sq-ft **Isla Cabo Blanco,** with pelicans, frigate birds, brown boobies, and an abandoned lighthouse. As a strict reserve, Cabo Blanco has no tourist facilities, although rangers will act as guides. ▨ $6. ⊙ *Daily 8–4.*

NICOYA AND THE TEMPISQUE RIVER DELTA

This northeastern section of the peninsula encompasses the parks in and around the Río Tempisque basin—prime places to watch birds and other wildlife—and Nicoya, the commercial and political hub of the northern Nicoya Peninsula. Besides providing the best access to the central Nicoya beach towns, Nicoya is also linked by a smooth, well-paved road to the artisan communities of Santa Cruz and Guaitil, to the northern Nicoya beach towns, and to Playa Naranjo and the southern peninsula by way of Carmona.

Palo Verde National Park and Lomas Barbudal Biological Reserve

❼ *Palo Verde is 28 km (17 mi) southwest of Bagaces; Lomas Barbudal is 20 km (12 mi) southwest of Bagaces.*

Bordered on the west by the meandering Río Tempisque, the territories in Parque Nacional Palo Verde and Reserva Biológica Lomas Barbudal extend over 95 sq km (36½ sq mi) of mainly flat terrain. Migrating herons, egrets, ducks, and grebes rest up on the Tempisque's abandoned oxbow lakes and lagoons. You can camp in both parks; meals and lodging are available by request at Palo Verde. For more information *see* Chapter 9. ☎ 671–1062. ▨ *$10 each park.* ⊙ *Daily 8–4.*

Lodging is also available at the **Organization for Tropical Studies** station (reserve through San José, ☎ 240–6696, ℻ 240–6783, ✉).

From Puerto Moreno, you can hire a motorboat to take you north up the river into Palo Verde park for a closer look at **Isla Pajaros** (Bird Island), home to thousands of birds from January to March. Boats are to the right of the ferry dock as you disembark. The trip takes roughly 45 to 60 minutes; the price is negotiable but will probably be in the neighborhood of $50. For this hefty price, however, you might see alligators, howler monkeys, and other wildlife on the way to the birds themselves. Bring something soft to put on your plank seat and something waterproof to wear—these are small fishing boats, not tour boats, and the river ride can be windy, bumpy, and wet.

There are two ways to reach the parks near the Río Tempisque: on the Río Tempisque passenger and car ferry, or by car from farther north. For the ferry, head north from San José on the Pan-American Highway, turn left about 48 km (30 mi) north of the Puntarenas turnoff, and drive 25 km (16 mi) to the ferry, which takes you across to Puerto Moreno. Note that the ferry gets extremely crowded during high season, and you may have to wait several hours to cross. The second option is to continue north another 42 km (26 mi) on the Pan-American Highway and turn left at the gas station in Bagaces, 15 km (9 mi) north of Cañas, which will lead you to the Lomas Barbudal Biological Reserve (after 15 km/9 mi) and the adjacent Palo Verde National Park (after 35 km/22 mi).

Outdoor Activities and Sports

CATA Tours (☎ 221–5455 or 690–1203) offers wildlife and bird-watching boating adventures down the Río Bebedero into Palo Verde from a starting point on the Pan-American Highway north of Cañas. The low-action adventure trips led by **Safaris Corobicí** (☎ FAX 669–1091) on the Río Corobicí cover some of the same wildlife-rich territory not far from Palo Verde and Lomas Barbudal; follow signs from the highway.

Barra Honda National Park

➑ *6 km (4 mi) west of Puerto Moreno.*

Parque Nacional Barra Honda covers almost 23 sq km (9 sq mi) north of the road that runs between the Nicoya–Carmona highway and Tempisque ferry. The limestone ridge rising from the surrounding savanna was once thought to be a volcano but was later found to contain an intricate network of caves, formed as a result of erosion once the ridge had emerged from beneath the sea. Some caves remain unexplored, and they're home to surprisingly abundant animal life, including bats, birds, blindfish, salamanders, snails, and rats. For details *see* Chapter 9. ☎ 233–5284. 🎟 $6. ☉ Daily 8–4.

In the dry season, with a week's notice, rangers will take you down a 60-ft steel ladder to the **Terciopelo Cave,** which shelters unusual formations shaped like fried eggs, popcorn, and shark's teeth, and sonorous columns collectively known as the organ. Travel companies no longer take tourists or speleologists deeper underground, but local groups have reportedly organized tours of the caves. Verify safety standards with park guards before venturing inside, and don't attempt to visit the caves on your own unless accompanied by a park guard.

You can climb **Barra Honda peak,** 1,082 ft high, from the northwest (the southern wall is almost vertical): follow in sequence the Ojoche, Trampa, and Terciopelo trails. From the summit plateau you have fantastic views over the islet-studded Gulf of Nicoya, and the plateau surface is pocked with orifices and white rocks eroded into odd shapes. Some of the ground feels dangerously hollow. Surface wildlife includes howler monkeys, skunks, coatis, parakeets, and iguanas, and the relatively open, deciduous-forest vegetation makes viewing the fauna easy. The park has camping facilities.

Nicoya

❾ *30 km (19 mi) west of Puerto Moreno.*

Though often referred to as Guanacaste's colonial capital, Nicoya is a typical provincial town, not really worth visiting unless you want a taste of everyday life. The Chorotegan chief Nicoya greeted the Spanish conquistadors upon their arrival here in 1523, and many of his people were converted to Catholicism. These days the culture and traditions of the Chorotegans are being emphatically revived. A Chinese population, descendants of 19th-century railroad workers, gives the place a certain cosmopolitanism, manifested in part by numerous Chinese restaurants. Its only colonial landmark is the whitewashed 16th-century church of **San Blas** in the central square, inside which a museum displays silver, bronze, and copper objects from pre-Columbian times.

Lodging

$ 🏨 **Hotel Yenny.** If you do need to stay in Nicoya, choose this sterile but adequate hotel. The rooms have white walls, wooden beds, tile floors, air-conditioning, and reasonable rates. ⊠ *1 block south of main square,* ☎ *685–5050,* 🖷 *686–6874. 24 rooms. Air-conditioning, laundry service. V.*

Guaitil

❿ *24 km (15 mi) north of Nicoya.*

Near the town of Santa Bárbara (look for the left-hand turn just south of Santa Cruz) is the sleepy country village of Guaitil. Artists here—most of them women in this matriarchal indigenous culture—have revived a vanishing tradition by producing clay pottery handmade in the manner of pre-Columbian Chorotegans. The town square is a soccer field, and almost every house facing it has a pottery shop out front and a round, wood-fired kiln in back. Pottery designs range from imitation Mexican to inspired Cubist abstractions. Every artisan's style is different, so take the time to wander from shop to shop. Prices are very reasonable, and although the pieces are rumored to crack rather too easily, they make wonderful keepsakes and gifts if you can get them home in one piece.

Santa Cruz

⓫ *14 km (9 mi) west of Guatil, 20 km (13 mi) north of Nicoya.*

The National Folklore City of Santa Cruz is dedicated to preserving Guanacaste's rich traditions and customs. Music and dance programs are still held here despite a fire that destroyed much of the town's center and the popular Casa de la Cultura. Santa Cruz is not a glamorous place, but it has a lively commercial center where you can get a feel for the daily life of the Guanacastecans.

Dining

$ ✕ **Coope-Tortillas.** Founded by a local women's cooperative to help create jobs, Coope-Tortillas has enjoyed resounding success. Watch tortillas baked the old-fashioned way—on thick, round plates on an open fire—by chatty women in blue uniforms. Family-style meals are served at a picnic table in a long, high-ceiling, corrugated-metal building that once housed electricity generators. This is one of the few places in the province that still serves traditional Guanacasteco foods: try the absolutely delicious *arroz de maíz,* a kind of corn stew. It's not that easy to find; go straight through the business district, past the plaza, and look for the peaked-roof metal structure. The restaurant is open daily 5 AM–7 PM. ⊠ *Near central plaza,* ☎ *680–0688. No credit cards.*

THE CENTRAL NICOYA BEACHES: PUNTA ISLITA TO NOSARA

Strung along the coast of the Nicoya Peninsula are sparkling sand beaches lined with laid-back fishing communities along with hotels and resorts in every price category. Don't be in a rush to get anywhere; take things one hour at a time and you'll soon be as mellow as the locals. Bus service connects the larger cities to each other and to the more popular beaches, but forget about catching a bus from beach to beach; you'll have to backtrack to the inland hubs of Nicoya, Carmona, or Santa Cruz. The road that leads southwest from Nicoya via Curime continues to Sámara, Nosara, Carrillo, Guiones, Punta Islita, and Ostional; it's smoothly paved all the way to the beach at Sámara except for a 100-meter stretch near Curime. The dirt roads between the beach towns are, however, subject to washouts and often passable only by four-wheel-drive vehicle. You literally have to drive through two rivers, for example, to get from Sámara north to Garza and Nosara (consider renting a four-wheel drive vehicle, especially for Nosara). There are airstrips at Carrillo and Nosara, so flying in from San José is worth considering.

Punta Islita

⑫ *8 km (5 mi) south of Carrillo.*

Hidden in a slender cove, Islita beach is rather rocky, but there's some good snorkeling near the point. The only hotel in the area has a private dry-forest nature preserve threaded with well-made trails.

Lodging

$$$$ 🏨 **Hotel Punta Islita.** This secluded inn overlooking the Pacific south
★ of Carrillo and Sámara may be the best in Guanacaste. Adobe-style bungalows with barrel-tile roofs and clay-color walls surround the main building, where a massive thatched dome tops the open-air restaurant. The French chef turns fresh seafood into inventive daily specials, and both the bar and restaurant open onto a blue-tile pool. The rustic bungalows have private porches and come complete with hammocks, big windows, terra-cotta tile floors, and rough-hewn wooden bedposts (not to mention hair dryers). Suites have private hot tubs and interior gardens. Boat tours to nearby beaches are easily arranged. Since the "road" to the hotel is passable only by a four-wheel-drive vehicle, most guests fly in and are picked up at the airstrip by the hotel staff. ⊠ *Just below Playa Camaronal, a few miles south of Playa Carrillo; San Jose office, Apdo. 242–1225, Plaza Mayor;* ☎ *656–0473 or, in San José, 231–6122;* FAX *656–0471 or, in San José, 232–2183. 24 bungalows, 3 villas, 9 suites. Restaurant, bar, air-conditioning, minibars, pool, driving range, 2 tennis courts, exercise room, spa, horseback riding, boating, fishing, mountain bikes, laundry service. AE, DC, MC, V.* 🐾

Playa Carrillo

⑬ *6 km (4 mi) south of Sámara.*

A long, reef-protected beach backed by an elegant line of swaying palms and sheltering cliffs, Carrillo is good for swimming, snorkeling, walking, and lounging. You can even camp here. This is one of the most beautiful and undeveloped beaches in Costa Rica—fly in and land at the airstrip, or head south on the dirt road from Sámara.

Lodging

$$$$ 🏨 **Hotel La Guanamar.** This used to be a private fishing club, and it
★ continues its tradition as a sportfishing mecca with two boats of its

own for use by hotel guests. Beautifully positioned above the southern end of Playa Carrillo, it occupies several levels connected by wooden terraces and steps, bringing to mind a luxury cruise liner. The white bedrooms have blue nightstands, patterned bedcovers, olive-green carpets, and amazing views. ✉ *Apdo. 71880, San José,* ☎ *656–0101 or, in San José, 239–2000;* FAX *656–0010 or, in San José, 239–2405;* ✉ *Costa Sol International, 2490 Coral Way, Suite 301, Miami, FL 33145,* ☎ *800/245–8420. 41 rooms. Restaurant, bar, air-conditioning, in-room safes, pool, horseback riding, laundry service. AE, MC, V.* ✎

Sámara

⑭ *29 km (18 mi) south of Nicoya.*

When you reach Sámara you'll see a sign proclaiming it the BEST BEACH IN AMERICA. This may be a slight overstatement, but only a slight one. Two forest-covered hills jut out on either side of the clean, white beach, forming one giant cove ideal for swimming. The coral reef 1½ km (1 mi) from shore is a snorkeler's nirvana. With a smooth road paved all the way from Nicoya, Sámara is flourishing these days, and the numerous hotels springing up around town cater to both Ticos and foreigners. Happily, Tico spirit still predominates.

Lodging

$$ 🏨 **Hotel Giada.** In a town of overpriced hotels, this little gem two blocks from the beach is an excellent deal. The interior walls—wash-painted in garish pinks, oranges, and yellows—are covered with Guatemalan and Nicaraguan tapestries. Guest quarters surround a fertile courtyard and a curvacious pool. The room are small, but they're tastefully decorated with bamboo furniture and tile floors. The hotel offers special packages in conjunction with the in-house tour agency; options include horseback riding, water sports, and dolphin-spotting boat trips. ✉ *Apdo. 84, Playa Sámara, Main strip, 150 m from beach,* ☎ *656–0132,* FAX *656–0131. 13 rooms. Breakfast room, pool, horseback riding, snorkeling, boating, fishing, laundry service. MC, V www.hotelgiada.net.*

Playa Garza

⑮ *16 km (10 mi) north of Playa Sámara.*

Playa Garza occupies a short, serene horseshoe-shape bay 16 km (10 mi) north of Sámara. The rustic fishing village of Garza is front and center, its fleet of fishing boats anchored offshore. Driving here is tough at times, as the approaches from both directions are badly maintained dirt roads, and you'll have to ford a river or two. Two-wheel drive can manage these rivers in the dry season, but don't try it without four-wheel drive in the rainy season.

Lodging

$$$–$$$$ 🏨 **Hotel Villaggio La Guaria Morada.** Don't be fooled by the rustic thatch: this is a luxury complex. The elegant, white, freestanding guest rooms form an arc around a landscaped tropical garden, and the restaurant serves inspired international cuisine in a new open-air dining area. The poolside lounging is top-notch, and there's a wide-screen satellite TV for sports-starved gringos. ✉ *Apdo. 860–1007, Centro Colón, San José,* ☎ *661–8119 or, in San José, 233–2476;* FAX *222–4073 in San José. 30 rooms. Restaurant, bar, pool, horseback riding, volleyball, snorkeling, fishing, laundry service. AE, MC, V.* ✎

Nosara

16 *10 km (6 mi) northeast of Garza.*

Set a bit inland, the minor and not very exciting town of Nosara is a good base of exploration for Playa Nosara and neighboring beaches as well as the nearby Ostional National Wildlife Refuge (☞ *below*), a haven for nesting turtles. This whole area of Guanacaste is currently being subdivided and settled by Europeans and Americans at a fairly rapid pace. (If you're thinking of buying land in Costa Rica and you want the security of other expats nearby, look into Nosara.) To approach from the north, you'll need to ford the Río Nosara; from the south, you're coming from Garza and will already have accomplished your river crossings.

Dining and Lodging

$-$$ ✕ **Olga's Bar.** Right behind Playa Pelada, Olga's serves local food at local prices. The open-air eatery has some rough wooden chairs and oilcloth-covered tables, a dirt floor, and a great beach right in front. This is a great place to eat fresh seafood after a day on one of the area's prettiest beaches. ⊠ *Playa Pelada,* ☎ *no phone. No credit cards.*

$$$ ⊞ **Hotel Rancho Suizo Lodge.** Proximity to tiny Playa Pelada, just 300 m away by forest trail, makes this one of the most attractive small hotels around Nosara. Monkeys are partial to the property's shady ambience. The Swiss operators are renowned for their hearty breakfasts, included in the room price, and they also barbecue on the beach occasionally. Turtle tours are run during the arribadas. ⊠ *Apdo. 14, Bocas de Nosara 5233,* ☎ *682–0057,* FAX *682–0055. 10 bungalows. Restaurant, 2 bars, hot tub, laundry service. V.* 🐢

$$$ ⊞ **Hotel Villas Taype.** Set roughly 100 m back from the long, lovely Playa Guiones, the Villas Taype's 19 rooms are in a low-rise building that forms a U shape around a pair of garden swimming pools. Seven freestanding bungalows have refrigerators and more privacy. The breakfast buffet is complimentary; dinner is served in a separate restaurant with its own street entrance. The German owners rent out surfboards, boogie boards, and snorkeling gear as well as bicycles and tennis racquets for the day-and-night tennis court; they can also arrange all local tours. ⊠ *Apdo. 8–5233, Nosara,* ☎ *682–0188,* FAX *682–0187. 19 rooms, 7 bungalows. Restaurant, 2 bars, breakfast room, air-conditioning, 2 pools, tennis court, Ping-Pong, beach, dance club, laundry service. AE, MC, V.* 🐢

$$$ ⊞ **Lagarta Lodge.** Named for the alligators that live in the delta of the Ríos Nosara and Montaña, which is visible from the bird- and beach-watching lobby area, this property has a magnificent promontory setting with views of the Ostional National Wildlife Refuge (☞ *below*). The rooms, which have private balconies, are in a separate building. A 125-acre private nature reserve flanks the banks of the Río Nosara; stairs lead to boats and riverside trails. Tours to Ostional can be arranged, and a 10-minute walk through a monkey-filled forest takes you out onto beautiful Playa Guiones. ⊠ *Apdo. 18, Nosara,* ☎ *682–0035,* FAX *682–0135. 7 rooms. Restaurant, pool, hiking, laundry service. V.* 🐢

Ostional National Wildlife Refuge

17 *7 km (4½ mi) north of Nosara.*

Apart from sun and sand, the main reason to come to the central Nicoya is to visit the Refugio Nacional de Fauna Silvestre de Ostional, with its top-notch turtle-watching. During the rainy season you'll probably need a four-wheel-drive vehicle to ford the river just north of Nosara;

a track then leads through shrubs to the reserve, which protects one of Costa Rica's major breeding grounds for olive ridley turtles. Locals run the reserve on a cooperative basis, and during the first 36 hours of the arribadas they harvest the eggs, on the premise that eggs laid during this time would likely be destroyed by subsequent waves of mother turtles. These eggs, believed by some to be powerful aphrodisiacs, are sold to be eaten raw in bars. Members of the cooperative take turns guarding the beach from poachers, but they're happy to let you watch the turtles. Turtle arrivals at this and most other nesting sites depend on the moon and tides as well as the time of year; nesting peaks between October and April. Before you go, ask some local about current conditions and try to get a sense of when, if ever, the turtles will arrive. For more information *see* Close Up: Tico Turtles *in* Chapter 7 *and* Santa Rosa National Park *in* Chapters 3 and 9.

LIBERIA AND THE NORTHERN NICOYA BEACHES

Highway 21, from Liberia south toward Nicoya, starts opposite Liberia's Hotel Bramadero on the Pan-American Highway and runs through cattle country sporadically shaded by guanacaste and tabebuia trees. Just past the village of Comunidad is the turnoff to Playas Hermosa, del Coco, and Ocotal. Continue toward Belén, and 5 km (3 mi) past Filadelfia you'll hit the Belén junction, where you turn right to get to the surfing hot spots of Tamarindo and Playa Grande. Some roads leading to the coast are intermittently paved. As you work your way toward the coast, pay close attention to the assorted hotel signs at intersections—they may be the only indicators of which roads to take to your lodging.

Liberia

⑱ *234 km (145 mi) northwest of San José.*

North of San José on the Pan-American Highway, Liberia is a low-rise, grid-plan cattle-market town with a huge central square dominated by an ugly modern church. The capital of Guanacaste province, it acts as the gateway to a northern route that encompasses Volcán Rincón de la Vieja, several spectacular and biologically important national parks, and a turtle-nesting site on the Pacific coast. The jet runway at Liberia's Daniel Oduber International Airport serves both national and international flights; if and when San José and Liberia sort out their differences on the economically volatile issue of air traffic, Liberia's proximity to the resort-oriented beaches of Guanacaste will make it the arrival point of choice for even more travelers. Though pleasant and prosperous, Liberia doesn't offer much to see or do. If you have extra time, visit the city's museum and get tourist information at the **Casa de Cultura.** ⊠ *3 blocks south of Parque Central,* ☎ *661–4527.* ⊙ *Weekdays 8–12 and 1:30–5, Sat. 8–12 and 1:30–4.*

Dining and Lodging

$$ ✕ **Pókopí.** Even in Costa Rica's cattle capital, Pókopí eclipses rival steak houses. You dine amid white walls with ranching memorabilia, wooden chairs and tables, and a Latin-cowboy atmosphere. Try the delicious chateaubriand with *salsa Barnesa* (béarnaise sauce, fresh vegetables, and a stuffed tomato). If you're less carnivorously inclined, dig into the *dorado* (sea bass) in white sauce with mushrooms, onions, green pepper, and white wine. ⊠ *150 m west of town entrance on Nicoya highway,* ☎ *666–1036. AE, MC, V.*

$$$ 📺 **Best Western Hotel El Sitio.** If you're stopping for a night in Liberia, consider El Sitio for its spacious, modern rooms and extensive facilities: an Italian restaurant, a casino, a volleyball court, two pools, a car-rental agency, tour planning, and walking trails. It's basically a nondescript roadside motel, but the conveniences redeem it. Breakfast is complimentary. ✉ *Apdo. 134–5000, across from Pókopí restaurant,* ☎ *666–1211,* FAX *666–2059. 52 rooms. Restaurant, air-conditioning, 2 pools, spa, horseback riding, volleyball, casino, laundry service, meeting rooms, car rental. AE, MC, V.* ♨

$$ 📺 **Hotel La Siesta.** The advantage of this modern hotel is its quiet location three blocks south of the central plaza. The rooms, surrounding a landscaped patio with a pool, have narrow, firm beds, white walls, and functional bathrooms that are beginning to show signs of age. The upstairs rooms are slightly larger and quieter. ✉ *Apdo. 15–5000,* ☎ *666–0678,* FAX *666–2532. 24 rooms. Restaurant, bar, air-conditioning, pool. AE, MC, V.*

Nightlife and the Arts

In late July, Liberia celebrates its annexation to Costa Rica (or its secession from Nicaragua) on Guanacaste Day, with folk dances, bullfights, and rodeos. Semana Cultural, or Cultural Week, brings a variety of arts events in the first week of September. Year-round, the Fiestas Bravas at the **Hacienda la Cueva Liberia** (☎ 666–5096) will appeal to the John Wayne, or the kitschy tourist, in you—hollering, whooping cowboys on horseback accompany the last stretch of your bus ride as you pull up to the working ranch and 1824 adobe farmhouse. Music, lasso shows, bull-riding, dancing, and a dinner of Guanacaste specialties all follow.

Playa del Coco

⑩ *35 km (22 mi) southwest of Liberia.*

Playa del Coco is a slightly seedy beachfront town that should suit those inclined toward noise, dance clubs, and general commotion. As one of the most accessible beaches in Guanacaste, Playa del Coco serves as a playground for Costa Rica's college kids, who, like students the world over, cannot always be trusted to clean up after themselves. The beaches are often littered with garbage, and the holiday season is impossibly crowded. But Coco's scruffy pier, slightly down-at-the-heels ambience, and trinket and souvenir stands are appealing if you like your resorts with some color.

Dining and Lodging

$$ ✕ **Papagayo.** Born and raised in Louisiana, owner and chef Bob Williams has imported his down-home Cajun seafood recipes and zydeco music to ensure one heck of a dining experience. The open and airy restaurant, complete with buoys hanging from the ceiling and portholes in the walls, has a large patio with simple, white plastic tables and chairs. The excellent fish-sampler platter includes four types of fresh fish, each prepared differently: with olive oil and fresh herbs, ginger and sesame, or macadamia pesto, or blackened Cajun style with pineapple-rum sauce. Other delectable treats include Cajun popcorn shrimp and jambalaya, made as spicy as you want. ✉ *Main strip, 250 m from beach,* ☎ *670–0882. AE, MC, V.*

$$ ✕ **Tequila Bar and Grill.** This popular gringo hangout with a concrete floor and old wooden tables is created in the image of a humble, almost grubby Mexican restaurant. The meals are also simple, but they're authentic and tasty, especially the fajitas, which come with chicken, beef, shrimp, or octopus. Bonus: The restaurant also delivers to hotels

in the vicinity. ⊠ *Main strip, 150 m from b*
credit cards.

$$–$$$ ⊡ **Villa Flores.** Weight-lifting, scuba-diving
res, a combination bed-and-breakfast and d
scuba trips and other water sports. Rooms
handsome hardwood building have fans, wh
have air-conditioning. The more luxurious
has a commodious bathtub. A well-equipped gym and a large pool add
to the fitness options, and the beach is a minute away. Italian dishes
are served in the three-square-meal restaurant. ⊠ *Apdo. 2,* ☎ FAX *670–*
0269. 9 rooms, 3 suites. Restaurant, air-conditioning, pool, exercise
room, laundry service. V.

$$ ⊡ **Villa del Sol.** The French-Canadian owners of this small B&B offer
seven quiet, spacious, light-filled rooms in a contemporary building with
a pool out front. Well away from Coco's main drag, the Villa del Sol
lies just 100 m from the quiet part of the beach. Views of the lush trop-
ical garden and the ocean (albeit slightly obscured by the trees) are best
from the upstairs balconies. The owners are happy to organize area
tours and activities. ☎ FAX *670–0085. 7 rooms, 5 with bath. Breakfast*
room, pool, laundry service. AE, MC, V. ⊛

$–$$ ⊡ **Cabinas Chale.** This place is nothing special—even run-down in some
parts—but it's one of the town's better budget deals. Many surfers stay
here, as it's only 50 m from the beach. Guest rooms are large and bright,
containing up to five beds, overhead fans, a refrigerator, and a porch
with a dining table and chairs. Three rooms have air-conditioning, but
none have hot water. ⊠ *Turn right when you see Tequila Bar and Grill*
on the left and head down the road. ☎ *670–0036,* FAX *670–0303. 25*
rooms. Pool, refrigerators, basketball. No credit cards.

Hermosa

㉛ *13 km (8 mi) east of Playa del Coco.*

Hermosa has a relaxed village atmosphere that recalls a Mexican
beach town. The full length of the village beach has long been occupied by hotels, restaurants, and homes, so the newer hotel behemoths
and other developments have been forced to set up shop off the beach
or on other beaches in the area. Hermosa's crescent of grayish sand
fronts a line of trees that provide a welcome respite from the heat of
the sun. At the north end of the beach, low tide creates wide, rock-
lined tidal pools.

Dining and Lodging

$$ ✕⊡ **Aqua Sport.** This beachfront hotel complex has a gift shop, min-
imarket, and water-sports equipment rental shop, but the main draw
is its casual open-air restaurant. The seafood platter of lobster, shrimp,
calamari, and oysters is highly recommended. ⊠ *Apdo. 100–5019, Playa*
del Coco, ☎ FAX *672–0050. 8 rooms, 1 apartment. AE, MC, V.*

$$$$ ⊡ **Blue Bay Village Papagayo.** Encompassing 78 hilly beachfront
acres, this resort is on the south shore of Bahía Culebra, a bit north of
Hermosa. Each of the freestanding villas houses two guest rooms with
private baths, marble floors, in-room satellite TV, and direct-dial
phones. Originality is at a minimum. The Blue Bay package is all-in-
clusive, covering meals and use of all facilities in one price per couple.
Water sports and tours are easily arranged. ⊠ *Playa Arenilla, Golfo*
de Papagayo, ☎ *672–0131 or, in San José, 233–8566;* FAX *672–0138*
or, in San José, 221–0739. 50 bungalows, 60 rooms. 2 restaurants, 3
bars, 2 snack bars, air-conditioning, in-room safes, 2 pools, hot tub,
tennis court, health club, beach, dance club, theater, laundry service.
AE, MC, V. ⊛

☒ **Hotel Occidental Costa Smeralda.** The grand scale of this all-inclusive resort is announced by its Mediterranean-style reception building, with its capacious lobby, enormous open-air buffet dining area, casino, and conference rooms. But the guest rooms counterpoint the oversize quality, as they're carefully distributed in smaller buildings heading down a long, gently sloping site toward a sliver of beach, amid gardens, lawns, and an appealing, amoeba-shape pool. Rooms are luxurious, especially the 48 new ones, but largely unimaginative. They have air-conditioning and full-length windows perfect for gazing at the ocean down below. Choose from a wide range of extracurricular activities. ☒ *Playa Panamá,* ☎ *672–0191,* FAX *672–0041. 120 rooms, 4 suites. 2 restaurants, snack bar, air-conditioning, pool, tennis court, beach, dive shop, snorkeling, casino, meeting rooms. AE, MC, V.*

$$$ ☒ **El Velero.** This elegant, two-story beachfront hotel has large, attractive
★ white rooms with arched doorways, terra-cotta tiles, bamboo furniture, and large windows. A boutique, a satellite-TV room, and resident caged toucans are among the perks. Along with the use of Jet Skis, sea kayaks, and a sailboat, the Canadian owners offer sunset cruises and all-day snorkeling trips. The sailboat also serves as a spare guest room on occasion—don't be afraid to ask if you like sleeping on board. In the restaurant, sample the jumbo shrimp with rice and vegetables, or anything with mashed potatoes—a rarity in Costa Rica. ☒ *Playa Hermosa,* ☎ *672–0036,* FAX *672–0016. 22 rooms. Restaurant, bar, air-conditioning, pool, snorkeling, boating, jet skiing, laundry service. AE, MC, V.* ✎

$$ ☒ **Hotel Cabinas Playa Hermosa.** A mischievous white-faced capuchin monkey is always on hand to welcome you to this simple beachfront lodging. Strict maritime laws prohibit major improvements to the one-story, pink brick units that house two guests rooms, so the rooms are in not in tip-top shape; each has a curious hodgepodge of cheap and nice furniture and art. The restaurant serves pasta, steak, and seafood. ☒ *Apdo. 117, Liberia,* ☎ FAX *672–0046. 22 cabinas. Restaurant, beach, laundry service. V.*

Outdoor Activities and Sports

SCUBA DIVING

Just off the beach at Hotel Sol Playa Hermosa (at the north end of Playa Hermosa), **Bill Beard's Diving Safaris** (☎ FAX 672–0012 or, in the U.S., 800/779–0055, FAX 954/351–9740 in the U.S.) offers a complete range of scuba activities, from beginner training to open-water certification courses and even multitank dives at more than 20 tantalizing sites off the coast of Guanacaste. His guides and trainers know underwater Guanacaste—alive with rays, sharks, fish, and turtles—as well as anyone. Prices range from $40 for a one-tank afternoon dive to $375 for a PADI (Professional Association of Diving Instructors) open-water certification course. On the beach below the dive shop, an independent **kiosk** rents boogie boards, plastic kayaks, Jet Skis, and other water toys.

Playa Ocotal

㉑ *3 km (2 mi) west of Playa del Coco.*

In spite of its proximity to student-thronged Coco, Playa Ocotal is a serene spot, with a lilliputian crescent of beach sheltered by rocks. Located at the entrance to the Gulf of Papagayo, it's a good place for sport-fishing enthusiasts to hole up between excursions. There's good diving at Las Corridas, just 1 km (½ mi) away.

Lodging

$$$–$$$$ ☒ **El Ocotal Beach Resort.** Three kilometers (2 miles) south of Playa
★ del Coco down a paved road, this luxury hotel with a sportfishing fleet

ONE LAST TRAVEL TIP:

Pack an easy way to reach the world.

123 456 7891 2345
J.D. SMITH

Wherever you travel, the MCI WorldCom Card℠ is the easiest way to stay in touch. You can use it to call to and from more than 125 countries worldwide. And you can earn bonus miles every time you use your card. So go ahead, travel the world. MCI WorldCom℠ makes it even more rewarding. For additional access codes, visit **www.wcom.com/worldphone**.

EASY TO CALL WORLDWIDE

1. Just dial the WorldPhone® access number of the country you're calling from.
2. Dial or give the operator your MCI WorldCom Card number.
3. Dial or give the number you're calling.

Country	Access Number
Argentina	0800-222-6249
Belize (A)	557 or 815
Brazil	000-8012
Chile	800-207-300
Colombia ◆	980-9-16-0001
Costa Rica (A) ◆	0800-012-2222
Ecuador ⋅⋅	999-170
Egypt ◆	7955770
El Salvador (A)	800-1567
Guatemala ◆	99-99-189
Honduras (A) ⋅⋅	8000-122
Israel	1-800-920-2727
Mexico	01-800-021-8000
Nicaragua	166
Panama (A)	00800-001-0108
Turkey ◆	00-8001-1177
Venezuela ◆ ⋅⋅	800-11140

(A) Calls back to U.S. only.   ◆ Public phones may require deposit of coin or phone card for dial tone.   ⋅⋅ Limited availability.

EARN FREQUENT FLIER MILES

Bureau de change

Cambio

外国為替

In this city, you can find money on almost any street.

NO-FEE FOREIGN EXCHANGE

The Chase Manhattan Bank has over 80 convenient
locations near New York City destinations such as:
  Times Square
  Rockefeller Center
  Empire State Building
  2 World Trade Center
  United Nations Plaza
Exchange any of 75 foreign currencies

 CHASE

THE RIGHT RELATIONSHIP IS EVERYTHING.®

and dive shop is perched above secluded Ocotal Bay. The upper rooms look north to the Peninsula Santa Elena and northwest to Rincón de la Vieja. Inside, the air-conditioned rooms have patterned bedspreads, white walls, watercolors, overhead fans, and huge French windows. The freestanding, triangular bungalows down the hill are larger and have polished wood floors. ⊠ *Apdo. 1, Playa del Coco,* ☎ *670–0321,* 🖷 *670–0083. 40 rooms, 3 suites, 12 bungalows. Restaurant, bar, air-conditioning, 3 pools, tennis court, horseback riding, boating, dive shop, laundry service. AE, MC, V.* 🍴

$$$ 🖸 **Villa Casa Blanca.** Surely one of the finest B&Bs in Costa Rica, the
★   Casa Blanca occupies a hillside Mediterranean-style building buried in a bower of tropical plantings. The intimate, junglelike setting attracts numerous colorful, talkative birds. Victorian-influenced rooms comfort you with air-conditioning, pleasant wood details and artwork, canopy beds, and enormous bathrooms with wall-covering mirrors. Secluded, romantic, and equipped with a pool, the Casa Blanca also turns out Guanacaste's heartiest breakfasts. For dinner, you can have specialties delivered from an area restaurant if you don't feel like moving. ⊠ *Apdo. 176–5019, Playa Ocotal,* ☎ *670–0518,* 🖷 *670–0448. 10 rooms, 5 suites. Breakfast room, air-conditioning, pool. AE, MC, V.* 🍴

Playa Pan de Azúcar

㉒ *8 km (5 mi) north of Playa Flamingo.*

Sugar Bread Beach, at the end of a hilly dirt road, lends its only hotel one quality that can be hard to come by in this area—privacy. There are good islands for snorkeling just offshore.

Lodging

$$$$ 🖸 **Hotel Sugar Beach.** Accessible via a dirt track 8 km (5 mi) north of
★   Flamingo, this hotel overlooks a thin, curving white-sand beach. Most of the nicely varied, air-conditioned rooms have idyllic ocean views, and each room's wooden door has a hand-carved image of a local bird or animal. You can rent a beach house with two bedrooms (or three, if you take the upstairs as well) by the day or week. The open-air rotunda restaurant serves good seafood dishes. The hotel offers a full complement of activities and area tours, from boat trips to surfing at Witches Rock to golf, horseback riding, and volcano tours. ⊠ *Apdo. 90, Santa Cruz,* ☎ *654–4242,* 🖷 *654–4239. 29 rooms, 1 beach house. Restaurant, bar, air-conditioning, pool, horseback riding, snorkeling, laundry service. AE, MC, V.* 🍴

Playa Potrero

㉓ *1 km (½ mi) north of Flamingo.*

Although Potrero has historically been known mostly for its views of nearby Flamingo, it has its own charm thanks to its wide, white-sand beach. There's excellent swimming at an island nearby, and the **Isla Santa Catalina** bird refuge is 10 km (6 mi) offshore.

Lodging

$$$$ 🖸 **Bahía Potrero Beach and Fishing Resort.** Fishing is the main activity at this squat white bungalow. The rustic-style rooms are equipped with air-conditioning and refrigerators, but they're showing signs of wear. The 16 new condos, eight with one room and the other eight with two, are ultramodern and quite luxurious: Each has a full kitchen, a washing machine, and dryer. The shady, open-air restaurant serves seafood, pizza, and pasta dishes. The beach is ideal for young kids, as the sea here is shallow and safe. ⊠ *Apdo. 45, Santa Cruz,* ☎ *654–4183,*

FAX 654–4093. *10 rooms, 16 condos. Restaurant, bar, air-conditioning, in-room safes, pool, fishing. AE, MC, V.*

$$ ⊞ **Casa Sunset.** A five-minute walk from the village of Potrero, on the inland side of the dirt road to Hotel Sugar Beach, the American-run Casa Sunset offers wonderful views of that sinking ball of fire from cabinas stacked up the steep hillside above the road. Each basic cabina has two single beds and one bunk bed, ceiling fans, and a bath with warm (not hot) showers. A sunbathing patio surrounds a pool near the top of the property, and a communal kitchen allows some on-site cooking. Secluded Playas Penca and Prieta are also within walking distance, as is the bustle of Flamingo Beach, about half an hour away. Breakfast is included. ⊠ *Apdo. 5111, Playa Potrero, Santa Cruz,* ☎ FAX *654–4265. 7 cabinas. Pool, horseback riding, boating, fishing, laundry service. No credit cards.*

Playa Flamingo

㉔   *39 km (24 mi) west of Filadelfia.*

Flamingo was one of the first of the northern Nicoya beaches to experience the wonders of overscale resort development, a fact immortalized in the huge Aurola Flamingo Beach Resort that dominates the landscape. The beach, however, is still a welcome oasis. If you like the anonymity that large, character-free hotels offer, this is as good a place as any.

Dining and Lodging

$$ ✕ **Marie's Restaurant.** Friendly Marie and her fresh food make this
★   place well worth a visit. Shortly after the road bends toward the north end of Flamingo, look for a veranda furnished with sliced-tree-trunk tables and settle back for generous helpings of fresh seafood at very reasonable prices. The ceviche is delightful, as is the house specialty, *plato de mariscos* (shrimp, lobster, and oysters served with garlic butter, potatoes, and salad), but do save room for the superb banana-chocolate bread pudding. ⊠ *Main road near north end of beach,* ☎ *654–4136. V.*

$$$$ ⊞ **Flamingo Marina Resort.** This hillside complex of pink buildings with orange, yellow, and maroon tile roofs has far more personality than the other large resorts in this area. The fashionably decorated rooms, wash-painted in a mango hue, have terra-cotta lamps, hand-carved wooden furniture, and shell-shape sinks. The luxurious condos have full modern kitchens and spacious sitting areas with leather couches. Nearly all rooms and condos have large verandas with excellent views of the sea below. ⊠ *Apdo. 321–1002 Paseo Estudiantes, San José,* ☎ *654–4141 or, in San José, 290–1858;* FAX *654–4035 or, in San José, 231–1858. 39 condos, 22 rooms, 18 suites. Restaurant, 2 bars, 3 pools, air-conditioning, in-room safes, minibars, tennis court, dive shop, laundry service. AE, DC, MC, V.* ✧

$$$ ⊞ **Mariner Inn.** Near the marina, this two-story white building is the cheapest hotel in Flamingo. The compact rooms, with small TVs built into the dressers, feel like boat cabins; all have air-conditioning, ceiling fans, and firm beds. The hotel arranges sportfishing trips. ⊠ *Apdo. 65, Santa Cruz,* ☎ *654–4081,* FAX *654–4024. 11 rooms, 1 suite. Restaurant, bar, air-conditioning, pool, laundry service. AE, MC, V.* ✧

Brasilito

㉕   *35 km (22 mi) west of Filadelfia.*

Around the town square of this fishing village (which doubles as the soccer field) huddles a ramshackle row of houses. Before high tide, boats line up just off a white-sand beach that is the equal of Flamingo minus the megahotels. The presence of the nearby Meliá hotel (☞ Playa Conchal, *below*), however, has begun to wear on the charm, infusing Brasilito with a tacky resort energy. Strung along the road through town, new shops and at least one gas-station market now sell overpriced sunglasses, T-shirts, and water toys.

Dining and Lodging

$–$$ ✕ **El Camarón Dorado.** This bar-restaurant derives much of its appeal from its shaded setting on Brasilito's beautiful beach, and no less from the small-vessel fishing fleet anchored offshore, assuring you of the freshness of seafood on the menu. The chef has a way with fresh-caught fish, from deep-fried to grilled to swathed in a savory sauce. Some tables are right on the beach, with the surf crashing just yards away as you dine beneath the stars. Thanks to its spectacular sunset views, this is a popular place for early-evening drinks. ⊠ *220 m north of Brasilito Plaza,* ☎ *654–4244. AE, MC, V.*

$$ ▦ **Hotel Brasilito.** This simple, intimate German-run establishment is just off the beach. Fronting the sea is the hotel's wooden, open-air restaurant, its tables and chairs arrayed beneath lazily turning ceiling fans. The sparely furnished but comfortable rooms occupy both floors of the old, two-story wooden building behind the restaurant; ask for one of the two rooms with unobstructed sea views. There is no hot water. ⊠ *Next to square and soccer field,* ☎ *654–4237,* FAX *654–4247. 17 rooms. Restaurant, snorkeling, laundry service. V.* ✧

Playa Conchal

㉖ *Immediately south of Playa Brasilito.*

Playa Conchal, one of Guanacaste's finest and most secluded beaches, is aptly named—it's sprinkled with shells that offer themselves up for easy collecting. The sprawling Meliá Playa Conchal Resort looms large here.

Lodging

$$$$ ▦ **Meliá Playa Conchal Beach & Golf Resort.** This resort is ideal for the golfing traveler who wants luxury in a remote locale. Standing in the enormous, open-air, marble-floored reception lobby, you'll see the massive grounds, encompassing almost 4 sq km (1½ sq mi) of manicured golf courses, bungalows, tennis courts, the largest pool in Central America, and a distant beach. The rooms, set in low-slung, colonial-style houses (four per bungalow), are large, luxurious, and air-conditioned, and the restaurants serve a range of international fare. ⊠ *Entrance less than 1 km (½ mi) south of Brasilito,* ☎ *654–4123 or, in the U.S., 800/336–3542;* FAX *654–4181. 310 bungalows. 6 restaurants, 4 bars, pool, air-conditioning, beauty salon, two 18-hole golf courses, 4 tennis courts, beach, surfing, jet skiing, bicycles, casino, dance club, laundry service, meeting rooms. AE, MC, V.* ✧

En Route   To get to Las Baulas Marine National Park, take the Pan-American Highway north to Liberia. From there head south to Santa Cruz, then west to the coast.

Las Baulas Marine National Park

㉗ *37 km (23 mi) west of Filadelfia, 3 km (2 mi) north of Tamarindo.*

Just north of Tamarindo, across an estuary, Parque Nacional Marino Las Baulas protects the long **Playa Grande**, an important nesting site for the leatherback sea turtle (☞ Chapter 9). It's a great surf spot as well. The owners of the Hotel Las Tortugas struggled for a decade to get the national park established and have a real understanding of the importance of balancing the oft-conflicting needs of locals, turtles, and tourists. An evening spent discussing ecotourism, ecopolitiçs, and related matters with them is a real education.

You can witness Guancaste's resort boom in this bucolic place—a few small hotels have opened not far from Hotel Las Tortugas, and a golf and country club has property for sale behind the adjacent estuary.

Lodging

$$–$$$ 🏨 **Hotel Las Tortugas.** Near the turtle-nesting beach, Las Tortugas stands at the edge of Las Baulas Marine National Park. Rooms are comfortable, with good beds and air-conditioning as well as stone floors and stucco walls. Owners Louis Wilson and Marianela Pastor—he American, she Costa Rican—offer a number of long-term rentals, including the apartments they call Greek 1, 2, and 3. The restaurant serves healthful, high-quality food. Beware: the beach surf break sometimes has dangerous rip currents, at which times you can retreat to the turtle-shape pool. Local guides escort you along the beach at night, and the hotel also offers canoe trips in the nearby Tamarindo Wildlife Refuge. ⊠ *Apdo. 164, Santa Cruz de Guanacaste,* ☎ *653–0423,* ☎ FAX *653–0458. 11 rooms. Restaurant, air-conditioning, pool, boating, laundry service. V.* 🐾

Tamarindo

28 *37 km (23 mi) west of Filadelfia.*

Tamarindo is a lively town with a great variety of restaurants, cabins, bars, and hotels at all price levels. Developmental hustle is everywhere, evidenced by the presence of condo projects and mini strip malls; still, Tamarindo remains appealing because it's virtually self-contained: Its beaches are great for snorkeling, boating, kayaking, diving, surfing, and just plain swimming; there are estuaries north and south of town for bird- and animal-watching; and there are two turtle-nesting beaches—Langosta to the south, Grande to the north—nearby. With an airstrip just outside town, Tamarindo is also a convenient base for exploring all of Guanacaste. Except for some sections through the middle of town, the road is in dire need of pavement.

Dining and Lodging

$$–$$$ ✕ **Nogui's.** Local gringos swear by this scruffy restaurant. Also known
★   as the Sunrise Café, Nogui's is considered by aficionados to have the freshest, best, and most reasonably priced seafood in all of Tamarindo. Only a dirt road separates Nogui's alfresco plastic tables and chairs from the beach, but when it gets crowded, some stand in the parking area eating on their feet rather than waiting for a table. The langostino is highly recommended, as is the swimsuit selection in the adjacent Nogui's shop. ⊠ *Just south of Zullymar on Tamarindo circle,* ☎ *653–0029. AE, MC, V.*

$$ ✕ **Trattoria Iguana Surf.** Inventive pasta and fish dishes are the forte of this Italian eatery. At dinnertime each table gets a scrumptious focaccia with grilled eggplant and tomato sauce. Hardly Italian-looking, the setting is nonetheless quite elegant; under a thatched roof, the eating area is softly lit with elegant wooden furniture, and a small, melodious fountain adds texture to the soundscape. Lunch is undistinguished, designed for tourists on the run. ⊠ *Below Iguana Surf,* ☎ *653–0148. No credit cards. Closed Sun.*

$–$$ ✕ **Bakery de Paris.** The owners of this bakery (formerly Johann's), on
★   the right side of the road near the entrance to town, also own the adjacent Cocodril Restaurant and Disco 24. At tables nicely distributed

on a shady, off-road patio you can enjoy all three meals of the day, especially great European pastries in the morning. Have a closer (but not too close) look at the pond behind the adjacent tire-repair shop: You may catch a glimpse of the rather fat crocodile that lives there, feeding, they say, on roast chickens from the Cocodril. ⊠ *Right side of main road just as you enter town,* ☎ *653–0255. No credit cards.*

$ ✕ **Frutas Tropicales.** Friendly waiters hose down the road to dampen
★ the dust that would otherwise smother this busy street-side eatery. The white plastic tables and chairs stay full for a reason—the restaurant dishes out Costa Rican food at Costa Rican prices to travelers of every shape and description. The food is nothing fancy, but the casados and other dishes are tasty and substantial. The menu includes U.S.-style items as well, and great *frutas tropicales* (tropical fruit drinks). ⊠ *Main road, toward north end of town,* ☎ *653–0041. AE, MC, V.*

$$ ✕🏨 **Arco Iris Restaurant & Cabinas.** A pair of spirited Italian sisters,
★ Laura and Simona Fillipini, run this wonderful Italian vegetarian restaurant and hotel on the hill behind the Tamarindo circle. Meals don't exceed $5, and the food is healthful and lovingly prepared. You do not have to be a guest to eat here. The four cheery, wildly imaginative cabinas are painted in primary colors and decorated along distinct themes. One has two bedrooms and a kitchen. You're welcome to join a karate session in the on-site dojo, and in case it all gets to be too much, there's also a masseuse. ⊠ *Follow signs past Hotel Pasatiempo (☞ below) and go up hill to the right,* ☎ *653–0330. 4 cabinas. Restaurant, massage. No credit cards.*

$$$$ 🏨 **El Jardín del Edén.** The only drawback to the Garden of Eden (this
★ one, anyway) is that it's not right on the beach. Set among lush hillside gardens, the two-tier pink building offers rooms with green interiors and elegantly styled bathrooms. All rooms have ocean views, air-conditioning, refrigerators, and fans. The thatched-roof restaurant prepares French and Italian food and outstanding steaks. Fishing packages are available. ⊠ *Apdo. 1094–2050, San Pedro,* ☎ *653–0137,* ℻ *653–0111. 18 rooms, 2 apartments. Restaurant, 2 bars, air-conditioning, refrigerators, 2 pools, hot tub, laundry service. AE, MC, V.*✎

$$$$ 🏨 **Hotel Capitán Suizo.** The "Swiss Captain" is Ruedi Schmid, who,
★ with his partner, Ursula Schmid, has created an elegant lodging at the south end of Tamarindo. Steps from a relatively quiet stretch of Tamarindo's gorgeous beach, these bungalows are set in a lushly landscaped garden around a pool. The stunning rooms have high, angled ceilings and exquisite contemporary artwork on the walls. The rather pricey restaurant serves international cuisine. Ruedi and Ursula can arrange horseback riding, kayaking, sportfishing, and diving trips. A lot of monkeys hang around the Swiss Captain's place as well, so the price of your room includes some "wildlife" in any case. ⊠ *Right side of road toward Playa Langosta (veer left before circle),* ☎ *653–0075,* ℻ *653–0292. 22 rooms, 8 bungalows. Restaurant, air-conditioning, in-room safes, pool, laundry service. AE, MC, V.*✎

$$$$ 🏨 **Hotel Tamarindo Diriá.** A shady tropical garden next to the beach
eliminates the need to stray far from Tamarindo's first high-end hotel, still a posh spot. Rooms in the contemporary three-story building have tile floors and modern furniture, and each has a spacious balcony overlooking treetops. The thatched rotunda bar and restaurant overlook a large rectangular pool. ⊠ *Apdo. 676–1000, San José,* ☎ *653–0031 or, in San José, 258–4224;* ℻ *653–0208. 82 rooms. Restaurant, bar, air-conditioning, in-room safes, minibars, pool, casino, laundry service. AE, MC, V.*✎

$$$–$$$$ 🏨 **Casa Cook.** These two one-bedroom, hardwood-detailed cabinas just
★ off Tamarindo's beach are owned by a retired American couple, Chuck and Ruthann Cook. Each has a full kitchen, its own water heater, a

queen-size sofa bed in the living room, a queen-size bed in the bedroom, ceiling fans, and screened doors and windows. The second story of the main house is the "villa," a 1,500-sq-ft, two-bedroom apartment with private baths, kitchen, dining area, living room, and large deck. ⊠ On road to Playa Langosta, north of the Hotel Capitán Suizo (☞ above), ☎ 653–0125 or, in the U.S., 925/846–0784; FAX 653–0753 or, in the U.S., 925/426–1141. 2 cabinas, 1 villa. Air-conditioning, in-room safes, pool. AE, MC, V. ✍

$$–$$$ 🏠 **Hotel Pasatiempo.** Steps from the beach and just off the dirt road to Playa Langosta, the Pasatiempo is one of the better bargains in Tamarindo. The cabinas, each named after a Guanacaste beach, are scattered around the nicely landscaped grounds and the pool; each is air-conditioned and has a hand-painted mural over the bed. The bar frequently hires live music—"grown-up rock-and-roll," says owner Ron Stewart—and a wide-screen satellite TV provides American sports fans with their periodic fix. ⊠ 200 m from beach behind the Tamarindo circle, ☎ 653–0096, FAX 653–0275. 11 cabinas. Restaurant, bar, air-conditioning, pool, laundry service. AE, MC, V. ✍

$$ 🏠 **Cabinas Marielos.** In high season Tamarindo presents few decent bargain rooms; among the best are those at Cabinas Marielos, across the main dirt road from the beach in what is more or less the town center. The cabinas are in two wings, flanking a courtyard set well back from the noise and dust of the road. The atmosphere is surprisingly serene. Note that the water doesn't get terribly hot. ⊠ Near the north of town, follow signs, ☎ FAX 653–0141. 16 cabinas. Laundry service. V.

Outdoor Activities and Sports

BOATING, SURFING, AND KAYAKING
Iguana Surf (☎ FAX 653–0148) rents surfboards and leads guided kayak tours into the bird-watching havens of the nearby San Francisco and Tamarindo estuaries. The San Francisco seems to have more birds, and a nature walk upriver might include an encounter with a troop of howler monkeys. The larger Tamarindo is a more exotic, overgrown, jungle-like estuary, with an African Queen–like ambience deep in the mangrove jungle.

SPORTFISHING
A number of fishing charters in Tamarindo cater to saltwater anglers. The best among them is probably **Tamarindo Sportfishing** (☎ 653–0090), run by Randy Wilson, who has led the way in developing new fish-saving catch-and-release techniques that go easy on the fish. Wilson has roamed and fished the Guanacaste waters for 25 years now, and he knows where the big ones lurk. His boat, the Talking Fish, is equipped with a marlin chair and a cabin with a shower. Full days run $875, half days $550.

Playa Langosta

㉙ 2 km (1 mi) south of Tamarindo.

Playa Langosta, a leatherback-turtle nesting beach, is less protected than the beach at Tamarindo. Informal viewings with private guides are a lot cheaper than the more organized Playa Grande turtle tours, but eggs are stolen in huge quantities. The arrangement will most likely be formalized in the near future. Big, well-shaped river-mouth waves near the north end of the beach make it popular with surfers. An oversize casino-condo-hotel complex is going up on the bluff overlooking the river mouth.

Lodging

$$$$ 🖫 **Sueño del Mar.** Gather a group of friends and take over American
★   Susan Money's dream of a B&B for a week—you'll love every minute.
The complex has swinging hammocks, lovely gardens, a pool, and intimate patios and is adorned throughout with hand-painted frescoes
and colorful antique tiles. The adobe-style buildings contain three
double rooms with air-conditioning, overhead fans, and Balinese-style
showers open to the sky. A casita with its own kitchen and veranda
sleeps four. Upstairs, the matrimonial suite offers even greater privacy.
Gourmet breakfast is served in the "community" room, where three-
course dinners are offered a few times a week. The lively Ms. Money
and her husband, surfing forester Greg Mullins, will help arrange
trips. ✉ *Playa Tamarindo, Santa Cruz,* ☎ ꜰᴀx *653–0284;* ✉ *Susan
Money, 4 Mountainview Ct., Burlington, VT 05401,* ☎ ꜰᴀx *802/658–
8041. 3 rooms, 1 suite, 1 casita. Restaurant, air-conditioning, pool,
horseback riding, snorkeling, surfing, boating, fishing, bicycles, laundry service. V.* 🐾

En Route   To reach Playa Avellanes, Negra, and Junquillal from the highway, turn
south toward Tamarindo at the Huacas junction, and when you reach
the village of Villarreal continue south 14 km (8½ mi) rather than turn
right toward Tamarindo. The road is in fairly good shape most of the
way. At the T-junction, turn right for Paraiso and Junquillal (the left
turn goes to Santa Cruz). From the junction it's about 12 km (7 mi)
to Paraiso along an alternately dirt and paved road. The dirt road north
from Paraiso to Playa Negra (6 km/4 mi) is funky but passable; the
road south from Paraiso, 2 km (1 mi) to the north end of Junquillal,
is in better shape. To reach Playa Avellanes, take the road past Villareal
via Hernandez and follow signs to Cabinas Las Olas.

Playa Avellanes

③⓪   *20 km (12 mi) south of Tamarindo.*

Avellanes is a beautiful 1-km (½-mi) stretch of pale-gold sand with rocky
outcroppings, a river mouth, and a mangrove swamp estuary. Locals
claim there are eight surf spots when the swell is strong.

Lodging

$$$ 🖫 **Cabinas Las Olas.** Frequented mainly by surfers on holiday pack-
ages from Brazil and Argentina, these spacious freestanding cabinas
in an airy forest behind Playa Avellanes should also appeal to bird-watch-
ers, animal lovers, and all manner of naturalists. Monkeys and other
critters lurk around this isolated spot. An elevated boardwalk leads from
the cabinas to the beach through a protected mangrove estuary. The
three-meal restaurant, complete with an adjacent outdoor video bar,
serves reasonably priced food. ✉ *Apdo. 1404–1250, Escazú,* ☎ *233–
4455,* ꜰᴀx *222–8685. 10 cabinas. Restaurant, bar, dive shop, bicycles,
laundry service. AE, MC, V.* 🐾

En Route   From Playa Avellanes, questionable roads lead south to Playa Negra;
sage drivers will only attempt this trip with four-wheel-drive vehicles.
It's better to double back to the T-junction on the main road from Vil-
larreal and head south again. After 21 km (12½ mi) you'll come to a
junction with a left turn to Santa Cruz (a terribly potholed road) and
a right to Paraiso and Junquillal. Turn right, and another 15 km (8 mi)
of alternating dirt and pavement gets you to the hamlet of Paraiso. From
here it's about 6 km (4 mi) north on an interesting but passable dirt
road to Playa Negra, and 2 km (1 mi) south on a better road to the
north end of Junquillal, which stretches south uninterrupted for about
3 km (2 mi).

Playas Negra and Junquillal

③¹ *44 km (27 mi) south of Playa Langosta.*

Americans—surfers at least—got their first look at Playa Negra in *The Endless Summer II,* which featured some dynamite sessions at this spectacular rock-reef point break. Surfing cognoscenti will dig the waves, which are almost all rights and often beautifully shaped. Junquillal (pronounced hoon-key-*yall*), to the south, is a long stretch of uninterrupted beach with calm surf and only one hotel on the beach side of the road. This is one of the quieter beaches in Guanacaste, and a real find for tranquillity-seekers.

Lodging

$$$$ 🏨 **Hotel Antumalal.** Set back off the beach at the south end of Junquillal, the resort of Atumalal is perhaps a bit too slick for its loca-
★ tion. On the other hand, why not play tennis, slide into the pool, and then have an Italian dinner near a perfect beach in the middle of nowhere? The grounds are pleasant, and the views of the sea from the main dining room, behind the reception area, are splendid. Breakfast is included. ⊠ *Apdo. 49, Santa Cruz, or reserve through 650 West Ave., Apt. 2409, Miami Beach, FL 33139,* ☎ 𝖥𝖠𝖷 *653–0425. 23 rooms, 8 suites. Restaurant, 2 bars, refrigerators, pool, tennis court. AE, DC, MC, V.*✍

$$$ 🏨 **Hotel Playa Negra.** For years, surfers and other adventurers roughed
★ it at assorted motley lodges and cabinas around here. All that changed when Lito Pedro Fernandez opened the Playa Negra in 1996. Behind the restaurant-bar facing the sea, a collection of round, bright-pastel, thatched-roof cabinas sits among lawns and plantings; inside, cooled by ceiling fans, the cabinas have built-in sofas and beautiful tile bathrooms. The ocean is good for swimming and snorkeling, with rock reefs providing shelter, tidal pools, and swimming holes. And for surfers, with a good swell running, this is paradise found. The restaurant serves Latin and European dishes, deftly prepared by the French and Costa Rican chefs. ⊠ *Go north on dirt road out of Paraiso and follow signs carefully at forks in the road,* ☎ *382–1301 or, in San José, 293–0332;* 𝖥𝖠𝖷 *382–1302. 10 cabinas. Restaurant, bar, in-room safes, pool, horseback riding, volleyball, surfing, laundry service. AE, MC, V.*✍

$$–$$$ 🏨 **Guacamaya Lodge.** Up on the hill a few hundred m off Playa Jun-
★ quillal (follow signs), the secluded Guacamaya offers expansive views and ideal bird-watching. Swiss brother and sister Alice and Bernie Etene have a delightful compound, with flocks of visiting parrots in the morning and a multitude of cranes visible in the estuary below. The three-meal restaurant is very reasonably priced. In addition to cabinas, there's a well-equipped house with a full kitchen for groups of three or four. ⊠ *Apdo. 6, Santa Cruz,* ☎ 𝖥𝖠𝖷 *653–0431. 6 cabinas. Restaurant, bar, pool, laundry service. AE, MC, V.*✍

$$–$$$ 🏨 **Hotel Iguanazul.** Spread out along the bluff at the north end of Playa
★ Junquillal, the Iguanazul is an isolated beachfront resort that has it all: cabinas, a pool, a three-meal restaurant and bar, and 3 km (2 mi) of beach stretching south. The fabulous surf of Playa Negra is 10 minutes away. Air-conditioned rooms cost more, but breakfast is free for all. ⊠ *Apdo. 130–5150, Santa Cruz,* ☎ *653–0124,* 𝖥𝖠𝖷 *653–0123. 24 cabinas. Restaurant, bar, in-room safes, pool, volleyball, recreation room, laundry service. AE, MC, V.*✍

$$ 🏨 **Hotel Playa Junquillal.** This funky little hotel has gained a reputation as a haven for low-budget wanderers in search of a secret. It's no longer all that cheap, however, and its ramshackle appearance may dishearten some. Others will be happy to trade amenities for the hotel's intangible charm and the 3-km (2-mi) stretch of beach in the front yard.

The hotel is run by a shifting cast of American partners, all very friendly and happy to share stories over cold beers. The restaurant sits on one side of the quasi-landscaped courtyard, with the sparsely furnished cabinas on the other. ✉ *Santa Cruz,* ☎ FAX *653–0432. 4 cabinas. Restaurant, bar, laundry service.* V.

$$ ⛵ **Mono Congo Lodge.** "Mono Congo" translates as howler monkey, and those noisy but endearing creatures are plentiful at this hotel on the road to Playa Negra. The hardworking American owners have transformed 10 acres of barren cattle pasture into a little gem, with extensive plantings surrounding a handsome three-story hardwood structure housing a restaurant, comfortable seating areas, and four guest rooms. If the waves go flat, take a different kind of ride: the owners lead horseback tours. Good food, good waves, boards for rent, and rustic, comfortable accommodations are available on demand, making this a potentially perfect spot for a surfing holiday. ✉ *Apdo. 177–5150, Santa Cruz,* ☎ FAX *382–6926. 5 rooms, 1 guest house. Restaurant, pool, tennis court, horseback riding, laundry service. No credit cards.*

THE NICOYA PENINSULA A TO Z

Arriving and Departing

By Boat
See Getting Around, *below.*

By Bus

PUNTARENAS TO CABO BLANCO
Buses (**Empresarios Unidos,** ☎ 222–1867) run from San José (C. 12 between Avdas. 7 and 9) to Puntarenas daily, a two-hour trip, every 40 minutes 6 AM–7 PM. Ferries (**Asociacion de Desarrollo Integral Paquera,** ☎ 661–0118) connect Puntarenas with Playa Naranjo and Paquera, with continuing bus service to Montezuma.

NICOYA AND THE TEMPISQUE RIVER DELTA REGION
Buses (**Empresa Alfaro,** ☎ 222–2666) run from San José (C. 14 between Avdas. 3 and 5) to Nicoya daily, including the Río Tempisque ferry leg, at 6 AM, 8 AM, and 2 PM. Buses run to Liberia at 6:30 and 10 AM and 1:30, 3, and 5 PM, from the same location. The trip takes four hours. Daily buses (**Tralapa,** ☎ 221–7202) to Santa Cruz leave from San José's Calle 14 between Avenidas 1 and 3 every hour from 7 AM to 1 PM and at 2, 4, and 6 PM. The trip lasts five hours.

CENTRAL NICOYA BEACHES: PUNTA ISLITA TO NOSARA
Buses (**Empresa Alfaro,** ☎ 222–2666) leave San José (C. 14 between Avdas. 3 and 5) daily at 6 AM for the six-hour trip to Nosara. Buses (**Empresa Alfaro,** ☎ 222–2750) leave from Calle 14 between Avenidas 3 and 5 for the 4½-hour trip to Sámara daily at 12:30 PM.

LIBERIA AND THE NORTHERN NICOYA BEACHES
From Calle 14 between Avenidas 1 and 3, San José, buses leave hourly 6 AM–8 PM for the four-hour trip to Liberia (**Pulmitan,** ☎ 222–1650). For Playa del Coco, a five-hour bus runs daily at 8 AM and 2 PM from Calle 14 between Avenidas 1 and 3. For the five-hour trip to Hermosa and Playa Panamá, a bus departs daily at 3:20 PM from Calle 12 between Avenidas 5 and 7 (**Empresa Esquivel,** ☎ 666–0042). Five-hour buses for Brasilito, Flamingo, and Potrero (**Tralapa,** ☎ 221–7202) leave daily from Calle 20 between Avenidas 3 and 5 at 8 and 10 AM. For Tamarindo, a 5½-hour trip, a bus leaves daily at 3:30 PM from Calle 14 between Avenidas 3 and 5 (**Empresa Alfaro,** ☎ 222–2666). For $19, you can ride on the comfortable, air-conditioned **Fantasy Tours** bus which connects San Jose, Liberia, and Tamarindo. The bus from San Joséto

Tamarindo and Liberia leaves daily at 8 AM. The return bus leaves
Tamarindo at 2 PM and passes through Liberia at 3:30 PM.

By Car
The northwest is accessed via the paved two-lane Pan-American Highway (CA1), which begins at the top of Paseo Colón in San José.

By Plane
Sansa (✉ C. 42 between Avdas. 3 and 5, San José, ☎ 221–9414, ⒻⒶⓍ
255–2176) and **Travelair** (✉ Aeropuerto Internacional Tobías Bolaños, Apdo. 8–4920, ☎ 220–3054, ⒻⒶⓍ 220–0413) fly to San José,
Liberia, Tamarindo, Carrillo, Punta Islita, and Tambor.

Getting Around

By Boat
Note that these schedules are subject to change, especially between the
high and low seasons. If possible, call ahead to verify schedules.

PUNTARENAS TO CABO BLANCO
The Puntarenas–Playa Naranjo **car ferry** (☎ 661–1069), which takes
1½ hours, departs daily at 3:15, 7, and 10:50 AM and 2:50 and 7 PM.
The 1¼-hour Puntarenas–Paquera ferry leaves six times daily between
5 AM and 8:15 PM, with an equal number of return trips. Two com-
peting companies ply this route, so don't be fooled by the signs with
only three departures listed. A passenger-only ferry leaves Puntarenas
daily at 6 AM, returning at 2:30 PM. Bus links and cabs are available
at the Nicoya end of the ferry lines. Pedestrian-only ferry service from
Montezuma to Paquera and Puntarenas is also available; just ask
around in town. Expect long waits on all car ferries in high season and
holiday weekends.

NICOYA AND THE TEMPISQUE RIVER DELTA REGION
The 20-minute Tempisque car ferry crosses continuously. Lines can get
very long in the dry season.

By Bus
PUNTARENAS TO CABO BLANCO
Buses currently run to Montezuma from Paquera six times daily between 6 AM and 6 PM, returning six times between 5:30 AM and 4 PM;
but inquire about the latest schedule for this route before you set off.

CENTRAL NICOYA BEACHES: PUNTA ISLITA TO NOSARA
Buses leave Nicoya for Nosara, Garza, and Guiones daily at 10 AM and
2 PM (**Empresa Rojas,** ☎ 232–1949); the same line runs from Nicoya
to Samara, Monday to Friday at 8 and 10 AM, noon, 3 and 4:15 PM,
and to Carrillo from Nicoya at 3 PM.

LIBERIA AND THE NORTHERN NICOYA BEACHES
Buses from Liberia leave daily for Hermosa and Panamá at 7:30 and
11:30 AM and 3:30, 5:30, and 7 PM (☎ 666–1249). There's a daily bus
from Santa Cruz to Junquillal at 6:30 PM.

By Car
Paved roads run down the spine of the Nicoya Peninsula all the way
to Playa Naranjo, with just a few unpaved stretches. Once you get off
the main highway, the pavement holds out only so far, and then dirt,
dust, mud, potholes, and other factors come into play. The roads to
Playa Sámara and Playa del Coco are paved all the way; every other
destination requires some dirt-road maneuvering. If you're headed
down to the coast via unpaved roads, be sure to get advance information
on road conditions. Take a four-wheel-drive vehicle if possible.

Contacts and Resources

Car Rentals

It's best to stick with the main rental offices in San José. **ADA** (✉ Avda. 18 between Cs. 11 and 13, ☎ 233–7733 or 800/CAR–RENT) offers pickup and car delivery in Liberia. **Sol Rentacar** (✉ In front of Hotel El Bramadero, ☎ 666–2222). **Budget** (✉ 10 km/6 mi west of airport, ☎ 223–3284). **Economy** (✉ Sabana Norte, ☎ 231–5410) now offers cars in Tamarindo. **Elegante** (✉ C. 10 between Avdas. 13 and 15, ☎ 221–0066) also offers cars in Tamarindo.

Emergencies

General (☎ 911). **Ambulance** (☎ 221–5818). **Fire** (☎ 118). **Police** (☎ 117 in towns; 127 in rural areas). **Traffic Police** (☎ 227–8030).

Guided Tours

In addition to the following major agencies, most hotels can organize guided tours for you.

ADVENTURE

The **Hotel Oasis del Pacific** (✉ Apdo. 200–5400, Puntarenas, ☎ FAX 661–1555) at Playa Naranjo coordinates riveting sea-kayaking trips along the coast and among the islands of the Gulf of Nicoya.

DAY TRIPS

Day trips to the idyllic Isla Tortuga in the Gulf of Nicoya are very popular, and **Calypso Tours** (✉ Avda. 2 between Cs. 1 and 3, San José, ☎ 256–2727, FAX 256–6767) has been leading them longer than anyone else.

SPECIAL-INTEREST TOURS

Tikal Tours (✉ Avda. 2, between Cs. 7 and 9, Apdo. 6398–1000, San José, ☎ 223–2811) runs highly informative weeklong tours of Carara Biological Reserve, Manuel Antonio National Park, Lomas Barbudal Biological Reserve, Playa Grande, Santa Rosa National Park, and Volcán Arenal. The excellent **Horizontes** (✉ *150 m north of Pizza Hut Paseo Colón, San José*, ☎ 222–2022) specializes in more independent tours with as few as eight people, including four-wheel-drive transport, naturalist guides, and guest lecturers.

Visitor Information

The tourist office in San José has information on Guanacaste. In Liberia, the **Casa de la Cultura** (✉ 3 blocks south of Parque Central, ☎ 661–4527, ☉ Mon.–Fri. 8–12, 1:30–5; Sat. 8–12, 1:30–4) has local tourist information.

5 THE CENTRAL PACIFIC COAST

It doesn't cover much ground, but Costa Rica's central Pacific coast has disproportionate natural assets. Playas Jacó, Hermosa, and Manuel Antonio promise sparkling surf and sun-baked sand, while the Carara Biological Reserve and Manuel Antonio National Park hold rare and beautiful wildlife species. And since it's so close to San José, this region lets you get quickly down to the business of rest and relaxation.

S MALL BUT VARIED, the region southwest of San José packs most of the attractions that probably drew you to Costa Rica: lush tropical forests, palm-lined beaches, and hospitable terrain for an array of outdoor activities. The region—and the Carara Biological Reserve in particular—is a transition zone between the tropical dry forest of the northwest and the wet forests of the Pacific coast farther south. Since most of its woodlands were cut years ago, however, the central Pacific landscape is dominated by steep coffee farms, vast oil-palm plantations, and rolling green pastures ideal for horseback riding. Manuel Antonio National Park protects an indented stretch of coastal rain forest and idyllic white-sand beaches. Despite the fact that the region's protected areas are among the smallest in the country, they are vibrant habitats with an amazing variety of flora and fauna, including such endangered species as the scarlet macaw and the Central American squirrel monkey. Decent snorkeling and world-class sportfishing are paramount in Playas Jacó and Manuel Antonio, thanks to abundant marine life. Ideal conditions for surfing, sea kayaking, horseback riding, rafting, hiking, and bird-watching also abound—all within just 160 km (100 mi) of San José.

Updated by
George
Soriano

Pleasures and Pastimes

Dining
Restaurants in Manuel Antonio and Jacó serve some of the best food in Costa Rica. They haven't cornered the dining market, however; a number of isolated lodges also serve delicious local food. Thanks to world-class fishing, seafood—from fresh-caught dorado and yellowfin tuna to crustaceans—is the forte of the area's best chefs.

Lodging
Accommodations here are as varied as the scenery, encompassing everything from beachside cement boxes to luxury hotels on verdant hillsides (including some of Costa Rica's premier establishments). Manuel Antonio has some of the priciest, charging more than $150 for a double during high season, but places in nearby Quepos rent rooms at backpackers' rates, and plenty of inns fall between the two extremes. As a rule, prices drop 20% to 30% during low season.

Outdoor Adventures
Several white-water rivers—Ríos Parrita, Naranjo, and the less accessible Savegre—flow northeast from the Cordillera de Talamanca chain. You can ride horseback just about everywhere, and two working ranches near Orotina (which double as hotels) have enough trails to keep you in the saddle for a week. Skin-diving is good in the Manuel Antonio area, and the offshore sportfishing is among the best in the world. Other options include surfing, sea kayaking, and ocean excursions ranging from wave-runner tours to dolphin-watching sunset cruises.

Exploring Central Pacific Costa Rica

Attractions lie conveniently close to each other, making it easy to combine beach time with forest exploration or country living with marine diversions. Every destination in this chapter is between two and four hours from San José by road. A winding mountain road passes through Atenas on the way to Orotina, from where the coastal highway, or Costanera, heads southeast to Tárcoles, Jacó, Playa Hermosa, and Quepos. The flight from San José to Quepos is speedy, a mere half hour.

Numbers in the text correspond to numbers in the margin and on the Central Pacific Costa Rica map.

Great Itineraries

Fly directly to ⬚ **Quepos** ⑧ and hit the beach at ⬚ **Manuel Antonio** ⑨. If you're driving, be sure to stop at **Carara Biological Reserve** ③ on your way to Manuel Antonio. Rise early the next day to spend the morning exploring **Manuel Antonio National Park** ⑩, and spend the afternoon horseback riding or relaxing on the beach. Dedicate the third morning to white-water rafting, skin-diving, or taking another tour; then catch an afternoon flight back to San José.

Spend your first two nights at one of the ranches near ⬚ **Orotina** ②, enjoying horseback riding, rafting, and bird-watching. From there explore the **Carara Biological Reserve** ③. On the third morning, head to either ⬚ **Tárcoles** ④, ⬚ **Jacó** ⑤, or ⬚ **Playa Hermosa** ⑥ to get your beach and/or surfing fix. On day four, go south to ⬚ **Manuel Antonio** ⑨ and spend the day fishing, skin-diving, rafting, horseback riding, or lounging on the beach. Visit **Manuel Antonio National Park** ⑩ early on day five; then drive back into the mountains to spend your last night in **Atenas** ①, just 40 minutes from the international airport. Alternately, since Quepos and Manuel Antonio have so much to offer, fly straight there and stay put. If you want more remote conditions, spend two days in the Manuel Antonio area and head south to the Osa Peninsula (☞ Chapter 6) for the last three days, catching a flight from Golfito back to San José.

When to Tour Central Pacific Costa Rica

The weather in the central Pacific region follows the same dry- and rainy-season weather patterns common to the rest of the Pacific slope, which means lots of sun from December to May and frequent rain from September to November. Since you'll have to share the area with other travelers in the dry season, consider touring the region at another time. The weather tends to be perfect in July and August, with lots of sunny days and occasional light rain.

THE CENTRAL PACIFIC HINTERLANDS

Beaches may be this region's biggest draw, but the countryside hides vast haciendas interspersed with patches of tropical wilderness where you might encounter any critter from the capuchin monkeys to the collared aracari, and estuaries where crocodiles lurk amid the mangroves. Because it's an ecological transition zone, the region is extremely diverse biologically, making it a boon for bird-watchers and other wildlife enthusiasts.

Atenas

❶ *42 km (26 mi) west of San José.*

National Geographic once listed Atenas as having one of the 12 best climates in the world, and that's pretty much this little town's only claim to fame. In addition to having spectacular weather, Atenas is a pleasantly quiet, traditional community that few foreigners visit, despite the fact that it's en route to the central Pacific beaches. Some well-kept wooden and adobe houses are scattered around a small church and central plaza, and surrounding the town are coffee farms, cattle ranches, and patches of forest. Just west of Atenas, the road to Orotina winds its way down the mountains past breathtaking views.

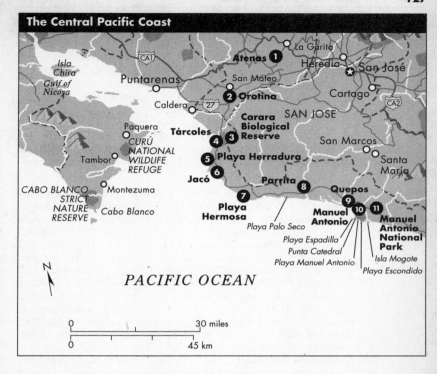

The Central Pacific Coast

PACIFIC OCEAN

0   30 miles

0   45 km

Dining and Lodging

$ ✕ **Guarumo Café.** This whimsical breakfast and lunch café doubles as an information center thanks to the helpful bilingual owner with a penchant for macrobiotic treats. Pick up some postcards or stock up on herbal teas as you wait for your American-style breakfast, energy-boosting Guarana (protein powder) fruit smoothie, cappuccino, or takeout lunch. The café is in an historic building off Atenas' central park. ✉ *Apdo. 110–4013, Atenas, 150 m east of Banco Nacional,* ☎ *446–6442. Reservations not accepted. No credit cards. Closed Christmas Day.*

$$$–$$$$ ⌂ **El Cafetal Inn.** The friendly owners of this B&B, a Salvadorean-Colombian couple, go out of their way to make you comfortable and help with your travel plans. Set on a hill amid a coffee farm, their two-story cement lodge offers simple accommodations. The tower rooms are larger, and have curved windows for panoramic views. Complimentary breakfast—including home-roasted coffee—is usually served on the patio out back. Trails through the surrounding countryside are perfect for hikes or horseback tours. El Cafetale is halfway between Grecia and Atenas, and is as close to the airport as San José. ✉ *Apdo. 105, Atenas, on hwy., 1 km (½ mi) west of Grecia, turn left just before bridge and follow signs,* ☎ *446–5785,* ℻ *446–7028. 10 rooms. Restaurant, bar, pool. AE, MC, V.* ⌂

$$ ⌂ **Villas de la Colina.** A colorful archway of bougainvillea guides you to rustic quarters at this mountain retreat. Sweeping views and an ample pool—also with a view—are the lodge's best assets, making it an ideal overnight stop on the way to the beach. The wood cabins are simple, but each has a private balcony with a comfortable hammock. The lodge is one of the few in the country to offer motorcycle tours. ✉ *Apdo. 165, Atenas, 6 km (4 mi) from Coopeatenas on road to Orotina,* ☎ *446–5015,* ℻ *446–6635, 6 cabins. Kitchenettes, pool, horseback riding, motorcycles. No credit cards.*

Orotina

❷ *24 km (15 mi) southwest of Atenas, 66 km (41 mi) southwest of San José.*

One of the central Pacific's oldest communities, Orotina is a laid-back commercial center and transportation hub in the heart of an important agricultural region. The town centers on an attractive park shaded by tall tropical trees, with a modern church towering over its eastern end. The market, a rickety building near the park, is a good place to pick up some locally grown fruits, such as mangoes. The main agricultural endeavor nearby, however, is cattle ranching, and the main reasons to stop here are the two haciendas west of town, now lovely hotels.

Lodging

$$$ ⊞ **Dundee Ranch.** Right up the road from Hacienda Doña Marta (☞
★ *below*), this 850-acre hacienda outside Orotino is something between a dude ranch and a nature lodge. The old ranch house and a newer building hold spacious, comfortable guest rooms with colorful bedspreads and ceiling fans; rooms open onto a portico surrounding a garden courtyard. You'll hear chittering wildlife from the rooms: monkeys, macaws, iguanas, and toucans abound in the Machuca River Canyon, and a shallow lagoon nearby is home to waterfowl and crocodiles. Two dozen tour options, including horseback trips, keep you busy. ⊠ *Apdo. 7812–1000, San José, 16 km (10 mi) west of Orotina, take Costanera toward Puntarenas, turn right at 3rd intersection, and look for ABOPAC factory,* ☎ *428–8776 or 267–6222,* FAX *267–6229. 23 rooms. Restaurant, air-conditioning, pool, horseback riding. AE, MC, V.* ✎

$$$ ⊞ **Hacienda Doña Marta.** Part cattle ranch, part romantic hideaway,
★ this little complex of wooden *cabinas* (cottages) surrounding a tiny pool shaded by *marañón* (cashew fruit) and coconut trees is a real find. Fine hardwoods and bamboo ceilings, cool tile floors, expansive bathrooms and showers, and sweet country-style appointments characterize the rooms, each of which is different and prettier than the last. The no-funny-business kitchen crew cooks stellar traditional meals, served in a handsome wood-beamed dining room where you'll also find handmade pottery for sale. Horseback riding among the hacienda's acres of woods, cattle pastures, and mango trees is a must, as is early-morning bird-watching. Note that the hotel closes when no rooms are reserved, so book in advance or you might find that no one is here to greet you. ⊠ *Apdo. 463–1000, San José (for directions ☞ Dundee Ranch, above),* ☎ *253–6514 or 428–8126,* FAX *234–0958. 6 cabinas, 2 rooms. Restaurant, pool, horseback riding. No credit cards.*

Carara Biological Reserve

❸ *21 km (13 mi) southwest of Orotina, 83 km (51 mi) southwest of San José.*

Situated between Costa Rica's drier northwest and the more humid south, the Reserva Biológica Carara is part of an ecological transition zone, which means, in effect, that it packs a tremendous variety of plants and animals. Much of the 47-sq-km (18-sq-mi) reserve is covered with primary forest on steep slopes, the massive trees laden with vines and epiphytes. The relatively sparse undergrowth makes wildlife easier to see here than in many other parks, albeit still tough; if you're lucky, you'll glimpse armadillos, basilisk lizards, blue-crowned motmots, scarlet macaws, iguanas, coatis, and any number of monkey species.

Look for the first trail on the left shortly after the bridge that spans the Río Tárcoles. This leads to a horseshoe lagoon—abandoned as an oxbow lake by the meandering Tárcoles, the lagoon is now almost entirely covered with water hyacinths and is home to such waterbirds as the northern jacana and boat-billed heron, as well as river turtles and crocodiles. The main ranger station is several miles farther south; from there another trail heads into the forest. Remember that the earlier in the morning you get here, the more likely you are to see animals. For more on Carara *see* Chapter 9. ☒ *Turn left off CA1 for Atenas and follow signs for Jacó; reserve is on left after you cross the Río Tárcoles.* ☒ *$6.* ☉ *Daily 8–4.*

Tárcoles

❹ *90 km (56 mi) southwest of San José.*

The town of Tárcoles doesn't warrant a stop, but it's the departure point for a crocodile-watching boat tour up the Río Tárcoles. There are two exceptional hotels nearby, as is a spectacular waterfall in a private nature reserve. If you pull over just after crossing the **Río Tárcoles bridge,** you can often spot such elegant birds as roseate spoonbills, great egrets, and baby-blue herons strutting through the shallows, as well as massive crocodiles lounging along the banks (bring binoculars). The entrance to Tárcoles is on the west side of the road, just south of the Carara Biological Reserve; across the highway is a dirt road that leads to the Hotel Villa Lapas and the waterfall reserve.

The **Manantial de Agua Viva** is a 600-ft waterfall in the heart of a private reserve across from Tárcoles. The waterfall flows into 10 natural pools, any of them perfect for a refreshing dip after the hike into the reserve. The forest surrounding the waterfall is home to parrots, monkeys, scarlet macaws, and most of the other animals found in the adjacent Carara Biological Reserve. A tough 2½-km (1½-mi) trail makes a loop through the woods, passing the waterfall and pools; it takes between 40 minutes and two hours to hike, depending on how much birdwatching you do. The entrance is 5 km (3 mi) from the coastal highway, up the same dirt road that leads to the Hotel Villa Lapas (☞ Lodging *below*). ☒ *$7.* ☉ *Daily 8–5.*

Lodging

$$$$ ☒ **Hotel Villa Lapas.** The grounds of this hotel, just a short drive from Carara and the waterfall reserve, are shaded by tall trees with a stream flowing by, making it a great place to bird-watch. A trail heads up the valley into a patch of protected forest. The white bungalows with barrel-tile roofs and small porches hold two rooms each; those nearest the restaurant have views of the stream and forest. All meals are included in the room price. ☒ *Apdo. 171–5400, Puntarenas,* ☎ *663–0811,* 𝐅𝐀𝐗 *663–1516. 46 rooms. Restaurant, bar, pool, 2 hot tubs, recreation room, meeting room. AE, MC, V.*

$$$$ ☒ **Villa Caletas.** Set on a promontory of lush slopes in the rain forest,
★ this elegant collection of villas may seem remote, but it's only minutes from Jacó and Carara. The architecture recalls Southeast Asia, but guest rooms are decorated in the French style, with fine antiques and art, black furniture, and sweeping drapes. France is also the predominant influence in the cuisine, which is served in an attractive open-air restaurant with a spectacular long-distance view of Puntarenas. The infinity pool appears to blend into the horizon, and a small amphitheater plays occasional host to live music. Enter on the west side of the road between Tárcoles and Jacó. ☒ *Apdo. 12358–1000, San José,* ☎ *257–3653 or 637–0161,* 𝐅𝐀𝐗 *222–2059. 8 rooms, 6 suites, 12 villas. Restaurant, bar, pool. AE, MC, V.*

Outdoor Activities and Sports

BOAT TRIPS

After hiking the trails of Carara, the most popular activity in the area is the river trip up the muddy Río Tárcoles to see ferocious crocodiles and colorful birds. **Jacó Adventures** (☎ 643–1049) runs a boat tour that guarantees close encounters of the crocodilian kind. Jacó's **Fantasy Tours** (✉ Best Western lobby, ☎ 643–3032) leads its own boat trip on the Río Tárcoles.

THE COAST NEAR SAN JOSÉ

Along this short stretch are some of Costa Rica's most accessible beaches and the popular Manuel Antonio National Park. Convenient to the capital city, this region is great for a quick overview of Costa Rica's rich natural splendor.

Playa Herradura

❺ *16 km (10 mi) south of Tárcoles.*

Large-scale development has put this once-secluded rocky beach on the map for both travelers and investors, who can opt for North American amenities in a tropical setting. The brand-new, multimillion-dollar Los Sueños Resort arrived hand in hand with an 18-hole, Ted Robinson–designed ecological golf course and luxury condos to the beach area.

$$$$ ✕🏨 **Marriott Los Sueños Beach and Golf Resort.** This palatial Spanish Colonial-style masterpiece was built to resemble a Latin American village. The design mixes modern elegance with such authentic touches as Nicaraguan terra-cotta tile roofing, painted Costa Rican floor tiles, Guatemalan textiles, and antique furniture. The enormous horizon pool has landscaped islands of its own, and several bars and restaurants ensure that companions of different tastes can relax together. The kids' club keeps youngsters occupied while their parents soak up the sun, play golf just off the beach, or just close out the world. ✉ *Playa Herradura , ☎ 630–9000, FAX 630–9090. 191 rooms, 10 suites. 3 restaurants, 2 bars, café, pool, sauna, 18-hole golf course, exercise room, baby-sitting, children's programs, travel services. AE, MC, V.* 🐾

Jacó

❻ *2 km (1 mi) south of Playa Herradura, 108 km (67 mi) southwest of San José.*

Relative proximity to San José coupled with the attractiveness of its wide sandy bay has made Jacó a popular and affordable beach getaway. More than 50 hotels and cabinas back its long gray-sand beach, and the cluttered appearance of the town's main drag makes it look distinctly overdeveloped; but from the water, the development is mostly hidden behind the palms. The beach itself is large enough to allow you to escape from the package tours and surfer dudes, except during major holidays. Aside from sunbathing and surfing, you can rent bicycles, ride horseback, or tour the nearby Carara Biological Reserve or Río Tárcoles.

The gray sand of Jacó's long, palm-lined **Playa Jacó** can burn the soles of your feet on a sunny afternoon. It's popular with surfers for the consistency of its waves, but riptides make the sea hazardous for swimmers when the waves are robust. If you're traveling with children, you might appreciate the **miniature golf** course on the town's main drag. Kids might also enjoy the **butterfly garden** across from the Best Western hotel.

Dining and Lodging

$$ ✕ **Chatty Cathy's.** This small, second-floor restaurant in the heart of Jacó is *the* place to go for breakfast. The friendly Canadian owners serve fast-breaking favorites—banana pancakes, bacon, hash browns, cinnamon buns—as well as some tasty inventions of their own and a small lunch menu. The name's no joke; Cathy will happily talk your ear off if you let her. ✉ *Across from Mas X Menos supermarket,* ☎ *no phone. No credit cards. Closed Mon.–Tues. and Apr. No dinner.*

$$ ✕ **Marisquería El Recreo.** This place has Jacó's most extensive seafood menu: If it swims in the sea, they probably serve it, with the possible exception of surfers and tourists. Sure, they have a few meat and vegetable dishes, but the menu is dominated by tuna, lobster, shrimp, and mahimahi, each prepared in a variety of ways. You dine beneath a thatched roof overlooking Jacó's main street; a colorful marine mural covers the only wall. ✉ *Across from Mas X Menos supermarket,* ☎ *643–1172. AE, MC, V.*

$$ ✕ **Rioasis.** The menu at this colorful, open-air restaurant just off the main drag is eclectic—burritos and other Tex-Mex treats, a few pastas, and salads—but the big draw is the pizza, with more than two dozen different pies baked in a wood-burning oven. You eat on the front patio or under a high roof hung with ceiling fans and backed by a long bar. This is also a good place to shoot pool or play darts during the happy hours (6 to 7 and 9 to 11). ✉ *Just north of Banco Nacional,* ☎ *643–3354. V.*

$$$–$$$$ 🏨 **Hotel Club del Mar.** It's easy to forget you're in busy Jacó if you stay
★ in this secluded spot on the extreme southern end of the beach. The bungalows are shaded by giant trees, and iguanas lounge on the lawn. The handsome "Superior" rooms have green tile floors, high ceilings, and wooden shutters that open onto porches or balconies with ocean or garden views; the smaller standard rooms in back have kitchenettes, sitting areas, and balconies. The restaurant is one of the few in Jacó with an ocean view, and it serves some of the best food in town, both Tico and international. ✉ *Apdo. 107–4023, follow Costanera south past main signposted entrances to Playa Jacó, then turn right at first street after service station,* ☎ FAX *643–3194. 18 rooms. Restaurant, bar, pool, some kitchenettes. AE, MC, V.* ✍

$$$ 🏨 **Tangerí Chalets.** Six of the rooms in these two-story cement building have ocean views, while the remaining eight overlook the hotel's lawn and two pools. Every room has a tile floor, high ceiling, two double beds, and a small balcony or porch. As an alternative, each eccentrically designed bungalow has a kitchen, covered patio, and eight beds—perfect for a family or group of friends. ✉ *Apdo. 622–4050, Alajuela, on main street between Jacó center and Best Western,* ☎ *643–3001,* FAX *643–3636. 14 rooms, 9 bungalows. 2 restaurants, air-conditioning, pool, basketball. AE, MC, V.*

$$–$$$ 🏨 **Aparthotel Flamboyant.** This small, quiet oceanfront hotel is a good
★ deal, especially if you take advantage of the cooking facilities. Every room has a kitchenette, breakfast bar, tile floor, ceiling fan, and a double and single bed. Small terraces with chairs overlook the verdant pool area, where there's a grill for your use. It's all just a few steps from the beach and Jacó's busy main strip. ✉ *Apdo. 018, Puntarenas, Jacó center behind Wishbone Restaurant,* ☎ *643–3146,* FAX *643–1068. 13 rooms. Kitchenettes, pool. AE, MC, V.*

$$ 🏨 **Mar de Luz.** It may be a few blocks away from the beach, and it doesn't look like much from the street, but Mar de Luz is a surprisingly pleasant place and one of the best deals in town. The Dutch owners are dedicated to cleanliness and details, such as the poolside grill and well-stocked kitchenettes. The older rooms, colored in pastels, have two queen-size beds and small porches; the newer, split-level newer rooms

are a bit larger, with attractive stone walls, white tile floors, and windows overlooking the gardens. ⊠ *50 m east of main road, across from Tangerí Chalets,* ☎ FAX *643-3259. 27 rooms. Kitchenettes, air-conditioning, pool. No credit cards.*

$–$$ 🏨 **La Cometa.** If you want clean, convenient rooms without expensive frills, this place delivers. Across the street from Jacó's strip of souvenir shops and restaurants, La Cometa fills with budget travelers, who can usually be found reading or lazing on the long patio that overlooks a parking lot camouflaged by a simple tropical garden. Ceiling fans in the rooms lend a bit of a breeze. ⊠ *Apdo. 116, Jacó, across from Restaurante Colonial,* ☎ FAX *643-3615. 10 rooms, 6 with bath. No credit cards.*

Nightlife and the Arts

In high season, Jacó gets lively when the sun goes down. Cut loose at the popular disco **La Central** (☎ 643-3076), on the beach opposite Tienda La Flor. Next door to La Central, you can also dance at **Los Tucanes** (☎ 643-3226). If you prefer to park it and watch a game, hit the **sports bar** by the pool at the Copacabana Hotel.

Outdoor Activities and Sports

HORSEBACK RIDING

Jacó Beach Equestrian Center (☎ 643-1904) offers two- to four-hour horseback rides with English or Western equipment. To get there, follow the signs at the bridge.

KAYAKING

Neil Kahn (☎ 643-1233) runs river- and sea-kayaking tours for both novices and seasoned adventurers.

SURFING

Jacó has several excellent beach breaks, all of which are best around high tide, and its reputation has spread far and wide. Surfboard-toting tourists abound here. Surfboard rentals are easy to arrange; one good outfitter is **Chosita del Surf,** which also repairs boards. The shop is on the main street just north of the Hacienda Restaurant. If you plan to spend more than a week surfing, it might be cheapest to buy a used board and sell it before you leave—**Mother of Fear** (☎ 643-2001), on the main street south of Tangerí Chalets, has the best selection of used surfboards in the country.

Playa Hermosa

➐ *5 km (3 mi) south of Jacó, 113 km (70 mi) southwest of San José.*

Just over the rocky ridge that forms the southern edge of Jacó is Playa Hermosa, a swath of gray sand stretching southeast as far as the eye can see. The beach's northern end is popular with surfers: because of its angle, it often has waves when Jacó and other spots are flat. But you don't have to be a surfer to enjoy Hermosa, a quiet alternative to Jacó; just keep mind, if you want to swim, that dangerous rip currents are common when the surf is up.

Dining and Lodging

$$$ ✕🏨 **Fuego del Sol.** A colorful tropical garden surrounds the pool area of this modern beachfront hotel with a top-notch gym. Next to the pool are a small, open-air sports bar and a simple restaurant with an ocean view. The guest rooms, all in a two-story cement building, have tile floors, ceiling fans, and rain-forest murals. Those upstairs have high wooden ceilings and balconies overlooking either the pool area or beach, and those downstairs have small terraces. The hotel offers an all-inclusive surf camp. ⊠ *Diagonally across from soccer field,* ☎

643–3737, FAX 643–3736. *18 rooms. Restaurant, bar, air-conditioning, pool, exercise room. AE, MC, V.*

$$ 🎿 **Ola Bonita.** Just a few steps from the surf break, this two-story building with a barrel-tile roof is a nicer alternative to Hermosa's other budget hotels. Rooms have red-tile floors, white stucco walls, simple kitchenettes, fans, and one bunk and double bed each. There's a tiny pool out front for quick post-ocean dips. ✉ *Playa Hermosa,* ☎ FAX *643–3990. 6 rooms. Kitchenettes, pool. No credit cards.*

Outdoor Activities and Sports
HORSEBACK RIDING

In case you tire of surf and sand, **Diana Trail Rides** (☎ 643–3808) runs a nice horseback tour through the countryside, taking in some waterfalls on the way.

SURFING

Most people who bed down at Playa Hermosa are here for the same reason. The surf is best at high tide. You can rent, repair, and purchase boards in nearby Jacó (☞ *above*).

Parrita

8 *45 km (28 mi) south of Jacó, 150 km (93 mi) southwest of San José.*

Set in the heart of an African-palm plantation, Parrita is a dusty town of painted wooden bungalows. First planted in 1945 by the United Fruit Company after its banana plantations were decimated by Panama disease, the palms are cultivated for their fruit, from which oil is extracted for margarine, cooking oil, scent, and soap. The town has little to offer travelers, but a dirt road heading west from the Costanera just south of town leads to **Playa Palo Seco,** a seemingly endless beach backed by palms and mangrove swamps.

Quepos

9 *23 km (14 mi) south of Parrita, 174 km (108 mi) southwest of San José.*

With a population of around 12,000, Quepos is the largest and most important town in this corner of Costa Rica. It owes its name to the tribe that inhabited the area when the first visiting Spaniard, Juan Vásquez de Coronado, rode through the region in 1563. It's not certain whether those Indians were called Quepos or Quepoa, but we do know that they lived by a combination of farming, hunting, and fishing until the violence and disease that accompanied the Spanish conquest wiped them out.

For centuries following the Spanish conquest, Quepos hardly existed, but in the 1930s the United Fruit Company put it on the map, building a banana port and populating the area with workers from other parts of Central America. The town thrived for a decade, until Panama disease decimated the banana plantations around 1945. The fruit company then switched to (less lucrative) oil palms, and the area slipped into a prolonged depression. Only in the last decade have tourism revenues lifted the town out of its slump—a renaissance owed to natural causes, the beauty of the nearby beach and Manuel Antonio National Park (☞ *below*).

En Route If you're traveling with children and/or have a keen interest in wildlife, you may want to visit the **Jardín Gaia,** a small zoo that rehabilitates former pets and injured animals and releases them back into the wild. The inhabitants are mostly parrots and macaws confiscated by government wildlife officials, and monkeys that were electric-shocked while playing on power lines. There's also an orchid garden. Admission is free for kids under 12. ⊠ *Left side of road to Manuel Antonio, 2½ km (1½ mi) from Quepos,* ☎ 777–0535. ⊡ *$5.* ☉ *Thurs.–Tues. 2–5.*

Dining and Lodging

$$–$$$ ✕ **El Gran Escape.** Situated on a corner of the town's waterfront strip,
★ with seating scattered between an old wooden building, patio, and second-floor bar, this is it for seafood in Quepos. El Gran Escape is a favorite with sportfishermen—"You hook 'em, we cook 'em." The menu ranges from broiled shrimp with a tropical sauce to the catch of the day prepared in any of a half dozen ways. The impressive array of appetizers includes crab cakes, unusual in Costa Rica, and a good selection of burgers and Tex-Mex standards. ⊠ *Waterfront,* ☎ 777–0395. *V. Closed Tues. and 2 wks in June.*

$$ ✕ **Restaurant Isabel.** One of the oldest restaurants in Quepos—run by the same family for three decades now—Isabel is famous for serving fresh seafood at palatable prices. It occupies the ground floor of an old wooden building on the busy waterfront road, with big windows and ceiling fans keeping things cool. The menu covers three meals a day, from cheap breakfasts to pepper steaks to pastas, but the specialty is fresh fish, such as mahimahi sautéed in garlic or grilled tuna served with a salad and potatoes. ⊠ *C. 2 and Avda. Central,* ☎ 777–0137. *AE, MC, V. Closed Wed. May–Dec.*

$–$$ 🏨 **Hotel Malinche.** One block west of the Quepos bus station, this small hotel has two kinds of rooms, both of which are a bargain. Newer, air-conditioned room are carpeted and have large tile baths with hot-water showers. The older rooms, cooled by ceiling fans, cost about half as much; those on the ground floor are nicer, with white tile floors and baths, while those on the second floor have wooden floors and are slightly smaller. ⊠ *Avda. Central, ½ block west of bus station,* ☎ FAX 777–0093. *29 rooms. AE, MC, V.*

Nightlife and the Arts

American expats gather beneath the ceiling fans of **El Banco Bar** (☎ 777–0478), on Avenida Central, to watch U.S. sports on TV or listen to live rock and roll. A popular watering hole with younger travelers is **La Boquita** (☎ no phone), upstairs behind the bus station, where wild murals cover the walls and reggae is usually blasting on the stereo. The popular disco **El Arco Iris** (☎ 777–0449), built over the estuary just north of the bridge, gets packed on weekends and holidays. The late-night dance scene is at large, glitzy **Maracas** (☎ 777–0707), south of town, next to the docks. There are small casinos on the ground floors of the **Hotel Kamuk** (☎ 777–0379), in Quepos, and in the **Hotel Divisamar** (☎ 777–0371), on the way to Manuel Antonio.

Outdoor Activities and Sports

HORSEBACK RIDING

Lynch Travel (⊠ Quepos, ☎ 777–1170) can arrange two horseback tours: a three-hour ride to a scenic overlook, and an all-day trip to the Catarata de Nara, a waterfall that pours into a natural swimming pool. **Rain Maker** (⊠ Hotel Si Como No, Manuel Antonio, ☎ 777–0777) leads a more exclusive excursion through the pristine rain forest of a private reserve in the mountains, as well as a fascinating walk through suspended bridges over the forest canopy. Other guided tours of the 1,500-acre reserve include hikes to waterfalls and natural pools.

SPORTFISHING

The southwest has some of Costa Rica's finest deep-sea fishing, and Quepos is one of the best points of departure. Fewer boats troll these waters than troll off Guanacaste, and they usually catch plenty of sailfish, marlin, wahoo, mahimahi, roosterfish, and yellowfin tuna. Some sportfishing operations in Quepos are: **Sportfishing Karahé** (☎ 777–0170), **Pacific Coast Charters** (☎ 777–1382), and **Lynch Travel** (☞ Horseback Riding, *above*).

WHITE-WATER RAFTING

There are three white-water rivers near Quepos, but they have rather limited seasons. The Parrita is a mellow route (class II–III), perfect for a first rafting trip; it's navigable in rafts from May to January, after which it drops so low that you can only float in two-person inflatable "duckies." The Naranjo (class III–IV) requires some experience and can only be run from June to December. The Savegre (class II–III) is fun: it flows past plenty of rain forest and wildlife and is passable from June to March, but landslides sometimes limit access. **Iguana Tours** (☎ 777–2052) is the oldest rafting outfitter in Quepos, and also runs sea-kayaking tours. **Amigos del Río** (☎ 777–0082) leads trips down all the area's rivers.

Manuel Antonio

❿ *3 km (2 mi) south of Quepos, 179 km (111 mi) southwest of San José.*

Once you're here, it's not hard to see why Manuel Antonio has become one of Costa Rica's most famous destinations: You need only contemplate one of its views of beach, jungle, and the shimmering Pacific dotted with rocky islets. Spread over the hill that separates Quepos from Manuel Antonio National Park (☞ *below*), the town of Manuel Antonio is surrounded by dozens of hotels and restaurants, scattered along the road between Quepos and the park. The best hotels are near the top of the hill, as the views are most spectacular; and since there is nearly as much rain forest around these hotels as in the nearby national park, most of the wildlife in the park can also be spotted near the hotels.

As the road approaches the national park, it skirts the lovely, palm-lined strand of **Playa Espadilla,** which stretches north from the rocky outcropping that borders the park. The beach is popular with sunbathers, surfers, volleyball players, and vacationing Ticos; just beware of deadly rip currents when the waves are large.

Dining and Lodging

$$$–$$$$ ✕ **Gato Negro.** Though seafood reigns here (as it does all over town), this open-air restaurant at the top of the hill stands out thanks to its Italian chef, who has a flair for international cooking. The extensive menu combines classic Italian preparations with innovative dishes like spaghetti *a lo scoglio* (mixed seafood pasta) and *penne con salmone e gamberi* (pasta with salmon and shrimp). Breakfast and lunch are also served in the Mediterranean-style dining room, which has a terra-cotta tile floor and white stucco walls and pillars. ⊠ *Next to Hotel Casitas Eclipse,* ☎ 777–1728. AE, MC, V.

$$$ ✕ **Karolas.** Nestled in the forest just below Barba Roja (☞ *below*), with tables on two simple patios surrounded by greenery, Karolas is easily Manuel Antonio's most attractive, intimate restaurant at night. At any time of day, it makes up for its lack of ocean view with quality cuisine, particularly fresh fish and shrimp dishes. The options extend to such entrées as chicken caribe, and the homemade desserts are top-notch—leave room for a piece of macadamia pie. Reservations are recommended. ☎ 777–1557. V.

$$–$$$ ✕ **Barba Roja.** Perched near the top of the hill, with sweeping views of the Manuel Antonio shoreline, Barba Roja is one of this town's oldest and most popular restaurants. The dining room is furnished with dark hardwoods and decorated with colorful prints. Food takes a close second to atmosphere; try the daily fish specials or, at lunchtime,

the excellent sandwiches. Desserts are delicious as well. Breakfast is popular, but the view is most impressive at sunset. ⊠ *Manuel Antonio,* ☎ *777–0331. V. No lunch Mon.*

$$ ✕ **Café Milagro.** The only place in town serving banana bread and home-roasted coffee, Café Milagro doubles as a souvenir shop and meeting place right off the road to the national park and Playa Espadilla. The atmosphere is decidedly North American, as are the prices, but the charm and consistently good breakfast food—available all day—keep locals and travelers coming back for seconds. The café also sells local and international newspapers here and at its sister locale in Quepos. ⊠ *Main road at top of hill, in front of Hotel Casa Blanca,* ☎ *777–1707. AE, MC, V.*

$$$$ 🛏 **Hotel Si Como No.** Designed to damage as little of the forest as possible, this attractive, eco-friendly place was built to use solar power, energy-efficient air-conditioning systems, and very little hardwood. The surrounding jungle is frequented by fearless monkeys and varied birds. Inside, the tasteful standard and deluxe rooms are decorated in pastels and have stained-glass windows in the bathrooms; luxury rooms have small kitchens and balconies. Two luxury rooms join to make a villa, a good deal for two couples or a family. The blue-tiled pool has an artificial cascade, water slide, and swim-up bar; there's also a poolside grill, a formal Costa Rican restaurant, and a small movie theater. ⊠ *Top of the hill,* ☎ *777–1250; 800/237–8201 in the U.S.;* 🖷 *777–1093. 38 rooms. 2 restaurants, 2 bars, air-conditioning, pool, cinema. AE, MC, V.* ✆

$$$$ 🛏 **Makanda by the Sea.** If you've got an occasion coming up, give your-
★   self the gift of a stay at Makanda, a secluded luxury retreat on a rain-forested hill, with its own infinity pool and ocean views through the trees. A handful of villas stud the landscape, hidden from each other by tropical fruit trees, which regularly attract troops of monkeys and colorful birds right off the villas' private oversize balconies. A footpath winds through the 14-acre wooded property to the hotel's small beach, a good place to snorkel. All villas have high roofs, ceiling fans, hammocks, couches, modern kitchenettes, phones, and modem lines. Villa 1 is completely open on the ocean side; the three "studios" below it are smaller and less expensive, but they're air-conditioned and equally attractive, with whitewashed walls, colorful upholstery, terra-cotta tile floors, and oversize windows. The poolside restaurant serves some of the best food in town, to which nonguests are welcome if they reserve in time. ⊠ *1 km (½ mi) west of La Mariposa,* ☎ *777–0442,* 🖷 *777–1032. 5 villas, 4 studios. Restaurant, kitchenettes, pool, beach. AE, MC, V.* ✆

$$$$ 🛏 **La Mariposa.** Set high on a promontory, Manuel Antonio's classi-
★   est hotel has the best view in town, perhaps in Costa Rica: a sweeping panorama of verdant hills, pale beaches, rocky islands, and the shimmering Pacific. The main building is a white, Spanish-style villa with an open-air dining room and pool area below. The older, split-level units are perched on the edge of the ridge and have sitting rooms, balcony bedrooms, and conservatory bathrooms alive with plants. The newer suites and deluxe rooms have hot tubs and cost slightly less; there are also a few smaller, less private rooms above the restaurant. ⊠ *Top of hill,* ☎ *777–0355,* 🖷 *777–0050. 6 rooms, 12 suites, 4 villas. Restaurant, bar, pool. MC, V.*

$$$–$$$$ 🛏 **Costa Verde.** The builders of this place were careful to damage the forest as little as possible, so the hotel is enveloped in lush foliage. You might well spot squirrel monkeys, sloths, and iguanas right outside your room. Two types of rooms are spread through five buildings: smaller efficiencies, short on privacy, and spacious studios, with tile floors, larger beds, tables, chairs, air-conditioning, and kitchenettes. All have ceil-

ing fans, lots of screened windows, and large balconies shared by two rooms each. The open-air restaurant serves good seafood and killer tropical drinks. ⊠ *Southern slope of hill, near park,* ☎ *777–0584,* FAX *777–0560. 44 rooms. 2 restaurants, bar, some air-conditioning, kitchenettes, 2 pools. AE, MC, V.* ✆

$$$ 🖭 **Hotel California.** Just uphill from the Villas Mymosa (☞ *below*), this lovely place features a 70-acre private reserve with waterfalls and observation towers. All guest rooms have kitchenettes, murals of Costa Rica's national parks, and balconies overlooking the large pool area or surrounding jungle. The hotel is painted in playful colors to contrast with its forested backdrop. A snack bar serves breakfast around the pool. ⊠ *Apdo. 159, Quepos,* ☎ *777–1234,* FAX *777–1062. 22 rooms. Snack bar, kitchenettes, pool. AE, MC, V.* ✆

$$$ 🖭 **Hotel Verde Mar.** Also known as La Casa del Sol, this whimsical hotel just off the main road borders the rain forest and offers direct access to the beach. The rooms, all in one long cement building, have colorfully artistic interiors and windows on each end overlooking surrounding gardens and wild foliage. There's a small pool in back, from which a wooden catwalk leads through the woods and out to the shore. ⊠ *Apdo. 348, Quepos, ½ km (¼ mi) north of park,* ☎ *777–1805,* FAX *777–1311. 20 rooms. Kitchenettes, pool, library, travel services. AE, MC, V.*

$$$ 🖭 **Villas Mymosa.** These tasteful, incredibly spacious condos are simple, clean, inviting and well worth the not-excessive price. Second-floor rooms have the best views of mountains and estuaries to the north; and high barrel-tile ceilings, clever, irregular architectural details, and oversize private balconies with tables and hammocks make the already commodious quarters feel even larger. All rooms have kitchenettes, futons or day beds, and air-conditioning. Outside, the grounds are less charming; there are no intimate spaces, and the large tiled pool is off the parking area, surrounded by a sparse garden. ⊠ *Apdo. 271–6350, Quepos, up side road from Hotel Mymosa,* ☎ FAX *777–1254. 8 rooms, 2 suites. Kitchenettes, pool. AE, MC, V.* ✆

$$$ 🖭 **Villas Nicolás.** There's a certain serenity to the rooms in these
★   Mediterranean-style villas that sets them apart from other options in this price range. Narrow walkways between whitewashed, garden-lined villas lead to attractive split-level rooms built on a cliff, the higher of which have wonderful views over the Pacific. The more private rooms at the bottom look out at the jungle, where some interesting creature is usually stirring. Half the units have well-equipped kitchens; all have terra-cotta floors and oversize balconies furnished with a dining table, chairs, and hammocks. Some connect to form larger units. Waterfalls unite two small pools. This is a tasteful, friendly place that has very competitive rates in the low season. ⊠ *Top of hill,* ☎ *777–0481,* FAX *777–0451. 18 rooms. Restaurant, kitchenettes, pool. V.* ✆

$$–$$$ 🖭 **Hotel Playa Espadilla.** A short walk from the beach and national park entrance, this small hotel has its own forest reserve. (The owners' land was declared part of the park decades ago, but they were never paid for it, so they petitioned the government to create a private preserve.) Two cement buildings hold simple but spacious rooms with tile floors and kitchenettes. A blue-tile pool and small bar are covered by a barrel-tile roof in back, and the surrounding lawn is bordered by the reserve's thick foliage. You can also opt for one of the smaller, cheaper cabinas across the street. ⊠ *1 block east of beach, Apdo. 195,* ☎ FAX *777–0903. 16 rooms, 16 cabins. Restaurant, bar, air-conditioning, kitchenettes, pool. AE, MC, V.* ✆

$$–$$$ 🖭 **Hotel Vela Bar.** Set just a hundred meters back from Playa Espadilla on a paved road, this small, low-key hotel has rooms of varying size and with various views; all have white stucco walls decorated with framed tapestries, terra-cotta floors, and ceiling fans. The bungalow (which

sleeps four) is a good value for small groups. The open-air restaurant set beneath a high, circular roof is popular with nonguests for its selection of fresh seafood, vegetarian, and meat entrées. ⊠ *Next to Hotel Playa Espadilla (☞ above)*, ☎ *777–0413*, FAX *777–1071. 9 rooms, 2 bungalows. Restaurant, bar. AE, MC, V.*

$$ 🏨 **La Colina.** The new cement tower of this small B&B on the Quepos side of Manuel Antonio's hill has the nicest rooms, with tile floors, ceiling fans, big windows, and balconies; two are air-conditioned. Smaller rooms without views are less expensive; there are also two cozy, air-conditioned apartments. Next to the small split-level pool is the thatch-roof, open-air restaurant, where complimentary breakfast, a light lunch menu, and nightly dinner specials are served. The friendly American owners are happy to book tours and help you with travel arrangements. ⊠ *North side of hill,* ☎ *777–0231,* FAX *777–1553. 11 rooms, 2 apartments. Restaurant, bar, pool. AE, MC, V.* 🐾

Nightlife and the Arts

Most of Manuel Antonio's nightlife is in nearby Quepos (☞ *above*), which has several bars and two full-fledged discotheques. **Mar y Sombra** (☎ 777–0510), the restaurant on the beach, becomes an open-air disco on weekend evenings. **Barba Roja** (☞ *above*) has a bit of a bar scene to complement the dining, as does **Billfish Billiards** (☎ 777–0411) at the Byblos Hotel, across from Villas Nicolás. There is a small casino in the **Hotel Divisamar** (☎ 777–0371), across from Barba Roja. The **Costa Verde** (☞ *above*) hosts live jazz in a roadsize bar–cum–Internet café across the street.

Outdoor Activities and Sports

HORSEBACK RIDING

Malboro Stables (☎ 777–1108) rents horses and leads a two-hour guided tour through the forest. **Equus** (☎ 777–0001) can provide mounts and lead you through the forest and beach.

SEA KAYAKING

Iguana Tours (☎ 777–1262) runs sea-kayaking adventures to the islands of Manuel Antonio National Park (☞ *below*), which requires some experience when the seas are high, and a mellower paddle to the mangrove estuary of Isla Damas, where you might see monkeys, crocodiles, and plenty of birds.

SKIN DIVING

Playa Manuel Antonio, inside the national park, is a good snorkeling spot, as is Playa Biesanz, near the **Hotel Parador** (600 m south of Makanda by the Sea). During high season, **Lynch Travel** (☎ 777–1170) offers scuba diving for experienced divers only around the islands in the national park.

SWIMMING

Manuel Antonio's safest swimming area is the sheltered second beach in the national park, Playa Manuel Antonio, which is also great for snorkeling. When the surf is up, rip currents are a dangerous problem on Playa Espadilla, the long beach north of the park. Riptides are characterized by a strong current running out to sea; the important thing to remember if you get caught in one of these currents is not to struggle against it, but instead to swim parallel to shore. If you can't swim out of it, the current will simply take you out just past the breakers, where its power dissipates. If you conserve your strength, you can then swim parallel to shore a bit, then back into the beach. Needless to say, the best general policy is not to go in deeper than your waist when the waves loom large.

Shopping

There's no shortage of shopping in this town, between the T-shirt vendors near the national park and the boutiques in major hotels. You'll find little in the way of local handicrafts, however; goods here are similar to those in San José, at slightly elevated prices. **La Buena Nota** (☎ 777–0345), to the right on the southern slope of the hill, is one of the oldest and largest souvenir shops in town; it also sells used books and international newspapers and magazines.

Manuel Antonio National Park

⑪ *5 km (3 mi) south of Quepos, 181 km (112 mi) southwest of San José.*

The white-sand beaches, turquoise waters, and verdant coastal forest of Parque Nacional Manuel Antonio have made it one of the most popular protected areas in Costa Rica (☞ Chapter 9). Though small—only 6½ sq km (2½ sq mi)—the park protects a remarkable stretch of coastline comprising three idyllic beaches and luxuriant rain forest where massive ficus, cow, kapok, and gumbo-limbo trees tower over trails. To this, mangrove swamps, marshland, and coral reefs add substantial biodiversity. Manuel Antonio is home to an endemic species of the endangered Central American squirrel monkey, as well as two- and three-toed sloths, green and black iguanas, capuchin monkeys, agoutis (large jungle rodents), and nearly 200 species of birds.

To enter the park, you have to cross a narrow estuary at the end of the road—waist-deep at high tide, ankle-deep at low tide. The first beach after the ranger station, **Playa Espadilla Sur,** is the longest and least crowded, since it can be rougher than the second beach. At its southern end is a tombolo (isthmus formed from sedimentation and accumulated debris) leading to a steep forested path that makes a loop over **Punta Catedral.** That trail passes a lookout from which you can gaze over the blue Pacific at some of the park's 12 islands; among them, **Isla Mogote** was the site of pre-Columbian Quepos Indian burials. The lovely strand of white sand east of the tombolo is **Playa Manuel Antonio,** a small, relatively safe swimming beach. At low tide you can see the remains of a Quepos Indian turtle trap on the right—the Quepos stuck poles in the semicircular rock formation, and these trapped turtles as the tide receded. This deep bay is good for snorkeling, with coral formations a mere shell's toss from the beach. Walk even farther east and you'll come to the rockier, more secluded **Playa Escondido.**

Be careful of manzanillo trees (indicated by warning signs)—their leaves, bark, and applelike fruit secrete a gooey substance that irritates the skin. And don't feed or touch the monkeys, who have seen so many tourists that they sometimes walk right up to them, and have been known to bite overfriendly visitors. Because the park is so popular, you'll want to get here as early as possible, especially during the dry season; the number of people allowed entrance on any given day is limited. Note that the park is closed on Monday. ☎ 777–0644. ☞ $6. ☉ Tues.–Sun. 7–4.

CENTRAL PACIFIC COAST A TO Z

Arriving and Departing

By Bus

THE CENTRAL PACIFIC HINTERLANDS

From San José, **Coopetransatenas** (✉ Coca-Cola bus station, C. 16 between Avdas. 1 and 3, ☎ 446–5767) buses leave for **Atenas** daily at 3:30 and every 30 minutes until 7. Buses to **Orotina** also leave the Coca-Cola station daily at 8, 9:30, and 11:15 AM and 12:30, 1:45, 2:45, and

4 PM. All buses heading *toward* San José can drop you off at the airport, but you need to ask the driver ahead of time. Buses to Jacó and Quepos (☞ Getting Around, *below*) can drop you off at the Carara Biological Reserve.

THE COAST NEAR SAN JOSÉ

Transporte Jacó (✉ Coca-Cola bus station, ☎ 223–1109) buses to Jacó leave from San José's Coca-Cola station daily at 7:30 AM, 10:30 AM, and 3:30 PM (2½-hr trip), returning at 5 AM, 11 AM, and 3 PM. There are direct, more-frequent buses on weekends, and buses to Quepos and Manuel Antonio National Park can also drop you off at **Jacó** or **Playa Hermosa. Fantasy Tours** (☎ 220–2126) runs a comfortable, if expensive, two-hour daily shuttle to Jacó from San José's Best Western Irazú at 9:30 AM, returning at 2 PM. Express buses piloted by **Transportes Delio Morales** (✉ Coca-Cola bus station, ☎ 223–5567) depart from San José's Coca-Cola bus station for the 3½-hour trip to **Quepos** and **Manuel Antonio National Park** at 6 AM, noon, and 6 PM, returning at 6 AM, noon, and 5 PM. If you're moving on to the southern Pacific region (☞ Chapter 6), buses leave Quepos for Dominical daily at 9 AM and 1:30, 4:30, and 6:30 PM, returning at 6 AM, 2 PM, and 2:45 PM (2½ hrs).

By Car

The quickest way to get to this region from San José is to take the Carretera Inter-Americana (Pan-American Highway, CA1) west past the airport to the turnoff for Atenas, turn left (south), and drive through Atenas to Orotina. The coastal highway, or Costanera, heads southeast from Orotina to Tárcoles, Jacó, Hermosa, and Quepos and is well marked and paved most of the way. A paved road connects Quepos to Manuel Antonio National Park.

By Plane

Most travelers find the 30-minute flight between San José and Quepos preferable to the three-hour drive or 3½-hour bus trip. **Sansa** (☎ 221–9414 or, in Quepos, 777–0683) flies eight times daily between San José and **Quepos** in the high season, four in the low season. **Travelair** (☎ 220–3054 or, in Quepos, 777–1170) also has eight daily flights between San José and **Quepos** in the high season, four in the low season, and Travelair flies once daily between Quepos and **Palmar Sur** (☞ Chapter 6).

Getting Around

By Bus

THE CENTRAL PACIFIC HINTERLANDS

Any bus traveling between San José and either Jacó or Quepos can drop you off at Orotina.

THE COAST NEAR SAN JOSÉ

Buses make the short trip from **Quepos** to **Manuel Antonio** every half hour from dawn till dusk, with a few more runs after dark. Buses leave **Puntarenas** for the three-hour trip to Quepos daily at 5 AM and 2:30 PM, returning at 10:30 AM and 3 PM; these stop at Hermosa and on the outskirts of Jacó.

By Car

The well-marked, newly paved Costanera connects Orotina with Carara Biological Reserve, Tárcoles, Jacó, Playa Hermosa, and Quepos. The drive from Quepos to Manuel Antonio National Park takes about 15 minutes.

Contacts and Resources

Car Rentals

Elegante (643–3224 in Jacó, 777–0115 in Quepos). **Economy** (643–3280 in Jacó).

Emergencies

General (☎ 911). **Ambulance** (☎ 777–0116). **Fire** (☎ 118). **Police** (☎ 117 in towns; 127 in rural areas). **Traffic Police** (☎ 222–9245).

Guided Tours

FROM SAN JOSÉ

The *Okeanos Aggressor* (⊠ 1–17 Plaza Colonial, Escazú, ☎ 289–3333, FAX 289–3737) makes all-inclusive 9- and 10-day guided dive trips to Cocos Island, one of the best dive spots in the world. Transfers to and from San José are provided from Puntarenas. **Cruceros del Sur** (⊠ Across from Colegio Los Angeles, Sabana Norte, San José, ☎ 232–6672, FAX 220–2103), offers a seven-day natural-history cruise through Costa Rica's central and south Pacific regions and some islands off Panama aboard the *Temptress,* a 63-passenger ship. The **Undersea Hunter** (⊠ San Rafael de Escazú, 600 m north and 50 m west of Rosti Pollos, ☎ 228–6535, FAX 289–7334) also leads 10-day dive trips to Cocos Island.

Any number of land-bound agencies can help you arrange tours. Try **Camino Travel** (⊠ Between Avdas. Central and 1, Calle 1, San José, ☎ 257–0107, FAX 257–0243), **Cosmos Tours** (⊠ 50 m north and 50 m east of Centro Cultural Norteamericano Coastarricense, ☎ 234–0607, FAX 253–4707), **Costa Rica Expeditions** (⊠ Avda. 3 and C. Central, San José, ☎ 222–0333, FAX 257–1665), and **Horizontes** (⊠ 150 m north of Pizza Hut Paseo Colón, ☎ 222–2022, FAX 255–4513).

THE COAST NEAR SAN JOSÉ

Fantasy Tours (⊠ Best Western Jacó Beach Hotel, ☎ 643–3032) leads an array of tours from Jacó, among them hikes in Carara Biological Reserve, boat trips on the Río Tárcoles, horseback rides, kayak outings, and cruises to Isla Tortuga. **Jacó Adventures** (☎ 643-1049) offers an unforgettable crocodile- and bird-watching tour.

In Quepos, **Lynch Travel** (⊠ Behind bus station, ☎ 777–1170) offers a wildlife-watching boat trip to the Isla Damas Estuary, guided tours of the national park, several horseback trips, river rafting, kayaking, sportfishing, and more. **Iguana Tours** (⊠ Across from soccer field, Quepos, ☎ 777–1262) specializes in sea kayaking and white-water rafting. The **Eco-Era Foundation** (⊠ Manuel Antonio, ☎ 777–1661) runs an invigorating jungle hike to a waterfall in its private reserve and a less strenuous bird-watching and conservation tour. **Rain Maker** (⊠ Hotel Si Como No, Manuel Antonio, ☎ 777–0850) leads horseback rides, hikes, and canopy tours in its private reserve.

Visitor Information

The tourist office in San José (☞ Visitor Information *in* Chapter 1) has information on the central Pacific region. In Quepos, **Lynch Travel** (☞ *above*) can also give general advice.

6 THE SOUTHERN PACIFIC COAST

Diverse and wild, Costa Rica's southern Pacific zone is marked by the cloud forests of the Cordillera de Talamanca and remote Osa Peninsula beaches. With isolated national parks, private biological preserves, comfortably rustic lodges, one of Latin America's finest botanical gardens, and sublime surfing, fishing, hiking, bird-watching, skin diving, and horseback riding, this terrain is seventh heaven for outdoors enthusiasts.

Updated by
George
Soriano

A TRIP TO THIS REGION REVEALS what most of Costa Rica looked like decades, or even centuries, ago. Because it was the last part of the country to be settled—a road into the region from San José wasn't completed until the 1950s—the southern Pacific zone retains a disproportionate percentage of its wilderness. Much of that nature lies within several of Costa Rica's largest national parks, and other patches are protected as private reserves. From the surprising highland scenery of the Cordillera de Talamanca, Costa Rica's highest mountain range, to the pristine beaches and coastal rain forest of the Osa Peninsula, the southern Pacific holds some of the most dramatic scenery and wildlife in Costa Rica.

In Chirripó National Park you can climb the highest mountain in the country, Cerro Chirripó, and wander lands ranging from rugged forest to glacial lakes. On the Osa Peninsula, the creation of Corcovado National Park put something of a halt to the furious logging and gold mining that was destroying the rain forest; the park now contains a wide range of habitats, including large areas of swamp, deserted beach, cloud forest, and luxuriant lowland rain forest, and houses most of the country's endangered species.

Conditions for a variety of outdoor sports are excellent here, including some of Costa Rica's best surfing breaks and the country's second-best skin-diving area. Anglers can fish the renowned Pacific waters. Rafters can take on the rambunctious Río General. Trekkers can climb Cerro Chirripó. Bird-watchers who go to the right places are almost guaranteed glimpses of the country's two most spectacular birds: the resplendent quetzal and scarlet macaw. Botany lovers, too, will find their jaws dropping here, especially at the Wilson Botanical Garden near San Vito, with its spectacular displays of both local and imported plant life.

Pleasures and Pastimes

Dining

This region is not renowned for its food, but there are still tasty meals to be had. Thanks to prime fishing off the coast, seafood is a staple. Apples, peaches, and plums are grown in profusion in the upper reaches of the Cordillera de Talamanca, and the lowlands are the source of those thirst-quenching pineapples. If you're here between June and August, try rambutans, locally called *mamones chinos,* their red spiky shells protecting a succulent white fruit very similar to a litchi.

Lodging

Accommodations here range from simple, low-budget oceanside *cabinas* (cottages) to tranquil mountain retreats and luxury rain-forest hotels. Remember that nature lodges may be less expensive than they initially appear, as the price of a room includes three hearty meals a day.

Outdoor Adventures

Outdoors enthusiasts may never want to leave these parts. This is hiking territory, with treks ranging from one-day jaunts through private reserves to more demanding multiday treks up Chirripó or into the Corcovado jungles. Simple horseback rides take you along spectacular beaches and forest trails. The lively habitat of the water surrounding Isla del Caño offers some of Costa Rica's best skin diving, and there's prime sportfishing off the entire southern Pacific coast. The surf whips up into a half dozen breaks, and you can navigate in the quieter waters of Golfo Dulce in a sea kayak.

Private Nature Preserves

In addition to celebrated national parks, this region has a growing number of private nature preserves, some of which run their own lodges. Dominical's Hacienda Barú, a 700-acre reserve, offers a number of ways to experience the rain forest, as does Lapa Ríos, on the southern tip of the Osa Peninsula, with its extensive protected rain forest. Cabinas Chacón, in San Gerardo de Dota, has a large cloud-forest reserve criss-crossed by footpaths.

Exploring the Southern Pacific Coast

This coastal area comprises the western slope of the Cordillera de Talamanca, the Valle de El General, and the Osa Peninsula. There are two routes into the region: the Costanera (Route 34), or coastal highway, and the Carretera Interamericana (Pan-American Highway, CA2). To take the Costanera, drive west from San José, turn off the highway at the road to Atenas, and turn south after Orotina toward Jacó and Quepos. This road is unpaved, and gets pretty rough south of Quepos. To reach the Valle de El General from the Pan-American Highway, drive east out of San José and turn south outside Cartago. The CA2 heads up through dense fog at the top of the Cordillera de Talamanca, then descends to cross the rolling hills of the Valle de El General all the way to Panama. The Costanera runs into the CA2 at Palmar Norte, south of which is the turnoff for Puerto Jiménez. Though a faithful translation of the Spanish, "highway" is really a misnomer for these neglected two-lane roads.

The good news is that Costa Rica's two domestic airlines offer regular flights from San José to Golfito, Palmar Sur, Puerto Jiménez, Pavones, Drake Bay, and Coto 47, and charter flights to more-isolated spots. Because the drive from San José to anywhere in this region takes six to eight hours, a one-hour flight is that much more attractive.

Numbers in the text correspond to numbers in the margin and on the Southern Pacific Coast map.

Great Itineraries

IF YOU HAVE 3 DAYS

Fly straight to the Golfo Dulce–Osa Peninsula area, where you can stay in a comfortable nature lodge in or near any of three pristine wilderness areas. You can fly direct to 🔲 **Playa Pavones** ⑩ on a charter arranged by the Tiskita Jungle Lodge, *or* fly to 🔲 **Puerto Jiménez** ⑪, a short drive from the lodges of 🔲 **Cabo Matapalo** ⑬ and the Tent Camp at the edge of 🔲 **Corcovado National Park** ⑫. The third option is to fly to Palmar Sur, where the taxi and boat trip to 🔲 **Drake Bay** ⑭ begins.

IF YOU HAVE 5 DAYS

In five days you can stretch out the three-day itinerary above or concentrate on inland areas. Drive south on the Pan-American Highway (CA2) into the cool mountain air and cloud forests of 🔲 **San Gerardo de Dota** ①, a perfect place to hike and bird-watch. The next day, drive up and hike down the Cerro de la Muerte, or simply explore the Dota Valley. On day three, head down out of the mountains to the coastal enclave of 🔲 **Dominical** ④ or the nearby 🔲 **Ballena Marine National Park** ⑤. Spend day four and the morning of day five enjoying the area's waterfalls, nature reserves, and beaches.

IF YOU HAVE 8 DAYS

Drive south on the CA2 to 🔲 **San Gerardo de Dota** ① for hiking and quetzal-watching. The next afternoon, work your way down to 🔲 **Dominical** ④, which deserves at least two nights. The morning of day four, drive to either 🔲 **Golfito** ⑧ or 🔲 **San Vito** ⑥; move on the following

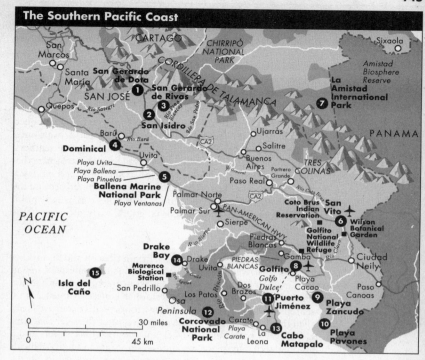

The Southern Pacific Coast

day to **La Amistad National Park** ⑦, 🔲 **Playa Zancudo** ⑨, or 🔲 **Playa Pavones** ⑩. If you're so inclined, slip into Panama for three days to explore the province of Chiriquí; if not, on day four you might go from Dominical straight out to the rain forests and isolated beaches of the Osa Peninsula for three nights. Drive or take a bus to 🔲 **Puerto Jiménez** ⑪ and 🔲 **Cabo Matapalo** ⑬, or park in Sierpe and take a boat to 🔲 **Drake Bay** ⑭.

When to Tour the Southern Pacific Coast

In the rainy season, it rains considerably more here than in the northwest, but in July and August you may catch a week without any serious precipitation. The Osa Peninsula and Talamanca highlands are especially susceptible to downpours, making this region the last place you want to visit during the October–November deluge.

THE GENERAL VALLEY

The Valle de El General is bounded to the north by the massive Cordillera de Talamanca and to the south by the Golfo Dulce, or Sweet Gulf (the name connotes tranquil waters). This area comprises vast expanses of highland wilderness, on the upper slopes of the Cordillera de Talamanca and the high-altitude *páramo* (shrubby ecosystem) of Chirripó National Park, as well as the isolated beaches and lowland rain forest of the Dominical and Golfito areas.

San Gerardo de Dota

❶ *80 km (50 mi) southeast of San José.*

Cloud forests, cool mountain air, pastoral imagery, and excellent birdwatching make San Gerardo de Dota one of Costa Rica's best-kept secrets. You'll find it in a narrow valley of the Río Savegre, 9 km (5½ mi) down a twisting track that descends abruptly to the west from the Pan-American Highway. The town's peaceful surroundings look more like the Rocky Mountains than like typical Central America, but hike down the waterfall trail and the vegetation quickly turns tropical again. Beyond hiking, activities include horseback riding and trout fishing, but you might well be content just to wander around the pastures and forests, marveling at the valley's avian inhabitants.

The damp, epiphyte-laden forest of giant oak trees, now broken up by bare patches strewn with stumps, is renowned for its high count of quetzals, for many the most beautiful bird in the Western world. Male quetzals are more spectacular than females, with metallic green feathers, bright crimson stomachs, helmetlike crests, and long tail streamers that look especially dramatic in flight. Quetzals commonly feed on *aguacatillos* (small avocado-like fruits) in the tall trees scattered around the valley's forests and pastures. The staff in your hotel can usually point you in the direction of some quetzal hangouts; early morning is the best time to spot them.

Lodging

$$$–$$$$ 🏨 **Cabinas Chacón.** Nearly 30 years ago, Efrain Chacón and his brother bushwhacked their way through the mountains to homestead in San Gerardo. Through hard work and business acumen, they built a successful dairy farm. Now a hotelier and staunch conservationist, Efrain aids researchers and leads quetzal-spotting tours on his extensive farm. Also called the Albergue de Montaña Savegre (after the river that runs past it), Chacón's hotel consists of clean, comfortable cabinas and a main building with a fireplace, veranda, restaurant, and bar. All meals are included, and the staff will pick you up from the turnoff on the Pan-American Highway or, for a fee, anywhere in Costa Rica. ⊠ *Apdo. 1636, Cartago,* ☎ 🖷 *771–1732. 26 cabinas. Restaurant, bar, hiking, horseback riding. AE, MC, V.* 🐾

$$$–$$$$ 🏨 **Trogon Lodge.** A collection of green cabins nestled in a secluded part
★   of an enchanting valley, the Trogon Lodge overlooks the cloud forest and boulder-strewn Río Savegre. Each cabin has two rooms with hardwood floors, colorful quilts, big windows, white-tile baths with hot showers, and small electric heaters for chilly mountain nights. Meals are served in a small dining hall and can be taken separately or as part of a package. The lodge can also provide a guide and/or transportation from San José. ⊠ *Apdo. 10980–1000, San José,* ☎ *223–2421 or 771–1266,* 🖷 *222–5463. 10 rooms. Restaurant. AE, DC, MC, V.*

Outdoor Activities and Sports

HIKING

The network of trails and country roads around San Gerardo de Dota can keep you on your feet days. Above the Trogon Lodge, a short trail heads through the forest and ends in a pasture; and miles of trails wind through the forest reserve belonging to Cabinas Chacón. The best trail in the General Valley is the one that follows the Río Savegre down to a **waterfall.** Follow the main road past Cabinas Chacón to a fork, where you veer left, cross a bridge, and head over the hill to a pasture that narrows to a footpath. The hike is steep and vigorous, especially near the bottom, and takes about three hours each way; it's well worth the effort if you're in shape. A longer, guided hike is offered by Cabinas Chacón: they drive you up to the páramo near **Cerro de la Muerte,** and you spend the day hiking from there back down through the forest into the valley.

San Isidro

❷ *54 km (34 mi) south of San Gerardo de Dota, 205 km (127 mi) northwest of Golfito.*

San Isidro has no attractions of its own, but it's not a bad place to get stuck spending a night, as it has friendly inhabitants and a fairly agreeable climate. The second-largest town in the province of San José, San Isidro has a bustling market and grid-plan streets of colorfully painted houses. The large central plaza is the town's hub, with a modern church towering to the east. A few blocks south is the market, where buses depart for San Gerardo de Rivas (☞ *below*), the starting point of the trail into Chirripó National Park. The regional office of the **National Parks Service** (✉ Across from Camara de Cañeros, ☎ 771–3155) can provide information about Chirripó and help you reserve lodging in the park's cabins. Buses to the nearby beach town of Dominical (☞ *below*) leave from a point near the fire station.

OFF THE
BEATEN PATH

LAS QUEBRADAS BIOLOGICAL CENTER – In a lush valley 7 km (4 mi) north of San Isidro, a community-managed nature reserve (*centro biológico*) protects 1,853 acres of dense forest in which elegant tree ferns grow in the shadows of massive trees and where colorful tanagers and euphonias flit about the foliage. A 3-km (2-mi) trail winds through the forest and along the Río Quebradas, which supplies water to San Isidro and surrounding communities. The Centro Biológico is 2 km (1 mi) north of the town of Las Quebradas; drive or take a taxi from San Isidro. ✉ *Apdo. 73–8257, San Isidro, Perez Zeledon,* ☎ *771–4131.* 🖃 *$4.* ☉ *Tues.–Sun. 8–2.*

Lodging

$$ 🏨 **Hotel del Sur.** The extensive grounds of this rambling complex, 6 km (4 mi) south of town on the Pan-American Highway, include a pool and tennis court. The rooms are spacious, and have large windows and tile floors. The bungalows in back are good for families and offer an escape from the drone of the highway; these have kitchenettes, bunks, and separate bedrooms. ✉ *Apdo. 4–8000, San Isidro, Perez Zeledon,* ☎ *771–3033,* FAX *771–0527. 48 rooms, 12 bungalows. Restaurant, bar, pool, tennis court, basketball. AE, MC, V.*

$$ 🏨 **Talari.** A 10-minute drive northeast from San Isidro on the road to San Gerardo di Rivas takes you to this family-run lodge on a small farm, where the gurgling of the Río General lulls you to sleep and dozens of bird songs awaken you. Simple rooms with big windows, tile floors, and porches are set in two cement buildings, with a small pool nearby. All meals are included in the room price. The surrounding fruit trees and forest patches make for good bird-watching, and the owners can arrange guided trips into Chirripó National Park. To get here, turn left off of the Pan-American Highway after the second bridge south of San Isidro. ✉ *Apdo. 517–8000, San Isidro, Perez Zeledon,* ☎ FAX *771–0341. 8 rooms. Restaurant, pool. AE, MC, V.*

Outdoor Activities and Sports

WHITE-WATER RAFTING

With the country's longest white-water run, the Río General makes for a rousing raft or kayak trip. The white water begins south of San Isidro, flowing through predominantly agricultural land before winding its way through a rocky canyon. Three-day camping expeditions on the Río General, a class III–IV river, are offered by San José's major rafting companies in the wettest months (September to November). In San Isidro, **Brunca Tours** (✉ 3 km/2 mi west of San Isidro on road to Dominical, ☎ 771–3100 or 771–0008) offers one- to three-day rafting trips on the Río General and nearby Río Coto Brus from May to January. Brunca Tours also leads snorkeling excursions to Isla del Caño and guided trips to Chirripó National Park, La Amistad Biosphere Reserve, the hot springs near San Gerardo de Rivas, and Wilson Botanical Garden (☞ *below*).

San Gerardo de Rivas

❸ *20 km (12 mi) northeast of San Isidro.*

The trail up to **Chirripó National Park** (Parque Nacional Chirripó; ☞ Chapter 9), home of the highest mountain in Costa Rica, begins above this scenic agricultural community. The climb to the park is grueling—six to 10 hours, depending on your physical condition—so try to head out of San Gerardo with the first light of day. If you aren't up for this adventure, San Gerardo de Rivas is still a great place to spend a day or two. Spread over steep terrain at the end of the narrow valley of the boulder-strewn Río Chirripó, the town offers a cool climate, good bird-watching, spectacular views, and an outdoor menu that includes hiking and horseback riding to waterfalls. A favorite stop is the **Aguas Termales,** small hot springs on a farm above the road to Herradura, about 1½ km (1 mi) after the ranger station.

Lodging

$–$$ ⊡ **El Pelicano.** Perched on a ridge south of town, this wooden lodge has an odd name for a mountain hotel—it refers to a chunk of wood that resembles a pelican—and that's not its only oddity. The restaurant, which has a gorgeous view of the valley below San Gerardo, is is decorated with dozens of idiosyncratic wooden statues carved by owner Rafael Elizondo out of tree roots. All the rooms upstairs have lots of wood, and share several clean, tiled bathrooms. ✉ *Apdo. 942–8000, San Gerardo de Rivas, Perez Zeledon,* ☎ *382–3000. 10 rooms. Restaurant, horseback riding. No credit cards.*

Dominical

❹ *22 km (14 mi) southwest of San Isidro.*

Fifty minutes southwest of San Isidro, Dominical, once a sleepy fishing village, is slowly being "discovered." It still has a mere fraction of the tourists that cover beaches like Tamarindo and Manuel Antonio, but not for want of natural attractions. Dominical's magic lies in its combination of terrestrial and marine wonders: the rain forest grows right up to the beach in some places, and the sea offers world-class surfing. The beaches here are long, practically empty, and perfect for strolling and shell collecting (just beware of rip currents when the waves are large).

There's also plenty to see and do inland as well. The local steep hillsides are covered with lush forest, much of it protected within private nature reserves. By leading hikes and horseback tours, several of these reserves are trying to finance preservation of the rain forest through ecotourism. Two reserves border the spectacular **Cataratas de Nauyaca** (Nauyaca Waterfalls), a massive double cascade that is one of the most spectacular sights in Costa Rica. The **Pozo Azul** is a considerably smaller waterfall in the jungle about 5 km (3 mi) south of town. Both are accessible on foot or on horseback (☞ Outdoor Activities and Sports, *below*).

Dining and Lodging

$$ ✕ **La Campanna.** A little slice of Italy near the beach, La Campanna
★   is the favorite restaurant of Dominical's many resident foreigners. Burlap sacks and palm fronds are about the only concessions the Italian owners have made to decor, but the food is first-rate. In addition to pizzas, they serve minestrone, marinated eggplant, baked squid stuffed with vegetables and Parmesan cheese, and a variety of fresh pasta dishes. ✉ *Main road,* ☎ *787–0072. No credit cards. Closed Mon.*

$$ ✕ **San Clemente Restaurant.** This is the local surfer hangout, most crowded whenever it's too dark or too flat to catch a wave. Dozens of broken surfboards ply the ceiling, and photos of the sport's early years adorn the walls. You can sit in a wooden booth next to the pool table, or out in the garden. The menu is dominated by fresh seafood (grilled outdoors for dinner), sandwiches, and Tex-Mex standards like burritos and nachos. Inventive breakfast items are also served. the satellite TV is tuned into U.S. sporting events and news, and the local post office, surf shop, and laundromat (rolled into one) are right next door. ✉ *Next to soccer field,* ☎ FAX 787–0055. AE, MC, V.

$$$ ☷ **Villas Río Mar.** Upriver from the beach on landscaped grounds, this hotel is the fanciest in town. The adobe-style bungalows have thatched roofs, white-tile floors, and cane ceilings. Rooms and bathrooms are on the small side, but each room has a porch with a hammock, wet bar with refrigerator, and mosquito-net curtains. The restaurant, with lots of plants and elegant table settings, is covered by a giant thatched roof. ✉ *Apdo. 1350–2050, San José,* ☎ *787–0052 or 257–1138,* FAX *787–0054. 40 rooms. Restaurant, bar, pool, tennis court, exercise room. AE, MC, V.*

$$–$$$ ☷ **Hacienda Barú.** These bungalows are part of a large private reserve, making them an ideal base for exploring the rain forest. The bungalows are basic, with red cement floors, bare white walls, small kitchens, sitting rooms, and two or three bedrooms (perfect for three or four people). You can linger for an hour or two on a platform in the hotel's rain-forest canopy, or stay overnight at a shelter in the heart of the forest. ✉ *Selva Mar, 1,000 m north of Dominical; Apdo. 215–8000, San Isidro, Perez Zeledon,* ☎ *771–4582 or 771–4579,* FAX *771–1903. AAA Express Mail, 1641 N.W. 79th Ave., Miami, FL 33126-1105. 8 bungalows. Restaurant, kitchenettes, hiking, horseback riding. AE, MC, V.*☜

$$–$$$ ☷ **Pacific Edge.** The forest grows right up to this small lodge, set on a
★ mountain ridge south of town, and the grounds are planted with flowers and fruit trees frequented by many a bird and butterfly. The four rustic but comfortable bungalows are surrounded by screened windows and have large, hammock-strung porches; each has a simple kitchen, which costs $5 a day to use, but the lodge's thatch-roof dining room serves great breakfasts and dinners, including some Thai dishes. The road up to Pacific Edge leaves the coastal highway 4 km (2½ mi) south of Dominical and requires a four-wheel-drive vehicle, but the hotel will pick you up in town with advance notice. Note that the reception desk closes at 6 PM. ✉ *Apdo. 531–8000, Dominical,* ☎ *381–4369, 771–4582,* FAX *771–8841. 4 bungalows. Restaurant. AE, MC, V.*

$–$$ ☷ **Cabinas San Clemente.** With a great location (just across the road from the beach) and a wide selection of accommodations, San Clemente has something for just about everyone. A two-story building overlooking a tropical garden holds the best rooms, which are spacious, bright, nicely decorated, well ventilated, and equipped with screened windows, ceiling fans, and small bathrooms. Several also have air-conditioning. Rooms in the building next door are smaller, darker, and warmer, but they're much cheaper. Management also rents several houses and some dorm-style rooms. ✉ *Across from beach,* ☎ *787–0158,* FAX *787–0055. 18 rooms. Air-conditioning, travel services. AE, MC, V.*

$ ☷ **Posada del Sol.** This little place offers simple, clean accommodations in a tranquil atmosphere at very reasonable rates. Rooms are on the ground floor of a cement building, opening onto a narrow porch with chairs and tables. In back is a little garden with a cement table and an area for washing clothes. The Costa Rican owners are friendly and helpful. ✉ *Main road,* ☎ FAX *787–0085. 4 rooms. No credit cards.*

Outdoor Activities and Sports

ECOTOURISM

Hacienda Barú (☞ Dining and Lodging, *above*) is definitely the best-organized ecotourism operation in Dominical, offering such unusual tours as a trip into the rain-forest canopy—which entails being hoisted up to a platform in the crown of a giant tree—and a night in a shelter in the woods.

INNER TUBING

A popular excursion here is an inner-tube trip down the green **Río Barú**, which flows into the Pacific south of town. Arrange a trip through your hotel or at the San Clemente Restaurant (☞ Dining and Lodging, *above*).

SPORTFISHING

Angling options range from expensive sportfishing charters to a trip in a small boat with a local fisherman. The folks at the information and room-reservation center **Tropical Waters** (⊠ 3½ km/2 mi north of Dominical on road to San Isidro, ☎ 787–0031) and the San Clemente Restaurant can arrange trips.

SURFING

Surfers have long flocked to Dominical for its consistent beach breaks. The surf shop next to the San Clemente Restaurant rents, sells, and repairs surfboards.

WATERFALLS

The easiest way to get to Nauyaca Waterfalls is with **Don Lulo** (⊠ 12 km/8 mi north of town, ☎ 771–3187). Lulo's horseback trips to the falls include swimming in the natural pools below the cascades, a light breakfast, and a hearty Costa Rican lunch. Reserve through your hotel, Tropical Waters (☞ *above*), or the San Clemente Restaurant. Alternately, traveling to the falls via the private reserve of the **Bella Vista Lodge** (☎ 771–1903) entails a longer horseback ride but takes you through much more rain forest. To hike to **Pozo Azul,** head up the road toward the Bella Vista lodges, and when it begins to climb the hill, look for a trail down to the river on your right.

Ballena Marine National Park

⑤ *20 km (12 mi) southeast of Dominical.*

One of Costa Rica's few marine parks, the Parque Nacional Marino Ballena (literally, Whale Marine National Park) protects several beaches, a small mangrove estuary, and a vast swath of ocean with rocky isles and islets. At the park's northern end, **Playa Uvita** stretches out into Punta Uvita, a long swath of sand, or *tombolo,* connecting a former island to the coast. **Playa Ballena,** to the southeast, is an even lovelier strand, backed by lush vegetation. Tiny **Playa Pinuelas** is set in a deep cove that serves as the local port. **Playa Ventanas,** just south of the park, is another beautiful beach that's popular for sea kayaking. The mountains that rise up behind all these beaches hold rain forest, waterfalls, and lots of wildlife. This is one of the only parks in the country that doesn't charge an admission fee; there are too many places to enter it.

Lodging

$$$ 🏨 **Villas Gaia.** Far from the beaten track, this tasteful lodge gives you
★ access to beaches and wilderness that few foreigners see. The hotel consists of a collection of colorful villas spread around the jungle on a ridge behind Playa Tortuga, just south of Playa Ventanas. Decorated with pastel colors and local hardwoods throughout, the villas have sliding

windows and doors and small balconies overlooking forested ravines. The blue-tile pool has an ocean view and an open-air bar. The restaurant serves some of the best food in this region. The Dutch owners rent mountain bikes and arrange horseback, mangrove, and sea-kayaking tours as well trips to Isla del Caño and Corcovado National Park. ✉ *Playa Tortuga,* ☎ *223–2240,* ☎ FAX *256–9996. 12 cabinas. Restaurant, pool. AE, MC, V.*

San Vito

6 *139 km (86 mi) southeast of San Isidro, 93 km (58 mi) northeast of Golfito.*

The little town of San Vito owes its 1952 founding to a government scheme whereby 200 Italian families were awarded grants to convert the rain forest into coffee, fruit, and cattle farms. It's now a busy, modern agricultural center near the Panama border, with little to offer travelers beyond the nearby botanical garden. Because of its proximity to the **Coto Brus Indian Reservation,** San Vito is one of the few towns in Costa Rica where you might see Ngwobe, or Guaymí, Indians, who are easy to spot thanks to the colorful dresses worn by the women.

Six kilometers (4 miles) south of San Vito is the extensive and enchanting **Wilson Botanical Garden,** 25 hillside acres converted from a coffee plantation in 1961 by U.S. landscapers Robert and Catherine Wilson. The Wilsons planted a huge collection of tropical species, including palms (an amazing 700 species), orchids, aroids, ferns, bromeliads, heliconias, and marantas, all linked by a series of neat grass paths; the gardens now hold around 3,000 native and 4,000 exotic species. The property was transferred to the Organization for Tropical Studies (OTS) in 1973, and in 1983 became part of **Amistad Biosphere Reserve** (☞ *below*). Wilson functions mainly as a research and educational center, but visitors and overnight guests are welcome; a night in the garden is a pleasure, if considerably pricier than sleeping in San Vito (☞ Dining and Lodging, *below*). ✉ *Apdo. 73–8257, San Vito,* ☎ *773–4004,* FAX *773–3665.* ▨ *$8 full day, $5 half day.* ☉ *Daily 8–4.*

OFF THE BEATEN PATH	**CIUDAD NEILY –** The 33-km (21-mi) road between San Vito and Ciudad Neily is twisting and spectacular, with views over the Coto Colorado plain to the Golfo Dulce and Osa Peninsula beyond. Much of this steep terrain is covered with tropical forest, making it an ideal route for bird-watching and photography.

Dining and Lodging

$ ✕ **Pizzeria Liliana.** A simple, small-town restaurant near San Vito's central plaza, the Liliana serves large portions of good food at remarkably low prices. Decor is basic, with wooden tables and a bar at one end, but the pastas and pizzas are delicious. If you don't feel like Italian, go for the baked chicken or the steak with mushroom sauce. ✉ *1½ blocks west of central square,* ☎ *773–3080. V.*

$$$–$$$$ ☷ **Wilson Botanical Garden.** A row of 12 rooms with hardwood floors, ★ high ceilings, and large balconies lines a ridge in the heart of this pretty garden. Four cabins have small sitting rooms and more windows but less-panoramic views. Room rates include three hearty, home-style meals and 24-hour access to the garden. Staying overnight is the easiest way to see the garden at dusk and dawn, a highly recommended experience. ✉ *Reserve through OTS, Apdo. 676–2050, San Pedro,* ☎ *240–6696 or 773–4004,* FAX *240–6783. 16 cabinas. Restaurant. AE, MC, V.*

$–$$ ☷ **Hotel El Ceibo.** Having arrived here from Italy at age two, owner Antonio Papili has some interesting stories about his early days in San

Vito. Guest rooms are pleasantly modern and clean, with foam-rubber mattresses their only drawback. Rooms at the back of the two-story buildings overlook a forested ravine. The airy restaurant, with its sloping wood ceiling, arched windows, and wine trolley, serves a solidly good mix of Italian and Costa Rican fare. All in all, it's quite a deal. ✉ *San Vito, behind Municipalidad,* ☎ 𝔽𝔸𝕏 *773–3025. 40 rooms. Restaurant, bar. MC, V.*

Shopping

In an old farmhouse on the east side of the road between San Vito and the botanical garden, a shop called **Cántaros** (✉ 3 km/2 mi south of San Vito, ☎ 773–3760) features crafts by local indigenous artisans as well as ceramics from San José artists. Profits help support the adjacent children's library.

La Amistad National Park

❼ *40 km (25 mi) northwest of San Vito.*

Comprising more than 1,980 sq km (765 sq mi), Parque Nacional La Amistad is by far the largest park in Costa Rica, yet it's actually a mere portion of the vast **Amistad Biosphere Reserve** (Reserve La Biósfera La Amistad)—a collection of protected areas stretching from southern Costa Rica into western Panama. The national park covers altitudes ranging from 700 to 11,600 ft and has an array of ecosystems that hold two-thirds of the country's vertebrate species. Unfortunately, the park is practically inaccessible, but it's a worthwhile excursion for the adventurous. The easiest part to visit is **Tres Colinas,** 23 km (14 mi) north of Potrero Grande, a small town just north of Paso Real. There's a ranger station in Potrero Grande, and from here a road suitable only for four-wheel-drive vehicles winds its bumpy way up into the mountains. Camping is allowed here; reserve space at the regional office in San Isidro (☎ 771–3155).

Golfito

❽ *339 km (211 mi) southeast of San José.*

Beautifully situated overlooking a small gulf (hence its name) and hemmed in by a steep bank of forest, Golfito has a great location and little else. The town consists of a pleasant older section and a long, ugly strip of newer buildings, dilapidated former workers' quarters, and abundant seedy bars. Golfito was a thriving banana port for several decades—United Fruit arrived in 1938—and a center of activity, with a dock that could handle 4,000 boxes of bananas per hour and elegant housing for its plantation managers. The northwestern end of town is the so-called **American Zone,** full of stilted wooden houses where the expatriate managers lived courtesy of United Fruit; these were purchased by Costa Ricans when the company departed. With several swimming pools and a golf course nearby, life here must have been more than bearable for the privileged few.

United Fruit pulled out in 1985 in response to labor disputes and rising export taxes, and Golfito promptly slipped into a state of poverty and neglect from which it has yet to recover completely. In an effort to inject some life into the town, the government declared it a duty-free port in 1990—the handful of shops called the **Depósito Libre** (Duty-Free Zone) is in a fenced compound in the former American Zone. It does much of its business the month before Christmas, at which time Costa Ricans come in droves, and it can be very difficult to find a room in Golfito.

Golfito doesn't have a beach of its own, but **Playa Cacao** is a mere five-minute boat ride across the bay. The beach has several restaurants and lodges, making it a convenient all-around option when the hotels in Golfito are full.

The hills behind Golfito are covered with the lush forest of the **Golfito National Wildlife Refuge** (Refugio Nacional de Vida Silvestre Golfito). Adjacent is **Piedras Blancas National Park** (Parque Nacional Piedras Blancas; literally, White Stones National Park), which lends the Golfito area some great birding. Follow the main road northwest through the old American Zone, past the airstrip and a housing project, and the place where a dirt road heads into the rain forest is ground zero for bird-watchers. If you have four-wheel drive, you can follow that dirt track through the heart of Piedras Blancas National Park to the community of **La Gamba,** the Esquinas Rain Forest Lodge, and Villa Briceño, on the Pan-American Highway. This back route can cut miles off a trip to or from the north, and it passes through some gorgeous wilderness.

Farther into the Golfo Dulce, accessible by boat, is **Casa Orquideas** (✉ Apdo. 69, Golfito), a mass of ornamental plants, palms, bromeliads, heliconias, cycads, orchids, and flowering gingers tended with care by American owners Ron and Trudy MacAllister. A two-hour tour (Saturday through Thursday at 8:30 AM) includes touching, tasting, and smelling, plus spotting toucans and hummingbirds. A cabin on the grounds rents expensive ($$$$) rooms; the price includes transport from Golfito.

Lodging

$$$$ 🕾 **Caña Blanca Beach and Rain Forest Lodge.** Don't be put off by the resident scarlet macaw's habit of swooping close to your head; it's harmless. Spread out on a truly idyllic beach on a cove in the lush, private Caña Blanca reserve are three open-air cabins and a lodge run by Bay Area natives Earl and Carol Crews. The cabins are made entirely of fine wood and have double or single beds, built-in benches, and lights covered with wicker, Asian-style paper, and the occasional shell. The package includes transport from Puerto Jiménez or Golfito, all drinks, three high-class meals, and a daily tour through the reserve, which is a verdant primary and secondary forest with cocoa and breadfruit trees and birds and mammals aplenty. You can also arrange individual day hikes for about $5, or $25 with transport. This place fills up, so reserve far in advance. ✉ *Puerto Jiménez, Península de Osa, 30 mins by boat from Golfito in Golfo Dulce,* ☎ *735–5062 or 383–5707,* FAX *735–5043. 3 cabins. Restaurant, bar, hiking, boating. Subject to closing periodically; call in advance.*

$$–$$$ 🕾 **Hotel Las Gaviotas.** Just south of town on the water's edge, this hotel has wonderful views over the inner gulf. Rooms have terra-cotta floors, teak furniture, fans and air-conditioning, and outside each one is a small veranda with two chairs overlooking the well-tended tropical gardens and the shimmering ocean beyond. An open-air restaurant looks onto the pool, whose terrace is barely divided from the sea. ✉ *Playa Tortuga, Apdo. 12, Golfito,* ☎ *775–0062,* FAX *775–0544. 18 rooms, 3 suites. Restaurant, bar, air-conditioning, pool. AE, DC, MC, V.*

Outdoor Activities and Sports
SPORTFISHING
Fishing is great in the waters off Golfito, either in the Golfo Dulce or out in the open ocean. The open ocean holds plenty of sailfish, marlin, and roosterfish during the dry months, as well as dolphin, tuna, and wahoo during the rainy season; there's excellent bottom fishing any time of year. Contact **Roy Ventura** (☞ Playa Zancudo, *below*).

CRUISING THE PACIFIC COAST

"**A** WOODPECKER," WHISPERED Max, binoculars trained on a tree wrapped with strangler figs and bromeliads. Cicadas chanted a hypnotic mantra, broken by the throaty call of the three-wattled bellbird and the crashing of waves. A morpho butterfly floated by, winking atomic blue. "No, it's a branch," Max sighed sheepishly, inspiring a collective chuckle.

Led by a naturalist guide, this group of 12 had sped to the beach in a dinghy at 6 AM for a hike through Caña Blanca (☞ Golfito, *above*), a privately owned patch of lush tropical jungle. They were part of an eco-adventure tour aboard the 185-ft *Temptress Explorer*, which nudges right up to the pristine islands, funky towns, and rain forests of the Pacific coast, some too remote for roads. From the shore, excellent rain-forest hikes, horseback riding, bird-watching, snorkeling, sea kayaking, and a visit to a luxuriant botanical garden are easily accessible.

On the trails, friendly Tico guides point out fascinating organisms in the forest—a cavalcade of leaf-cutter ants, the coveted treasure of a cacoa tree—and such critters as the scarlet macaw and white-faced Capuchin monkey. At sunset, drinks sprouting paper umbrellas are shared amid lively chatter and folks like Max—happy that the other branch wasn't a poisonous snake. For more information, *see* **Temptress Adventure Cruises** *in* The Southern Pacific Coast A to Z, *below,* and Cruise Travel *in* Smart Travel Tips A to Z.

Shopping

Most Costa Rican travelers in Golfito are drawn by duty-free bargains on such imported items as TV sets, stereos, linens, and tires. You can shop in the **Depósito Libre,** but you won't find things too much cheaper than they are back home. To buy anything in the Depósito you have to spend the night, which means you register in the afternoon with your passport and shop the next morning. Shopping is sheer madness in December.

Playa Zancudo

9 *32 km (20 mi) south of Golfito.*

Playa Zancudo, a long, palm-lined beach fronting the tiny fishing village of Zancudo, is accessible by car or by boat, the latter of which you can hire at the municipal dock in Golfito. Zancudo has a good surf break, but it's nothing compared with Playa Pavones (☞ *below*). There are also some good swimming areas, and if you get tired of playing in the surf and sand you can arrange a boat trip to the nearby mangrove estuary to see birds and crocodiles. Zancudo is also home to the area's best sportfishing operation, headquartered at Roy's Zancudo Lodge (☞ *below*).

Lodging

$$–$$$ 🏨 **Roy's Zancudo Lodge.** Most people who stay at Roy's are anglers on all-inclusive sportfishing packages, but the hotel is a good choice even if you've never caught anything more exciting than a cold. It's right on the beach, its ample, verdant grounds surrounding a pool and an open-air restaurant that serves buffet meals. Guest rooms have hardwood floors, firm beds, ceiling fans, air-conditioning, and ocean views. You can rent lodgings on their own, or with three meals and

open bar included. ✉ *Playa Zancudo, Apdo. 41, Zancudo,* ☎ *776–0008,* FAX *776–0011. 10 rooms, 4 cabins. Restaurant, bar, air-conditioning, kitchenettes, pool. DC, V.* ✇

$$ 🏨 **Cabinas Sol y Mar.** This group of beachside cabins is a 20-minute walk south of where you disembark from the Golfito boat. Some of the rooms were designed to resemble polyhedral space modules, with elegant charcoal-clay tiles, wooden beds, and white canvas sofas. People love the large, stone-and-tile bathrooms with skylights. The staff can arrange boat transportation from the dock if you call ahead. ✉ *Playa Zancudo, Apdo. 87, Golfito,* ☎ *776–0014,* FAX *776–0015. 5 cabinas, 1 house. Restaurant, bar. V.* ✇

Outdoor Activities and Sports
SPORTFISHING

If you've got your own gear, you can do some good shore fishing from the beach or the mouth of the mangrove estuary, or hire one of the local boats to take you out into the gulf. **Roy Ventura** (☞ Roy's Zancudo Lodge, *above*) runs the best charter operation in the area, with 10 boats ranging in length from 22 to 32 ft. Packages include room, food, and drink, and you can arrange to be picked up in Golfito or Puerto Jiménez.

Playa Pavones

⑩ *45 km (28 mi) south of Golfito.*

On the southern edge of the mouth of Golfo Dulce stands Pavones, a windswept beach town at the end of a dirt road. Famous among surfers for having one of the longest waves in the world, the town also has pristine beaches and virgin rain forest in its favor. It's not close to anything in particular, but the rain forest, beaches, horseback riding, and a small arboretum make it a worthwhile destination for adventurous types.

Lodging

$$$$ 🏨 **Tiskita Jungle Lodge.** Peter Aspinall has planted 100 different fruit trees from all over the world as a kind of research exercise into alternative exports. For you he has built wooden cabins on stilts, surrounded by screens and lush vegetation, and equipped with rustic furniture and open bathrooms from which you can look right out at the fauna. Trails invite you to explore the jungle and the wide variety of wildlife lured by the fruit trees' fine pickings. Most people fly here, but you can reach the lodge with a four-wheel-drive vehicle. ✉ *Costa Rica Sun Tours, 4 km (2½ mi) north of Pavones, Apdo. 1195–1250, Escazú,* ☎ *255–2011,* ☎ FAX *233–6890. 16 cabinas. Dining room, pool, hiking, horseback riding, snorkeling. AE, DC, MC, V. Closed Sept.–Oct.* ✇

THE OSA PENINSULA

Some of Costa Rica's most breathtaking scenery and wildlife thrives on the Osa Peninsula, one-third of which is covered by Corcovado National Park. A paradise for backpackers, who can hike into the park on any of three routes, Corcovado also works for day trips from nearby nature lodges, most of which lie within private preserves that are home for much of the same wildlife you might see in the park. And to complement the peninsula's lush forests and pristine beaches, the sea around it offers great sportfishing and skin diving.

En Route   If you're driving from San José, you've got an eight-hour trip: Take the Pan-American Highway (CA2) south to Piedras Blancas, and turn right for the rough road into the Osa Peninsula.

Puerto Jiménez

⓫ *127 km (79 mi) west of Golfito, 364 km (226 mi) southeast of San José.*

There isn't much to write home about in Puerto Jiménez, but it's the largest town on the Osa Peninsula and can make a convenient base for exploring some of the nearby wilderness. You won't be dodging any pigeons in this urban center, but you are likely to see scarlet macaws flying noisily over the rooftops or perching in the Indian almond trees. Most people spend a night here before or after visiting Corcovado National Park (☞ *below*), as Puerto Jiménez has the best access to the park's two main trailheads. The town also lies just 40 minutes by car from spectacular Cabo Matapalo (☞ *below*), where virgin rain forest meets the sea at a rocky point.

The headquarters of the **National Parks Service** (☎ 735–5440) are at the southern end of town, opposite the Texaco gas station. Check in here to enter Corcovado, or just to inquire about hiking routes and trail conditions. In the dry season, call the same number well ahead of time to reserve camping space, meals, or accommodations at the **Sirena ranger station**. You may be asked to deposit money into the Environment Ministry's account in the Banco Nacional to reserve space.

Dining and Lodging

$ ✕▥ **Restaurante Carolina.** It doesn't look like much, but this simple
★   restaurant in the heart of Puerto Jiménez serves what is widely considered the best food in town, especially fresh seafood. The five small guest rooms in back make this a good rest stop for backpackers entering or leaving Corcovado; rooms are your basic cement boxes, with private bathrooms and cold running water, but they're clean and convenient. The truck to Carate leaves daily from the market next door. ⊠ *Center of town, 2 blocks south of soccer field,* ☎ *735–5185. 5 rooms. No credit cards.*

$–$$ ▥ **Cabinas Los Manglares.** Though fairly basic, this small lodge provides the most comfortable accommodations in Puerto Jiménez proper, and you can see an amazing amount of wildlife in the surrounding mangrove forest. Cabins have tile floors, pastel-color walls, fans, and simple wooden furniture. Five stand by the parking lot, and five are scattered around a lawn on the other side of the mangroves, which are crossed by a catwalk. The thatch-roof restaurant serves an unexciting selection of meat and seafood. ⊠ *Puerto Jiménez, across from the airport,* ☎ *735–5705,* ℻ *735–5002. 10 cabins. Restaurant, bar. No credit cards.*

Outdoor Activities and Sports

HIKING

A truck carries hikers to **Carate** and its nearby beach from the Mini Mercado El Tigre every morning at 6 AM. If you have four-wheel drive, it's just a 30-minute ride to **Dos Brazos** and the Tigre sector of the park, which few hikers explore.

RAFTING AND SEA KAYAKING

Hire a taxi to the **Río Rincón,** near Los Patos. Puerto Jiménez is a good base for boat or sea-kayaking trips on the **Golfo Dulce** and the nearby mangrove rivers and estuaries.

Corcovado National Park

⓬ *From Puerto Jiménez: 1-hr four-wheel drive to Carate plus 20-min walk to La Leona; 20-min drive to Río Rincón plus 2- to 3-hr hike to Los Patos.*

Comprising 435 sq km (168 sq mi), the Parque Nacional Corcovado is one of the largest and wildest protected areas in Costa Rica (☞ Chapter 9). Much of the park is covered with virgin rain forest, where massive *espavel* and *nazareno* trees tower over the trails, thick lianas hang from the branches, and animals such as toucans, spider monkeys, scarlet macaws, and poison dart frogs abound. There are three entrances: San Pedrillo to the north, Los Patos to the east, and La Leona to the south. The park has no roads, however, and the roads that approach it are dirt tracks that require four-wheel drive most of the year. Travelers often arrive by boat on day trips from the nature lodges in Drake Bay (☞ *below*), but the best way to explore the park is to sling on a backpack and hike into the wilds.

Camping

$$$ **Corcovado Lodge Tent Camp.** This rustic lodge and the surrounding 400-
★   acre forest reserve are owned by Costa Rica Expeditions. The 20 tents, each with two single beds, are pitched on wooden platforms just off the beach. Bathrooms are communal, and a bar-restaurant serves family-style meals. Resident naturalist guides will lead you through the jungle and hoist you into the forest canopy via a platform 100 ft high. Bring a flashlight (there's electricity only a few hours each day) and insect repellent. Charter planes leave San José for Carate, a 20-minute walk from here, several times a week, but it's cheaper to fly to Puerto Jiménez and take a cab to Carate. ✉ *Apdo. 6941–1000, San José,* ☎ *222–0333,* 🖷 *257–1665. 20 tents. Restaurant, bar. AE, MC, V.* ⬡

Outdoor Activities and Sports

HIKING

There are three hiking routes to Corcovado, two beginning near Puerto Jiménez and the other in Drake Bay, which follows the coast down to San Pedrillo. You can hire a taxi in Puerto Jiménez for the Los Patos trailhead, or at least to the first crossing of the Río Rincón (from which you hike a few miles upriver to the trailhead). The beach route, via La Leona, starts in Carate, about 37 km (23 mi) southwest of Puerto Jiménez. A four-wheel-drive truck carries hikers to Carate every day from Puerto Jiménez, departing at 6 AM and returning at 10:30 AM; for information call the **Mini Mercado El Tigre** (☎ 735–5075) in Puerto Jiménez.

Cabo Matapalo

⓭ *16 km (10 mi) south of Puerto Jiménez.*

The southern tip of the Osa Peninsula retains the kind of natural beauty that people travel halfway across the country to experience. From its ridges you can look out on the blue Pacific Ocean, sometimes spotting schools of dolphin and whales in the distance. The forest is tall and dense, its giant trees draped with thick lianas and its branches covered with aerial gardens of bromeliads and orchids. The name Cabo Matapalo means "Cape Strangler Fig," a reference to the fig trees that germinate in the branches of other trees and eventually grow to smother them with their roots and branches. Strangler figs are common in this area, as they are nearly everywhere else in the country, but Matapalo's greatest attractions are its rarer species, such as the brilliant scarlet macaw and the *gallinazo* tree, which bursts into yellow blossom as the rainy season draws to an close.

A forested ridge extends east from Corcovado down to Matapalo, where the foliage clings to almost-vertical slopes and waves crash against the black rocks below. This continuous forest corridor is protected within a series of private preserves, which means that Cabo Matapalo has most of the same wildlife as the national park—even the big cats. Most of the point itself lies within the private reserves of the area's two main hotels, and that forest is crisscrossed by footpaths, some of which head to tranquil beaches or to waterfalls that pour into small pools.

Lodging

$$$$ 🏨 **Bosque del Cabo.** The 200-acre grounds of this nature lodge, more
★   than half of them covered with primary forest and home to all kinds of wild critters (the lodge's name means "Forest of the Cape"), encompass the tip of Capo Matapalo. Comfortably rustic bungalows are scattered along the edge of a wide lawn, affording breathtaking views of the ocean through the foliage. Each bungalow is slightly different, but all have wood floors, private baths, solar energy, and porches with hammocks. Delicious meals are served family-style in a simple, open-air restaurant. Trails wind down through the forest to two secluded beaches and a waterfall with a natural swimming pool; other distractions include sport-fishing, sea kayaking, bird-watching, and horseback riding. ✉ *Matapalo, Apdo. 15, Puerto Jiménez,* ☎ FAX *735–5206. 8 bungalows. Restaurant, pool. V.*

$$$$ 🏨 **Lapa Ríos.** Spread along a ridge in the jungle, within its own nature
★   reserve, Lapa Ríos is more than just one of Costa Rica's finest hotels—it's part of an innovative conservation project engineered by owners Karen and John Lewis to preserve endangered wildlife. You can explore the pristine wilderness on foot or on horseback, accompanied by one of several resident naturalist guides, but you're quite likely to spot toucans, sloths, iguanas, and other animals from the restaurant and bungalows themselves. The spacious, airy villas, built of local hardwood and embellished with thatched roofs, four-poster beds draped with mosquito nets, and large balconies, suggest how Tarzan might live on Bill Gates's budget. The restaurant's food is excellent. ✉ *Apdo. 100, Puerto Jiménez,* ☎ *735–5130,* FAX *735–5179. Box 025216, SJO 706, Miami, FL 33102-5216. 14 bungalows. Restaurant, bar, pool, hiking, horseback riding. AE, MC, V.* 🐾

Outdoor Activities and Sports

WATER SPORTS

On the eastern side of the point, waves break over a platform that creates a perfect right, drawing surfers from far and wide. This area also has excellent sea kayaking, and both Lapa Ríos and Bosque del Cabo can arrange horseback excursions, guided tours to Corcovado, or deep-sea fishing trips.

Drake Bay

⓮   *10 km (6 mi) north of Corcovado, 40 km (25 mi) southwest of Palmar Sur.*

Bahía Drake was named after Sir Francis Drake (1540–96), the British explorer who is supposed to have anchored here more than four centuries ago. The rugged coast that stretches south from the mouth of the Río Sierpe to Corcovado probably doesn't look much different than it did in Drake's day: small beaches backed by thick jungle, cropped by rocky points, and overlooking dark, igneous islets. The tiny villages and nature lodges scattered along the coast are hemmed in by the rain forest, which is home to troops of monkeys, inconspicuous sloths, striking scarlet macaws, and hundreds of other bird species.

A trip here is a real tropical adventure, with plenty of hiking and some rough boat rides. Most people reach this isolated area by boat via the Río Sierpe, but direct flights are now available, and backpackers occasionally hike north out of Corcovado (two hours from Marenco, four from Drake Bay). Another option is to come here with **Temptress Adventure Cruises,** whose 185-ft Costa Rican ship runs three-, four-, and seven-night nature trips to Drake Bay, Corcovado, and Isla del Caño (☞ The Southern Pacific Coast A to Z, *below,* and Close-Up: Cruising the Pacific Coast, *above*); a four-day cruise sails from Golfito.

The town of **Drake,** scattered along the bay, has the cheapest accommodations, and there are several nature lodges—Drake Bay Wilderness Camp, Aguila de Osa Inn, and La Paloma Lodge—near the Río Agujitas on the bay's southern end (☞ Lodging, *below*), all of which offer comprehensive packages including trips to Corcovado and Isla del Caño as well as horseback tours, scuba dives, and deep-sea fishing trips. Lodges farther south, such as the Marenco Beach and Rainforest Lodge and Casa Corcovado (☞ *below*), offer the same excursions from even wilder settings.

Lodging

All package tours mentioned in the reviews below include round-trip transportation from San José.

$$$$ 🏠 **Aguila de Osa Inn.** Just because you're out in the woods doesn't mean you have to rough it. In the tradition of great fishing lodges, this inn (the "Eagle of Osa") offers plenty of comfort and good food. Sportfishing is the specialty—the inn has a four-boat fleet and extensive tackle room—but scuba diving, snorkeling, and other excursions are easily arranged. The spacious rooms are in a series of cement buildings spread along a ridge, with views of Drake Bay through the bamboo and unusual details like hand-carved doors and large tile baths. Meals centered on fish, perhaps one you caught, are served in a handsome thatch-roof restaurant. ⊠ *Apdo. 10486–1000, San José,* ☎ *232–7722,* FAX *296–2190. 14 rooms. Restaurant, horseback riding, fishing. No credit cards. Closed Oct.* 🐾

$$$$ 🏠 **Casa Corcovado.** The advantage to this place is its parkside location: since a trail leads right into Corcovado National Park from here, you can explore its forests hours before anyone else arrives if you get moving early enough. Guest rooms are spread around a garden surrounded by the rain forest, into which trails lead, and there's a sunset bar down the hill. The modern cement rooms have bright tile floors, large bathrooms, screened walls, and ceiling fans. There's plenty of room for relaxation: you can navigate a tropical cocktail at the second bar, overlooking the jungle and a small pool, or plot your next move from one of the hammocks or chairs on the beach below. ⊠ *Apdo. 1482-1250, Escazú, northern border of Corcovado,* ☎ *256–3181,* FAX *256–7409. 10 rooms. 2 bars, dining room, pool, hiking, horseback riding, beach, snorkeling, boating. AE, MC, V. Closed Sept.–mid-Nov.* 🐾

$$$$ 🏠 **La Paloma Lodge.** Sweeping views and a sense of jungle seclusion
★   make these deluxe bungalows the best in the area. Scattered on a forested hill south of Drake Bay, the airy wooden villas have bedroom lofts and large porches complete with hammocks. The smaller standard rooms, not nearly as nice, are farther up the hill. The tiled pool, overlooking forest and ocean, is an important plus, and the hotel offers skin diving and trips to Corcovado and Isla del Caño. The restaurant serves guests only. ⊠ *Apdo. 97–4005, San Antonio de Belen, Heredia,* ☎ *239–2801,* FAX *239–0954. 4 rooms, 5 bungalows. Restaurant, pool, horseback riding, fishing. MC, V.* 🐾

$$$$ 🏠 **Marenco Beach and Rainforest Lodge.** Bordering a wildlife refuge
★   that protects almost 52 sq km (20 sq mi) of rain forest along the coast between Drake Bay and Corcovado National Park, Marenco was one of Costa Rica's first ecotourism enterprises. Resident biologist guides interpret the wonders of tropical nature on a series of well-marked trails

through the forest. Overlooking the forest and ocean from a high ridge are breezy, wooden bungalows with large balconies; some smaller rooms; and an open-air dining hall. It's a bit rustic—there's no hot water—but the contact with nature can't be topped. All-inclusive packages include excursions to Corcovado and Isla del Caño. ⊠ *Apdo. 4025–1000, San José, 11 km (7 mi) southwest of Drake Bay,* ☎ *258–1919,* FAX *255–1346. 25 rooms. Restaurant, hiking, horseback riding, beach, snorkeling. MC, V.*

$$$–$$$$ 🏕 **Drake Bay Wilderness Camp.** Spread over a grassy point between the Río Agujitas and the ocean, at the southern end of the bay, the Wilderness Camp is one of the best deals around, especially if you stay for a while. The rooms are in cement buildings scattered around manicured grounds; inside, each has tile floors, a ceiling fan, and a small porch. The tent cabins (large tents on cement platforms) share bath facilities and are a bit cramped, but they're considerably less expensive and have great ocean views. Most guests come here to see the rain forest, but you can also opt for scuba diving, sportfishing, horseback riding, canoeing, and sea kayaking. Charter flights direct to Drake Bay make this lodge the quickest, easiest place to reach. ⊠ *Apdo. 98–8150, Palmar Norte,* ☎ *256–7394,* ☎ FAX *770–8012,* FAX *221–4948. 20 rooms, 5 tent cabins without bath. Restaurant, bar, pool, horseback riding, boating, fishing. MC, V.* 🐾

Isla del Caño

⑮ *19 km (12 mi) off Osa Peninsula, due west of Drake Bay.*

Most of this uninhabited isle (2½ sq km, or 1 sq mi) and its biological reserve are covered in evergreen forest comprising fig, locust, and rubber trees. Coastal Indians used it as a burial ground, and the numerous bits and pieces unearthed here have prompted archaeologists to speculate about pre-Columbian long-distance maritime trade. The island's main attraction now is the ocean around it, which offers superb scuba diving and snorkeling. The snorkeling is excellent around the rocky points flanking the island's main beach; if you're a certified diver, you'll want to explore Bajo del Diablo and Paraiso, where you're guaranteed to encounter thousands of good-size fish. Lodges in Drake Bay (☞ *above*) offer day trips here.

THE SOUTHERN PACIFIC COAST A TO Z

Arriving and Departing

By Boat
Drake Bay is usually connected by boat to Sierpe, south of Palmar Norte, but you can also arrange direct boat trips from Dominical (contact Tropical Waters, ☎ 232–6672) or from **Villas Gaia,** near Ballena Marine National Park.

By Bus
GENERAL VALLEY
Musoc buses from San José (⊠ C. 16 and Avdas. 1 and 3, ☎ 222–2422) to San Isidro, a three-hour trip, depart almost every hour between 5:30 AM and 5 PM, returning at the same times. **Transportes Blanco** buses from San Isidro to Dominical (☎ 771–4744 or, in San José, 257–2141) leave a point 125 m east of the church at 7 AM, 9 AM, 1:30 PM, and 4 PM. Buses to Ballena Marine National Park via Quepos leave San José's Coca-Cola Station daily (a six-hr trip) at 5:30 AM and 3 PM, returning at 5:30 AM and 2 PM.

Tracopa-Alfaro buses leave San José (Calle 14 between Avenidas 3 and 5) for the eight-hour trip to Golfito daily at 7 AM and 3 PM, returning at 5 AM and 1 PM. Tracopa buses from San José (also Calle 14 between Avenidas 3 and 5) to San Vito, a seven-hour trip, leave daily at 5:45 AM, 8:15 AM, 11:30 AM, and 2:45 PM.

OSA PENINSULA

Transportes Blanco-Lobo (☎ 257–4121) buses from San José to Puerto Jiménez, a nine-hour trip, leave Calle 12 between Avenidas 7 and 9 at noon and return at 5 AM and 11 AM. Tracopa Alfaro buses from San José to Palmar Norte (a six-hr trip) depart from Calle 14 between Avenidas 5 and 7 daily at 5, 7, and 10 AM and 1 and 2:30 PM; buses to Golfito, Puerto Jiménez, and San Vito also stop here. In Palmar Norte, you can hire a taxi to Sierpe, the port for boats to Drake Bay.

By Car

The quickest way to reach the Costanera, or coastal highway, which leads past Jacó and Quepos (☞ Chapter 5) to Dominical and the rest of the southern Pacific zone, is to take the Carretera Interamericana (Pan-American Highway, CA1) west past the airport to the turnoff for Atenas, turn left, and drive through Atenas to Orotina, where you head south on the coastal highway. You can also get to this region by taking the Pan-American Highway south (CA2) past Cartago and over the Cerro de la Muerte—where you'll pass the turnoff for San Gerardo de Dota—to San Isidro, Valle de El General, and the Osa Peninsula. Foggy conditions atop Cerro de la Muerte make it best to cross the mountains as early in the day as possible.

By Plane

Sansa (✉ C. 42 between Avdas. 3 and 5, San José, ☎ 506/221–9414 or 506/441–8035, FAX 506/255–2176) has several flights daily from San José to Golfito and some daily flights to Palmar Sur (for Drake Bay), Puerto Jiménez, and Coto 47 (for Panama). Travelair (✉ Aeropuerto Tobias Bolaños, Pavas, ☎ 220–3054, FAX 506/220–0413) has daily flights to Golfito, Palmar Sur, and Puerto Jiménez. Both airlines also have daily flights from Quepos to Palmar Sur—the quickest way to move between the central (☞ Chapter 5) and southern Pacific coasts. Costa Rica Expeditions (☎ 222–0333, FAX 257–1665) runs several charter flights weekly to Carate, a 40-minute hike from the company's Corcovado Tent Camp. Drake Bay Wilderness Camp (☎ FAX 770–8012) runs its own daily charter flights from Drake Bay.

Getting Around

By Boat

A small ferry crosses the Golfo Dulce, leaving Puerto Jiménez daily at 6 AM and returning from Golfito at 11:30 AM. Boat transport to Zancudo or the more distant Pavones can be arranged through the Coconut Cafe (✉ Golfito, ☎ 775–0518), which doubles as a general information center and Internet café. Drake Bay is usually accessed by boat from Sierpe, south of Palmar Norte. Travel between the Drake Bay lodges, Corcovado, and Isla del Caño is most commonly accomplished in small boats owned by the major lodges.

By Bus

GENERAL VALLEY

Buses run by Transportes Blanco (☎ 771–2550) leave San Isidro for the one-hour trip to Dominical daily at 5:30 and 7 AM and 1:30 and 3 PM; and for San Gerardo de Rivas, the trailhead for Chirripó, at 5 AM and 2 PM.

OSA PENINSULA

From San Isidro, buses leave for the five-hour trip to Puerto Jiménez at 9 AM and 3 PM. A truck for hikers leaves Puerto Jiménez daily at 6 AM for Carate, returning at 10:30 AM.

By Car

The coastal highway gets a bit rough south of Dominical, but it can take you all the way to Palmar Sur on the Pan-American Highway (CA2). The Pan-American Highway also has some potholes, but most of it is paved. From San Isidro, good roads head northeast to San Gerardo de Rivas and west to Dominical. The Pan-American Highway continues southeast from San Isidro to the turnoffs for San Vito, Puerto Jiménez, and Golfito before reaching Paso Canoas and the border of Panama. The turnoff for the back road to Golfito (four-wheel drive only) is on the right at Villa Briceño; look for signs to La Gamba and the Esquinas lodge. The road from the Pan-American Highway into the Osa Peninsula was in rough shape at press time; four-wheel drive is recommended.

By Plane

Aerotaxi Alfa Romeo (☎ 735–5178, FAX 735–5112) offers charter flights to Carate, Drake Bay, Puerto Jiménez, Sirena ranger station (☞ Puerto Jiménez, *above*), Tiskita Jungle Lodge (☞ Playa Pavones, *above*), and anywhere else you want to go. You have to charter the whole plane, which is expensive, so it's best to fill it with the maximum capacity of five.

Contacts and Resources

Car Rentals

See Contacts and Resources *in* San José A to Z, Chapter 1.

Emergencies

Ambulance (☎ 221–5818). **Fire** (☎ 118). **Police** (☎ 117 in towns; 127 in rural areas). **Traffic Police** (☎ 227–8030).

Guided Tours

CRUISES

Temptress Adventure Cruises (✉ 351 N.W. LeJeune Rd., Penthouse 6, Miami, FL 33126, ☎ 305/643–4040, FAX 305/643–6438) runs three-, four-, and seven-day adventure cruises on the *Temptress Explorer* that visit Corcovado National Park, Drake Bay, Isla del Caño, and Manuel Antonio National Park (☞ Chapter 5). Activities include hiking through national parks and refuges, bird-watching, nature walks, snorkeling, horseback riding, fishing, and diving accompanied by excellent naturalist guides (☞ Close-Up: Cruising the Pacific Coast, *above*). The ship sails from Puntarenas (three- or seven-day cruises) and Golfito (four-day cruises), with transport to and from the airport in San José. Contact Temptress directly or reserve through **Cruceros del Sur** (✉ Across from Colegio Los Angeles, Sabana Norte, San José, ☎ 232–6672, FAX 220–2103), which also offers 10-day skin-diving expeditions to distant Coco Island on the *Okeanos Agressor.* The smaller vessel **Undersea Hunter** (☎ 228–6535, FAX 298–7334) makes similar dive trips to Coco Island.

HIKES

Brunca Tours (☎ 771–3100) leads hikes and nature tours to Chirripó and other areas. In Dominical, **Hacienda Barú** (✉ 1 km/½ mi north of Dominical, ☎ 771–4582) offers a number of guided hikes through the rain forest. **Ecole Travel** (✉ C. 7 between Avdas. Central and 1, San José, ☎ 223–2240, FAX 223–4128) runs inexpensive guided hikes into Chirripó and Corcovado national parks.

From San José, **Costa Rica Sun Tours** (⊠ C. 36 at Avda. 4, San José, ☎ 255–2011, FAX 233–6890) runs tours to its remote Tiskita Jungle Lodge. **Costa Rica Expeditions** (⊠ Avda. 3 at C. Central, San José, ☎ 222–0333, FAX 257–1665) runs guided tours to its Corcovado Tent Camp (☞ Corcovado National Park, *above*).

In Puerto Jiménez, **Escondido Trex** (⊠ Restaurante Carolina, Apdo. 9, Puerto Jiménez, ☎ 735–5210) organizes sea-kayaking tours that range from a sunset paddle to a one-week trip around the entire Golfo Dulce. Other adventures include rappelling down waterfalls.

Visitor Information

The tourist office in San José (☞ San José A to Z, Chapter 1) has information on the southern Pacific coast. In Dominical, contact **Tropical Waters** (⊠ 3½ km/2 mi north of Dominical on road to San Isidro, ☎ 787–0031).

7 THE ATLANTIC LOWLANDS AND CARIBBEAN COAST

Inhabited by African-Caribbean, Spanish, and indigenous peoples, the Atlantic lowlands mix wild outposts, banana and cacao plantations, and dense primary jungle. Too hot and humid to be anything but laid-back, they're a world unto themselves. Along the Caribbean coast, it's turbulent rivers, verdant national parks, easy-going villages, and coral-fringed beaches.

D OMINATED BY CLOUD FORESTS, sprawling banana plantations, and thick tropical jungle, the Atlantic lowlands lie in the provinces of Heredia and Limó on the Caribbean Sea. This expansive, largely untamed region stretches from the eastern slope of the Cordillera Central up to the Sarapiquí area northeast of San José (home to the private Rara Avis and La Selva reserves), east through banana-growing country, and down to the pristine beaches at Cahuita and Puerto Viejo de Limón on the southern Caribbean coast. The region also stretches north to the Nicaraguan border, encompassing the coastal jungles and canals of Tortuguero National Park and Barra del Colorado Wildlife Refuge, on whose beaches turtles arrive by the thousands to lay their eggs. The occasional caiman can be spotted here, sunning on a bank or drifting like a log down a jungle waterway; and farther north still, sportfishing fans will find tarpon and snook to detain them off the shores of Barra del Colorado.

Updated by
Brad Weiss

Roughly a third of the people in Limón province are Afro-Caribbeans, descendants of early-19th-century turtle fishermen and the West Indians who arrived in the late 19th century to build the Atlantic Railroad and remained to work on banana and cacao plantations. Some 4,000 Jamaicans are reputed to have died of yellow fever, malaria, and snakebites during construction of the first 40 km (25 mi) of railroad to San José. They were paid relatively well, however, and gradually their lot improved: By the 1930s many had obtained their own small plots of land, and when the price of cacao rose in the 1950s they emerged as comfortable landowners employing landless, migrant Hispanics. Until the Civil War of 1948, Afro-Caribbeans were forbidden from crossing into the Central Valley lest they upset the country's racial balance, and they were thus prevented from following work when United Fruit abandoned many of its blight-ridden plantations in the 1930s for green-field sites on the Pacific plain. Although Jamaicans brought some aspects of British colonial culture with them, such as cricket and the maypole dance, these habits have long since given way to reggae and salsa, soccer and baseball. Many Atlantic-coast Ticos are bilingual, speaking fluent English and Spanish, and around Puerto Viejo de Limón you may even hear some phrases derived from the language of the indigenous peoples, among them the Kekóldi, the Bribri, and the Cabecar.

A note on crime: in the 1990s, some of the cocaine flowing from Latin America into the United States spilled into the area near Puerto Viejo de Limón and Cahuita, resulting in a drug-related crime problem. Up near the Nicaraguan border, Nicaraguan refugees have become rather aggressive in their efforts to squat on and claim land, some belonging to American and European investors. Costa Rica is still far safer for travelers than most countries, but the dangers are real: two Europeans were kidnapped in 1996. (Ransoms were paid, and no one was hurt in the end.) If you're eager to experience Costa Rica's Caribbean beaches and jungles but want to avoid the potentially more dangerous towns, take a boat or plane directly to Tortuguero or Barra del Colorado, or drive south through Puerto Viejo de Limón to savor the seaside jungle experience holed up in one of the many lodges, hotels, and tent camps along the road between Puerto Viejo de Limón and Manzanillo.

Pleasures and Pastimes

Dining

A flurry of new upscale hotels, lodges, and restaurants has introduced this region to an even more varied international cuisine. Still, much of the cooking along the Caribbean coast has its roots in old Jamaican

recipes. *Rondon,* for example, is a traditional Jamaican stew that requires hours of preparation. Rice and beans are flavored with coconut; meat is fried with hot spices to make *paties* (pies); and fish or
meat, yams, plantains, breadfruit, peppers, and spices are boiled in coconut milk. Johnnycakes and *panbón* (a heavy, spicy fruit bread) are
popular baked goods. Various medicinal herbal teas are ubiquitous in
the lowlands. Seafood is, of course, readily available, as is a wide variety of fresh fruit.

Fishing
World-class tarpon and snook attract serious sportfishermen to the northern Caribbean shore in and off the Tortuguero and Barra del Colorado
national parks. The months between January and May are best for tarpon, August through November for snook.

Hiking and Jungle Boating
From the beach hikes of Cahuita National Park to the more leisurely
jungle-boat cruises arranged by the lodges near Tortuguero National
Park, opportunities for plunging into tropical jungle and rain forest
abound in the Atlantic lowlands. Farther inland, on the eastern slope
of the mountains, Braulio Carrillo's cloud- and rain-forested mountains offer scenic trails, and the private lowland reserves of La Selva
and Rara Avis beckon with excellent jungle terrain. In the southeastern part of this region, the remote and little-visited Hitoy Cerere Biological Reserve lays out both easy and difficult hiking trails as the jungle
climbs into the hills of the Talamanca range; look for waterfalls, swimming holes, and an encyclopedic variety of Costa Rican flora and
fauna.

Lodging
The Atlantic lowlands have little in the way of luxury hotels, though
a number of relatively upscale, self-proclaimed ecotourist lodges and
some other, pricier accommodations have opened along the highway
south of Puerto Limón and (especially) on the beach road south of Puerto
Viejo de Limón. Most lodgings here are rustic *cabinas* (cottages) or nature lodges. Often isolated in the jungle—accessible only by boat or
strenuous hike—the lodges can be rough, no-frills places or can verge
on the luxurious. Because it's hard to haul supplies to these places, you'll
pay a hefty price if you insist on hot showers and cold beers in the middle of the jungle.

Snorkeling and Scuba Diving
Costa Rica's largest coral reef is off the coast of Cahuita National Park,
and although it has been severely damaged by pollution, there's plenty
still to admire. Other dive spots include the coral reef at Uvita Island
(Isla Uvita) off Puerto Limón, the many reefs off the beaches of the Gandoca-Manzanillo Wildlife Refuge, and the sea caverns off Puerto Viejo
de Limón. The water is clearest during the dry season. Snorkeling and
diving are both excellent in and around Bastimentos Island Marine National Park, near Bocas del Toro in nearby Panama (☞ Chapter 8).

Surfing
Though some point breaks were badly affected by coastal uplift in 1991,
new ones were created—a left at Punta Cocles and a right at Punta Uva.
You can still ride Puerto Viejo de Limón's famous and formidable Salsa
Brava, but its spectacular waves are really only for the experienced and
fearless surfer. Less hairy spots include Playa Negra, Cahuita, the
beach break just south of Puerto Viejo, Playa Bonita north of Puerto
Viejo de Limón, and Uvita Island, 20 minutes from Puerto Limón by
boat. You must always beware of riptides. This coast is best surfed from
December to March and June to August.

Turtle-Watching

Costa Rica's Caribbean shore is one of the few places in the world where the green sea turtle nests: great groups of them descend on Tortuguero National Park from July to October each year. Three other turtle species—the hawksbill, loggerhead, and giant leatherback—also nest here; *see* ☞ Close-Up: Tico Turtles, *below.*

Exploring the Atlantic Lowlands and Caribbean Coast

Below the cloud- and rain-forested mountains and foothills of the Central and Talamanca ranges lie fertile plains and dense tracts of primary tropical jungle. Much of this land has been cleared and given over to farming and ranching, but vast expanses are still inaccessible by car. No roads lead to Barra del Colorado or Tortuguero; you have to fly from San José or take a jungle boat from Móin, an alluring prospect if it's solitude you crave. Coastal Talamanca, the region to the south, however, is accessible by car via the Carretera Guápiles.

Keep in mind that there are two towns called Puerto Viejo in this region. One, Puerto Viejo de Sarapiquí, is a former river port in the more northerly, inland section of the lowlands; the other, Puerto Viejo de Limón, is on the coast not far from the Panamanian border. Keeping the two straight can be confusing, as locals often call both of them "Puerto Viejo." To compound the problem, plain old Puerto Limón (often called Limón) is north along the coast from Puerto Viejo de Limón.

Numbers in the text correspond to numbers in the margin and on the Atlantic Lowlands and Caribbean Coast map.

Great Itineraries

You need at least a week to cover this territory, but three days are enough to sample its charms if you plan your time judiciously. In addition to the difficulties of getting around, remember that the Atlantic lowlands offer various activities requiring different levels of physical endurance and commitment, ranging from seaside lounging to rain-forest trekking. If your time, energy, and stomach for discomfort—mud, mosquitoes, and rain, for starters—are limited, you'll have to make choices. Another consideration is travel time. The Rara Avis preserve, for example, is a great place to visit, but because it's so hard to reach—via two- to four-hour tractor haul into the park—the lodge obliges you to stay for at least two nights. Note that many lodges require reservations.

IF YOU HAVE 3 OR 4 DAYS: THE BEACH

Hop on an early flight from San José to 🔟 **Tortuguero** ⑥ or 🔟 **Barra del Colorado** ⑦ for a jungle-boat tour, turtle-watching session, or fishing trip. The next morning take the boat down to **Móin** ⑩ and then head to **Puerto Limón** ⑨. Drive or take a bus south to 🔟 **Cahuita** ⑪ and/or 🔟 **Puerto Viejo de Limón** ⑬, where you can relax on the beach, play in the surf, snorkel, or hike in Cahuita National Park. Camp at Puerto Vargas or stay a few nights in Cahuita, Puerto Viejo de Limón, Punta Uva, or farther south along the beach road that terminates at the bird-filled jungles and deserted beaches of the **Gandoca-Manzanillo National Wildlife Refuge** ⑭.

IF YOU HAVE 3 OR 4 DAYS: THE RAIN FOREST

Wake early in San José and drive or take a bus over the Guápiles Highway to hike in **Braulio Carrillo National Park** ① or ride the **Rain Forest Aerial Tram.** (Get here early, as the people in the first gondolas see the most wildlife.) Then drive or take a bus to 🔟 **La Selva Biological Station** ③ (a 2-km/1-mi walk from the road to the entrance; pack lightly if you're not driving) and spend the afternoon hiking its network of trails. Spend a night here, then move to one of the lodges in

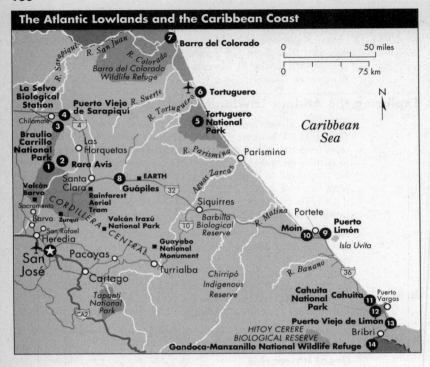

The Atlantic Lowlands and the Caribbean Coast

the ✈ **Puerto Viejo de Sarapiquí** ④ area, most of which offer hikes, jungle excursions on horseback, kayaking trips, and white-water rafting adventures. Alternately: after a night at La Selva, drive or take a bus early the next morning back to Las Horquetas to meet the 9 AM tractor to ✈ **Rara Avis** ②, and settle in there for two nights.

IF YOU HAVE 7 DAYS

Throw in some variations on the above two themes: add an overnight rafting trip down the Río Pacuare, near Turrialba (☞ Chapter 2), or take a multi-day fishing trip out of **Barra del Colorado** ⑦ or **Tortuguero** ⑥. Arrange to visit the Bribri, Cabecar, or Kekoldi Indian reservations in the hills west of **Puerto Viejo de Limón** ⑬; hike into the remote Hitoy Cerere Biological Reserve. If you fancy snorkeling amid pristine coral reefs, allow two or three days to wander off to Panama's Bocas del Toro and Bastimentos Island Marine National Park (☞ Chapter 8). From Changuinola, two hours by water taxi and bus gets you to Bocas, and an eight-hour bus ride gets you back to San José.

When to Tour the Atlantic Lowlands and Caribbean Coast

In three words: when it's dry. This realm absorbs 200 or more inches of rain a year, so unless you want to watch turtles lay their eggs on the beach (each species has its own schedule), you'll want to avoid the worst of it. Chances are you'll be rained on no matter when you go, but your best bets for good weather are the Atlantic coast's two short "dry" seasons—September and October and March and April—which unfortunately do not correspond to the dry season in the rest of the country. If you don't mind rain, come in the rainy season: in exchange for being waterlogged, you'll pay lower prices and see few tourists.

BRAULIO CARRILLO NATIONAL PARK AND THE NORTHERN LOWLANDS

The immense Braulio Carrillo National Park, northeast of San José, protects virgin rain forest on either side of the highway to Guápiles. You can get a feel for it as you pass through on the highway, but inside it's another world: everywhere you look, green things sprout, twist, and bloom. Bromeliads and orchids cling to arching trees while white-faced monkeys and blue morpho butterflies creep, climb, and flutter. Adjacent to the park is a private reserve where you can explore the flora and fauna of the rain-forest canopy from gondolas, a creation known as the Rain Forest Aerial Tram.

After threading through Braulio Carrillo, the Guápiles Highway branches at Santa Clara, having completed its descent onto the Caribbean plain, and continues southeast to Puerto Limón and the Caribbean coast. If you turn left and head north, the smoothly paved road (Highway 4) leads through flat, deforested pasture and pockets of old-growth forest toward two preserves, Rara Avis and La Selva. Just north are the old river-port town of Puerto Viejo de Sarapiquí and the forest-clad hills of the eastern slope of the Cordillera Central.

Braulio Carrillo National Park

❶ *30 km (19 mi) north of San José.*

In a country where deforestation is still rife, Parque Nacional Braulio Carrillo provides a rare opportunity to witness dense, primary tropical cloud forest as far as the eye can see (☞ Chapter 9). The park owes its foundation to the public outcry provoked by the construction of the highway through this region in the late 1970s—the government bowed to pressure from environmentalists, and, somewhat ironically, the park is the most accessible one for travelers from the San José area thanks to the highway running through it. Covering 443 sq km (171 sq mi), Braulio Carrillo's extremely diverse terrain ranges from 100 to more than 9,500 ft above sea level and extends from the central volcanic range down the Atlantic slope to La Selva research station near Puerto Viejo de Sarapiquí. Six thousand tree species, 500 bird species, and 135 mammal species have been cataloged here.

The **Zurquí ranger station,** where hikes begin, is to the right of the road, half a kilometer (¼ mi) before the Zurquí tunnel. Hikes here are steep, and the trails inevitably involve a lot of ups and downs; wear hiking boots on the trails to protect yourself from mud, slippage, and possible snakes. The main trail through primary forest, 1½ km (1 mi) long, culminates in a mirador (lookout point), but alas, the highway mars the view. Monkeys, tapirs, jaguars, kinkajous, sloths, raccoons, margays, and porcupines all live in this forest, and resident birds include the quetzal and the eagle. Orchids, bromeliads, heliconias, fungi, and mushrooms are less bashful than any of the animals; you can spot them throughout. From the **Carrillo ranger station,** 22 km (14 mi) northeast along the highway from Zurquí, the trails are less steep, making for easier hiking. For access to the 9,500-ft **Volcán Barva,** you need to start from Sacramento, north of Heredia. The walk to the crater takes two to three hours, but your efforts are rewarded by great views as long as you start early, preferably before 8 AM, to avoid the mist that sometimes obscures views of the summit. ☎ *283–8004 for Sistemas de Areas de Conservación in San José; 192 for National Parks toll-free hot line.* 🔲 *$6.* ☉ *Daily 7–4.*

Rain Forest Aerial Tram

Adjacent to Braulio Carrillo, a 4-sq-km (2½-sq-mi) preserve houses a privately owned and operated engineering marvel: a series of gondolas strung together in a modified ski-lift pulley system. (To lessen the impact on the jungle, the support pylons were flown into place by helicopter, with the chopper and pilot rented from neighboring Nicaragua's Sandinista Army.) The tram gives students, researchers, and travelers like you a new way of seeing the rain-forest canopy and its spectacular array of epiphyte plant life and birds from just above, a feat you could otherwise accomplish only by climbing the trees yourself. The founder, Dr. Donald Perry, who owns the preserve, also developed a less elaborate system of canopy touring at nearby Rara Avis; of the two, this is user-friendlier. Though purists might complain that it treats the rain forest like an amusement park, it's an entertaining way to learn the value and beauty of rain-forest ecology.

The 21 gondolas hold five people each, including a bilingual biologist-guide equipped with a walkie-talkie to request brief stops for gaping or snapping pictures. The ride covers 2½ km (1½ mi) in 1½ hours. The price includes a biologist-guided walk through the area for ground-level orientation before the tram ride; the walk starts at 7 AM (after 9 on Monday), the tram ride at 8. There are simple facilities for researchers and students and a breakfast and lunch café on site. You can arrange a personal pickup in San José; alternately, there are public buses (on the Guápiles line) every half hour. ☎ 257–5961, 🖷 257–6053 *for reservations.* 🖾 *Guided walk and tram $49. AE, MC, V.* ☉ *Mon. 9–3:30, Tues.–Sun. 7–3:30.*

Rara Avis

❷ *Las Horquetas: 17 km (11 mi) north of Santa Clara, 100 km (62 mi) north of San José.*

Toucans, sloths, green macaws, howler and spider monkeys, vested anteaters, and tapirs may be on hand to greet you when you arrive at Rara Avis, one of Costa Rica's most popular private reserves. Ecologist Amos Bien founded Rara Avis with the intent of combining research, tourism, and the sustainable extraction of forest products. Bilingual guides take you along the muddy trails and canopy observation platforms and help point out wildlife. Bring a camera: the reserve's lacy double waterfall is one of Costa Rica's most photogenic sights. Rara Avis is open only to overnight guests (☞ Lodging, *below*).

The town of **Las Horquetas** is the jumping-off point for the 13-sq-km (8-sq-mi) private reserve. The 16-km (10-mi) trip from Horquetas to the reserve can be accomplished in three hours on horseback, two to three hours by tractor (leaves daily at 8:30 AM), or one hour by four-wheel-drive vehicle, plus a rough 3-km (2-mi) hike up to the lodge proper. The trails are steep and rugged, but the flora and fauna en route are remarkable. Note: some readers have complained that, although the reserve itself is lovely, they found the guides and services considerably less impressive. From Braulio Carrillo, turn left at signs for Puerto Viejo de Sarapiquí and go 17 km (11 mi) to Las Horquetas.

Lodging

$$$ 🏨 **Rara Avis.** The reserve operates two lodges. The Waterfall Lodge, named for the 180-ft waterfall nearby, contains hardwood-paneled rooms with chairs, firm beds, balconies, and hammocks. Despite the prices, these are rustic accommodations with minimal amenities and no electricity. El Plástico Lodge used to be a prison and has more-rustic coed bunk rooms, with price reductions for International Youth Hostel

Federation members, students, and scientists. All rates include transport from Horquetas, guides, and three meals a day. The minimum stay is two nights. ✉ *Las Horquetas, Apdo. 8105–1000, San José,* ☎ *710–6872, 253–0844, or 764–3131;* FAX *253–0844 or, in San José, 764–4187. 13 rooms, 8 with bath. Restaurant. AE, MC, V.* ✉

La Selva Biological Station

❸ *14 km (9 mi) north of Rara Avis, 79 km (49 mi) northeast of San José.*

Sitting at the confluence of the Puerto Viejo and Sarapiquí rivers, La Selva is a biologist's paradise, its 15 sq km (6 sq mi) packing about 420 bird species, 460 tree species, and 500 butterfly species. Spottings might include the spider monkey, poison dart frog, agouti, collared peccary, and dozens of other rare creatures. If you want to see wildlife without having to rough it, La Selva is much more agreeable than Rara Avis. Run by the **OTS (Organization for Tropical Studies)**, the research station is designed for scientists but welcomes visitors in the daytime and offers basic lodging in the beautiful Selva Verde Lodge. Extensive, well-marked trails and swing bridges connect habitats as varied as tropical wet forest, swamps, creeks, rivers, secondary regenerating forest, and pasture. To see the place, you must take an informative 3½-hour nature walk with one of La Selva's guides, who are some of the best in the country. Reserve a walk and lunch ($5 additional) in advance. To get here, take a public bus or use the OTS van, which leaves San José on Monday at 7 AM and returns on Monday at 3 PM. The cost is $10. ✉ *OTS, Apdo. 676–2050, San Pedro, look for sign on west side of road,* ☎ *766–6565 or, in San José, 240–6696,* FAX *766–6535.* ▣ *Nature walk $20, lunch $5.* ☾ *Walks 8 AM and 1:30 PM.*

Lodging

$$$–$$$$ 🏨 **La Selva Verde Lodge.** Other lodges provide more comfort for the money, but none can match La Selva's tropical nature experience. The dorm-style rooms have large bunk beds, ceiling fans, tile floors, and lots of screened windows. The restaurant, something like a school cafeteria, serves decent food but has a very limited schedule (reserve ahead). For $60 per person ($75 per person in single room), you get three meals and a guided nature walk. ✉ *OTS, Apdo. 676–2050, San Pedro,* ☎ *766–6565 or, in San José, 240–6696,* FAX *240–6783. 60 bunk beds, 3 cabins. Restaurant, hiking, coin laundry. AE, MC, V.*

Puerto Viejo de Sarapiquí

❹ *6½ km (4 mi) north of La Selva.*

In the 19th century, Puerto Viejo de Sarapiquí was a thriving river port and the only link with the coastal lands straight east, now Barra del Colorado National Wildlife Refuge and Tortuguero National Park. Fortunes nose-dived with the construction of the coastal canal from the town of Moín, and today Puerto Viejo has a slightly run-down air. The activities of the Nicaraguan Contras made this an actual danger zone in the 1980s, but now that the political situation has improved, boats once again ply the old route up the Río Sarapiquí to the Río San Juan on the Nicaraguan frontier, from where you can travel downstream to Barra del Colorado or Tortuguero. There's not much here to grab your attention, but a few companies now offer river tours with up to class III rapids, (☞ Guided Tours *in* The Atlantic Lowlands and Caribbean Coast A to Z, *below*), and there's plenty of wildlife around.

Lodging

$$$$ ⊞ **Selva Verde Lodge.** This expansive ranch-style complex in Chilamate stands on the edge of a 2-sq-km (1-sq-mi) private reserve of tropical rain forest. Built on stilts over the Río Sarapiquí, it caters primarily to natural-history tours. The buildings have wide verandas strung with hammocks, and the rooms come with polished wood paneling, fans, and mosquito blinds. Activities include guided walks, boat trips, canoeing, rafting, and mountain biking. Room prices include all meals. ✉ *7 km (4 mi) west of Puerto Viejo de Sarapiquí; reserve through Apdo. 55, Chilamate, Heredia,* ☎ *766–6800,* 𝔽𝔸𝕏 *766–6011. 40 rooms, 5 bungalows. Restaurant, horseback riding, boating, fishing, hiking, library, laundry service. AE, MC, V.*

$$–$$$ ⊞ **El Gavilán Lodge.** Erstwhile hub of a fruit and cattle farm, this two-
★   story lodge is fronted by a veranda. The comfortable rooms have white walls, terra-cotta floors, fans, and decorative crafts. Beautiful manicured gardens run down to the river, and colorful tanagers and three types of toucan feast in the citrus trees. The food, Costa Rican *comida típica* (typical fare), has earned its good reputation. Most guests are with tours, having been picked up in San José; prime activities are horseback jungle treks and boat trips up the Río Sarapiquí. Flash this book for a free breakfast. ✉ *1 km/½ mi southeast of comando atlántico (naval command); reserve through Apdo. 445–2010, Zapote, San José,* ☎ *766–6743 or 234–9507,* 𝔽𝔸𝕏 *253–6556. 13 rooms. Restaurant, hot tub, horseback riding, fishing. AE, MC, V.* 🐾

$$ ⊞ **Hotel Bambú.** Unlike the many isolated properties in this region, Bambú is in the heart of Puerto Viejo de Sarapiquí. The rooms are simple but comfortable, nothing special. Nine have air-conditioning. A dense cluster of tall bamboo stalks climbs like Jack's bean stalk out of the garden, lending shade for the bar and restaurant, the latter of which serves Costa Rican–influenced Chinese food at reasonable prices. ✉ *Main street across from town square/soccer field; reserve through Apdo. 151–A–2100, Guadeloupe,* ☎ *766–6005,* 𝔽𝔸𝕏 *766–6132. 11 rooms. Restaurant, bar, laundry service. MC, V.*

$$ ⊞ **Rancho Leona.** Built by owners Ken and Leona Upcraft largely to accommodate kayaking tours, this roadside ranch has small, rustic dormitories with shared bath facilities. The restaurant, which is open to the public, serves tasty, reasonably priced food including numerous vegetarian dishes and such Italian classics as eggplant parmigiana and chicken cacciatore. Dazzling works of stained glass are crafted in the adjacent studio. Activities include kayaking on the Sarapiquí, hiking to a 30-ft waterfall, and swimming in the river. ✉ *La Virgen de Sarapiquí, Heredia, 17 km (11 mi) southwest of Puerto Viejo,* ☎ 𝔽𝔸𝕏 *761–1019. 5 rooms without bath. Restaurant, sauna, hiking, boating, library. MC, V.* 🐾

TORTUGUERO AND BARRA DEL COLORADO

Tortuguero means "turtle region," and indeed this northeastern sector remains one of the prime places in the world to watch the awesome life cycle of sea turtles. The stretch of beach between the Colorado and Matina rivers was first mentioned as a nesting ground for sea turtles in a 1592 Dutch chronicle, and because the area is so isolated—there's no road to this day—the turtles nested virtually undisturbed for centuries. By the mid-1900s, however, the harvesting of eggs and catching of turtles had reached such a level that the turtles faced extinction. In 1963 an executive decree regulated the hunting of turtles and the gathering of eggs, and in 1970 the government established Tortuguero

National Park (☞ Chapter 9). Not far from here is the watery Barra del Colorado Wildlife Refuge.

Tortuguero National Park

❺ *50 km (31 mi) northwest (3 hrs by boat) of Puerto Limón.*

At various times of the year, green, hawksbill, loggerhead, and giant leatherback turtles lumber up the beaches of Parque Nacional Tortuguero and deposit their eggs for safekeeping—a fascinating natural ritual (☞ Close Up: Tico Turtles, *below*). Freshwater turtles inhabit Tortuguero's rivers, as do crocodiles—most populous in the Río Agua Fría—and the endangered *vacas marinas,* or manatees. Manatees consume huge quantities of aquatic plants and are endangered mainly because their lack of speed makes them easy prey for hunters. You might catch glimpses of tapirs (watch for these in jolillo groves), jaguars, anteaters, ocelots, howler monkeys, collared and white-lipped peccaries, raccoons, otters, skunks, and coatis. Some 350 species of birds and countless butterflies, including the iridescent blue morpho, also call this area home. At a station deep in the Tortuguero jungle, a few volunteers from the **Canadian Organization for Tropical Education and Rainforest Conservation** manage a butterfly farm, catalog plants and animals, and explore sustainable forest practices.

Tortuguero

❻ *There are no roads to Tortuguero. Travel time is 30 mins by plane from San José, 3 hrs by boat from Moín.*

North of the national park, the hamlet of Tortuguero is a pleasant little place to spend an hour or two, with its 600 inhabitants, two churches, three bars, and two souvenir shops. Pick up information on the park, turtles, and other wildlife at the kiosk in the town center. You can also take a stroll on the 32-km (20-mi) beach, but swimming is not recommended due to strong riptides and the presence (not threatening, say the locals) of large numbers of bull sharks and barracuda.

The **Caribbean Conservation Corporation** (CCC) runs a visitor's center and museum here. Displays include excellent animal photos, a video in which actor Cliff Robertson narrates local history, and detailed discussions of the latest ecological goings-on and what you can do to help. There's a souvenir shop next door, and at least one other store in Tortuguero sells local crafts. ✉ *Apdo. 246–2050, Tortuguero, San Pedro, from beach, walk north along path and watch for sign,* ☎ *710–0547 or, in San José, 224–9215.* 🖼 *$1.* ☉ *Mon.–Sat. 10–noon and 2–5, Sun. 2–5.*

For the committed ecotourist, the **Casa Verde Green Turtle Research Station** (✉ Near airport, across canal from Tortuga Lodge, ☎ 352/ 373–6441 in the U.S.) has camping areas as well as dorm-style quarters with a communal kitchen. If you want to get involved in the life of the turtles, arrange a stay through the CCC (☞ *above*).

OFF THE BEATEN PATH **COASTAL CANALS –** The jungle life that you'll see on a three-hour boat trip through the combination of natural and man-made canals between Tortuguero and Moín is awesome, a kind of real-life Indiana Jones adventure. As you swoop through the sinuous turns of the natural waterways, your driver-guide will spot monkeys, snakes, caiman, mud turtles, sloths, and dozens of bird species, including flocks of bright and noisy parrots, kingfishers, aracaris, and assorted herons. The densely layered greenery is highlighted by brilliantly colored flowers, and the visual impact is doubled by the jungle's reflection in the mirror-smooth surface of the water.

TICO TURTLES

COSTA RICA'S TURTLE VISITA-TIONS are renowned among devoted ecotourists. An array of species makes predictable yet astonishing annual visits to beaches on both the Pacific and the Atlantic-Caribbean coasts, many set aside to protect them. Nesting turtles come ashore at night, plowing an uneven furrow with their flippers to propel themselves past the high-tide line, then using their hind flippers to scoop out a hole in which to lay their eggs. A few months later, hatchlings struggle out of the nests and make their perilous journey back, in effect, to the sea.

In spite of this protection, their "endangered" classifications, and the earnest ecologists and well-meaning animal lovers looking after them, turtle populations remain seriously threatened: poachers have for generations harvested the eggs—a rumored aphrodisiac—and the meat and shells; beachfront development, with its bright lights, can disorient the turtles; and longline fishermen's hooks and lines entangle and drown them.

On Costa Rica's east coast, four species of turtles nest at Tortuguero National Park: the green turtle, hawksbill, loggerhead, and giant leatherback. Green turtles reproduce in large groups from July to October. A green turtle lays eggs on average every two to three years and produces two or three clutches each time; between those times, the turtles feed as far afield as Florida and Venezuela. Small in comparison with their peers, hawksbills are threatened by hunters because of their shells, a transparent brown hide much sought-after for jewelry making in, among other countries, Japan. Loggerheads, as their name implies, have outsize heads and shorter fins and make rare appearances at Tortuguero. The giant leatherback is the largest of all

turtle species—individuals grow up to 6½ ft long and can weigh in at up to 1,000 pounds—and has a tough outer skin rather than a shell, hence the name. From mid-February through April, leatherbacks nest mainly in Tortuguero's southern sector.

Olive ridleys are the smallest sea turtles—the average carapace, or hardback shell, is 21 to 29 inches long—and the least shy. During mass nestings, or *arribadas*, thousands of olive ridley turtles take to the Pacific shores at night, plowing the sand as they move up the beach sniffing for the high-tide line. An estimated 200,000 of the 500,000 turtles that nest in Costa Rica each year choose Playa Nancite, a gray-sand beach in Guanacaste's Santa Rosa National Park, backed by dense hibiscus and button mangroves. This is the world's only totally protected olive ridley arribada.

EASIER TO REACH IS THE OSTIONAL National Wildlife Refuge, near Nosara on the Nicoya Peninsula. Locals harvest the eggs in the early stages of the arribada—turtle visits run from August to December and peak in September and October—because the later arrivals invariably destroy the earlier nests. More accessible is Playa Grande, also on Nicoya, stomping ground of the mammoth, ponderous, exquisitely dignified leatherback turtles from November to April. Marino Las Baulas National Park was created specifically to protect the leatherbacks, who also show up in smaller numbers at Playas Langosta and Junquillal.

To help save these gentle giants, you can volunteer with turtle research and protection at such organizations as ATEC (☞ The Atlantic Lowlands and Caribbean Coast A to Z, *below*).

Lodging

$$$$ 🏨 **Jungle Tarpon Lodge.** Nestled on 100 acres at the Parsimina River lagoon, this intimate lodge specializes in sportfishing packages (it has a sister program in Alaska's Lake Clark National Park) and also arranges eco-adventure activities, turtle-watching, and custom tours. Though small, the lodge is a deluxe affair, crafted in fine wood with large rooms, modern tiled bathrooms, and beamed ceilings. Savory lócal cuisine—heavy on fish, of course—is served in the dining room; some meals are enjoyed riverside. Transfers to San José, meals, and charters are included. *May–mid-Oct.:* ✉ *Great Alaska, 33881, Sterling Hwy., Sterling, AK 99672,* ☎ *800/544–2261 or 907/262–4515,* FAX *907/262–8797; mid-Oct.–Apr.:* ✉ *Great Alaska Box 2670, Poulsbo, WA 98370,* ☎ *360/697–6454,* FAX *360/697–7850. 4 rooms. Restaurant, hiking, boating, fishing. AE, MC, V.* ✎

$$$$ 🏨 **Mawamba Lodge.** Nestled between the river and the ocean,
★ Mawamba is the perfect place to kick back and relax. Once you're whisked from Moín in a 2½-hr launch, you stay in comfortable rustic cabinas with hot water, garden views, and fans, taking meals in the spacious dining room. Packages include all meals, transfers, and guided tours of the jungle and canals; trips to turtle-heavy beaches cost $10 extra. ✉ *500 m north of Tortuguero on ocean side of canal; reserve through Apdo. 10980–1000, San José,* ☎ *710–7282 or, in San José, 223–2421,* FAX *222–5463. 54 cabinas. Restaurant, bar, pool, volleyball, beach, laundry service, meeting room. AE, MC, V.* ✎

$$$$ 🏨 **Pachira Lodge.** This is the prettiest and most luxurious of Tortuguero's
★ lodges. Set amid lush, well-manicured gardens, each almond-wood cabina contains four guest rooms, each of which, in turn, has high-ceilings, an overhead fan, king-size beds, and lovely bamboo furniture. The stunning new pool is shaped like a giant sea turtle: The head is a hot tub, the left paw is a kiddie pool, and the right paw is equipped for swimmers with disabilities. The only drawback is that you have few options at night, as there is no cross-river transport into town. Package deals include transport from San José, a jungle tour, and all meals. ✉ *Across river from Mawamba Lodge; reserve through Apdo. 1818–1002, San José,* ☎ *382–2239 or, in San José, 256–7080,* FAX *223–1119 in San José. 48 rooms. Restaurant, bar, pool, laundry service. AE, MC, V.* ✎

$$$$ 🏨 **Tortuga Lodge.** Owned by Costa Rica Expeditions, this thatched riverside lodge is surrounded by lush lawns, orchids, and tropical trees and renowned for its tarpon- and snook-fishing packages. The second-largest tarpon ever caught in Costa Rica, weighing 182 pounds, was reeled in here in 1987. Guest rooms are comfortable, with fans and mosquito blinds—much needed, as the mosquitoes can be voracious. Wear repellent and long sleeves on the hiking trails. Considering that most of the restaurant ingredients are flown in, the chefs do an excellent job preparing hearty food. The lodge is across the river from the airstrip, 2 km (1 mi) from Tortuguero. ✉ *20 mins north by boat from Tortuguero National Park or 35 mins by plane from San José; reserve through Apdo. 6941–1000, San José,* ☎ *257–0766 or, in San José, 222–0333,* ☎ FAX *710–6861,* FAX *257–1665. 24 rooms. Bar, dining room, pool, hiking, fishing. AE, MC, V.* ✎

$$ 🏨 **El Manatí.** Simple and reasonably priced, El Manatí is popular with budget travelers and researchers, some of whom study the lodge's namesake—the endangered manatee. The comfortable but slightly run-down rooms have firm beds, mosquito screens, and fans. The contiguous terraces look across a narrow lawn to the river, where you can kayak and canoe. Chestnut-beaked toucans, poison dart frogs, and three types of monkey hang out in the surrounding jungle. The price of a stay includes breakfast. ✉ *Across river, about 1 km (½ mi) north of Tortuguero,* ☎ FAX *383–0330. 8 rooms. Restaurant, Ping-Pong, boating. No credit cards.*

Barra del Colorado

❼ *25 km (16 mi) northwest of Tortuguero.*

Farther up the coast from Tortuguero is the ramshackle hamlet of Barra del Colorado, a sportfishing paradise characterized by plain, stilted wooden houses, dirt paths, and a complete absence of motorized land vehicles (though some locals have added outboard motors to their hand-hewn canoes). Bordered to the the north by the Río San Juan and the frontier with Nicaragua is the vast, 905-sq-km (350-sq-mi) **Barra del Colorado Wildlife Refuge** (Refugio Nacional de Fauna Silvestre Barra del Colorado; ☞ Chapter 9), really the only local attraction for nonanglers. Most people approach by air or boat from San José or Tortuguero; you can also come from Puerto Viejo de Sarapiquí up the Sarapiquí and San Juan rivers. Transport once you get here is almost exclusively waterborne, as there are virtually no paths in this swampy terrain. The list of species that you're likely to see from your boat is virtually the same as that for Tortuguero; the main difference here is the feeling of being farther off the beaten track.

Lodging

$$$$ ☶ **Río Colorado Lodge.** This jungle lodge caters almost exclusively to sportfishing folk, complete with a modern fleet of 16- and 23-ft sport-fishing vessels. Guest rooms have twin beds with patterned bedspreads, paneled ceilings, white curtains, and basket lamp shades. The pricey all-inclusive tours include airport pickup, all meals, and fishing trips; alternately, some fly-in, boat-out nature-tour packages include Tortuguero National Park at lower prices. ⌧ *35-min flight from San José via Travelair; reserve through Apdo. 5094–1000, San José,* ☎ *710–6879 or, in San José, 232–8610; in the U.S., 800/243–9777;* ℻ *231–5987. 18 rooms. Restaurant, bar, air-conditioning, fishing, laundry service. AE, MC, V.* ☙

COASTAL TALAMANCA

The quickest route from San José to the Atlantic coast runs through the magnificent cloud forest of Braulio Carrillo National Park on its way to the Caribbean Sea and the lively and sometimes dangerous port town of Puerto Limón. The 160-km (100-mi) trip along the Guápiles Highway to the coast takes about 2½ hours if all goes well; the highway is carved out of mountainous jungle and is susceptible to landslides. Make sure it's not blocked before you set off. As the highway descends and straightens toward Guápiles, you'll enter the province of Limón, where cloud forest gives way to banana plantations and partially deforested pastureland. (Note well that the highway gives way to potholes, some big enough to swallow an entire wheel and ruin your car's suspension.) Many of the crystal-clear green rivers running through this region have bathing pools. Local farms produce cocoa, exotic export plants, and macadamia nuts. After passing through villages with names like Bristol, Stratford, and Liverpool, you'll arrive in the provincial capital, Puerto Limón.

Guápiles

❽ *60 km (38 mi) east of San José.*

You may not see any reason to stop in the Guápiles area—the town itself is off the main road—other than weariness or the need for a fuel fix, automotive or gastronomic. This farm and forest area is a crossroads of a sort: more or less equidistant are the palm beaches of the Caribbean shore, the jungles to the north, and the rain-forested moun-

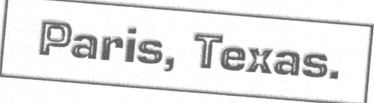

When it Comes to Getting Local Currency at an ATM, Same Thing.

Whether you're in Yosemite or Yemen, using your Visa® card or ATM card with the PLUS symbol is the easiest and most convenient way to get local currency. For example, let's say you're in France. When you make a withdrawal, using your secured PIN, it's dispensed in francs, but is debited from your account in U.S. dollars. This makes it easy to take advantage of favorable exchange rates. And if you need help finding one of Visa's 627,000 ATMs in 127 countries worldwide, visit **visa.com/pd/atm**. We'll make finding an ATM as easy as finding the Eiffel Tower, the Pyramids or even the Grand Canyon.

It's Everywhere You Want To Be.®

SEE THE WORLD
IN FULL COLOR

Fodor's Exploring Guides bring all the great sights vividly to life with hundreds of photographs, fascinating historical background, and colorful anecdotes. Detailed maps and practical information keep you headed in the right direction.

Pair a **Fodor's** Exploring Guide with your trusted Gold Guide for a complete planning package.

tains looming in the west. For this reason it's not a bad place to linger for a day or two, day-tripping in any of three directions. Guápiles is home to several major biological-research facilities as well as commercial producers of tropical plants.

Lodging

$$ 🏨 **Hotel Río Palmas.** Think of it a hacienda motel. Proximate to EARTH (☞ *below*), the Rio Palmas grabs your eye as you're speeding by on the Guápiles Highway thanks to the red-tile roof topping its open-air restaurant. Behind an arched, whitewashed entry gate, one-story, tile-roof whitewashed cabinas wrap around a central courtyard with a fountain and plants. The guest rooms inside have ceiling fans. Exotic plantings abound (the hotel is actually on an ornamental-plant farm), and the staff can arrange hikes, farm and jungle tours, and horseback rides to private waterfalls. ⊠ *Guápiles Hwy.,* ☎ 760–0305, 𝐅𝐀𝐗 760–0296. 32 rooms, 24 with bath. Restaurant, pool, hiking, horseback riding, laundry service. AE, MC, V.

EARTH

15 km (9 mi) east of Guápiles on Guápiles Highway.

Agriculture and ecology buffs will want to check out EARTH (Escuela de Agricultura de la Region Tropical Humeda), a nonprofit research center emphasizing the hands-on study and production of less pesticide-dependent bananas and other forms of sustainable agriculture, as well as medicinal plants. (You'll see EARTH's elegant stationery and other paper products made from banana stems in many tourist shops.) The property encompasses a banana plantation and a forest reserve with nature trails. You're welcome to stay in the school's 50-person lodging facility, replete with private bathrooms, hot water, and ceiling fans, for $20 to $30 a night, including the use of a swimming pool and exercise equipment.

En Route   If you're bypassing Puerto Limón entirely en route south to Cahuita and Puerto Viejo de Limón, a right turn via Moín 3 km (2 mi) shy of Puerto Limón will give you an alternate route—a smooth road that weaves through the hills. Look for the white road sign indicating a right turn to Sixaola and other points south.

Puerto Limón

➒ *130 km (81 mi) southeast of Braulio Carrillo National Park, 100 km (62 mi) southeast of Guápiles.*

Puerto Limón inherited its promontory setting, overlooking the Caribbean, from the ancient Indian village of Cariari, which lay close to Uvita Island, where Christopher Columbus lay anchor on his final voyage in 1502. The colorful Afro-Caribbean flavor of Costa Rica's most important port (population 50,000) is the first sign of life for seafaring visitors to Costa Rica's east coast. Puerto Limón is a lively, if shabby, town with a 24-hour street life. The wooden houses are brightly painted, but the grid-plan streets look rather worn, due largely to the damage caused by the 1991 earthquake. Street crime, including pickpocketing and nighttime mugging, is common here, and staying overnight is not recommended. There are, however, several appealing hotels at Portete, just north of Limón town, with easy access to the docks at Moín.

On the left side of the highway as you enter Puerto Limón is a large **Chinese cemetery,** Chinese having made up a large part of the ill-starred railroad-construction team that worked here. Follow the railroad as far as the palm-lined **promenade** that runs around the Parque Vargas. From the promenade you can see the raised dead coral left stranded by the quake. Nine or so Hoffman's two-toed sloths live in the trees of **Parque Vargas**; ask a passerby to point them out, as spotting them requires a trained eye. From the park, find the lively **market** on Avenida 2, between Calles 3 and 4, where you can buy fruit for the road ahead.

Dining and Lodging

$–$$ ✕ **Springfield.** Protected from the street by a leafy conservatory, this Caribbean kitchen whips up tasty rice-and-bean dishes. Decor consists of wood paneling, red tablecloths, and a white-tile floor. Bring your dancing shoes: the huge dance floor out back creaks to the beat of soca, salsa, and reggae on weekends. ⊠ *On road north from Puerto Limón to Portete, left opposite hospital,* ☎ 758–1203. *AE, MC, V.*

$$$ 🏨 **Hotel Maribú Caribe.** Perched on a cliff overlooking the Caribbean
★   Sea between Puerto Limón and Portete, these white conical thatched huts have great views and hot water, and most are air-conditioned. Green lawns, shrubs, palm trees, and a large, kidney-shape pool dominate the lovely gardens. The poolside bar discourages exertion. Breakfast is complimentary. ⊠ *On Guápiles Hwy. to Portete; reserve through Apdo. 623–7300, San José,* ☎ 758–4010, ℻ 758–3541. *52 rooms. Restaurant, bar, snack bar, some air-conditioning, pool, laundry service. AE, MC, V.*

$$$ 🏨 **Hotel Matama.** If you're coming from San José and planning to catch an early boat north out of Moín, this is a great place to get your first taste of the Caribbean. Across the street from the beach, the property has a pool and bar in close proximity, and the grounds are gorgeously landscaped with botanical trails. The open-air restaurant has lovely views of the gardens. ⊠ *Apdo. 606, Limón,* ☎ 758–1123 *or* 758–4409; ℻ 758–4499. *16 rooms. Restaurant, bar, air-conditioning, pool, dance club, meeting room, laundry service. AE, MC, V.*

Moín

➓   *5 km (3 mi) north of Puerto Limón.*

The docks at Moín are a logical next stop after neighboring Puerto Limón, especially if you want to take a boat north to explore the Caribbean coast. You'll probably be able to negotiate a waterway and national-park tour with a local guide, and if you call in advance or just get lucky, you'll find the man considered the best guide on the Caribbean coast: Modesto Watson, legendary for his bird- and animal-spotting skills as well as his howler-monkey imitations (☞ Guided Tours *in* The Atlantic Lowlands and the Caribbean Coast A to Z, *below*).

En Route   As you head south from Puerto Limón, the Caribbean character of the Atlantic lowlands becomes powerfully evident in the surf rolling shoreward on your left; the hot, humid stir of the Caribbean trade winds; and the laid-back pace of the people you meet. This is tropical Central America, and it feels like another country, its slow, somewhat sultry atmosphere far removed from the business and bustle of San José. The coast is lined with gorgeous black- and white-sand beaches fringed with palm trees, and you can see white-water breaks far offshore, where the waves crash over coral reefs. Watch carefully for the left turn to Cahuita about 44 km (27 mi) out of Puerto Limón; then turn right at the end of the first of three entrance roads to reach Cahuita's main drag.

Cahuita

⓫   *44 km (27 mi) southeast of Puerto Limón.*

Dusty Cahuita, its main dirt street flanked by wooden-slat cabins, is a backpackers' holiday town with something of a seedy reputation, a hippie hangout with a dash of Afro-Caribbean spice tossed in. The town's image as a dangerous drug center is only partially deserved; like Puerto Viejo de Limón, Cahuita has its share of junkies, but the locals don't seem them as a threat, nor should you. That said, the town's image was not helped by the March 2000 gun murders of two young American women, who were found on the highway nearby. Time will tell whether, or how, the tragedy affects tourism in this part of Costa Rica.

Lively regga, soca, and samba blast from the turquoise **Salón Vaz** bar 24 hours a day, and the assemblage of dogs dozing on its veranda illustrates the rhythm of local life. Turn left at the main intersection for the **Turística Cahuita** information center (☎ 755–0071), where Joaquin Fuentes can set you up with any of various adventures including tours of the canals, Indian reservations, and mountains; river rafting and kayaking; and bike and snorkeling-equipment rentals. He can also reconfirm flights and make lodging reservations. At the southern end of Cahuita's main street is the start of **Cahuita National Park** (☞ *below*).

Dining and Lodging

$$ ✕ **Cha Cha Cha.** The French-Canadian chef-owner of this excellent new restaurant calls his eclectic menu "world cuisine," and indeed you can order anything from Thai shrimp salad to Tex-Mex fajitas. Another delectable specialty is *langosta cha cha cha*, lobster in a white-wine garlic sauce with fresh basil. Paintings by local artists hang on the light-blue walls of the candlelit outdoor dining area, separated from the street by miniature palm trees. ⊠ *One block south of bus station on main strip,* ☎ *394–4153. MC, V. Closed Mon. No lunch.*

$$ ✕ **Miss Edith.** Miss Edith is revered for her flavorful Caribbean cook-
★ ing, vegetarian meals, and herbal teas for whatever ails you. You won't be fed in a hurry—most dishes are made to order—but the rondon and spicy jerk chicken are worth the wait. You dine on the front porch of Miss Edith's house, located on an easy-to-miss side street at the north end of town. ⊠ *From bus station, follow main road north and turn right at police station,* ☎ *755–0248. No credit cards. Closed Sun.*

$$$ 🏨 **Aviarios del Caribe.** Luís and Judy Arroyo built this lodge and bird-
★ watching sanctuary from the rubble of the 1991 earthquake. More than 285 bird species have been spotted here, many with the help of the telescope on the wide second-floor deck. The spacious guest rooms have white walls, blue-tile floors, and fresh flowers. Buttercup, the resident three-toed sloth (our cover girl), oversees the proceedings in the upstairs open-air dining room. For $3 you can hike the adjoining wildlife refuge, and $30 will get you an unforgettable 3½-hour riverboat tour guided by Luís himself. ⊠ *South of city, follow hotel signs on Río Estrella delta, 9 km (5 mi) north of Cahuita; reserve through Apdo. 569–7300, Puerto Limón,* ☎ *710–8101 (cell),* ☎ FAX *382–1335. 6 rooms, 16 beds in 2 dormitories. Breakfast room, hiking, laundry service. AE, MC, V.*

$$$ 🏨 **Hotel Jaguar.** Canadian owner Paul Vigneault proffers his own 50-page guide to the flora and fauna in the Jaguar's 17 acres of botanical gardens. Guest rooms are significantly less colorful than the outdoor menagerie, however; the spaciousness of these sterile, white concrete quarters only highlights the lack of decoration or furniture. Moreover, cobwebs and mosquitoes betray a certain openness to the elements. If you don't stay here, do come for the food: using goodies from the on-site herb garden, Vigneault turns out a popular *dorada en salsa de hierbas* (dorado fish in an herb sauce). ⊠ *300 m north of soccer field, across from Playa Negra; reserve through Apdo. 7046–1000, San José,* ☎ *755–0238 or, in San José, 226–3775,* FAX *226–4693. 45 cabinas. Restaurant, bar, pool, hiking, laundry service. AE, DC, MC, V.* ✒

$$$ 🏨 **Magellan Inn.** The owners sailed the seas for 20 years before land-
★   ing here around 1990 to build this group of bungalows, perhaps the
most elegant lodging around. Graced with tile-floored terraces facing
a pool and gardens growing on an ancient coral reef, the carpeted rooms
have original paintings, custom-made wooden furniture, and ceiling
fans. Feast on intensely flavored French and Creole seafood special-
ties in the Casa Creole, a freestanding coral-pink structure with an out-
door dining room, and don't miss the house pâté or the homemade ice
cream. The hotel's enticing open-air bar rocks to great blues and jazz
recordings in the evenings and mellows with classical music at break-
fast. ⊠ *Apdo. 1132, Puerto Limón, 2 km (1 mi) north of Cahuita at
far end of Playa Negra,* ☎ ℻ *755–0035. 6 rooms. Restaurant, bar,
pool. AE, DC, MC, V.* ✎

$$–$$$ 🏨 **Atlántida Lodge.** Atlántida's main assets are its attractively landscaped
grounds, the beach across the road, and the large pool. You're welcomed
to your room with a lovely assortment of fresh and dried flowers; the
rooms themselves have tile floors and pretty terraces. Enjoy complimentary
breakfast in the pleasant thatch-roof restaurant or cook your own food
in the communal kitchen. ⊠ *Next to soccer field at Playa Negra,* ☎
755–0115, ☎ ℻ *755–0213. 30 rooms. Restaurant, pool, hot tub, mas-
sage, laundry service, meeting rooms. AE, MC, V.* ✎

$$ 🏨 **El Encanto B&B.** Zen Buddhists Pierre and Patricia Leon have culti-
★   vated a serene and beautiful environment here, ideal for physical and
spiritual relaxation. Set in an enchanting garden, the three comfortable bungalows are decorated with art from all over the globe. Amenities include queen-size beds, ceiling fans, hot water, and secure parking.
The owners plan to host meditation workshops in the future. ⊠ *Apdo.
1234, Limón,* ☎ ℻ *755–0113. 3 bungalows. AE, MC, V.* ✎

$$ 🏨 **Kelly Creek Hotel-Restaurante.** Owners Andres and Marie-Claude de
Alcalá of Madrid have created a wonderful budget option in this hand-
some wooden hotel, which sits on the creek bank across a short pedes-
trian bridge from the park entrance. Each of the four hardwood-finished
guest rooms is big enough to sleep a small army. Señor de Alcalá bar-
becues meat and fresh fish on an open-air grill, and also cooks paella
and other Spanish specialties. Caiman come to the creek bank in search
of snacks, and the monkeys, parrots, jungles, and beaches of the national
park are just yards away, as is the lively center of Cahuita. ⊠ *Next to
park entrance,* ☎ *755–0007. 4 rooms. Restaurant. AE, MC, V.*

Cahuita National Park

⓬   *Puerto Vargas is 5 km (3 mi) south of Cahuita.*

Parque Nacional Cahuita starts at the southern edge of Cahuita town.
The park's lush rain forest extends right to the edge of its curving, 3-
km (2-mi), utterly undeveloped white-sand beach. Roughly parallel to
the coastline, a 7-km (4-mi) trail passes through the forest to Cahuita
Point, encircled by a 2½-sq-km (1½-sq-mi) coral reef. Blue parrot fish
and angelfish weave their way among the various equally colorful
species of coral and sponge. The reef escaped the 1991 earthquake with
little damage, but biologists are worried that the coral has stopped grow-
ing due to silt and plastic bags washed down the Río Estrella from ba-
nana plantations upstream. To see this aquatic garden, take a ride in a
glass-bottom boat from Cahuita (visibility is best in September and Oc-
tober) or, to snorkel independently, swim out from the beach on the Puerto
Vargas side. Five kilometers (3 miles) south of Cahuita on the left is the
road to park headquarters at Puerto Vargas, which include a ranger sta-
tion and a camping area where campsites carved out of the jungle dot
the beach. ☎ *755–0302.* ▨ *Donation requested at Cahuita entrance,
$6 at Puerto Vargas entrance.* ⊙ *Mon.–Fri. 8–4, Sat.–Sun. 7–5.*

Outdoor Activities and Sports

BICYCLING

You can bike through Cahuita National Park, but the trail gets pretty muddy at times, and you'll run into logs, river estuaries, and other obstacles. Nevertheless, mountain bikes are a good way to get around on the dirt roads and trails surrounding Cahuita and Puerto Viejo de Limón, and there are several rental outlets. **Caribbean Flavor** (☎ 755–0017), in the center of town, charges a mere $1 an hour.

HIKING

A hiking trail extends as far as Puerto Vargas. If you stay in Cahuita, you can take a bus or catch a ride into Puerto Vargas and hike back around the point in the course of a day. If you camp at Puerto Vargas, you can also hike south along the beach to Puerto Viejo de Limón and bus or cab it back to the park. Be sure to bring plenty of water, food, and sunscreen. Along the trail you might spot howler and white-faced monkeys, coatis, armadillos, and raccoons. Swimming is prohibited here because of the extremely strong current.

SNORKELING

Cahuita's reefs are just one of several high-quality dive spots around here. You can rent snorkeling gear in Cahuita or Puerto Viejo de Limón or through your hotel; most hotels will also organize dive trips. Staff at the friendly storefront **Turística Cahuita,** at the convergence of the two beach roads, can assist with tourist information, travel arrangements, snorkeling and surfing-equipment rental, and horseback-riding and other tours. ATEC (☞ Outdoor Activities and Sports *in* Puerto Viejo de Limón, *below*) does the same and more down the road in Puerto Viejo de Limón. It's wise to work with a guide, as the number of good dive spots is limited and they're not always easily accessible.

En Route   Look for the left turn for Puerto Viejo de Limón 8 km (5 mi) before Bribri. Beyond Puerto Viejo, the road south to Punta Cocles and Punta Uva is of deeply pocked dirt; it ends a mile or so south of Manzanillo.

Puerto Viejo de Limón

⑬   *16 km (10 mi) south of Cahuita.*

Puerto Viejo de Limón was once quieter than Cahuita, but no more—it's one of the hottest spots on the international surfpunk circuit. This muddy, colorful little town swarms with surfers, New Age hippies, beaded and spangled punks, would-be Rastafarians of all colors and descriptions, and wheelers and dealers both pleasant and otherwise. Time was when most kids came here with only one thing on their mind: surfing. Today, many seem to be looking only for a party, with or without surf. (Nevertheless, the waves are at their best between December and April and again in June and July.) Some locals bemoan the loss of their town's innocence, as the ravages of crack cocaine and other evils have surfaced, but only in small doses: this is still a fun town to visit, with a great variety of hotels, cabinas, and restaurants in every price range. Heading south from Puerto Viejo de Limón to Punta Cocles and Punta Uva, you'll see some of the region's first luxury tourist developments and some interesting new ecotourist lodges. Things move slowly in Talamanca—numerous hotels are still negotiating their phone lines and credit-card contracts, so note that phone numbers and our listings of acceptable credit cards are subject to change.

Dining and Lodging

$$–$$$ ✕ **The Garden.** Transplanted to Costa Rica from Trinidad by way of
★   Toronto, chef-owner Vera Maron incorporates her Indian heritage into her beautifully prepared and presented Asian-Caribbean food. Col-

orful decor—candlelight, linen, and flowers—highlights the round, wood- and thatch-roof open-air building enveloped in a flowering garden. The Cabinas Jacaranda, on the same property, also belong to Vera Maron. ⊠ *Follow signs near beach,* ☎ *750–0069. AE, MC, V. Closed Mon. and mid-Mar.–mid Dec.*

\$\$–\$\$\$ ✕ **Salsa Brava.** The restaurant at Salsa Brava—with sublime surf vistas—has taken the name of this famed surfing locale. Opt for casual counter service or grab a seat at one of the colorful roadside tables. Breakfast is served from 8 AM to noon; dinner, centering on and barbecued fresh fish and meat, follows a long siesta. ⊠ *Salsa Brava,* ☎ *750–0241. No credit cards. Closed Mon. No lunch in low season.*

\$–\$\$ ✕ **Bambú.** This funky little waterfront bar serves cocktails in view of Salsa Brava's world-class surf, which you can see beyond a quarter-mile expanse of Caribbean laced with wicked-looking reefs and treacherous crosscurrents. Unremarkable snack foods are also served. ⊠ *Outside town on ocean road,* ☎ *no phone. No credit cards.*

\$–\$\$ ✕ **Restaurant Tamara.** This unpretentious, two-story restaurant on the beachfront strip serves tasty, authentic Caribbean food at reasonable prices. Diners in the nondescript indoor seating area are cooled by a fan and entertained by TV; the outdoor seating area—with a large image of Bob Marley on red, yellow, and green walls—has a Jamaican motif. You can't lose with the chicken in Caribbean sauce or virtually any of the fresh fish dishes. ⊠ ☎ *750–0148. AE, MC, V.*

\$\$\$–\$\$\$\$ ▥ **Shawandha Lodge.** Shawandha's refined, spacious, beautifully de-
★   signed bungalows nestle in remote jungle settings well back from the road through Punta Uva. The bungalows feature elegant hardwoods, custom furniture, and large verandas with hammocks—and their bathrooms, replete with gorgeous tile work, were designed by French ceramicist Filou Pascal. Well-known local chef Madame Oui Oui lovingly crafts her distinctive French-Caribbean cuisine in the open-air restaurant; a hearty breakfast is complimentary. A white-sand beach protected by a coral reef lies 200 meters away. All regional tours and activities are available. ⊠ *6 km (4 mi) from town on road to Manzanillo,* ☎ *750–0018,* 𝔽𝔸𝕏 *750–0037. 10 bungalows. Restaurant, hiking, horseback riding, snorkeling, surfing, boating, laundry service. AE, MC, V.*

\$\$\$ ▥ **Almonds & Corals.** Buried in a dark, densely atmospheric beachfront jungle within the Gandoca-Manzanillo Wildlife Refuge, Almonds & Corals takes tent camping to a new level. The "campsites" are freestanding platforms raised on stilts and linked by boardwalks lit by kerosene lamps. Each is protected by a peaked roof, enclosed in mosquito netting, and equipped with electric lamps, fans, beds, hammocks, and a private (cold-water) bath. A fine, three-meal restaurant is tucked into the greenery halfway down to the property's exquisite, secluded beach. Your wake-up call is provided by howler monkeys and gossiping parrots. ⊠ *Near end of road south from Puerto Viejo to Manzanillo; reserve through Apdo. 681–2300,* ☎ *272–2024 or 272–4175,* 𝔽𝔸𝕏 *272–2220. 20 tent cabins. Restaurant, beach, snorkeling, laundry service. AE, DC, MC, V.*🕭

\$\$\$ ▥ **Hotel La Perla Negra.** The owners' previous experience as designers is evident in the fine construction of this handsome, two-story wooden structure across a tiny dirt road from Playa Negra. All rooms have balconies, half with ocean views, half with jungle views. The three-meal restaurant features grilled meats and fish. Between the building and the beach is a spacious, inviting pool. ⊠ *North of Puerto Viejo on Playa Negra,* ☎ *750–0111,* 𝔽𝔸𝕏 *750–0114. 24 rooms. Restaurant, pool, tennis court, laundry service. No credit cards.*

\$\$\$ ▥ **Villas del Caribe.** Set right on the beach north of Punta Uva, Del
★   Caribe's multiroom villas are commodious and comfortable, if somewhat pedestrian in design. Each has a blue-tile kitchen with stove and refrigerator, a small sitting room with low-slung couches, a plant-

filled bathroom, and a patio with excellent views of the beach. Upstairs are one or two spacious bedrooms with a wooden deck. Though coffee is served at the reception counter, the nearest restaurant is several hundred meters away—which may not seem far, but when it rains it pours, and the road is unlit and full of potholes. If you bring your own edibles, you're set, as the hotel rents all kinds of water-sports equipment and will arrange any kind of divertissement. ⊠ *Puerto Viejo, Limón,* ☎ *750–0203 or, in San José, 233–2200,* FAX *221–2801 in San José. 12 villas. Kitchenettes. AE, DC, MC, V.* ✆

$$$ ▥ **Yaré.** The sound of the jungle is overpowering, especially at night, as you relax in your brightly painted Yaré cabina. All cabinas have fans, hot water, and verandas with hammocks; four have kitchenettes. The restaurant is open for breakfast, lunch, and dinner, and the owner organizes all kinds of tours. ⊠ *4 km (2½ mi) on right side of road to Manzanillo,* ☎ *232–7866 in San José,* ☎ FAX *750–0106 or 284–5921. 10 rooms, 8 cábinas. Restaurant, laundry service. AE, MC, V.*

$$–$$$ ▥ **Cariblue Bed & Breakfast.** Cariblue's finely crafted all-wooden bun-
★ galows are spaciously arrayed on the edge of the jungle, across the road from the splendid black- and white-sand beaches of Punta Cocles. Cabinas are linked to the main ranch-style building by paths that meander through a gently sloping lawn shaded with enormous trees. The youthful Italian owners serve a complimentary Continental breakfast. Expansive verandas and beautiful bathroom-tile mosaics add an air of refinement. ⊠ *Across road from beach, south of Puerto Viejo on road to Manzanillo,* ☎ FAX *750–0057. 11 bungalows. Breakfast room, laundry service. AE, MC, V.* ✆

$$–$$$ ▥ **El Pizote Lodge.** El Pizote observes local architectural mores while offering more than most in the way of amenities. All standard rooms have polished wood paneling, reading lamps, mirrors, mats, firm beds, and a fan, and the four deluxe rooms are air-conditioned. Each of the two-room bungalows sleeps six. The restaurant serves breakfast, dinner, and drinks all day. Guanabana and papaya grow on the grounds, and hiking trails lead off into the jungle. ⊠ *Right side of road into Puerto Viejo, 500 m before town; reserve through Apdo. 230–2200,* ☎ *750–0227 or, in San José, 221–5915,* FAX *750–0226 or, in San José, 223–8838. 8 rooms, 4 with bath; 6 bungalows; 1 cabin. Restaurant, bar, pool, volleyball, laundry service. V.* ✆

$$ ▥ **Playa Chiquita Lodge.** Elevated a few feet above the damp jungle floor and set 100 m back from the beautiful, secluded Chiquita beach near Punta Uva, these wooden cabinas are tastefully furnished and have spacious verandas. The property is run by German-born Wolf Bissinger and his talented Talamancan-born wife, Wanda Patterson-Bissinger. ⊠ *6 km (4 mi) from Puerto Viejo on left side of road,* ☎ *750–0048,* ☎ FAX *750–0062,* FAX *223–7479. 11 cabinas. Restaurant, bar, laundry service. MC, V.*

$–$$ ▥ **Casa Verde.** This Swiss-run property is one of the finest moderately priced accommodations in Puerto Viejo itself. Set back a few blocks from the waterfront hustle, the comfortable cabinas are decorated with an interesting variety of items such as shell mobiles, Oriental rugs, watercolor paintings, and indigenous tapestries. Exotic birds flutter constantly through the lush plantings that screen the cabinas from the street. The six rooms with private bathrooms also have refrigerators. ⊠ *Apdo. 1115, Puerto Limón,* ☎ *750–0015,* FAX *750–0047. 14 rooms, 6 with bath. Restaurant, laundry service. AE, DC, MC, V.* ✆

Outdoor Activities and Sports

ECOTOURISM

Founded in 1990, **ATEC**—the Talamanca Association for Ecotourism and Conservation—plays an increasingly important role in Talamanca's ecotourism movement. The agency's small office in the middle of

Puerto Viejo di Limón also serves as a fax and phone center, a post office, and a general travel-information center for the town and the region. Under ATEC's auspices you can arrange walks focusing on Afro-Caribbean or indigenous culture; rain-forest hikes; coral-reef snorkeling or fishing trips; bird-watching; night walks; and adventure treks. ATEC is also an excellent source for information on volunteer vacations. Of the money collected for tours booked through the agency, 15%–20% goes to local organizations and wildlife refuges. ⊠ *Puerto Viejo de Talamanca, Limón*, ☎ ⨳ 750–0191. ☉ *Daily 7 AM–9 PM, except when closed for lunch (hrs vary).*

SURFING

Surfing is the name of the game in Puerto Viejo. There are a number of breaks here, most famously Salsa Brava, which breaks rather far offshore and requires maneuvering past some tricky currents and a shallow reef. Hollow and primarily right-breaking, Salsa Brava is one gnarly wave when it gets big. If it gets *too* big, or not big enough, check out the breaks at Punta Uva, Punta Cocles, or Playa Chiquita. Boogieboarders and bodysurfers will also dig the beach-break waves at various points along this tantalizingly beautiful coast.

Gandoca-Manzanillo National Wildlife Refuge

⓮ *15 km (9 mi) south of Puerto Viejo de Limón.*

The Refugio Nacional de Vida Silvestre Gandoca-Manzanillo (☞ Chapter 9) comprises orey and jolillo swamps, 10 km (6 mi) of beach where four species of turtles lay their eggs, and almost 3 sq km (2 sq mi) of cativo forest and coral reef. The Gandoca estuary is a nursery for tarpon and a wallowing spot for crocodiles and caimans. The administrators of the park, Benson and Florentino Grenald, can tell you more and recommend a local guide; inquire when you enter Manzanillo village and the locals will point you toward them. From the frontier with Panama, retrace your steps to the main road and head southwest through Bribri to Sixaola, the border town. Nearby Indian reservations protect the domains of the Bribri, Cabecar, and Kekoldi tribes.

Dining

$–$$$ ✕ **Restaurant Maxie's.** Cooled by sea breezes and shaded by tall, stately palms, this two-story, brightly painted wooden building offers weary travelers cold beer, potent cocktails, and great seafood at unbeatable prices after a day's hike in the refuge. Locals and expatriates alike—and even chefs from Puerto Viejo's fancier restaurants—come here for their lobster fix, and the fresh fish is wonderful, too. Locals tend to congregate in the rowdy but pleasant downstairs bar, where reggae seems to throb forth 24 hours a day. ⊠ *Main town road, Manzanillo*, ☎ *no phone. No credit cards.*

OFF THE
BEATEN PATH
HITOY CERERE NATIONAL PARK The remote, 90-sq-km (56-sq-mi) Reserve Biológica Hitoy Cerere occupies the head of Valle de la Estrella (Star Valley). The park's limited infrastructure was badly damaged by the 1991 quake, whose epicenter was precisely here. Paths that do exist are very much overgrown due to limited use—travelers scarcely come here. Jaguars, tapirs, peccaries, porcupines, anteaters, and armadillos all carry on, however, along with more than 115 species of birds. Watch for Jesus Christ lizards, which walk on water. The moss-flanked rivers have clear bathing pools and spectacular waterfalls. To get here, catch a bus in Puerto Limón for Valle de la Estrella and get off at Finca Seis; then rent a four-wheel-drive vehicle and you'll come within 1 km (½ mi) of the reserve. Check with the park service in San José if you want to stay overnight. ☎ *283–8004.*

THE ATLANTIC LOWLANDS AND CARIBBEAN COAST A TO Z

Arriving and Departing

By Bus

Buses from San José to Guápiles (**Empresarios Guapileños,** ☎ 222–0610) can drop you off in Braulio Carrillo National Park, a nine-hour trip; they leave every half hour between 7:30 AM and 7 PM and at 8 and 10 PM from the Gran Terminal del Caribe on Calle Central, next to the Kamakiri Restaurant. Buses also go to Río Frío and Puerto Viejo de Sarapiquí (a two-hour trip, with stops at Rara Avis and La Selva en route) via Braulio Carrillo from Avenida 9 and Calle 12; they depart daily at 8, 10, and 11:30 AM and 1:30, 3:30, and 4:30 PM (**Autotransportes Sarapiqui,** ☎ 258–2734). Buses also travel from San José to Puerto Viejo de Sarapiquí via Vera Blanca—a four-hour trip that does *not* pass through Braulio Carrillo—at 6:30 AM, noon, and 3 PM.

Coopelimon (☎ 223–7811) offers daily direct service from San José to Puerto Limón, a 2½-hour trip, departing the Gran Terminal del Caribe on Calle Central at 6 AM, 8, 10:30, noon, 1, 2, and 4. A second, nondirect line (☎ 256–4248) goes from San José to Puerto Limón with stops in Siquerres and Guápiles. **Transportes Mepe** (☎ 257–8129) runs daily service to Cahuita and Sixaola, a four-hour trip, from the Gran Terminal del Caribe at 6 AM, and 1:30 PM and 3:30 PM. **Transportes Mepe** (☎ 257–8129) also serves Puerto Viejo de Limón from the Gran Terminal del Caribe, a 4½-hour trip departing 6 AM and 10 AM, and 1:30 and 3:30 daily. **Fantasy Bus** (☎ 800/326–8279) stops in Cahuita on its daily service between San José and Puerto Viejo de Limón; these comfortable, air-conditioned buses leave San José at 8 AM and return at 2 PM. Tickets cost $19 and must be reserved a day in advance.

By Car

The Carretera Guápiles (Guápiles Highway) passes the Zurquí and Quebrada González sectors of **Braulio Carrillo National Park,** whereas the Barva sector lies to the north of Heredia. The roads in the Sarapiquí part of the Atlantic lowlands are mostly paved, with the usual rained-out dirt and rock sections; road quality depends on the time of year, the length of time since the last visit by a road crew, and/or the amount of rain dumped by the latest tropical storm.

The paved two-lane Guápiles Highway runs from Calle 3 in San José to Puerto Limón, a distance of about 160 km (100 mi).

By Plane

Travelair (✉ Aeropuerto Internacional Tobías Bolaños, Apdo. 8–4920, ☎ 506/220–3054 or 506/232–7883, FAX 506/220–0413) flies from San José to Tortuguero daily at 6:45 AM. **Sansa** (✉ C. 24 between Avdas. Central and 1, San José, ☎ 506/221–9414 or 506/441–8035, FAX 506/255–2176) flies to Barra del Colorado daily at 6 AM. Several tour companies, such as **Costa Rica Eco Adventure Services** (☎ 222–0333, FAX 257–0766), offer regular or charter flights into Tortuguero and/or Barra del Colorado in conjunction with stays in their lodges.

Neither of Costa Rica's two domestic airlines, Travelair and Sansa, flies to Puerto Limón on a scheduled basis; but charter flights may be an option, as there's a good landing strip just south of town.

Getting Around

By Boat

From Puerto Viejo de Sarapiquí, boats ply the old route up the Río Sarapiquí to the Río San Juan on the Nicaraguan border. From here you can travel downstream to Barra del Colorado or Tortuguero, but departure times vary—contact El Gavilán Lodge (☞ Puerto Viejo de Sarapiquí, *above*) or negotiate your own deal dockside. Many private operators will take you from the docks at Moín, just outside of Puerto Limón, to Tortuguero, but there is no scheduled public transportation. Show up to the docks early and expect to pay around $100 round-trip for up to four people. Modesto Watson (☞ Guided Tours, *below*), an eagle-eyed Miskito Indian guide, will take you upstream if he has room on his boat. You can also hire boats to travel between Tortuguero and Barra del Colorado, but prices are quite high.

By Bus

Buses (**Transportes Mepe**, ☎ 758–1572) leave from in front of Distribuidora Tropigas Victor Chin on the west side of Calzado Mary in Puerto Limón for Cahuita (one hour), Puerto Vargas, Puerto Viejo de Limón (1½ hours), and Sixaola daily at 5, 8, and 10 AM and 1, 4, and 6 PM.

By Car

You cannot drive to Tortuguero (☞ By Boat, *above, and* Arriving and Departing–By Plane, *above*).

South of Puerto Limón, a paved road covers the roughly 40 km (25 mi) to Cahuita, then passes the Cahuita turnoff and proceeds for roughly 16 km (10 mi) toward Puerto Viejo de Limón, passing Bribri and Sixaola. It remains navigable as far as Punta Uva year-round (and as far as Manzanillo in the dry season). Four-wheel drive is always preferable, but the major roads in this region are generally passable by any car. Just watch for potholes and unpaved sections—they can appear on any road at any time, without marking or warning.

Contacts and Resources

Car Rentals

See Contacts and Resources *in* San José A to Z, *in* Chapter 1.

Emergencies

Ambulance (Cruz Roja, ☎ 128). **Fire** (☎ 118). **Police** (☎ 117 in towns; 127 in rural areas). **Traffic Police** (☎ 227–8030).

Guided Tours

Both **Desafio** (✉ Apdo. 37–4417, La Fortuna, ☎ 479–9464, FAX 479–9178) and **Sunset Tours** (✉ La Fortuna, ☎ 479–9415, FAX 479–9099) run tours to Puerto Viejo de Sarapiquí.

Tortuguero tours are usually packaged with one- or two-night stays in local lodges. **Cotur's** (✉ Paseo Colón and C. 38, San José, ☎ 233–0133) offers three-day, two-night tours, including bus and boat transport from San José to the Jungle Lodge in Tortuguero, for about $230. **Mawamba** (✉ San José, ☎ 223–2421) leads a slightly more expensive version of the same tour, with nights at the Mawamba Lodge, or a less expensive version with nights in Cabinas Sabina. **Costa Rica Expeditions** (✉ C. Central and Avda. 3, San José, ☎ 222–0333, ℻ 257–1665) flies you straight to its rustically charming Tortuga Lodge for three days and two nights, at about $380 a head. **Fran and Modesto Watson** (☎ ℻ 226–0986) are experts on the history and ecology of the area; among other tours, they offer a two-day tour on their *Riverboat Francesca,* with the overnight at Laguna or Manati Lodge. The cost is about $180 per person, including meals and transfers.

PUERTO VIEJO DE LIMÓN

ATEC (✉ Across from Soda Tamara, Puerto Viejo de Limón, ☎ 750–0191) conducts such special-interest tours as "Sustainable Logging," "Yorkin Indigenous Tour," and assorted bird-watching, turtle-watching, indigenous culture, and ecologically oriented excursions. **Atlántico Tours** (✉ Waterfront, Puerto Viejo de Limón, ☎ 750–0004) leads you around Tortuguero and Gandoca-Manzanillo Wildlife Refuge as well as renting surfboards, bicycles, boogie boards, and snorkeling gear.

Visitor Information

The **tourist office** in San José has information on the Atlantic lowlands (☞ Visitor Information *in* San José A to Z, *in* Chapter 1). The **ATEC** (☎ ℻ 750–0191) office in Puerto Viejo de Limón is a great source of information on local tours, guides, and interesting activities.

8 EXCURSIONS TO PANAMA AND NICARAGUA

The verdant valleys and mountains of Panama's Chiriquí province beckon with lush cloud forests, raging rivers, and Volcán Barú. The islands of Bocas del Toro feature stunning coral reefs, palm-lined beaches, and a tumbledown provincial capital. On the other end of Costa Rica, slip across the border from Guanacaste into southwestern Nicaragua to see a vast freshwater lake, active and inactive volcanoes, miles of pristine beaches, and a jewel of a colonial city, Granada.

PANAMA

Updated by
George
Soriano and
Brad Weiss

AMERICANS' THOUGHTS OF PANAMA are usually restricted to
the canal Teddy Roosevelt dug here, a dictator named Manuel
Noriega, and the invasion George Bush launched to put Noriega behind U.S. bars. Are we myopic or merely uninformed? Probably
a bit of both. Look beyond that controversial canal and you'll find vast,
biologically amazing expanses of jungle, proud indigenous cultures
preserving centuries-old traditions, idyllic islands ringed with coral
reefs, and exuberant mountain forests filled with colorful birds and other
creatures. And since Panama has only begun to receive the attention it
deserves, you won't have to share its attractions with hordes of tourists.

Several destinations in western Panama are worth a detour from Costa
Rica. The tranquil province of Chiriquí, for example, has two small
agricultural communities set in lush valleys, surrounded by dense cloud
forests, with a massive, extinct volcano towering over them. The isolated islands of the Bocas del Toro archipelago, on the other hand, are
all about long, deserted beaches lined with coconut palms and washed
by aquamarine waters that hide an incredible diversity of marine life.

Pleasures and Pastimes

Dining
Western Panama is unlikely to become an epicurean mecca anytime
soon, but the region does have a few upscale restaurants and plenty
of inexpensive eateries. Panamanian food tends to be a bit greasy, but
the kitchens of the mountains of Chiriquí practice more northern
(though still fried) preparations. Plenty of fresh seafood is lured from
the sea near Bocas del Toro, and though local cooks aren't terribly inventive with it, a few resident foreigners are: Chinese and Italian foods
are available on the islands. Note that, unlike Costa Rican restaurants,
those in Panama do not add a service charge to the bill—a 10% gratuity is expected.

Festivals
David's Feria Internacional, a commercial exposition of little interest
to travelers (and perhaps worth avoiding), takes place in late March.
Boquete's extensive fairgrounds on the east bank of the Río Caldera
host the annual Feria de las Flores (Flower Festival) in mid-January, a
colorful, noisy affair with folk music, dancing, and disco music aplenty.
The Feria del Mar (Festival of the Sea) hits the beach north of Bocas
del Toro in late September; it's a sort of Caribbean version of Boquete's
Flower Festival.

Lodging
Since tourism has yet to take off here, your choice of accommodation
in the western provinces is limited. Still, Chiriquí has some of Panama's
nicest hotels. The most charming inns are nestled in stunning mountain valleys, one in the middle of a forest. Reservations are a must during Panamanian holidays (☞ When to Tour Panama, *below*). A recent
tourist boom has left the town of Bocas del Toro with an overabun-
dance of hotel rooms and relatively low rates; the two oldest inns are
in former banana-company homes. An even more idyllic alternative
to Bocas is Bastimentos, just across the bay.

National Parks
Chiriquí's two national parks, Volcán Barú and Amistad, lie within the
binational Amistad Biosphere Reserve, a collection of protected areas

that together cover the better part of the Cordillera de Talamanca range. Although most of Amistad—contiguous with the Costa Rican park of the same name—lies in the province of Bocas del Toro, Chiriquí has the best access to this protected area. The two sectors of the park accessible from Cerro Punta consist of cloud forest, which is home to the emerald toucanet, resplendent quetzal, three-wattled bellbird, nearly a dozen types of hummingbirds, and several hundred other avian species. Volcán Barú National Park covers the northern slope and upper reaches of Panama's only volcano, whose peak allows views of two oceans on those rare clear mornings. That park is home to much of the same wildlife found in Amistad (which it borders) as well as the rare volcano-junco bird.

Skin Diving

Whether you're an experienced scuba diver itching to plumb the depths or are thrilled by the very thought of snorkeling, Bocas del Toro has what you need. The points, cays, and submerged reefs in this vast lagoon host an array of marine life that ranges from lugubrious sea turtles to hyperactive tropical fish. The ocean off Panama's Caribbean coast is home to almost 75 different species of coral and an even greater variety of sponges, around which lurk countless vibrantly colored invertebrates, rays, lobsters, and hundreds of fish species.

White-Water Rafting

Two rambunctious rivers wind their way down out of the Chiriquí highlands, inviting white-water rafting year-round. The Río Chiriquí, which pours down from Fortuna Lake northeast of David, has Class III rapids during the dry season and works well even if you have no rafting experience. In the wettest months, October to December, the water level rises and the river gets wilder, with some of the rapids becoming Class IV. The Chiriquí Viejo, which begins in the mountains above Cerro Punta and flows through the western end of the province, provides an invigorating Class IV white-water trip that's really only appropriate if you have some rafting experience.

Exploring Panama

The Panamanian province of Chiriquí is a short trip from San Vito and Golfito. From San José, it's an eight-hour drive or a one-hour flight. From Cahuito or Puerto Viejo, it takes about four hours to reach Bocas del Toro on a sequence of bus, taxi, and water taxi.

Numbers in the text correspond to numbers in the margin and on the Chiriquí Province and the Bocas del Toro Archipelago map.

Great Itineraries

After the long haul to get to Panama, you'll want to spend at least a few days in either Chiriquí or Bocas del Toro before turning around. There's plenty to keep you busy.

IF YOU HAVE 3 DAYS—CHIRIQUÍ

You won't want to spend too much time in **David** ①; head for the mountain air of ⊡ **Boquete** ②, which has a good selection of lodging. Get up early the next morning, either for a bird-watching walk or for the predawn drive up Volcán Barú to catch the sunrise from the summit. Stay the second night in Boquete or move on to ⊡ **Cerro Punta** ⑤, which is higher and thus cooler. Whether you spend one or two nights in Cerro Punta, explore the forests of Amistad International Park. You can go white-water rafting from either town, but Boquete is a bit more convenient for this sport. Other diversions include horseback riding, hiking, and mountain biking.

Chiriquí Province and the Bocas del Toro Archipelago

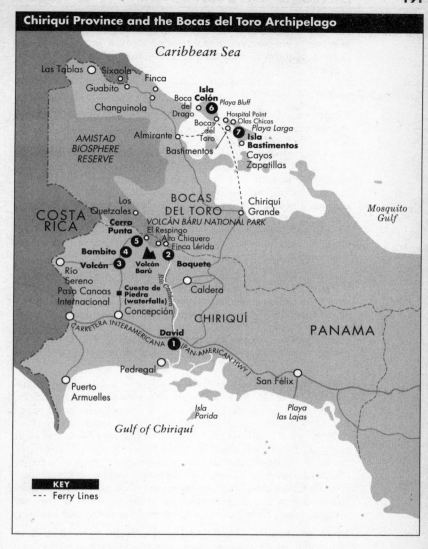

IF YOU HAVE 3 DAYS—BOCAS DEL TORO

Spend your first day wandering the town of 🏨 **Bocas del Toro** on **Isla Colón** ⑥. That afternoon, relax completely or rent a bike and ride out to Playa Bluff. On day two, wake up early and make for a long beach day on 🏨 **Isla Bastimentos** ⑦, Hospital Point, or Cayos Zapatillas, where you can dive or snorkel. On day three, take a boat trip to Isla de Pajaros and nearby Boca del Drago or visit an indigenous community.

When to Tour Panama

Costa Rica and Panama have identical religious holidays but different political holidays. Reserve well ahead of time for travel during any of the these, especially the last week of December, Holy Week (the week before Easter Sunday), and Carnival Week (just before Lent; about six weeks before Holy Week).

The massive Cordillera de Talamanca divides western Panama into Atlantic and Pacific slopes, and the weather can differ considerably between its two provinces. Chiriquí is most pleasant during its dry season, from December to May, and enjoys some sunny days in July and August. It rains pretty much year-round in Bocas del Toro, though spells of dryness sometimes occur in September–October and March–April. Since most of this rain falls at night, however, it's not bound to ruin your trip.

Chiriquí Province

Panama's southwest corner is a land of rolling plains, green mountain valleys, raging rivers, and luxuriant forests. It's dominated by the peaks of the Cordillera de Talamanca, which extends southeast from Costa Rica into Panama and defines the province's northern edge. The upper slopes of this range are covered with thick cloud forest, kept wet by the mist that the trade winds regularly push over the continental divide. That mist not only keeps the landscape green, it creates the perfect conditions for rainbows and feeds countless streams and boulder-strewn rivers. Two valleys set high on either side of Volcán Barú—Panama's highest peak—offer cool mountain climates and intense exposure to nature, while the rolling lowlands are hot and almost completely deforested.

Much of Chiriquí is home to cowboys and Indians—vast haciendas cover the better part of the lowlands, and Indian villages are scattered along the eastern highlands—whereas agricultural communities like Boquete, Volcán, and Cerro Punta are dominated by the descendants of European immigrants. The province consequently reflects Panama's varied cultural spectrum, which includes half a dozen indigenous ethnicities, a mestizo majority, and the descendants of immigrants from all over the world.

During the colonial era, Chiriquí was still the realm of indigenous peoples, who descended from various ethnicities but whom the Spanish invaders collectively dubbed the Guaymí—a name that has stuck to this day. The Spaniards introduced cattle to the region, and as ranching took hold the area's forests receded. In the 19th century, banana and sugar plantations were established in the lowlands, and the rich soil of the mountain valleys was dedicated to more lucrative crops such as coffee, fruit, and vegetables. This agricultural development meant that Indian territory shrank considerably—the majority of Chiriquí's indigenous inhabitants now live in the mountains to the east—but it made the province fairly affluent and gave it a certain amount of independence.

Most immigrants came to Chiriquí via the Panama Canal area, which was an important transit route long before the U.S. government started digging that famous ditch. Some of the resident foreigners were contract laborers who never went home; some were businessmen drawn by the opportunities presented by interoceanic transit; and others were simply travelers who got sidetracked. Though most immigrants stayed in the center of the country, some drifted west to Chiriquí. Distance from the Panamanian capital and canal probably has something to do with the independent nature of the Chiricanos, a hardworking, traditional people with a rich folkloric heritage. You may be fortunate enough to experience some local folk music and dance in Chiriquí, and you're almost certain to hear some popular Panamanian *típica* music, which is similar to Colombian *cumbia* but adds accordions and ululating vocals.

David
❶ *37 km (23 mi) east of Costa Rican border.*

The provincial capital of David is of little aesthetic use to travelers, but it is the local transportation hub. Serving as political and economic center for a vast agricultural area, the town is well equipped with banks, car-rental agencies, and a small airport. Not only do Chiriquí's scattered inhabitants come here to take care of business, but Costa Ricans sometimes travel to David on shopping trips, as most imported items are considerably cheaper in Panama than in Costa Rica; thus, the busy boulevards near the town center are lined with a variety of modern shops and other enterprises. Wander past some of the clothing and department stores and you may notice a peculiar habit of Panamanian salesmen: clapping and shouting about the merchandise and walking along next to passersby, telling them personally to come into the store and buy something.

Though David was founded almost 400 years ago, no buildings survive from the colonial era; there's hardly even anything left from the 19th century. This is a fairly modern, grid-plan city centered on the shady Parque Cervantes and skirted by the Pan-American Highway. It's not terribly attractive, and its lowland location makes for steamy temperatures, but David can be a convenient base for one-day whitewater rafting trips, boat tours of the mangroves and islands in the Gulf of Chiriquí, or day hikes on Los Quetzales Trail through the forest on the northern slope of Volcán Barú.

If you have some extra time here, pop into the **Museo José de Obaldía,** which has displays on Chiriquí's pre-Columbian cultures and colonial history. ⊠ *Avda. 8 Este and C. A Norte,* ☎ *507/775–7839.* ⚏ *$1.* ☉ *Tues.–Sat. 8:30–4:30.*

DINING AND LODGING

$$–$$$ ✕ **Mar del Sur.** The best seafood in David is served at this Peruvian restau-
★ rant. Owned by the same people who run San José's popular Machu Picchu, it's in a former home on the north end of town, a few blocks from the bus station. The dining area has tile floors, wooden ceilings, arched doorways, and a few posters and paintings of Peru. Appetizers include ceviche, *chicharón de calamar* (deep-fried squid), and *papas a la huancaina* (boiled potatoes in a cream sauce). The entrées, like the *picante de langostinos* (prawns in a spicy cream sauce) and the corvina prepared six different ways, are delicious. ⊠ *C. 7 Norte, just west of Avda. 4,* ☎ *507/775–0856. AE, MC, V. Closed Sun. and daily 3–6.*

$–$$ ✕ **Churrascos Place.** This open-air restaurant one block from Parque Cervantes serves a good selection of inexpensive food and is open 24 hours a day. Plants line two sides of the dining room, which has a red-tile floor, a high sloping ceiling, and a bar on one end. The menu is pretty basic, with several cuts of beef, fish fillets, rice with chicken, soups, and sandwiches. Main courses come with a simple salad. ⊠ *Avda. 2 Este and C. Central,* ☎ *507/774–0412. AE, MC, V.*

$–$$ ✕ **Pizzería Hotel Nacional.** Across the street from the Hotel Nacional (in the same building as the hotel's discotheque), this place serves decent pizza and an ample selection of meat, seafood, and pasta dishes. Decor is pretty basic, but the place is clean and air-conditioned, and service is good. The hotel's nearby multi-cinema makes this complex a hot spot at night; the hotel itself has questionable management and is not recommended for overnight stays. ⊠ *Avda. Central and C. Central,* ☎ *507/775–1042. AE, MC, V.*

$–$$ ☷ **Hotel Madrid.** Right on the bus route to Boquete and Cerro Punta, and close to a supermarket and some local bars, this hotel is one of the most convenient in town. The rooms, though basic, are clean, air-conditioned, and comfortable if you don't mind monochrome peach decor. Public areas are more tasteful, their concrete walls painted teal and beige. A cafeteria-style restaurant serves good Panamanian food, natural fruit juices, and desserts that might send you into sugar shock. Small balconies at the ends of second-floor hallways overlook one of the quieter streets in town. ⊠ *C. F Norte; reserve through Box 741, David,* ☎ *507/775–2051,* FAX *507/774–1849. 36 rooms. Restaurant, bar, air-conditioning. MC, V.*

$-$$ ⚏ **Hotel Alcalá.** The Alcalá stands on a busy street near the market, a few blocks from Parque Cervantes. Its shiny, modern rooms have little in the way of personality, but they're air-conditioned, equipped with phones, and decorated with some exceptionally tacky photos. ⊠ *Avda. 3 Este at C. D Norte,* ☎ *507/774–9020,* FAX *507/774–9021. 57 rooms. Restaurant, bar, air-conditioning. AE, MC, V.*

$ ⚏ **Hotel Occidental.** Step back into the 1970s at this budget hotel fronting Parque Cervantes. The Occidental's cafeteria jumps at lunchtime, with locals traveling from across town for hearty Panamanian food at a great price. Complete with mini-casino, the hotel has kindly retained its harvest-gold leather furniture and orange-and-brown detail, giving the interior a relatively clean look. The beige guest rooms are air-conditioned. ⊠ *C. 4, in front of Parque Cervantes; reserve through Box 27-B, David,* ☎ *507/775–4068,* FAX *507/775–7424. 60 rooms. Cafeteria, air-conditioning, casino. AE, MC, V.*

OUTDOOR ACTIVITIES AND SPORTS

The vast Gulf of Chiriquí offers world-class sportfishing; book charters through the **Marina de Pedregal** (☎ 507/721–0071) or **Marco Devilio** (☎ 507/775–3830).

To escape the heat, head to the *balneario* (swimming hole) just north of town, across the bridge from the *cervecería* (brewery) on the road to Boquete. This simple hole in the Río David is fed by a small waterfall and, in a different way, an open-air bar. It's packed on weekends and holidays but is usually quiet the rest of the week.

Boquete
❷ *38 km (24 mi) north of David.*

This pleasant little town of wooden houses and colorful gardens sits 3,878 ft above sea level in the verdant valley of the Río Caldera. Trade winds blow over the mountains and down through this valley during much of the year, often bringing a mist that keeps the area green and makes rainbows a common sight. The mountains above town still have plenty of trees on them, great for bird-watching, and the roads and trails heading into the hills can be explored on foot, mountain bike, horseback, or four wheels.

Thanks to its rich soil, Boquete has become an important agricultural center for coffee, oranges, flowers, strawberries, and apples. The combination of good farming conditions and pleasant climate has drawn many Europeans and North Americans to settle here over the years, which is why you see plenty of fair-skinned people and architecture that differs significantly from that of the lowlands. You'll also probably see Ngwóbe, or Guaymí, Indians, who migrate here from the eastern half of Chiriquí to work the orange and coffee harvests, which together span the period from September to April. Tidy homes and abundant blossoms make Boquete a nice place for a stroll; you can make a short loop by walking north until you come to a fork in the road, where you veer right, passing the Hotel Panamonte and crossing the Río Caldera. Turn right after crossing the river and follow it south past the flower-filled fairgrounds to another bridge, which you cross to return to the town square. If you drive to Boquete, be sure to stop at the Tourist Information Center, on the hill south of town, for information on local sights and a splendid view of the Boquete Valley. Look for it on the right as you climb the hill into town.

Just north of town—veering left at the sign for the Hotel Panamonte—is **Mi Jardin es su Jardin** (My Garden is Your Garden), the private-yet-public garden of an eccentric millionaire. Cement paths wind past flower beds ablaze with color, and all kinds of bizarre statues of animals and cartoon characters make this place a minor monument to kitsch. ⊠ ½ km (¼ mi) north of town, just south of Café Ruiz, ☎ no phone. ☞ Free. ⊙ Daily 9–5.

The processing plant of **Café Ruiz,** also north of town, offers a 15-minute tour of its roasting and packaging operations and a taste of its coffee. If you have a deep interest in coffee, call ahead of time and reserve a private tour of the family farm in the mountains above town, where you'll get a close look at the cultivation, harvest, and processing of the golden bean. Not surprisingly, this is the best place in Boquete to buy coffee. ⊠ Just north of Mi Jardin es Su Jardin, ☎ 507/720–1392. ☞ Free. ⊙ Mon.–Sat. 8–11:30 and 1:30–4.

The biggest attraction—literally—in this area lies a bit higher than Boquete. The road to the top of **Volcán Barú National Park** begins in town; a large sign marks the route one block north of the main road. It's paved for the first 7 km (4½ mi), after which it becomes a rough and rocky dirt track that requires four-wheel drive for the remaining 14 km (9 mi) to the summit. Tours to the summit are expensive; cheaper guided hikes include transportation to and from the end of the paved road (☞ Outdoor Activities and Sports, below). A four-wheel-drive-only road winds its way up to the top of the volcano from Boquete; a footpath heads up the other side, beginning near Bambito and Volcán; and another footpath loops through the cloud forest on the volcano's northern side, connecting the tiny agricultural outposts of El Respingo and Alto Chiquero above Cerro Punta and Boquete, respectively. ☞ $5.

Other distractions include bird-watching, horseback riding, and mountain biking in the hills above town; hiking through the forest to several waterfalls; white-water rafting; and visiting the hot springs and pre-Columbian petroglyphs in the nearby village of **Caldera.**

DINING AND LODGING

$$ ✕ **La Casona Mexicana.** Run by a local woman who lived in Mexico for many years, this colorful place serves a limited selection of popular Toltec taste treats. The burritos are pretty standard, but the tacos are made with soft corn tortillas; tostadas and sopas have fried tortillas. The setting is an attractive old wooden house, its rooms painted wild colors and decorated with Mexican souvenirs. The building is on the left as you enter town. ⊠ Avda. Central, ☎ no phone. No credit cards.

$ ✕ **Pizzeria La Volcanica.** This simple restaurant on Boquete's busy main drag serves decent pizza at amazingly low prices. You can build your own pie with impunity, as they charge only by size, not by number of toppings. Note that the attraction ends there; the premises have all the ambience of a prison block. ⊠ Avda. Central, 50 m south of Parque Central, ☎ no phone. No credit cards. Closed Mon.

$$$ 🏠 **La Montaña y el Valle.** These three charming chalets offer peace, ★ privacy, luxuriant surroundings, and the best view in Boquete. Each chalet has a spacious sitting room with a dinner table and fully stocked kitchenette. The large bedrooms have firm, comfortable beds and dehumidifiers to keep mold and mildew away. Abundant windows and a ample balconies with lounge chairs frame vistas of the forested valley below and of massive Volcán Barú. Expertly designed footpaths wind their way through tropical gardens, coffee plants, and forest patches— prime bird-watching territory. The friendly Canadian owners can help plan your peregrinations, and serve delicious dinners (with vegetarian options) by candlelight in your chalet. They also have three campsites.

This place is often full, so reserve well in advance. ✉ *Jaramillo Arriba (in hills northeast of town, near El Explorador; follow signs),* ☎ FAX *507/720–2211. 3 chalets. Dinner service, kitchenettes. MC, V.*

$$$ 🏨 **Panamonte.** It's easier to picture this country inn in rural New England than on this quiet Central American street near the Río Caldera; but the Collins family, of North American origin, have been pleasantly surprising their guests since they opened the hotel in 1946. Painted baby-blue, the wooden main building has a lobby with a small collection of colonial art, an elegant restaurant, a bar, and several guest rooms; rooms in the newer cement units behind it are more spacious and private, though not nearly as charming. The yellow house across the street has a few more rooms. The restaurant is exceptional, and the large bar in back has a fireplace and garden views. Mountain bikes are available for general use, and the in-house tour company offers bird-watching on the family farm, Finca Lérida; a sunrise trip to Barú's summit; horseback riding; a coffee tour; and more. ✉ *Avda. 11 de Abril, right at fork after town; reserve through Box 4-086, Boquete,* ☎ *507/720–1327,* FAX *507/720–2055. 15 rooms, 4 suites. Restaurant, bar, horseback riding, mountain bikes, travel services. AE, MC, V.*

$$–$$$ 🏨 **Villa Marita.** Spread along a ridge about five minutes north of Boquete, these attractive yellow *cabañas* share a gorgeous view of the valley, volcano, and nearby coffee farms through bay windows. Inside, each has two bright rooms: a bedroom and a smaller sitting room with a couch that doubles as an extra bed. The dining room is on the second floor of a cement building behind the bungalows. Interestingly, rates drop $10 after your first night. Hiking and horseback tours are available. ✉ *Alto Lino, 4 km (2½ mi) north of Boquete,* ☎ *507/720–2164,* FAX *507/720–2164. 7 bungalows. Restaurant. MC, V.*

$–$$ 🏨 **Hotel Rebequet.** This small hotel on a quiet corner two blocks east of the main road is good for those who like to cook—it offers public kitchen facilities and an adjoining dining area. Guest rooms surround a small courtyard and are relatively large, with parquet floors, windows, wood ceilings, blue-and-green tiled bathrooms, and small refrigerators. ✉ *C. 6 Sur,* ☎ *507/720–1365. 9 rooms. No credit cards.*

$–$$ 🏨 **Pensión Topas.** Owned by a young German couple, this small lodge sits in the corner of their backyard. Rooms are spacious and attractive, with tile floors, large windows, firm beds, posters, and original paintings. Four rooms open onto a covered terrace with a few tables where you can enjoy a hearty German breakfast overlooking the yard and small pool. The separate mountain house–cum–art studio houses a few guest rooms and a small café with views of the Pacific coast. ✉ *Behind Texaco station (turn right after station, then right at first corner); reserve through Box 47, Boquete,* ☎ *507/720–1005. 7 rooms, 5 with bath. Pool. No credit cards.*

$ 🏨 **Pensión Marilos.** The small, clean rooms in this family-run lodge are the best deal in Boquete, perhaps in all of Panama. All have tile floors and windows, and all but two have private bathrooms. Access to kitchen facilities, the Internet, and a small library help you feel right at home, and the hospitable, friendly owner is quick to help arrange tours. The *pensión* is on the corner of two quiet side streets a few blocks south of Parque Central. ✉ *C. 6 Sur,* ☎ *507/720–1380. 7 rooms, 5 with bath. No credit cards.*

OUTDOOR ACTIVITIES AND SPORTS

Bird-Watching. The forested hills above Boquete are perching grounds for abundant and varied avian life, including such polychrome critters as collared redstarts, emerald toucanets, sulfur-winged parakeets, and about a dozen species of hummingbirds and their relatives. This is one of the best places in the world to see the legendary resplendent quet-

zal, most easily accomplished between January and May. The cattle
pastures, coffee farms, and orchards that surround the town actually
facilitate bird-watching, since birds are easier to see when they leave
the forest for open areas. The Panamonte (☞ Dining and Lodging, *above*)
offers bird-watching on its private farm, where you're practically guaranteed to see a quetzal during the dry season. The waterfall hike offered by Expediciones Tierras Altas (☞ *below*) also passes through prime
quetzal territory. The trip to the top of **Volcán Barú** takes you to higher
life zones with bird species not present in Boquete.

Hiking. Plenty of hiking routes are easily accessible, and some are just
as suitable for horseback or mountain-bike exploration. You can hike
either of the two paved loops above town; note that the one you reach
by veering left at the fork is considerably longer and steeper, but passes
more forest and has spectacular views. Find the **Sendero los Quetzales,** the footpath to Cerro Punta, by following the road to Alto Chiquero. The trail heads through the forest along Río Caldera, crossing
the river several times, and then over a ridge to El Respingo in the hills
above Cerro Punta. This 6-km (4-mi) hike is easier if you start in
Cerro Punta, and a guided trip offered by **Expediciones Tierras Altas**
(☎ 507/720–1342) includes transportation to El Respingo and pickup
at Alto Chiquero. If you want to make the hike on your own, catch
one of the first buses to David, then a bus to Cerro Punta, then hire a
four-wheel-drive taxi to take you to El Respingo. The trail is not
marked—keep your eyes open for a left turn in a clearing about 1½
km (1 mi) into it, shortly after which you should turn right at a gate,
where the trail heads back into the forest. Arrange to have a taxi pick
you up in Alto Chiquero in the evening.

The hike to the summit of **Volcán Barú** is considerably more demanding, more than twice as long, and much steeper than the Sendero los
Quetzales. Leave a car or arrange to be dropped off and picked up at
the entrance to the national park, 14 km (9 mi) from the summit. Bring
lots of water and warm, waterproof clothing. Expediciones Tierras Altas
(☞ *above*) offers guided hikes up Barú and, as an alternative, a much
easier tour on a farm above town, where you visit several waterfalls
hidden in the forest. **Río Monte Ecological Tours** (☎ 507/720–1327)
also arranges hikes up Barú. If you're not up to the hike, you can still
opt for sunrise jeep tour that deposits you on the summit.

Volcán

❸ *60 km (36 mi) northwest of David, 16 km (10 mi) south of Cerro Punta.*

A breezy little town at a crossroads, Volcán is spread along the road
on a plain south of Barú, in an area that lost its forests long ago. The
highland towns of Boquete, Bambito, and Cerro Punta are all so close
to the volcano that you can't see it in its entirety from any of them;
but from Volcán, weather permitting, you can often admire that massive peak and the mountains beyond it. Like Bambito and Cerro Punta,
Volcán was settled largely by immigrants from Switzerland and Yu-
goslavia in the early 20th century. It's a good place to stay if you want
to hike up the volcano's southern side, a grueling trip for which you'll
want to get up before dawn. If that's not your cup of tea, use Volcán
as a base for day trips to the Cerro Punta area, which has much more
to see and do. Though it's often windy, Volcán tends to be warmer than
either nearby Bambito or Cerro Punta, which can get very chilly at night.

Several miles south of Volcán, a few small lakes known as Las Lagunas are surrounded by some of the last bits of standing forest in the
area. These are too remote to reach on foot, however, and the last stretch
of road is too rough for anything but a vehicle with four-wheel drive.

OFF THE
BEATEN PATH

CUESTA DE PIEDRA WATERFALLS – There are several waterfalls in a valley below Cuesta de Piedra, a small community on the road to Volcán about 20 km (12 mi) north of Concepción. Since the cascades are in a restricted area belonging to the national electric institute, IHRE, you can only visit them with a guide from Cuesta de Piedra. Hire one through the **Restaurante Porvenir** (☎ 507/770–6088)—talk to Eneida or Leonel, and be prepared to haggle over the price (aim for around $30 a day). If you're driving, the **Mirador Alanher,** on the left side of the road shortly after Cuesta de Piedra, is a good place to stop for a *batido* (fruity milk drink)—papaya and *zarzamora* (blackberry) are the usual flavors—hot chocolate, or coffee. Just don't forget to climb the stairs to the *mirador* (lookout) itself.

LODGING

$$
★
Hotel Dos Ríos. This two-story wooden building west of town houses Volcán's nicest hotel: large rooms have wood floors, walls, and ceilings and small tile baths. Two larger suites on the far end of the building have sitting areas and lots of windows and are well worth the extra $6. A large restaurant in front serves basic meat and seafood dishes, and the bar next door is a bit on the ugly side, but a large window lets you gaze at the volcano while you sip your martini. The hotel can arrange early morning transport to the foot of the volcano and a guide to the summit. ✉ *2 km (1 mi) west of Volcán,* ☎ *507/771–4271. 14 rooms, 2 suites. Restaurant, bar. AE, MC, V.*

Bambito

4 *6 km (4 mi) north of Volcán, 10 km (6 mi) south of Cerro Punta.*

It's not really a town . . . Bambito consists of a series of farms and homes scattered along the narrow valley on the western side of Volcán Barú, down which the Río Chiriquí Viejo winds. The terrain is marked by sheer rock walls, trees clinging to steep hillsides, and suspension bridges spanning the boulder-strewn river. trade winds whip down through the valley for much of the dry season, keeping it fairly cool, but it gets more sun than the Cerro Punta area. Small coffee and vegetable farms line much of the road, and several roadside stands sell local vegetables and fruit preserves. This is a lovely spot, and makes a good base for exploring the mountains around Cerro Punta or rafting on the Río Chiriquí Viejo.

LODGING

$$$$
Hotel Bambito. This full-service resort has a great position at the entrance to the Bambito Valley, and all of its rooms overlook a massive rock wall, draped with foliage, that towers over the Río Chiriquí Viejo. Rooms have hardwood floors, high ceilings, picture windows, and large tile bathrooms, though their chrome furniture is resoundingly incongruous. Junior suites have balconies, and master suites have bedroom lofts. The lobby features a fireplace and a small exhibit of pre-Columbian art; next door are a spacious, plush restaurant and cocktail lounge. The large, heated pool is enclosed in a greenhouse of sorts. Motor scooters and mountain bikes are available, and naturalist guides can take you bird-watching and hiking in the nearby national parks. ✉ *Bambito,* ☎ *507/771–4265,* FAX *507/771–4207. 37 rooms, 10 suites. Restaurant, bar, pool, spa, 2 tennis courts, exercise room, hiking, horseback riding, mountain bikes. AE, DC, MC, V.*

Cerro Punta

5 *78 km (48 mi) northwest of David, 16 km (10 mi) north of Volcán.*

This bowl-shape valley in the shadow of the Cordillera de Talamanca holds some of the most fertile dark volcanic soil in the country. That soil has been a mixed blessing—it's a boon for farmers, but it has also led them to deforest most of the valley. Still, Cerro Punta has some splendid pastoral scenery with its patchwork of vegetable farms, some clinging to steep slopes, and an extensive ranch that raises dairy cattle and Thoroughbred horses. Several foliage-clad rocky formations tower over the rolling landscape, one of which gives the valley its name ("Pointy Hill"). The upper slopes of the mountains that ring the valley still have most of their forest cover, and it's home to countless birds and other wildlife. Since the trade winds regularly push clouds over the continental divide and into the valley, Cerro Punta is often swathed in mist, which keeps it verdant year-round and makes for frequent rainbow sightings.

Because it's considerably higher than Boquete, Cerro Punta can get rather chilly when the sun goes down or gets stuck behind the clouds. The temperature sometimes drops down near 40°F at night, so you'll want to bring warm clothes and a waterproof jacket. The cool climate no doubt played a part in the decision of many Swiss and Yugoslavian families to settle here early in the 20th century; you might also see full-blooded Ngwóbe, or Guaymí, Indians in Cerro Punta, most of them temporary farm laborers.

The pastoral landscapes, distant mountains, colorful farmhouses, and abundant flowers in these parts are impressive enough, but if you fancy bird-watching or hiking, you have even more reason to come here. The paved road that enters the valley makes a small loop, and several dirt roads branch off it heading farther up into the mountains—these dirt roads follow small streams past farms and patches of forest, which make them ideal routes for bird-watching. There are also several footpaths into the mountains around town.

Two trails lead into the forest near the headquarters of **Amistad International Park,** a 20-minute drive along a dirt track that ventures into the mountains above Cerro Punta. Turn left after the Hotel Cerro Punta, then left at the next intersection, then follow that road to the park, keeping to the left after you drive through the gate. The road is rough, and fit only for vehicles with four-wheel drive; if you don't have one, hire a four-wheel-drive taxi to take you to the park entrance (it should cost about $3). **Hotel Bambito** (☎ 507/771–4265; ☞ Bambito, *above*) can arrange guided tours.

Another way to explore that park's forest is to visit the private reserve belonging to **Los Quetzales** (☞ Dining and Lodging, *below*), which lies up a rough, four-wheel-drive-only road from the Guadelupe neighborhood. You must be accompanied by one of the reserve's guides, who charge each person $3 per hour; they can take you to waterfalls and possibly help you spot quetzals. The reserve entrance is about a 30-minute hike from where the bus stops; ask for directions at the hotel.

Anyone with even the slightest interest in orchids will want to visit **Finca Dracula** (☎ 507/721–2223), home of one of the largest orchid collections in Latin America. Named after the Dracula orchid, one of the many rare species found here, the farm has a series of shade and green houses filled with hundreds of orchids from different parts of Panama and the world, as well as a laboratory where rare orchids are reproduced using micro-propagation methods. The farm is usually open to the public for a small fee and is on the road to Los Quetzales reserve, which can help arrange visits.

DINING AND LODGING

$$ ✕▥ **Los Quetzales.** Cerro Punta's best hotel has something for everyone, not least some unique accommodations. Hidden from the world on a private 600-acre reserve in the Amistad cloud forest are a pair of two-story wood cabins, each with several beds and futons, a kitchen, a woodstove, a gas-heated shower, kerosene lanterns, lots of windows, and no electricity. Preceding them, at the edge of the forest, a cement duplex (a good deal for a small group) holds a pair of two-bedroom apartments that are similarly equipped and cheaper, but not as spectacularly situated. All cabins are a bumpy 20-minute jeep ride from the main hotel over two small rivers. The hotel itself offers contains various suites with kitchenettes and fireplaces; standard rooms; and dormitories, all with hardwood floors and a ski-lodge atmosphere. The ample public areas are hung with the paintings of one of Panama's most acclaimed artists, who also happens to be the owner's brother. The spacious restaurant serves the best food in town, specializing in pizza and international cuisine, and there's a full-service spa near the river. ⊠ *Altos de Guadelupe; reserve through Box 55-0039, Panama City,* ☎ *507/771–2182,* FAX *507/771–2226. 17 rooms, 5 suites, 4 cabins. Restaurant, bar, hot tub, sauna, hiking, horseback riding. MC, V.* ✎

$–$$ ⊡ **Hotel Cerro Punta.** This cozy lodge across from the Shell gas station has great views of the surrounding farms and distant peaks, along with hearty food. Rooms are on the small side, with worn wooden floors, picture windows, and tiled baths. The restaurant serves basic Panamanian food; daily specials are your best bet. The grounds are planted with flowers, which attract an amusing cast of hummingbirds to the scene you take in from comfortable patio chairs. ⊠ *C. Principal,* ☎ FAX *507/ 771–2020. 10 rooms. Restaurant, bar. MC, V.*

OUTDOOR ACTIVITIES AND SPORTS

Bird-Watching. Cerro Punta is surrounded by high-altitude mountain forests that are home to a large and diverse bird population. The region's various feathered friends can be spotted all around the bowl-shape valley, especially near the streams and rivers that flow into and out of it. Several roads head off the main loop around the valley floor, all leading to prime bird-watching territory. The trails into the national parks bring you to the vast expanses of wilderness that border the valley, but the best birding area in Cerro Punta is probably the private Los Quetzales nature reserve (☞ *above*).

Hiking. A decent selection of trails head into the mountains around Cerro Punta, ranging from short paths through the woods to the six-hour trek around the back of Volcán Barú to Boquete. Several trails also explore the cloud forests of **Amistad International Park,** both near the ranger station and within the private reserve at Los Quetzales. The most challenging and rewarding hike out of Cerro Punta is the 6-km (4-mi) trek over the northern slope of **Volcán Barú,** from El Respingo to Alto Chiquero, high in the hills above Boquete. The hardest part, in fact, might be getting back to Cerro Punta, which lies about four hours by bus from Boquete. The last buses from Boquete and David leave at 6 PM, which means it's safer to take the hike while based in David, since it gives you a few more hours to get back to your hotel. Guides are available for this hike, as is transport back to Cerro Punta, though it can be expensive.

Chiriquí Province A to Z

ARRIVING AND DEPARTING

By Bus. Several buses make the trip between San José and David every day, but be warned that it's a 10-hour trip. **Tracopa** (☎ 506/221–4214 in San José; 507/775–0585 in David) has daily buses from San José to David, departing San José from Calle 14 and Avenida 5 at 7:30 AM and departing David daily from the main terminal at 8:30 AM.

By Car. Since you can't cross an international border with a car rented in Costa Rica, you can only drive to Panama in a private car. The Carretera Interamericana (Pan-American Highway, CA2) enters Panama at Paso Canoas, about 15 km (9 mi) before the turnoff to Volcán and Cerro Punta, and 37 km (23 mi) before David.

By Plane. The Panamanian airline **Aeroperlas** (☎ 506/296–0909 [Lacsa] in San José; 507/721–1195 in David) has seven flights weekly between San José and David, with direct connections to Bocas del Toro and Panama City. Those flights depart David weekdays at 8:15 AM, returning from San José at 8:45 AM. Another quick, and less-expensive, way to travel between Chiriquí and San José is to take the daily **Sansa** (☎ 506/221–9414 or 506/783–3275) flight to **Coto 47** (☎ 506/783–3275), an airstrip in an oil-palm plantation a 20-minute drive from the border town of Paso Canoas. If you fly to Coto 47, you'll want to call and arrange to have a taxi from **Paso Canoas** (☎ 506/732–2355) meet you at the airstrip. When traveling back to San José, try to confirm your reservation the day before. Another option is to fly either Sansa or **Travelair** (☎ 506/296–1102) to Golfito, where taxis and buses to the border abound.

GETTING AROUND

By Bus. Buses travel regularly between David and the following destinations: Paso Canoas (on the Costa Rican border) every 20 minutes from 5 AM to 7 PM, a one-hour trip; Cerro Punta, Bambito, and Volcán every 30 minutes from 5 AM to 6 PM, a two-hour trip; and Boquete, every 30 to 60 minutes from 5 AM to 6 PM, a 90-minute trip.

By Car. Renting a car is the best way to explore Chiriquí, as the roads are in good repair and David has several rental agencies. Moreover, it costs a lot less to rent a car in Panama than it does in Costa Rica. The road to Boquete heads straight north out of David, no turns required. To reach Volcán, drive west on the Pan-American Highway to the town of Concepción—a collection of modern buildings 24 km (15 mi) west of David—where you turn right. The road to Bambito and Cerro Punta, on the right in Volcán, is well marked.

By Plane. Aeroperlas (☎ 506/296–0909 [Lacsa] in San José; 507/721–1195 in David) flies several times a week between David, Changuinola, and Bocas del Toro and daily between those three towns and Panama City.

CONTACTS AND RESOURCES

Car Rentals. Rental agencies (all of which offer four-wheel-drive vehicles) with offices in David include: **Hertz** (✉ Avda. 20 at C. F Sur, ☎ 507/775–6828), **Dollar** (✉ Avda. 7 Oeste at C. F Sur, ☎ 507/775–1667 or 507/774–3385), **Avis** (☎ 507/774–7075), and **National** (☎ 507/774–3462).

Emergencies. Ambulance (☎ 507/775–2161). **Fire** (☎ 103). **Hospital** (☎ 507/775–4221, David). **Police** (☎ 104).

Guided Tours. Boquete's **Expediciones Tierras Altas** (☎ 507/720–1342) offers a variety of day trips including bird-watching, hiking, taking jeep trips up Volcán Barú, and visiting the nearby hot springs and pre-Columbian sites of Caldera. **Río Monte Ecological Tours** (☎ 507/720–1327), also in Boquete, offers bird-watching tours to Finca Lérida and four-wheel-drive-vehicle trips up Barú Volcano. **Chiriquí River Rafting** (☎ 507/720–1505; 507/225–8949 in Panama City, FAX 507/720–1506) is the local specialist in white-water rafting.

Telephones. International operator (☎ 106). To pay for calls in cash, go to the **Cable and Wireless** office (✉ C. C Norte and Avda. Cincuentenaria).

Visitor Information. The **regional tourist office** (✉ Avda. 3 de Noviembre and C. A Norte, David, ☎ 507/775–5120), on the second floor of a corner building across from Parque Cervantes, is open weekdays 8:30–4:30.

Bocas del Toro Archipelago

The isolated cluster of islands known as Bocas del Toro—in the northwest corner of Panama, in a province of the same name—has some spectacular scenery, a wealth of natural assets, and a laid-back, Caribbean atmosphere. The province includes a large piece of the mainland as well, but this part of mainland Panama is nothing special—it's the Chiquita Republic, an area virtually blanketed with banana plantations. The real interest for travelers lies offshore, on the islands where you'll find the capital city, also called Bocas del Toro.

The archipelago was "discovered," or at least visited, by Christopher Columbus in 1502. The islands' original inhabitants were Guaymí Indians, and they're still around in isolated villages and intermingled with African-Caribbeans and Hispanics in the larger towns. The language, too, is an interesting mix called Guari-Guari, a patois English with traces of Spanish and indigenous languages. The source of the region's odd name, which translates as "Mouths of the Bull," is lost to legend. One theory is that the area was named after an Indian chief called something like Bokatoro, who ruled the area when the first Europeans arrived.

Bocas del Toro is experiencing something of a tourist boom that may actually have had bureaucratic beginnings: thousands of foreigners living in Costa Rica on tourist visas have to leave the country for 72 hours every 90 days, and nearly all of them eventually wind up on Bocas. These temporary refugees quickly discover that the islands are a very cool place: offbeat, out of the way, and possessed of great beaches, supreme diving, and mellow locals. Now the word is very much out.

Isla Colón

❻ *21 km (13 mi) north of Chiriquí Grande.*

A look at a map of the archipelago shows what an odd piece of geography is Isla Colón, named after the explorer himself (Cristóbal Colón). The town of **Bocas del Toro,** sometimes called Bocas, sits on a little headland connected to the island's main bulk by an isthmus that gets no wider than a hundred yards. In the early 20th century, Bocas del Toro was the third-largest city in Panama; it was the hub of the banana business in those days, and the elegant wooden homes of banana barons lined the town's waterfront and main streets. That prosperity was ephemeral, however: when a fungal disease began to destroy the region's banana crop during the 1930s, the fruit company abandoned the region for nearly two decades. Bocas slipped into economic decline, and even when the banana company returned to the province in the 1950s, it built its offices on the mainland, near the plantations.

The town's slow fade into disrepair and obscurity was hastened by several fires and the disastrous earthquake of 1991, which wrecked many buildings and left many others teetering precariously. Dozens of the structures still functioning in Bocas would be condemned anywhere in the United States, and as you ascend a tilting staircase you might occasionally have the sensation of entering an amusement-park fun house. Still, many of the town's older buildings are lovely, if dilapidated, with carved porch rails, fretwork, and trim.

Only in recent years has Bocas del Toro begun to pull out of an extended period of economic depression. The renaissance has largely been the result of a tourist boom. Take time to wander around town, checking out the classic, beautifully kept, circa-1926 **fire engine** in the fire-department garage. Another strange element: a few hundred yards offshore from Hotel Las Brisas, a **little sunken island** slid a few feet below water during the 1991 earthquake. The entire island is still underwater, but parts of it are less than a foot beneath the surface. You can paddle a kayak or swim out there and walk around; there's even an underwater tennis court.

During the annual **Feria,** normally held in September or October, Panamanians crowd into Bocas by the hundreds. Along the right side of the isthmus road are dozens of simple structures that house beer shacks, restaurants, and exhibits during the Feria, standing empty the rest of the year. Behind those shacks is the **town beach,** which is unfortunately sometimes littered. The island has much nicer beaches, though you'll want to rent a bike or hire a taxi to visit them.

If you follow the road for several miles, veering right at the fork, you'll reach **Playa Bluff,** a long swath of golden sand backed by thick foliage and washed by aquamarine waters. Four species of endangered sea turtles nest here from March to October, including the leatherback turtle, one of the largest reptiles in the world. Local guides can take you to the beach at night during nesting season (☞ Outdoor Activities and Sports, *below*).

Veer left at the fork and you'll cross the middle of the island to the other side, where there's a little village called **Boca del Drago.** Between the two villages called Bocas, the island is mainly jungle. The rain forest here is home to such animals as armadillos, pacas, several types of frogs, boa constrictors, two- and three-toed sloths, raccoons, coatis, and monkeys. At the center of the island is a large grotto with bats and a shrine to the Virgin Mary—bring a flashlight! The island is pretty big, so plan on a long bike ride to cross it, or take a taxi, which should cost about $30.

Bocas is a good place to catch a boat out to the real draw of these islands: the diving in and around **Isla Bastimentos Marine National Park.** There are dozens of great diving and snorkeling spots around here, especially around the two **Cayos Zapatillas,** and the richness and variety of sea life—the diversity of sponges and coral, for starters—are amazing. Panama's **National Authority on the Environment (ANAM)** charges a $10 admission fee for the Cayos Zapatillas, which you should pay at their office on First Street in Bocas before leaving for the cays. Since that fee increases the cost of an excursion considerably, most of the boat drivers in Bocas take people to other good dive spots that lie outside the park but hold much the same marine life as the Cayos Zapatillas; these include **Hospital Point, Coral Island,** and **Olas Chicas,** on Isla Bastimentos.

DINING AND LODGING

$$–$$$ ★ ✕ **Buena Vista Bar & Grill.** The deck at the back of this wooden building, which sits right over the water, is the most pleasant place in town to have a meal. Ceiling fans turn above the tables, plants hang here and there, and the view over the water is splendid. The menu features such gringo favorites as pork chops, filet mignon, sandwiches made with imported meats and cheeses, and the only cheesecake in town. You can also order a box lunch to carry over to the national park. Sports events play on a large TV over the bar, which in turn is famous for its frozen margaritas; the bar is popular with the area's growing population of expatriate Americans. ⊠ C. 1, *where it splits from C. 3 (main street),* ☎ 507/757–9035. MC, V. Closed Tues.

$$–$$$ ✕ **La Ballena.** Just behind the Municipalidad, La Ballena ("The Whale") is a popular little joint were Christmas lights brighten the entrance at night and the colorful interior is usually enhanced by good music. A few tables in front overlook one of this little town's somnambulant side streets and a garden patio next door. The Italian owners prepare some superb food, offering an ample selection of salads, pastas, and fresh seafood; dishes include pasta with a lobster sauce and steak *a la pizzaiola* (in a tomato sauce). They also rent bicycles, arrange horseback tours, rent apartments, and give general travel advice. ✉ *Avda. F between Cs. 3 and 2,* ☎ *507/757–9089. No credit cards.*

$$ ✕ **Alberto's.** This unassuming little restaurant serves some of the best Italian food in a town, not an easy task in a place brimming with Italian eateries. What sets Alberto's apart is the friendly service and authentic menu, which changes depending on what's fresh. Adding to its charm, the restaurant is housed in a century-old building, with seating on a rustic wooden balcony overlooking Simón Bolívar Park. Dine on pasta carbonara or seafood pasta with fresh-baked bread, and finish with a warm brownie topped with ice cream. ✉ *Across from central park,* ☎ *507/757–9066. No credit cards.*

$–$$ ✕ **Heike's.** The eponymous German chef-owner of this small restau-
★ rant on the main drag serves a limited menu of delicious items at very reasonable prices. Heike happily whips up everything from chicken curry to a tasty meatless dish to which she's given the mysterious name "Vegetarian Food." The restaurant itself is a narrow affair with a colorful interior, two tables overlooking the street, and a few more on a tiny garden patio in back. Heike and her Panamanian husband only serve dinner, but they stay open until the last person leaves. ✉ *C. 3, across from Municipalidad,* ☎ *507/757–9708. No credit cards. No lunch.*

$–$$ ✕ **Kuna.** Don't let its ramshackle appearance fool you; this place serves great food, especially breakfast, at excellent prices. The Kuna Indian family that runs the joint knows what its northern clientele wants, and has mastered the art of pancake and omelet preparation. Instead of toast, they serve a puff of fried dough, the perfect accompaniment to coffee. The cooks are wizards with seafood and specialize in lobster dishes. Large groups should stop in to place orders a few hours in advance. ✉ *Avda. Norte, C. 3,* ☎ *no phone. No credit cards.*

$$$ 🏨 **Hotel Swan's Cay.** The newest, biggest, and fanciest hotel in Bocas, Swan's Cay was built by an Italian family that also has an inn on the Lago di Garda. It's an extensive, two-story wooden complex with attractive interior courtyards and a bit of artwork that evokes old Italy. The furniture in the carpeted guest rooms was also brought over from the old country. All rooms are air-conditioned and have tiled, hot-water baths; the nicest ones have small balconies. The large restaurant serves international cuisine. ✉ *C. 3 between Avdas. F and G,* ☎ *507/757–9090,* 📠 *507/757–9027. 40 rooms, 3 suites. Restaurant, bar, air-conditioning, pool, bicycles. AE, MC, V.*

$$–$$$ 🏨 **Mangrove Inn.** A short boat trip from town takes you to this collection of buildings propped over the water on stilts at the edge of a mangrove forest, connected to each other by a series of docks. Primarily a dive resort, with all the equipment and a resident dive master, the inn is just a short swim from a decent reef; dive packages include meals and boat transportation to the best dive sites in the province. This is, however, a good spot even if you just want to snorkel, swim, and relax. The blue-and-white wooden cabins have bunks, double beds, and small bathrooms. ✉ ☎ 📠 *507/757–9594. 4 cabins with bath. Restaurant, bar, snorkeling, dive shop. No credit cards.*

$$ 🏨 **Cocomo on the Sea.** This small, homey place offers Bocas's best wa-
★ terside accommodations. Its spacious rooms have day beds, hardwood floors, and white walls decorated with tropical prints. All rooms have

air-conditioning, but ceiling fans and lots of windows give you the option of letting the ocean breeze cool things down. The breeziest spot here is the porch in back, which protrudes over the water and is well furnished with chairs and hammocks. The friendly Canadian owners serve a sumptuous complimentary breakfast on the veranda, and will arrange tours. ⊠ *Avda. Norte at C. 6,* ☎ FAX *507/757–9259. 4 rooms. Air-conditioning. MC, V.*

$–$$ ★ 🏨 **Hotel La Veranda.** This delightful inn one block from the water embodies all the charm of its Caribbean setting, from the playful sponge-painted patterns on the walls to the vintage furniture, high wood-paneled ceiling, and oversize windows. The veranda—complete with a kitchen—overlooks a small tropical garden and a quiet neighborhood street. The artistic Canadian owner pays great attention to detail, using braided-rope rugs, bamboo blinds, and other accessories to create a true-to-form Caribbean retreat. Guest rooms vary in size, personality, and privacy, so ask what's available when you reserve. All rooms have fans and comfortable beds draped in mosquito netting. Bathrooms are light and airy, with tiled showers and large vanities. ⊠ *Avda. G at C. 7,* ☎ FAX *507/757–9211. 4 rooms, 2 with bath. Travel services. No credit cards.* 🍃

$$ 🏨 **Hotel Laguna.** With its carved wooden balconies and sidewalk café, the Hotel Laguna looks like it was picked up from an Alpine village and dropped into the heart of Bocas. For reasonable prices you get such amenities as air-conditioning and firm mattresses. The rooms have local-hardwood furniture, modern black fixtures, closets, and small windows. Downstairs rooms have tile floors; upstairs rooms, wood floors. The brightest and nicest quarters are the suites and the one standard room that face the street. ⊠ *C. 3 between Avdas. D and E,* ☎ *507/757–9091,* FAX *507/757–9092. 16 rooms, 1 suite. Restaurant, bar. AE, MC, V.*

$–$$ 🏨 **Casa Max.** The namesake for this revamped two-story home across the street from the water is the family bull terrier, who greets you at the gate. Whimsical details such as colorful toucan plant pots and chameleon-shape window frames give the place an upbeat feel. The small but comfortable rooms are painted in shades of mango, papaya, and other bright hues, and a raised porch seems designed for lazing the day away. The Dutch owners have a boat and can advise you on tour options. ⊠ *Where Avda. Norte splits onto Avda. G ,* ☎ FAX *507/757–9120. 10 rooms. Travel services. No credit cards.* 🍃

OUTDOOR ACTIVITIES AND SPORTS

Snorkeling and Scuba Diving. There are three dive centers on Isla Colón and at least half a dozen people who lead snorkeling excursions. Though you might not encounter as many fish and big marine life here as in other parts of the world, Bocas has a great variety of coral—almost 75 different species—sponges, and small invertebrates. You're also likely to see rays, colorful tropical fish, and sometimes sea turtles or even dolphins. The most famous snorkel spot is the reef around the **Cayos Zapatillas,** which is vast and packed with varied marine life; but the $10 parks fee makes this the most expensive option. A cheaper alternative to Cayos Zapatillas is **Coral Island,** a smaller isle outside the national park. Another option not far from Bocas, good if you're short on time or money, is **Hospital Point,** where an impressive coral and sponge garden extends down a steep wall into the blue depths. **Olas Chicas,** on the northern coast of Isla Bastimentos, is another sublime spot. If you stay in Bocas, it's cheaper to bike or hike out to the reef off Paunch or, better yet, the point on the far end of Playa Bluff.

Bocas Water Sports (⊠ C. 3, ☎ 507/757–9541) offers a variety of boat dives and nonscuba excursions, including trips to its Red Frog camping area on a beach on Isla Bastimentos. **J & J Boat Tours** (⊠ C. 3, ☎ 757–9565) leads trips to about a dozen dive spots, and can customize private tours. **Starfleet Eco-Adventures** (✉ C. 1, ☎ FAX 507/757–9630) offers scuba and snorkeling excursions on a private catamaran and inexpensive certification courses. Note that you can also negotiate a ride to any local attraction with one of the dozens of freelance boatmen in and around town, though you might want to get a small group together to make it affordable. Dive trips usually cost about $15 a head if you go with a group.

Surfing. There are a few surfers in Bocas but no boards for rent, so you have to bring your own. The point off Isla Colón's Playa Paunch—a meager beach on the road to Bluff—has a good left that breaks over a coral platform when the ocean gets undulant. Another good left breaks over the reef on the northern tip of Isla Carenero. The first beach on Isla Bastimentos, across the island from the town of Bastimentos, has a nice beach break that's less dangerous than the others and is surfable when the swell is small. Bocas hosts an international surf competition in December.

Turtle-Watching. For information on turtle-watching in these parts, contact **CARIBARU** (✉ C. 3, ☎ 507/757–9488), a local conservation group with a small office in front of the town library. They run nightly guided tours to Playa Bluff during peak nesting season (March–October) for a small donation. When you're out turtle-watching, be as quiet as possible, don't use a flashlight once you're on the beach, and don't subject the turtles to flashlights or cameras.

Isla Bastimentos

7 *24 km (15 mi) north of Chiriquí Grande.*

A large part of Isla Bastimentos, just across the lagoon from Bocas, lies within the boundaries of **Isla Bastimentos Marine National Park** (Parque Nacional Marina Isla Bastimentos), which protects an important seaturtle nesting beach and a significant expanse of rain forest that houses plenty of birds, an abundance of colorful poison dart frogs, and various other interesting creatures. **Playa Larga,** the park's long beach, is an important nesting area for several species of sea turtles, which arrive here at night from March to September to bury their eggs in the sand. Unfortunately, this beach is almost impossible to visit at night, which makes Isla Colón's Playa Bluff the best option for turtle-watching.

An easy place to visit is the funky little town of **Bastimentos,** also called Old Bank, on the island's southwestern end. Its hundreds of small houses are packed together on a hillside overlooking a quiet bay, populated by friendly, Guari-Guari–speaking residents. Among other things, Bastimentos is the home of an authentic little calypso band with a not-too-original name: the Beach Boys of Bastimentos (there is actually another calypso band in Bocas, also called the Beach Boys, which is considerably better but performs much less regularly). When the Beach Boys aren't blasting their music over the bay, Bastimentos is a tranquil, unspoiled place, with a few small hotels that provide interesting alternatives to staying in Bocas. Small boats regularly carry people between the towns of Bocas and Bastimentos, leaving Bocas from the dock next to the Commercial Chow Kai store and Bastimentos from the fruit-company dock. The ride costs $2 each way.

Bastimentos's greatest attraction is probably the golden beach on the island's northern side, a 30-minute hike from town on a dirt path. Known locally as the **First Beach,** this lovely strand, backed by thick vegetation, is a surf spot when the ocean is rough, and has decent snorkeling around the point to the left when the ocean is calm. It's just one of several sparkling beaches that line the island's northern shore, all but one of which lie outside the national park. If you set aside a day and carry lots of water, you can follow that coast east to those deserted beaches; it takes almost four hours to walk to Playa Larga, which marks the beginning of the national park.

The northern coast of Bastimentos Island also has one of the region's best dive sites: **Olas Chicas,** also known as Polo's Beach after Polo, the friendly hermit who lives here (and who is, in turn, also known as "Beach Doctor"). Boat operators in Bastimentos and Bocas offer snorkeling trips to Olas Chicas, which can even include a lunch of fresh-caught seafood prepared by Polo for $6.

LODGING

$ ⚇ **Pensión Bastimentos.** Housed in a wooden building over the water, ★ this small, German-owned inn has the nicest accommodations in Bastimentos, which doesn't say much. Rooms are simple but comfortable—though only one has a private bath—and the deck out back has a lovely view over the bay. Delicious meals are served on the deck. The owners lead a variety of snorkeling and hiking trips. ✉ *Bastimentos,* ☎ *no phone. 4 rooms, 1 with bath. Restaurant, travel services. No credit cards.*

Bocas del Toro Archipelago A to Z

ARRIVING AND DEPARTING

By Boat. Water taxi is the most common means of transport between Almirante, Bocas del Toro, and Chiriquí Grande. Water taxis make the 20-minute trip between Almirante and Bocas del Toro approximately every hour from 6 AM to 6 PM. There are two companies, headquartered about 100 yards apart in Almirante; and the 20-passenger boats leave once they fill up, so it's worth investigating each one and signing up at one that has more people waiting. In Bocas, taxis leave from a cement dock near the police station on Calle 1 and from another dock a few blocks south of Le Pirate Restaurant.

Daily water taxis also shuttle regularly between Almirante and Chiriquí Grande, stopping in Bocas if three or more people want to get on or off there; otherwise, you have to take a separate taxi to and from Almirante. These are run by the same companies that connect Almirante with Bocas, and the schedule varies according to demand (check ahead). A **car ferry** runs between Almirante and Bocas every Wednesday, Friday, and Sunday, but it's much slower than a water taxi, and putting a car on it is pricey.

By Bus. A direct bus departs San José, Costa Rica (☎ 506/556–1432), for **Changuinola,** Panama, daily at 10 AM from the bus terminal at Calle 14 between Avenidas 5 and 7. It's a seven-hour trip each way. Buses depart Changuinola for the port of **Almirante** every 20 minutes; from here water taxis run hourly to Bocas del Toro. Several daily buses (☎ 506/257–8129) also travel between San José and the border town of **Sixaola;** these leave San José from the **Gran Terminal del Caribe** (✉ C. Central at Avda. 15) at 6 AM, 10 AM, 1:30 PM, and 3:30 PM; they pick up passengers in Cahuita 3½ hours later, and at the entrance to Puerto Viejo 20 minutes after that, and arrive at Sixaola six hours after departing San José. Buses leave Sixaola for San José at 5, 7:30, and 9:30 AM and 2:30 PM. There are also six buses a day between **Puerto Limón** and Sixaola, all of which stop at Cahuita and Puerto Viejo di Limón. From Sixaola, you hike across the railroad bridge into the Panamanian town of Guabito, where you can catch a bus or taxi to nearby Changuinola for $1.

By Plane. The Panamanian airline **Aeroperlas** (☎ 507/757–9341 or 506/ 296–0909 [Lacsa] in San José) has weekday flights from San José to both David and Bocas. Daily flights also connect Bocas to Panama City.

GETTING AROUND

By Bike. Several places in town rent bicycles—Hotel Swan's Cay, Hotel Laguna, and La Ballena Restaurant (☞ Dining and Lodging *in* Isla Colón, *above*)—providing a good way to reach the island's beaches.

By Boat. This is the main mode of transport here. Individually chartered, motorized dugouts are the usual means of interisland travel, though there's at least one sailboat for charter in town. Boats to Bastimentos leave fairly regularly from the dock next to the Commercial Chow Kai store, charging $2 per person.

By Bus. A small bus crosses Isla Colón every Monday, Wednesday, and Friday, leaving Boca del Drago at 7 AM and Bocas del Toro at 1 PM. It sometimes makes the trip on weekends as well, but the schedule is not set in stone.

By Car. You won't see much in the way of auto traffic here, though a few cabs cruise around town. You can take a taxi from Bocas to Boca del Drago for about $25 round-trip, or to the closer Playa Bluff for about $10 round-trip. You can also rent a car in Changuinola and bring it over on the car ferry, but this is not recommended, as the most desirable spots can only be reached by boat.

CONTACTS AND RESOURCES

Bank. There's a branch of the **Banco Nacional de Panama** in Bocas, on Avenida F between Calles 1 and 2; they'll cash traveler's checks but cannot give cash advances on credit cards. An ATM machine next to the Taxi 25 building allows cash withdrawals from Visa, MasterCard, and Cirrus- and Plus-affiliated bank accounts. The accepted currency is the American dollar, also called the balboa.

Communication. Connect to one of four computers at **Internet Don Chichos** (⊠ C. 3, ☎ FAX 507/757–9829) in Bocas del Toro, next to the restaurant of the same name. You pay 10¢ a minute.

Emergencies. Fire (⊠ Corner of C. 1 and Avda. Norte, ☎ 103). **Hospitals** (Bocas, ☎ 507/757–9201; Changuinola, ☎ 507/758–8295; Panama City, ☎ 507/263–6060). **Police** (⊠ next to IPAT building on waterfront, ☎ 104).

Guided Tours. Three dive shops and several local fishermen offer one-day excursions to the Cayos Zapatillas, Hospital Point, Olas Chicas, and other popular snorkeling sites for about $15 per person including equipment. Some other boatmen dock next to the Chow Kai store and are usually willing to negotiate a price. Always confirm that there are life vests on board before you set out.

Temptress Adventure Cruises (⊠ 351 N.W. LeJeune Rd., Penthouse 6, Miami, FL 33126, ☎ 305/643–4040, FAX 305/643–6438) offers seven-day adventure cruises that stop in Hollandaise Cayes, Portobelo, Panama Canal, Darién, and Islas Perlas; activities include national-park hikes, sea kayaking, trips to indigenous villages, bird-watching, and snorkeling. **Turtle Divers** (☎ FAX 507/757–9594) leads boat trips to Isla de Pajaros, Boca del Drago, a Teribe Indian village in the rain forest, and a Guaymí Indian village. **Transparente Tours** (☎ FAX 507/757–9172 or 507/757–9600) specializes in snorkeling excursions to all the local dive sites. **Starfleet Eco-Adventures** (☎ FAX 507/757–9630) features diving and snorkeling excursions on a private catamaran, as well as hiking on Isla Bastimentos. **Bocas Water Sports** (☎ 507/757–9541) has a variety of dive trips and a day trip to their Red Frog camp on Isla Bastimentos.

Telephones. Information (☎ 102). **International operator** (☎ 106). There are public telephones scattered throughout town including Bocas's airport, Parque Simón Bolívar, Hotel Bahía, Hotel ANCON, the Cable and Wireless office, and near the fire department on Calle 1.

Visitor Information. The **Panamanian Tourist Board (IPAT)** is in Bocas, on Avenida D at Calle 1. The organization updates its Web site (🖰) regularly. For information on Isla Bastimentos Marine National Park, stop by **ANAM** (✉ C. 1, ☎ 507/757–9244). The **Immigration Office** is in the back of the Government House overlooking Parque Simón Bolívar.

NICARAGUA

After decades of war, revolution, and political and economic struggle, Nicaragua appears at last to have achieved enough stability to merit consideration as a travel destination for pleasure and enlightenment (as opposed to the political causes that drew many idealistic Americans here in the 1980s). For better or worse, democratic capitalism had taken hold, and both foreign investors and exiled Nicaraguans of all political persuasions are buying or reclaiming property all over the country. You will not find riots, hooligans toting machine guns, or gangs of thieves. You will find a poor but friendly country, where travelers are still rare enough to incite curiosity. Roads are therefore pleasantly uncrowded, or are crowded with bicycles, oxcarts, and horses rather than cars. The tourist industry, though lacking in infrastructure—and still grappling with the devastating effects of Hurricane Mitch (1998) on much of the country—is getting off the ground. If you have an adventurous spirit and open mind, slip across the Costa Rican border into southwestern Nicaragua to see the pristine beauty of the beach towns at Nicaragua Lake and the dusty colonial city of Granada.

Pleasures and Pastimes

Beaches

A few miles from the Costa Rican border, San Juan del Sur is a pretty, slightly run-down beach town tucked into a perfect little bay with high headlands providing shelter to the north and south. From here, enterprising travelers can book boat or four-wheel-drive trips to dozens of magnificent deserted beaches for great surfing, fishing, diving, turtle-watching, and sunbathing.

Dining

Nicaraguan food is comparable to that of Costa Rica, minus the international options inspired by the tourist influx. Like Ticos, Nicaraguans favor rice and beans with meat, fish, or chicken; salads are usually made of cabbage with tomatoes and a vinaigrette-style dressing; and rice and beans usually reappear as *gallo pinto* (a mixture of rice and beans) at breakfast the next day. A favorite dish to which you may not be accustomed is *mondongo,* tripe (beef stomach) cooked with beef knuckles. Near the coast, fresh fish is abundant and relatively cheap. Fresh fruit and fruit juices are plentiful and cheap.

Lodging

Upscale lodging in Nicaragua is limited to a few hotels in the larger cities and some beachfront resorts, none of which are in the southwest. You'll find a reasonable selection of medium-priced hotels and *hospedajes,* the Nicaraguan version of cabinas, in the cities and small towns.

National Parks and Volcanoes

Southwestern Nicaragua has one major national park, Volcán Masaya, which features an active volcano, an enormous visitor center, and several hiking trails. The dormant Volcán Mombacho, a designated natural reserve, has an excellent trail through the unique cloud forest surrounding its forested crater. Two volcanoes on Madera, Concepción and Madera, offer still other prime hiking opportunities.

Shopping

Great buys can be had all over Nicaragua, but the best shopping town is Masaya, where the lively, scruffy old market competes with a more sterile but easier-to-navigate new one. In both places, look for shoes, leather goods, pottery, and paintings—the country is full of artists making lively, colorful paintings in the style first developed in the Solentiname archipelago in Lake Nicaragua, where Father Ernesto Cardenal (later Minister of Culture in the Sandinista government), founded a commune and trained farmers and laborers in various crafts.

Exploring Nicaragua

The most populous region in Nicaragua, the Pacific lowlands of southwestern Nicaragua look much like the dry country of northern Guanacaste, with rolling agricultural plains and relatively sparse vegetation. The road north from the Costa Rican border follows a level, unhindered, fairly straight route to Managua. Public transportation is easily accessible and very cheap; buses ranging from diesel-belching antique American school buses to sleek minivans connect most of the towns and cities. You can bring a privately owned car or take a bus across the border; driving rental cars across the border is not permitted, so it's best to rent a car in Managua. The primary roads are in good shape, better than Costa Rica's in many ways.

Numbers in the text correspond to numbers in the margin and on the Southwestern Nicaragua map.

Great Itineraries

You can explore this small slice of Nicaragua in four or five days, depending on how you enter and move around the country. If time were no object, however, you could comfortably spend several weeks exploring the volcanoes, colonial towns, surf, and sun.

IF YOU HAVE 4 OR 5 DAYS

This itinerary is appropriate if you're crossing the border by private car or bus rather than flying into Managua and heading south. If you fly into Managua, simply reverse the itinerary. Get an early-morning start and negotiate the border at Peñas Blancas (Costa Rica) and Sapoa (Nicaragua); then grab a bus or taxi and head for ⛱ **San Juan del Sur** ⑧. Spend a day and a half exploring the beaches in this area. On day two, head to Rivas and take the ferry from nearby San Jorge to ⛱ **Isla Ometepe** ⑨; tour the island and check out balmy Playa Santa Domingo. Spend a night and get an early start on an all-day hike to one of the island's two volcanic craters. Catch a late ferry, or an early one the next day, and bus up to ⛱ **Granada** ⑩, about an hour away, on day four. Spend one or two nights at the wonderful old Hotel Alhambra, devoting a day to soaking up the colonial ambience, touring the historic buildings, and boat-cruising Las Isletas. This leaves time for a morning shopping session in **Masaya** ⑫ and an afternoon at **Volcán Masaya National Park** ⑬. A trip up to **Catarina** ⑪ to have lunch at the spectacular mirador makes a perfect close to an intoxicating five-day trip. From here, the Costa Rican border is about two hours away.

When to Tour Nicaragua

This region shares the climate of northwestern Costa Rica, so it's intensely hot at lower elevations in the dry season, from late November to April. The rainiest month is usually October. It's always cooler up in the mountains near the volcanoes. With tourism still in an infant state in all of Nicaragua, there's no reason to avoid the height of the

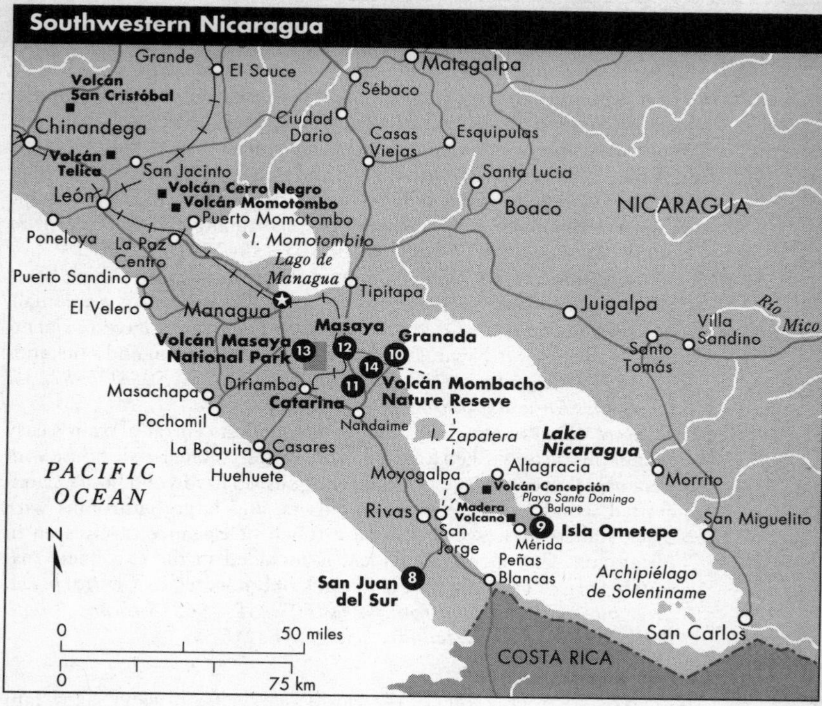
Southwestern Nicaragua
Grande
El Sauce
Matagalpa
Volcán San Cristóbal
Sébaco
Chinandega
Ciudad Dario
Casas Viejas
Esquipulas
Volcán Telica
San Jacinto
Santa Lucia
León
Volcán Cerro Negro
Volcán Momotombo
Boaco
NICARAGUA
Puerto Momotombo
Poneloya
La Paz Centro
I. Momotombito
Lago de Managua
Puerto Sandino
Tipitapa
El Velero
Managua
Juigalpa
Río Mico
Villa Sandino
Masaya
Granada
Santo Tomás
Volcán Masaya National Park
13
12
10
14
11
Masachapa
Diriamba
Volcán Mombacho Nature Reseve
Catarina
Pochomil
Nandaime
I. Zapatera
Lake Nicaragua
La Boquita
Casares
Altagracia
Huehuete
Moyogalpa
Morrito
PACIFIC OCEAN
Volcán Concepción
Playa Santo Domingo
Balque
Rivas
Madera Volcano
San Miguelito
San Jorge
9
Isla Ometepe
Mérida
N
Peñas Blancas
San Juan del Sur
8
Archipiélago de Solentiname
0
50 miles
San Carlos
COSTA RICA
0
75 km

dry season, though the limited number of rooms at the beach might cause some crowding around the Christmas and Easter holidays.

Southwestern Nicaragua

Just north of Costa Rica's Guanacaste province, southwestern Nicaragua combines genuinely warm people, a wealth of natural beauty, dependable road and boat access to major destinations, and one town—Granada, just north of Lake Nicaragua—with more historic and architectural richness than all of Costa Rica put together. The oldest city in the Americas, Granada is a quiet, colorful jewel of a town and serves as a wonderful base of exploration. This relatively untouristed region offers a quieter, less-expensive alternative—or accompaniment—to the pleasures of Guanacaste.

San Juan del Sur

8 After a brief stay in San Juan del Sur, Ernest Hemingway complained that the beer was warm, the music was lousy, and the women were ugly. Most present-day travelers will leave considerably more satisfied. San Juan del Sur and its pretty half-moon beach are tucked between two high headlands, offering shelter for a sweet but ramshackle little town, a small fishing fleet, and the odd pleasure craft. In the last few years a minor influx of European backpackers has inspired the beginnings of a tourist infrastructure, centered on Ricardo's Bar. The beachfront boulevard is lined with open-air seafood restaurants, with a few small hotels across the street. This is the place to make your plans for all area activities, from surfing to sportfishing—dozens of pristine beaches lie within half an hour by car or boat. Think of this as Costa Rica 20 years ago, on the brink of discovery.

DINING AND LODGING

$$ ✕ **Ricardo's Bar.** Owners Marie and Richard sold the legendary Marie's Bar to move to this prettier locale on the beach. Ricardo's is a logical first stop in town, as it proffers reliable tourist information, Internet use, boogie-board rental, an English-language book exchange, and good food. Recommended dishes include seafood crepes and Ricardo's special, a chicken breast with shrimp and a cheese sauce. Day and night, the atmosphere is endlessly lively, as travelers' chatter mixes with the sound of the music videos playing on the satellite TV. ⊠ *Waterfront road, 3 blocks north of bus stop,* ☎ *505/458–2502. AE, MC, V.*

$$–$$$ ⊞ **Casablanca Hotel.** We recommend the upstairs suite, which has a balcony overlooking the sea across the street. The other rooms are small, though comfortable and air-conditioned. Five rooms have refrigerators. It's pricey for Nicaragua, but has a great location and outstanding, personalized service. ⊠ *San Juan del Sur,* ☎ FAX *505/045–82135. 13 rooms. Air-conditioning, pool, laundry service. AE, MC, V.* ✎

$$ ⊞ **Hotel Villa Renata.** From the town's modest central plaza it's easy
★ to spot this distinguished hotel—it's the white, colonial-style house with a colorful flower garden out front. The polished hardwood floors, handcrafted wood furniture, walk-in closets, and large bathrooms with black Italian tiles give this hotel a touch of elegance rarely seen in Nicaragua. Continental breakfast is included in the extremely reasonable price. The only flaw is the lack of hot water. ⊠ *Central plaza, three blocks from oceanfront,* ☎ FAX *505/458–2568. 5 rooms, 3 with bath. Breakfast room, laundry service AE, MC, V.*

Lake Nicaragua

Lago de Nicaragua, one of the world's larger fresh-water lakes, laps Granada's northern shores and stretches south almost to Costa Rica. Once upon a time, bull sharks swam up the San Juan River from the Caribbean to live part-time here, though they're rarely, if ever, seen these days. A ferry from the port of San Jorge (about halfway down the lake just east of the town of Rivas) delivers people, animals, and goods to Moyogalpa on magical Ometepe, a figure-eight-shape island in the lake with a volcano rising out of each roughly circular half.

Isla Ometepe

⑨ With about 35,000 residents and 300 cars, Isla Ometepe is a quiet, pastoral place, worth visiting for a few reasons: to ascend through virgin rain forest to the tops of volcanoes Concepción and Madera; to kick back and relax at the beach of Santa Domingo; or to explore archaeological sites where ancient petroglyphs have been discovered. The ferries are small and usually crowded, and Ometepe's roads are marginally passable. With taxis and tours available at the ferry dock, we recommend leaving the car behind. There's a secure parking garage at San Jorge.

On the northern, or Concepcíon, half of the island, the two main towns are **Moyogalpa,** to the west, and **Altagracia,** to the northeast. Contrary to what most maps indicate, the coastal road encircling this upper half of the island no longer goes all the way around; a lava flow took out a section several years ago, and it has not been repaired. But it's still relatively easy to get around. Heading south and then east on the dirt road from Moyogalpa, you'll soon reach the turnoff for **Playa Santa Domingo,** the island's longest beach. From Playa Santa Domingo, Altagracia is just a few minutes' drive north—a trip worth taking for the petroglyphs alongside the road by Altagracia's town square. Another area with dozens of petroglyphs is near **Balque,** the main town on the southern half of the island, dominated by Volcán Madera. Come see the volcanoes, beach, green lagoon where crocodiles live, and the little towns on this southern half of the island. The rest is pleasant country sightseeing, walking, biking, or bouncing along the bad roads with the locals.

LODGING

$$ ⊞ **Villa Paraiso.** Facing east across Lake Nicaragua from Playa Santo Domingo, the Paraiso has basic, comfortable accommodations—six rooms in the main building and 11 cabinas, the latter with private baths. The hotel's shady bar and restaurant overlook the lake, and the staff can help organize volcano, petroglyph, and other island tours. ⊠ *Playa Santo Domingo,* ☎ FAX *505/453–4675. 6 rooms, 11 cabinas. Restaurant, bar, horseback riding, boating, laundry service. AE, MC, V.*

$–$$ ⊞ **Cari Hotel y Marina.** You can see the Cari from the ferry as you dock in Moyogalpa. Like all of Ometepe's hotels and hospedajes, it offers small, clean rooms, some with private baths, at rock-bottom prices. In addition, this hotel rents cars and canoes and offers island tours. If you're feeling lackadaisical, hang out in the open-air restaurant-bar and watch island women do their laundry on washing platforms in the lake. ⊠ *Moyogalpa,* ☎ FAX *505/459–4263. 22 rooms. Restaurant, air-conditioning, laundry service, car rental. AE, MC, V.*

$ ⊞ **Castillo Hotel.** Señor Castillo serves as tour guide emeritus, unofficial historian, and general source of relevant Ometepe information. His one-story hotel encircling a quiet courtyard has clean, comfortable little rooms, some with private baths, within walking distance of Altagracia's petroglyph collection. ⊠ *1 block south and half a block west of Parque Central, Altagracia,* ☎ *505/552–8744. 13 rooms, 7 with bath. Restaurant, horseback riding. AE, MC, V.*

OUTDOOR ACTIVITIES AND SPORTS

Hiking. Beyond exploring the pastoral towns and beaches, the main activity on Ometepe is hiking the two volcanoes. The trail to the top of Concepción starts near Altagracia and takes about five hours each way. Another trail of similar length and difficulty begins near Moyogalpa. The trail up Madera Volcano, beginning at Balque, takes roughly four hours each way. The use of a guide is highly recommended for both volcano hikes, as the trails are arduous and not always easy to follow. Wildlife abounds—monkeys, birds, sloths—and the views are remarkable from both peaks. Your hotel can arrange a guide; otherwise, ask around at the dock, or contact **Ometepe Tours** (☎ 505/453–4779).

Granada

⓪ Founded in 1524, prosperous for centuries, and ravaged by the gringo maniac William Walker in the mid-19th century, Granada (about 102 km/63 mi north of the Costa Rican border) has survived, and even prospered, through Nicaragua's troubled history. In the 1990s the entire city was declared a museum, meaning that no tall buildings will ever be erected in or near the colonial-era downtown. Additionally, every building renovation must follow strict design guidelines intended to maintain the integrity of the existing colonial architecture. Though Nicaragua is impoverished, efforts are under way to restore Granada's finest public buildings; Nicaraguans and investors from Europe, the United States, Costa Rica, and elsewhere have been buying up the city's elegant 18th- and 19th-century homes, renovating them, and transforming them into restaurants, hotels, inns, and private homes. There's a quiet little boom going on.

Surrounded by blocks of low-rise, pastel-hue colonial buildings, Granada holds many charms, beginning with the **Parque Central,** or central plaza, surrounded by the **Palacio Episcopal, Palacio Municipal, Palacio de la Cultura,** and wonderful old **Hotel Alhambra** (☞ Dining and Lodging, *below), the* place to stay overnight.

The plaza is dominated by the **cathedral** on its eastern side. Walker burned the original cathedral down in 1857; this structure was completed in 1910. It's a rather imposing example of neoclassical architecture, worth a visit to explore the vivid, slightly tacky examples of religious art within. ⊠ *Parque Central.* ⊙ *Daily 8–6.*

Two blocks east, beyond the **Plaza de los Leones,** the church of **San Francisco,** dating from the 1520s, has a Baroque facade with a system of pediments and symmetrical oval windows. Next door, the old convent serves as a **museum,** with a collection of stunningly carved stone artifacts dating from around AD 800, gathered on the Ometepe and Zapatera islands in Lake Nicaragua. ⊠ *C. Arsenal and Avda. Miguel Cervantes (2 blocks east of cathedral).* ⊙ *Daily 9–6.*

Stroll or take one of the ubiquitous, low-cost horse-carriage cabs (the painfully thin horses are a sorry sight, but locals say it's a parasite, not starvation, that gives them that bony look) down Calle la Calzada to the lakeshore, and head south to the **Centro Turistico,** a long, shady waterfront park lined with discos, restaurants, and other diversions. From here it's a few miles farther south to **Puerto Aseses** (☎ 055/552–2269) where you can book a boat tour and spend an hour or two cruising through Granada's famed Las Isletas, the 360-odd tiny, plant-bedecked islands that lie offshore. Most are privately owned, but others protect bird reserves or feature small hotels or restaurants.

DINING AND LODGING

$$–$$$ ✕ **Mediterraneo.** Hostess-owner Enriqueta, unfailingly gracious and
★   well informed, hails from Spain, Canada, Morocco, New York, and elsewhere. Her worldliness, which includes a command of seven languages, shines through on the Spanish menu infused with international accents. The paellas are exceptional. A wonderfully romantic atmosphere pervades; the elegantly furnished dining room, done in rosy terra-cotta tones, flanks a lovely interior garden, enhanced by with candlelight, plants, and quietly flowing fountains. This is, hands down, the finest restaurant in Granada. ⊠ *C. El Caimito,* ☎ *505/552–6764. AE, MC, V. Closed Mon.*

$$ ✕ **Café del Pêss.** Antonio and Vera Moro prepare Italian food the old-fashioned way: with pasta made by hand every morning, meats marinated for four days, and homemade sauces of only the freshest ingredients. All are served with warm ciabatta and focaccia loaves fresh out of the oven. The delicious *ravioli café del pêss* is served in a tomato cream sauce with onions, garlic, carrots, and bacon. You can dine indoors, at elegant tables surrounded by pictures of Italy's Lake Como region, or outdoors, on a patio facing a small garden. ⊠ *1 km (½ mi) from city center on highway to Masaya,* ☎ *505/552–2237. AE, MC, V. Closed Wed.*

$$–$$$ ▣ **Hotel Alhambra.** A jewel on Granada's shady Parque Central, the
★   two-story Alhambra is slightly run-down but still highly recommended as the essential Granada spot. The colonnaded, comfortably furnished lobby wraps around an interior courtyard garden with a pleasantly murmuring fountain. Guest rooms are filled with a hodgepodge of modern desks, lamps, and the like, matched with old carved-wooden cabinets, double beds, and atmospheric pieces. All rooms are air-conditioned, and some have hot water some of the time, but other aspects vary. The second-story rooms overlooking the plaza are simply wonderful, except for the very noisy cathedral bells, which ring at the strangest times; rooms overlooking the pool in back are smaller but quieter. ⊠ *West of Parque Central,* ☎ *505/552–4486,* ℻ *505/552–2035. 60 rooms. Restaurant, café, air-conditioning, pool, laundry service, meeting rooms. AE, MC, V.*

$–$$ ✿ Posada Don Alfredo. Two blocks off the Parque Central, the Ger-
★ man-run Posada offers huge, high-ceilinged rooms with multiple beds
at great prices in an exquisitely restored 165-year-old colonial building. The dining and lounging area is invitingly comfortable, with a small
library and satellite TV. Don Alfredo spends two hours every morning preparing an out-of-this-world breakfast for anyone who's interested—it's a bit expensive, but guests pay less. You can also rent
kayaks here for $10 a day. ⊠ *C. 14 de Septiembre,* ☎ *505/552–4455,*
FAX *505/552–4455. 6 rooms, 2 with bath. Restaurant, bicycles, laundry service. No credit cards.* ✿

Catarina

⓫ Watch for the turnoff to Catarina, 16 km (10 mi) along the road from
Granada to Masaya—it takes you up to a spectacular mirador, or lookout, in this colorful little town overflowing with attractive plant stores.
On the back side of town, past the cathedral, a cluster of gaudy souvenir stands (one sells respectable paintings by the young artist man-
ning the stand) and a row of restaurants line the edge of a cliff overlooking
the crater lake called Laguna de Apoyo. The restaurants are pricey by
Nicaraguan standards, but well worth the view of Lake Apoyo, Masaya,
Granada, and, stretching into the distance, Lake Nicaragua. A different road off the main highway—at Kilometer 38—leads to **Lake Apoyo**
itself, where the swimming is safe and pleasant. Just across the road from
Catarina lies the entrance to the village of **Niquinohomo,** birthplace of
fabled Nicaraguan revolutionary Augusto Sandino.

Masaya

⓬ Twenty minutes (about 24 km/15 mi) northwest of Granada by car,
the city of Masaya offers great shopping, pleasant strolling, and not
much else. A half-day trip from Granada should give you enough time
to prowl the two markets for hammocks, leather goods, weavings, pottery, paintings, and other crafts, and to explore the town. The original crafts market is within the labyrinthine confines of the main city
market, five blocks east of the main plaza, known as the **Parque 17
de Octobre.** A spanking-new arts-and-crafts complex, **Nuevo Mercado,** is closer to the center of town. Remember to bring dollars or córdobas, the Nicaraguan currency; leave your Costa Rican colones
behind.

Volcán Masaya National Park

⓭ Five kilometers (3 miles) farther north along the main highway from
Granada, heading toward Managua, is the turnoff to Parque Nacional
Volcán Masaya (☞ Chapter 9). Stop first at the expansive **visitor center and museum** for an overview of the region's cultural and geological history; there's a lot of fascinating information here, though most
of the text is in Spanish. Ascending into volcanic terrain, it's just a few
feet from the parking lot to the edge of the smoldering **Santiago Crater,**
one of four that compose the Masaya volcano. The viewpoint from
which you can actually see the fire below has been closed, but the steaming, sulphurous crater is still an awesome sight. Hike up the long staircase to the overlook, where a cross—a replica of one put up in the 16th
century—keeps the devil in his hole, or so thought the Spaniards who
erected the first one, as they called this place Boca del Infierno—the
"Mouth of Hell." ⊠ *Carretera Masaya–Managua, Km 23, Apdo. NI-
1, Nindiri,* ☎ *505/522–5415.* ⌨ *$3.50.* ☉ *Daily 9–5.*

Volcán Mombacho Nature Reserve

⓮ This unique cloud-forest reserve (the Reserva Natural Volcán Mombacho) was opened to the public in 1999 with the support of USAID
and the British Embassy, the latter of which is building a biological research station here. A well-marked, 2-km-long (1-mi-long) hiking trail

surrounds the verdant crater of this dormant volcano, and numerous signs (in Spanish) explain the reserve's diverse flora and fauna—over 450 species of plants, 87 varieties of orchids, and 118 species of birds—some of which exist nowhere else. At 1,345 m (4,440 ft) above sea level, the park has excellent views of the valley and lakes below. The reserve is only 10 km (6 mi) and a cheap taxi ride from Granada; on the Nandaime highway, turn right at the park's entrance and continue another 1½ km (1 mi) to the park entrance. From here it's another 5 km (3 mi) to the trail—hike up through pretty coffee plantations or get a free ride in the park's jeep at 8:30 AM, 10, 1, or 3. ☎ *505/552–5858.* 🖃 *$5.* ☉ *Thurs.–Sun. 8–5.*

Southwestern Nicaragua A to Z

ARRIVING AND DEPARTING

Getting to Nicaragua is slightly complicated by the fact that you cannot take rental cars across the border from Costa Rica, but planes, private cars, buses, boats, and taxis do the trick.

By Car. Nicaragua's only car-rental agencies are in Managua, beyond the reach of this chapter. The numerous agencies at Managua's Sandino International Airport and in Managua city offer a good selection of cars for $25 a day and up, much cheaper than in Costa Rica. A few major names with branches at Managua's airport: **Budget** (☎ 505/266–6226, FAX 505/222–5567). **Hertz** (☎ 505/233–1237, FAX 505/266–8400). **Lugo** (☎ 505/266–2387, FAX 505/266–4477).

By Bus. You can reserve a bus seat in San José; the **Transnica** (🖃 C. 22 between Avdas. 3 and 5, ☎ 221–0953 in San José or ☎ 505/278–2090 in Managua) line runs between San José and Managua three times daily. You can also catch a bus in front of the Hotel Guanacaste in Liberia, provided you've either reserved a seat in advance or there happens to be space. Ask the driver to drop you off in Rivas or Granada once across the border. The fare is around $20 round-trip from either starting point.

By Plane. Grupo Taca (☎ 505/266–3136 in Managua or 506/296–0909 in San José) offers two flights a day from San José to Managua and back. The cost is about $200 per person plus a $20 exit tax at each end. Flights leave San José at 6:30 AM and 2 PM.

GETTING AROUND

By Boat. Ferries to Ometepe's Moyogalpa run daily from San Jorge, near Rivas. Boats from Granada and San Jorge run three times a week. Weekend hydrofoil service operates from Granada. For ferry information call 505/552–2966.

By Bus. There are plentiful buses, ranging from low-cost locals—usually recycled American school buses—to pricier air-conditioned expresses.

By Car. Most of Nicaragua's main roads are in good shape, so four-wheel drive is not necessary.

CONTACTS AND RESOURCES

Embassies. Canada (🖃 Apdo. 25, Managua, ☎ 505/268–0433). **U.K.** (🖃 Plaza Churchill Reparto Los Robles, Apdo. A-169, Managua, ☎ 505/278–0014). **U.S.** (🖃 Carretera Sur, Km 4½, Managua, ☎ 505/266–6010).

Emergencies. Ambulance (Granada, ☎ 505/552–2711; Masaya, ☎ 505/522–2870). **Hospitals** (Granada, 🖃 San Juan de Dios, ☎ 505/552–2719; Isla Ometepe, Moyagalpa, 🖃 Del Parque, 3 C. al Sur, ☎ 505/459–4247). **Police** (Granada, ☎ 505/552–4399; Masaya, ☎ 505/522–4222).

Careli Tours. If you'd rather leave the arrangements to someone else: **Careli Tours** (☎ 505/278–2572) and **Tours Nicaragua** (☎ 505/884–1712) offer complete packages with a car and bilingual driver-guide. **Ome-tepe Tours** (☎ 505/453–4779), near the dock in San Jorge, will set up an Ometepe island tour, complete with car and driver to greet you at the Moyogalpa end of the one-hour ferry ride. Stop in and see the jaws on the office walls—they come from sharks caught in the lake. Check out the bulletin board at **Ricardo's Bar** in San Juan del Sur (☎ 505/458–2502; ☞ *above*) for the names and numbers of every tour operator in the area, from sailing boats such as *Pelican Eyes* (☎ 505/458–2110) to express buses to Managua (☎ 505/453–3783).

Travel Agencies. *See* **Careli Tours** and **Tours Nicaragua,** *above.*

Visitor Information. Granada (✉ Parque Central, next to cathedral, ☎ 505/552–6858). **Isla Ometepe** (contact Ometepe Tours, ✉ San Jorge, near dock, ☎ 505/453–4779; ✉ Moyogalpa, ☎ 505/459–4116).

9 NATIONAL PARKS AND BIOLOGICAL RESERVES

A selective primer on the best protected areas in Costa Rica, Panama, and Nicaragua—eternal homes of spectacular wildlife, flora, coral, and volcanoes.

By David
Dudenhoefer
and Justin
Henderson

THE WEALTH OF NATURAL ASSETS in Costa Rica and Panama is almost unfathomable to anyone who doesn't live there. The breathtaking scenery in these two countries encompasses barren mountain peaks, lush forests, and vibrant, multihued coral reefs, and the native population of wildlife includes more species of plants and animals than scientists have been able to count.

Fortunately, the governments of both nations have had the foresight to protect a significant portion of this ecological wealth in national parks and biological preserves. Flora and fauna also benefit from some degree of protection in wildlife refuges, forest reserves, and Indian reservations. The conservation effort is particularly remarkable when you remember that Costa Rica and Panama are relatively poor countries with limited infrastructures. Just three decades ago, there was hardly a protected area in either nation; today Costa Rica's parks cover about 13% of the national territory, and Panama's parks and reserves cover 17% of its terrain (though the Panamanian areas tend to be less protected than those in Costa Rica).

Let's hope the winds of change keep blowing in Nicaragua: with decades of political upheaval only recently drawn to a close, Nicaragua has had little spare money or energy for the development of a national-park system. The country's only officially designated national park is that of Volcán Masaya, established in 1979; several other areas in the country have attained unofficial park or reserve status and will probably become national parks eventually.

During the first decades of Costa Rica's and Panama's park systems, conservationists raced against rampant deforestation to protect as much of their countries' vital wildlands as possible. Parks were created and maps were drawn, but protecting the flora and fauna within them turned out to be a daunting task for the underfunded government agencies in charge. Thanks to the foresight of local conservationists and ample assistance from abroad, these parks and reserves now contain examples of nearly all the region's ecosystems: mangrove estuaries, lowland rain forests, tropical dry forests, cloud forests, caves, active volcanic craters, transition forests, freshwater swamps and lagoons, and various marine ecosystems including pristine beaches and coral reefs.

The Costa Rican Ministry of the Environment and Energy (MINAE) and the Panamanian Institute of Renewable Natural Resources (INRENARE) are now focusing on consolidating park management and improving park infrastructure. Many parks are accessible only by four-wheel-drive vehicles; only a few have paved roads; and some can only be visited by boat, on horseback, or on foot. Most parks still don't have visitor centers, and walking trails aren't always well marked.

Indeed, because its wildlife *is* so outstanding, Costa Rica faces a relatively new conservation challenge—controlling the crowds that now flock to its best-known protected areas. Some Costa Rican parks get so many visitors in high season that it can be worth your while to opt for less popular protected areas, as you'll probably have a more private and natural experience. In addition to national parks, a growing number of private nature reserves are open to the public, many of which have their own lodges. Nearly all tour companies offer trips to national parks and reserves, some with more experience in ecotourism than others.

Responsible Tourism
Economic pressures still cause some Ticos and Panamanians to cut down trees and hunt endangered animals. These citizens are slowly coming to

realize that conservation pays; and whenever you visit a park or reserve, you send a positive message to both the government and the marketplace at large. But your contribution to wilderness protection can go well beyond the payment of an entrance fee. Whether you travel on your own or with a tour group, try to make your visit beneficial to those who live near protected areas: use local guides or services, eat in local restaurants, and buy local crafts or produce. To ensure land preservation for future generations, you can also donate to local conservation groups; and in addition to these, a few foreign environmental organizations—including Conservation International, the Nature Conservancy, and the World Wide Fund for Nature—aid ecological efforts in Costa Rica and Panama.

Eye on Wildlife

Needless to say, the protected areas are packed with amazing scenery and wildlife, including such endangered species as jaguars, tapirs, and giant anteaters. Don't be disappointed, however, if you don't come face to face with these animals. Despite their frequent appearances in advertisements and brochures, jaguars, for example, are practically impossible to see in the wild, given their scarcity, shyness, and nocturnal schedules. Don't give up hope: if you take the time to explore a few protected areas, you're almost certain to spy some monkeys, iguanas, sloths, parrots, toucans, and dozens of other interesting critters.

Travelers are often surprised by how hard it can be to see animals in the rain forest. Between the low density of mammals and the fact that thick vegetation often obstructs your view, you must be patient and stay attentive. Because the tropical dry forest is less overgrown than the rain forest, it's one of the best life zones for animal observation; river trips, too, can make for great viewing.

Visitor Information and Admission Fees

In August 1994, Costa Rica's Environment Ministry raised the cost of entry for foreign visitors to all national parks, biological reserves, and national monuments from less than $2 to $15, a decision that infuriated many in the tourism industry. The country's environment minister claimed the drastic increase was needed to accomplish two important goals: raising the money to patrol the parks effectively and improve infrastructure, and decreasing the traffic into some of the more heavily visited parks. Money was raised and visitation decreased, but representatives from the country's tourism sector insisted that the high fees were hurting that vital industry, and in 1996 the price of admission to national parks was reduced to $6 per day. The Panamanian government currently charges entrance fees ranging from $3 to $10.

For specific information on Costa Rican parks and protected areas, call the environment ministry's **national-park information line** (☎ 192)—the well-informed, bilingual operators can quickly answer most questions. For specific requests, such as reserving camping or cabin space, call the regional office of the park in question. Practical information on parks, including limited literature, are available at the **Fundación de Parques Nacionales** (⊠ 300 m south and 300 m east of Church of Santa Teresita, San José, ☎ 506/257–2239).

In Panama, **INRENARE** is supposed to fax you written permission to visit a park after you contact the main office in Panama City (☎ 507/232–7228), but it's much easier to go straight to the park itself: rangers are always happy to help visitors, who are still relatively scarce.

For information on the Masaya Volcano national park and other refuges in Nicaragua, contact the **Dirección de Silvestres y Faunas** (⊠ Km 12½, Carretera Norte, Apdo. 5123, Managua, ☎ 505/31112–31595, FAX 505/31112–31596).

THE CENTRAL VALLEY: AROUND SAN JOSÉ

Because the Central Valley was one of the first parts of Costa Rica to be settled and is now home to more than half of its burgeoning population, Mother Nature has had to retreat to the mountaintops and a few isolated river valleys. Parks here have good access via paved (albeit somewhat potholed) roads, and most are feasible for travelers who can't walk long distances. Because the floor and lower slopes of the Central Valley are covered with coffee plantations, towns, and cities, the region's parks are predominantly cloud-forest ecosystems at high elevations—extremely luxuriant, and often shrouded in thick mist.

Volcán Irazú National Park

Parque Nacional Volcán Irazú protects little more than the summit of Volcán Irazú, Costa Rica's highest volcano at 11,260 ft. The landscape at the top of the crater is bleak but beautiful; it's still scarred from the volcano's violent eruptions between 1962 and 1965, when several feet of ash covered the Central Valley. Head up Irazú as early in the morning as possible—before the summit is enveloped in clouds—so you can catch a glimpse of its cream-of-asparagus crater lake and, if you're lucky, views of nearby mountains and either the Pacific or the Caribbean in the distance. There are no trails or visitor centers at the summit, but a paved road leads all the way to the top through pastoral landscapes suggesting the Alps more than prototypical Central America.

Tapantí National Wildlife Refuge

The Río Grande de Orosí flows through the middle of Refugio Nacional de Fauna Silvestre Tapantí, a protected cloud forest that covers the mountain at the southern end of the Orosí Valley. The emerald waters of that boulder-strewn river pour into some brisk but inviting swimming holes near the park's picnic area. There's a modest visitor center by the entrance, and 1½ km (1 mi) up the road is a parking area with trails that head into the woods off both sides of the street. The Sendero Oropéndola trail leads to two loops, one that passes the picnic and swimming areas and another that winds through the forest nearby. The trail across the road forms a loop along a forested hillside, and La Pava trail, 2½ km (1½ mi) farther up on the right, leads down a steep hill to the riverbank. Several miles farther up the road from La Pava is a view of a long, slender cascade on the far side of the valley. Camping is not permitted.

Guayabo National Monument

True, the ruins here don't compare with those of Guatemala and Mexico, but Monumento Nacional Guayabo is Costa Rica's most important archaeological site. Most of the original buildings were made of wood, so only their bases remain. Rangers give guided tours (in Spanish) of the ruins, which include stone roads and a communal well fed by a pre-Columbian aqueduct. On your own, you can hike a trail that loops through the surrounding rain forest and perhaps do a little birdwatching. Camping is allowed near the ranger station. Guayabo is closed to visitors on Monday.

NORTHERN GUANACASTE AND ALAJUELA

Parks in the province of Guanacaste protect some of the last remnants of the Mesoamerican tropical dry forest that once covered the Pacific lowlands from Costa Rica to the Mexican state of Chiapas. Because Spanish colonists found the climate on the Pacific slope of the isthmus more hospitable than its humid Atlantic side, most of the development that followed the conquest of Central America took a toll on the Pacific forests; hardly any wilderness now remains on that half of the land bridge. Consequently, the protected dry forests of Guanacaste are of extreme importance to conservationists. The institution of new national parks is a work in progress: Volcán Tenorio is now protected, but has no infrastructure as of yet.

Guanacaste's daily deluges of rain subside in December, and the lush landscape enters a transition: as the dry season progresses, most trees drop their foliage and the region resembles a desert. Many trees flower in the dry season, however, and the yellow, white, and pink blossoms of the *tabebuia* add splashes of color to the leafless landscape.

Because of their sparse foliage and partial deforestation, Costa Rica's dry-forest parks are some of the best places in the country to see wildlife. Many animals native to North America are common in Guanacaste's protected areas—white-tailed deer, coyotes, magpie jays, diamondback rattlesnakes—but you might also see some predominantly South American animals, such as collared peccaries, armadillos, parrots, and broad-beaked hawks called caracaras. Because the northwest is so expansive, parks in this region tend to lie away from bus routes, which means you're better off traveling to most of them in a rental car or on a tour.

Juan Castro Blanco National Park

Most of the once-jungle-covered land on the upper level of the Atlantic plain, where foothills mark the transition from the coastal lowland to the central mountains, has been cleared for cattle and dairy farming. There are, however, a number of biological preserves here, plus Parque Nacional Juan Castro Blanco. East of Ciudad Quesada (locally known as San Carlos), this 142-sq-km (88-sq-mi) park was created to protect large tracts of virgin forest around the headwaters of the Platanar, Tora, Aguas Zarcas, Tres Amigos, and La Vieja rivers. Unfortunately, the park has no facilities of any kind at present.

Caño Negro National Wildlife Refuge

The river trip to Refugio Nacional de Vida Silvestre Caño Negro can be an interesting alternative to the Tortuguero canal trip. A lowland rain-forest reserve, Caño Negro has suffered severe deforestation over the years; but most of the Río Frío is still lined with trees, so the boat trip up the river to the reserve helps you spot a variety of wildlife. The lagoon at the heart of the reserve also attracts numerous waterfowl from November to January. Caño Negro is most easily accessed from the Nuevo Arenal–La Fortuna area.

Rincón de la Vieja National Park

Parque Nacional Rincón de la Vieja was created to protect the upper slopes of this volcano, with forests that stay greener than those in the drier lowland and a series of steam geysers, bubbling mud pots, hot springs, and cascades. The extensive protected area has entrances at

Hacienda Santa María and Las Pailas. There's a camping area by the old farmhouse of Santa María, and a 2-km (1-mi) hike from here is Bosque Encantado, where the Río Zopilote pours over a cascade in the forest to form an enticing pool. Three kilometers (2 miles) farther is a hot sulfur spring, and 4 km (2½ mi) beyond that are bubbling, boiling mud pots and fumaroles in an area called Las Pailas. Respect the fences, and don't get too close to the mud pots—their edges are brittle, and several people have slipped in and been severely burned. The trail to the summit heads into the forest above Las Pailas, but it's a trip for serious hikers, best done in the dry season with preparation for cold weather at the top.

A less strenuous option is to hike the 3-km (2-mi) loop, along which you'll see fumaroles, a *volcáncito* (baby volcano), and Las Pailas. Possible critter sightings include armadillos, howler monkeys, and semidomesticated, raccoonlike coatis looking for handouts (a plea you should ignore: a cardinal rule of wildlife encounters is not to feed the animals).

Santa Rosa National Park

Parque Nacional Santa Rosa is one of Costa Rica's most impressive protected areas. The dry forest covering much of the park draws biologists and nature lovers; and whereas one of the park's beaches (Nancite) is a vital nesting area for the olive ridley sea turtle, the beach next to it (Naranjo) is well known among surfing cognoscenti for its world-class waves.

You can see the forested slopes of Volcán Orosí, protected within Guanacaste National Park, from the Carretera Interamericana (Pan-American Highway) as you approach Santa Rosa's entrance. A few miles after you enter Santa Rosa, a scenic overlook on the right grants your first good look at the park's dry forest. La Casona Hacienda, an old farmhouse and former battle site, houses a small museum with exhibits on the area's ecology and the battle between ill-equipped Costa Ricans and American mercenary William Walker. A small nature trail loops through the woods, and there's a large camping area nearby. (To reserve a site, call park headquarters at 666–5020. The road that passes the campground heads to Playa Naranjo, a pristine beach with great surfing and animal-spotting. Playa Naranjo has a camping area, but it provides no potable water and can only be reached in a four-wheel-drive vehicle or via a 12-km (7-mi) hike from La Casona. Note that Santa Rosa's campgrounds, which can sleep 150 people, sometimes fill up during the dry season, especially in the first week of January and during Holy Week (Palm Sunday–Easter Sunday).

If you can't make it to Playa Naranjo, try one of two good animal-watching trails that branch off the road before it gets too steep for anything but four-wheel-drive vehicles. The Patos Trail, on the left a few miles after the campgrounds, heads through the forest past a water hole and several scenic overlooks. A kilometer (½ mile) farther down the road on the right is a short trail leading to an overlook from which you can see distant Playa Naranjo and, offshore, the massive Witches Rock. Nancite, north of Naranjo, is an important turtle-nesting beach, and the *arribadas* (mass nestings) for which Nancite is famous also occur at Ostional National Wildlife Refuge (Refugio Nacional de Fauna Silvestre Ostional), near Nosara.

Guanacaste National Park

East of the Pan-American Highway but contiguous with Santa Rosa National Park, comprising a mosaic of ecologically interdependent protected areas, parks, and refuges, Parque Nacional Guanacaste stretches up to the cloud forests atop Volcán Cacao. The park is still in fragments; the goal is to create a single Guanacaste megapark to accommodate the natural migratory patterns of myriad creatures from jaguars to tapirs. As things stand there are 300 different birds and more than 5,000 species of butterflies here. Camping is reportedly possible at the biological stations, and there are a few highly rustic lodges; call park headquarters in advance (☎ 506/661–8150).

THE NICOYA PENINSULA

Out on this sunny protrusion, monkeys howl in the dry tropical forests, coatimundis caper, and turtles ride in on the evening high tide to deposit their eggs in the sand in one of the world's most fascinating biological rites.

Palo Verde National Park and Lomas Barbudal Biological Reserve

Parque Nacional Palo Verde and Reserva Biológica Lomas Barbudal protect significant expanses of deciduous dry forest, and because both receive fewer visitors than Santa Rosa, they offer a more natural experience. Palo Verde's major attraction is its swampland, a temporary home for thousands of migratory birds toward the end of the rainy season. An important part of these lagoons lies near the ranger station, where a raised platform aids bird-watchers; between December and March you can see dozens of species of aquatic birds in these parts, including several kinds of herons, ducks, wood storks, and elegant roseate spoonbills.

Palo Verde's forests are alive with species inhabiting Santa Rosa, and the road that leads to the ranger station from the town of Bagaces passes some wooded patches where you're bound to glimpse birds and mammals if you drive slowly. Trails also head away from the ranger station—one short path into the hills behind it, and a longer one to the river. The 28-km (17-mi) road south from Bagaces is fairly rough and passes a lot of pasture. An alternative route between Palo Verde and the Pan-American Highway passes through Lomas Barbudal (meaning it traverses more forest), but it's a longer haul. The ranger station in Lomas Barbudal stands by the Río Cabuya, which has a small swimming hole, and the road across the stream becomes a trail that winds around the forested hillside. The road north from Lomas is pretty bad, but it deposits you on the highway after only 15 km (9 mi). Lodging options in Palo Verde are limited to camping and rustic dorm facilities.

Barra Honda National Park

Rocky hills that contain an extensive network of caves dominate Parque Nacional Barra Honda, an area of protected dry forest. Local guides lower spelunkers into the caverns using ropes and a climber's ladder—a descent into darkness that's inadvisable for the fainthearted but rewarding for the adventurous. If you're not up for the drop, you can trek into the forest-covered hills, full of wildlife and blessed with scenic overlooks featuring the Gulf of Nicoya and surrounding countryside. The two- to three-hour Cascada Trail begins near the ranger's office and makes a loop near the caves; serious hikers will want to continue to the Boquete Trail, which brings the round-trip length to the better part of a day. A community tourism association provides guides and climbing equipment and runs a simple restaurant and lodge, Las Delicias, by the park entrance. Camping is permitted.

Marino Las Baulas National Park

Playa Grande, protected within Parque Nacional Marino Las Baulas, near Tamarindo, is an important turtle-nesting beach. Dedicated in 1991 and officially designated a park in 1995, Las Baulas is visited by thousands of leatherback turtles—the largest in the world—every year during their nesting season, October to March. The adjacent Tamarindo wildlife refuge, although under some developmental pressure, protects a mangrove estuary with some excellent bird-watching. Just south of Tamarindo, accessible by dirt road, is the Río San Francisco, with its own estuary system. Beyond this river lies Playa Langosta, added to the protected-areas list but not nearly as well organized as Las Baulas (turtle tours here are less formal and less expensive). The San Francisco estuary is rich in bird life and, unlike the Tamarindo refuge, free of motorboats. Playa Langosta, like Playa Grande–Las Baulas, is a nesting site for leatherbacks.

THE CENTRAL PACIFIC COAST

Thanks to its proximity to San José, the central Pacific coast has two of Costa Rica's most popular protected areas—home to such endangered species as the scarlet macaw and the squirrel monkey. Set off for either one as early in the morning as possible.

Carara Biological Reserve

The Reserva Biológica Carara, on the road between Puntarenas and Playa Jacó, protects one of the last remnants of a transition zone between the dry forests of the northern Pacific lowlands and the humid forests of the southwest. Tall trees don't drop their foliage during the dry season here, but the sylvan scenery is much less luxuriant than what you'd see farther south. Carara is one of two places in Costa Rica where you can see scarlet macaws, easiest to spot in the early morning or late afternoon. The Río Tárcoles, which defines the park's northern border, is a good place to see crocodiles, and you might also come upon monkeys, coatis, and an array of birds as you wander the forests.

Carara's proximity to San José and Jacó means that tour buses pull in daily in high season, with the perhaps unsurprising result that animals are frightened into the depths of the forest by midday. If you catch Carara very early or late in the day, however, you can see a lot. The trail that starts near the ranger station makes a one-hour loop through the forest; a longer trail, a few miles to the north, is better for animal-watching, but cars parked at that trailhead have been broken into. Camping is not permitted in Carara.

Manuel Antonio National Park

It's only natural that Parque Nacional Manuel Antonio is high on travelers' lists—it mixes exuberant forests with idyllic beaches and coral reefs. But the assets of this beautiful patch of wilderness may have made it too popular for its own good. The road between the park and the town of Quepos is lined with hotels, and when their guests head to the park en masse, its magic wanes. In an attempt to keep crowds at bay, the park service limits visitors to 600 a day (though they almost never get *that* many); and the park is closed on Monday.

Because it's relatively small, Manuel Antonio doesn't have a great deal of wildlife, but along with Corcovado it's one of only two places in Costa Rica where you can see squirrel monkeys. It's also a good place to see agoutis, sloths, and capuchin monkeys, which come so close that they sometimes bite people who attempt to pet them. A tropical storm that hit Manuel Antonio several years ago toppled many of the park's largest trees, but there is plenty to see in the coves, which hold submerged rocks, coral formations, and abundant marine life.

The park entrance is on the beach, just across a little estuary (don't swim here—it's polluted) from the end of the road. A trail leads into the forest just behind the beach; you can also walk on the sand. Another trail makes a loop on Punta Catedral, the steep point at the end of the beach, offering a good look back at the rain forest. The beach on the other side of the point is tucked into a deep cove safe for swimming and good for snorkeling. From here, one trail leads to the nearby cove of Puerto Escondido and a lookout point beyond; a second, the Perezoso, heads back through the forest to the park's entrance. Camping is not allowed in the park, but you can camp just outside it.

THE SOUTHERN PACIFIC COAST

Vast and wild, the southwest hides ecosystems ranging from the reefs off Caño Island to the highland *páramo* (a landscape of shrubs and herbs) of Chirripó peak. This is one of the best places to see such animals as scarlet macaws, spider monkeys, toucans, and coatis, and some equally spectacular forest vegetation.

Chirripó National Park

Surrounding the Parque Nacional Chirripó is a wild and scenic area that's unique in Costa Rica. Because it's so remote, there is no easy way in; hikers usually spend one night in San Gerardo de Rivas, which has several inexpensive lodges. From San Gerardo it's a grueling climb up to the park—six to 10 hours, depending on your physical condition. Try to head out of San Gerardo with the first light of day. You hike through pastures, then forests, and then the burnt remains of forest fires. There are extensive cabin facilities near the top, where you'll want to spend at least two nights, as it's from here that you hike up to the peaks, glacier lakes, and *páramo*—a highland ecosystem common to the Andes that consists of shrubs and herbaceous plants. Trails lead to the top of Chirripó—the highest point in Costa Rica—and the nearby peak of Terbi. The park's new hostel consists of small rooms with four bunks each, cold-water baths, and a cooking area; they rent camp stoves and blankets, but you'll need to bring food, water for the hike, a good sleeping bag, and plenty of warm clothes. At press time there was talk of a cafeteria in the park, which would mean having to pack less food; inquire when you call to reserve space.

Camping is not allowed at Chirripó, and it's wise to reserve a bed in the 40-hiker cabin well ahead of time during the dry season. Contact the environment ministry's regional office in San Isidro (☎ 506/771–3155)—if space is available on your chosen dates, they'll give you the number of a Banco Nacional account into which you must deposit admission and lodging fees to confirm your reservation. Be prepared for very cold weather on top.

Corcovado National Park

A tranquil expanse of wilderness covering one-third of the Osa Peninsula, Parque Nacional Corcovado safeguards virgin rain forest, deserted beaches, jungle-edged rivers, and a vast, inaccessible swamp. Corcovado is home to boa constrictors, jaguars, anteaters, tapirs, and if you're lucky enough to encounter one of these rare creatures anywhere in Costa Rica, it's most likely to happen here. You'll definitely see flocks of scarlet macaws, troops of spider monkeys, colorful poison dart frogs, toucans, and agoutis.

The easiest way to visit remote Corcovado is on a day trip from one of the lodges in the nearby Drake Bay area, or from the Corcovado Tent Camp; but if you have a backpack and strong legs, you can spend days deep in its wilds. A limited number of bunks are available at the Sirena station—you'll need sheets and a good mosquito net—and meals can be arranged at any one of the stations if you reserve in advance. Only 35 people are allowed to camp at any given ranger station, so reservations are essential in high season; the environment ministry's regional office in Puerto Jiménez (☏ 506/735–5036) starts taking reservations for each month on the first day of the preceding month. Be sure to reconfirm your reservation a few days before you enter the park.

There are several trails into Corcovado, taking you along the beach starting from La Leona or San Pedrillo ranger stations or through the forest from Los Patos ranger station. Hiking is always tough in the tropical heat, but the forest route is easier than the beach hikes, and the latter are accessible only at low tide. The longer hike between San Pedrillo and Sirena is only passable in the dry season, as the rivers get too high to cross in the rainy months. You can hire a boat in Sierpe to take you to San Pedrillo or Drake Bay; from Drake it's a four-hour hike to San Pedrillo. Alternately, a taxi in Puerto Jiménez will take you most of the way to Los Patos; and a truck leaves Puerto Jiménez every morning at 6 for Carate, a short hike from La Leona. The hike between any two stations takes all day, and the one between San Pedrillo and Sirena is especially long. There is potable water at every station; don't drink stream water. Be sure to bring insect repellent, sunblock, rain gear, a pair of good boots, a first-aid kit, and either a mosquito net and sheets or a tent and sleeping bag. All that said, try to pack light.

THE ATLANTIC LOWLANDS AND CARIBBEAN COAST

The parks of Costa Rica's Caribbean coast—with their humid, greenhouse-like climate and lush vegetation—are precisely what you probably picture when you hear the word "jungle." In these Atlantic forests are South American species you won't find anywhere else in Costa Rica—poison dart frogs, crab-eating raccoons, and great green macaws.

The most popular protected areas in the Atlantic region are its coastal parks, where the rain forest meets the beach. Here you'll find marine wonders as well as jungle flora and fauna. Aside from the surf and sand, the prime natural attractions on the southern portion of the Caribbean coast are coral reefs; the northern beaches are famous for the sea turtles that show up at night to lay their eggs in the sand.

The protected areas on the Caribbean side have the added advantage of proximity to good dining and lodging. Moreover, the trip here can be an adventure in its own right, as the highway to the Atlantic coast passes through the heart of Braulio Carrillo National Park, and the boat trip up the canals to Tortuguero is one of the best wildlife-spotting opportunities in the country.

Braulio Carrillo National Park

This amazing, and accessible, wild expanse is one of Costa Rica's largest protected areas (443 sq km/171 sq mi). Stretching from the misty mountaintops north of San José to the Atlantic lowlands, Parque Nacional

Braulio Carrillo protects a series of ecosystems ranging from the cloud forests covering the park's upper slopes to the tropical wet forest of the Magsasay sector. The Guápiles Highway, the main route to the Atlantic coast, cuts through one of Braulio's most precipitous areas, passing endless breathtaking views of the rugged landscape. There's a ranger station just after the Zurquí Tunnel, where a short trail loops through the cloud forest; another trail leads into the forest to the right about 17 km (11 mi) after the tunnel, where it follows the Quebrada González, a stream with a cascade and swimming hole, into the rain forest. The vegetation is lovely around the highway, and you may see a few of the park's 350 bird species. (Although Braulio is home to most of the mammals found in Costa Rica, they tend to avoid the area near the highway.) There are no campsites in this part of the park.

Hikers will want to explore the Volcán Barva sector, with its trail through the cloud forest to two crater lakes. You can camp at the Barva ranger station, which is far from any traffic and thus is a good place to watch birds and animals. Quetzals appear during the dry season (the only time you'll want to camp here anyway), but this a good place for a morning hike just about any time of year. Stay on the trail when hiking anywhere in Braulio; it's easy to get lost in the cloud forest, and the rugged terrain makes wandering through the woods very dangerous.

Tortuguero National Park and Barra del Colorado Wildlife Refuge

Parque Nacional Tortuguero (*tortuga* means "turtle") was created expressly to protect the sea turtles that nest by the thousands on its beach. The park's palm-lined beach stretches off as far as the eye can see, and its additional ecosystems include lowland rain forest, estuaries, and swampy areas covered with *yolillo* palms. You can wander the beach independently, but rip currents make swimming dangerous, and shark rumors persist. The beach is even more intriguing at night, when four species of endangered sea turtles nest here. If you want to watch them, contact your hotel or the parks office to hire a certified local guide. You won't be allowed to use a camera on the beach and must cover your flashlight with red plastic, as lights can deter the turtles from nesting.

The jungle-lined canals that lead to Tortuguero have been called the Amazon of Costa Rica, and the boat trip up to the park (leaving from the docks at Moín) is a great way to see the local wildlife, which includes several species of kingfishers and herons, sloths, monkeys, and crocodiles. Hire a dugout canoe and a guide to explore some of the rivers flowing into the canal; these waterways bear less boat traffic and, often, more wildlife. You can also continue up the canals to the Refugio Nacional de Fauna Silvestre Barra del Colorado, an immense protected area that's connected to the park via biological corridor. Barra del Colorado is less visited than Tortuguero.

Cahuita National Park

The nearly 2½-sq-km (1½-sq-mi) coral reef surrounding Punta Cahuita is a natural treasure. The purpose of Parque Nacional Cahuita is to protect the reef's 35 species of coral and even-more-numerous sponges and seaweeds, which provide food and refuge for the myriad tropical fish and crustaceans. The reef alone is ample attraction, but most travelers come here to see Cahuita's luxuriant coastal forest and idyllic palm-lined beaches, which you may think you've seen on a poster back home.

The 7-km (4-mi) path that winds in and out of the forest along the beach—from the town of Cahuita around the point to Puerto Vargas—

gives you a good look at the park's coastal and jungle wonders. The hike takes only a few hours; just note that you have to ford several rivers on the way—check conditions beforehand, as they can be prohibitive in the rainy season. The forest and swamps are home to troops of monkeys, kingfishers and herons, sloths, snakes, crabs, and lizards. The beach nearest the town of Cahuita has a regular riptide, so hold the swimming urge until you're farther into the park, where the beach curves toward the point. This is also a good snorkeling area, though the best diving is off the point. Sadly, the park's coral reef is slowly being killed by sediment, runoff from deforested areas such as the banana plantations in the nearby Estrella Valley. This process was intensified by the earthquake of 1991, as many riverbank trees in the nearby jungle foothills were felled by the quake, exposing riverbank soil to the erosive effect of tropical deluges and sending trees, soil, leaves, shrubs, and everything else seaward. After the quake, local divers estimated that the reef was 80% dead, but don't despair: you can in any case enjoy a good snorkel. Just use a local guide to find the best reefs, and don't dive for a few days after it rains, as the water is sure to be murky.

Gandoca-Manzanillo National Wildlife Refuge

Though less pristine than Cahuita National Park, the Refugio Nacional de Vida Silvestre Gandoca-Manzanillo stretches along the southeastern coast from the town of Manzanillo to the Panamanian border, bearing plenty of rain forest and many a good dive spot. Because of weak laws governing the conservation of refuges and the value of coastal land in this area, Gandoca-Manzanillo has suffered steady environmental degradation over the years and continues to be developed. For now, the easiest way to explore it is to hike along the coast south of Manzanillo, which also has some good snorkeling offshore. You can hike back out the way you came in, or arrange in Puerto Viejo de Limón to have a boat pick you up at Monkey Point (a three- to four-hour walk from Manzanillo) or Gandoca (six to eight hours). Boat trips to dive spots and beaches in the refuge can also be arranged in Puerto Viejo de Limón and Manzanillo.

PANAMA

Panama's national-park network protects an array of ecosystems as impressive as Costa Rica's, but since Panamanian tourism lags far behind that of its neighbor, Panamanian parks tend to have limited infrastructure. The advantage is that you don't have to share Panama's protected areas with big crowds. Panama's Renewable Resources Institute, **INRENARE** (☎ 507/232–7228), charges entrance fees between $3 and $10.

The Cordillera de Talamanca extends from eastern Costa Rica into western Panama, and much of this massive range is protected within a series of parks and reserves that together form La Amistad Biosphere Reserve (☞ *below*). Most of the biosphere reserve covers the mountains' Atlantic slopes, but its most accessible areas are on the Pacific side, several in western Panama. The trails and roads winding into the mountains of Chiriquí, Panama's southwestern province, not only pass unforgettable panoramas but lead to luxuriant cloud forests inhabited by quetzals, toucans, tiny venomous toads, and other colorful creatures.

Most of the isolated Bocas del Toro Archipelago is covered with jungle. Much of this green land is protected within national parks, forest reserves, and Indian reservations, but the bulk of it is barely accessible. Adventurers with jungle gear and time to spare may want to head back into mountain refuges such as Palo Seco Forest Reserve, Teribe Indian Reservation, and the Atlantic sector of La Amistad; casual travelers will have to settle for the region's most accessible protected area, Isla Bastimentos.

Volcán Barú

The Chiriquí countryside is dominated by this long-extinct volcano. Rising to a massive 11,450 ft above sea level, it positively invites hiking and bird-watching enthusiasts to ascend. The upper slopes and summit are protected within Volcán Barú National Park, which encompasses significant patches of cloud forest as well as the rugged peak. Inside the cloud forest is a wealth of bird life, including three-wattled bellbirds and resplendent quetzals; the rare volcano junco lives up top. There are two routes to the summit: a footpath that winds up the western slope from near the town of Volcán, and a road (four-wheel drive only) that heads up the eastern slope from Boquete. Along the northern slope, a dirt trail leads through the forest between Cerro Punta and Boquete, a good day hike. There are no facilities at the summit, and although camping is allowed, you'll need plenty of water and warm clothes—temperatures regularly drop to freezing.

Marino Isla Bastimentos National Park

Centered on Bastimentos Island, the Parque Nacional Marino Isla Bastimentos is a jewel of a seaside park, comprising coral reefs, white-sand beaches, and dozens of small cays and islets. Among the diversions are fantastic skin diving, beachcombing, copious wildlife, sea-turtle nesting events, and, potentially, windsurfing and surfing. There are communities on its western and eastern ends, but most of Isla Bastimentos is covered with lush forests that house ospreys, iguanas, parrots, and tiny poison dart frogs. The long, palm-lined beaches of the island's northern coast are as beautiful as they are ecologically important, and the waters to the south and west of the island hide some extensive coral reefs.

The best place to skin-dive within the park is around the Zapatillas Cays—two atolls southeast of Bastimentos. When the ocean is calm, visibility is quite good around the cays, revealing an impressive array of sponges and corals that includes immense brain-coral formations. Of course, such a colorful coral garden is home to countless tropical fish, from tiny angels to larger parrot and trigger fish, and a great diversity of rays. The caves at the reef's edge often attract massive snappers, drums, moray eels, and sometimes sleeping sharks; and if you have time to look closer you may discover delicate starfish, shrimp, octopuses, and still other interesting invertebrates.

But the cays are delightful enough above the water to please those without any desire to don a mask and submerge themselves. Lined with lanky coconut palms and washed by aquamarine waters, their pale sand belongs on postcards and in the dreams of northern winter nights. The long beach on Bastimentos Island is equally impressive, though harder to access, and from April to September it's visited by nesting sea turtles on a nightly basis. That beach is backed by thick forest that adventurous travelers may want to take the time to explore, as it's packed with wildlife. You can reach Bastimentos Island and the Zapatillas Cayes by boat from the regional capital, Bocas del Toro, a pleasant town with a small selection of lodges and a few decent restaurants.

La Amistad International Park

This is the single largest protected area within La Amistad Biosphere Reserve: It covers more than 2,007 sq km (775 sq mi) from cloud forests down to sultry lowland jungles. The name Amistad—Spanish for "friendship"—refers to the park's binational status; Panama's Parque Internacional La Amistad is contiguous with Costa Rica's Parque Nacional La Amistad, slightly smaller than its Panamanian twin and harder to visit. The ranger station at Las Nubes, in the hills above Cerro Punta, is the park's main entry point, a quiet spot at the edge of the forest with a few houses and a grassy area where you can camp. A 2-km (1-mi) trail makes a loop through the forest, and a second trail scales a ridge, complete with views of the Cerro Punta valley, en route to a nearby waterfall (roughly two hours round-trip). If you spend a night or two here, you may be able to accompany one of the rangers up Cerro Picacho, a four- to five-hour hike deep into the forest.

NICARAGUA

Blessed with natural beauty rivaling that of its more celebrated Central American neighbors, Nicaragua has few of the necessary resources for a national-park system in the wake of decades of political turmoil. Hurricane Mitch, which slammed Nicaragua and Honduras in 1999, heightened the nation's challenge to protect its wildlife, volcanoes, forests, and beaches and waters. Nicaragua's only designated national park is Volcán Masaya National Park, established in 1979, which encompasses roughly 20 sq km (12 sq mi), including the volcano's multiple craters and Lake Masaya. Several other areas have unofficial park or reserve status, which will probably be "upgraded" to national-park status at some point; these include the volcanoes on Ometepe Island—Madera and Concepcíon—and Volcán Mombacho, not far from Granada. An official wildlife refuge, Chococente, has been established to protect a turtle nesting site on the Pacific coast north of San Juan del Sur. Tours of this refuge during turtle nesting periods can be arranged through Marie's Bar in San Juan del Sur (☞ Chapter 8); for information on this and other Nicaraguan refuges, contact the **Dirección de Silvestres y Faunas** (✉ Km 12½, Carretera Norte, Apdo. 5123, Managua, ☎ 505/31112–31595, ℻ 505/31112–31596).

Volcán Masaya National Park

The evocative landscapes of Volcán Masaya, also known as Popogatepe ("Mountain That Burns"), suggest a moon with shrubbery—these sterile lava fields slowly turn fertile and are invaded by native vegetation, bedecked with thousands of colorful flowers, even orchids, during the dry season. Along with the plants come animals, including coyotes, skunks, raccoons, deer, iguanas, rabbits, and monkeys. Birds are plentiful as well, with flocks of parakeets gamboling within the craters' otherwise toxic confines. Look for them in the late afternoon, along with motmots, magpie jays, and woodpeckers. The Coyote Trail offers intrepid hikers a 5⅓-km (3½-mi) trek featuring views of petrified lava beds and bird-filled forests en route from the craters' edges to the shores of Lake Masaya. Don't miss the San Fernando Crater, inactive for 200 years and now home to a lush forest, or the Bobadilla Cross, at the top of 200 stairs, a replica of one erected by Spanish priests in the 16th century to exorcise the devil. Best of all, park your car at the Plaza de Oviedo, and stroll up to the Santiago Crater lip (fenced off, thankfully) for a look into what those Spanish priests were convinced was nothing less than the Boca del Infierno—the Mouth of Hell. The visitor center and museum give an insightful overview of regional cultural and geological history, with most of the documentation in Spanish. ✉ Km 23, Carretera Masaya–Managua, Apdo. NI-1, Nindiri, ☎ 505/0522–5415. ☞ $3.50. ☉ Daily 9–5.

10 BACKGROUND AND ESSENTIALS

Portrait of Costa Rica

Wildlife Glossary

Books and Films

Smart Travel Tips A to Z

A BIOLOGICAL SUPERPOWER

Costa Rica may lack oil fields and coal deposits, but it's not without natural assets. The country's ecological wealth includes fertile volcanic soil, sun-swathed beaches, massive trees whose thick branches support elevated gardens of orchids and bromeliads, and hundreds of colorful bird species—the kind of priceless commodities that economists have long ignored. Bankers may wonder how this tiny nation ended up with so pretentious a name as "Rich Coast," but many a barefoot Indian, grizzled biologist, and binocular-toting traveler understands where the republic's wealth lies hidden.

Costa Rica's forests hold an array of flora and fauna so vast and diverse that scientists haven't even named many of the plant and insect species therein; and of the species that have been identified, few have been thoroughly studied. These forests are among the most diverse and productive ecosystems in the world: Although tropical forests cover a mere 7% of the earth's surface area, they hold more than half the planet's plant and animal species, and few countries offer better exposure to tropical biological treasures than Costa Rica.

About half the size of the U.S. state of Kentucky, Costa Rica covers less than 0.03% of the earth's surface, yet it contains nearly 5% of the planet's plant and animal species. The variety of native flora and fauna is astonishing even if you're not professionally acquainted with the norms: Costa Rica contains at least 9,000 plant species, more than 1,100 varieties of orchids, in excess of 2,000 different butterflies, and at least 850 bird species (more birds than the United States and Canada combined). But such numbers don't begin to convey the awe you can feel when you're staring up the convoluted trunk of a centennial strangler fig, listening to the roar of a howler monkey reverberate through the foliage, or watching a delicate hummingbird drink nectar from a multicolored heliconia flower.

All these plants and animals are as beautiful as they are intriguing, and their habitats as complex as they are fascinating. It may be hard to apprehend the richness of a Costa Rican forest at first glance—the overwhelming verdure of the rain forest, for instance, can give the false impression of uniformity—but look closely and you'll come to understand why scientists have dubbed Costa Rica a "biological superpower."

Costa Rica's biological diversity is the result of its tropical location (on a slip of land connecting North and South America), its varied topography, and the many microclimates resulting from the combination of mountains, valleys, and lowlands. But to understand why Costa Rica is so biologically important today, we need to look back to prehistoric times, to a world that human eyes never saw but that scientists have at least partially reconstructed.

Just a Few Dozen Millennia Ago

In geological terms, Costa Rica is relatively young, which explains why there are precious few valuable minerals beneath its soil. Five million years ago, this patch of land didn't even exist: North and South America were separated by a canal the likes of which Teddy Roosevelt—father of the Panama Canal—couldn't have conjured up in his wildest dreams. In the area now occupied by Panama and Costa Rica, the waters of the Pacific and Atlantic oceans flowed freely together. Geologists have named that former canal the Straits of Bolívar, after the Venezuelan revolutionary who wrested much of South America from Spain.

Far beneath the Straits of Bolívar, the incremental movement of tectonic plates slowly created the Central American isthmus. Geologists speculate that a chain of volcanic islands appeared in the gap around 30 million years ago; a combination of volcanic activity and plate movement caused the islands to grow and rise from the water, eventually forming a connected ridge. The land bridge was completed around 3 million years ago, closing the interoceanic canal and forming a corridor, biological and otherwise, between the Americas.

Because several tectonic plates do meet beneath Central America, the region has long been geologically unstable, experiencing occasional earthquakes, frequent tremors, and regular volcanic eruptions. While it seems a curse to be hit by one of these natural disasters, there actually wouldn't be a Costa Rica were it not for such frightening phenomena. What is now the country's best soil was once spewed from the bowels of the volcanoes that dominate its landscape, and the jarring adjustments of adjacent tectonic plates actually pushed most of today's Costa Rica up out of the sea. A recent example of this movement was the earthquake of 1991—7.2 on the Richter scale—which thrust Costa Rica's southern Caribbean coastline up several feet, leaving portions of some coral reefs literally high and dry. When the shallow coral platforms around the points of Limón and Cahuita were thrust from the water, as many as 30 yards of land were added to some oceanfront property. For humans, that quake was a devastating natural disaster, damaging or destroying almost half the homes along the Caribbean coast, yet it was but a tiny adjustment in the incremental tectonic process that created the country in the first place.

The intercontinental connection completed 3 million years ago had profound biological consequences: It separated the marine life of the Pacific and Atlantic oceans, and it created a pathway for interchange between North and South America. Though hardly the kind of lapse that excites a geologist, 3 million years is a long time by biological standards, and the region's plants and animals have changed considerably since the inter-American gap was stopped up. Whereas evolution took different paths in the waters that flank the isthmus, organisms that had evolved on separate continents were able to make their way into the opposite hemisphere, and the resulting interaction determined what lives in the Americas today.

Mind-Boggling Biodiversity

Costa Rica's outdoor menagerie is in many ways the result of the intercontinental exchange, but the country's flora and fauna actually add up to more than what has passed between the continents. Although it is a biological corridor, the isthmus also acts as a filter, a hospitable haven to many species that couldn't complete the journey from one hemisphere to the other. The rain forests of Costa Rica's Atlantic and southwestern lowlands, for example, are the most northerly home of such southern species as the crab-eating raccoon and a dreaded jungle viper known as the bushmaster. The tropical dry forests of the northern Pacific slope, on the other hand, are the southern limit for such North American species as the white-throated magpie jay and the Virginia opossum. In addition to species whose range extends only as far as Costa Rica in one direction, and those whose range extends into both North and South America, such as the white-tailed deer and the gray hawk, Costa Rica's many physical barriers and microclimates have fostered the development of indigenous plants and animals, such as the mangrove hummingbird and mountain salamander.

What all this biological balderdash means to travelers is that they might spot a North American pale-billed woodpecker and a howler monkey (of South American descent) in the branches of a rain tree, which is native to Central America. And then there are the tourists—migrants, that is—such as the dozens of northern bird species that spend winter holidays in Costa Rica, among them the Tennessee warbler, western tanager, and yellow-bellied sapsucker. In addition to recognizing some of the birds that migrate here, you'll no doubt be at home with some of the plants, like the orchids and impatiens that grow wild in the country but cost a pretty penny in the garden shop back home. But while Costa Rica has plenty of oak trees, squirrels, and sparrows, most of its flora and fauna look decidedly tropical. Not only are such common plants as orchids, palms, and ficuses unmistakably tropical, but many of the resident animals are distinctly neotropical—found only in the American tropics—including sloths, poison dart frogs, toucans, and monkeys with prehensile tails.

The wildlife is spread through an array of ecosystems, which biologists have divided into a dozen "life zones" but which actually consist of a biological continuum almost too multifarious for classification. Though the existence of specific flora and fauna in any given life zone are determined by various physical conditions, the two most important are altitude and rainfall. Average temperatures in the tropics change very little from month to month, but they do change a good bit during the course of the day, especially in the mountains. The Costa Rican highlands are consistently cooler than the lowlands, which means you can spend a morning sweating in a sultry coastal forest, then drive a few hours into the mountains and find yourself needing a warm jacket.

In more temperate parts of the world, cold weather hits the mountaintops a month or two before the lowlands, with Old Man Winter eventually getting his icy grip on everything. In the tropics, only the tops of the highest mountains freeze, so high-altitude flora tends to look completely different from that of even nearby valleys. Altitude also plays a substantial role in regulating humidity, since clouds accumulate around mountains and volcanoes, providing regular precipitation as well as shade, which in turn slows evaporation. These conditions lead to the formation of luxuriant cloud forests on the upper slopes of many mountains. In general, the higher you climb, the more lush the vegetation, except for the peaks of the highest mountains, which often protrude from the cloud cover and are thus fairly arid.

While you may associate the tropics with rain, precipitation in Costa Rica varies considerably depending on where you are and when you're there. This is a result of the mountainous terrain and regional weather patterns. A phenomenon called rain shadow—when one side of a mountain range receives much more rain than the other—plays an important ecological role in Costa Rica. Four mountain ranges combine to create an intercontinental divide that separates the country into Atlantic and Pacific slopes; and thanks to the trade winds, the Atlantic slope receives much more rain than the Pacific. The trade winds steadily pump moisture-laden clouds southwest over the isthmus, where they encounter warm air or mountains, which make them rise. As the clouds rise, they cool, lose their ability to hold moisture, and eventually dump most of their liquid luggage on the Caribbean side.

During the rainy season—mid-May to December—the role of the trade winds is diminished, as regular storms roll off the Pacific Ocean and soak the western side of the isthmus. Though it rains all over Costa Rica during these months, it often rains more on the Pacific side of the mountains than on the Atlantic. Come December, the trade winds take over again, and hardly a drop falls on the western side until May. The dry season is most intense in northwestern Costa Rica (the province of Guanacaste), where most trees drop their foliage and the forests take on a desert visage. That region quickly regains its verdure once the rains return in May, marking the beginning of a springlike season that Costa Ricans nonetheless refer to as winter.

Climate variation within the country results in a mosaic of forests, from those that receive only a few feet of rain each year to those that soak up several yards of precipitation annually. The combination of humidity and temperature helps determine what grows where; but while some species have very restricted ranges, others seem to thrive just about anywhere. Plants such as strangler figs and bromeliads grow all over Costa Rica, and animals such as the collared peccary and coati—a long-nosed cousin of the raccoon—can pretty much live wherever human beings let them. Other species have extremely limited ranges, such as the mangrove hummingbird, restricted to the mangrove forests of the Pacific coast, and the volcano junco, a gray sparrow that lives only around the highest peaks of the Cordillera de Talamanca.

It's a Jungle Out There

Costa Rica's incredible natural spectrum is part of what makes it such an invigorating vacation spot, but the landscape that travelers most want to see is the tropical rain forest. The protected areas of the Atlantic and southern Pacific lowlands hold tracts of virgin rain forest where massive tropical trees tower more than 100 ft over the forest floor. The thick branches of these jungle giants are covered with an abundance of epiphytes (plants that grow on other plants but are not parasites) such as ferns, orchids, bromeliads, mosses, vines, and aroids; and most of the rain forest's plant and animal species are clustered in the arboreal garden of the canopy.

Although life flourishes in the canopy, the intense sunlight that quickly dries the treetops after downpours results in a recurrent water shortage. Consequently, plants that live up here have developed ways to cope with aridity: Many orchids have thick leaves that resist evaporation and spongy roots that can quickly soak up large amounts of water when it rains. Tank bromeliads have a funnel shape that enables them to collect and hold water at the center of their leaves. Acting as miniature oases, these plants attract arboreal animals to drink from, hunt at, or—in the case of certain insect larvae and tree-frog tadpoles—live in their pools. In exchange for vital water, the waste and carcasses of these animals give the plant valuable nutrients, which are also scarce in the canopy.

Many animals spend most or all of their time in the canopy, which can be frustrating for people who come to the jungle in search of wildlife. Peering through binoculars, you might glimpse the still, furry figure of a sloth or the brilliant regalia of a parrot; and it's hard to miss the arboreal acrobatics of monkeys, who leap from tree to tree, hang from branches, throw fruit or sticks, and generally make spectacles of themselves. For a closer look at the canopy, you may want to take a ride on the Rain Forest Aerial Tram, near the Guápiles Highway, or linger on a tree platform at Hacienda Barú in Dominical, or the Corcovado Lodge Tent Camp, both in the southern Pacific region.

Because little sunlight reaches the ground, the rain-forest floor is a dim, quiet place, with not nearly as much undergrowth as you saw in those old Tarzan movies. Still, plants from aroids to palm trees have adapted to this shady world. The light level inside a virgin rain forest is comparable to that of the average North American living room or shopping mall, and indeed some of the plant species that grow here have become popular houseplants up north. And the vegetation is not always sparse: Whenever an old tree falls, there's a riot of growth as plants fight over the newfound sunlight.

Few travelers are disappointed by the tropical forest, but some are frustrated by the difficulty of spotting animals. Hikers occasionally encounter such earthbound creatures as the coati or the agouti, a terrier-size rodent that resembles a giant guinea pig, and in most areas you're likely to see iridescent blue morpho butterflies, hyperactive hummingbirds, brightly colored poison-dart frogs, and tiny lizards standing guard on tree trunks. Most forest critters, however, spend much of their time and energy trying *not* to be seen, and the thick foliage aids them in that endeavor. An untrained eye can miss the details, which is why a naturalist guide is invaluable here: In addition to spotting and identifying both plants and animals, a good guide can explain some of relationships that weave them together in one of the planet's most complicated ecosystems.

The rain forest is characterized by intense predation. Its inhabitants dedicate most of their resources to the essential tasks of finding their next meal and avoiding *becoming* a meal in the process. Whereas animals must often hide or flee when in danger, plants have developed such survival tactics as thorns, prickly hairs, and toxic substances that make their leaves unappetizing. Because of the relative toxicity of most rain-forest foliage, many insects eat only a small portion of a leaf before moving on to another plant, so as not to ingest a lethal dose of any one poison. You can see the results of this practice by looking up into the canopy—almost every leaf is full of little holes.

Camouflage is another popular animal defense. The tropical rain forest is full of insects that have evolved to resemble the leaves, bark, moss, and leaf litter around them. Some bugs have adopted the colors of certain flowers, or even the mold that grows on plants. They're a chore to spot, but camouflaged critters are incredibly intriguing.

Some creatures go to the opposite extreme and advertise themselves with bright colors. Some hues are meant to help find a mate amid the mesh of green; others serve as a warning to potential predators. Some species of caterpillars, for example, are not only immune to the toxins of the plant on which they live, but they actually sequester that poison within their bodies, making themselves toxic as well. In certain areas you might see brightly colored frogs hopping around the forest floor—their skins are laced with such poisonous secretions that some Indian tribes use them to poison their own darts and arrows. This frog's typical warning pattern mixes bright colors with black, a coloration that conveys a simple message to predators: Eat me and die.

Mimicry can scare off predators as well—certain edible caterpillars look like venomous ones, and some harmless serpents have markings similar to those of the deadly coral snake. Such acts of deception often reach amazing levels of intrigue. The cocoons of certain butterflies not only resemble the head of a viper, but if disturbed, they begin to move back and forth just as a snake's head would. One large butterfly has spots on its wings that look like eyes, so that when it opens them it resembles an owl; another butterfly species looks exactly like a wasp.

In addition to avoiding predators, plants and animals must compete with other species that have similar niches—the biological equivalents of jobs. This competition fosters cooperation between noncompetitive organisms. Plants need to get their pollen and seeds distributed as far as possible, and every animal requires a steady food supply, which brings us to everyone's favorite subject: the birds and the bees.

Although butterflies and bees do most of the pollinating up north, tropical plants are pollinated by everything from fruit flies and hummingbirds to beetles and bats. The flowers of such plants are often designed so that their nectar is readily available to pollinators but protected from freeloaders. The beautiful hibiscus flower is designed to dust a hummingbird's forehead with pollen and collect any pollen that's already there while the tiny bird drinks the nectar hidden deep in its base; the flower is too long for a butterfly, and the nectar is held too deep for a bee to reach. No system is perfect, though: You may see a bananaquit—a tiny bird with a short beak—biting holes in the bases of a hibiscus flower in an effort to drink its nectar without getting anywhere near its pollen.

Intense competition for limited resources keeps the rain forest's trees growing taller, roots reaching farther, and everything mobile working on a way to get more for less. The battle for light sends most of the foliage sky-high, and the battle for nutrients speeds to a breakneck pace the process of decay and recycling that follows every death in the forest. One result of this high-speed decomposition is that most of the nutrients in a rain forest are present in living things, while the soil beneath them retains few essential elements. Rain-forest soils tend to be nutrient-poor, less than ideal for farming.

A Gorgeous Mosaic

Though the rain forest is most iconic, Costa Rica has other types of forests that are equally rich in life and well worth exploring. The tropical dry forests of the northwestern lowlands are similar to rain forests during the rainy season, but once the daily deluges subside, the dry forest changes profoundly: Most trees lose their leaves, and some burst simultaneously into full, colorful flower. The yellow-blossomed buttercup tree and the pink tabebuia, among others, brighten up the arid northwestern landscape in the dry season. The dry forest contains many of the plants, animals, and exclusive relationships found in the rain forest, but it's also home to species often associated with the forests and deserts of Mexico and the southwestern United States, such as cacti, coyotes, and diamondback rattlesnakes. Because dry forests are less dense than rain forests, it can be easier to see animals in them; this is especially true in the dry season, when foliage is sparse, and animals often congregate around scarce water sources and around trees with fruit or flowers.

The cloud forests on the upper reaches of many Costa Rican mountains and volcanoes are even more luxuriant than rain forests, so deeply lush that it can be hard to find the bark on a cloud-forest tree for all the growth on its trunk and branches. Plants grow on plants that grow on still other plants: Vines, orchids, ferns, aroids, and bromeliads are everywhere, and mosses and liverworts cover the vines and leaves of other epiphytes. Because of the steep terrain, a cloud forest's trees grow on slightly differ-ent levels, and the canopy is less continuous than that of a lowland rain forest. Because more light reaches the ground, there is plenty of undergrowth, including prehistoric-looking tree ferns, a wealth of flowering plants, and "poor man's umbrellas"— made up of a few giant leaves.

Cloud forests are home to a multitude of animals, ranging from delicate glass frogs, whose undersides are so transparent that you can see many of their internal organs, to the resplendent quetzal, a bird considered sacred by the ancient Maya. The male quetzal has a crimson belly and iridescent green back, wings, and tail feathers, the last of which can grow longer than 2 ft. Those tail feathers float behind the quetzal when it flies, a splendid sight that no doubt inspired its ancient name, "the plumed serpent." Although the tangle of foliage and almost constant mist make it hard to see cloud-forest wildlife, you should still catch glimpses of such colorful birds as the emerald toucanet, collared redstart, and various hummingbirds.

Humidity protects the cloud-forest canopy from the water shortage that often plagues lowland rain forests. In fact, the cloud forest's canopy is usually soaking wet. During most of the year, a moisture-laden mist moves through the cloud forest, depositing condensation on the plants; this condensation causes a sort of secondary precipitation, with droplets forming on the epiphytic foliage and falling regularly from the branches to the forest floor. Cloud forests thus function like giant sponges, soaking up humidity from the clouds and sending it slowly downhill to feed the streams and rivers on which many regions and communities depend for water.

On top of high ridges, and near the summits of volcanoes, the cloud forest is transformed by strong, steady winds that topple tall trees and regularly break off branches. The resulting collection of small, twisted trees and bushes is known as an elfin forest. On the upper slopes of the Cordillera de Talamanca, Costa Rica's highest range, the cloud forest gives way to the *páramo,* a high-altitude ecosystem composed of shrubs, grasses, and hardy herbs. Most of these plants are common in the heights of South America's Andes; the Costa Rican páramo defines their most northerly distribution.

On the other extreme, along both coasts, are river mouths and estuaries with extensive mangrove forests. These primeval-looking, often flooded profusions grow in tidal zones all over the tropics. Many of the trees in a mangrove forests grow on "stilt" roots, which prop their leaves up out of the saltwater and help them absorb carbon dioxide when the tide is high. The roots also lend protection to various small fish and crustaceans, and are often covered with barnacles, mussels, and other shellfish.

Mangrove forests are fairly homogeneous, with stands of one species of tree stretching off as far as the eye can see. They are also extremely productive ecosystems that play an important role as estuaries: Many marine animals, such as shrimp, spend the early stages of their lives in mangrove estuaries, and some species, such as certain kinds of snappers, are born and die there. Vital to the health of the ocean beyond them, mangroves are attractive sites for animals that feed on marine life, especially fish-eating birds like cormorants, herons, pelicans, and ospreys.

The forests that line the Caribbean canals, along Costa Rica's northeastern coast, are dominated by the water-resistant *yolillo* palm. This area is home to many of the same animals found in the rain forest—monkeys, parrots, iguanas—as well as river dwellers, such as turtles, otters, and anhingas. A boat trip up the canals is thus a great opportunity to observe wildlife, as are similar excursions on jungle rivers such as the Río Frío and the Río Sarapiquí. Seasonal swamps like Caño Negro and the *lagunas* of Palo Verde, which disappear during the dry months, are also excellent places to see birds. There's also a vast swamp in the heart of Corcovado National Park, which never dries up

but is virtually impenetrable because of the thick, thorny vegetation surrounding it.

In addition to its varied forests, Costa Rica has 1,224 km (760 mi) of coastline, which consists of beaches separated by rocky points. The points are home to a variety of marine life, but even more remarkable, most of the country's beaches are important nesting spots for endangered sea turtles. And submerged in the sea off both coasts are extensive coral reefs, inhabited by hundreds of species of colorful fish, crustaceans, and other invertebrates. With its vertiginous biological variety, the coral reef could well be the marine equivalent of the rain forest.

Where Have All the Jungles Gone?

All this lush forest notwithstanding, you'll soon see that Costa Rica's predominant landscapes are not cloud and rain forests but the coffee and banana plantations that have replaced them. The country's pre-Columbian cultures may have revered the jaguar and the harpy eagle, but today's inhabitants seem to put more stock in less-illustrious beasts: the cow and the chicken.

In the last half century, more than two-thirds of Costa Rica's original forests have been destroyed, cut at a rate of between 362 sq km (140 sq mi) and 765 sq km (295 sq mi) per year. Forests have traditionally been considered unproductive land, and their destruction was for a long time synonymous with development. In the 1970s and 1980s, international and domestic development policies fueled the destruction of large tracts of wilderness. Fortunately, Costa Rican conservationists grew alarmed by this deforestation, and in the 1970s they began creating what has since grown to become the best national-park system in the region.

In addition to protecting vast expanses of wilderness—between 15 and 20% of the national territory—the Costa Rican government has made progress in curbing deforestation outside the national parks. The rate of de-

Portrait

struction has dropped significantly, but poaching and illegal logging continue to be serious problems that, if left uncorrected, will eventually wipe out many important species and wild areas.

Deforestation not only spells disaster for the jaguar and the eagle, but it can also have grave consequences for human beings. Forests absorb rain and release water slowly, playing an important role in regulating the flow of rivers—which is why severely deforested regions often suffer floods during the rainy season and drought during the dry months. Tree covers also prevent topsoil erosion, thus keeping the land fertile and productive; in many parts of the country, erosion has left once-productive farmland almost worthless. Finally, hidden within Costa Rica's endless living species are countless unknown or under-studied substances that might eventually be extracted to cure diseases and serve humankind. The destruction of this country's forests is a loss for the entire world.

Responsible Travel

With each passing year, more and more Costa Ricans are coming to realize how valuable and imperiled their remaining wilderness is. Costa Ricans visit their national parks in significant numbers, and they consider those protected areas vital to the national economy, both for the natural resources they preserve and for their commercial role as tourist attractions. Local conservationists, however, are

still a long way from achieving their goal of involving communities in the protection of the parks around them.

Costa Ricans who cut trees and hunt endangered animals usually do so out of economic necessity, and alas, the people who live near protected areas are often the last to benefit from the tourism that wilderness attracts. When you visit a park or reserve, your entrance fee helps pay for the preservation of Costa Rica's wildlife; but you can also make your visit beneficial to the people living nearby by hiring local guides, horses, or boats; eating in local restaurants; and buying things (other than wild-animal products, of course) in local shops.

You can go a few steps further by making donations to local conservation groups or to such international organizations as Conservation International, the Nature Conservancy, the Rainforest Alliance, and the World Wildlife Fund, all of which support important conservation efforts in Costa Rica. It's also helpful to stray from the beaten path: Explore private preserves, and stay at lodges that contribute to environmental efforts and to nearby communities. By planning your visit with an eye toward grassroots conservation efforts, you join the global effort to save the earth's tropical ecosystems and help ensure that the treasures you traveled so far to see remain intact for future generations.

— David Dudenhoefer

WILDLIFE GLOSSARY

An astonishing array of creatures has evolved in tiny Costa Rica, sandwiched between the two great American continents. Thanks in part to the protection of the park and refuge system, many are not terribly hard to see. Here is a rundown of some of the most common and attention-grabbing mammals, birds, reptiles, amphibians, and even a few insects that you might encounter. We give the common Costa Rican names so you can understand the local wildlife lingo as well as the latest scientific terms.

Agouti (*guatusa*; *Dasyprocta punctata*): A 20-inch tailless rodent with small ears and a large muzzle, the agouti is reddish-brown on the Pacific side, more of a tawny orange on the Caribbean slope. It sits on its haunches to eat large seeds and fruit.

Anteater (*oso hormiguero*): Three species of anteater inhabit Costa Rica—the giant (*Myrmecophaga tridactyla*), silky (*Cyclopes didactylus*), and collared, or vested (*Tamandua mexicana*). Only the latter is commonly seen, and too often as roadkill. This medium-size anteater, 30 inches long with an 18-inch tail, laps up ants and termites with its long, sticky tongue and has long sharp claws for ripping into insect nests.

Aracaris (*cusingo*): These slender toucans, with their trademark bills, travel in groups of six or more and eat ripe fruit. The collared aracaris (*Pteroglossus torquatus*) on the Caribbean side has a chalky upper mandible; the fiery-billed (*Pteroglossus frantzii*) aracaris on the southern Pacific coast has an orange-red upper mandible.

Armadillo (*cusuco*; *Dasypus novemcinctus*): The species found in the southern United States is widespread in Costa Rica. Mostly nocturnal and solitary, this edentate roots in soil with long muzzle for varied diet of insects, small animals, and plant material.

Caiman (*cocodrilo*): The spectacled caiman (*Caiman crocodilus*) is a small crocodilian (to 7 ft) inhabiting freshwater, subsisting mainly on fish. Most active at night (it has bright-red eyeshine), it basks by day. It is distinguished from the American crocodile (☞ *below*) by a sloping brow and smooth back scales.

Coati (*pizote*; *Nasua narica*): This is a long-nosed relative of the raccoon, its long tail often held straight up. Lone males or groups of females with young are active during the day, on the ground or in trees. Opportunistic and omnivorous, coatis feed on fruit, invertebrates, and small vertebrates.

Cougar (*puma*; *Felis concolor*): Mountain lions are the largest unspotted cats (to 5 ft, with 3½-inch tail) in Costa Rica. Widespread but rare, they live in essentially all-wild habitats and feed on vertebrates ranging from snakes to deer.

Crocodile (*lagarto*; *Crocodylus acutus*): The American crocodile, up to 16 ft in length, is found in most major river systems, particularly the Tempisque and Tárcoles. Despite its size and appearance, it seldom attacks humans, preferring fish and birds. It's distinguished from the caiman (☞ *above*) by a flat head, narrow snout, and spiky scales.

Ctenosaur (*garrobo*; *Ctenosaura similis*): A.k.a. the black, or spiny, iguana, this is a large (up to 18 inches long with 18-inch tail), tan lizard with four dark bands on its body and a tail ringed with sharp, curved spines. Terrestrial and arboreal, it sleeps in burrows or tree hollows. Though mostly vegetarian, it consumes small creatures. It lives along the coast in the dry northwest and in wetter areas farther south.

Dolphin (*delfin*): Several species, including bottlenose dolphins (*Tursiops truncatus*), frolic in Costa Rican waters. Frequently observed off Pacific shores are spotted dolphins (*Stenella attenuata*), which are small (up to 6 ft), with pale spots on the posterior half of the body; they often travel in groups of 20 or more and like to play around vessels and in bow wakes.

Frigatebird (*tijereta del mar*; *Fregata magnificens*): A large, black soaring bird with slender wings and forked tail, this is one of the most effortless and agile fliers in the avian world. More common on the Pacific coast, it doesn't dive or swim but swoops to pluck its food.

Frog (*rana*): Some 120 species of frogs exist in Costa Rica; most are nocturnal, except for brightly colored poison-dart frogs (*Dendrobates* spp.), whose coloration, either red with blue or green hind legs or charcoal black with fluorescent green markings, warns potential predators of their toxicity. Red-eyed leaf frogs (*Agalychnis* spp.) are among the showiest of nocturnal species. Large, brown marine toads (*Bufo marinus*) come out at night.

Howler Monkeys (*mono congo*; *Alouatta palliata*): These dark, chunky-bodied monkeys (to 22 inches long with 24-inch tail) with black faces travel in troops of up to 20. Lethargic mammals, they eat leaves, fruits, and flowers. The males' deep, resounding howls serve as communication among and between troops.

Iguana (*iguana*): Mostly arboreal but a good swimmer, the iguana is Costa Rica's largest lizard: Males can grow to 10 ft, including tail. Only young green iguanas (*Iguana iguana*) are bright green; adults are much duller, females dark-grayish, and males olive (with orange-ish heads in breeding season). All have round cheek scales and smooth tails.

Jacana (*gallito de agua*; *Jacana spinosa*): These birds are sometimes called "lily trotters" because their long toes allow them to walk on floating vegetation. Feeding on aquatic organisms and plants, they're found in almost any body of water. They expose yellow wing feathers in flight. The "liberated" females lay eggs in several nests tended by different males.

Jaguar (*tigre*; *Panthera onca*): The largest New World feline (to 6 ft, with 2-ft tail), this top-of-the-line predator is exceedingly rare but lives in a wide variety of habitats, from dry forest to cloud forest. It's most common in the vast Amistad Biosphere Reserve.

Jesus Christ Lizard (*gallego*): Flaps of skin on long toes enable this spectacular lizard to run across water. Costa Rica has three species: the lineated basilisk (*Basiliscus basiliscus*) on the Pacific side is brown with pale lateral stripe; the emerald basilisk (*Basiliscus plumifrons*) in the Caribbean lowlands is marked with turquoise and black on a green body; the striped basilisk (*Basiliscus vittatus*), also on the Caribbean side, resembles the lineated basilisk. Adult males grow to 3 ft (mostly tail), with crests on head, back, and base of tail.

Kinkajou (*martilla*; *Potos flavus*): This nocturnal, arboreal relative of the raccoon (to 20 inches, with 20-inch prehensile tail) has light-brown fur and yellow-green eyeshine. It forages actively, often noisily, for fruit, insects, and nectar.

Leaf-Cutter Ant (*zompopas*; *Atta* spp.): Found in all lowland habitats, these are the most commonly noticed neotropical ants. Columns sometimes extend for several hundred yards from an underground nest to plants being harvested; clipped leaves are fed to the cultivated fungus that the ants eat.

Macaw (*lapas*): Costa Rica's two species are the scarlet macaw (*Ara macao*), on the Pacific side (Osa Peninsula and Carara Biological Reserve), and the great green macaw (*Ara ambigua*) on the Caribbean side, where the population is severely threatened. These are huge, raucous parrots with long tails; their immense bills are used to rip fruit apart to reach the seeds. They nest in hollow trees and are victimized by pet-trade poachers and deforestation.

Magpie Jay (*urraca; Calocitta formosa*): This southern relative of the bluejay, with long tail and distinctive topknot (crest of forward-curved feathers), is found in the dry northwest, where it's often commensal (omnivorous) with humans. Bold and inquisitive, with amazingly varied vocalizations, these birds travel in noisy groups of four or more.

Margay (*caucel; Felis wiedii*): Fairly small, this spotted nocturnal cat (22 inches long, with 18-inch tail) is similar to the ocelot (☞ *below*) but has a longer tail and is far more arboreal: mobile ankle joints allow it to climb down trunks head-first. It eats small vertebrates.

Morpho (*morfo*): Three Costa Rican species of this spectacular large butterfly have a brilliant-blue upper wing surface, one of which (*Morpho peleides*) is common in moister areas; one has an intense ultraviolet upper surface; one is white above and below; and one is brown and white. Adults feed on rotting fallen fruit; they never visit flowers.

Motmot (*pajaro bobo*): Most of these handsome birds of the understory have "racquet-tipped" tails. Nesting in burrows, they sit patiently while scanning for large insect prey or small vertebrates. Costa Rica has six species.

Ocelot (*manigordo; Felis pardalis*): Mostly terrestrial, this medium-size spotted cat (33 inches long, with 16-inch tail) has a shorter tail than the margay (☞ *above*). Active night and day, it feeds on rodents and other vertebrates. Forepaws are rather large in relation to the body, hence the local name, which means "fat hand."

Oropéndola (*oropendola; Psarocolius* spp.): This crow-size bird in the oriole family has a bright-yellow tail and nests in colonies, in pendulous nests (up to 6 ft long) built by females in isolated trees. Males make unmistakable, loud, gurgling liquid call. The bird is fairly omnivorous, eating much fruit, and far more numerous on Caribbean side.

Parakeet and Parrot (*pericos,* parakeets; *loros,* parrots): There are 15 species in Costa Rica (plus two macaws, ☞ *above*), all clad in green, most with a splash of a primary color or two on the head or wings. They travel in boisterous flocks, prey on immature seeds, and nest in cavities.

Peccary: Piglike animals with thin legs and thick necks, peccaries travel in small groups (larger where the population is still numerous); root in soil for fruit, seeds, and small creatures; and have a strong musk odor. Costa Rica has two species: the collared peccary (*saíno, Tayassu tajacu*) and the white-lipped peccary (*chancho de monte, Tayassu pecari*), the latter now largely exterminated.

Pelican (*pelícano*): Large size, a big bill, and a throat pouch make the brown pelican (*Pelecanus occidentalis*) unmistakable in coastal areas (it's far more abundant on the Pacific side). Pelicans often fly in V formations, and dive for fish.

Quetzal (*quetzal*): One of the world's most exquisite birds, the resplendent quetzals (*Pharomachrus mocinno*) was revered by the Maya. Glittering green plumage and the male's long tail coverts draw thousands of people to highland cloud forests for sightings from February to April.

Roseate Spoonbill (*garza rosada; Ajaia ajaja*): Pink plumage and a spatulate bill set this wader apart from all other wetland birds; it feeds by swishing its bill back and forth in water while using its feet to stir up bottom-dwelling creatures. Spoonbills are most common around Palo Verde and Caño Negro.

Sea Turtle. *See* Close-Up: Tico Turtles, *in* Chapter 7.

Sloth (*perezoso*): Costa Rica is home to the brown-throated, three-toed sloth (*Bradypus variegatus*) and Hoffmann's two-toed sloth (*Choloepus hoffmanni*). Both grow to 2 ft, but two-toed (check forelegs) sloths often look bigger due to longer fur, and are the only species in the highlands. Sloths are herbivorous; accustomed to a low-energy diet; and well camouflaged.

Spider Monkey (*mono colorado, mono araña; Ateles geoffroyi*): Lanky and long-tailed, these are the largest monkeys in Costa Rica (to 24 inches, with 32-inch tail). Moving in groups of two to four, they eat ripe fruit, leaves, and flowers. Incredible aerialists, they can swing effortlessly through branches using long arms and legs and prehensile tails. Caribbean and southern Pacific populations are dark reddish-brown; northwesterners are blond.

Squirrel Monkey (*mono tití; Saimiri oerstedii*): The smallest of four Costa Rican monkeys (11 inches, with 15-inch tail), this one has a distinctive facial pattern (black cap and muzzle, white mask). The species travels in noisy, active groups of 20 or more, feeding on fruit and insects. Found only around Manuel Antonio National Park and parts of the Osa Peninsula, it may have been introduced by humans in pre-Columbian times.

Tapir (*danta; Tapirus bairdii*): The largest land mammal in Costa Rica (to 6½ ft), the tapir is something like a small rhinoceros without armor. Adapted to a wide range of habitats, it's nocturnal, seldom seen, but said to defecate and sometimes sleep in water. Tapirs are herbivorous, and use their prehensile snouts to harvest vegetation.

Toucan (*tucán, tucancillo*): This bird is familiar to anyone who's seen a box of Froot Loops cereal. The aracaris (☞ *above*) is one; keel-billed (*Ramphastos sulfuratus*) and chestnut-mandibled toucans (*Ramphastos swainsonii*) are the largest (18 inches and 22 inches), black with bright-yellow "bibs" and multihued bills. The smaller, stouter emerald toucanet (*Aulacorhynchus prasinus*) and yellow-eared toucanet (*Selenidera spectabilis*) are aptly named. All eat fruit, with some animal matter, and nest in cavities.

Whale (*ballenas*): Humpback whales (*Megaptera novaeanglia*) appear off the Pacific coast between November and February; they migrate from California and as far as Hawaii.

White-Faced Capuchin Monkey (*mono carablanca; Cebus capuchinus*): Medium-size and omnivorous, this monkey (to 18 inches, with 20-inch tail) has black fur and a pink face surrounded by a whitish bib. Extremely active foragers, they move singly or in groups of up to 20, examining the environment closely and even coming to the ground.

WHAT TO READ & WATCH BEFORE YOU GO

Books

For insight on local culture, pick up *Costa Rica: A Traveler's Literary Companion,* edited by Barbara Ras (Consortium), a collection of translated short stories by the country's best writers. For a factual rundown, consult *Inside Costa Rica,* by Tom Barry and Silvia Lara (Interhemispheric Resource Center). David Rains Wallace's *The Quetzal and the Macaw: The Story of Costa Rica's National Parks* (Sierra Club Books) is an entertaining and informative account of Costa Rica's exemplary conservation efforts.

Some of the most popular books on this country feature its rich natural history. *A Guide to the Birds of Costa Rica* (Cornell), by F. Gary Stiles and Alexander F. Skutch (Cornell), is a first-rate field guide. Alexander Skutch has also written some entertaining chronicles combining natural history, philosophy, and anecdote, among them *A Naturalist in Costa Rica* (University Press of Florida).

The *Costa Rica: Eco-Traveller's Wildlife Guide,* by Les Beletsky (Academic Press), gives an overview of the most common fauna. For an in-depth look at local ecology, read *Tropical Nature,* by Adrian Forsyth and Ken Miyata (Macmillan).

Costa Rica has a rich literary tradition, but few of its writers have been translated into English. Those who have can be hard to find in the United States; *Years Like Brief Days* (Dufour Editions) is one of the most popular novels of Fabián Dobles, famous for his humorous depiction of life in rural Costa Rica in the early 20th century. *The Lonely Men's Island* (Editorial Escritores Unidos, Mexico), the first novel of José León Sánchez, recounts the author's years on Isla San Lucas—the Costa Rican version of Alcatraz—where he was sent for stealing the country's patron saint, La Virgin de los Angeles (☞ Cartago *in* Chapter 2).

Films

Jurassic Park (1993) was set on Costa Rica's isolated Cocos Island, but the film was actually shot in Hawaii. Oddly enough, much of the film version of *Congo* (1995), another Michael Crichton novel, was shot in Costa Rica. Most of Ridley Scott's *1492: Conquest of Paradise* (1992) was filmed on Costa Rica's Pacific coast. If you're more interested in the waves that break off that coast, check out the surf classic *The Endless Summer* (1966), both the original and remake of which have Costa Rica footage.

ESSENTIAL INFORMATION

AIR TRAVEL

BOOKING

When you reserve, **look for nonstop flights** and **remember that "direct" flights stop at least once.**

FROM NORTH AMERICA

Costa Rica's main tourist season—corresponding roughly with the dry season, from mid-December to April—coincides with Thanksgiving (in the U.S.), Christmas, and Easter, so book your airline tickets well ahead of time. During this time, weekly charter flights serve Costa Rica from half a dozen United States and Canadian ports, most landing in Liberia, Guanacaste. Ask a travel agent about charter options.

➤ MAJOR AIRLINES: **American** (☎ 800/433–7300). **Continental** (☎ 800/231–0856). **Delta** (☎ 800/221–1212). **United** (☎ 800/241–6522). **US Airways** (☎ 800/428–4322).

➤ SMALLER AIRLINES: **Lacsa** (☎ 800/225–2272). **LTU** (☎ 800/888–0200). **Mexicana** (☎ 800/531–7921). **Nica** (☎ 800/831–6422). **Grupo TACA** (☎ 800/535–8780).

WITHIN CENTRAL AMERICA

Given Central America's often difficult driving conditions—distances that appear short on a map can represent hours of driving on dirt roads pocked with craters—**consider domestic flights.** Because car-rental rates are so steep, flying is actually cheaper than driving as well.

Costa Rica has two domestic airlines, Sansa and Travelair. Panama's domestic airline, Aeroperlas, connects major cities in that country and flies five times a week to Costa Rica. **Sansa** flies from Juan Santamaría International Airport, near Alajuela, to the following Costa Rican destinations: Barra del Colorado, Coto 47, Golfito, La Fortuna, Liberia, Nosara, Palmar

Sur, Puerto Jiménez, Punta Islita, Quepos, Samara, Tamarindo, Tambor, and Tortuguero. Sansa also flies between Quepos and Palmar Sur and between La Fortuna and Tamarindo. One-way fares range from U.S. $40 to U.S. $60. **Travelair** has daily flights from Tobias Bolaños Airport, in the San José suburb of Pavas, to Carrillo, Golfito/Puerto Jiménez, La Fortuna, Liberia, Palmar Sur, Punta Islita, Quepos, Tamarindo, Tambor, and Tortuguero. More than a dozen flights also run between those destinations, saving you the trouble of returning to San José. Prices range from $50 for a one-way hop between San José and Quepos to $92 for a one-way trip to Liberia.

Note that domestic flights on both Sansa and Travelair technically impose a luggage weight limit of 25 lbs. (*including* carry-ons) on their domestic flights, as the planes are tiny. Excess weight is charged by the pound.

Panama's **Aeroperlas** has five direct weekday flights between David and San José ($171 round trip), with connections to Bocas del Toro, Changuinola, and Panama City. Aeroperlas also flies daily between David, Changuinola, Bocas del Toro, and Panama City, from which flights depart to Contadora and the Darien Gap. **Aerotaxi** has daily flights to about a dozen airstrips in the San Blas Islands region.

Grupo Taca flies twice daily between San José and Managua, Nicaragua, leaving San José at 6:30 AM and 2 PM. The cost is about $200 per person plus a $20 exit tax at each end.

➤ AIRLINES: **Aeroperlas** (Costa Rica, ☎ 506/296–0909; Panama ☎ 507/269–4555). **Aerotaxi** (Panama, ☎ 507/264–8844). **Grupo Taca** (Costa Rica ☎ 506/296–0909, Nicaragua 505/266–3136; **Panama**, ☎ 507/265–

7825 or 507/265–7814). **Sansa** (✉ Costa Rica, ☎ 506/221–9414 or 506/441–8035). **Travelair** (Costa Rica, ☎ 506/220–3054).

CHARTER FLIGHTS

Several charter companies in San José, Travelair included, offer charter flights to places not served by scheduled flights. Helinorte and Helitur provide helicopter service.

➤ CHARTER COMPANIES: **Aero Costa Sol** (☎ 506/440–1444). **Aerolineas Turisticas** (☎ 506/232–1125). **Aeronaves** (☎ 506/282–4033 in San José, ☎ 506/775–0278 in **Golfito**). **Helinorte** (☎ 506/232–7534).**Helitur** ☎ 506/220–3940

FROM THE U.K.

American Airlines flies from Heathrow to Miami and **Virgin Atlantic** flies from Gatwick to Miami, where you can connect with flights to San José. **British Airways** flies weekly from Gatwick to San José via Puerto Rico. You can also fly from London to San José on **Iberia**, but you have to change planes in Madrid and Miami. **United Airlines** flies from Heathrow to Washington, D.C., where another flight serves Costa Rica via Mexico.

➤ AIRLINES: **American Airlines** (☎ 0345/789–789). **British Airways** (☎ 0345/222–111). **Iberia** (☎ 0171/830–0011). **Virgin Atlantic** (☎ 01293/747747).

CHECK-IN & BOARDING

Airlines ask passengers on international flights to **check in two hours before departure.** If you arrive less than an hour before your flight is scheduled to leave, you may not be allowed to board. Note that when you fly out of Costa Rica, you'll have to pay a $17 airport departure tax at Juan Santamaría Airport (☞ Taxes, *below*).

Airlines routinely overbook planes, presuming that not everyone who bought a ticket will show up. When everyone does, airlines ask for volunteers to give up their seats. In return, these volunteers usually get a certificate for a free flight and are rebooked on the next flight out. If there are not enough volunteers, the airline must choose who will be denied boarding,

and the first to get bumped are passengers who checked in late and those flying on discounted tickets—so **get to the gate and check in as early as possible,** especially during peak periods.

Always **bring a government-issued photo I.D. to the airport.** You may be asked to show it before you're allowed to check in.

CUTTING COSTS

The least-expensive airfares must usually be purchased in advance and are nonrefundable. **Call a number of airlines, and when you're quoted a good price, book it on the spot**—the same fare may not be available the next day. Always **check different routings** and look into using different airports. In addition to fares for direct flights to San José, check fares for routes that connect in a U.S. gateway city; the latter can be cheaper.

Travel agents, especially low-fare specialists (☞ Discounts & Deals, *below*), can be helpful. Consolidators are another good source; they buy tickets for scheduled international flights at reduced rates from the airlines, then sell them at prices that beat the best fare available directly from the airlines, usually without restrictions. Sometimes you can even get your money back if you need to return the ticket. Carefully read the fine print detailing penalties for changes and cancellations, and **confirm your consolidator reservation with the airline.**

➤ CONSOLIDATORS: **Cheap Tickets** (☎ 800/377–1000). **Discount Airline Ticket Service** (☎ 800/576–1600). **4Great Fares** (☎ 877/735–9540, ✆). **Unitravel** (☎ 800/325–2222). **Up & Away Travel** (☎ 212/889–2345). **World Travel Network** (☎ 800/409–6753).

ENJOYING THE FLIGHT

For more legroom, **request an emergency-aisle seat.** Don't sit in the row in front of the emergency aisle or in front of a bulkhead, where seats may not recline. If you have dietary requirements such as vegetarian, low-cholesterol, or kosher food, **ask for special meals when booking.** To fight jet lag on long flights, try to maintain a normal routine: at night, **get some sleep.** By day, **eat light meals, drink water** (not alcohol), and **move around the cabin** to stretch your legs.

FLYING TIMES

From New York, flights to San José last 5½ hours nonstop, 6–7 hours via Miami; from Los Angeles, 8½ hours via Mexico; from Houston, 3½ hours nonstop; from Miami, 3 hours.

HOW TO COMPLAIN

If your baggage goes astray or your flight goes awry, complain right away. Most carriers require that you **file a claim immediately.**

➤ AIRLINE COMPLAINTS: U.S. Department of Transportation **Aviation Consumer Protection Division** (⊠ C-75, Room 4107, Washington, DC 20590, ☎ 202/366–2220, ✇). **Federal Aviation Administration Consumer Hotline** (☎ 800/322–7873).

RECONFIRMING

Note well: before leaving Costa Rica, Panama, or Nicaragua you must **reconfirm your flight by phone within 72 hours of departure.** Failure to do so may result in cancellation of your reservation.

AIRPORTS

➤ AIRPORT INFORMATION: **Aeropuerto Internacional Juan Santamaría** (San José, ☎ 506/443–2682). **Aeropuerto Internacional Daniel Oduber** (Liberia, ☎ 506/668–1032). **Aeropuerto Internacional Tobías Bolaños** (Pavas, 3 km/2 mi west of San José, ☎ 232–2820).

DUTY-FREE SHOPPING

San José's Aeropuerto Internacional Juan Santamaría has several duty-free shops, which sell mostly liquor and perfume.

BIKE TRAVEL

You can rent mountain bikes in many resort areas, and they're actually a great way to get around town as well as explore off-road trails. The regional topographical maps sold at the San José department stores Universal and Lehmann include unpaved roads that are often perfect for mountain biking.

For a list of bike tour operators, *see* Outdoors & Sports, *below.* Several companies lead organized mountain-bike tours, which take you to less-traveled areas and usually provide lunch and refreshments.

➤ BIKE MAPS: **Universal** (⊠ Avda. Central between Cs. 0 and 1, San José). **Lehmann** (⊠ Avda. Central between Cs. 1 and 3, San José).

BIKES IN FLIGHT

Most airlines accommodate bikes as luggage provided they're dismantled and boxed. The Costa Rican airlines Sansa and Travelair usually allow disassembled mountain bikes (and 7-ft surfboards) on board for $15, space permitting. For bike boxes—often free at bike shops—you'll pay about $5 (and at least $100 for bike bags) from airlines. International travelers can sometimes substitute a bike for a piece of checked luggage at no charge; otherwise, the cost is about $100. U.S. and Canadian airlines charge $25–$50 on domestic flights.

BOAT & FERRY TRAVEL

WITHIN COSTA RICA

Regular passenger and/or car ferries connect Puntarenas with Playa Naranjo, Tambor, and Paquera, on the south end of the Nicoya Peninsula. A car ferry crosses the Río Tempisque, about a one-hour drive northwest from Puntarenas, every 20 minutes from 5 AM to 7 PM. Note that during holidays and high season, waits of up to three hours are common for the 15-minute trip. The Arco Iris Passenger Ferry makes daily runs between Golfito and Puerto Jiménez, and the Zancudo ferry makes a daily round-trip to Golfito.

➤ INFORMATION: **Puntarenas–Playa Naranjo Ferry** (☎ 506/661–1069).

WITHIN PANAMA

Water taxis travel regularly between Almirante and Bocas del Toro, and several times daily between Almirante and Chiriquí Grande. A daily car ferry also connects Almirante and Chiriquí Grande, stopping at Bocas del Toro twice a week; but water taxis make the same trip in a fraction of the time. Several ferries run daily between Panama City and the island of Taboga.

WITHIN NICARAGUA

Ferries to Ometepe's Moyogalpa run from San Jorge, near Rivas, six days a week. Boats from Granada and San Jorge run three times a week, and there's regular weekend hydrofoil service from Granada.

➤ INFORMATION: **Lake Nicaragua ferry** (☎ 505/552–2966).

BUS TRAVEL

WITHIN COSTA RICA

Reliable, inexpensive bus service covers much of the country. A patchwork of private companies leaves San José from a variety of departure points. For schedules and departure locations for your destination of choice, *see* Getting Around *in* the A to Z sections of the appropriate chapter.

Tickets are sold at bus stations and on the buses themselves. The only way to reserve a seat is to buy your ticket ahead of time or, depending on the route, simply show up early for departure. On longer routes, buses stop midway at modest restaurants. Near the ends of their runs many nonexpress buses turn into large taxis, dropping passengers off one by one at their destinations; to save time, take a *directo* (express) bus.

➤ BUS COMPANIES: Central Valley: **Empresarios Unidos** (☎ 506/222–0064). **Rapiditos Heredianos** (☎ 506/233–8392). **Sacsa** (☎ 506/233–5350). **Transtusa** (☎ 506/556–0073). **Tuasa** (☎ 506/222–5325). Northern Guanacaste and Alajuela: **Tralapa** (☎ 506/221–7202). **Transportes La Cañera** (☎ 506/222–3006). **Transportes Tilarán** (☎ 506/222–3854). Nicoya Peninsula: **Empresa Alfaro** (☎ 506/685–5032). **Empresarios Unidos** (☎ 506/222–0064). **Pulmitan** (☎ 506/222–1650). Central Pacific: **Transportes Delio Morales** (☎ 506/223–5567). **Transportes Jacó** (☎ 506/223–1109). Southern Pacific: **Alfaro Tracopa** (☎ 506/221–4214). **Musoc** (☎ 506/222–2422). **Transportes Blanco Lobo** (☎ 506/257–4121). Atlantic Lowlands and Pacific Coast: **Autotransportes Sarapiqui** (☎ 506/

259–8571). **Empresarios Guapilenos** (☎ 506/222–0610). **Transportes Caribeños** (☎ 506/221-2596). **Transportes Mepe** (☎ 506/257–8129).

WITHIN PANAMA

Microbuses provide frequent service between most Panamanian towns. Buses depart about every 30 minutes between Changuinola and Almirante, slightly less frequently between Changuinola and the border with Costa Rica. About five buses a day connect Chiriquí Grande with David, from which buses leave every 20 minutes for the Costa Rican border, Volcán and Cerro Punta, and Boquete. Old Greyhound buses leave every hour for the seven-hour trip between David and Panama City. There's also daily direct service from Panama City and Chiriquí Grande, departing Panama City at 5 AM and Chiriquí Grande at 1 PM, when the ferry arrives from Almirante.

Tica Bus buses leave Panama City daily at noon and arrive in San José at 5 AM the next morning; in the other direction, they leave San José for Panama at 10 PM and arrive the following day at 4 PM. Round-trip fare is about $34. **Panaline** has a daily luxury express service that departs from the Hotel Cocorí at 1 PM and arrives in Panama City at 6 AM the next day, returning from Panama City at 1 PM and arriving in San José at 5 AM. Round-trip fare is about $42. **Tracopa** buses leave San José from the Hotel Cocorí daily at 7:30 AM, arriving at David, Panama, at 5:30 PM. From there, buses depart every hour for Panama City, seven hours farther. The round-trip fare is around $14. **Panaline** also runs a daily bus from San José to Changuinola, in northwest Panama, at 10 AM. Leaving from the Hotel Cocorí, the eight-hour trip costs about $6 each way.

➤ BUS INFORMATION: **Alico** (☎ 507/775–2923). **Panaline** (✉ Hotel Cocorí, C. 16 between Avdas. 3 and 5, ☎ 506/255–1205). **Tica** (✉ C. 9 and Avda. 4, San José, ☎ 506/221–8954). **Tracopa** (✉ Hotel Cocorí, C. 16 between Avdas. 3 and 5, ☎ 506/221–4214). **Union de Buses Panamericana** (☎ 507/229–6333).

WITHIN NICARAGUA

Buses in Nicaragua range from low-cost locals—usually recycled American schoolbuses—to pricier air-conditioned express vehicles. The transportation hub of southwest Nicaragua is Granada, from which buses regularly leave for the nearby beaches, Lake Nicaragua, Granada, and Managua. Tica offers regular bus service from San José to Managua, with a stop in Liberia.

➤ BUS INFORMATION: **Tica** (☎ 506/221–8954, 506/255–4771, or 505/222–6094).

PAYING

Bus companies in all these countries accept cash only.

RESERVATIONS

In high season, bus tickets to most popular beaches should be purchased ahead of time. Reservations are not taken over the phone; you have to buy a ticket in person.

BANKS & OFFICES

Most state banks in Costa Rica and Panama are open weekdays 9 to 3, and many are open Saturday morning. Several branches of Banco Nacional are open until 6. The growing cadre of private banks tend to keep longer hours, and are usually the best places to change dollars and traveler's checks. Bank hours in Nicaragua are 8:30 to 4:30 on weekdays, 8:30 to noon on Saturday.

GAS STATIONS

There are 24-hour gas stations near most cities, especially along the Pan-American Highway. Most other stations are open from about 7 to 7, sometimes until midnight.

MUSEUMS & SIGHTS

Most of Costa Rica's public museums are closed on Monday.

SHOPS

Most shops in Costa Rica and Panama are open 8 to 6 Monday to Friday and 8 to 1 Saturday. Shops in Nicaragua are open roughly 9 to 6 weekdays and 9 to 5 Saturday.

CAMERAS & PHOTOGRAPHY

The *Kodak Guide to Shooting Great Travel Pictures* is an excellent tool and is available in bookstores or from Fodor's.

➤ PHOTO HELP: **Kodak Information Center** (☎ 800/242–2424). *Kodak Guide to Shooting Great Travel Pictures* ($16.50 plus $4 shipping); contact Fodor's Travel Publications (P 800/533–6478.

EQUIPMENT PRECAUTIONS

Always **keep your film and videotape out of the sun,** and carry an extra supply of batteries. In airports, be prepared to turn on your camera or camcorder to prove to security personnel that the device is real. **Ask for hand inspection of film,** which may become clouded after repeated exposure to airport X-ray machines, and **keep videotapes away from metal detectors.**

FILM & DEVELOPING

Most **film costs at least 20 percent more in Costa Rica** than in the United States, so try to bring enough for your trip. Plenty of shops in San José develop film, usually the same day, but they tend to change the chemicals less often than they should, so you risk getting prints of poor quality. Kodachrome slide film cannot be developed in Costa Rica.

➤ LOCAL LABS: **Dima Color** (✉ 325 m east of U.S. Embassy, Pavas, ☎ 506/231–4130). **Rapi Foto** (✉ C. Central at Avda. 5, San José, ☎ 506/223–7640).

CAR RENTAL

Many travelers shy away from renting a car in Costa Rica, if only for fear of the road conditions. Indeed, this is not an ideal place to drive—in San José, traffic is bad and car theft is rampant (look for guarded parking lots or hotels with lots); in rural areas, roads are often unpaved or dotted with potholes. The greatest deterrent of all might be the extremely high rental rates (☞ *below*) and gas prices (about $1.50/gallon).

Still, having your own wheels gives you more control over your itinerary and the pace of your trip. If you decide to go for it, you'll have to choose which type of vessel to rent: a standard vehicle, fine for most destinations, or a *doble-tracción* (four-wheel-drive), often essential to reach the more remote parts of the country, especially during the rainy season. These can cost roughly twice as much as an economy car and should be booked well in advance. If you plan to rent any kind of vehicle between December 15 and January 3, or during Holy Week, **reserve several months ahead of time.**

Costa Rica has around 50 international and local car-rental firms, the larger of which have several offices around San José. At least a dozen rental offices line San José's Paseo Colón, and most large hotels have representatives. Panama and Nicaragua have fewer rental agencies, but rates are often lower than in Costa Rica. For a complete listing, look in the local phone directory once you arrive, under *alquiler de automóviles.*

➤ MAJOR AGENCIES: **Alamo** (☎ 800/ 522–9696; 0181/759–6200 in the U.K.). **Avis** (☎ 800/331–1084; 800/ 879–2847 in Canada; 02/9353–9000 in Australia; 09/525–1982 in New Zealand). **Budget** (☎ 800/527–0700; 0144/227–6266 in the U.K.). **Dollar** (☎ 800/800–6000; 0181/897–0811 in the U.K., where it is known as Eurodollar; 02/9223–1444 in Australia). **Hertz** (☎ 800/654–3001; 800/263–0600 in Canada; 0181/897– 2072 in the U.K.; 02/9669–2444 in Australia; 03/358–6777 in New Zealand). **National** (☎ 800/227– 3876; 0345/222525 in the U.K.).

RATES

At press time, high-season rates in San José began at $45 a day and $290 a week for an economy car with air-conditioning, manual transmission, unlimited mileage, and obligatory insurance; but rates fluctuate considerably according to demand, season, and company. Rates for a four-wheel-drive vehicle during high season are $80 a day and $500 per week. When renting a car in San José, **ask whether the rate includes the mandatory $15 daily fee for collision insurance.**

CUTTING COSTS

To get the best deal, **book through a travel agent who will shop around.** Also **look into wholesalers,** companies that do not own fleets but rent in bulk from those that do and often offer better rates than traditional rental agencies. Prepayment is required.

➤ SAN JOSÉ AGENCIES: **Ada** (☎ 506/ 233–7733). **Adobe** (☎ 506/233– 9937). **Avis** (☎ 506/293–2222). **Budget** (☎ 506/223–3284). **Dollar** (☎ 506/257–1585). **Economy** (☎ 506/231–5410). **Elegante** (☎ 506/ 257–0026). **Hertz** (506/221–1818). **Hola** (☎ 506/231–5666). **National** (☎ 506/290–8787).

➤ PANAMA CITY AGENCIES: **Alamo** (☎ 507/260–0822). **Avis** (☎ 507/ 264–0722). **Budget** (☎ 507/263– 8777). **Dollar** (☎ 507/225–3455). **Hertz** (☎ 507/226–7110). **National** (☎ 507/264–8277).

➤ MANAGUA AGENCIES: **Budget** (☎ 505/266–6226). **Hertz** (☎ 505/233– 1237). **Lugo** (☎ 505/263–2368).

INSURANCE

When driving a rental car, you are generally responsible for any damage to or loss of the vehicle as well as for any property damage or personal injury that you may cause. Insurance issued by car-rental agencies in Costa Rica usually has a very large deductible. Before you rent, **see what coverage you already have** under the terms of your personal auto-insurance policy and credit cards.

REQUIREMENTS & RESTRICTIONS

To rent a car in Costa Rica and Panama you need a driver's license, a valid passport, and a credit card. In Nicaragua you need a driver's license and a credit card with at least $500 in credit; you must also be at least 25 years of age.

SURCHARGES

Before you pick up a car in one city and leave it in another, **ask about drop-off charges or one-way service fees,** which can be substantial. Note, too, that some rental agencies charge extra if you return the car *before* the time specified in your contract. To avoid a hefty refueling fee, **fill the tank just before you turn in the car,** remembering that gas stations near the rental outlet may overcharge.

CAR TRAVEL

Driving in a developing nation can be a challenge, but it's a great way to explore certain regions, especially Guanacaste, the Atlantic Lowlands, and the Caribbean Coast (apart from Tortuguero and Barra del Colorado). Keep in mind that mountains and poor road conditions make most trips take longer than you'd normally expect. If you want to visit a few different far-flung areas, domestic flights (☞ Air Travel, *above*) might be a better option.

AUTO CLUBS

➤ IN AUSTRALIA: **Australian Automobile Association** (☎ 02/6247–7311).

➤ IN CANADA: **Canadian Automobile Association** (CAA, ☎ 613/247–0117).

➤ IN NEW ZEALAND: **New Zealand Automobile Association** (☎ 09/377–4660).

➤ IN THE U.K.: **Automobile Association** (AA, ☎ 0990/500–600). **Royal Automobile Club** (RAC, ☎ 0990/722–722 for membership; 0345/121–345 for insurance).

➤ IN THE U.S.: **American Automobile Association** (AAA, ☎ 800/564–6222).

DRIVING OVER THE BORDER

You can drive over Costa Rica's borders into Panama and Nicaragua, but not in a rental car—vehicles rented in one country cannot be taken into the next.

EMERGENCIES

In Costa Rica, 911 is the nationwide number for accidents. Traffic police are scattered around the country, but Costa Ricans are very good about stopping for people with car trouble. Local car-rental agencies can give you with a list of numbers to call in case of accidents or car trouble. In Panama dial 104; in Nicaragua 119.

GASOLINE

Gas costs about $1.50 per gallon.

PARKING

Car theft is rife in Costa Rica, Panama, *and* Nicaragua. **Park overnight in a locked garage or guarded lot, as Central American insurance may hold you liable if your rental car is stolen.** Most hotels, barring the least expensive, offer secure parking with a guard or locked gates.

ROAD CONDITIONS

Road conditions in Costa Rica are lamentable: you'll run into plenty of potholes and long stretches with no pavement at all. Roads are considerably better in Panama and Nicaragua.

RULES OF THE ROAD

There are plenty of questionable drivers on Costa Rican and Panamanian highways; **be prepared for harebrained passing on blind corners, tailgating, and failures to signal.** Watch, too, for two-lane roads that feed into one-lane bridges with specified rights of way. And finally, look out for potholes, even in the smoothest sections of the best roads. The highway speed limit in Costa Rica is usually 90 km (54 mi) per hour, which drops to 60 kph (36 mph) in residential areas. Seat belts are required in Panama and Costa Rica, but drunk-driving laws tend to be less severe than in other parts of the world. You may not drive out of Costa Rica in a rental car.

CHILDREN IN COSTA RICA

Thanks to its generally high safety and health standards, Costa Rica is popular with traveling families. Most of the health problems you might associate with the tropics are rare or nonexistent in Costa Rica (though not in Nicaragua), and the country's most popular destinations have plenty to offer kids. However, many popular beaches have dangerous currents when the surf is up.

If your kids are small and you decide to rent a car, don't forget to **arrange for a car seat** when you reserve.

FLYING

If your children are two or older, **ask about children's airfares.** As a general rule, infants under two not occupying a seat fly at greatly reduced fares or even for free. When booking, **confirm** carry-on allowances if you're traveling with infants. In general, for babies charged 10% of the adult fare you are allowed one carry-on bag and a collapsible stroller; if the flight is full, the stroller may have to be checked or you may be limited to less.

Experts agree that it's a good idea to use safety seats aloft for children weighing less than 40 pounds. Airlines set their own policies; U.S. carriers usually require that the child be ticketed, even if he or she is young enough to ride free, since the seats must be strapped into regular seats. **Check your airline's policy about using safety seats during takeoff and landing.** And since safety seats are not allowed everywhere in the plane, get your seat assignments early.

When buying plane tickets, **request children's meals or a freestanding bassinet** if you need them; just note that bulkhead seats, where you must sit to use the bassinet, may lack an overhead bin or storage space on the floor.

LODGING

Most hotels in Costa Rica allow children under a certain age to stay in their parents' room at no extra charge, but others charge for them as extra adults. **Ask the cutoff age for children's discounts.**

SIGHTS & ATTRACTIONS

Throughout this book, places that are especially appealing to kids are indicated by a rubber-duck icon (🐤) in the margin.

COMPUTERS ON THE ROAD

Many hotels in Costa Rica have data ports. Batteries and stabilizers are hard to come by, however, and since the current fluctuates significantly in these countries, a stabilizer is usually necessary. It's best to call your hotel in advance for details.

Cyber cafés are popping up all over metropolitan San José; ask around for the one nearest you. The ones we list below are centrally located and accustomed to international travelers.

➤ INTERNET CAFÉS: CyberCafé Search-costarica.com (Avda. 2 between Cs. 1 and 3, ground floor of Las Arcadas building, San José, ☎ 506/233–3310). Y2K Net Café Costa Rica (200 meters east of Universidad Latina, San Pedro, ☎ 506/283–4829). Internet Café Costa Rica (50 meters west of the Banco Popular, San Pedro, ☎ 506/224–7295). Racsa office (C. 1 at Avda. 5, San José, ☎ 506/287–0087).

CONSUMER PROTECTION

Whether you're purchasing goods or travel services in Costa Rica, **pay with a major credit card** so you can cancel payment or get reimbursed if there's a problem. If you're doing business with a travel company for the first time, **contact your local Better Business Bureau and the attorney general's offices** in your own state and the company's home state, as well. Have any complaints been filed? Finally, if you're buying a package or tour, always **consider travel insurance** that includes default coverage (☞ Insurance, *below*).

➤ BBBs: **Council of Better Business Bureaus** (✉ 4200 Wilson Blvd., Suite 800, Arlington, VA 22203, ☎ 703/276–0100, FAX 703/525–8277 ✉).

CRUISE TRAVEL

Cruises are the most restful way to travel. The U.S.–Costa Rica cruise season runs September–May, with trips lasting from three days to a week. A travel agent can explain prices, which range from $1,000 to $5,000. Luxury liners equipped with pools and gyms sail from Fort Lauderdale, Florida, to Limón, or through the Panama Canal to Caldera, south of Puntarenas. Some cruises sail from Los Angeles to Caldera, continuing to the canal. On board the ship you can sign up for shore excursions and tours. Cruise packages include the cost of flying to the appropriate port.

➤ CRUISE LINES: **Carnival** (☎ 800/327–9501). **Crystal Cruises** (☎ 800/446–6645). **Cunard** (☎ 800/221–4770). **Holland America** (☎ 800/426–0327). **Ocean Cruise** (☎ 800/556–8850). **Royal Viking** (☎ 800/422–8000). **Seabourn** (☎ 800/351–9595). **Sitmar Cruise** (☎ 305/523–1219). **Temptress Adventure Cruises** (☎ 800/872–6400 or 800/336–8423). **Temptress Adventure Cruises** (☎ 800/872–6400 or 800/336–8423).

CUSTOMS & DUTIES

When shopping, **keep receipts for all purchases.** Upon reentering your home country, **be ready to show customs officials what you've bought.** If you feel a duty is incorrect or object to the way your clearance was handled, note the inspector's badge number and ask to see a supervisor; if the problem is not resolved, write to the appropriate authorities, beginning with the port director at your point of entry.

COSTA RICA

Visitors entering Costa Rica may bring in 500 &del;grams of tobacco, 3 liters of wine or spirits, 2 kilograms of sweets and chocolates, and the equivalent of $100 worth of merchandise. Two cameras, six rolls of film, binoculars, and electrical items for personal use only are also allowed. Customs officials at San José's international airport rarely examine tourists' luggage, but if you enter by land, they'll probably look through your bags.

Visitors entering Panama may bring in 500 cigarettes, 3 liters of wine or spirits, two cameras, and personal electronic equipment. As in Costa Rica, luggage inspection is rare at the airport but standard at land crossings.

Visitors entering Nicaragua may bring 3 cartons of cigarettes, 3 liters of wine or spirits, one camera, and one more piece of personal electronic equipment.

AUSTRALIA

Residents 18 or older may bring home $A400 worth of souvenirs and gifts (including jewelry), 250 cigarettes or 250 grams of tobacco, and 1,125 ml of alcohol (including wine, beer, and spirits). Residents under 18 may bring back $A200 worth of goods. Prohibited items include meat products. Seeds, plants, and fruits need to be declared upon arrival.

➤ INFORMATION: **Australian Customs Service** (Regional Director, ✉ Box 8, Sydney, NSW 2001, ☎ 02/9213–2000, FAX 02/9213–4000).

CANADA

Residents who have been out of Canada for at least 7 days may bring home C$500 worth of goods duty-free. If you've been away less than 7 days but more than 48 hours, the duty-free allowance drops to C$200; if your trip lasts 24–48 hours, the allowance is C$50. You may not pool allowances with family members. Goods claimed under the C$500 exemption may follow you by mail; those claimed under the lesser exemptions must accompany you. Alcohol and tobacco products may be included in the 7-day and 48-hour exemptions but not in the 24-hour exemption. If you meet the age requirements of the province or territory through which you reenter Canada, you may bring in, duty-free, 1.14 liters (40 imperial ounces) of wine or liquor *or* 24 12-ounce cans or bottles of beer or ale. If you are 16 or older you may bring in, duty-free, 200 cigarettes and 50 cigars. Check ahead of time with Revenue Canada or the Department of Agriculture for policies regarding meat products, seeds, plants, and fruits.

You may send an unlimited number of gifts worth up to C$60 each to Canada duty-free; label the package UNSOLICITED GIFT—VALUE UNDER $60. Alcohol and tobacco are excluded.

➤ INFORMATION: **Revenue Canada** (✉ 2265 St. Laurent Blvd. S, Ottawa, Ontario K1G 4K3, ☎ 613/993–0534; 800/461–9999 in Canada, FAX 613/957–8911, ✉).

NEW ZEALAND

Homeward-bound residents 17 or older may bring back $700 worth of souvenirs and gifts. Your duty-free allowance also includes 4.5 liters of wine or beer; one 1,125-ml bottle of spirits; and either 200 cigarettes, 250 grams of tobacco, 50 cigars, or a combination of the three up to 250 grams. Prohibited items include meat products, seeds, plants, and fruits.

➤ INFORMATION: **New Zealand Customs** (Custom House, ✉ 50 Anzac Ave., Box 29, Auckland, New Zealand, ☎ 09/359–6655, FAX 09/359–6732).

UNITED KINGDOM

From Costa Rica and other countries outside the EU, residents may bring home, duty-free, 200 cigarettes or 50 cigars; 1 liter of spirits or 2 liters of fortified or sparkling wine or liqueurs; 2 liters of still table wine; 60 ml of perfume; 250 ml of toilet water; plus £136 worth of other goods, including gifts and souvenirs. Prohibited items include meat products, seeds, plants, and fruits.

➤ INFORMATION: **HM Customs and Excise** (✉ Dorset House, Stamford St., Bromley, Kent BR1 1XX, ☎ 0171/202–4227).

UNITED STATES

Residents who have been out of the country for at least 48 hours (and who have not used the $400 allowance or any part of it in the past 30 days) may bring home $400 worth of foreign goods duty-free. U.S. residents 21 and older may bring back 1 liter of alcohol duty-free. In addition, regardless of your age, you are allowed 200 cigarettes and 100 non-Cuban cigars. Antiques, which the U.S. Customs Service defines as objects more than 100 years old, enter duty-free, as do original works of art done entirely by hand, including paintings, drawings, and sculptures.

You may also send packages home duty-free: up to $200 worth of goods for personal use, with a limit of one parcel per addressee per day (except alcohol or tobacco products or perfume worth more than $5); label the package PERSONAL USE and attach a list of its contents and their retail value. Do not label the package UNSOLICITED GIFT or your duty-free exemption will drop to $100. Mailed items do not affect your duty-free allowance on your return.

➤ INFORMATION: **U.S. Customs Service** (✉ 1300 Pennsylvania Ave. NW, Washington, DC 20229, www.customs.gov; inquiries ☎ 202/354–1000; complaints ✉ Office of Regulations and Rulings; registration of equipment ✉ Resource Management, ☎ 202/927–0540).

DINING

Though Costa Rican, Panamanian, and Nicaraguan food don't quite compare with the world's great cuisines, all three countries have interesting local dishes. There are also plenty of foreign-owned restaurants serving everything from French and Italian to Cantonese and Peruvian cuisine.

The restaurants we list are the cream of the crop in each price category.

CATEGORY	COST*
$$$$	over $20
$$$	$10–$20
$$	$5–$10
$	under $5

*for dinner entrée and nonalcoholic beverage.

MEALTIMES

Dining hours in Costa Rica, Panama, and Nicaragua are usually noon–3 and 7–10. Unless otherwise noted, the restaurants listed in this book are open daily for lunch and dinner.

PAYING

Cash is the rule at local restaurants. In Costa Rica, 23% is added to all menu prices—13% for tax and 10% for service. Because the gratuity is included, there is no need to tip, but if service is good, it's nice to add a little money to the obligatory 10%. Restaurants in Panama do not charge for service, so a 10% gratuity is expected. The rule of thumb for tips in Nicaragua is 10%, and the tip is often included in the bill (look for the word *servicio*).

RESERVATIONS

Reservations are always a good idea; we mention them only when they're essential or not accepted. Reserve as far ahead as you can, and reconfirm when you arrive in Costa Rica.

WINE, BEER & SPIRITS

Costa Rica's one brewery makes half a dozen brands of beer, including the popular Imperial, a dark brew called Steinbrau, and a local version of Heineken. All wine is imported; the best deals are usually from Chile and Argentina, particularly the Chilean Castillero del Diablo and Sangre de Toro. Costa Rica's best rum is Centenario, and the cheaper Nicaraguan rum, Flor de Caño, is just as good, but most Ticos drink a rot-gut rum called *guaro*. All of the above is served at restaurants and bars, and sold in supermarkets and liquor stores.

DISABILITIES & ACCESSIBILITY

Accessibility in Central America is extremely limited. Wheelchair ramps are practically nonexistent, and streets are often unpaved outside major cities, making wheelchair travel difficult. Exploring most attractions involves walking down cobblestone streets, steep trails, or muddy paths. Buses are not equipped to carry wheelchairs, so people using wheelchairs should hire a van to get around and bring someone along to help out. There is a growing awareness of the needs of people with disabilities, and some hotels and attractions in Costa Rica have made the necessary provisions; the **Costa Rican Tourist Institute**, known locally as the ICT, has more information.

➤ LOCAL RESOURCES: **Costa Rican Tourist Institute** (✉ Avda. 4 and Cs. 5 and 7, 11th floor, San José, Costa Rica, ☎ 506/223–1733).

LODGING

Very few hotels in Costa Rica are equipped for travelers in wheelchairs. In San José, the Hampton Inn and Hacienda El Rodeo, both near the international airport, have some wheelchair accommodations; and Wilson Botanical Gardens, in San Vito (Southern Pacific) has one room equipped for a wheelchair.

RESERVATIONS

When discussing accessibility with an operator or reservations agent, **ask hard questions.** Are there any stairs, inside *or* out? Are there grab bars next to the toilet *and* in the shower/tub? How wide is the doorway to the room? To the bathroom? For the most extensive facilities meeting the latest legal specifications, **opt for newer accommodations.**

SIGHTS & ATTRACTIONS

Unfortunately, most Costa Rican attractions are inaccessible for travelers with wheelchairs, as are restaurant bathrooms. Volcán Poás National Park is probably the most wheelchair-friendly site, with Volcán Irazú the runner-up. The Orosi Valley and Sarchí also have limited exploring options for wheelchair travelers. The Rain Forest Aerial Tram is a real challenge, but might be a possibility for some.

TRANSPORTATION

Developed areas, especially San José and the Central Valley, can be managed in a wheelchair more easily than rural areas. The tour company **Vaya con Silla de Ruedas** (Go with Wheelchair) provides transportation and guided tours.

➤ COMPLAINTS: **Disability Rights Section** (✉ U.S. Department of Justice, Civil Rights Division, Box 66738, Washington, DC 20035-6738, ☎ 202/514–0301 or 800/514–0301; TTY 202/514–0301 or 800/514–0301, FAX 202/307–1198) for general complaints. **Aviation Consumer Protection Division** (☞ Air Travel, *above*) for airline-related problems. **Civil Rights Office** (✉ U.S. Department of Transportation, Departmental Office of Civil Rights, S-30, 400 7th St. SW, Room 10215, Washington, DC 20590, ☎ 202/366–4648, FAX 202/366–9371) for problems with surface transportation.

TRAVEL AGENCIES

In the United States, the Americans with Disabilities Act requires that travel firms serve the needs of all travelers. Some agencies specialize in working with people with disabilities.

➤ TRAVELERS WITH MOBILITY PROBLEMS: **Access Adventures** (✉ 206 Chestnut Ridge Rd., Rochester, NY 14624, ☎ 716/889–9096), run by a former physical-rehabilitation counselor. **Flying Wheels Travel** (✉ 143 W. Bridge St., Box 382, Owatonna, MN 55060, ☎ 507/451–5005 or 800/535–6790, FAX 507/451–1685, ✍). **Hinsdale Travel Service** (✉ 201 E. Ogden Ave., Suite 100, Hinsdale, IL 60521, ☎ 630/325–1335, FAX 630/325–1342).

➤ TRAVELERS WITH DEVELOPMENTAL DISABILITIES: **New Directions** (✉ 5276 Hollister Ave., Suite 207, Santa Barbara, CA 93111, ☎ 805/967–2841 or 888/967–2841, FAX 805/964–7344, ✍).

DISCOUNT RESERVATIONS

To save money, **look into discount reservations services** with toll-free numbers, which use their buying power to get better prices on hotel rooms, airline tickets, even car rentals. Ask hotels about special packages or corporate rates.

When shopping for hotel rooms and car rentals, **look for guaranteed exchange rates,** which protect you against a falling dollar. With your rate locked in, you won't pay more, even if the price goes up in the local currency.

➤ AIRLINE TICKETS: ☎ 800/FLY–4–LESS.

PACKAGE DEALS

Don't confuse package vacations with guided tours. When you buy a package, you travel on your own, just as though you had planned the trip yourself. Fly/drive packages, which combine airfare and car rental, are often a good deal.Ecotourism

Ecotourism, green tourism, environmental tourism: the buzzwords have been flying around Costa Rica for more than a decade. Many of the tour companies that operate in Costa Rica and Panama have incorporated a high level of environmental awareness into their business practices. **Find out whether or not your prospective tour company has "eco-friendly" policies,** such as hiring and training locals as guides, drivers, managers, and office workers; teaching people as much as possible about the plant and animal life, geography, and history that surrounds them; controlling the numbers of people allowed daily onto a given site; restoring watersheds and anything else damaged by trail-building, visiting, or general overuse; and discouraging wildlife feeding or any other unnatural or disruptive behavior (i.e., making loud noises to scare birds into flight). All these practices can mitigate the effects of intense tourism. After all, it's better to have a hundred people walking through a forest than to cut the forest down.

There are numerous environmental organizations in Costa Rica and Panama, most of them heavily dependent on private donations and dedicated volunteers. To obtain a list of Costa Rican groups that might need a hand or a donation, consult the *Directorio de Organizaciones, Institu-*

ciones y Consultores en El Sector de Recursos Naturales en Costa Rica, published in Spanish by the Costa Rican Federation for the Preservation of the Environment (FECON). For locally generated advice on ecotourism, consult the *Sustainable Tourism Newsletter,* published by the Eco-Institute of Costa Rica.

COSTA RICA

Costa Rica Expeditions has won awards for its commitment to conservation and the quality of its tours. **Horizontes** is an award-winning natural-history tour operator with some of the country's best guides. **Sun Tours** owns several properties with private nature reserves. **Tikal Tours** specializes in nature tours for small groups. **Temptress Adventure Cruises** offers multi-day natural-history cruises along the Southern Pacific coast aboard the 185-ft *M/V Temptress.*

➤ TOUR OPERATORS: **Costa Rica Expeditions** (☎ 506/222–0333, FAX 506/257–1665). **Horizontes** (☎ 506/222–2022, FAX 506/255–4513). **Sun Tours** (☎ 506/255–2011, FAX 233–6890). **Tikal Tours** (☎ 506/223–2811, FAX 506/223–1916). **Temptress Adventure Cruises** (☎ 506/220–1679 or 506/232–6672; 800/336–8423 in the U.S.).

➤ ENVIRONMENTAL ORGANIZATIONS: **AECO** (☎ 506/233–3013). **ANAI** (☎ 506/224–6090). **APREFLOFAS** (☎ 506/240–6087). **Neotropica Foundation** (☎ 506/253–2130).

PANAMA

Ancon Expeditions, owned by Panama's largest environmental group, has several field stations around the country, including one in Bocas del Toro, and offers a variety of multi-day packages. **Pesántez Tours,** a pioneer in bird-watching tours, leads trips throughout Panama. **Turtle Divers,** in Bocas del Toro, runs tours to dive sites, islands, and indigenous communities, and supports environmental education in local schools. **Río Monte Ecological Tours,** in Boquete, is run by the Collins family, which has been involved in ecotourism since long before the term was coined. **Expediciones Tierras Altas,** in Boquete, is a small outfit offering low-budget nature and hiking tours.

➤ CONTACTS: **Ancon Expeditions** (☎ 507/269–9415). **Expediciones Tierras Altas** (☎ 507/720–1342). **Pesántez Tours** (☎ 507/263–8771). **Río Monte Ecological Tours** (☎ 507/720–1327). **Turtle Divers** (☎ ℻ 507/757–9594).

ELECTRICITY

The electrical current in Central America is 110 volts (AC), and plugs are the same as in the United States. No converter or adapter is required.

EMBASSIES

Most embassies are on the western end of San José or in nearby suburbs. Citizens of Australia and New Zealand should contact the British Embassy.

➤ CANADA: (✉ Sabana Sur, next to tennis club, ☎ 506/296–4149).

➤ UNITED KINGDOM: (✉ Centro Colón, Paseo Colón between Cs. 38 and 40, ☎ 506/258–2025).

➤ UNITED STATES: (✉ Pavas, ☎ 506/220–3939).

EMERGENCIES

Costa Ricans are usually quick to respond in emergencies. In a hotel or restaurant, the staff would offer immediate immediate assistance, and in a public area, passersby can be counted on to stop and help.

➤ COSTA RICA: **General emergencies** (☎ 911). **Ambulance** (☎ 128). **Police** (☎ 117; 127 outside cities).

➤ PANAMA: **Fire** (☎ 103).**Police** (☎ 104).

➤ NICARAGUA: **Fire** (☎ 115). **Police** (☎ 119).

ENGLISH-LANGUAGE MEDIA

English is practically everywhere in Costa Rica, from abundant publications to the cable TV beamed into most San José hotels.

BOOKS

Several San José bookstores carry a good selection of new and used English-language books, at prices slightly higher prices than those in the United States. Some large hotels and other shops also sell English-language books, particularly titles on the tropical outdoors.

Major Bookstores: **7th Street Books** (✉ C. 7 between Avdas. Central and 1, San José, ☎ 506/256–8251). **Lehmann** (✉ Avda. Central between Cs. 1 and 3, San José, ☎ 506/223–1212). **Librería Internacional** (Barrio Dent, 300 m west of Taco Bell, ☎ 506/253–9553

NEWSPAPERS & MAGAZINES

American newspapers and magazines are widely distributed at newsstands and hotels in San José, and sold in some resorts outside the capital. The English-language weekly *The Tico Times,* published every Friday, has local news and information on entertainment and travel.

RADIO & TELEVISION

Most mid- to high-priced hotels in San José have cable TV in guest rooms, with at least a dozen English-language channels. Some hotels outside the capital have satellite dishes. Local TV is in Spanish and not worth writing home about. There is one exclusively English-language radio station, which plays rock (107.5 FM); a few others (99.5 and 102.3 FM) play some tunes in English.

ETIQUETTE & BEHAVIOR

On the whole, Costa Ricans are extremely polite, quick to shake hands and place a soft kiss on the left cheek. At the same time, an unsettlingly large portion of Costa Rican men make a habit of ogling or making gratuitous comments when young women pass on the street. Panamanians and Nicaraguans are perhaps a bit less gregarious, and correspondingly less given to harassment.

As you would anywhere, **dress and behave respectfully when visiting churches.**

BUSINESS ETIQUETTE

Northerners are bound to find business meetings friendlier and more relaxed in Costa Rica and its neighbors than at home. Dress is usually casual, and tardiness is common.

FLIGHTSEEING

San José–based pilot **Jenner Rojas** (506/385–5425) will take you anywhere in Costa Rica for "flightseeing" and photography. The rate is $230 hour, or less if you arrange a trip of several hours' duration.

GAY & LESBIAN TRAVEL

While harassment of gays and lesbians is infrequent in Costa Rica, Panama, and Nicaragua, so are public displays of affection. Discretion is advised. As a result of its history of tolerance, Costa Rica has attracted many gays from other Latin American nations, and consequently has a large gay community. San José and Manuel Antonio are probably the most gay-friendly towns, with plenty of bars and hangouts in this vein. The beach at the northern end of Playa Espadilla in Manuel Antonio National Park is a small, secluded cove known as a gay nude beach. There are no anti-gay laws.

Panama and Nicaragua do not have as large a gay population as Costa Rica, but discreet gay travelers should not encounter problems here, either.

➤ GAY- & LESBIAN-FRIENDLY TRAVEL AGENCIES: **Different Roads Travel** (⊠ 8383 Wilshire Blvd., Suite 902, Beverly Hills, CA 90211, ☎ 323/651–5557 or 800/429–8747, FAX 323/651–3678). **Kennedy Travel** (⊠ 314 Jericho Turnpike, Floral Park, NY 11001, ☎ 516/352–4888 or 800/237–7433, FAX 516/354–8849, ✍). **Now Voyager** (⊠ 4406 18th St., San Francisco, CA 94114, ☎ 415/626–1169 or 800/255–6951, FAX 415/626–8626, ✍). **Skylink Travel and Tour** (⊠ 1006 Mendocino Ave., Santa Rosa, CA 95401, ☎ 707/546–9888 or 800/225–5759, FAX 707/546–9891, ✍) serves lesbian travelers.

➤ LOCAL CONTACTS: **1 en 10** (C. 1 between Avdas. 9 and 11, ☎ 506/258–4561). **Abraxas** (⊠ Apartado Postal 1619–4050, Alajuela). **Asociacion Triangulo Rosa** (C. 11 at Avda. 2, San José, ☎ 506/234–2411). **Costa Rica Human Rights Commission** (San Pedro, ☎ 506/226–2658 or 506/226–2081).

HEALTH

ENGLISH-SPEAKING DOCTORS

Many of the doctors at San José's Clinica Biblica and Clinica Catolica speak English well, and some studied medicine in the United States.

➤ LOCAL MEDICAL HELP: **Clinica Biblica** (Avda. 14 at C. 1, San José, ☎ 506/221–3922). **Clinica Catolica** (San Antonio Guadalupe, ☎ 506/283–6616).

FOOD & DRINK

Most Costa Rican and Panamanian food and water are sanitary. In rural areas, you run a mild risk of encountering drinking water, fresh fruit, and vegetables contaminated by fecal matter, which causes intestinal ailments known variously as Montezuma's Revenge (traveler's diarrhea) and leptospirosis (another disease borne in contaminated food or water that can be treated by antibiotics if detected early). **Watch what you eat**—avoid ice, uncooked food, and unpasteurized milk (including milk products), and **drink bottled water.** Health standards in Nicaragua are lower than in Costa Rica or Panama, so it's best to stick exclusively to bottled water there, and avoid unpeeled fruits and vegetables. Mild cases of Montezuma's Revenge may respond to Imodium (known generically as loperamide) or Pepto-Bismol (not as strong), both of which can be purchased over the counter. Paregoric, another antidiarrheal agent, requires a doctor's prescription in Costa Rica. Drink plenty of purified water or tea; chamomile is a good folk remedy. In severe cases, rehydrate yourself with a salt-sugar solution (½ teaspoon salt and 4 tablespoons sugar per quart of water).

MEDICAL PLANS

No one plans to get sick while traveling, but it happens, so **consider signing up with a medical-assistance company.** Members get doctor referrals, emergency evacuation or repatriation, hotlines for medical consultation, cash for emergencies, and other assistance.

➤ MEDICAL-ASSISTANCE COMPANIES:
International SOS Assistance (✉ 8
Neshaminy Interplex, Suite 207,
Trevose, PA 19053, ☎ 215/245–4707
or 800/523–6586, FAX 215/244–9617,
www.internationalsos.com; ✉ 12
Chemin Riantbosson, 1217 Meyrin 1,
Geneva, Switzerland, ☎ 4122/785–
6464, FAX 4122/785–6424, www.inter-
nationalsos.com; ✉ 331 N. Bridge
Rd., 17-00, Odeon Towers, Singapore
188720, ☎ 65/338–7800, FAX 65/
338–7611, ✏).

OVER-THE-COUNTER REMEDIES

Most drugs for which you need a
prescription back home are sold over
the counter in Central America.
Pharmacies (*farmacias*) are abundant,
and most sell aspirin and sunscreen in
a wide range of SPFs, though the
latter is relatively pricey.

HAZARDS

Mild insect repellents, like the ones in
some skin softeners, are no match for
the intense mosquito activity in the
hot, humid regions of the Atlantic
Lowlands. Moreover, perfume, after-
shave, and other lotions and potions
can actually attract mosquitoes. Poisonous snakes, scorpions, and other
pests pose a small (overrated) threat.

The greatest danger to your person
actually lies off this region's popular
beaches—riptides are common wherever there are waves, and several
tourists drown in them every year. If
you see waves, ask the locals where it's
safe to swim; and if you're uncertain,
don't go in deeper than your waist. If
you get caught in a rip current, swim
parallel to the beach until you're free
of it, then swim back to shore.

SHOTS & MEDICATIONS

According to the U.S. Centers for
Disease Control, travel to Central
America poses a limited risk of
malaria, hepatitis A and B, dengue
fever, typhoid fever, rabies, and *E.
coli*. Travelers in most urban or easily
accessible areas need not worry; but if
you plan to visit remote regions or
stay for more than six weeks, check
with the CDC for detailed health
advisories (☞ Health Warnings,
below). In areas with malaria and

dengue, both of which are carried by
mosquitoes, **bring mosquito nets,
wear clothing that covers your body,
apply repellent containing DEET, and
use insect spray in living and sleeping
areas.**

Dengue and malaria are less of a
problem in Panama, but they do arise,
especially in the country's western and
eastern extremes and along the Atlantic coast. The threat of malaria is
worst in Panama during the rainy
season, May to mid-December. In
Nicaragua, travelers run a somewhat
higher risk of contracting dengue fever
or malaria, particularly in jungle areas.

Children traveling to Central America
should have current inoculations
against measles, mumps, rubella, and
polio.

➤ HEALTH ADVISORIES: **National
Centers for Disease Control** (CDC;
National Center for Infectious Diseases, Division of Quarantine, Traveler's Health Section, ✉ 1600 Clifton
Rd. NE, M/S E-03, Atlanta, GA
30333, ☎ 888/232–3228, FAX 888/
232–3299, ✏).

HOLIDAYS

National holidays are known as
feriados. On these days government
offices, banks, and post offices are
closed, and public transport is restricted. Religious festivals are characterized by colorful processions.
Panama's annual carnival celebrations
feature spectacular costumes.

2001 dates: January 1, New Year's
Day; January 9, Day of the Martyrs
(Panama only); February 27, Shrove
Tuesday; February 27, Carnival
Tuesday (Panama); April 11, Juan
Santamaría Day (Costa Rica); April
13–15, Good Friday–Easter Sunday;
May 1, Labor Day; July 25, Annexa-
tion of Guanacaste (Costa Rica);
August 2, Virgin of the Angels (Costa
Rica's patron saint); September 15,
Independence Day (Costa Rica);
October 12, Columbus Day (Día de la
Raza); November 3, Independence
from Colombia (Panama); November
10, Call for Independence (Panama);
November 28, Independence from
Spain (Panama); December 25,
Christmas.

INSURANCE

The most useful travel-insurance plan is a comprehensive policy that includes coverage for trip cancellation and interruption, default, trip delay, and medical expenses (with a waiver for preexisting conditions).

Without insurance, you will lose all or most of your money if you cancel your trip, regardless of the reason. Default insurance covers you if your tour operator, airline, or cruise line goes out of business. Trip-delay insurance covers expenses that arise from bad weather or mechanical delays. Study the fine print when comparing policies.

If you're traveling internationally, a key component of travel insurance is coverage for medical bills incurred if you get sick on the road. Such expenses are not generally covered by Medicare or private policies. British and Australian citizens need extra medical coverage when traveling overseas. U.K. residents can buy a travel-insurance policy valid for most vacations taken during the year in which it's purchased (but check coverage for pre-existing conditions).

Always **buy travel policies directly from the insurance company**—if you buy them from a cruise line, airline, or tour operator that goes out of business you probably will not be covered for the agency or operator's default, a major risk. Before making any purchase, **review your existing health and home-owner's policies** to see what they cover away from home.

➤ TRAVEL INSURERS: In the U.S.: **Access America** (⊠ 6600 W. Broad St., Richmond, VA 23230, ☎ 804/285–3300 or 800/284–8300, FAX 804/673–1583, ✒), **Travel Guard International** (⊠ 1145 Clark St., Stevens Point, WI 54481, ☎ 715/345–0505 or 800/826–1300, FAX 800/955–8785, ✒). In Canada: **Voyager Insurance** (⊠ 44 Peel Center Dr., Brampton, Ontario L6T 4M8, ☎ 905/791–8700; 800/668–4342 in Canada).

➤ INSURANCE INFORMATION: In the U.K.: **Association of British Insurers** (⊠ 51–55 Gresham St., London EC2V 7HQ, ☎ 0171/600–3333, FAX 0171/696–8999, ✒). In Australia:

Insurance Council of Australia (☎ 03/9614–1077, FAX 03/9614–7924).

LANGUAGE

Spanish is the official language of Costa Rica, Panama, and Nicaragua, although some people also speak English, especially along the Caribbean coast. You'll have a better time in Central America if you learn some basic Spanish before you go, and bring a phrase book with you. At the very least, **learn the rudiments of polite conversation**—niceties like *por favor* (please) and *gracias* (thank you) will be warmly appreciated.

➤ PHRASE BOOK & LANGUAGE TAPES: *Fodor's Spanish for Travelers* (P 800/733–3000 in the U.S.; 800/668–4247 in Canada; $7 for phrase book, $16.95 for audio set).

SPANISH-LANGUAGE PROGRAMS

Thousands of people travel to Costa Rica every year to study Spanish. Dozens of schools in and around San José offer professional instruction and home stays, and there are several smaller schools outside the capital.

➤ CONTACTS: **Conversa** (⊠ Apdo. 17–1007, Centro Colon, San José, ☎ 506/221–7649; 800/354–5036 in U.S./Canada) also has a school in Santa Ana, west of San José. **IPEE** (⊠ 25 m. south of Pops, Curridabat, ☎ 506/283–7731; 813/988–3916 in U.S.). **ILISA** (⊠ Dept. 1420, Box 25216, Miami, FL 33102, ☎ 506/225–2495; 800/454–7248 ext. 3000 in U.S.). **La Escuela D'Amore** (⊠ Apdo. 67, Quepos, ☎ 506/777–1143) is in beautiful Manuel Antonio.

LODGING

Hotels are going up fast in Costa Rica, thanks to the country's skyrocketing popularity with travelers. Development is slower in Panama and Nicaragua. At Costa Rica's popular beach and mountain resorts and Panama's Chiriquí highlands, **reserve well in advance for the dry season** (mid-December–April). You'll need to give credit-card information or send a deposit to confirm the reservation. During the rainy season, May to mid-December, most hotels drop their rates considerably, which sometimes sends them into a lower price category than the one we indicate.

Luxury international hotels are found mainly in San José. Many travelers prefer the smaller, one-of-a-kind hotels set in former homes with verdant courtyards in and around San José, particularly in the historic Amón and Otoya neighborhoods. Except for the most popular Pacific beaches, lodging in outlying areas is usually in smaller, simpler hotels, often called *cabinas* (cabins) in Costa Rica, *cabañas* in Panama, and *hospedajes* in Nicaragua. Cabinas range from basic cement boxes with few creature comforts to flashier units with all the modern conveniences. Costa Rica and Panama also have an abundance of nature lodges (often within private biological reserves) with an emphasis on ecology; most of these are entirely rustic, but a few of the newest are quite luxurious. About half the national parks in this region have campgrounds with facilities.

Hotels operate on the **European Plan** (EP, with no meals) unless we specify otherwise.

The lodgings we review are the cream of the crop in each price category. We always list facilities, but we don't specify whether they cost extra—when pricing hotel rooms, always ask what's included and what costs extra.

CATEGORY	COST*
$$$$	over $90
$$$	$50–$90
$$	$25–$50
$	under $25

for a double room, excluding service and tax (16.4% in Costa Rica, 10% in Panama, 15% in Nicaragua)

APARTMENT & VILLA RENTALS

If you want a home base that's big enough for a family or group and comes with cooking facilities, **consider a furnished rental.** In addition to accommodating your crowd, these can save you money. Look through classified ads in the Real Estate section of Costa Rica's English-language weekly, *The Tico Times.* Home-exchange directories sometimes list rentals as well as exchanges. Costa Rica Rentals International has rental homes and apartments in the San José

area and elsewhere; Tropical Waters arranges short-term rentals in the Dominical area. Marina Trading Post, an affiliate of Century 21, arranges house and condominium rentals near Playa Flamingo.

➤ INTERNATIONAL AGENTS: **Europa-Let/Tropical Inn-Let** (✉ 92 N. Main St., Ashland, OR 97520, ☎ 541/482–5806 or 800/462–4486, ℻ 541/482–0660). **Hideaways International** (✉ 767 Islington St., Portsmouth, NH 03801, ☎ 603/430–4433 or 800/843–4433, ℻ 603/430–4444 www.hideaways.com; membership $99).

Vacation Home Rentals Worldwide (✉ 235 Kensington Ave., Norwood, NJ 07648, ☎ 201/767–9393 or 800/633–3284, ℻ 201/767–5510, ✍). **Villas International** (✉ 950 Northgate Dr., Suite 206, San Rafael, CA 94903, ☎ 415/499–9490 or 800/221–2260, ℻ 415/499–9491, ✍).

➤ LOCAL AGENTS: **Costa Rica Rentals International** (✉ Apdo. 1136–1250, Escazú, ☎ 506/228–6863). **Tropical Waters** (✉ 3km north of Dominical, ☎ 506/787–0031). **Marina Trading Post** (✉ Suites Presidenciales, Playa Flamingo, Guanacaste, ☎ 506/654–4004).

CAMPING

Many national parks have camping areas; it's best to contact the park rangers for information. Some popular beaches, including Manuel Antonio, Jacó, Sámara, Tamarindo, and Puerto Viejo, have private camping areas with bathrooms and showers. If you camp on the beach or in other unguarded areas, **don't leave belongings unattended in your tent.**

HOSTELS

No matter what your age, you can **save on lodging costs by staying in hostels.** In Costa Rica, information and reservations for any of the country's six hostels are available at the Toruma Youth Hostel in San José (☞ Chapter 2). In some 5,000 locations in more than 70 countries around the world, Hostelling International (HI), the umbrella group for a number of national youth-hostel associations, offers single-sex, dorm-style beds and, in many cases, rooms for couples and family accommodations. Membership in any HI national hostel association, open to travelers of all ages, allows you to stay in HI-affiliated hostels at member rates; one-year membership is about $25 for adults (C$26.75 in Canada, £9.30 in the U.K., $30 in Australia, and $30 in New Zealand); hostels run about $10–$25 per night. Members have priority if the hostel is full and are eligible for various discounts, even on rail and bus travel in some countries.

➤ ORGANIZATIONS: **Hostelling International—American Youth Hostels** (✉ 733 15th St. NW, Suite 840, Washington, DC 20005, ☎ 202/783–6161, ℻ 202/783–6171, ✍). **Hostelling International—Canada** (✉ 400–205 Catherine St., Ottawa, Ontario K2P 1C3, ☎ 613/237–7884, ℻ 613/237–7868, ✍). **Youth Hostel Association of England and Wales** (✉ Trevelyan House, 8 St. Stephen's Hill, St. Albans, Hertfordshire AL1 2DY, ☎ 01727/855215 or 01727/845047, ℻ 01727/844126, ✍). **Australian Youth Hostel Association** (✉ 10 Mallett St., Camperdown, NSW 2050, ☎ 02/9565–1699, ℻ 02/9565–1325, ✍). **Youth Hostels Association of New Zealand** (✉ Box 436, Christchurch, New Zealand, ☎ 03/379–9970, ℻ 03/365–4476, ✍).

HOTELS

There are a few large hotels on the outskirts of San José and on some of the more popular beaches, but most Costa Rican hotels are smaller, with more personalized service. Outside San José, rooms are in great demand between the week after Christmas and the week before Easter; reserve one to three months in advance for those times. Most hotels drop their rates during the "green season" (May to December), and during this time—barring July—it's quite feasible to show up without reservations and haggle over rates, a process that can bring your hotel budget down to nearly half what it might be in the high season. All hotels listed have private bathrooms unless we indicate otherwise. If you want a double bed, request a *cama doble.*

MAIL & SHIPPING

Mail from the U.S. or Europe can take two to three weeks to arrive in Costa Rica (occasionally it never arrives at all). Within the country, mail service is even less reliable. Outgoing mail is marginally quicker, with delivery in five days to two weeks, especially when sent from San José. **Always use airmail for overseas cards and letters.** Mail theft is a chronic problem, so **do not mail checks, cash, or anything else of value.**

OVERNIGHT SERVICES

If you need to send important documents, checks, or other noncash valuables, you can use an international courier service, such as Federal Express, DHL, or Jetex, or any of various local courier services with offices in San José. (Look in the yellow pages under "Courier.") If you've worked with international couriers before, you won't be surprised to hear that, for any place farther away than Miami, "overnight" is usually a misnomer—shipments to most North American cities take two days, to Britain, three, and to Australia and New Zealand, four or five.

POSTAL RATES

Letters from **Costa Rica** to the United States and Canada cost the equivalent of U.S. 22¢, postcards U.S. 18¢; to the United Kingdom, letters cost 29¢, postcards 23¢; and to Australia or New Zealand, letters cost 33¢, postcards 28¢. From **Panama,** letters to the U.S. cost 35¢; to Canada 40¢; to the U.K., Australia, and New Zealand, 45¢. A letter from **Nicaragua** to the U.S. or Canada costs 60¢ (52¢ to Miami), to the U.K. 81¢, and to Australia and New Zealand $1.

RECEIVING MAIL

You can have mail sent poste restante (*lista de correos*) to any Costa Rican post office. There is no house-to-house mail service—indeed, no house numbers—in Costa Rica; most residents pick up their mail at the post office itself. In written addresses, *apartado,* abbreviated *apdo.,* indicates a P.O. box.

Anyone with an American Express card or traveler's checks can receive mail at the American Express office in San José.

SHIPPING PARCELS

Packages can be sent from any post office, with rates spanning U.S. $6–$12 per kilogram and shipping time ranging from a week or a month, depending on destination. A quicker, more expensive alternative is United Parcel Service, which has offices in Costa Rica, Panama, and Nicaragua—prices are about 10 times what you'd pay at the post office, but packages arrive in a matter of days.

MONEY

Here's an idea of the cost of living in Costa Rica: 750-ml (¾-liter) bottle of Coca-Cola, U.S. 65¢–95¢; cup of coffee, 65¢–95¢; bottle of beer, $1–$1.50; sandwich, $2–$3; daily U.S. newspaper, $1.25–$2.25. At sights and parks, we list admission prices for adults only; reduced fees are almost always available for children, students, and senior citizens. For information on taxes *see* Taxes, *below*.

ATMS

ATMs on the Plus system can be accessed at branches of the Banco Popular in Alajuela, Cartago, Heredia, Limón, Puntarenas, Quepos and half a dozen other cities. In San José, the main Banco Popular is at Avenida 2 and Calle 1, near the National Theater. Cash advances are also available in the Credomatic office, on Calle Central between Avenidas 3 and 5, or the Banco de San José, across the street, which also has an American Express office on the third floor. All offices of the Banco de San José (in Liberia, Puerto Limón, San Isidro, and other towns) have ATMs on the Cirrus system, and the bank has more than a dozen locations in San José, including the Centro Omni, one block north of the Gran Hotel Costa Rica.

In Panama, you can get cash advances on MasterCard and Visa cards at the Banco del Istmo, which has branches in Changuinola and David. The Bocas del Toro branch of the Banco Nacional de Panama has an ATM on the Plus and Cirrus systems.

ATMs in Nicaragua are rare outside Managua. You can use them for cash advances as well as straight cash, but the former carries a hefty service charge. Don't count on this option; bring sufficient cash into the country.

CREDIT CARDS

Barring only Panama's Bocas del Toro, credit cards are accepted at most major hotels and restaurants in this book. As the phone system improves and expands, many budget hotels, restaurants, and other properties have begun to accept plastic; but plenty of properties, some in the expensive range, still require payment in cash. **Don't count on using plastic all the time**—once you venture outside San José **carry enough cash or traveler's checks** to patronize the many businesses without credit-card capability. Note that some hotels, restaurants, tour companies, and other businesses add a surcharge (around 5%) to the bill if you pay with a credit card, or give you a 5%–10% discount if you pay in cash.

The following abbreviations are used throughout this book,: **AE**, American Express; **DC**, Diner's Club; **MC**, MasterCard; **V**, Visa.

➤ REPORTING LOST CARDS: **American Express** (☎ 910/333–3211 collect to U.S.). **Diner's Club** (☎ 702/797–5532 collect to U.S.). **MasterCard** (☎ 0800/011–0184 toll-free to U.S.). **Visa** (☎ 0800/011–0030 toll-free to U.S.).

CURRENCY

All prices in this book are quoted in U.S. dollars.

The Costa Rican currency, the colón (plural: colones), is subject to continual, small devaluations. At press time, the colón had topped 300 to the dollar, 480 to the pound sterling, 210 to the Canadian dollar, 194 to the Australian dollar, and 151 to the New Zealand dollar.

Panama's national currency is the balboa, which has been out of print for decades—Panamanians use the U.S. dollar instead, and simply call it a balboa. The Panamanian government mints its own coins, the same size as U.S. coins, and circulates these with their American counterparts. Since the greenback is legal tender in Panama, and most businesses accept traveler's checks, there is little need to go to the bank. Carry lots of $10 and

$20 bills; an abundance of counterfeit dollars has forced many businesses to stop accepting $50 and $100 bills.

Note that you cannot change Costa Rican colones to Panamanian balboas (U.S. dollars) in Panama. If you take cash to Panama, take U.S. dollars only.

The Nicaraguan unit of currency is the córdoba (plural: córdobas), but U.S. dollars are widely accepted here, too. At press time, the exchange rate was 12 córdobas to the U.S. dollar, 8 to the Canadian dollar, 19 to the pound sterling, 7 to the Australian dollar, and 6 to the New Zealand dollar.

CURRENCY EXCHANGE

For the best exchange rates, **change money in banks.** You won't do as well at exchange booths in airports, hotels, restaurants, or stores, though their hours are undeniably convenient. Remember that **exchange booths in U.S. airports offer extremely unfavorable rates**—and since the cabbies at Costa Rica's international airport accept dollars and most hotels change them, you need not buy colones before you leave for Costa Rica. While ATM transaction fees may be higher abroad than at home, ATM *rates* are excellent, as they're based on wholesale rates offered only by major banks.

Avoid people on the city streets who offer to change money. San José's outdoor money-changers are notorious for shortchanging people and passing counterfeit bills. The guys who change money at the airport aren't quite as shady, but they might not be above shortchanging you, and they don't offer great rates in any case.

➤ EXCHANGE SERVICES: **International Currency Express** (☎ 888/278–6628 for orders, ✎). **Thomas Cook Currency Services** (☎ 800/287–7362 for phone orders and retail locations, ✎).

TRAVELER'S CHECKS

Traveler's checks are widely accepted in cities. If you'll be staying in small towns or rural areas, bring extra cash. Lost or stolen checks can usually be replaced within 24 hours. To ensure a speedy refund, buy your own traveler's checks—don't let someone else pay for them—and make the call yourself if you need to request a refund. Irregularities can cause delays.

If you have an American Express card and can draw on a U.S. checking account, you can buy dollar traveler's checks at the American Express office in San José for a 1% service charge.

OUTDOORS & SPORTS

BIKING

Much of this region is mountainous, but there are plenty of cycle-friendly flatlands in Costa Rica. Sun Tours (☞ Ecotourism, *above*) can arrange guided mountain-biking tours from San José through a number of local companies; tours can be simple day trips or dedicated week-long bike vacations. You can also rent bikes in most Costa Rican and Panamanian mountain and beach resorts.

➤ TOUR OPERATORS: **BiCosta Rica** (Atenas, ☎ 506/446–7585). **Desafío** (La Fortuna, ☎ 506/479–9464 or 202/647–0518). **Río Escondido Mountain Bikes** (Rock River Lodge, Tilarán, ☎ 506/695–5644).

BIRD-WATCHING

➤ TOUR OPERATORS: **Ancon Expeditions** (☎ 507/269–9415). **Costa Rica Expeditions** (☎ 506/222–0333). **Horizontes** (☎ 506/222–2022). **Pesántez Tours** (☎ 507/263–8771).

WATER SPORTS

Costa Rica and Panama are worth visiting for their water sports alone. Wild rivers churn plenty of white water for rafting, and Lake Arenal is one of the best places in the world to windsurf. You can make skin-diving excursions from Drake Bay, Playa Flamingo, Playa Ocotal, and Playa del Coco, but Costa Rica's best dive spot, Cocos Island, can only be visited on a 10-day scuba safari on the *Okeanos Aggressor* or *Undersea Hunter.* Panama has even more diving options, with three dive operations in Bocas del Toro alone. Both Costa Rica and Panama also have excellent surf—especially Costa Rica, where popular surfing beaches include Tamarindo, Jacó, Hermosa and Dominical. Airlines generally allow surfboards on board for a nominal fee of around $15.

➤ DIVE OPERATORS—COSTA RICA: **Bill Beard's Diving Safaris** (Playa Hermosa, ☎ 506/672–0012). **El Ocotal Diving Safaris** (Playa del Ocotal, ☎ 506/670–0321). *Okeanos Agressor* Plaza Colonial, Escazú, P 506/289–3333). **Undersea Hunter** (600 m north and 200 m west of Rosti Pollos, San Rafael de Escazú, P 506/228–6535).

➤ DIVE OPERATORS—PANAMA: **Scuba Panama** (Panama City, ☎ 507/261–3841). **Starfleet Eco-Adventures** (Bocas del Toro, ☎ 507/757–9630). **Turtle Divers** (Bocas del Toro, ☎ 507/757–9594).

➤ RAFTING OUTFITTERS: **Aventuras Naturales** (☎ 506/225–3939). **Chiriquí River Rafting** (☎ 507/720–1505). **Costa Rica Expeditions** (☎ 506/222–0333). **Ríos Tropicales** (☎ 506/233–6455).

➤ WINDSURFING OUTFITTERS: **Tilawa** (Lake Arenal, ☎ 506/695–5050).

PACKING

Pack light. Bring comfortable, hand-washable clothing. T-shirts and shorts are acceptable near the beach and in tourist areas; loose-fitting long-sleeve shirts and trousers are good in smaller towns (where immodest attire is frowned upon) and to protect your skin from ferocious sun and mosquitoes. **Bring a large hat to block the sun from your face and neck.** Pack a light sweater or jacket for cool nights, early mornings, and trips up volcanoes; you'll need even more clothes for trips to Chirripó National Park or Volcán Baru and overnight stays in San Gerardo de Dota or La Providencia Lodge. Sturdy sneakers or hiking boots are essential for sightseeing on foot. Waterproof hiking sandals such as Tevas are good for boat rides, beach walks, streams (should you need to ford one), and light hiking trails.

Insect repellent, sunscreen, sunglasses, and umbrellas (during the rainy season) are crucial. Other handy items—especially if you'll be camping—include toilet paper, facial tissues, a plastic water bottle, and a flashlight (for occasional power outages or use at campsites). Snorkelers staying at budget hotels should consider bringing their own equip-

ment; otherwise, you can rent gear at most beach resorts. Some beaches, such as Playa Grande, do not have shade trees, so if you're planning to linger at the beach you might consider investing in a sturdy tarpaulin. For long-term stays in remote rural areas, *see* Health, *above*, for more tips on what to bring.

In your carry-on luggage, **pack an extra pair of eyeglasses or contact lenses** and **enough of any medication you take** to last the entire trip. You might also ask your doctor to write a spare prescription using the drug's generic name, since brand names may vary from country to country. **Never pack prescription drugs or valuables** in luggage to be checked. To avoid delays at customs, carry medications in their original packaging. Finally, don't forget to carry with you the addresses of offices that handle refunds of lost traveler's checks.

CHECKING LUGGAGE

Your airline decides how many bags you can carry onto the plane. Most allow two, but not all, so make sure that everything you carry aboard will fit under your seat or in the overhead bin, and line up for boarding early for the best dibs on bin space. Note that if you have a seat at the back of the plane, you'll probably board first, while the overhead bins are still empty.

Note that baggage allowances on overseas flights might be determined not by piece but by weight—generally 88 pounds (40 kilograms) in first class, 66 pounds (30 kilograms) in business class, and 44 pounds (20 kilograms) in economy. If you plan to fly within Central America, note that weight limits are stricter on such flights, since the planes are much smaller; ☞ Air Travel, *above*, and plan accordingly.

Airline liability for baggage on international flights amounts to $9.07 per pound or $20 per kilogram for checked baggage (roughly $640 per 70-pound bag) and $400 per passenger for unchecked baggage. You can buy additional coverage at check-in for about $10 per $1,000 of coverage, but it excludes a rather extensive list of items, shown on your airline ticket.

Label each of your bags with your name, address, and phone number (if you use your home address, cover it so potential thieves can't see it readily). **Pack a copy of your itinerary** inside each piece of luggage. When you check in, **make sure that each bag is correctly tagged** with the destination airport's three-letter code. If your bags arrive damaged or fail to arrive at all, file a written report with the airline *before* leaving the airport.

PASSPORTS & VISAS

Carry your passport even if you don't need one (it's always the best form of I.D.) and **make two photocopies of the data page,** one for someone at home and another for you, carried separate from your passport. If you lose your passport, promptly call the nearest embassy or consulate and the local police.

U.S. CITIZENS

Although U.S. citizens technically do not need a valid passport to enter Costa Rica for stays of up to 30 days, the only alternative is to get a tourist card upon entry, which requires a photo ID and copy of your birth certificate. **Bring your passport—** for passage from Costa Rica into Panama, for emergencies, for longer stays, and because it's an indisputable form of identification for changing currency, renting hotel rooms, and just about any other transaction. U.S. citizens with valid passports may stay in Costa Rica for 90 days, after which they must leave for at least 72 hours.

You do need a valid passport to visit Panama, enhanced with either a visa issued by a Panamanian embassy or consulate (free of charge) or a tourist card that you can buy at the border, airport, or tourist offices in Paso Canoas for $5. Travelers without visas must also purchase a $10 stamp card at the Banco General and get it stamped at the immigration office in Bocas del Toro or Changuinola. In Costa Rica, you can get a Panamanian visa free of charge from the **Panamanian Consul** in San Pedro (☎ 506/221–4784)—you'll need a round-trip ticket (to and from Panama, or your airline ticket to and from Costa Rica) and a photocopy of the photo

page of your passport. Drop these items off on a weekday morning and your visa will be ready the next business day.

To visit Nicaragua, you need a valid passport with a tourist card (5$), which you can purchase at the airport or border, and a return ticket.

AUSTRALIAN AND NEW ZEALAND CITIZENS

Citizens of Australia and New Zealand need only a valid passport to enter Costa Rica for stays of up to 30 days (and once you're here, you can go to the Migracion office in La Uruca and extend the visa to 90 days). You can buy a 30-day Panamaniam visa for US$10 at a Panamanian consulate (☞ U.S. Citizens, *above*). Tourist cards, also good for 30 days, are sold for $5 at the border, airport, Paso Canoas, or Sixaola. To visit Nicaragua, Australian and New Zealand citizens need a valid passport with a tourist card (5$), which can be purchased at the airport or border, and a return airline ticket.

CANADIAN CITIZENS

Canadians need only a valid passport to enter Costa Rica for stays of up to 90 days. You can buy a 30-day Panamanian visa for $10 U.S. at a Panamanian consulate (☞ U.S. Citizens, *above*). Tourist cards, also good for 30 days, are sold for $5 at the airport of Paso Canoas border. To visit Nicaragua, Canadian citizens need a valid passport with a tourist card (5$), available at the airport or border, and a return airline ticket.

U.K. CITIZENS

Citizens of the United Kingdom need only a valid passport to enter Costa Rica for up to 90 days, and to enter Panama for stays of up to 30 days. To visit Nicaragua, you need a valid passport with a tourist card (5$), which you can buy at the airport or border, and a return airline ticket.

PASSPORT OFFICES

The best time to apply for a passport, or to renew an old one, is in fall and winter. Before any trip, check your passport's expiration date, and, if necessary, renew it as soon as possible.

➤ AUSTRALIAN CITIZENS: **Australian Passport Office** (☎ 131–232, 🖂).

➤ CANADIAN CITIZENS: **Passport Office** (☎ 819/994–3500 or 800/567–6868, 🖂).

➤ NEW ZEALAND CITIZENS: **New Zealand Passport Office** (☎ 04/494–0700, 🖂).

➤ U.K. CITIZENS: **Passport Agency** (☎ 0990/210410, http://www.ukpa.gov.uk/ukpass.htm).

➤ U.S. CITIZENS: **National Passport Information Center** (☎ 900/225–5674; 35¢ per minute for automated service, $1.05 per minute for operator service; 🖂).

SAFETY

Rural areas tend to be safe, but crime is a problem in San José, where scammers and thieves prey on tourists. A drug addict tells tales of having been recently robbed, then asks you for donations; a distraction artist squirts you with cream or chocolate sauce, then tries to clean you off while his partner steals your backpack; pickpockets and bag slashers work buses and crowds; and street money changers pass off counterfeit bills. To top it all off, car theft is rampant. Beware of anyone who seems overly friendly, aggressively helpful, or disrespectful of your personal space.

WOMEN IN COSTA RICA

Latin machismo means that, in cities anyway, young women have to deal with ogling and suggestive comments from men on the street. Local women tend to ignore this harrassment, avoiding eye contact; and the men are rarely aggressive enough to threaten anyone's safety. Rape is as common in these countries as it is at home, but perhaps a bit more so: the date-rape drug Rohypnol is still afoot, so never leave a drink unattended.

All that said, hundreds of thousands of women visit Costa Rica every year, many of them alone, and have a fabulous time.

SENIOR-CITIZEN TRAVEL

Older travelers may encounter more challenges to mobility than they do at home—especially on those muddy jungle trails—but should otherwise find Costa Rica most hospitable.

To qualify for age-related discounts, **mention your senior status up front** when reserving hotel rooms (not when checking out) and before you're seated in restaurants (not when paying the bill). When renting a car, ask about promotional discounts, which can be cheaper than senior-citizen rates.

➤ EDUCATIONAL PROGRAMS: **Elderhostel** (🖂 75 Federal St., 3rd floor, Boston, MA 02110, ☎ 877/426–8056, FAX 877/426–2166, 🖂). **Interhostel** (🖂 University of New Hampshire, 6 Garrison Ave., Durham, NH 03824, ☎ 603/862–1147 or 800/733–9753, FAX 603/862–1113, 🖂).

SHOPPING

Needless to say, the coffee and rum are quite good. Costa Rica has few artisans, however, so many of the crafts sold here were made in other countries. Interesting crafts include balsa-wood masks and intricately carved dried gourds made by indigenous peoples; you'll also find jewelry, leather goods, and wooden items. Nicaragua has similar products at better prices, as well as interesting ceramics and woven mats that make good wall hangings. Panama's indigenous peoples produce some colorful handicrafts, such as the woven bags of the Gaymí and the Kuna's *molas,* or fabric pictures.

STUDENTS IN COSTA RICA

Central America is fantastic for students and young people on a budget. Although prices are on the rise, you can still travel on $25 or $30 a day if you put your mind to it. There are youth hostels all over Costa Rica, and though Panama and Nicaragua lack hostels, they have their share of inexpensive hotels. One of the cheapest ways to spend the night in this region is to camp: as long as you have your own tent, it's easy to set up house anywhere. (Of course, if you're near someone's home, inquire first). Still, don't ever leave your belongings unattended.

➤ IDs & SERVICES: **Council Travel** (CIEE; 🖂 205 E. 42nd St., 14th floor, New York, NY 10017, ☎ 212/822–2700 or 888/268–6245, FAX 212/822–

2699, ✎) for mail worders only, in the U.S. **Travel Cuts** (✉ 187 College St., Toronto, Ontario M5T 1P7, ☎ 416/979–2406 or 800/667–2887, ✎) in Canada.

STUDYING ABROAD

The University of Costa Rica has exchange programs with at least half a dozen American universities, the oldest of which is the University of Kansas program. Many private language institutes offer Spanish courses for college credit (☞ Language Study Programs, *above*).

TAXES

When you fly out of Costa Rica, you'll have to pay a $16.50 airport departure tax at Juan Santamaría Airport. People may offer to sell you the exit stamp as you climb out of taxis and buses—look for airport-employee identification, and **make sure you get the appropriate stamps in exchange for your dollars or colones.**

VALUE-ADDED TAX

All Costa Rican businesses charge a 13% sales tax, and hotels charge an extra 4% tourist tax. Sales tax in Panama is 5%, and the hotel tax is another 5%. Sales tax in Nicaragua is 15%. Tourists do not get refunds on sales tax paid in Central American countries.

TELEPHONES

The Costa Rican, Panamanian, and Nicaraguan phone systems are all very good by Third World standards. Calls within each country are very cheap.

COUNTRY CODES

The country code for Costa Rica is 506; for Panama, 507; and for Nicaragua, 505. There are no area codes. Phoning home: the country code for the United States and Canada is 1, Australia 61, New Zealand 64, and the United Kingdom 44.

DIRECTORY & OPERATOR ASSISTANCE

In Costa Rica, dial ☎ 113 for domestic directory inquiries and ☎ 110 for domestic collect calls. In Panama dial ☎ 102, and in Nicaragua, ☎ 112.

INTERNATIONAL CALLS

Costa Rica's *guía telefónica* (phone book) lists the rates for calling various countries. To call overseas directly, dial 00, then the country code (☞ *above*), the area code, and the number. Calls to the United States and Canada are discounted on weeknights between 10 PM and 7 AM and on weekends; calls to the United Kingdom are only discounted on weekends, from Friday at 10 PM to Monday at 7 AM.

It's cheapest to call from a pay phone using an international phone card, sold in shops; call from a pay phone using your own long-distance calling card; or call from a telephone office. Dialing directly from a hotel room is very expensive, as is recruiting an international operator to connect you.

LOCAL CALLS

Pay phones are abundant, though they always seem to be in use. Some phones accept coins; others require phone cards, which are sold in various shops.

LONG-DISTANCE SERVICES

AT&T, MCI, and Sprint access codes make calling long distance relatively-convenient, but you may find the local access number blocked in many hotel rooms. If this happens, ask the hotel operator to connect you; if he or she can't comply, ask for an international operator, or dial the international operator yourself. (One way to improve your odds is to travel with more than one company's calling card; a hotel may block Sprint, for example, but not MCI.) If you can't make it work from your hotel room, take your calling card to a pay phone or telephone office (☞ International Calls, *above*).

➤ ACCESS CODES: **AT&T Direct** (☎ 0800/011–4114 from Costa Rica; 109 from Panama; 800/435–0812 for other areas). **MCI WorldPhone** (☎ 0800/012–2222 from Costa Rica; 108 from Panama; 800/444–4141 for other areas). **Sprint International Access** (☎ 0800/013–0123 from Costa Rica; 800/877–4646 for other areas).

➤ TELEPHONE OFFICES: **Radiográfica Costarricense** (✉ Avda. 5 between Cs. 1 and 3), open daily 7 AM–10 PM, also has phone, fax, and Internet facilities.

PHONE CARDS

Costa Rica has two kinds of phone cards: domestic cards, which record what you spend, and international cards, which have codes that you have to punch into the telephone. Both cards are sold in an array of shops.

TIME

Costa Rica and Nicaragua lie in the Central Standard time zone, but move into the Mountain time zone during Daylight Saving Time (April to October). Panama is in the Eastern Standard time zone, but moves into the Central Standard time zone during Daylight Saving Time.

TIPPING

Restaurant bills in Costa Rica include a 13% tax and 10% service charge—sometimes these amounts are included in prices on the menu, and sometimes they aren't. Additional gratuity is not expected, especially in cheap restaurants; but people often leave something extra when service is good.

In Panamanian restaurants, only a 5% tax is added, so you're expected to leave at least 10% gratuity. It's also customary to tip 10% in Nicaraguan restaurants, but check the bill first, as the tip (*servicio*) is often added.

TOURS & PACKAGES

Because everything is prearranged on a guided tour or package vacation, you spend less time planning—and often get the whole trip for a reasonable price.

TRAVEL AGENTS

Agents are excellent resources. Do collect brochures from several, however, as some agents' suggestions may be influenced by relationships with tour and package firms that reward them for volume sales. If you have a special interest, **find an agent with expertise in that area**; ASTA (☞ Travel Agencies, *below*) has a database of specialists worldwide.

Make sure your travel agent is familiar with the rooms and other services in any hotel he or she recommends. Ask about the hotel's location, room size, beds, and whether the hotel has any specific amenities you need. Has your agent been there in person or sent others whom you can contact?

Do some homework on your own, too: local tourism boards can provideinformation about lesser-known and small-niche operators, some of which may sell only direct.

BUYER BEWARE

Every year consumers are stranded or lose their money when tour operators—even large ones with excellent reputations—go out of business. **Check out the operator**—ask several travel agents about its reputation, and try to **book with a company that has a consumer-protection program.** (Look for information in the company's brochure.) In the United States, members of the National Tour Association and the United States Tour Operators Association are required to set aside funds to cover your payments and travel arrangements in the event that the company defaults. It's also a good idea to choose a company that participates in the American Society of Travel Agents' Tour Operator Program (TOP); ASTA will act as mediator in any disputes between you and your tour operator.

Remember that the more your package or tour includes, the better you can predict the total cost of your vacation. Make sure you know exactly what's covered; **beware of hidden costs.** Are taxes, tips, and transfers included? Entertainment and excursions? These can add up.

➤ TOUR-OPERATOR RECOMMENDATIONS: **American Society of Travel Agents** (☞ Travel Agencies, *below*). **National Tour Association** (NTA; ✉ 546 E. Main St., Lexington, KY 40508, ☎ 606/226–4444 or 800/682–8886, 🍷). **United States Tour Operators Association** (USTOA; ✉ 342 Madison Ave., Suite 1522, New York, NY 10173, ☎ 212/599–6599 or 800/468–7862, FAX 212/599–6744, 🍷).

TRAIN TRAVEL

Costa Rica's train system has been defunct for years due to recurring earthquakes.

TRANSPORTATION WITHIN
COSTA RICA

The most common form of public transportation is the bus. All Costa Rican towns are connected by regular, inexpensive bus service. Buses can, however, be a slow and uncomfortable way to travel, making domestic flights a desirable and practical option. Most major destinations are served by daily domestic flights, most costing a reasonable US$35–US$60 one way (round trips are double the one-way fare). Renting a car gives you the most freedom, but rates can be expensive, especially since you'll probably (depending on where you're headed) need four-wheel drive.

TRAVEL AGENCIES

A good travel agent puts your needs first. Look for an agency that has been in business at least five years, emphasizes customer service, and has someone on staff who specializes in your destination. In addition, **make sure the agency belongs to a professional trade organization.** The American Society of Travel Agents (ASTA), with 27,000 agents in some 170 countries, is the largest and most influential in the field. Operating under the motto "Integrity in Travel," it maintains and enforces a strict code of ethics and will step in to help mediate any agent-client disputes if necessary. ASTA also maintains a Web site that includes a directory of agents. (If a travel agency is also acting as your tour operator, *see* Buyer Beware *in* Tours & Packages, *above*.)

➤ LOCAL AGENT REFERRALS: **American Society of Travel Agents** (ASTA; ☎ 800/965–2782 24-hr hot line, FAX 703/684–8319, ✍). **Association of British Travel Agents** (✉ 68–71 Newman St., London W1P 4AH, ☎ 0171/637–2444, FAX 0171/637–0713, ✍). **Association of Canadian Travel Agents** (✉ 1729 Bank St., Suite 201, Ottawa, Ontario K1V 7Z5, ☎ 613/521–0474, FAX 613/521–0805). **Aus-**tralian Federation of Travel Agents (✉ Level 3, 309 Pitt St., Sydney 2000, ☎ 02/9264–3299, FAX 02/9264–1085, ✍). **Travel Agents' Association of New Zealand** (✉ Box 1888, Wellington 10033, ☎ 04/499–0104, FAX 04/499–0827).

VISITOR INFORMATION

➤ COSTA RICA—U.S. AND CANADA: **Costa Rica Tourist Board** (☎ 800/343–6332).

➤ COSTA RICA—U.K.: **Costa Rica Tourist Services** (✉ 47 Causton St., London SW1P 4AT, ☎ 0171/976–5511, FAX 0171/976–6908).

➤ TRAVEL ADVISORIES: **U.S. Department of State** (✉ Overseas Citizens Services Office, Room 4811 N.S., 2201 C St. NW, Washington, DC 20520, ☎ 202/647–5225 for interactive hot line, 301/946–4400 for computer bulletin board, FAX 202/647–3000 for interactive hot line). If you write, enclose a self-addressed, stamped, business-size envelope.

VOLUNTEER & EDUCATIONAL
TRAVEL

A few Costa Ricans have, in recent years, realized the need to preserve their country's precious biodiversity. Both Ticos and far-flung environmentalists have founded volunteer and educational concerns to this end, and you, too, can have an impact.

➤ OPERATORS: The **Caribbean Conservation Corporation (CCC)** (✉ 4424 Northwest 13th St., Suite A-1, Gainesville, FL 32609, ☎ 800/678–7853) is devoted to the preservation of sea turtles. The **Earthwatch Institute** (✉ 680 Mt. Auburn St., Box 9104, Watertown, MA 02272–9104, ☎ 800/776–0188) leads science-based trips. The **Talamancan Association of Ecotourism and Conservation (ATEC)** (✉ Puerto Viejo de Limón,, ☎ 506/750–0191) designs short group and individual outings centered on Costa Rican wildlife and indigenous culture.

WEB SITES

Do check out the World Wide Web when you're planning. You'll find everything from current weather forecasts to virtual tours of famous

Smart Travel Tips A to Z

cities. Fodor's Web site, www.fodors.com, is a great place to start your on-line travels. When you see a 🕸 in this book, go to www.fodors.com/urls for an up-to-date link to that destination's site.

➤ COSTA RICA: Start with **www.costarica.tourism.co.cr** and **www.info-costarica.net/english** for general information. For current events, check out the English-language Tico Times online: **www.ticotimes.net**. To explore nature-tour options, see the commercial sites **www.horizontes.com** and **www.expeditions.co.cr**.

WHEN TO GO

The most popular time to visit Costa Rica is the dry season, which runs from mid-December through April. From mid-December until early February in particular, you have the combined advantages of good weather and lush vegetation. Of course, hotels are more likely to be full during this time of year, making advance planning all but essential; and some areas, especially Guanacaste, are dry and dusty by April, for lack of enriching rains.

In the rainy season, beaches are often wet in the afternoon but sunny and dry in the morning. Much of Costa Rica gets some sunny weather in July, August, and early September; and the Caribbean coast around Cahuita and Bocas del Toro tends to enjoy a short dry season in September and October, while the Pacific slope is being drenched by daily storms.

To avoid crowds and high prices, come to Costa Rica in the rainy season, which is sometimes promoted as the "Green" season. Green it is—the vegetation is lush and most gorgeous—

but some roads, especially those without asphalt, are washed out, and require four-wheel drive and patience. Come in July or August, when the storms let up a bit, or mid-December, when the rains are tapering off but the high tourist season has yet to kick in. While some rural hotels shut down for the rainiest months, September and October, most stay open and have rooms to spare. You'll even have the beaches to yourself.

It can be useful to know that Costa Ricans call their dry season (mid-December–April) *verano* (summer), and the rainy season (May–mid-December) *invierno* (winter).

CLIMATE

Central America's climate varies greatly between the lowlands and the mountains. Tropical temperatures generally hover between 70°F and 85°F; high humidity, especially in the dense jungle of the Caribbean coast, is the true culprit in any discomfort. Guanacaste, on the more arid Pacific coast, is perhaps Costa Rica's hottest region, with frequent temperatures in the 90s during the dry season. Drink plenty of bottled water to avoid dehydration.

➤ FORECASTS: **Weather Channel Connection** (☎ 900/932–8437), 95¢ per minute from a Touch-Tone phone.

SAN JOSÉ

San José's climate is similar to that of other highland towns, such as Monteverde and Panama's Boquete, but are warmer than San Gerardo de Dota and Panama's Cerro Punta.

Average daily high and low temperatures:

Jan.	75F	24C	May	80F	27C	Sept.	79F	26C
	58	14		62	17		61	16
Feb.	76F	24C	June	79F	26C	Oct.	77F	25C
	58	14		62	17		60	16
Mar.	79F	26C	July	77F	25C	Nov.	77F	25C
	59	15		62	17		60	16
Apr.	79F	26C	Aug.	78F	26C	Dec.	75F	24C
	62	17		61	16		58	14

GOLFITO

Positioned at sea level, Golfito has a climate similar to that of most coastal and lowland towns, such as Manuel Antonio, Jacó, Puntarenas, most of Guanacaste, and Panama's David.

Average daily high and low temperatures:

Jan.	91F	33C	May	91F	33C	Sept.	91F	33C
	72	22		73	23		72	22
Feb.	91F	33C	June	90F	32C	Oct.	90F	32C
	72	22		73	23		72	22
Mar.	91F	33C	July	90F	32C	Nov.	91F	32C
	73	23		72	22		72	22
Apr.	91F	33C	Aug.	90F	32C	Dec.	91F	33C
	73	23		72	22		72	22

Costa Rica

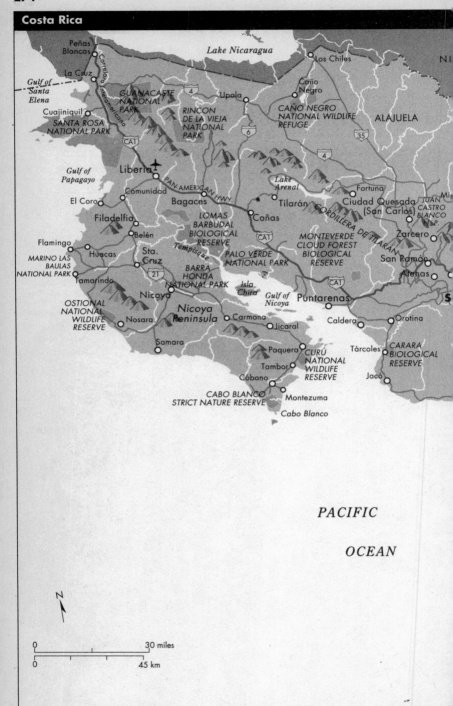

Peñas Blancas

Lake Nicaragua

Los Chiles

NI

La Cruz

Carretera Interamericana

Gulf of Santa Elena

GUANACASTE NATIONAL PARK

4

Upala

Caño Negro

CAÑO NEGRO NATIONAL WILDLIFE REFUGE

ALAJUELA

Cuajiniquil

RINCON DE LA VIEJA NATIONAL PARK

6

35

SANTA ROSA NATIONAL PARK

CAT

Gulf of Papagayo

Liberia

PAN-AMERICAN HWY

Lake Arenal

Fortuna

Ciudad Quesada (San Carlos)

JUAN CASTRO BLANCO N.P.

Mi

El Coro

Comunidad

Bagaces

Tilarán

4

Zarcero

Filadelfia

LOMAS BARBUDAL BIOLOGICAL RESERVE

Cañas

CORDILLERA DE TILARÁN

San Ramón

Belén

CAT

MONTEVERDE CLOUD FOREST BIOLOGICAL RESERVE

Flamingo

Huacas

Sta. Cruz

Tempisque

PALO VERDE NATIONAL PARK

Arenas

MARINO LAS BAULAS NATIONAL PARK

21

BARRA HONDA NATIONAL PARK

Isla Chira

CAT

S

Tamarindo

Nicoya

Gulf of Nicoya

Puntarenas

OSTIONAL NATIONAL WILDLIFE RESERVE

Nosara

Nicoya Peninsula

Carmona

Jicaral

Caldera

Orotina

Samara

Paquera

CURÚ NATIONAL WILDLIFE RESERVE

Tárcoles

CARARA BIOLOGICAL RESERVE

Tambor

Cóbano

Jacó

CABO BLANCO STRICT NATURE RESERVE

Montezuma

Cabo Blanco

PACIFIC

OCEAN

N

0   30 miles

0   45 km

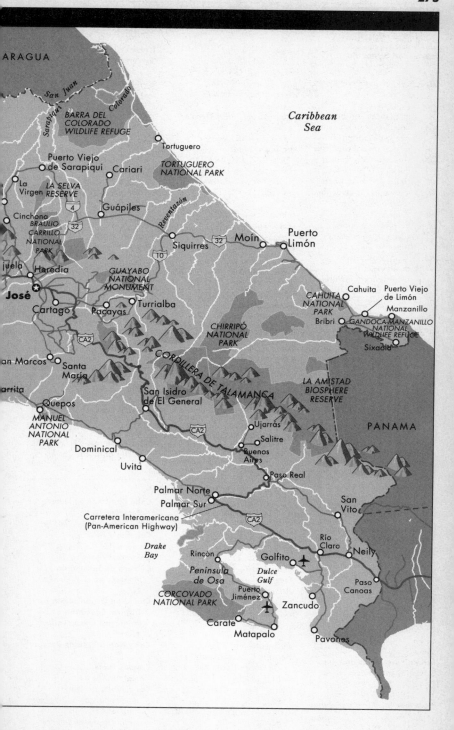

INDEX

Index

281

Southern Pacific Costa Rica,
150, 158
Swimming. ☞ Beaches

T

Tabacón Resort, *72–73*
Taller Eloy Alfaro e Hijos
(ox-cart factory), *54*
Tamarindo, *116–118*
Tambor, *101*
Tapirs, *83, 85, 169, 173,*
184
Tárcoles, *129–130*
Taxis, *38–39, 64*
Teatro Nacional, *25–26*
Tercipelo Cave, *104*
Theater, *24, 25–26, 35*
Thermal pools, *59*
Tilarán, *78–79*
Tortuguero, *173, 175*
Tres Colinas, *152*
Turrialba, *60–62*
Turtles
Atlantic Lowlands and the
Caribbean Coast, 167,
172–173
Nicoya Peninsula, 95–96,
108–109, 115, 118
Northern Guanacasta and
Alajuela, 85
Panama, 203, 206

U

Ujarrás, *58*

V

Valle de la Estrella, *184*
Venado Caves, *73*
Volcán (Panama), *197*
Volcán Arenal, *76*
Volcán Barú (Panama), *192,*
197, 230

Volcán Barva, *49–50, 169*
Volcán Cacao, *86*
Volcán Irazú, *57*
Volcán Mombacho Nature
Reserve, *215*
Volcán Orosí, *86*
Volcán Poás, *52*
Volcán Rincón de la Vieja, *84*
Volcanoes, *43, 68, 209.* ☞
Also specific volcanoes

W

Waterfalls
Atlantic Lowlands and the
Caribbean Coast, 170, 184
Central Pacific Costa Rica,
129
Northern Guanacaste and
Alajuela, 73, 86
Nicoya Peninsula, 102
Panama, 197–198
Southern Pacific Costa Rica,
146, 148, 150
Water sports, *88, 158*
Whales, *157*
White-water rafting,
Central Pacific Costa Rica,
135
Central Valley, 61–62
Northern Guanacaste and
Alajuela, 75
Panama, 190
San José, 37
Southern Pacific Costa Rica,
147, 156
Wildlife glossary, *241–244*
Wildlife refuges, *218–231*
Barra del Colorado Wildlife
Refuge, 176, 228
Cabo Blanco Strict Nature
Reserve, 102–103
Caño Negro Wildlife Refuge,
76, 222

Centro Biológico Las
Quebradas, 147
Curú National Wildlife
Refuge, 100–101
Gandoca-Manzanillo National
Wildlife Refuge, 184, 229
Golfito National Wildllife
Refuge, 153
Isla Bolaños, 88
La Selva Biological Station,
171
Los Quetzales, 199
Ostional National Wildlife
Refuge, 108–109
private nature preserves, 129,
144, 148, 170, 199
Rara Avis, 170–171
Reserva Biológica Carara,
128–129, 225
Reserva Biológica Hitoy
Cerere, 184
Reserva Biológica Lomas
Barbudal, 103–104, 224
Reserva La Biósfera La
Amistad, 151, 152
Reserva Natural Volcán
Mombacho (Nicaragua),
215–216
Tapantí National Wildlife
Refuge, 221
Wilson Botanical Gardens,
151
Windsurfing, *68, 79, 88*

Z

Zarcero, *71–72*
Zoo Ave (bird zoo), *51*
Zoos, *25, 27, 51, 133–134*
Zurqui ranger station, *169*

NOTES

NOTES

NOTES

NOTES

NOTES

FODOR'S COSTA RICA 2001

EDITOR: Christine Cipriani

Editorial Contributors: George Soriano, Brad Weiss

Editorial Production: Tom Holton

Maps: Bob Blake, *map editor*

Design: Fabrizio La Rocca, *creative director;* Guido Caroti, *art director;* Jolie Novak, *photo editor;* Melanie Marin, *photo researcher*

Cover Design: Pentagram

Production/Manufacturing: Robert B. Shields

SPECIAL SALES

Fodor's Travel Publications are available at special discounts for bulk purchases for sales promotions or premiums. Special editions, including personalized covers, excerpts of existing guides, and corporate imprints, can be created in large quantities for special needs. For more information contact your local bookseller or write to Special Markets, Fodor's Travel Publications, 280 Park Avenue, New York, NY 10017. Inquiries from Canada should be directed to your local Canadian bookseller or sent to Random House of Canada, Ltd., Marketing Department, 2775 Matheson Boulevard East, Mississauga, Ontario L4W 4P7. Inquiries from the United Kingdom should be sent to Fodor's Travel Publications, 20 Vauxhall Bridge Road, London, England SW1V 2SA.

PRINTED IN THE UNITED STATES OF AMERICA

10 9 8 7 6 5 4 3 2 1

IMPORTANT TIP

Although all prices, opening times, and other details in this book are based on information supplied to us at press time, changes occur all the time in the travel world, and Fodors cannot accept responsibility for facts that become outdated or for inadvertent errors or omissions. So always confirm information when it matters, especially if you're making a detour to visit a specific place.

PHOTOGRAPHY

Buddy Mays, cover *(sloth).*

Leslie Anderson, *2 bottom center, 14D.*

Axiom: *Ian Cumming, 13C.*

Jan Butchofsky-Houser, *11B.*

Corbis: *Gary Braasch, 16. Jeremy Horner, 13B. Danny Lehman, 13A. Joel W. Rogers, 4-5. Martin Rogers, 10B. Kevin Schafer, 14J. Kennan Ward, 8B.*

Hilary Duffy, *2 upper left.*

Fundación Catedral Metropolitana: *Carlos Jinesta Urbini, 3 upper left, 6A.*

Hotel Grano de Oro, *14G.*

Hotel Le Bergerac, *14F.*

Hotel Punta Islita, *2 upper right, 14B.*

Dave G. Houser, *6C, 7A, 8A, 12B.*

The Image Bank: *Macduff Everton, 14C. Sharon Guynup, 12C.*

Jardin Lankester, *2 bottom left, 3 bottom right.*

La Mariposa, *14E.*

Sheila McKinnon, *7 top right.*

Rios Tropicales, *3 upper right, 7 bottom left.*

Elle Schuster, *14H, 14I.*

Tony Stone Images: *Nick Gunderson, 6B. Kevin Schafer, 1, 9 bottom left. Larry Ulrich, 9A.*

Travel Stock: *Buddy Mays, 7B, 8C, 10 top, 10A, 11A, 11C, 12A.*

Nik Wheeler, *9B.*

Xandari Plantation, *2 bottom right, 3 bottom left, 14A.*

ABOUT OUR WRITERS

Every trip is a significant trip. So if there was ever a time you needed excellent travel information, it's now. Acutely aware of that fact, we've pulled out all stops in preparing *Fodor's Costa Rica 2001* To help you zero in on what to see in Costa Rica, we've gathered some great color photos of the key sights in every region. To show you how to put it all together, we've created great itineraries and neighborhood walks. And to direct you to the places that are truly worth your time and money this year, we've rallied the team of endearingly picky know-it-alls we're pleased to call our writers. Having seen all corners of the regions they cover for us, they're real experts. If you knew them, you'd poll them for tips yourself.

A perpetual tourist, Miami native **George Soriano** began exploring Costa Rica three years ago and hasn't stopped yet. Based in San José, he is an editor at the English-language *Tico Times*, and has written for several publications on Central America and Mexico. His travels have given him a taste for simple pleasures—including isthmian brew—and the chance to pursue another of his passions, photography.

Brad Weiss has become one of Fodor's most versatile Latin American correspondents. After graduating from Haverford College with a degree in Spanish literature, Brad spent a year teaching English at the University of Cuenca, Ecuador, then moved to São Paulo, where he worked at the financial newspaper *Gazeta Mercantil*, led tours, and wrote the Amazon chapter of *Fodor's Brazil*. Since returning—in a manner of speaking—to the U.S., he has written for Fodor's guides to Argentina and Los Cabos, Mexico, as well as Costa Rica.

Don't Forget to Write

Keeping a travel guide fresh and up-to-date is a big job. So we love your feedback—positive and negative—and follow up on all suggestions. Contact the Costa Rica editor at editors@fodors.com or c/o Fodor's, 280 Park Avenue, New York, New York 10017. And have a wonderful trip!

Karen Cure

Karen Cure
Editorial Director